THE FACTS

PART I—an alphabetical listing of composers that includes the chronology of their works, the age of the composer at the time of composition, and his/her nationality.

THE SCOPE

PART II—an ingenious calendar of music history that shows exactly what was happening in the musical world in any given year.

THE PERSPECTIVE

PART III—an invaluable timeline that graphically illustrates the life span of each composer and his contemporaries, indicating interrelations and possible influences.

THE DICTIONARY OF
COMPOSERS
and their Music

EVERY LISTENER'S COMPANION
Arranged Chronologically and Alphabetically

Eric Gilder
June G. Port

BALLANTINE BOOKS · NEW YORK

Library of Congress Catalog Card Number: 77-15998

ISBN 0-345-28041-5

This edition published by arrangement with Paddington Press
Ltd.

Manufactured in the United States of America

First Ballantine Books Edition: April 1979

*To those who speak the only truly international
language, between whom there are no barriers
of space or time, race or creed; to the makers of
music, this book is humbly dedicated.*

We have lectured for many years on music appreciation and history. We found that we needed to carry to the classroom about twenty bulky volumes in order to answer most of the questions thrown at us. Biographies of composers are legion, but in years of searching we could find no one book that contained all the information required. Many others to whom we spoke all admitted the same difficulty.

What was obviously required was complete factual information about who wrote what, and when, all between the covers of one book. This would be of lasting value as a permanent reference, not only to the academic student, but also to the vast numbers of interested laymen—the music-lovers, the concert-goers, the record-collectors, the listeners.

Our original intention has now become Part One of the present book. This is an alphabetical list of composers with their music arranged chronologically. Each composition is dated and the composer's age is supplied.

To have called this "A Complete List of Everything Ever Composed by Anybody" would have been far too rash a boast. All composers must have their jottings, tentative pieces, trifling things that have been discarded as unworthy, mere exercises. Some of these have been preserved, and may be seen in museums in the composer's own handwriting; but their contribution to the world's musical treasury is too inconsiderable to make them worthy of special mention. There are some works that composers themselves would not wish to be immortalized. (Dukas, for example, who was his own severest critic, burned all his unpublished compositions when in his early forties and, although still composing, published no more.)

Omissions are therefore inevitable, and we have used our own discretion. However, we feel that every work of importance by the 275 composers represented is included. There are countless others, but in such a book as this the line must be drawn somewhere, and the reader must forgive us if some favorite composer or work does not appear. The composers chosen are those whose works may be heard in the concert hall, the opera or ballet house, and the church. Many of these composers have also written incidental music and music for the theater which is included here; but a complete list of works for the theater could fill a large book by itself and, in general, composers who wrote for that medium alone have been omitted.

Where does such a book begin? Not until the sixteenth century did composers emerge who began to develop music as a serious art form, and music as we know it can be said to date from this time. An exact date cannot be provided, for there was a long period of evolution; but one can say definitely that the birth of "modern" music took place in Europe, and the first composer mentioned in this book is Thomas Tallis, who was born about 1505.

It was during the compiling of Part One that the ideas for Parts Two and Three emerged, and for us these became the most fascinating sections in some respects.

Part Two is a chronological survey, enabling the reader to turn to any year from 1554 through 1975 and see exactly what music was written, which composers were born and which died. Such an historical overview can perhaps best be appreciated if one sticks a pin somewhere in the calendar. Take the year 1847. That was the year Mendelssohn died. Spontini the indestructible was still prolifically writing opera in the classical mold. Bizet, Dvořák, Fauré, Grieg. Mussorgsky, Rimsky-Korsakov, Sullivan and Tchaikovsky were toddlers. Donizetti, whose operas were well rooted in tradition, still had a year to live, whereas in that year Verdi wrote *Macbeth* and Wagner was already working on *Lohengrin,* to be produced three years later. It was a good year for opera, contributions coming from Balfe, Dargomizhsky, Flotow and Schumann. Berwald, Meyerbeer and Rossini were all writing with middle-aged maturity, while the fourteen-year-old Borodin produced his Flute Concerto. Glinka, called the Father of Russian Music, wrote *Greetings to the Fatherland,* Berlioz was in his forties, Liszt his thirties, and Chopin was an ailing man of thirty-seven with only two years to live. Offenbach and Franck were both twenty-five years of age and already established as powers in the musical world. Lalo, the elegant Frenchman of Spanish descent, was already writing the music of Spanish flavor which was to influence Falla, Debussy and Ravel. Smetana was twenty-three and was later to establish the great nationalist school of Czech music, and to conduct the Czech Opera in which Dvořák played the viola. Brahms, Saint-Saëns and Balakirev were as yet unfledged children.

When Spontini was born, Boyce was still alive; when Boyce was born, Corelli was still alive; and Corelli was born a mere ten years after Monteverdi died. In this year of 1847 Spontini still had four more years to live; by the time he died, d'Indy was born, and *he* lived until 1931, by which time Boulez was very much alive. So with the names of five men—Corelli, Boyce, Spontini, d'Indy and Boulez—who could just have met each other, we span the whole of musical composition from the glees, motets and madrigals to the music of today, a matter of something over three hundred years. Music as we know it is a very young art indeed.

Part Three of this book is a timeline, enabling one to see at a glance which composers were contemporaries, when each was born and died. It is a visual aid to gaining a clear perspective of musical history.

Research for this book brought up copious anomalies. Standard books on the subject have often been at variance with each other in the matter of dates. This is sometimes quite understandable. Certain modern composers, for example, were only accepted by publishers or by performing or copyright organizations quite late in their composing careers, and a large collection of early works bears only the date of such acceptance. Not all manuscripts bear a date in the composer's handwriting. If one of the present compilers, himself a composer, were asked the date of a certain one of his works, he might easily say, "Oh, about twenty years ago," and be unable to be any more accurate.

Many composers did not give their works opus numbers, and some who did seemed to be unable to count! Köchel's catalog of the works of Mozart can be accepted as definitive. For the rest, we have been ruled by the greatest consensus of opinion.

There has been a great variety of spellings of the names and works of Russian composers. The only accurate way to spell them, of course, is in the original Russian; any other spelling must be purely phonetic. This book incorporates spellings that are generally accepted in the Western world. In a similar way, the titles of works given are the titles by which they are best known, be they translated or in the original language.

Special mention must be made of the list of works by Johann Sebastian Bach. To begin with, his works can generally only be dated according to the years he spent in various appointments; i.e., during the nine years between 1708 and 1717 while at Weimar, as court organist, chamber musician and finally Concertmeister, he composed most of his great organ works. Then at Cöthen, between 1717 and 1723 as Kapellmeister and conductor of the court orchestra, he wrote the Brandenberg Concerti, the suites for orchestra, the violin concerti and much chamber music. From 1723 until his death in 1750, he was Cantor of the Leipzig Thomasschule, and there he composed approximately 265 church cantatas, as well as compositions for one of the Leipzig musical societies of which he was conductor.

Our obvious sources of information were such standard works as Grove's *Dictionary of Music and Musicians*, the Oxford *Histories*, Scholes's *Oxford Companion to Music*, the *International Cyclopaedia of Music and Musicians*, and Anderson's *Contemporary American Composers*, from all of which we had to choose a mere handful from the thousands listed. The British *Performing Rights Society* and the American

ASCAP contributed much information on contemporary British and American composers; for the rest, the reference books in French, German and Italian, and the biographies of composers, have been too numerous for us to be able to remember them. However, to all these and to the many composers who took the time to answer our letters of inquiry, for the great excitement over years of research, we give our grateful thanks.

Eric Gilder
June G. Port

In this alphabetical listing of composers, their music is arranged in chronological order. The dates, next to which appear the composers' ages, are those when the music is first mentioned. It is not always possible to ascertain whether these dates refer to the commencement or to the completion of a piece of music. Where possible, both dates are given, as Stravinsky: *Les Noces* (1917–1923). In some cases, the first information available is a mention of a first performance, in which case the name of the work is prefaced with the letters *f.p.;* in others, the first information may refer to the date of publication, when the letter *p.* is used. For some works, the letter *c.* for *circa* prefaces the nearest approximation. *Posthumous* in the age column indicates that the work was published, or first performed, after the composer's death. When dates of some of a composer's music cannot be traced, those works are listed at the end of the entry and undated.

Collections of short works are sometimes not listed individually. Consider the five hundred chamber cantatas of Alessandro Scarlatti, or the two hundred songs of Charles Ives: to list all such music would require many volumes. Instead, in such cases, works are referred to as so many "songs," "piano pieces," "cantatas," etc.

Key signatures are generally given in full, such as, *Rhapsody* in C♯ minor. However, if a number of works of the same kind were written in any one year, keys are abbreviated: e.g., Four string quartets in Dm: C: A: F♯m, indicating works in D minor, C major, A major and F♯ minor.

In the section for Bach, a number of works bear the

suffix *(& continuo)*. This indicates that the continuo is not generally used in modern performance.

A few composers, although generally considered as being of a particular nationality, were born in another country. In these instances both countries are listed: e.g., U.S.A. (b. Germany). In cases where the country of a composer's birth no longer exists, the modern equivalent is also included: Bohemia (Czechoslovakia).

As explained in the preface, works are given the names by which they are best known to English-speaking people.

ADAM, Adolphe/1803–1856/France

1832 (29) *Faust*, ballet
1834 (31) *Le Châlet*, opera
1836 (33) *Le Postillon de Longjumeau*, opera
1839 (36) *La Jolie fille de Gand*, ballet
1841 (38) *Giselle*, ballet
1849 (46) *Le Toréador*, opera
1852 (49) *Si J'étais roi*, opera
1856 (53) *Le Corsaire*, ballet
Adam also composed a total of 39 operas, as well as many ballets, choruses, songs and much church music.

ALBÉNIZ, Isaac/1860–1909/Spain

1893 (33) *The Magic Opal*, opera
1894 (34) *San Antonio de la Florida*
1895 (35) *Enrico Clifford*, opera
1896 (36) *Pepita Jiménez*, opera
1899 (39) *p. Catalonia*, orchestral rhapsody
1906–09 (46–49) *Iberia*, piano cycle
Albéniz also composed:
Merlin, opera
Piano Concerto
Navarra
Cantos de Espana
Espana
Recuerdof de Viaje

Suite Espanola
Torre Bermeja
Rapfodia Espana

ALBINONI, Tommaso/1671–1750/Italy

1694 (23) *Zenobia, regina di Palmireni,* opera
1707 (36) Sinfonie e Concerti a 5
1710 (39) Concerti a 5
*c.***1716** (*c.*45) 12 Concerti a 5
*c.***1722** (*c.*51) 12 Concerti a 5
Albinoni composed many works of concerto grosso
type, as well as more than 50 operas.

ALFVÉN, Hugo/1872–1960/Sweden

1896 (24) "Sonata" and "Romance", for violin and
                      piano
1897 (25) Symphony No. 1 in F minor
1898–99 (26) Symphony No. 2 in D major
                      Elegy, for horn and organ
1904 (32) Swedish Rhapsody No. 1 *Midsommervaka*
1905 (33) Symphony No. 3 in E major
                      En Skargardssagen, symphonic poem
1907 (35) Swedish Rhapsody No. 2, *Uppsalarapsodi*
1912 (40) *Sten Sture,* cantata for male voices
1918–19 (46) Symphony No. 4 in C minor
1923 (51) *Bergakungen,* pantomime drama
1928 (56) *Manhem,* cantata for male voices
1932 (60) *Spamannen,* incidental music
                      Vi, incidental music
1937 (65) Swedish Rhapsody No. 3, *Dalarapsodi*
1942 (70) Symphony No. 5 in A minor
Between 1898 and 1937 Alfvén wrote a number of
piano pieces, and between 1900 and 1928 he wrote 10
cantatas, for solo voices, chorus and orchestra.

ALWYN, William/b.1905/Great Britain

1927 (22) Five Preludes for orchestra

1930 (25) Piano Concerto
1936 (31) *Marriage of Heaven and Hell,* choral work
1939 (34) Violin Concerto
Rhapsody, for piano quartet
Sonata-Impromptu, for violin and viola
1940 (35) *Masquerade,* overture
Divertimento for solo flute
1942 (37) Concerto Grosso No. 1
1943 (38) *Pastoral Fantasia,* for viola and strings
1945 (40) Concerto for oboe, harp and strings
1946 (41) Suite of Scottish Dances
1947 (42) *Manchester Suite,* for orchestra
Three Songs (Louis MacNeice)
Piano Sonata
1948 (43) *Three Winter Poems,* for string quartet
1949 (44) Symphony No. 1
1951 (46) Festival March
Concerto Grosso No. 2
1953 (48) Symphony No. 2
The Magic Island, symphonic prelude
1954 (49) *Lyra Angelica,* for harp and strings
1955 (50) *Autumn Legend,* for English horn and
strings
1956 (51) Symphony No. 3
1957 (52) *Elizabethan Dances,* for orchestra
1959 (54) Symphony No. 4
1964 (59) Concerto Grosso No. 3
1966 (61) *Derby Day,* overture
1970 (65) Sinfonietta for strings
1973 (68) Symphony No. 5, *Hydriotaphia*

ANTHEIL, George/1900–1959/U.S.A.

1922 (22) *Airplane Sonata,* for piano
Sonata Sauvage, for piano
Symphony No. 1
1923 (23) *Ballet Mecanique* (1923–24, revised 1953)
Violin Sonata No. 1
1926 (26) *Jazz Symphonietta,* for twenty-two
instruments
1928–29 (28) *Transatlantic,* opera
1931 (31) *Helen Retires,* opera

1935 (35) *Dreams,* ballet
1936 (36) *Course,* dance score
1942 (42) Symphony No. 4
1947–48 (47) Symphony No. 5
1948 (48) Symphony No. 6
                McKonkey's Ferry, overture for orchestra
                Serenade, for string orchestra
                Piano Sonata No. 4
                Songs of Experience (Blake poems), for
                  voice and piano
1950 (50) *Volpone,* opera
1951 (51) *Eight Fragments from Shelley,* for chorus
1953 (53) *Capital of the World,* ballet
1955–56 (55) *Cabezza de Vacca,* cantata

ARENSKY, Antony/1861–1906/Russia

1890 (29) *fp. A Dream on the Volga,* opera
1894 (33) *fp. Raphael,* opera
1899 (38) *Nal and Damayanti,* opera (completed)
Arensky also composed:
Egyptian Night, ballet
The Wolf, for bass voice and orchestra
2 Symphonies, in B minor and A minor
Nearly 100 piano pieces, including 3 suites for 2
    pianos and 6 pieces for four hands
Many string quartets, songs, vocal duets and cantatas,
    as well as music for unaccompanied chorus
Fantasia on Russian Folk Songs, for piano and
    orchestra.

ARNE, Thomas (Dr. Arne)/1710–1778/Great Britain

1733 (23) *Rosamund,* opera
                Opera of Operas, opera
                Dido and Aenas, opera
1736 (26) *Zara,* incidental music
1738 (28) *Comus,* a masque
1740 (30) *Alfred,* a masque (in which occurs "Rule,
                  Britannia")
                The Judgment of Paris, opera

1743 (33) *Eliza*, opera
            Britannia, a masque
1744 (34) *Abel*, oratorio
1750 (40) *p.* Seven trio sonatas for two violins with
            figured bass
1762 (52) *Artaxerxes*, opera
            Love in a Village, pasticcio
1764 (54) *Judith*, oratorio (possibly 1761)
            Olimpiade, opera
1775 (65) *Caractacus*

ARNELL, Richard/b.1917/Great Britain

1939 (22) String Quartet No. 1
1940 (23) Violin Concerto
1941 (24) String Quartet No. 2
1942 (25) Symphony No. 2
1943 (26) Symphony No. 1
1944 (27) Symphony No. 3
1945 (28) String Quartet No. 3
1946 (29) Piano Trio
            Piano Concerto
1947 (30) *Punch and the Child*, ballet
            Harpsichord Concerto
1948 (31) Symphony No. 4
1950 (33) Symphony No. 5
            String Quintet
1951 (34) *Harlequin in April*, ballet
            String Quartet No. 4
1953 (36) *The Great Detective*, ballet
            Lord Byron, a symphonic portrait
1955 (38) *Love in Transit*, opera
1956 (39) *Landscape and Figures*, for orchestra
1957 (40) *The Angels*, ballet
1958 (41) *Moonflowers*, opera
1959 (42) *Paralyzed Princess*, operetta
1961 (44) Brass Quintet
1962 (45) String Quartet No. 5
1963 (46) *Musica Pacifica*
1966 (49) *Robert Flaherty*, a symphonic portrait
1967 (50) *Sections*, for piano and orchestra

1968 (51) *Food of Love*, overture
Nocturne "Prague-1968", for mixed media
1971 (54) *I Think of All Soft Limbs*, for mixed media
1973 (56) *Astronaut One*, for mixed media

ARNOLD, Malcolm/b.1921/Great Britain

1943 (22) *Beckus the Dandipratt*, overture
Larch Trees, symphonic poem
1944 (23) Horn Concerto
Variations on a Ukrainian Folksong, for
piano
1946 (25) Symphony for strings
1947 (26) Violin Sonata No. 1
Viola Sonata
Children's Suite, for piano
1948 (27) *The Smoke*, overture
Festival Overture
Symphonic Suite
Sonatina for flute and piano
1949 (28) Clarinet Concerto
1950 (29) Symphony No. 1
Serenade for small orchestra
Eight English Dances
String Quartet No. 1
1951 (30) *Sussex*, overture
Concerto for piano duet and strings
Sonatina in three movements for clarinet
and piano
Sonatina in three movements for oboe and
piano
1952 (31) *Curtain Up*
Three Shanties for wind quintet
1953 (32) Symphony No. 2
Oboe Concerto
Homage to the Queen, ballet
Violin Sonata No. 2
Sonatina for recorder and piano
1954 (33) Harmonica Concerto
Concerto for organ and orchestra
Concerto for flute and strings

Sinfonietta No. 1, for two oboes, two
    horns and strings
"The Tempest", incidental music

1955 (34) *Tam O'Shanter*, overture
Little Suite for Orchestra, No. 1
John Clare Cantata, for voices and piano
    duet
Serenade for guitar and strings

1956 (35) *The Dancing Master*, opera
The Open Window, opera
Solitaire, ballet suite
A Grand Overture, for orchestra

1957 (36) *Toy Symphony*
Four Scottish Dances, for orchestra
Symphony No. 3

1958 (37) Sinfonietta No. 2, for flutes, horns and
    strings

1959 (38) Guitar Concerto
Oboe Quartet
"Five Songs of William Blake", for voice
    and strings

1960 (39) Symphony No. 4
Rinaldo and Armida, ballet
Song of Simeon, nativity play, with chorus,
    brass, harp, percussion, celesta and
    strings

1961 (40) Symphony No. 5
Divertimento No. 2, for full orchestra

1962 (41) Concerto for two violins and strings

1963 (42) Little Suite for Orchestra, No. 2

1964 (43) Sinfonietta No. 3, for strings and wind
Water Music

1965 (44) Fantasy, for bassoon
Fantasy, for clarinet
Fantasy, for horn
Fantasy, for flute
Fantasy, for oboe

1967 (46) Symphony No. 6
Peterloo, for orchestra
Trevelyan Suite, for wind band
Concert Piece, for piano and percussion

1973 (52) Symphony No. 7

AUBER, Daniel/1782–1871/France

1828 (46) *Muette de Portici* (also called *Masaniello*), opera
1830 (48) *Fra Diavolo*, opera
1835 (53) *The Bronze Horse*, opera (revised 1857)
1837 (55) *Domino Noir*, opera
1841 (59) *Les Diamants de la couronne*, opera
1846 (64) fp. *Manon Lescaut*, opera
1858 (76) p. Piano Trio in D major, Op. 1

AUBERT, Louis/1877–1969/France

1892 (15) "Sous bois", song
1894 (17) "Vielle chanson Espagnole"
1896 (19) *Rimes tendres*, song cycle
1897 (20) *Les Noces d'Apollon et d'Urainie*, cantata
1899 (22) Fantaisie for piano and orchestra
1900 (23) "Suite Brève", for two pianos
         (orchestrated and revised 1913)
        "Trois esquisses", for piano
        "La Lettre", vocal work
1902 (25) *La Légende du Sang*
1903 (26) *La Momie*, ballet
1904 (27) *Chrysothemis*, ballet
        The Blue Forest, opera (1904–10)
1908 (31) *Crépuscules d'Automne*, song cycle
1911 (34) *Nuit Mauresque* (possibly 1907)
1913 (36) *Sillages*, three pieces for piano
1917 (40) *Six poèmes Arabes* (possibly 1907)
        Tu es Patrus, for chorus and organ
1919 (42) *La Habanera*, symphonic poem
1921 (44) *Dryade*, symphonic poem
1923 (46) *La nuit ensorcelée*, ballet
1925 (48) *Capriccio*, for violin and orchestra
1927 (50) p. *Noel Pastoral*, for piano and orchestra
        p. Violin Sonata in D minor and D major
1930 (53) *Feuilles d'images*
1937 (60) *Les fêtes d'été*
1947 (70) *Offrande*

1948 (71) *Le Tombeau de Chateaubriande*
1952 (76) *Cinéma*

BACH, Carl Phillip Emmanuel/1714–1788/Germany

1731 (17) Trio in B minor
1742 (28) *Prussian* Sonata
1743 (29) Clavier Sonata, *Wurtemburgian*
1747 (33) Sonata in D major
1762 (48) Harp Sonata in B minor
1770 (56) *Passion Cantata*
              Solfeggio in C minor
              Duo in E minor
1773 (59) Fantasia in C minor
1775 (61) *The Israelites in the Wilderness*, oratorio
1780 (66) Symphony in F major
1787 (73) *The Resurrection and Ascension of Jesus,*
              oratorio
1788 (74) Concerto in E♭, for harpsichord,
              fortepiano and strings
              Quartet in G major

C.P.E. Bach's works include 210 solo clavier pieces,
52 concertos with orchestral accompaniment, 22
passions, many cantatas, sonatas for violin and piano,
and trios.

BACH, Johann Christian/1735–1782/Germany

1761 (26) *fp. Artaserse*, opera
              fp. Catone in Utica, opera
1762 (27) *fp. Allessandro nell'Indie,* opera
1763 (28) *Orione,* opera
              Zanaida, opera
1765 (30) *Adriano in Siria,* opera
1767 (32) *Carattaco,* opera
1770 (35) *Gioas, re di Giuda,* oratorio
1772 (37) *Endimione,* cantata
              Temisocle, opera
1776 (41) *Lucio Silla,* opera
1779 (44) *Amadis des Gaules,* opera

J.C. Bach also composed symphonies, opera overtures, concertos, sextets, quintets, quartets, trios, piano and violin sonatas, violin duets, piano sonatas, military marches, etc.

BACH, Johann Sebastian/1685–1750/Thuringia (Germany)

1700–08 (15–23) Five Fantasies in Bm: C: Cm: G: G for organ

Fantasy and Fugue in A minor for organ

Three Fugues in Cm: D: G for organ

Four Preludes in Am: C: C: G for organ

Four Preludes and Fugues in Am: C: Cm: Em (Short) for organ

Toccata and Fugue in E for organ

Variations on Chorales (Partitas) for organ:

    1) "Christ, der du bist der helle Tag"

    2) "O Gott, du frommer Gott"

    3) "Sei gegrüsset, Jesu gütig"

Fantasy in C minor for clavier

Fantasy (on a Rondo) in C minor for clavier

Fughetta in C minor for clavier

Five Fugues in C: Cm: Dm: Dm: Em for clavier

Two Preludes (Fantasies) in Am: Cm for clavier

Four Preludes and Fughettas in Dm: Em: F: G for clavier

Prelude and Fugue in A minor for clavier

Sonata in A minor (one movement) for clavier

Five Toccatas in D: Dm: Em: G: Gm for clavier

*c.***1704** (*c.*19) Sonata in D for clavier

*c.***1705** (*c.*20) *Quodlibet,* for four voices and continuo

1708–17 (23–32) "Alla breve pro organo pleno" in D for organ

Four organ concertos (after Vivaldi and others) in Am: C: C: G

Two Fantasies and Fugues in Cm: Gm
for organ
Fantasy in C minor for organ
Four Fugues in Bm: Cm: G "Jig":
Gm for organ
"Passacaglia" in C minor for organ
"Pastorale" in F for organ
Nine Preludes and Fugues in A: Am
(Great): C: Cm (Great): D: Fm: G
(Great): Gm for organ
Eight Short Preludes and Fugues in C:
Dm: Em: F: G: Gm: Am: B♭ for organ
Four Toccatas and Fugues in C: Dm
(Dorian): Dm: F for organ
Three Trios in Cm: Dm: F (Aria) for
organ
Fantasy in G minor for clavier
Fantasy (Prelude) in A minor for clavier
Five Fugues in A: A: A (on a theme by
Albinoni): Am: Bm for clavier
Suite in A minor for clavier
Suite in E♭ for clavier
Suite ("Ouverture") in F for clavier
*c.*1714 (*c.*29) "Canzona" in D minor for organ
1717 (32) Orgelbüchlein, for organ
1717–23 (32–38) Violin Concerto in A minor with
strings (& continuo)
Violin Concerto in D with strings (&
continuo)
Concerto in D minor for two violins with
strings (& continuo)
Fugue in G minor for violin and continuo
Sonata in E minor for violin and continuo
Sonata in G for violin and continuo
Three sonatas for flute and continuo:
No. 1 in C. No. 2 in E minor. No. 3
in E
Sonata in C for two violins and continuo
Sonata in C minor for flute, violin and
continuo (?1717–23)
Sonata in G for flute, violin and continuo
Sonata in G for two flutes and continuo

Three Sonatas for clavier and flute:
No. 1 in B minor. No. 2 in E♭. No. 3
in A minor
Three Sonatas for clavier and viola da
gamba: No. 1 in G. No. 2 in D. No. 3
in G minor
Six Sonatas for clavier and violin: No. 1
in B minor. No. 2 in A. No. 3 in E.
No. 4 in C minor. No. 5 in F minor.
No. 6 in G
Suite in A for clavier and violin
Fantasy and Fugue in A minor for clavier
Twelve Little Preludes, for clavier
Prelude and Fugue in A minor for clavier
Six Preludes for Beginners, for clavier
Suite in D for clavier (possibly not by
Bach)
Two Toccatas in Cm: F♯m for clavier

c.1720 (c.35) Six Sonatas (Partitas) for solo violin:
No. 1 in G minor. No. 2 in A minor.
No. 3 in C. No. 4 in B minor. No. 5
in D minor. No. 6 in E
Six Suites (Sonatas) for solo cello:
No. 1 in G. No. 2 in D minor. No. 3 in
C. No. 4 in E♭. No. 5 in C minor. No. 6
in D

1720 (35) "Clavierbüchlein vor Wilhelm Friedemann
Bach"

1720–23 (35–38) Chromatic Fantasy and Fugue, in
D minor for clavier

1721 (36) The "Brandenburg" Concerti:
No. 1 in F for violino piccolo, three
oboes, two horns, bassoon, strings
(& continuo)
No. 2 in F for violin, flute, oboe,
trumpet, strings (& continuo)
No. 3 in G for strings (& continuo)
No. 4 in G for violin, two flutes, strings
(& continuo)
No. 5 in D for clavier, violin, flute,
strings (& continuo)
No. 6 in B♭ for strings (without violins
and continuo)

1722 (37) "Clavierbüchlein vor Anna Magdalena
Bachin"
Six Suites ("French"), in Dm: Cm: Bm:
Eb: G: E for clavier (*c*.1722)
The Well-Tempered Clavier, Book I
1723 (38) Magnificat in D, for solo voices, chorus,
orchestra and continuo (?1723)
Motet: "Jesu, meine Freude", for five-part
chorus
Passion according to St. John, for soprano,
contralto, tenor and bass soli, chorus,
organ and continuo
"Sanctus" in D, for eight-part chorus,
orchestra and organ (*c*.1723)
Five Preludes and Fugues, in Bm (Great):
C (Great): Dm: Eb (St. Anne): Em
(Great or "The Wedge") (1723–39)
Variations on Chorale (Partita) "Vom
Himmel hoch da Komm' ich her"
(1723–50)
1725 (40) "Notenbuch vor Anna Magdalena
Bachin", for clavier
Five songs from Anna Magdalena Bach's
"Notenbuch"
Six Suites ("English"), in A: Am: Gm:
F: Em: Dm for clavier
***c*.1726** (*c*.41) Motet: "Fürchte dich nicht", for eight-
part chorus
1727–36 (42–51) Concerto in C for two claviers with
strings
Concerto in C minor for two claviers with
strings (identical to the concerto for
two violins in D minor, 1717–23)
Concerto in C minor for two claviers with
strings
1729 (44) Motet: "Der Geist hilft unsrer Schwachheit
auf", for eight-part chorus with
accompaniment
Passion according to St. Matthew, for
soprano, contralto, tenor and bass soli,
double chorus, double orchestra and
continuo

1729–33 (44–48) Six sonatas (trios) in E♭: Cm:
Dm: Em: C: G for organ

1729–36 (44–51) Clavier Concerto in A with strings
(& continuo)

Clavier Concerto in D with strings
(& continuo) (identical to violin
concerto in E)

Clavier Concerto in D minor with strings
(& continuo) (probably originally
a violin concerto)

Clavier Concerto in E with strings
(& continuo)

Clavier Concerto in F with two flutes,
strings (& continuo) (identical to
Brandenburg Concerto No. 4 in G)

Clavier Concerto in F minor with strings
(& continuo)

Clavier Concerto in G minor with strings
(& continuo) (identical to violin
concerto in A minor)

*c.***1730** (*c.*45) Concerto in A minor for clavier, flute
and violin with strings

1731 (46) Six Partitas for clavier, in B♭: Cm: Am:
D: G: Em

*c.***1733** (*c.*48) Concerto in C for three claviers with
strings

Concerto in D minor for three claviers
with strings

Concerto in A minor for four claviers with
strings (transcription of Concerto for
four violins by Vivaldi)

1733–?38 (48–?53) Mass in B minor for two
sopranos, contralto, tenor, bass, chorus,
orchestra and continuo

1734 (49) Christmas Oratorio (six cantatas) for solo
voices, chorus, orchestra and organ

1735 (50) Concerto in the Italian Style, for clavier,
in F

Ascension Oratorio (Cantata No. 11
"Lobet Gott in seinen Reichen")
(1735–36)

Partita (Ouverture) in B minor for clavier

1736 (51)   Easter Oratorio for solo voices, chorus, orchestra and organ

*c.***1737–40** (*c.*52–55) Lutheran Masses for solo voices, chorus, orchestra and organ: No. 1 in F: No. 2 in Gm: No. 3 in Am: No. 4 in G

*c.***1738** (*c.*53)   Fantasy (with unfinished Fugue) in C minor for clavier

1739 (54)   Catechism Preludes (Clavierübung, Vol. III):

      1)   Kyrie: Christie: Kyrie
      2)   do.   ("alio modo")
      3)   Allein Gott in der Höh' sei Ehr'
      4)   do.
      5)   do.   (fughetta)
      6)   Dies sind die heil'gen zehn Gebot'
      7)   do.   (fughetta)
      8)   Wir glauben all' an einem Gott
      9)   do.   (fughetta "Giant" fugue)
    10)   Vater unser in Himmelreich
    11)   do.
    12)   Christ unser Herr zum Jordan kam
    13)   do.
    14)   Aus tiefer Not schrei ich zu dir
    15)   do.
    16)   Jesus Christ unser Heiland
    17)   do.   (fugue)

Clavier Duets (two-part pieces for one player)

1742 (57)   Aria with thirty variations, "Goldberg Variations" for double-keyboard harpsichord

1744 (59)   *The Well-Tempered Clavier,* Book II

1747 (62)   *A Musical Offering,* for flute and violin, with continuo:
      "Ricercare a tre voci"
      "Canon perpetuus super thema regium"
      "Canones diversi 1–5"
      "Fuga canonica in Epidiapente"
      "Ricercare a sei voci"
      Two canons

*c.***1747–50** (*c.*62–65)   Schübler's Book, for organ

1748–50 (63–65)   *The Art of Fugue,* for unspecified instruments:

<pre>
          1–14 Contrapunctus I–XIV
         15–18 Four Canons
         19–20 Two Fugues for two keyboards
            21 Unfinished Fugue on three
                  subjects
</pre>
dates unknown: Overtures (Suites):
<pre>
          1) in C for woodwind, strings
                (& continuo)
          2) in B minor for flute, strings
                (& continuo)
          3) in D for oboes, bassoons, trumpets,
                timpani, strings (& continuo)
          4) in D for oboes, bassoons, trumpets,
                timpani, strings (& continuo)
</pre>
Bach also composed:
2 psalms:
  "Lobet den Herrn, alle Heiden", for four-part
    chorus
  "Singet dem Herrn ein neues Lied", for eight-part
    chorus
Fantasy and Fugue in A minor for clavier, after 1717
Prelude and Fugue in E♭ for clavier, after 1723
198 church cantatas
23 secular cantatas
Shorter keyboard works, including 15 two-part
inventions and 15 "symphonies", known today as
three-part inventions.

BALAKIREV, Mily/1837–1910/Russia

1852 (15) *Grand Fantaisie on Russian Folksongs,*
                  for piano and orchestra
               Septet for flute, clarinet, strings and piano
1854 (17) String Quartet, *Quatour original russe*
                  (1854–55)
*c.***1855** (*c.*18) Piano Concerto No. 1 in F♯ minor
               "Three Forgotten Songs"
1855–6 (18) Octet for flute, oboe, horn, strings and
                  piano
1858 (21) Overture on Russian Themes
1858–65 (21–28) Twenty songs

                        17

1861 (24) Piano Concerto No. 2 begun; resumed
               1909; completed by Liadov
1866–98 (29–61) Symphony No. 1 in C major
1867 (30) *Overture on Czech themes*
              Thamar, symphonic poem (1867–82)
1869 (32) *fp. Islamey*, for piano
1884 (47) *Russia*, symphonic poem
1895–96 (58) Ten songs
1903–04 (66) Ten songs
1905 (68) Piano Sonata in B minor
1907–08 (70) Symphony No. 2 in D minor
1910 (73) Suite on pieces by Chopin

BALFE, Michael/1808–1870/Great Britain

1829 (21) *I rivali de se stesso*, opera
1830 (22) *Un avvertimento ai gelosi*, opera
1833 (25) *Enrico IV al Passo della Marna*, opera
1835 (27) *The Siege of Rochelle*, opera
1836 (28) *Maid of Artois*, opera (based on *Manon
              Lescaut*)
1837 (29) *Catherine Grey*, opera
              Joan of Arc, opera
1838 (30) *Falstaff*, opera
              Diadeste, opera
1841 (33) *Keolanthe*, opera
1843 (35) *The Bohemian Girl*, opera
              Geraldine, opera
1844 (36) *The Castle of Aymon*, opera
              Daughter of St. Mark, opera
1845 (37) *The Enchantress*, opera
1846 (38) *The Bondman*, opera
1847 (39) *Maid of Honour*, opera
1852 (44) *The Devil's in it*, opera
              The Sicilian Bride, opera
1857 (49) *Rose of Castille*, opera
1860 (52) *Bianca*, opera
1861 (53) *The Puritan's Daughter*, opera
1863 (55) *The Armourer of Nantes*, opera
              Blanche de Nevers, opera
1864 (56) *The Sleeping Queen*, opera
1874 (posthumous) *fp. Il Talismano*, opera

BANTOCK, Sir Granville/1868–1946/Great Britain

1892 (24) *Aegypt,* ballet
              Fire Worshippers
1899 (31) String Quartet in C minor
1900 (32) Tone Poem No. 1, *Thalaba the Destroyer*
1901 (33) Tone Poem No. 2, *Dante*
              Tone Poem No. 3, *Fifine at the Fair*
1902 (34) Tone Poem No. 4, *Hudibras*
              Tone Poem No. 5, *Witch of Atlas*
              Tone Poem No. 6, *Lalla Rookh*
              The Time Spirit
1903 (35) Serenade for four horns
1906 (38) *Omar Khayyam*
1915 (47) *Hebridean* Symphony
1918 (50) *Pibroch,* for cello and piano (or harp)
1919 (51) Viola Sonata in F major, *Colleen*
1922 (54) *Song of Songs*
1923 (55) *Pagan* Symphony
1924 (56) *The Seal-woman,* opera
1928 (60) *Pilgrim's Progress*
1937 (69) *King Solomon*
1938 (70) *Aphrodite in Cyprus,* symphonic ode
Bantock also composed a setting of Swinburne's
"Atalanta in Calydon"; "Fantastic Poem" and "Celtic
Poem", for cello and piano; "Hamabdil", for cello and
harp (or piano).

BARBER, Samuel/b.1910/U.S.A.

1929 (19) Serenade for string orchestra, or string
              quartet
1931 (21) *School for Scandal,* overture
              Dover Beach, for voice and string quartet
1932 (22) Cello Sonata
1933 (23) *Music for a Scene from Shelley*
1936 (26) Symphony No. 1, in one movement
              String Quartet No. 1
              Adagio for Strings, arranged from String
                  Quartet No. 1
1937 (27) First Essay for Orchestra

1939 (29)	Violin Concerto
1940 (30)	*A Stop-watch and an Ordnance Map,* for male chorus and orchestra
1942 (32)	Second Essay for Orchestra
1944 (34)	Symphony No. 2 (revised 1947)
	Capricorn Concerto, for flute, oboe, trumpet and strings
	Excursions, for piano
1945 (35)	Cello Concerto
1946 (36)	*Medea: The Cave of the Heart,* ballet
1947 (37)	*Knoxville: Summer of 1915,* ballet suite for voice and orchestra
1948 (38)	Piano Sonata
	String Quartet No. 2
1953 (43)	*Souvenirs,* ballet suite
1954 (44)	*Prayers of Kierkegaard,* for soprano, chorus and orchestra
1956 (46)	*Summer Music,* for woodwind quintet
1958 (48)	*Vanessa,* opera (libretto by Gian-Carlo Menotti, *q.v.*)
1959 (49)	*A Hand of Bridge,* opera, for four solo voices and chamber-orchestra
1960 (50)	*Toccata Festiva,* for organ and orchestra
1961 (51)	*Dies Natali,* choral preludes for Christmas on "Silent Night"
1962 (52)	Piano Concerto
	Andromache's Farewell, for soprano and orchestra
1966 (56)	*Antony and Cleopatra,* opera
1969 (59)	*Despite and Still,* song cycle
1971 (61)	*The Lovers,* for baritone, chorus and orchestra
1973 (63)	*fp.* String Quartet

BARTÓK, Béla/1881–1945/Hungary

1902 (21)	Scherzo for orchestra
1903 (22)	*Kossuth,* tone poem
	Violin Sonata
1904 (23)	*Rhapsody,* for piano and orchestra
	Burlesca
	Piano Quintet

1905 (24) Suite No. 1
Suite No. 2 (1905–07, revised 1943)
1907 (26) Hungarian Folksongs, for piano
1908 (27) *Portraits,* for orchestra (1907–08)
Violin Concerto No. 1
String Quartet No. 1 in A minor
1909 (28) *For Children,* for piano
1910 (29) Four Dirges, for piano
Deux Images, for orchestra
1911 (30) *Duke Bluebeard's Castle,* opera
Allegro Barbaro, for piano
Three Burlesques, for piano
1912 (31) Four Pieces for Orchestra
1914 (33) Fifteen Hungarian Peasant Songs
(1914–17)
The Wooden Prince, ballet (1914–16)
1915 (34) Roumanian Folk Dances, for piano
Twenty Roumanian Christmas Songs
String Quartet No. 2 in A minor
(1915–17)
1916 (35) Suite for piano
1918–19 (37) *The Miraculous Mandarin,* ballet
1920 (39) Eight Improvisations on Peasant Songs
1921 (40) Violin Sonata No. 1 (Atonal)
1922 (41) Violin Sonata No. 2
1923 (42) Dance Suite, for orchestra
1924 (43) *Five Village Scenes* (Slovak folk songs),
for female voices and piano
1926 (45) Piano Concerto No. 1
Cantata Profana, for tenor and baritone
soli, mixed chorus and orchestra
Piano Sonata
Nine Little Pieces, for piano
Out of Doors, suite
Three Village Scenes, for chorus and
orchestra
Mikrokosmos, Books I–VI, 150 small
pieces for piano, arranged in order of
technical difficulty (1926–37)
1927 (46) String Quartet No. 3
1928 (47) *Rhapsody* No. 1 and No. 2, for violin and
orchestra

Rhapsody No. 1, for cello and piano
String Quartet No. 4
1930–31 (49) Piano Concerto No. 2
1931 (50) Forty-four Duos for two violins
1934 (53) String Quartet No. 5
1936 (55) *Music for Strings, Percussion and Celesta*
Petite Suite, for piano
1938 (57) Violin Concerto No. 2
Sonata for two pianos and percussion
Contrasts, trio for clarinet, violin and piano, the violinist using two instruments, one of normal tuning, the other tuned: G♯, D, A, E♭
1939 (58) Divertimento for strings
String Quartet No. 6
1941 (60) Concerto for two pianos and percussion (also orchestra)
1943 (62) *Concerto for Orchestra*
1944 (63) Sonata for unaccompanied violin
1945 (64) Piano Concerto No. 3
Viola Concerto

BAX, Sir Arnold/1883–1953/Great Britain

1906 (23) Piano Trio in E major, in one movement
1907 (24) *Fatherland,* for two sopranos, chorus and orchestra
1908 (25) *Lyrical Interlude,* for string quartet
1909 (26) Christmas Carol
Enchanted Summer, for tenor, chorus and orchestra
1910 (27) *In the Faery Hills,* symphonic poem
Violin Sonata No. 1 (1910–15)
1912 (29) *Christmas Eve on the Mountains,* for orchestra
Nympholept, for orchestra
1913 (30) Scherzo for orchestra
1914–15 (31) Piano Quintet in G minor
1915 (32) *Légende,* for violin and piano
Violin Sonata No. 2
The Maiden with the Daffodils, for piano
Winter Waters, for piano

1916 (33)   *Ballade,* for violin and piano
             Dream in Exile, for piano
             Elegy, trio for flute, viola and harp
1917 (34)   Symphonic Variations for piano and
                orchestra
             Tintagel, symphonic poem
             November Woods, symphonic poem
             An Irish Elegy, for English horn, harp
                and strings
             Moy Well (An Irish Tone Poem), for
                two pianos
             Between Dusk and Dawn, ballet
1918 (35)   String Quartet No. 1 in G major
             Folk Tale, for cello and piano
1919 (36)   Piano Sonata No. 1 in F♯ minor
             Piano Sonata No. 2 in G major
             Harp Quintet in F minor
             What the Minstrel Told Us, for piano
1920 (37)   *The Truth About Russian Dancers,* ballet
             The Garden of Fand, symphonic poem
             Summer Music, for orchestra
             Phantasy, for viola and orchestra
             Four pieces for piano: "Country Tune",
                "Hill Tune", "Lullaby" and
                "Mediterranean"
1921 (38)   Mater Ora Filium, for unaccompanied
                chorus
             Of a Rose I Sing, for small chorus, harp,
                cello and bass
             Viola Sonata
             Symphony No. 1 in E♭ major and minor
                (1921–22)
1922 (39)   *The Happy Forest,* symphonic poem
1923 (40)   *Romantic Overture,* for small orchestra
             Saga Fragment, for piano, strings, trumpet
                and cymbals
             Piano Quartet
             Oboe Quintet in G
             Cello Sonata in E minor
1924 (41)   *Cortège,* for orchestra
             Symphony No. 2 in E minor and C major
                (1924–25)

	String Quartet No. 2 in E minor (1924–25)
1927 (44)	Violin Sonata No. 3 in G minor
1928 (45)	Sonata for viola and harp
	Sonata for two pianos
	Symphony No. 3 in C major (1928–29)
1929 (46)	*Legend,* for viola and piano
	Overture, Elegy and Rondo, for orchestra
1930 (47)	Symphony No. 4 in E♭ (1930–31)
	Winter Legends, for piano and orchestra
	Overture to a Picaresque Comedy, for orchestra
1931 (48)	*The Tale the Pine Trees Knew,* symphonic poem
	Nonet for flute, oboe, clarinet, harp and strings
	String Quintet in one movement
	Symphony No. 5 in C♯ minor (1931–32)
1932 (49)	*A Northern Ballad,* for orchestra (1932–33)
	Sinfonietta
	Cello Concerto in G minor
	Piano Sonata No. 4 in G major
1933 (50)	Sonatina in D, for cello and piano
1934 (51)	Symphony No. 6 in C major
	Concerto for flute, oboe, harp and string quartet
	Octet for horn, strings and piano
	Clarinet Sonata in D major
1935 (52)	*The Morning Watch,* for chorus and orchestra
	Overture to Adventure, for orchestra
1936 (53)	Concerto for bassoon (or viola), harp and string sextet
	String Quartet No. 3 in F major
1937 (54)	Violin Concerto
	A London Pageant, for orchestra
	Northern Ballad No. 2, for orchestra
1939 (56)	Symphony No. 7 in A♭
1943 (60)	*Work in Progress,* overture
1944 (61)	*Legend,* for orchestra
1945 (62)	*Legend-Sonata,* for cello and piano in F♯ minor

1946 (63)   Te Deum, for chorus and organ
             Gloria, for chorus and organ
1947 (64)   *Epitholamium,* for chorus and organ
             Two Fanfares for the wedding of Princess
                Elizabeth and Prince Philip
             Morning Song, for piano and small
                orchestra
1950 (67)   Concertante for orchestra with piano
                (left hand), written for Harriet Cohen
1953 (70)   Coronation March

BEDFORD, David/b.1937/Great Britain

1963 (26)   *Two Poems,* for chorus
             Piece for Mo, for percussion, vibraphone,
                accordion, three violins, cello and
                double bass
1964–65 (27)   *A Dream of the Seven Lost Stars,* for
                mixed chorus and chamber ensemble
1965 (28)   *This One for You,* for orchestra
             Music for Albion Moonlight, for soprano
                and instruments
             "O Now the Drenched Land Awakes",
                for baritone and piano duet
1966 (29)   *That White and Radiant Legend,* for
                soprano, speaker and instruments
             Piano Piece I
1967 (30)   *Five,* for two violins, viola and two cellos
             Trona for 12, for instrumental ensemble
             18 Bricks Left on April 21st, for two
                electric guitars
1968 (31)   *Gastrula,* for orchestra
             Pentomino, for wind quintet
             Piano Piece II
             "Come In Here Child", for soprano and
                amplified piano
1969 (32)   *The Tentacles of the Dark Nebula,* for
                tenor and instruments
1970 (33)   *The Garden of Love,* for instrumental
                ensemble
             The Sword of Orion, for instrumental
                ensemble

1971 (34) *Star Clusters, Nebulae and Places in Devon,* for mixed double chorus and brass

Nurse's Song with Elephants, for ten acoustic guitars and singer

With 100 Kazoos, for instrumental ensemble and one hundred kazoos played by the public

"Some Stars Above Magnitude 2.9", for soprano and piano

1972 (35) *Holy Thursday with Squeakers,* for soprano and instruments

When I Heard the Learned Astronomer, for tenor and instruments

An Easy Decision, for soprano and piano

Spillihpnerak, for viola

1973 (36) *A Horse, His Name Was Hunry Fencewaver Walkins,* for instruments

Jack of Shadows, for solo viola and instruments

Pancakes, with Butter, Maple Syrup and Bacon and the T.V. Weatherman, for wind quintet

Variations on a Rhythm by Mike Oldfield, for percussion (three players, eighty-four instruments and conductor)

1974 (37) *Star's End,* for rock instruments and orchestra

Twelve Hours of Sunset, for mixed choir and orchestra

The Golden Wine is Drunk, for sixteen solo voices

Because He Liked to be at Home, for tenor (doubling recorder) and harp

---

BEETHOVEN, Ludwig van/1770–1827/Germany

1780 (10) Nine variations on a March by Dressler, in C minor for piano, Op. 176

1781 (11) "Schilderung eines Mädchen", song, Op. 229

1782–1802 (12–32) Seven Bagatelles for piano,
in E♭: C: F: A: C: D: A♭, Op. 33
1783 (13) Menuet in E♭ for piano, Op. 165
p. Three piano sonatas, in E♭: Fm: D,
Op. 161 (composed very early)
1784 (14) *p.* "An einem Säugling", song, Op. 230
p. Rondo, allegretto in A major, for
piano, Op. 164
1785 (15) Piano Quartets No. 1–3 in E♭: D: C,
Op. 152
Piano Trio No. 9 in E♭, Op. 153
Prelude in F minor, for piano, Op. 166
1786 (16) Trio in G major, for piano, flute and
bassoon, Op. 259
1789 (19) Two preludes through all twelve major
keys, for piano or organ, Op. 39
1790 (20) "Musik zu einem Ritterballet", Op. 149
Twenty-four variations on Righini's air
"Venni amore", for piano, Op. 177
Cantata on the death of Emperor Joseph
II, Op. 196a
Cantata on the ascension of Leopold II
"Er schlummert", Op. 196b
1791 (21) Thirteen variations on Dittersdorf's air
"Es war einmal", Op. 178
1792 (22) Allegro and menuetto in G major, for two
flutes, Op. 258
1793 (23) *p.* Twelve variations in F major on "Se
vuol ballare", for violin and piano,
Op. 156
1794 (24) Trio for two oboes and English horn,
Op. 87
Rondo allegro in G major, for violin
and piano, Op. 155
p. Variations in G major on a theme by
Count von Waldenstein, for piano
(four hands), Op. 159
1795 (25) *p.* Three piano trios, in E♭: G: Cm, Op. 1
Piano Concerto No. 2 in B♭, Op. 19
"Adelaide", song, Op. 46
p. Twelve Deutsche Tänze, Op. 140
Six minuets for piano, Op. 167

Six allemandes for violin and piano,
    Op. 171
p. Nine variations on Paisello's air "Quant
    è più bello", Op. 179
Twelve variations on minuet from ballet
    "Le nozze disturbate", Op. 181
"Der Freie Mann", song, Op. 233
"Die Flamme lodert", opferlied, Op. 234
"Seufer eines Ungeliebten" and
    "Gegenliebe", songs, Op. 254

1796 (26) Twelve variations on a Russian Dance
    from Wianizky's "Waldmachen",
    Op. 182
"Ah, perfido", scena and aria for soprano
    and orchestra, Op. 65
p. Six variations on Paisello's duet "Nel
    cor più", for piano, Op. 180
"Farewell to Vienna's citizens", song,
    Op. 231

1797 (27) *p.* Piano Sonatas No. 1–3 in Fm: A: C,
    Op. 2
p. String Trio in E♭, Op. 3
p. String Quintet in E♭, Op. 4
p. Cello Sonatas No. 1 and 2, Op. 5
p. Sonata in D, for piano (four hands),
    Op. 6
p. Piano Sonata No. 4 in E♭, Op. 7
p. Serenade in D for string trio, Op. 8
Quintet for piano, oboe, clarinet, bassoon
    and horn, Op. 16
p. Rondo for piano, Op. 51
p. Twelve variations in G on "See, the
    conquering hero comes", for cello and
    piano, Op. 157
War Song of the Austrians, Op. 232
Symphony in C, *Jena* (authenticity
    doubtful), Op. 257

1798 (28) *p.* Three string trios, in G: D: Cm, Op. 9
p. Piano Sonatas Nos. 5–7, in Cm: F:
    D, Op. 10
p. Trio in E♭ for piano, clarinet (or violin)
    and cello, Op. 11

    p. Twelve variations on "Ein Mädchen"
     for violin and piano, Op. 66
    p. Twelve minuets, Op. 139
    p. Six easy variations in F on a Swiss air,
     for piano or harp, Op. 183
    p. Eight variations in C on Grétry's air
     "Une fièvre brûlante", Op. 184

1799 (29) *p*. Violin Sonatas Nos. 1–3, Op. 12
    p. Piano Sonata No. 8 in Cm, *Pathétique,*
     Op. 13
    p. Piano Sonatas Nos. 9–10 in E: G,
     Op. 14
    p. Seven Ländler Dances, in D, Op. 168
    Ten Variations on Salieri's air "La stessa,
     la stessissima", Op. 185
    p. Seven variations on Wonter's "Kind,
     willst du", Op. 186
    Eight variations on Sussmayer's Trio
     "Tandeln und scherzen", Op. 187
    "Der Wachtelschlag", song, Op. 237

1800 (30) Sonata for piano and horn (or violin),
     Op. 17
    String Quartets No. 1–6 in F: G: D:
     Cm: A: B♭, Op. 18
    Septet in E♭, for violin, viola, horn,
     clarinet, bassoon, cello and double-
     bass, Op. 20
    Symphony No. 1 in C
    Piano Sonata No. 11 in B♭, Op. 22
    Sonata for piano, violin and viola, Op. 23
    Mount of Olives, oratorio, Op. 85
    Piano Concerto No. 3 in C minor, Op. 37
    Air with six variations on "Ich denke
     dein", Op. 160
    Six Very Easy Variations on an original
     theme, for piano, Op. 188

1801 (31) *p*. Piano Concerto No. 1 in C, Op. 15
    p. Violin Sonata No. 5 in F, *Spring,*
     Op. 24
    String Quintet in C, Op. 29
    fp. The Creatures of Prometheus
     (Numbers 1–16) ballet, Op. 43

1802 (32)   *p*. Serenade for flute, violin and viola,
            Op. 25
            p. Piano Sonata No. 12 in A♭, Op. 26
            p. Piano Sonata No. 13 in E♭, *Sonata
            quasi una fantasia,* Op. 27
            p. Piano Sonata No. 14 in C♯ minor,
            Moonlight, Op. 27
            p. Piano Sonata No. 15 in D, *Pastoral,*
            Op. 28
            Violin Sonatas No. 6–8 in A: Cm: G,
            Op. 30
            Six variations in F on an original theme,
            for piano, Op. 32
            Fifteen variations with a fugue on a
            theme from "Prometheus" for piano,
            Op. 35
            Symphony No. 2 in D, Op. 36
            Violin Sonata No. 9, *Kreutzer,* Op. 47
            Two Easy Sonatas (Nos. 19–20) in Gm:
            C for piano, Op. 49
            p. Rondo for piano, Op. 51
            Terzetto, *Tremate,* Op. 116
            Opferleid, Op. 121b
            p. Seven variations on "Bei Mannern"
            for cello and piano, Op. 158
            p. Six Ländler Dances in D (No. 4 in D
            minor), Op. 169
            Piano Sonatas No. 16–18 in C: D: E♭,
            Op. 31 (1802–4)
1803 (33)   Romance in G, for violin and orchestra,
            Op. 40
            p. Six songs for soprano, Op. 48
            Fidelio, opera (commenced 1803, last
            revision 1814), Op. 72
            p. "Das Glück der Freundschaft", song,
            Op. 88
            p. Twelve Kontretänze for orchestra,
            Op. 141
            p. "Zärtliche Liebe", song, Op. 235
            p. "La Partenza", song, Op. 236
            Six songs, Op. 75 (1803–10)
1804 (34)   *p*. Fourteen variations in E♭ for piano
            trio, Op. 44

              p. Three Grand Marches, for piano four
                   hands, Op. 45
              Piano Sonata No. 21, *Waldstein,* Op. 53
              Symphony No. 3, *Eroica,* Op. 55
              Triple Concerto in C for piano, violin,
                   cello and orchestra, Op. 56
              Piano Sonata No. 23 in F minor,
                   Appassionata, Op. 57
              Andante favori in F, for piano, Op. 170
              p. Seven variations on "God save the
                   King", for piano, Op. 189
              p. Five variations on "Rule, Britannia"
                   for piano, Op. 190
1805 (35) *p.* "An die Hoffnung", song, Op. 32
              p. Romance in F for violin and orchestra,
                   Op. 5
              p. Eight songs, Op. 52
              Piano Concerto No. 4 in G, Op. 58
              Symphony No. 5 in C minor, Op. 67
1806 (36) *p.* Piano Sonata No. 22 in F, Op. 54
              Symphony No. 4 in B♭, Op. 60
              Violin Concerto in D (also same
                   arranged for piano and orchestra),
                   Op. 61
              Thirty-two variations in C minor for
                   piano, Op. 191 (1806–07)
1807 (37) *Coriolanus,* overture, Op. 62
              Mass in C, Op. 86
               Leonore No. 1 overture, Op. 138
              "In questa tomba oscura", arietta,
                   Op. 239
              String Quartets Nos. 7–9, *Rasumovsky*
                   in F: Em: C, Op. 59
1808 (38) *p.* "Sehnsucht", songs with piano, Op. 241
1809 (39) *p.* Symphony No. 6 in F, *Pastoral,*
                   Op. 68
              p. Cello Sonata No. 3 in A, Op. 69
              p. Trios Nos. 4–5, for piano, violin and
                   cello, Op. 70
              Piano Concerto No. 5 in E♭, *Emperor,*
                   Op. 73
              String Quartet No. 10 in E♭, *Harp,* Op. 74

Military March in F, Op. 145
p. "Als die Geleibt sich trennan wollt",
    song, Op. 238
"Als mir hoch", song, Op. 242
"Turteltaube", song, Op. 255

1810 (40) *p.* Wind Sextet, Op. 71 (early work)
    p. Six variations in D for piano, Op. 76
    p. Fantasy in G minor for piano, Op. 77
    p. Piano Sonata No. 24 in F♯, Op. 78
    p. Piano Sonata No. 25 in G, Op. 79
    p. Sextet in E♭ for two violins, viola,
        cello and two horns, Op. 81b
    p. Three songs for soprano and piano,
        Op. 83
    Egmont, incidental music, Op. 84
    String Quartet No. 11 in Fm. *Quartett*
        serioso, Op. 95
    p. "Andenken", song, Op. 240
    p. "Welch ein wunderbares Leben", song,
        Op. 243
    p. "Der Frühling entbluhet", song,
        Op. 244
    "Gedenke mein! ich denke dein", song,
        Op. 256

1811 (41) *p.* Choral Fantasia in C minor for piano,
        orchestra and chorus (theme
        Beethoven's song "Gegenliebe"),
        Op. 80
    p. Piano Sonata No. 26 in E♭, *Les Adieux,*
        Op. 81a
    p. Four ariettas and duet, for soprano
        and tenor with piano, Op. 82
    Piano Trio No. 6 in B♭, *Archduke,* Op. 97
    The Ruins of Athens, overture and eight
        numbers, Op. 113
    King Stephen, overture and nine numbers,
        Op. 117
    "O dass ich dir", song, Op. 247

1812 (42) Symphony No. 7 in A, Op. 92
    Symphony No. 8 in F, Op. 93
    Violin Sonata No. 10 in G, Op. 96
    Piano Trio No. 10 in B♭, Op. 154

1813 (43) *Wellington's Victory* (or *Battle of Vittoria*), for orchestra, Op. 91
Triumphal March in C, for orchestra, Op. 143
"Dort auf dem hohen Felsen", song, Op. 248

1814 (44) Polonaise in C, for piano, Op. 89
Piano Sonata No. 27 in E minor, Op. 90
"Merkenstein", duet, Op. 100
Overture in C, *Namensfeier,* Op. 115
Elegiac Song, Op. 118
Der glorreiche Augenblick, cantata, Op. 136
p. "Germania", bass solo, Op. 193
Leonore Prohaska, incidental music, Op. 245
p. Twenty-five Irish songs, Op. 223 (1814–16)
p. Twenty Irish songs, Op. 224 (1814–16)
p. Twelve Irish songs, Op. 225 (1814–16)

1815 (45) Cello Sonatas Nos. 4–5 in C: D, Op. 102
Calm Sea and Prosperous Voyage, for chorus and orchestra, Op. 112
Three Duos, for clarinet and bassoon, Op. 147
p. "Es ist vollbracht", bass solo, Op. 194
Twelve Songs of varied nationality, Op. 228
"Wo bluht das Blumchen", song, Op. 250
Twenty-five Scotch songs for one and sometimes two voices and small orchestra, Op. 108 (1815–16)
"Der stille Nacht", song, Op. 246 (1815–16)

1816 (46) "An die Hoffnung", song, Op. 94
"Wenn ich ein Voglein war", song, Op. 249
An die ferne Geliebte, song cycle, Op. 98
p. "Der Mann van Wort", song, Op. 99
Military March in D, Op. 144

1817 (47) *p.* Piano Sonata No. 28 in A, Op. 101
String Quintet in Cm, (arranged from Op. 1, No. 3), Op. 104

Fugue in D, Op. 137
Song of the Monks, from "William Tell",
    Op. 197
p. Twenty-six Welch Songs, Op. 226
"Nord oder Sud", song, Op. 251
"Lisch aus, mein Licht", song, Op. 252
Symphony No. 9, *Choral,* Op. 125
    (1817–23)

1818 (48) *Missa Solemnis* in D, Op. 123
"Ziemlich Lebhaft" in B♭ for piano,
    Op. 172
Six very easy themes varied, for piano,
    flute or violin, Op. 105 (1818–19)
Piano Sonata No. 29 in B♭,
    Hammerklavier, Op. 106
    (1818–19)
Ten National Themes with Variations,
    for flute or violin and piano, Op. 107
    (1818–20)

1820 (50) Piano Sonata No. 30 in E, Op. 109
Allegro con brio in C, for violin and
    orchestra, Op. 148
"Wenn die Sonne nieder sinket", song,
    Op. 253

1821 (51) Piano Sonata No. 31 in A♭, Op. 110
p. Bagatelles for piano, Op. 119

1822 (52) *Consecration of the House,* overture,
    Op. 124
"The Kiss", arietta, Op. 128
"Bundeslied", Op. 122 (1822–23)

1823 (53) Piano Sonata No. 32 in C minor, Op. 111
Bagatelles for piano, Op. 126
p. Bagatelles for piano, Op. 119
Variations on a Waltz by Diabelli,
    Op. 120
"Minuet of Congratulations", Op. 142
Cantata in E♭, Op. 199

1824 (54) *p. The Ruins of Athens,* march and chorus,
    Op. 114
p. Variations on "Ich bin der Schneider
    Kakadu", Op. 121a
String Quartet No. 12 in E♭, Op. 127

1825 (55)   Great Fugue in E♭ for violins, viola and
                cello, Op. 133
               Rondo a capriccio in G, for piano, Op.
                129 (1825–26)
               String Quartet No. 13 in B♭, *Scherzoso*,
                Op. 130
1826 (56)   String Quartet No. 14 in C♯ minor, Op. 131
               String Quartet No. 15 in A minor, Op. 132
               String Quartet No. 16 in F, Op. 135
               Andante maestoso in C for piano, Op. 174

Other works:

Op. 38	Trio, arranged from Op. 25
Op. 41	Revision of Op. 25
Op. 42	Notturno in D, arranged from Op. 8
Op. 63	Arrangement of Op. 4 for piano trio
Op. 64	Arrangement of Op. 3 for cello and piano
Op. 134	Great Fugue in B♭ for piano (four hands), arrangement of Op. 133
Op. 150	(MS) Sonatina and Adagio in C minor, for mandolin and cembalo
Op. 163	Two sonatinas for piano (doubtful authenticity)
Op. 173	*Für Elise* in A minor, for piano
Op. 195	(no details)
Op. 198	"O Hoffnung", chorus (4 bars), *c.*1818
Op. 201	(no details)
Ops. 203–222	Canons and small incidental pieces
Op. 247a	Another setting of Op. 247

Published posthumously:

1828	Op. 119	Bagatelles for piano
1829	Op. 151	Rondo in B♭ for piano and orchestra
	Op. 146	Rondino in E♭ (composed very early)
1830	Op. 162	Piano Sonata in C, called "Easy"
1831	Op. 192	Eight variations in E♭ on "Ich habe ein kleines Huttchen nur"
1834	Op. 103	Octet in E♭, for two oboes, two clarinets, two horns, two bassoons (original of Op. 4)
1836	Op. 175	Ten cadenzas to the piano concertos
1841	Op. 227	Twelve Scottish Songs
1865	Op. 200	Cantata in E♭, "Graf, graf, lieber graf"

BELLINI, Vicenzo/1801–1835/Italy

1825 (24) *Adelson e Salvina*, opera
             Bianca e Fernando, opera
1827 (26) *Il Pirata*, opera
1829 (28) *La Straniera*, opera
             Zaira, opera
1830 (29) *I Capuleti ed i Montecchi*, opera
1831 (30) *La Sonnambula*, opera
             Norma, opera
1833 (32) *Beatrice di Tenda*, opera
1835 (34) *I Puritani*, opera

BENJAMIN, Arthur/1893–1960/Australia

1920 (27) "Three Impressions", for voice and string
             quartet
1924 (31) *Pastoral Fantasy*, for string quartet
             Sonatina for violin and piano
1925 (32) *Three Mystical Songs*, for unaccompanied
             chorus
1928 (35) *Concerto quasi una fantasia*, for piano
             and orchestra
1931 (38) *The Devil Take Her*, comic opera
1932 (39) Violin Concerto
1933 (40) *Prima Donna*, comic opera
1935 (42) *Heritage*, for orchestra
             Romantic Fantasy, for violin, viola and
             orchestra
1937 (44) *Nightingale Lane*, for two voices and piano
             Overture to an Italian Comedy, for
             orchestra
1938 (45) Two Jamaican Pieces for Orchestra,
             "Jamaican Song" and "Jamaican
             Rumba"
             Sonatina for cello and piano
             Cotillon Suite of English Dance Tunes,
             for orchestra
1940 (47) Sonatina for chamber orchestra
1942 (49) Concerto for oboe and strings

1944–45 (51) Symphony No. 1
1945 (52) *From San Domingo*, for orchestra
           Red River Jig, for orchestra
           Elegy, Waltz and Toccata, for viola and
             orchestra
1946 (53) *Caribbean Dance*, for orchestra
1947 (54) Ballade for strings
1949 (56) *The Tale of Two Cities,* opera (1949–50)
           Valses Caprices, for clarinet (or viola)
             and piano
1951 (58) *Orlando's Silver Wedding*, ballet

BENNETT, Richard Rodney/b.1936/Great Britain

1954 (18) Piano Sonata
           Sonatina for flute
1957 (21) Five Pieces for orchestra
           String Quartet No. 3
           Violin Sonata
           Sonata for solo violin
           Sonata for solo cello
           "Four Improvisations", for violin
1959 (23) *The Approaches of Sleep*
1960 (24) *Journal*, for orchestra
           Calendar, for chamber ensemble
           Winter Music, for flute and piano (also
             for orchestra)
1961 (25) *The Ledges*, one-act opera
           Suite Française, for small orchestra
           Oboe Sonata
1962 (26) *London Pastoral Fantasy*, for tenor and
             chamber orchestra
           Three Elegies, for chorus
           Fantasy for piano
           Sonata No. 2 for solo violin
1964 (28) *The Mines of Sulphur*, opera
           Jazz Calendar, ballet in seven scenes
           Aubade, for orchestra
           String Quartet No. 4
           Nocturnes for piano
1965 (29) Symphony No. 1

Trio for oboe, flute and clarinet
Diversions for piano
1966 (30) *Epithalamion,* for voices and orchestra
Childe Rolande, for voice and piano
1967 (31) *A Penny for a Song,* opera
Symphony No. 2
Wind Quintet
The Music That Her Echo Is, song cycle
1968 (32) Piano Concerto
All the King's Men, children's opera
Crazy Jane, for soprano, clarinet, cello
and piano
1969 (33) *A Garland for Marjory Fleming,* for
soprano and piano
1970 (34) Guitar Concerto
1972 (36) *Commedia* II, for flute, cello and piano
1973 (37) Concerto for Orchestra
Viola Concerto, for viola and chamber
orchestra
Commedia III, for flute/piccolo, oboe/
English horn, bass clarinet, horn,
trumpet, two percussion, piano/celesta,
violin and cello
Commedia IV, for two trumpets, horn,
trombone and tuba
Alba, for organ
Scena I, for piano
Scena II, for cello
1974 (38) *Spells,* for soprano, chorus and orchestra
Love Spells, for soprano and orchestra
Sonnet Sequence, for tenor and strings
Four-piece Suite, divertimento for two
pianos
Time's Whiter Series, for counter-tenor
and lute
1975 (39) Violin Concerto in two movements
Oboe Quartet

BERG, Alban/1885–1935/Austria

1905–08 (20–23) Seven "Frühe-Lieder" for soprano
and piano, or orchestra

1906–08 (21–23) Piano Sonata
1908 (23) *An Leukon*
1909–10 (24) Four Songs for medium voice and
piano
1910 (25) String Quartet
1912 (27) Five Orchestra Songs to Picture Postcard
Texts by Peter Altenberg
1913 (28) Four pieces for clarinet and piano
Three orchestral pieces (1913–14)
1917–21 (32–36) *Wozzeck,* opera
1923–25 (38–40) Chamber Concerto, for piano,
violin and thirteen wind instruments
1925–26 (40) *Lyric Suite,* for string quartet
1928–34 (43–49) *Lulu,* opera
1929 (44) Three pieces for orchestra
Der Wein, concert aria for soprano and
orchestra (possibly 1920)
1935 (50) Violin Concerto, "in memory of an angel"
(i.e. Manon Gropius, eighteen-year-old
daughter of Mahler's widow by her
second husband)

BERIO, Luciano/b.1925/Italy

1936 (11) Pastorale
1946–47 (21) Four Popular Songs, for female voice
and piano
1947 (22) Petite Suite for piano
1949 (24) *Magnificat,* for two sopranos, mixed
chorus and instruments
1950 (25) Concertino for solo clarinet, solo violin,
harp, celeste and strings
Opus Number Zoo, for woodwind quintet
and narrator (revised 1970)
1951 (26) Two pieces for violin and piano
1952 (27) *Allez Hop—story for voice, mime and
dance,* for mezzo-soprano, eight mimes,
ballet and orchestra
Five variations for piano (1952–53)
1953 (28) *Chamber Music,* for female voice, clarinet,
cello and harp
1954 (29) *Nones,* for orchestra

Variations for chamber orchestra
Mutations, electronic music
1956 (31) *Allelujah* I, for orchestra
Allelujah II, for orchestra
String Quartet
Perspectives, electronic music
1957 (32) Divertimento for orchestra (with Bruno
Maderna)
Serenata, for flute and fourteen instruments
El Mar la Mar, for soprano, mezzo-
soprano and seven instruments
Momenti, for electronic sound
1958 (33) *Tempi Concertati,* for flute, violin, two
pianos and other instruments
(1958–59)
Differences, for five instruments and tape
Sequence I, for flute
Theme (Homage to Joyce), electronic
music
1959 (34) *Quaderni* I, II and III from "Epifanie", for
orchestra (1959–63)
1960 (35) *Circles,* for female voice, harp and two
percussion
1961 (36) *Visage,* electronic music with voice
1962 (37) *Passaggio,* messa in scena for soprano, two
choirs and instruments
1963 (38) *Sequence* II, for harp
Sincronie, for string quartet (1963–64)
1965 (40) *Laborintus* II, for voices, instruments and
tape
Rounds, for cembalo
Sequence III, for solo voice
1966 (41) *Il combattimento di Tancredi e Clorinda,*
for soprano, baritone, tenor, three
violins and continuo
Sequence IV, for piano
Sequence V, for trombone
1967 (42) *Rounds,* for piano
Sequence VI, for viola
O King, for voice and five players
1968 (43) Sinfonia
Questo vuol dire che, for three female
voices, small choir and tape

1969 (44) *Opera,* opera in four acts
Sequence VII, for oboe
"The Modification and Instrumentation
    of a Famous Hornpipe as a Merry and
    Altogether Sincere Homage to Uncle
    Alfred", for five instruments

1970 (45) *Memory,* for electric piano and electric
    cembalo

1971 (46) *Bewegung,* for orchestra
Bewegung II, for baritone and orchestra
Ora, for soprano, mezzo-soprano, flute,
    English horn, small chorus and
    orchestra
Amores, for sixteen vocalists and fourteen
    instrumentalists
Agnus, for two sopranos and three
    clarinets
*Autre Fois—Berceuse Canonique pour
    Igor Stravinsky,* for flute, clarinet
    and harp

1972 (47) *E Vó—Sicilian Lullaby,* for soprano and
    instruments
Concerto for two pianos and orchestra
    (1972–73)
Recital I (for Cathy), for mezzo-soprano
    and seventeen instruments

1973 (48) *Still,* for orchestra
Eindrücke, for orchestra
... Points on the Curve to Find ..., for
    piano and twenty-two instruments
Linea, for two pianos, vibraphone and
    marimbaphone

1974 (49) *Per la dolce memoria di quel giorno,*
    ballet
Apres Visage, for orchestra and tape
Chorus, for voices and instruments
Calmo, for soprano and instruments

1975 (50) *Il Malato Immaginario,* incidental music
La Ritirata Notturna di Madrid, for
    orchestra
Sequence VIII, for percussion
Sequence IX, for violin

41

1925 (22) "The Thresher", for medium voice and
                piano
*c.***1933** (*c.*30) Violin Sonata No. 2
1934 (31) Polka, for piano
                Three pieces for two pianos (Polka,
                    Nocturne, Capriccio) (1934–38)
1935 (32) *Jonah,* oratorio
                Overture for Orchestra
                String Quartet No. 1
                "How Love Came In", for medium voice
                    and piano
                Étude, Berceuse and Capriccio, for piano
1936 (33) Five short pieces for piano
1937 (34) *Domini est Terra,* for chorus and
                    orchestra
                Mont Juic—Suite of Catalan Dances,
                    for orchestra (with Britten *q.v.*)
1938 (35) *The Judgement of Paris,* ballet
                Introductions and Allegro, for two
                    pianos and orchestra
1939 (36) Serenade for string orchestra
                Five songs for solo voice and piano
                    (1939–40)
1940 (37) Symphony No. 1
                Sonatina for recorder (flute) and piano
                Four Concert Studies, Set I, for piano
                Five Housman Songs, for tenor and
                    piano
1942 (39) String Quartet No. 2
                Sonatina for violin and piano
1943 (40) Divertimento for orchestra
                String Trio
1944 (41) "Lord, when the Sense of Thy sweet
                    Grace", for mixed choir and organ
1945 (42) Piano Sonata
                Violin Sonata
                Six Preludes for piano
                Festival Anthem for mixed choir and
                    organ
1946 (43) Introduction and Allegro, for solo violin

Nocturne, for orchestra
Five Songs (de la Mare) for high voice
and piano
1947 (44) Piano Concerto
Four Poems of St. Teresa of Avila, for
contralto and strings
Stabat Mater, for six solo voices and
twelve instruments
"The Lowlands of Holland", for low
voice and piano
1948 (45) Concerto for two pianos and orchestra
1949 (46) *Colonus' Praise,* for chorus and orchestra
Three Mazurkas for piano
Scherzo for piano
1950 (47) Sinfonietta for orchestra
Elegy for violin and piano
Toccata for violin and piano
Theme and variations for solo violin
1951 (48) *Gibbons Variations,* for tenor, chorus,
strings and organ
Three Greek Songs, for medium voice
and piano
1952 (49) Flute Concerto
Four Ronsard Sonnets, Set 1, for two
tenors and piano
1953 (50) Suite for orchestra
*c.*1954 (*c.*51) *A Dinner Engagement,* opera in one
act
Nelson, opera in three acts
Trio for violin, horn and piano
Sonatina for piano duet
1955 (52) Concerto for flute, violin, cello and
harpsichord (or piano)
Suite from "Nelson", for orchestra
Sextet for clarinet, horn and string
quartet
Crux fidelis, for tenor and mixed choir
Salve regina, for unison voices and organ
Look up sweet Babe, for soprano and
mixed choir
Concert study in E♭ for piano
1956 (53) *Ruth,* opera in three scenes
1957 (54) Sonatina for guitar

"Sweet was the song", for mixed choir
and organ
1958 (55) Concerto for piano and double string
orchestra
Five poems of W.H. Auden, for medium
voice and piano
1959 (56) Overture for Light Orchestra
Sonatina for two pianos
"So sweet Love seemed", for medium
voice and piano
1960 (57) *A Winter's Tale,* suite for orchestra
Improvisation on a Theme of Falla, for
piano
Prelude and Fugue, for clavichord
Missa Brevis, for mixed choir and organ
"Thou hast made me", for mixed choir
and organ
1961 (58) Concerto for violin and chamber
orchestra
Five pieces for violin and orchestra
1962 (59) Sonatina for oboe and piano
Batter my Heart, for soprano, mixed
choir, organ and chamber orchestra
"Autumn's Legacy", for high voice and
piano
1963 (60) *Four Ronsard Sonnets—Set 2,* for tenor
and orchestra
Justorum Animae, for mixed choir
"Counting the Beats", for high voice and
piano
"Automne", for medium voice and piano
1964 (61) *Diversions,* for eight instruments
"Songs of the Half-light", for high voice
and guitar
Mass for five voices
1965 (62) Partita for chamber orchestra
Three songs for four male voices
1966–68 (63–65) Three pieces for organ
1967 (64) *Castaway,* opera in one act
Signs in the Dark, for mixed choir and
strings
Oboe Quartet
Nocturne for harp

1968 (65)   "The Windhover", for mixed choir
            Theme and Variations for piano duet
1969 (66)   Symphony No. 3
            Windsor Variations, for piano duet
1970 (67)   *Dialogues,* for cello and chamber
            orchestra
            String Quartet No. 3
            Theme and variations for guitar
1971 (68)   "Palm Court Waltz", for orchestra/piano
            duet
            In Memoriam Igor Stravinsky, for string
            quartet
            "Duo", for cello and piano
            Introduction and Allegro, for double-bass
            and piano
            "Chinese Songs", for medium voice and
            piano
1972 (69)   *Four Concert Studies, Set II,* for piano
            Three Latin Motets, for five-part choir
            "Hymn for Shakespeare's Birthday", for
            mixed choir and organ
1973 (71)   Sinfonia Concertante for oboe and
            orchestra
            Antiphon, for string orchestra
            Voices of the Night, for orchestra
1974 (72)   Suite for strings
            Guitar Concerto
            Herrick Songs, for high voices and harp
1975 (73)   Quintet for piano and wind

BERLIOZ, Hector/1803–1869/France

1827 (24)   *Waverley,* overture
            Les Francs-Juges, overture
            La Mort d'Orphée, cantata
1828 (25)   *Herminie,* cantata
1829 (26)   *Cléopâtra,* cantata
            Huit scènes de Faust, cantata
            Irlande, five songs with piano (1829–30)
1830 (27)   *Symphonie Fantastique* (revised 1831)
            Sardanapale, cantata

1831 (28) *Le Corsaire,* overture (revised 1855)
King Lear, overture
1832 (29) *Le Cinq Mai,* cantata (1830–32)
1834 (31) *Harold in Italy,* for viola and orchestra
Sara la baigneuse, for three choirs, with
orchestra
Les Nuits d'été, song cycle for soprano
and orchestra
1837 (34) *Grande Messe des Morts,* requiem
1838 (35) *Benvenuto Cellini,* opera (1834–38)
Roméo et Juliette, dramatic symphony
for solo voices and chorus (1838–39)
1839 (36) *Rêverie and Caprice,* for violin and
orchestra
1840 (37) *Symphonie Funèbre et Triomphale,* for
chorus, strings and military band
1844 (41) *Roman Carnival,* overture (from material
from "Benvenuto Cellini")
1846 (43) *Damnation of Faust,* dramatic cantata
(in which occurs Berlioz's arrangement
of the Rákóczy March)
1848 (45) *La Mort d'Ophelie,* for two-part female
chorus (also for voice and piano)
1854 (51) *L'Enfance du Christ,* oratorio (1850–54)
1856–59 (53–56) *The Trojans,* opera (Part II
produced 1863; Part I produced 1890)
1862 (59) *Béatrice et Bénédict,* opera (1860–62)

BERNSTEIN, Leonard/b.1918/U.S.A.

1941 (23) Clarinet Sonata (1941–42)
Symphony No. 1, *Jeremiah* (1941–44)
1942–43 (24) *Seven Anniversaries,* for piano
1943 (25) *I Hate Music,* song cycle for soprano
1944 (26) *Fancy Free,* ballet
On the Town, dance episodes
1945 (27) *Hashkivenu,* for cantor, chorus and organ
1946 (28) *Facsimile,* ballet
1947 (29) Five Pieces for piano (1947–48)
Symphony No. 2, *The Age of Anxiety,*
for piano and orchestra (1947–49)
1948 (30) *Four Anniversaries,* for piano

46

1949 (31) *La Bonne Cuisine,* song cycle
Two Love Songs
1950 (32) *Prelude, Fugue and Riffs,* for jazz combo
and orchestra
1951 (33) "Afterthought", song
1952 (34) *Trouble in Tahiti,* one-act opera
Wonderful Town
1954 (36) Serenade for violin, strings and percussion
Five Anniversaries, for piano
On the Waterfront, film score
1956 (38) *Candide*
1957 (39) *West Side Story,* score for stage musical
and film
1960 (42) *Symphonic Dances* on "West Side Story"
1963 (45) Symphony No. 3, *Kaddish*
1965 (47) *Chichester Psalms,* for chorus and
orchestra
1971 (53) *Mass,* a theater piece for singers, players
and dancers
1974 (56) *Dybbuk,* ballet
1975 (57) Suite No. 1 from "Dybbuk"
Seven Dances from "Dybbuk"

BERWALD, Franz Adolf/1796–1868/Sweden

1816 (20) Theme and Variations, for violin and
orchestra
1817 (21) Double Concerto, for two violins and
orchestra (now lost)
Septet, for violin, viola, cello, clarinet,
bassoon, horn and oboe
1819 (23) Quartet, for piano, clarinet, bassoon and
horn
1820 (24) Symphony No. 1
Violin Concerto in C♯ minor
1825 (29) Serenade, for tenor and six instruments
1827 (31) *Gustav Wasa,* opera
Concertstücke, for bassoon and orchestra
1842 (46) Symphony No. 2, *Sérieuse*
Symphony No. 3
(Symphony No. 4 is lost)

47

1844 (48)   *A Country Wedding,* for organ, four
                    hands
1845 (49)   Symphony No. 5, *Singulière*
                    Symphony No. 6
                    Five piano trios
1852–54 (56–58)   Three piano trios
1855 (59)   Piano Concerto in D major
1856–58 (60–62)   Two piano quintets (possibly
                    1853–54)
1859 (63)   *p.* Cello Sonata
1862 (66)   *Estrella de Soria,* opera
1887 (posthumous)   *p.* String Quartet in E♭ major
1905 (posthumous)   *p.* String Quartet in A minor
Berwald also composed Violin Sonata in E♭.

BIRTWISTLE, Harrison/b.1934/Great Britain

1957 (23)   *Refrains and Choruses,* for flute, oboe,
                    clarinet, bassoon and horn
1959 (25)   *Monody for Corpus Christi,* for soprano,
                    flute, horn and violin
                    Preçis, for piano
1960 (26)   *The World is Discovered,* for instrumental
                    ensemble
1962–63 (28)   Chorales for orchestra
1964 (30)   Three Movements with Fanfares, for
                    orchestra
                    Entr'Actes and Sappho Fragments, for
                    soprano and instruments
                    Description of the Passing of a Year,
                    narration for mixed choir a cappella
1965 (31)   *Tragoedia,* for instrumental ensemble
                    Ring a Dumb Carillon, for soprano,
                    clarinet and percussion
                    Motet: *Carmen Paschale,* for mixed choir
                    and organ
1966 (32)   *Verses,* for clarinet and piano
                    Punch and Judy, opera (1966–67)
1968 (34)   *Nomos,* for four amplified wind
                    instruments and orchestra
                    Linoi, for clarinet and piano

1969 (35) *Down By The Greenwood Side*, dramatic
pastoral
Verses for Ensembles, for instrumental
ensemble
Ut Heremita Solus, arrangement of
instrumental motet
Hoquetus David (Double Hoquet),
arrangement of instrumental motet
Medusa, for instrumental ensemble
(1969–70)
Cantata, for soprano and instrumental
ensemble
1970 (36) *Prologue*, for tenor and instruments
Nenia on the Death of Orpheus, for
soprano and instruments
Four Interludes from a Tragedy, for
clarinet and tape
1971 (37) *An Imaginary Landscape*, for orchestra
Meridian, for mezzo-soprano, six-part
choir and ensemble
The Fields of Sorrow, for two sopranos,
eight-part mixed choir and instruments
Chronometer, for eight-track electronic
tape
1972 (38) *The Triumph of Time*, for orchestra
Tombeau—in memoriam Igor Stravinsky,
for flute, clarinet, harp and string
quartet
Dinah and Nick's Love Song, for three
soprano saxophones and harp (or three
English horns and harp)
La Plage—Eight Arias of Remembrance,
for soprano, three clarinets, piano and
marimba
Epilogue—"Full Fathom Five", for
baritone and instruments
1973 (39) *Grimethorpe Aria*, for brass band
Chanson de Geste, for solo sustaining
instrument and tape
Five Choral Preludes arranged from Bach,
for soprano and instrumental ensemble
1974 (40) *Chorales from a Toyshop*, in five parts
with variable orchestration

BIZET, Georges/1838–1875/France

1854 (16) *La Prêtresse,* one-act opera
1855 (17) Symphony in C (was not performed until
           1935)
1857 (19) *Le Docteur Miracle,* operetta
         Clovis et Clothilde, cantata
1859 (21) *Don Procopio,* opera
1863 (25) *The Pearl Fishers,* opera
1865 (27) *Chasse Fantastique,* for piano
         Ivan the Terrible, opera (withdrawn,
           thought lost, recovered 1944, produced
           1946 in Würtemburg)
1866 (28) Trois esquisses musicales, for piano or
         harmonium
1867 (29) *The Fair Maid of Perth,* opera
1868 (30) Symphony in C, *Roma*
         Marche Funèbre, for orchestra
         Variations Chromatiques, for piano
         Marine, for piano
1869 (31) *Vasco da Gama,* symphonic ode with
         chorus
1871 (33) Petite Suite d'Orchestre
         Jeux d'enfants, twelve pieces for piano
          duet (later five were made into an
          orchestral suite)
1872 (34) *L'Arlésienne,* incidental music
         Djarmileh, opera
1873 (35) *Patrie,* overture
1875 (37) *fp. Carmen,* opera

BLISS, Sir Arthur/1891–1975/Great Britain

*c.*1915 (*c.*24) Piano Quartet in A minor
         String Quartet in A major
1916 (25) Two pieces for clarinet and piano
1918 (27) *Madam Noy,* for soprano, flute, clarinet,
         bassoon, harp, viola and double-bass
1919 (28) *As You Like It,* incidental music for two
         solo violins, viola, cello and singers
         Rhapsody, (wordless) for mezzo-soprano,

> > tenor, flute, English horn, string quartet
> > and double-bass
> > Piano Quintet (unpublished, MS lost)
1920 (29) *Rout,* for soprano and chamber orchestra
> > (revised version for full orchestra
> > written at the invitation of Diaghilev,
> > *fp.* 1921)
> > *Conversations,* for chamber orchestra
> > Two Studies for orchestra
> > Concerto for piano and tenor voice, strings
> > and percussion (revised 1923; revised
> > as Concerto for two pianos and
> > orchestra, 1924)
1920–21 (29) *The Tempest,* overture and interludes
1921 (30) *Mêlée Fantasque,* for orchestra (revised
> > 1965)
> > *A Colour Symphony* (1921–22, revised
> > 1932). Movements are headed Purple,
> > Red, Blue and Green, and are
> > interpreted in the light of their
> > heraldic associations
1923 (32) *Ballads of the Four Seasons* (Li-Po),
> > for medium voice and piano
> > String Quartet (1923–24) (MS lost)
> > *The Women of Yueh* (Li-Po), song cycle
> > for voice and chamber ensemble
1924 (33) *Masks* I–IV, for piano
1926 (35) Introduction and Allegro for orchestra,
> > revised 1937
> > *Hymn to Apollo,* for orchestra, revised
> > 1965
1927 (36) Four Songs, for high voice and violin
> > Oboe Quintet
1928 (37) *Pastoral: Lie Strewn the White Flocks,* for
> > mezzo-soprano, chorus, flute, drums
> > and string orchestra
1929 (38) *Serenade,* for baritone and orchestra
1930 (39) *Morning Heroes,* symphony for orator,
> > chorus and orchestra
> > *Fanfares for Heroes,* for three trumpets,
> > three trombones, timpani and cymbals
1931 (40) Clarinet Quintet
1933 (42) Viola Sonata

1934–35 (43) *Things to Come,* suite for orchestra
from music for the film
1935 (44) Music for Strings
1936 (45) *Kenilworth Suite,* for brass
1937 (46) *Checkmate,* ballet
1938 (47) Piano Concerto
1940 (49) *Seven American Poems,* for low voice
and piano
1941 (50) String Quartet in B♭ major
1943 (52) Three Jubilant and Three Solemn
Fanfares, for three trumpets, three
trombones and tuba, or full military
band
1944 (53) *Miracle in the Gorbals,* ballet
The Phoenix. "Homage to France—August
1944", orchestral march
"Auvergnat" for high voice and piano
1945 (54) *Baraza,* concert piece for piano and
orchestra with men's voices ad lib
1946 (55) *Adam Zero,* ballet
1948–49 (57) *The Olympians,* opera
1950 (59) String Quartet No. 2
1952 (61) *The Enchantress,* scena for contralto and
orchestra
Piano Sonata
1953 (62) Processional, for full orchestra and organ
(composed for performance in
Westminster Abbey at the Coronation
of Her Majesty Queen Elizabeth II)
1954 (63) *A Song of Welcome,* for soprano,
baritone, chorus and orchestra
1955 (64) Violin Concerto
Meditations on a Theme of John Blow,
for orchestra
Elegiac Sonnet, for tenor, string quartet
and piano
1956 (65) *Edinburgh Overture,* for full orchestra
1957 (66) *Discourse,* for orchestra (recomposed
1965)
1958 (67) *The Lady of Shalott,* ballet
1960 (69) *Tobias and the Angel,* opera in two acts
1962 (71) *The Beatitudes,* cantata for soprano, tenor,
chorus, orchestra and organ

1963 (72) *Mary of Magdala*, cantata for contralto,
bass, chorus and orchestra
Belmont Variations, for brass band
A Knot of Riddles, for baritone and eleven
instruments

1964 (73) *Homage to a Great Man (Winston
Churchill)*, march for orchestra
The Golden Cantata, for tenor, mixed
chorus and orchestra

1966 (75) Fanfare Prelude, for orchestra

1967 (76) *River Music*, for unaccompanied choir

1969 (78) *The World is Charged with the Grandeur
of God*, for chorus and wind
instruments
Angels of the Mind, song cycle for soprano
and piano
Miniature Scherzo for piano

1970 (79) Cello Concerto

1971 (80) Two Ballads, for women's chorus and
small orchestra
Triptych, for piano

1972 (81) Three Songs for voice and piano
Metamorphic Variations, for orchestra

1974 (83) *Prelude "Lancaster"*, for orchestra

1975 (84) *Shield of Faith*, cantata for soprano,
baritone, chorus and organ

BLOCH, Ernest/1880–1959/Switzerland

1900–29 (20–49) *Helvetia*, a symphonic fresco for
orchestra

1901–02 (21) Symphony in C♯ minor

1904–05 (24) *Hiver*, symphonic poem
Printemps, symphonic poem

1906 (26) *Poèmes d'Automne*, for voice and
orchestra

1910 (30) *fp. Macbeth*, opera (written possibly
1903–9)

1912 (32) Prelude and Two Psalms, for high voice
(1912–14)
Israel Symphony, with two sopranos, two
altos and bass (1912–16)

1913 (33) *Trois Poèmes Juifs,* for orchestra
1915–16 (35) *Schelomo—Hebrew Rhapsody,* for cello and orchestra
1916 (36) String Quartet No. 1 in B minor
1918–19 (38) Suite for viola
Suite for viola and piano
1920 (40) Violin Sonata No. 1
1921–23 (41–43) Piano Quintet
1922 (42) *In the Night,* for piano
Poems of the Sea, for piano (1922–24)
1923 (43) *Baal Shem,* for violin and piano
Melody, for violin and piano
Enfantines, for piano
Five Sketches in Sepia, for piano
Nirvana, for piano
1924 (44) Concerto Grosso for strings with piano obbligato (1924–25)
In the Mountains (Haute Savoie), for string quartet
Night, for string quartet
Three Landscapes, for string quartet
Three Nocturnes for piano trio
Violin Sonata No. 2, *Poème mystique*
Exotic Night, for violin and piano
From Jewish Life, for cello and piano
Méditation Hébraïque, for cello and piano
1925 (45) *Prélude (Recueillement),* for string quartet
1926 (46) *America: an Epic Rhapsody,* for orchestra
Four Episodes, for chamber orchestra
1929 (49) *Abodah,* for violin and piano
1933 (53) *Avodath Hakodesh,* sacred service, for baritone, chorus and orchestra
1934–36 (54–56) *A Voice in the Wilderness,* symphonic poem for cello and orchestra
1935 (55) Piano Sonata
1937 (57) *Evocations,* symphonic suite
Violin Concerto (1937–38)
1938 (58) Piece for string quartet
1944 (64) Suite Symphonique
1945 (65) String Quartet No. 2
1946–48 (66–68) *Concerto Symphonique,* for piano

1949 (69) *Scherzo fantasque,* for piano
1950 (70) Concertino for viola, flute and strings
Piece for string quartet
1951 (71) *Cinq pièces Hébraïque,* for viola and
piano
String Quartet No. 3 (1951–52)
1952 (72) Sinfonia Brève
Concerto Grosso for string quartet and
string orchestra

BLOW, John/1649–1708/Great Britain

---

c.1684 (*c.*35) *Venus and Adonis,* a masque
Ode for St. Cecilia's Day—"Begin the
Song"
1697 (48) "My God, my God, look upon me",
anthem
1700 (51) *Amphion Anglicus,* collection of songs
and vocal chamber music
Blow also composed many harpsichord pieces, odes
for state occasions, secular songs and catches, 110
anthems, 13 services, etc.

BOCCHERINI, Luigi/1743–1806/Italy

1765 (22) *La Confederazione,* opera
1786 (43) *La Clementina,* opera
1801 (58) Stabat Mater
Boccherini also composed:
4 cello concerti
20 symphonies, including 8 concertantes
21 sonatas for piano and violin
6 sonatas for violin and bass
6 sonatas for cello and bass
6 duets for two violins
48 trios for two violins and cello
12 trios for violin, viola and cello
18 quintets for flute or oboe, violins, viola and cello
12 quintets for piano, two violins, viola and cello
112 quintets for two violins, viola and two cellos
12 quintets for two violins, two violas and cello
16 sextets for various instruments

2 octets for various instruments
Vocal works, totaling 467 in all, including a Mass for
    four voices and instruments; a Christmas cantata;
    and 14 concert arias and duets with orchestra
1 suite for full orchestra
102 string quartets

BOËLLMANN, Léon/1862–1897/France

1877 (15) Piano Quartet
Boëllmann wrote many works for organ, including:
Fantaisée dialogue, for organ and orchestra
Gothic Suite for organ
Fantasia in A major, for organ
Heures mystiques, for organ
Boëllmann also composed:
Symphony in F major
Symphonic Variations, for cello and orchestra
Piano Trio
Cello Sonata

BOÏELDIEU, François/1775–1834/France

1793 (18) *La Fille coupable,* opera
1795 (20) Harp Concerto in G major
1800 (25) *Calife de Bagdad,* opera
1803 (28) *Ma Tante Aurore,* opera
1812 (37) *Jean de Paris,* opera
1825 (50) *La Dame blanche,* opera

BORODIN, Alexander/1833–1887/Russia

1847 (14) Concerto for Flute in D major and minor,
        with piano
1862–67 (29–34) Symphony No. 1 in E♭ major
1867 (34) *The Bagotirs,* opera-farce
1869–76 (36–43) Symphony No. 2 in B minor
1869–87 (36–54) *Prince Igor,* opera (left unfinished
        and completed by Rimsky-Korsakov and
        Glazunov, *q.v.*)

1875–79 (42–46) String Quartet No. 1 in A major
1880 (47) *In the Steppes of Central Asia,* orchestral
  "picture"
1881 (48) String Quartet No. 2 in D major
1885 (52) Petite Suite, for piano
  Scherzo in A♭, for piano
1886 (53) *Serenata alla Spagnola,* a movement for
  the string quartet "B-la-F" (the other
  movements were by Rimsky-Korsakov,
  Liadov and Glazunov, *q.v.*)

BOULEZ, Pierre/b.1925/France

1946 (21) *Visage Nuptial,* for soprano, alto and
  chamber orchestra (first version)
  Piano Sonata No. 1
  Sonatina for flute and piano
1947–48 (22) *Soleil des eaux,* for voices and
  orchestra
  Piano Sonata No. 2
1949 (24) *Livre pour cordes,* for string orchestra
  Livre pour quatuor, for string quartet
1951 (26) *fp. Polyphonie* X, for eighteen instruments
  Second version of *Visage Nuptial,* for
  soprano, alto, choir and orchestra
1952 (27) *fp. Structures,* Book I, for two pianos
1954 (29) *Le Marteau sans maître,* for alto voice
  and six instruments
1955 (30) *Symphonie Mecanique,* music for the film
1957 (32) *Doubles,* for three orchestral groups divisi
  Poésie pour pouvoir, for reciter, orchestra
  and tape
  Deux Improvisations sur Mallarmé, for
  soprano and instrumental ensemble
  Piano Sonata No. 3
1959 (34) *fp. Tombeau,* for orchestra
1960 (35) *fp. Pli selon pli,* Portrait de Mallarmé
  (Don; Improvisations I, II, III;
  Tombeau), for soprano and orchestra
1961 (36) Structures, Book II, for two pianos
1964 (39) *fp. Figures-Doubles-Prismes,* for orchestra
  Éclat, for fifteen instruments

1968 (43) *fp. Domaines,* for clarinet and twenty-
one instruments
1970 (45) *Multiples,* for orchestra
fp. Cummings ist der Dichter, for sixteen
mixed voices and instruments
1972–74 (47–49) *... Explosante-Fixe ...,* for
ensemble and live electronics
1974–75 (49) *Rituel, in memoriam Maderna,* for
orchestra in eight groups

BOYCE, William/1710–1779/Great Britain

---

*c.***1750** (*c.*40) *p.* Eight Symphonies in Eight Parts
... Opera Seconda
1758 (48) Ode to the New Year
1769 (59) Ode to the King's Birthday
1772 (62) Ode to the New Year
1775 (65) Ode to the King's Birthday
*c.***1785** (posthumous) *p.* Ten voluntaries for organ
or harpsichord
1786 (posthumous) *p.* Ode to the King's Birthday
1790 (posthumous) *p.* "Oh where shall wisdom be
found?", anthem
Boyce also composed church and stage music and
songs.

BRAHMS, Johannes/1833–1897/Germany

1851 (18) Scherzo in E♭ minor, for piano, Op. 4
Six songs for tenor or soprano, Op. 7
(1851–53)
1852 (19) Piano Sonata No. 1 in C major, Op. 1
(1852–53)
Piano Sonata No. 2 in F♯ minor, Op. 2
Six songs for tenor or soprano, Op. 3
(1852–53)
Six songs for tenor or soprano, Op. 6
(1852–53)
1853 (20) Piano Sonata No. 3 in F minor, Op. 5
Piano Trio No. 1 in B major, Op. 8
(1853–54)

1854 (21)	Variations on a Theme by Schumann, for piano, Op. 9
	Four Ballades for piano, in Dm: D: B: Bm, Op. 10
	Piano Concerto No. 1 in D minor, Op. 15
1855–68	Seven Songs, Op. 48
1855–75	Piano Quartet No. 3 in C minor, Op. 60
1855–76	Symphony No. 1 in C minor, Op. 68
1856 (23)	"Lass dich nur nichts dauern", sacred song, Op. 30
	Variations on an original theme, for piano, Op. 21/1
	Variations on a Hungarian theme, for piano, Op. 21/2
1857–58 (24)	Serenade for orchestra in D major, Op. 11
1857–60	Serenade for orchestra in A major, Op. 16
1857–68	Four Songs, Op. 43
	German Requiem, Op. 45
1858 (25)	"Ave Maria", for women's chorus, orchestra and organ, Op. 12
	"Funeral Hymn", for mixed chorus and wind orchestra, Op. 13
	Eight Songs and Romances, Op. 14
1858–59	Five Songs, Op. 19
1858–60	Three Duets for soprano and alto, Op. 20
1858–68	Five Songs, Op. 47
1859 (26)	*Marienlieder,* for four-part mixed choir, Op. 22
	The 13th Psalm, for three-part women's chorus and organ, Op. 27
1859–60	Three Quartets for solo voices with piano, Op. 31
1859–61	Three Songs, Op. 42
1859–63	Three Sacred Choruses, Op. 37
	Twelve Songs and Romances, Op. 44
1859–73	String Quartet No. 1 in C minor, Op. 51
	String Quartet No. 2 in A minor
1860 (27)	Part-Songs, for women's chorus, two horns and harp, Op. 17
	String Sextet No. 1 in B♭ major, Op. 18

	Two Motets, for five-part mixed choir a cappella, Op. 29
1860–62	Four Duets for alto and baritone, Op. 28
1861 (28)	Variations and Fugue on a theme by Handel, for piano, Op. 24
	Piano Quartet No. 1 in G minor, Op. 25
	Piano Quartet No. 2 in A major, Op. 26
1861–62	"Soldaten Lieder", five songs, Op. 41
1861–68	Fifteen Romances from "Magelone", Op. 33
1862–63 (29)	Piano Studies (Variations on a theme by Paganini) Books I and II, Op. 35
1862–65	Cello Sonata No. 1 in Em, Op. 38
1862–74	Three Quartets for solo voices, Op. 63
1863 (30)	Song, for alto, viola and piano, Op. 91
1863–68	*Rinaldo,* cantata, Op. 50
1863–77	Two Motets, Op. 74
1863–90	Thirteen Canons, Op. 113
1864 (31)	Fourteen German folk songs, for four-part choir
	Piano Quintet in F minor, Op. 34
	Four Songs, Op. 46
1864–65	String Sextet No. 2 in G major, Op. 36
1864–68	Five Songs, Op. 49
1865 (32)	Trio for piano, violin and horn, in E♭ major, Op. 40
1869 (36)	*Liebeslieder Waltzer* (words, Daumer), Op. 52
	p. Piano Studies in Five Books, Books I–II
1870 (37)	Alto Rhapsody, for alto, male chorus and orchestra, Op. 53
1870–71	*Triumphlied,* for chorus and orchestra, Op. 55
1871 (38)	*Schicksalied (Song of Destiny),* Op. 54
	Eight Songs, Op. 57
	Eight Songs, Op. 58
1871–73	Eight Songs, Op. 59
1871–78	Eight piano pieces in two books: Nos. 1, 2, 5 and 8 are Capriccios. Nos. 3, 4, 6 and 7 are Intermezzi, Op. 76
1873 (40)	Variations on a theme by Haydn, *St. Anthony,* for orchestra, Op. 56a

Violin Sonata No. 2 in A major,
Meistersinger, Op. 100

Five Songs, Op. 105

Five Songs, Op. 106

Five Songs, Op. 107

1886–88 Violin Sonata No. 3 in D minor, *Thuner-
Sonate,* Op. 108

Deutsche Fest- und Gedenkspruche,
Op. 109

1887 (54) Double Concerto for violin, cello and
orchestra in A minor, Op. 102

Zigeunerliede, Op. 103

1888 (55) Five Songs, Op. 104

1888–91 Six Vocal Quartets, Op. 112

1889 (56) Three Motets, Op. 110

1890 (57) String Quintet No. 2 in G major, Op. 111

1891 (58) Trio for piano, violin and clarinet in
A minor, Op. 114

Clarinet Quintet in B minor, Op. 115

1892 (59) *Fantasien,* for piano, in two books,
Op. 116

Three Intermezzi for piano, Op. 117

Six Piano Pieces (intermezzi, ballade,
romance), Op. 118

Four Piano Pieces (three intermezzi,
one rhapsody), Op. 119

1894 (61) Sonata No. 1 in F minor, for piano and
clarinet, or viola, Op. 120

Sonata No. 2 in E♭ major, for piano and
clarinet, or viola, Op. 120

1896 (63) Four Serious Songs, Op. 121

BRIDGE, Frank/1879–1941/Great Britain

1902 (23) *Berceuse,* for violin and small orchestra

1904 (25) *Novelleten,* for string quartet

Violin Sonata

1905 (26) Piano Quintet

Phantasie Quartet in F♯ minor

Norse Legend, for violin and piano

1906 (27) Three Idylls for string orchestra

String Quartet in E minor
Nine Miniatures, for cello and piano
1907 (28) *Isabella*, symphonic poem
Trio No. 1 in C minor, *Phantasie*
1908 (29) *Dance Rhapsody*, for orchestra
Suite for strings
1909 (30) *Dance Poem*, for orchestra
1911 (32) *The Sea*, suite for orchestra
1912 (33) String Sextet
1914 (35) *Summer*, tone poem
1915 (36) *The Open Air*, poem for orchestra
The Story of My Heart, poem for
orchestra
Lament, for strings
String Quartet in G minor
1916 (37) "A Prayer", for chorus
1917 (38) Cello Sonata in D minor and D major
1919–29 (40–50) *The Christmas Rose*, opera
1922 (43) *Sir Roger de Coverley*, for string quartet
or orchestra
Piano Sonata (1922–25)
1926 (47) String Quartet No. 3
1927 (48) *Enter Spring*, for orchestra
1928 (49) *Rhapsody*, for two violins and viola
1929 (50) Trio No. 2
1930 (51) *Oration "concert elegiaco"*, for cello and
orchestra
1931 (52) *Phantasm*, rhapsody for piano and
orchestra
1937 (58) String Quartet No. 4
1940 (61) *Rebus*, for orchestra
Vignettes de Danse, for small orchestra
Divertimento for flute, oboe, clarinet and
bassoon

BRITTEN, Benjamin/1913–1976/Great Britain

1930 (17) Hymn to the Virgin
1932 (19) Sinfonietta, for chamber orchestra
Phantasy Quartet, for oboe and string trio
1933 (20) *A Boy Was Born*, choral variations for

men's, women's and boy's voices
unaccompanied with organ ad lib
Two Part-songs for chorus and piano
Friday Afternoons, twelve children's
songs with piano (1933–35)

1934 (21) *Simple Symphony,* for string orchestra
(based entirely on material which the
composer wrote between the ages of
9 and 12)
Suite, for violin and piano (1934–35)
Holiday Diary, suite for piano
Te Deum in C major

1936 (23) *Our Hunting Fathers,* song cycle
Soirées musicales, suite

1937 (24) *Mont Juic, suite of Catalan Dances,* for
orchestra (with Berkeley, *q.v.*)
Variations on a Theme of Frank Bridge,
for strings
On This Island, song cycle

1938 (25) Piano Concerto No. 1 (revised 1945)
1939 (26) Violin Concerto (revised 1958)
Canadian Carnival, for orchestra
Ballad of Heroes, for high voice, choir
and orchestra
Les Illuminations, song cycle

1940 (27) *Diversions on a Theme,* for piano (left
hand) and orchestra
Paul Bunyan, operetta (*c.*1940–41,
revised 1974)
Sinfonia da Requiem
Seven Sonnets of Michelangelo, for tenor
and piano

1941 (28) *Scottish Ballad,* for two pianos and
orchestra
Matinées musicales, for orchestra
String Quartet No. 1

1942 (29) Hymn to St. Cecilia, for five-part chorus
with solos unaccompanied
A Ceremony of Carols, for treble voices
and harp

1943 (30) *Rejoice in the Lamb,* a Festival Cantata
Prelude and Fugue, for strings

> *Serenade*, song cycle for tenor, horn and strings

1944 (31) Festival Te Deum, for chorus and organ

1945 (32) *Peter Grimes*, opera
The Holy Sonnets of John Donne, for high voice and piano
String Quartet No. 2

1946 (33) Variations and Fugue on a Theme of Purcell *(Young Person's Guide to the Orchestra)*, for speaker and orchestra
The Rape of Lucretia, opera

1947 (34) *Albert Herring*, opera
Canticle No. 1, "My Beloved is Mine"
Prelude and Fugue on a Theme of Vittoria, for organ

1948 (35) *St. Nicholas*, for tenor, choir, strings, piano and percussion
The Beggar's Opera, by John Gay realized from original airs

1949 (36) *The Little Sweep (Let's Make an Opera)*
Spring Symphony, for three solo singers, mixed choir, boys' choir and orchestra
A Wedding Anthem, for soprano, tenor, chorus and organ

1950 (37) *Lachrymae*, for viola and piano
Five Flower Songs, for unaccompanied chorus

1951 (38) *Billy Budd*, opera
Six Metamorphoses After Ovid, for solo oboe

1952 (39) Canticle No. 2, "Abraham and Isaac", for contralto, tenor and piano

1953 (40) *Gloriana*, opera
Winter Words, songs

1954 (41) *The Turn of the Screw*, opera
Canticle No. 3, "Still Falls the Rain", for tenor, chorus and piano

1955 (42) *Alpine Suite*, for recorder trio
Hymn to St. Peter, for choir and organ

1956 (43) *The Prince of the Pagodas*, ballet
Antiphon, for mixed choir and organ

1957 (44) *Noye's Fludde*, mystery play with music

Songs from the Chinese, for high voice
and guitar
1958 (45) *Nocturne,* song cycle for tenor, seven
obbligato instruments and strings
Sechs Hölderlin-Fragmente, song cycle
1959 (46) Missa Brevis
Cantata Academica, Carmen Basiliense,
for soprano, alto, tenor and bass soli,
chorus and orchestra
1960 (47) *A Midsummer Night's Dream,* opera
1961 (48) *War Requiem,* for soprano, tenor and
baritone soli, chorus, orchestra,
chamber orchestra, boys' choir,
and organ
Cello Sonata in C major
1963 (50) Symphony for cello and orchestra
Cantata misericordium, for tenor, baritone,
string quartet, string orchestra, piano,
harp and timpani
Nocturnal, after John Dowland, for guitar
1964 (51) *Curlew River,* parable for church
performance
Cello Suite No. 1
1965 (52) *Gemini Variations,* for flute, violin and
piano (four hands)
Songs and Proverbs of William Blake
Voices for Today, anthem for chorus
The Poet's Echo, for high voice and piano
1966 (53) *The Burning Fiery Furnace,* parable for
church performance
The Golden Vanity, for boys and piano
1967 (54) Cello Suite No. 2
The Building of the House, overture, with
or without chorus
1968 (55) *The Children's Crusade,* for children's
voices and orchestra
The Prodigal Son, parable for church
performance
1969 (56) Suite for harp
"Who are these children?", for tenor and
piano
1970 (57) *Owen Wingrave,* opera

1971 (58)   Cello Suite No. 3
              Canticle No. 4, "Journey of the Magi"
1973 (60)   *Death in Venice,* opera
1974 (61)   Canticle No. 5, "The Death of St.
              Narcissus", for tenor and harp
              Suite on English folk tunes, for orchestra
              A Birthday Hansel, for voice and harp
1975 (62)   *Phaedra,* dramatic cantata for mezzo-
              soprano and small orchestra
              String Quartet No. 3

BROWN, Earle/b.1926/U.S.A.

1952 (26)   *Folio and Four Systems,* for piano and
              orchestra
              Music for violin, cello and piano
1953 (27)   Twenty-five Pages—from one to twenty-
              five pianos
1961 (35)   *Available Forms* II, for ninety-eight
              players and two conductors
1962 (36)   *Novara,* for instrumental ensemble
1963 (37)   *From Here,* for chorus and twenty
              instruments (chorus optional)
              Times Five, for flute, trombone, harp,
              violin, cello and four-channel tape
1964 (38)   *Corroborree,* for two or three pianos
1965 (39)   *Nine Rarebits,* for one or two harpsichords
              String Quartet
1966 (40)   *Modules 1 and 2,* for orchestra
1967–68 (41)   *Event-Synergy II,* for instrumental
              ensemble
1969 (42)   *Modules 3,* for orchestra
1970 (43)   *Syntagm III,* for instrumental ensemble
1972 (45)   *Time Spans,* for orchestra
              New Piece: Loops, for choir and/or
              orchestra
              Sign Sounds, for instrumental ensemble
1973 (46)   *Centering,* for solo violin and ten
              instruments

BRUCH, Max/1838–1920/Germany

1856 (18) String Quartet in C minor
1857 (19) Piano Trio in C minor
1858 (20) *Scherz, List und Rache,* opera
1860 (22) String Quartet in E major
1863 (25) *Die Lorely,* opera
*c.***1864** (*c.*26) *Frithjof-Scenen,* for solo voices, chorus and orchestra
1868 (30) Violin Concerto No. 1 in G minor
1870 (32) Symphony No. 1 in E♭ major
              Symphony No. 2 in F minor
1872 (34) *Hermione,* opera
              Odysseus, cantata
1878 (40) Violin Concerto No. 2 in D minor
1881 (43) *p. Kol Nidrei,* for cello and piano, or orchestra
1887 (49) Symphony No. 3 in E major
1891 (53) Violin Concerto No. 3 in E major
1905 (67) Suite on a popular Russian melody
1911 (73) Concertstücke for violin, in F♯ minor

BRUCKNER, Anton/1824–1896/Austria

1849 (25) Requiem in D minor
1854 (30) Solemn Mass in B♭ major
1863 (39) Symphony in F minor (known as No. 00)
              Overture in G minor
              Germanenzug, for chorus and brass
1864 (40) Symphony in D minor (known as No. 0, revised 1869)
              Mass No. 1 in D minor
              "Um Mitternacht", for male-voice chorus
1866 (42) Symphony No. 1 in C minor (revised 1891)
              Mass No. 2 in E minor
1868 (44) Mass No. 3 in F minor, *Grosse Messe* (revised 1871 and 1890)
1869 (45) "Locus iste", motet
1871 (47) "Os uisti", motet

68

1872 (48)   Symphony No. 2 in C minor (revised 1891)
1873 (49)   Symphony No. 3 in D minor, *Wagner* (revised 1877 and 1888)
1874 (50)   Symphony No. 4 in E♭ major, *Romantic* (revised 1880)
1877 (53)   Symphony No. 5 in B♭ major (revised 1878)
1878 (54)   *Abendzauber,* for baritone and male chorus
1879 (55)   String Quartet
1881 (57)   Symphony No. 6 in A major
1883 (59)   Symphony No. 7 in E major
1884 (60)   Symphony No. 8 in C minor, *Apocalyptic* (possibly 1887, revised 1890)
                Te Deum
1894 (70)   Symphony No. 9 in D minor (unfinished, *fp.* 1903)

BULL, John/1563–1628/Great Britain

No details of Bull's works are available. He is included in this book because of his importance in the history of music as a composer for the virginals, and because he ranks as one of the founders of the keyboard repertory.

BUSONI, Ferruccio/1866–1924/Italy

1880–81 (14–15)   String Quartet No. 1 in C major
1882 (16)   *Spring, Summer, Autumn, Winter,* for male voice and orchestra
                Il Sabato del villagio, for solo voices, chorus and orchestra
                Serenata, for cello and piano
1883 (17)   Piano Sonata in F minor
1886 (20)   String Quartet in C minor
                Little Suite, for cello and piano
1888 (22)   Symphonic Suite
                Konzert-Fantasie, for piano and orchestra:

69

later (1892) called "Symphonisches Tongedicht"
1889 (23) String Quartet No. 2 in D minor
1890 (24) Konzertstücke for piano
Violin Sonata No. 1
1895 (29) Orchestral Suite No. 2
1896–97 (30) Violin Concerto in D major
1897 (31) *Comedy Overture*
1898 (32) Violin Sonata No. 2
1903–04 (37) Piano Concerto (using male choir)
1907 (41) *Élégien*, for piano
1908–11 (42–45) *The Bridal Choice*
1909 (43) *Berceuse élégiaque*
1912 (46) *Nocturne Symphonique*
1913 (47) *Indian Fantasy*, for piano and orchestra
1914–16 (48–50) *Arlecchino*, opera
1916–24 (50–58) *Doktor Faust*, opera (completed by Jarnach after Busoni's death and produced in Dresden in 1925)
1917 (51) *Turandot*, opera
Die Brautwahl, orchestral suite
1919 (53) Concertino for clarinet and small orchestra
1920 (54) Divertimento for flute and orchestra
Sonatina No. 6 for piano (chamber fantasy on Bizet's *Carmen*)
1921 (55) Romance and Scherzo for piano
Elegy for clarinet and piano
1923 (56) Ten variations on a Chopin prelude
Busoni also composed many piano solos and a *Fantasia Contrappuntista* for two pianos, based on Bach's *Art of Fugue*.

BUTTERWORTH, George/1885–1916/Great Britain

1909 (24) "I Fear Thy Kisses", song
1911 (26) Six Songs from Housman's "A Shropshire Lad"
Two English Idylls, for small orchestra
"Requiescat", song
1912 (27) *A Shropshire Lad*, rhapsody for orchestra
On Christmas Night, for chorus

> *We Get Up In The Morn,* arranged for
> male chorus
> *In The Highlands,* arranged for female
> voices and piano
> "Bredon Hill" and other songs
> Eleven folk songs from Sussex
> *p.* "Love Blows as the Wind Blows", for
> baritone and string quartet

1913 (28) *Banks of Green Willow,* idyll for orchestra

BUXTEHUDE, Dietrich/1637–1707/Denmark

1671 (34) Wedding Arias
1678 (41) Wedding Arias
1692 (55) Sonata in D major, for viola da gamba,
            cello and harpsichord
1696 (59) Seven Trio Sonatas for violin, gamba and
            basso continuo, Op. 1
            Seven Trio Sonatas for violin, gamba and
            basso continuo, Op. 2
1705 (68) Wedding Arias

BYRD, William/1543–1623/Great Britain

1575 (32) *p.* Seventeen Motets
*c.***1586** (*c.*43) *p.* A Printed Broadside for six voices
1588 (45) *p.* Psalms, Sonnets and Songs
1589 (46) *p.* Cantiones sacrae, Book I: twenty-nine
            motets for five voices
            p. Songs of Sundrie Natures
1591 (48) *p.* Cantiones sacrae, Book II: twenty
            motets for five voices; twelve motets
            for six voices
1605 (62) *p.* Gradualia, Book I: thirty-two motets
            for five voices; twenty motets for four
            voices; eleven motets for three voices
1607 (64) *p.* Gradualia, Book II: nineteen motets
            for four voices; seventeen motets for
            five voices, nine motets for six voices
1611 (68) *p.* Psalmes, Songs and Sonnets

71

1933 (21) Sonata for solo clarinet
1934 (22) Six Short Inventions for seven instruments
1938 (26) *Metamorphosis*, for piano
1939 (27) *First Construction (In Metal),* for
          percussion sextet
          Imaginary Landscape No. 1, for two
          variable-speed phono-turntables,
          frequency recordings, muted piano
          and cymbal
1941 (29) *Double Music,* for percussion
1942 (30) *Wonderful Widow of 18 Springs,* for
          voice and closed piano
1943 (31) *She is Asleep,* for twelve tom-toms, voice
          and prepared piano
          Amores, for prepared piano and
          percussion
          Perilous Night, suite for prepared piano
          (1943–44)
1944 (32) *A Book of Music,* for two prepared pianos
          Three Dances for two amplified prepared
          pianos (1944–45)
1946–48 (34–36) Sonatas and Interludes for
          prepared pianos
1950 (38) String Quartet in Four Parts
1951 (39) Concerto for prepared piano and chamber
          orchestra
          Music of Changes, for piano
          Imaginary Landscape No. 4, for twelve
          radios, twenty-four players and
          conductor
1952 (40) *Water Music,* for pianist with accessory
          instruments
          Williams Mix, for eight-track tape
          4' 33" (tacet), for piano, in four
          movements
1953–56 (41–44) *Music for piano "4–84 for 1–84*
          pianists"
1954 (42) *34' 46.776" for a pianist,* for prepared
          piano
1955 (43) *26' 1.1499" for a string player*

1957 (45) *Winter Music,* for one to twenty pianists
Concerto for piano and orchestra, for
piano and one to thirteen instrumental
parts
1958 (46) *Variations* I, for any kind and number
of instruments
Fontana Mix: a) a score for the
production of one or more tape tracks
or for any kind and number of
instruments
b) prerecorded tape material to be
performed in any way
1960 (48) *Cartridge music*
Theater Piece, for one to eight performers
1961 (49) *Music for Carillon,* No. 4
Variations II
Atlas eclipticalis, for orchestra
1963 (51) *Variations III*
Variations IV
1965 (53) *Variations V*
1966 (54) *Variations VI*
1967–69 (55–57) *H P S C H D,* for seven
harpsichords and fifty-two computer-
generated tapes (with Lejaren Hiller)
1969 (57) *Cheap Imitation,* for piano

CAMPIAN (CAMPION), Thomas/1562–1620/
Great Britain

1601 (39) *p.* A Book of Airs to be Sung to the Lute
1607 (45) *p.* Songs for a Masque to celebrate the
Marriage of Sir James Hay
1613 (51) *p.* Songs for a Masque to celebrate the
marriage of Princess Elizabeth
Campian composed more than 100 songs to lute
accompaniment.

CARPENTER, John Alden/1876–1951/U.S.A.

1904 (28) "Improving Songs for Anxious Children"
1912 (36) Violin Sonata

1913 (37) *Gitanjali*, song cycle on poems of Tagore
1915 (39) *Adventures in a Perambulator*, for
orchestra
Concertino for piano and orchestra
(revised 1947)
1917 (41) Symphony No. 1
1918 (42) Four Negro Songs
1919 (43) *Birthday of the Infanta*, ballet
1920 (44) *A Pilgrim Vision*, for orchestra
1921 (45) *Krazy Kat*, ballet
1925 (49) *Skyscrapers*, ballet
1928 (52) String Quartet
1932 (56) *Patterns*, for piano and orchestra
Song of Faith, for chorus and orchestra
1933 (57) *Sea Drift*, symphonic poem
1934 (58) Piano Quintet
1935 (59) *Danza*, for orchestra
1936 (60) Violin Concerto
1940 (64) Symphony No. 2
1941 (65) *Song of Freedom*, for chorus and
orchestra
1942 (66) Symphony No. 3
1943 (67) *The Anxious Bugler*, for orchestra
1945 (69) *The Seven Ages*
1948 (72) *Carmel Concerto*

CASELLA, Alfredo/1883–1947/Italy

1901 (18) *Pavana*, for piano
1903 (20) *Variations sur une chaconne*, for piano
1904 (21) Toccata for piano
1905–6 (22) Symphony No. 1
1907 (24) Cello Sonata No. 1
1908 (25) Sarabande for piano, or harp
Symphony No. 2 (1908–09)
1909 (26) *Italia*, orchestral rhapsody
Notturnino, for piano
Berceuse Triste, piano
Orchestral Suite in C major (1909–10)
1910 (27) *Barcarola*, for piano
1912–13 (29) *Le Couvent sur l'eau*, ballet
1913 (30) *Notte di Maggio*, for voice and orchestra

1914–17 (31–34) *Siciliana* and *Burlesca*, for piano
              trio
1916 (33) *Pupazzetti*, for nine instruments
              Pagine di Guerra
              Elegia eroica
1920 (37) Five pieces for string quartet
1921 (38) *A Notte alta*
1923–24 (40) Concerto for string quartet
1924 (41) *La Giara*, ballet
              Partita for piano
1926 (43) *Concerto Romano*, for organ and
                orchestra
              Introduction, Aria and Toccata, for
                orchestra
              Adieu à la vie, for voice and orchestra
              Scarlattiana
1927 (44) Cello Sonata No. 2
              Concerto for Strings
1928 (45) Violin Concerto in A minor
              La Donna Serpente, opera (1928–31)
1930 (47) Serenade for small orchestra
1931–35 (48–52) *Introduction, corale e marcia*,
              for woodwind
1932 (49) *La Favola d'Orfeo*, opera
              Sinfonia for clarinet, trumpet and piano
1933 (50) Concerto for violin, cello, piano and
                orchestra
1934 (51) *Notturno e Tarantella*, for cello
              Cello Concerto
1937 (54) Concerto for Orchestra
              Il Deserto Tentato, oratorio
1939–40 (56) Sinfonia
1942 (59) *Paganiniana*
1943 (60) Concerto for strings, piano and percussion
              Harp Sonata
1944 (61) Missa Solemnis "Pro Pace"

CASTELNUOVO-TEDESCO, Mario/1895–1968/
Italy

1915 (20) *Copias*, for guitar (orchestra version
              1967)

1920 (25) *Cipressi*
          La Mandragola, opera
1921–25 (25–29) Thirty-three Shakespeare Songs
1925 (29) *Le Danze del re David,* for piano
1927 (32) Piano Concerto No. 1
1933 (38) Sonata for Guitar, *Homage to Boccherini*
1936 (41) Tarantella
          Concerto for two guitars and orchestra
          Concertino for harp and chamber
            orchestra
1938 (43) *Aucassin et Nicolette,* for voice,
            instruments and marionettes
1939 (44) Guitar Concerto
          Violin Concerto No. 2, *The Prophets*
1956 (61) *All's Well that Ends Well,* opera
1958 (63) *The Merchant of Venice,* opera
          Saul
1963 (68) *Song of Songs*
1966 (71) Sonata for cello and harp
Castelnuovo-Tedesco also composed:
Violin Concerti Nos. 1 and 3
Piano Concerto No. 2
Concerto Italiano
Symphonic Variations for violin and orchestra
An American Rhapsody
In Toscana, opera
Many oratorios.

CATALANI, Alfredo/1854–1893/Italy

1883 (29) *Dejanire,* opera
1886 (32) *Edmea,* opera
1890 (36) *Lorely,* opera
1892 (38) *La Wally,* opera

CHABRIER, Emanuel/1841–1894/France

1860 (19) Impromptu in C, for piano
1877 (36) *L'Étoile,* opera
1879 (38) *Une Éducation manquée*
1880 (39) Dix pieces pittoresques, for piano

1883 (42) *fp. España*, orchestral rhapsody
Trois Valses romantiques, for piano duo
1885 (44) *Habanera*, for piano
1886 (45) *Gwendoline*, opera
1887 (46) *Le Roi malgré lui*, opera
1888 (47) *Marche Joyeuse*, for orchestra

CHAMINADE, Cécile/1857–1944/France

1888 (31) *Callirhoe*, ballet
Chaminade also composed:
Concertstücke, for piano and orchestra
2 orchestral suites
Le Sevillane, opera-comique
2 piano trios
Many songs and piano pieces.

CHARPENTIER, Gustave/1860–1956/France

1890 (30) *Impressions d'Italie*, orchestral suite
1892 (32) *La Vie du poète*, cantata
1894 (34) *Poèmes chantées*, for voice and orchestra
1895 (35) *Impressions fausses*, for voice and
orchestra
1896 (36) *Sérénade à Watteau*, for voice and
orchestra
1900 (40) *Louise*, opera
1913 (53) *Julien*, opera

CHAUSSON, Ernest/1855–1899/France

1880 (25) *Les Caprices de Marianne*, opera
Joan of Arc, for chorus
1882 (27) *Viviane*, symphonic poem
Piano Trio in G minor
Poème de l'amour et de la mer, for voice
and piano (1882–92)
1884–85 (29) *Hélène*, opera
1886 (31) *Hymne Védique*, for chorus and orchestra
Solitude dans les bois, for orchestra

1887 (32) *Chant Nuptial*
1890 (35) Symphony in B♭ major
1891 (36) Concerto for piano, violin and string
           quartet
1896 (41) *Poème,* for violin and orchestra
1897 (42) *Chant Funèbre*
           Ballata
           Piano Quartet in A major
1898 (43) *Soir de fête*
1899 (44) String Quartet in C minor, unfinished
1903 (posthumous) *fp. Le Roi Arthur*

CHÁVEZ, Carlos/b.1899/Mexico ·

1920 (21) Symphony
           Piano Sonata No. 1
1921 (22) *El Fuego Nuevo,* ballet
           String Quartet No. 1
1923 (24) Piano Sonata No. 2
1924 (25) Sonatina for violin and piano
           Sonatina for cello and piano
1925 (26) *Energia,* for nine instruments
1926 (27) *Los cuatro soles,* ballet
1927 (28) *H.P.* (*i.e.,* Horsepower), ballet
1930 (31) Sonata for horns
1932 (33) String Quartet No. 2
1933 (34) Symphony No. 1, *Sinfonia di Antigone*
           Cantos de Mexico
           Soli No. 1, for oboe, clarinet, trumpet
             and bassoon
1935 (36) Symphony No. 2, *Sinfonia India*
           Obertura Republicana
1938 (39) Concerto for four horns
1939 (40) Four Nocturnes for voice and orchestra
1940 (41) Piano Concerto
           Antigona, ballet
           Xochipili-Macuilxochitl (the Aztec God
             of Music), for Mexican orchestra
1942 (43) Toccata for percussion instruments
1944 (45) *Hija de Colquide* (Daughter of Colchis),
           ballet
1945 (46) *Piramide*

1948–50 (49–51) Violin Concerto, in eight sections
played without a break (revised 1962)
1951 (52) Symphony No. 3
1953 (54) Symphony No. 4, *Sinfonia Romantica*
Symphony No. 5, *Symphony for Strings*
1958 (59) *Inventions* No. 1, for piano
1960 (61) *Love Propitiated,* opera
1961 (62) Symphony No. 6
Soli No. 2, for wind quintet
1964 (65) *Resonancias,* for orchestra
Tambuco, for six percussion
1965 (66) *Soli* No. 3, for bassoon, trumpet, viola,
timpani and orchestra
Violin Concerto No. 2
Inventions No. 2, for violin, viola and cello
1966 (67) *Soli* No. 4, for brass trio
1967 (68) *Inventions* No. 3, for harp
1969 (70) *Clio,* symphonic ode
Discovery, for orchestra
Fuego Olimpico, suite for orchestra

CHERUBINI, Luigi/1760–1842/Italy

1778 (18) *Demophon,* opera
1788 (28) *Ifigenia in Aulide,* opera
1797 (37) *Médée,* opera
1800 (40) *Les Deux journées,* opera
1803 (43) *Anacreon,* opera
1814 (54) String Quartet No. 1 in E♭ major
1815–29 (55–69) String Quartet No. 2 in C major
String Quartet No. 3 in D minor
1833 (73) *Ali Baba,* opera
1835 (75) String Quartet No. 4 in E major
String Quartet No. 5 in F major
String Quartet No. 6 in A minor
1836 (76) Requiem Mass in D minor
1837 (77) String Quartet in E minor

CHOPIN, Frederic/1810–1849/Poland

1817 (7) Polonaises No. 13 in G minor, and No. 14
in B♭ major

1821	(11)	Polonaise No. 15 in A♭ major
1822	(12)	Polonaise No. 16 in G minor
1825	(15)	Polonaise No. 8, Op. 71/1
1826	(16)	Three écossaises
		Polonaise No. 11 in B♭ minor
		Introduction and variations in E minor, on *Der Schweizerbub*
1827	(17)	Nocturne No. 19, Op. 72
1828	(18)	*Krakowiak,* concert rondo for orchestra
		Fantasia on Polish Airs, in A major, for piano and orchestra
		Rondo in C major, for two pianos
		Piano Sonata No. 1 in C minor
		Polonaises Nos. 9 and 10, Op. 71
1829	(19)	Piano Concerto No. 2 in F minor
		Introduction and Polonaise in C major, for cello and piano
		Twelve Grande Studies for piano (No. 5 "Black Keys", No. 12 "Revolutionary")
		Polonaise No. 12 in G♭ major
		Variations on a Theme by Paganini, in A major
		Waltz No. 10, Op. 69/2
		Waltz No. 13, Op. 70/3
1830	(20)	Piano Concerto No. 1, in E minor
1830–31		Nocturnes, Nos. 1–3, Op. 9
		Nine Mazurkas
1830–33		Nocturnes, Nos. 4–6, Op. 15
1831	(21)	Waltz No. 1 in E♭ major
		Waltz No. 3
1831–34		Andante Spianoto, and Grande Polonaise Brilliant, in E♭
1832	(22)	Allegro de Concert in A major (sketched, completed 1841)
		Scherzo No. 1
1833	(23)	Bolero in C major
		Introduction and Variations on a Theme by Hérold, in B♭ major
1834	(24)	Fantaisie Impromptu in C♯ minor
		Prelude No. 26 in A♭ major
1834–35		Polonaises, Nos. 1–2
1834–36		Études, Nos. 13–14
1835	(25)	Nocturnes, Nos. 7–8

                    Waltz No. 2
                    Waltz No. 9
                    Waltz No. 11
                    Ballade, Op. 23
1836–37 (26) Nocturnes, Nos. 9–10
1836–39 Ballade, Op. 38
             Preludes, Nos. 1–24
1837 (27) Impromptu, Op. 29
               Scherzo No. 2
               Nocturne in C minor (*p.* posthumous)
1838 (28) Waltz No. 4
1838–39 Nocturnes, Nos. 11–12
             Polonaises, Nos. 3–4
1839 (29) Études, Nos. 25–27 in Fm: A♭: D♭
               Impromptu, Op. 36
               Scherzo No. 3
               Piano Sonata No. 2 in B♭ minor
1840 (30) Waltz No. 5
1840–41 (30–31) Ballade, Op. 47
                     Fantasia in F minor
1841 (31) Nocturnes, Nos. 13–14
               Polonaise No. 5
               Prelude No. 25
               Waltz No. 12
1842 (32) Impromptu, Op. 51
               Polonaise No. 6
               Scherzo No. 4
               Ballade, Op. 52
1843 (33) Berceuse in D♭ major (revised 1844)
               Nocturnes, Nos. 15–16
1844 (34) Piano Sonata No. 3 in B minor
1845–46 (35) Cello Sonata in G minor
                  Barcarolle in F♯ minor
                  Polonaise No. 7
1846 (36) Nocturnes, Nos. 17–18
1846–47 (36) Waltzes, Nos. 6–8

CILÈA, Francesco/1866–1950/Italy

1886 (20) Piano Trio
1887 (21) Suite for orchestra
1889 (23) *Gina,* opera

1892 (26) *La Tilda*, opera
1894 (28) Cello Sonata
1897 (31) *L'Arlesiania*, opera
1902 (36) *Adriana Lecouvreur*, opera
1907 (41) *Gloria*, opera
1913 (47) *Il Canto della vita,* for voice, chorus and
           orchestra
1931 (65) Suite for orchestra

CIMAROSA, Domenico/1749–1801/Italy

1772 (23) *Le stravaganze del conte*, opera
1778 (29) *L'Italiana in Londra*, opera
1780 (31) *Giuditta*, oratorio
1781 (32) *Il pittore parigino*, opera
           Il Convito, opera
1782 (33) *La ballerina amante*, opera
           Absalon, oratorio
1784 (35) *L'Olimpiade*, opera
           Artaserse, opera
1786 (37) *L'Impresario in Angustie*, opera
1789 (40) *Cleopatra*, opera
1792 (43) *Il matrimonio segreto,* opera (this won
           wide fame for its combination of
           dramatic and musical values, in a
           style near Mozart's)
1793 (44) *I Traci amanti*, opera
           Concerto for two flutes and orchestra
1794 (45) *Penelope*, opera
1796 (47) *Gli Orazi e Curiazi*, opera

CLEMENTI, Muzio/1752–1832/Italy

1773–1832 (21–80) One hundred sonatas, including
                   sixty for piano

COLERIDGE-TAYLOR, Samuel/1875–1912/
Great Britain

1896 (21) Symphony in A minor

1898 (23) *Hiawatha's Wedding Feast,* cantata
          (words by Longfellow)
          Ballade in A minor, for orchestra
1899 (24) *Death of Minnehaha,* cantata
          (Longfellow)
          Solemn Prelude
1900 (25) *Hiawatha's Departure,* cantata
          (Longfellow)
1901 (26) *The Blind Girl of Castel-Cuille*
          Toussaint l'ouverture, concert overture
          Idyll
1902 (27) *Meg Blane*
1903 (28) *The Atonement,* oratorio
1905 (30) Five Choral Ballads
1906 (31) *Kubla Khan*
1909 (34) *Bon-Bon* suite
1910 (35) *Endymion's Dream,* for chorus
1911 (36) *A Tale of Old Japan,* cantata
          Bamboula, rhapsodic dance
          Violin Concerto in G minor

Coleridge-Taylor also composed chamber music and
many piano solos.

COPLAND, Aaron/b.1900/U.S.A.

1923 (23) *As it Fell Upon a Day,* for soprano, flute
          and clarinet
1924 (24) Symphony for organ and orchestra
1925 (25) *Grogh,* ballet
          Dance Symphony (1922–25)
          Music for the Theater, suite for small
          orchestra
1926 (26) Piano Concerto
1928 (28) Symphony No. 1 (an orchestral version
          of the Symphony for organ, minus
          organ)
1929 (29) Symphonic Ode (revised 1955)
          Vitebsk, study on a Jewish theme, for
          piano trio
1930 (30) Piano Variations
1933 (33) Symphony No. 2, *Short Symphony*

1934	(34)	*Statements*, for orchestra
		Hear Ye! Hear Ye!, ballet
1936	(36)	*El Salon Mexico*, for orchestra
1938	(38)	*An Outdoor Overture*
		Billy the Kid, ballet (also orchestral suite)
1940	(40)	*Quiet City*, orchestral suite for trumpet, English horn and strings
1941	(41)	Piano Sonata
1942	(42)	*Danzon Cubano*
		Rodeo, ballet
		fp. *A Lincoln Portrait*, for narrator and orchestra
1943	(43)	Violin Sonata
1944	(44)	*Appalachian Spring*, ballet (also orchestral suite)
1946	(46)	Symphony No. 3
1948	(48)	Concerto for clarinet and strings, with harp and piano
1950	(50)	Piano Quartet
		Twelve Poems of Emily Dickinson, for voice and piano
1951	(51)	*Pied Piper*, ballet
1954	(54)	*The Tender Land*, opera in three acts
1955	(55)	Symphonic Ode
		A Canticle of Freedom, for mixed chorus and orchestra (revised 1965)
1957	(57)	Orchestral Variations
		Piano Fantasy
1959	(59)	*Dance Panels*, ballet in seven sections (revised 1962)
1960	(60)	Nonet for strings
1962	(62)	*Connotations*, for orchestra
		Down a Country Lane, for orchestra
1964	(64)	*Music for a Great City*, for orchestra
		Emblems for a Symphonic Band
1967	(67)	*Inscape*, for orchestra
1971	(71)	Duo for flute and piano
1972	(72)	Three Latin-American Sketches

CORELLI, Arcangelo/1653–1713/Italy

1681 (28) *p*. Sonatas in three parts (Twelve Sonatas da Chiesa)
1685 (32) *p*. Sonatas in three parts (Twelve Sonatas da Camera)
1689 (36) *p*. Sonatas in three parts (Twelve Sonatas da Chiesa)
1694 (41) *p*. Sonatas in three parts (Twelve Sonatas da Camera)
1700 (47) *p*. Sonatas for violin and violone or harpsichord. The first six of these are "da Chiesa"; the next five, "da Camera"; and the last, the famous set of variations on "La Folia"
c.**1714** (*c*.54) *p*. Concerti Grossi

COUPERIN, François/1668–1733/France

1690 (22) Pièces d'orgue en deux messes:
Messe pour les Paroisses, twenty-one organ pieces
Messe pour les Couvents, twenty-one organ pieces
Messe Solenelle
1692 (24) Trio Sonata, *La Steinkerque*
1709 (41) Messe à l'usage des Couvents
1713 (45) Harpsichord Works, Book I
1715 (47) Leçons de ténèbres, for one and two voices
1717 (49) Harpsichord Works, Book II
1722 (54) Harpsichord Works, Book III
Four "Concerts Royeaux" for harpsichord, strings and wind instruments
1724 (56) *Les Goûts-Réunis,* ten concerts for various instruments
1730 (62) *p*. Harpsichord Works, Book IV

CUI, César/1835–1918/Russia

1857 (22) Scherzo for orchestra, Nos. 1 and 2
1858 (23) *The Caucasian Prisoner,* opera

1859 (24) Tarantella
The Mandarin's Son, opera
1869 (34) *William Ratcliffe*, opera
1875 (40) *Angelo*, opera
1881 (46) Marche Solenelle
1883 (48) *Suite Concertante*, for violin and orchestra
1886 (51) *Deux Morceaux*, for cello and orchestra
1888–89 (53) *Le Filibustier*, opera
1890 (55) String Quartet in C minor
String Quartet in D major
String Quartet in E♭ major
1897 (62) *p.* Five Little Duets, for flute and violin
with piano
1899 (64) *The Saracen*, opera
1903 (68) *Mlle. Fifi*, opera
1907 (72) *Matteo Falcone*, opera
1911 (76) *The Captain's Daughter*, opera
p. Violin Sonata in D major
Cui also composed:
Petite Suite for violin and piano
12 miniatures for violin and piano.

DALLAPICCOLA, Luigi/1904–1975/Italy

1937–38 (33) *Volo di Notte*, opera
1938–41 (34–37) *Canti di Prigionia*, for chorus and
instruments
1942 (38) *Cinque Frammente di Saffo*, for soprano
and chamber orchestra
Marsia, ballet
1943 (39) *Sex carmina Alcaei*, for soprano and
instruments
1944–45 (40) *Due liriche di Anacreonte*, for soprano
and instruments
1944–48 *Il Prigioniero*, opera
1945 (41) Ciaccona, Intermezzo e Adagio, for cello
1946–47 (42) Two pieces for orchestra
1948 (44) *Quattro liriche di Antonio Machado*,
for soprano and piano
1949 (45) *Tre poemi*, for soprano and chamber
orchestra

1949–50	*Job*, mystery play, for narrator, solo voices, chorus and orchestra
1951–55 (47–51)	*Canti di Liberazione*, for chorus and orchestra
1952 (48)	*Quaderno musicale di Annalibera*, for piano
	Goethe-Lieder, for mezzo-soprano and three clarinets (1952–53)
1954 (50)	*Piccola musica notturna*, for orchestra
1955 (51)	*An Mathilde*, cantata
1956 (52)	*Cinque canti*, for baritone and eight instruments
	Concerto per la notte di natale dell'anno, for soprano and chamber orchestra
1957–58 (53)	*Requiescat*, for chorus and orchestra
1959–60 (55)	*Dialoghi*, for cello and orchestra
1960–68 (56–64)	*Ulisse*, opera
1962 (58)	*Preghiere*, for baritone and chamber orchestra
1964 (60)	*Parole di San Paolo*, for voice and instruments
	Quattro liriche di Antonio Machado, version for soprano and orchestra
1970 (66)	Sicut umbra, for mezzo-soprano and twelve instruments
	Tempus aedificandi
1971 (67)	Tempus destruendi

DARGOMIZHSKY, Alexander/1813–1869/Russia

1847 (34)	*Esmeralda*, opera (possibly c.1839)
1856 (43)	*fp. Rusalka*, opera
1861–63 (48–50)	*Baba-Yaga*, fantasy for orchestra
1867 (54)	*The Triumph of Bacchus*, opera-ballet
1872 (posthumous)	*fp. The Stone Guest*, opera (completed by Cui, orchestrated by Rimsky-Korsakov, *q.v.*)

Dargomizhsky also composed:
About 90 songs
15 vocal duets
Tarentelle Slav, for piano, four hands
Finnish Fantasy

Kosachok, Ukrainian Dance
The Dance of the Mummers

DAVIES, Peter Maxwell/b.1934/Great Britain

1955 (21) Trumpet Sonata
             Stedman Doubles, for clarinet and
                percussion (revised 1967)
1956 (22) Five Pieces for Piano
1957 (23) *St. Michael* Sonata, for seventeen wind
                instruments
             Alma redemptoris Mater, for six wind
                instruments
1958 (24) Sextet
             Stedman Caters, for chamber ensemble
                (revised 1968)
1959 (25) *Prolation,* for orchestra
             Five motets, for soloists, choir and
                instruments
             Ricercare and Doubles on "To Many a
                Well", for eight instruments
1960 (26) *O Magnum Mysterium,* four carols for
                chorus, with instrumental sonatas and
                a fantasia for organ
1961 (27) Te Lucis Ante Terminium, for choir and
                chamber orchestra
             String Quartet
1962 (28) First Fantasia on an "In Nomine" of
                John Taverner, for orchestra
             Leopardi Fragments, for soprano,
                contralto and instruments
             Sinfonia for chamber orchestra
1963 (29) Veni Sancte Spiritus, for soloists, chorus
                and small orchestra
             Seven "In Nomine", for instruments
                (1963–65)
1964 (30) Second Fantasia on John Taverner's "In
                Nomine", for orchestra
             Shakespeare Music, for chamber ensemble
1965 (31) *The Shepherd's Calender,* for young
                singers and instrumentalists

Revelation and Fall, for soprano solo
   and instruments
Ecce Manus Tradentis, for mixed choir
   and instruments
Shall I Die for Mannes Sake, carol for
   soprano and alto voices and piano
1966 (32) Five Carols for soprano and alto voices
   unaccompanied
Notre Dame des Fleurs, for soprano,
   mezzo-soprano, counter-tenor and
   instruments
1967 (33) *Antechrist*, for chamber ensemble
Hymnos, for clarinet and piano
1968 (34) *L'Homme Armé*, for speaker (or singer)
   and chamber ensemble (revised 1971)
1969 (35) *St. Thomas Wake*, Foxtrot for orchestra
   on a Pavan by John Bull
Eight Songs for a Mad King, for male
   singer and chamber ensemble
Worldes Bliss, for orchestra
Eram quasi Agnus, instrumental motet
Vesalii Icones, for dancer, solo cello and
   ensemble
1970 (36) *Taverner*, opera
1971 (37) *From Stone to Thorn*, for mezzo-soprano
   and instrumental ensemble
1972 (38) *Blind Man's Buff*, a masque
Fool's Fanfare, for speaker and
   instrumental ensemble
Hymn to St. Magnus, for soprano and
   chamber ensemble
Tenebrae super Gesualdo, for mezzo-
   soprano, guitar and chamber ensemble
Canon in memory of Igor Stravinsky,
   for instrumental ensemble
1973 (39) *Stone Litany*, for mezzo-soprano and
   orchestra
Scottish Dances for instrumental ensemble
Fiddlers at the Wedding, for mezzo-
   soprano and chamber orchestra
   (1973–74)
1974 (40) *Dark Angels*, for soprano and guitar

> *Miss Donnithorne's Maggot,* for mezzo-
> soprano and chamber ensemble
> *All Sons of Adam,* motet for instrumental
> ensemble

1975 (41) Ave Maris Stella, for instrumental
ensemble

DEBUSSY, Claude/1862–1918/France

1876–79 (14–17) Trio in G minor
1880 (18) *Danse bohémienne,* for piano
Andante for piano
La Belle au bois dormant, song
(1880–83)
1881 (19) Fugue for piano
1882 (20) Two four-part fugues, for piano
Triomphe de Bacchus, for piano duet
Intermezzo, for orchestra
Printemps, for women's choir and
orchestra
1883 (21) *Invocation,* for male voice choir and
orchestra
Le Gladiateur, cantata
1884 (22) *L'Enfant prodigue,* cantata
Diane au bois, for chorus
Divertissement I, for orchestra
Suite for Orchestra, No. 1
1885 (23) *Almanzor,* for chorus
1887–88 (25) *The Blessed Damozel (La Damoiselle
élue),* cantata (on a French translation
of Rossetti's poem)
1887–89 Cinq poèmes de Baudelaire, songs
1888 (26) *Petite Suite,* for piano, four hands:
"En bateau"
"Cortège"
"Menuet"
"Ballet"
Arabesques I and II, for piano
Ariettes oubliées, songs
1889–90 (27) *Fantaisie,* for piano and orchestra
1890 (28) *Suite Bergamasque,* for piano:
"Prélude"

"Menuet"
"Clair de Lune"
"Passepied"
Tarentelle Styrienne (Danse), for piano
Ballade, for piano
Rêverie, for piano
Valse romantique, for piano
1891 (29) *Mazurka*, for piano
Marche écossaise
Trois mélodies de Verlaine, songs
Deux Romances, songs
Rodrigue et Chimène, opera in three acts
(unfinished)
1892 (30) *Fêtes galantes*, songs (first series)
1893 (31) String Quartet in G minor
Proses lyriques, songs
1894 (32) *Prélude à l'après-midi d'un faune*, for
orchestra
1897 (35) *Chansons de Bilitis*, songs
1900 (38) *Nocturnes*, for orchestra:
"Nuages"
"Fêtes"
"Sirenes", with wordless female chorus
1901 (39) *Pour le piano:* (possibly 1896)
"Prélude"
"Sarabande"
"Toccata"
1902 (40) *Pelléas et Mélisande*, opera
1903 (41) *Estampes:*
"Pagodas"
"Soirée dans Grenade"
"Jardins sous la pluie"
Danse sacrée et danse profane, for harp
and strings
D'un cahier d'esquisses, for piano
Le Diable dans le beffroi, libretto and
musical sketches
1903–05 (41–43) *Rhapsodie*, for saxophone,
contralto and orchestra
1904 (42) *L'Isle Joyeuse*, for piano
Trois chansons de France
Masques, for piano

La Mer, three symphonic sketches
Fêtes Galantes, songs (second series)
1905 (43) Images, for piano, Book I:
    "Reflets dans l'eau"
    "Hommage à Rameau"
    "Mouvement"
1907 (45) Images, for piano, Book II:
    "Cloches à travers les feuilles"
    "Et la lune descend sur la temple qui fut"
    "Poissons d'or"
1908 (46) Children's Corner, for piano:
    "Doctor Gradus ad Parnassum"
    "Jumbo's Lullaby"
    "Doll's Serenade"
    "Snow is Dancing"
    "Little Shepherd"
    "Golliwog's Cake-walk"
    Ibéria (No. 2 of Images for orchestra)
    Trois chansons de Charles d'Orléans,
      for unaccompanied chorus
    The Fall of the House of Usher (sketches
      for libretto and vocal score, unfinished,
      1908–10)
1909 (47) Rondes de Printemps (No. 3 of Images
      for orchestra)
    Homage à Haydn, for piano
1909–10 Préludes for piano, Book I (12 préludes)
    Trois ballades de François Villon, songs
    Petite piece en B♭, for clarinet and piano
    La plus qui lente, for piano
    Le Promenoir des deux amants, three songs
    Rhapsody for clarinet, No. 1
1911 (49) Martyrdom of St. Sebastian, incidental
      music to d'Annunzio's mystery-play
1912 (50) Gigues (No. 1 of Images for orchestra)
    Jeux, poème dansé, for orchestra
    Khamma, ballet
    Syrinx, for solo flute
1913 (51) La Boîte à Joujoux, ballet music for piano
    Préludes for piano, Book II (12 préludes)
    Trois poèmes de Mallarmé, songs
1914 (52) Berceuse héroïque, for piano

1915 (53) Cello Sonata in D minor
En Blanc et noir, piano duet
Twelve Etudes for piano
Six Épigraphes Antiques
Noël des enfants, for chorus
1916 (54) Sonata for flute, viola and harp, in G minor
Ode à la France, for chorus (1916–17)
1917 (55) Violin Sonata in G minor and G major

DELIBES, Léo/1836–1891/France

1866 (30) *La Source (Nalla)*, ballet
1870 (34) *Coppélia*, ballet
1876 (40) *Sylvia*, ballet
1882 (46) *Le Roi s'amuse*, incidental music
1883 (47) *Lakmé*, opera

DELIUS, Frederick/1862–1934/Great Britain

1886 (24) *Florida Suite*, for orchestra
1888 (26) *Marche Caprice*, for orchestra
Sleigh Ride, for orchestra
1892 (30) *Irmelin*, opera
1895 (33) *Over the Hills and Far Away*, tone poem
1899 (37) *Paris—The Song of a Great City*,
nocturne for orchestra
1902 (40) *Appalachia*, for orchestra, with final
chorus
1903 (41) *Sea Drift*, for baritone, chorus and
orchestra
1904 (42) *Koanga*, opera
1905 (43) *A Mass of Life*, for soloists, chorus and
orchestra, text from Nietzsche's *Thus
Spake Zarathustra*
1906 (44) Piano Concerto in C minor
1907 (45) *Brigg Fair—an English Rhapsody*, for
orchestra
Songs of Sunset
A Village Romeo and Juliet, opera (from
which comes the "Walk to the Paradise
Garden")

1908 (46)   Dance Rhapsody No. 1, for orchestra
In a Summer Garden
1912 (50)   *On Hearing the First Cuckoo in Spring,*
     for orchestra
Summer Night on the River, for orchestra
Song of the High Hills, for wordless
     chorus and orchestra
1914 (52)   *North Country Sketches,* for orchestra
1916 (54)   Violin Concerto
Dance Rhapsody No. 2, for orchestra
1917 (55)   *Eventyr,* for chorus and orchestra
1918 (56)   *A Song Before Sunrise*
1919 (57)   *Fennimore and Gerda,* opera
1920 (58)   *Hassan,* incidental music
1922 (60)   *A Pagan Requiem* (possibly 1914–16)
1925 (63)   *Caprice and Elegy,* for cello and orchestra
1930 (68)   *A Song of Summer*
1932 (70)   *Prelude to Irmelin* (based on themes from
     the earlier opera)
1934 (72)   *Songs of Farewell,* for choir and orchestra

DIAMOND, David/b.1915/U.S.A.

1935 (20)   Partita, for oboe, bassoon and piano
1936 (21)   *Psalm,* for orchestra
Sinfonietta
TOM, ballet
Concerto for string quartet
Violin Concerto No. 1
Cello Sonata
1937 (22)   Variations for small orchestra
Quintet for flute, string trio and piano
1938 (23)   *Heroic Piece,* for small orchestra
Elegy in memory of Ravel, for brass,
     harps and percussion
Music, for double string orchestra, brass
     and timpani
Cello Concerto
Piano Quartet
1940 (25)   Concerto for small orchestra
Symphony No. 1
Quartet No. 1

1941 (26) *The Dream of Audubon*, ballet
1942 (27) Symphony No. 2
Concerto for two solo pianos
1943 (28) Quartet No. 2
1944 (29) *The Tempest*, incidental music
Rounds, for string orchestra
1945 (30) Symphonies Nos. 3 and 4
1946 (31) Quartet No. 3
Violin Sonata
1947 (32) Violin Concerto No. 2
Romeo and Juliet, incidental music
Piano Sonata
1948 (33) *Chaconne*, for violin and piano
1949 (34) *L'Âme de Debussy*, song cycle
Timon of Athens, symphonic portrait
1950 (35) Piano Concerto
Chorale for chorus
Quintet for two violas, two cellos and
clarinet
1951 (36) Quartet No. 4
Symphony No. 6
Mizmor l'David, sacred service for tenor,
chorus, orchestra and organ
The Midnight Meditation, song cycle
Piano Trio
1954 (40) Sinfonia Concertante
Sonata for solo violin
1956 (41) Sonata for solo cello
1957 (42) *The World of Paul Klee*
1958 (43) Woodwind Quintet
1959 (44) Symphony No. 7
1960 (45) Symphony No. 8
Quartet No. 5
1961 (46) Nonet for three violins, three violas and
three cellos
1962 (47) *This Sacred Ground*, for baritone, chorus,
children's chorus and orchestra
Quartet No. 6
1963 (48) Quartet No. 7
1964 (49) Quartet No. 8
We Two, song cycle
1966 (51) Quartets Nos. 9 and 10

1967 (52) *To Music,* choral symphony for tenor,
bass-baritone, chorus and orchestra
Hebrew Melodies, song cycle
Violin Concerto No. 3
1969 (54) Music for chamber orchestra
1974 (59) *fp.* Quartet No. 10

DITTERSDORF, Carl Ditters von/1739–1799/
Germany

1767 (28) *Amore in Musica,* opera
1770 (31) *Il Viaggiatore americano,* opera
1771 (32) *L'Amore disprezzato,* opera
1773 (34) *Il Tutore e la Pupilla,* opera
1774 (35) *Il tribunale de Giove,* opera
1775 (36) *Il finto pazzo per amore,* opera
Il maniscalco, opera
Lo Sposo burlato, opera
1776 (37) *La contadina felice,* opera
La moda, opera
Il barone di Rocca Antica, opera
1777 (38) *L'Arcifanfano, re de' matti,* opera
1786 (47) *Doktur und Apotheker,* opera
Betrug durch Aberglauben, opera
1787 (48) *Democrito corretto,* opera
Die Liebe in Narrenhaus, opera
1789 (50) *Hieronimus Knicker,* opera
1790 (51) *Das rote Käppchen,* opera
1791 (52) *Hokus Pokus,* opera
1794 (55) *Des Gespeust mit de Trommel,* opera
1795 (56) *Don Quixote der Zeite,* opera
Gott Mars, opera
Schach vom Schiras, opera
1796 (57) *Ugolino,* opera
Die Lustigen Weiber von Windsor, opera
Der Durchmarsch, opera
1797 (58) *Der Terno secco,* opera
Der Mädchenmarkt, opera
Dittersdorf also composed church music, symphonies,
and string quartets.

DOHNÁNYI, Ernst von/1877–1960/Hungary

1895 (18) *fp.* Piano Quintet in C minor (Op. 1, published 1902)
1896 (19) *Zrinyi,* overture
1897 (20) Symphony No. 1 in F major
1903 (26) *p.* String Quartet in A major
            p. Cello Sonata in B♭ minor
1904 (27) *p.* Serenade in C major, for string trio
1907 (30) *p.* String Quartet in D major
1910 (33) *Der Schlier der Pierette,* ballet
            p. Piano Quintet in E♭ major
1913 (36) *p.* Violin Sonata in C♯ minor
            Tante Simona, opera
1915 (38) Violin Concerto No. 1
1916 (39) *Variations on a Nursery Song,* for piano and orchestra
1919 (42) Suite in F♯ minor
1920 (43) *Hitvallas,* for tenor, choir and orchestra
1922 (45) *The Tower of the Voivod*
1929 (52) *A Tenor,* opera
1941? (?64) Cantus Vitae, cantata
1946 (69) Piano Concerto No. 2
1950 (73) Twelve Studies for Piano
1952 (75) Violin Concerto No. 2
            Harp Concerto
1953 (76) Stabat Mater
1954 (77) *American Rhapsody*
Dohnányi also composed:
Symphony No. 2 in D minor, (Op. 9)
Concertstücke for Cello, (Op. 12)
Ruralia Hungarica, for piano (later orchestrated) (Op. 33)
Symphony No. 3 in E major
No details are available of Dohnányi's work from 1929 until he went to the United States in 1946.

DONIZETTI, Gaetano/1797–1848/Italy

1830 (33) *Anna Bolena,* opera
1832 (35) *L'Elisir d'Amore,* opera

1833 (36) *Lucrezia Borgia,* opera
1834 (37) *Rosmonda d'Inghilterra,* opera
1835 (38) *Lucia di Lammermoor,* opera
1840 (43) *La Favorita,* opera
              La Fille du régiment, opera
1842 (45) *Linda de Chamounix,* opera
1843 (46) *Maria de Rohan,* opera
              Don Pasquale, opera
              Don Sébastien, opera
Donizetti composed more than 60 operas, some in
French.

DOWLAND, John/1563–1626/Great Britain

1597 (34) *p.* First book of Songes or Ayres
1600 (37) *p.* Second book of Songes
1603 (40) *p.* Third book of Songes or Ayres
1604 (41) *p. Lachrymae*
1612 (49) *p.* Fourth book of Songes, *A Pilgrimes
              Solace*

DUKAS, Paul/1865–1935/France

1892 (27) *Polyeucte,* overture
1896 (31) Symphony in C major
1897 (32) *The Sorcerer's Apprentice,* symphonic
              poem
1901 (36) Piano Sonata in E♭ minor
1903 (38) Variations, Interlude and Finale on a
              Theme by Rameau, for piano
1906 (41) *Villanelle,* for horn and piano
1907 (42) *Ariadne and Bluebeard,* opera
1909 (44) *Prélude élégiaque,* for piano
              Vocalise
1912 (47) *La Péri—poème dansé,* for orchestra
              (possibly 1921)
1921 (56) *La Plainte, au loin, du faune,* for piano
1924 (59) *Sonnet de Ronsard,* for voice and piano

DURUFLÉ, Maurice/b.1902/France

1926 (24) Scherzo, for organ
1927 (25) *Triptyque,* for piano
1928 (26) *Prélude, récitatif et variations,* for flute,
 viola and piano
1929 (27) Prélude, Adagio and Chorale Variations
 on "Veni, Creator", for organ
1930 (28) Suite (Prélude, Sicilienne and Toccata)
 for organ
1935 (33) Three Dances for orchestra
1940 (38) Andante and Scherzo, for orchestra
1942 (40) *Prélude et Fugue sur l'nom Alain,* for
 organ
1947 (45) *Requiem,* for mezzo-soprano, bass, choir,
 orchestra and organ
1960 (58) Four Motets on Gregorian themes, for
 choir a cappella
1967 (65) Mass "Cum Jubilo", for baritone solo,
 choir, orchestra and organ

DVORAK, Antonin/1841–1904/Bohemia
 (Czechoslovakia)

1857–59 (16–18) Mass in B♭ major
1861 (20) String Quintet in A minor
1862 (21) String Quartet No. 1 in A major
1865 (24) Symphony No. 1 in C minor
 Symphony No. 2 in B♭ major
 Cello Concerto in A major
 Clarinet Quintet
 The Cypresses, ten love songs for string
 quartet
1870 (29) *Alfred*
 Dramatic (Tragic) Overture
 Notturno, in B major, for strings
 String Quartet in B♭ major
 String Quartet in D major
 String Quartet in E minor
1871 (30) *King and Charcoal Burner,* opera (1st
 version)

           Rosmarine
           Overture in F major
           Piano Trios, Nos. 1 and 2
           Cello Sonata
1872 (31) Patriotic Hymn
           May Night, Nocturne for orchestra
           Piano Quintet in A major
1873 (32) Symphony No. 3 in E♭ major
           Romance, for violin and orchestra
           String Quartet in F minor
           String Quartet in A minor
           Octet *Serenade*
           Violin Sonata in A minor
1874 (33) Symphony No. 4 in D minor
           Rhapsody for orchestra, in A minor
           String Quartet in A minor
1875 (34) Symphony No. 5 in F major (old
              numbering: No. 3)
           Serenade for strings, in E major
           String Quintet, with double-bass, in G
              major
           Piano Quartet in D major
           Piano Trio in B♭ major
           Moravian Vocal Duets
1876 (35) Piano Concerto in G minor
           Stabat Mater
           String Quartet in E major
           Piano Trio in G minor
           Four songs for mixed choir
1877 (36) *The Cunning Peasant,* opera
           Symphonic Variations for orchestra
           String Quartet in D minor
1878 (37) *Slavonic Dances,* for orchestra (first series)
           Slavonic Rhapsodies, for orchestra
           Serenade in D minor, for orchestra
           String Sextet in A major
           Bagatelles, for two violins, cello and
              harmonium (or piano)
1879 (38) Violin Concerto in A minor (1879–80)
           Festival March
           Czech Suite in D major
           Mazurka, for violin and orchestra

		String Quartet in E♭ major
		Polonaise in E♭ major
1880	(39)	Symphony No. 6 in D major (old numbering: No. 1)
		Violin Sonata in F major
		Gipsy Songs
1881	(40)	*Legends,* for orchestra
		String Quartet in C major
1882	(41)	*My Home,* overture
1883	(42)	*Husitska,* overture
		Scherzo Capriccioso, for orchestra
		Piano Trio in F minor
1885	(44)	Symphony No. 7 in D minor (old numbering: No. 2)
		The Spectre's Bride, cantata
1886	(45)	*Slavonic Dances* for orchestra (second series)
		St. Ludmila, oratorio
1887	(46)	Piano Quintet in A major
		Piano Quartet in E♭ major
		Terzetto for two violins and viola
1889	(48)	Symphony No. 8 in G major (old numbering: No. 4)
1890	(49)	Gavotte, for three violins
		Piano Trio, *Dumka* (1890–91)
1891	(50)	*Nature, Life and Love,* cycle of overtures:
		"Amid Nature"
		"Carnival"
		"Othello" (1891–92)
		Rondo, for cello and orchestra
		Forest Calm, for cello and orchestra
1892	(51)	Te Deum
1893	(52)	Symphony No. 9 in E minor, *From the New World* (old numbering: No. 5)
		String Quartet in F major, *American*
		String Quartet in E♭ major
1895	(54)	Suite for orchestra
		Cello Concerto in B minor
		String Quartet in A♭ major
		String Quartet in G major
1896	(55)	Four Symphonic Poems:
		The Watersprite
		The Noonday Witch

> The Wood Dove
> The Golden Spinning-wheel

1897 (56) Heroic Song
1901 (60) *fp. Rusalka,* opera

ELGAR, Sir Edward/1857–1934/Great Britain

1878 (21) *Romance,* for violin and piano (also
arrangement for violin and orchestra)
Promenades, six pieces for wind
instruments
1879 (22) *Harmony Music,* seven pieces for wind
instruments (No. 7 1881)
Intermezzos for Wind, five pieces
1883 (26) *Une Idyll,* for violin and piano (*c.*1883)
Fugue in D minor, for oboe and violin
1890 (33) *Froissart,* concert overture
1891 (34) *La Capriceuse,* for violin and piano
1892 (35) *Serenade for Strings*
The Black Knight, cantata
1894–95 (37) *Scenes from the Saga of King Olaf,*
cantata
1895 (38) Organ Sonata in G major
1896 (39) *The Light of Life (Lux Christi),* oratorio
1897 (40) Imperial March
The Banner of St. George, a ballad for
soprano, chorus and orchestra
Sea Pictures, five songs for contralto and
orchestra
1898 (41) *Caractacus,* cantata for soprano, tenor,
baritone and bass soli, chorus and
orchestra
Variations on an Original Theme, *Enigma,*
for orchestra (1898–99)
1899 (42) *Sérénade Lyrique,* for orchestra
In the South (Alassio), concert overture
1900 (43) *The Dream of Gerontius,* oratorio
1901 (44) *Cockaigne* overture *(In London Town)*
Concerto allegro for piano
Introduction and Allegro for strings
(1901–05)

              Pomp and Circumstance Marches 1–4
                 (1901–07)
1902 (45) Coronation Ode
              Dream Children, two pieces for piano or
                 small orchestra
              Falstaff, symphonic study in C minor
                 (1902–13)
1903 (46) *The Apostles,* oratorio
*c.***1903**–10 (*c.*46–53) Symphony No. 2 in E♭ major
1906 (49) *The Kingdom,* oratorio
              The Wand of Youth, Suites 1 and 2, for
                 orchestra—final version 1906–07
                 (begun in 1867, 1869, or 1871; revised
                 1879–81; revised again *c.*1902)
1907 (50) Symphony No. 1 in A♭ major (1907–08)
1909 (52) Violin Concerto (*c.*1909–10)
              Elegy, for string orchestra
1910 (53) *Romance,* for bassoon and orchestra
1912 (55) *The Music Makers,* for contralto, chorus
                 and orchestra
1914 (57) *Carillon,* recitation with orchestra
              p. Sospiri, for orchestra
1915 (58) *Polonia,* symphonic prelude
              Une Voix dans le desert, recitation with
                 orchestra
1917 (60) *fp. The Spirit of England,* three pieces for
                 voices and orchestra:
                      No. 1 *The Fourth of August* (finished
                        1917)
                      No. 2 *To Women* (1915)
                      No. 3 *For the Fallen* (1915)
               Le Drapeau Belge, recitation with
                  orchestra
               Fringes of the Fleet, song cycle
1918 (61) Violin Sonata in E minor
              String Quartet in E minor
               Piano Quintet in A minor (1918–19)
1919 (62) Cello Concerto in E minor
1923 (66) *fp. King Arthur,* incidental music
1924 (67) *fp. Pageant of Empire*
1928 (71) *fp. Beau Brummel,* incidental music
1930 (73) *Severn Suite,* for brass band, also
                 arranged for orchestra

> *Pomp and Circumstance*, March No. 5
> for orchestra

1931 (74)   *p. Nursery Suite* for orchestra (dedicated
> to T.R.H. Princesses Elizabeth and
> Margaret Rose)

ENESCO, Georges/1881–1955/Rumania

1895 (14)   *Ouverture tragica e ouverture trionfale*
> Four *Sinfonie scolastiche* (1895–96)
1897 (16)   *Rumanian Poem*
1898 (17)   p. Violin Sonata No. 1
1899 (18)   *Fantaisie Pastorale*
1901 (20)   *Rumanian Rhapsody*, No. 1
> *Symphonie Concertante*, for cello and
> orchestra
> p. Violin Sonata No. 2
1902 (21)   *Rumanian Rhapsody*, No. 2
1903 (22)   Suite for orchestra
1905 (24)   Symphony No. 1 in E♭ major
> p. String Octet in C major
1911 (30)   Symphony No. 2 in A major
1915 (34)   Suite for Orchestra
1919 (38)   Symphony No. 3 with organ and chorus
1921 (40)   Violin Concerto
> *Oedipus*, opera (begun *c.*1921)
1937 (56)   *Suite Villageoise*, for orchestra
1950 (69)   *Vox Maris*, symphonic poem

FALLA, Manuel de/1876–1946/Spain

1908 (32)   *Pièces espagnoles*, for piano
1909 (33)   *Trois mélodies*, songs
> *Nights in the gardens of Spain*, for piano
> and orchestra (1909–15)
1913 (37)   *fp. La Vida brève*, opera
1915 (39)   *fp. El Amor Brujo*, ballet
1919 (43)   *fp. The Three-cornered Hat*, ballet
> *Fantasia bética*, piano solo
1921 (45)   *Homage pour la Tombeau de Debussy*,
> for guitar

104

1922 (46) *El Retablo de Maese Pedro,* opera
Seven Spanish Popular Songs
1923–26 (47–50) Concerto for harpsichord, flute, oboe, clarinet, violin and cello
1934 (58) Fanfare for wind and percussion
1935 (59) *Pour le Tombeau de Paul Dukas,* for piano
1940 (64) *Homenajes,* orchestral version of "Homage pour le Tombeau de Debussy"

FARNABY, Giles/*c.*1560–*c.*1600/Great Britain

1598 (*c.*38) Canzonets to Foure Voyces
Farnaby also composed over 50 pieces in the
Fitzwilliam Virginal Book.

FAURÉ, Gabriel/1845–1924/France

1870 (25) "Puisqu'ici-bas", duet for two sopranos
"Tarentella", duet for two sopranos
1873 (28) *Cantique de Jean Racine*
1875 (30) *Les Djinns,* for chorus and orchestra
Suite for Orchestra
Allegro Symphonique, for orchestra
1876 (31) Violin Sonata in A major
1878 (33) Violin Concerto
1879 (34) Piano Quartet No. 1 in C minor
1880 (35) *Berceuse,* for violin and piano
1881 (36) Ballade, for piano and orchestra
Le Ruisseau
1882 (37) *Romance,* for violin and orchestra
Le Naissance de Venus
1883 (38) *Élégie* in C minor
Four Valse-Caprices, for piano (1883–94)
Five Impromptus (1883–1910)
Thirteen Nocturnes (1883–1922)
Thirteen Barcarolles (1883–1921)
1884 (39) Symphony in D minor (unpublished)
1886 (41) Piano Quartet No. 2 in G minor

1887 (42) Requiem
Pavane, with chorus ad lib
1888 (43) *Caligula*, incidental music
1889 (44) *Shylock*, incidental music
Petite Pièce, for cello and piano
1890 (45) Cinq mélodies de Verlaine, songs
1891–92 (46) *La Bonne Chanson*, nine songs
1893 (48) *Dolly Suite*, for piano duet
1895 (50) *Romance*, for cello and piano
1897 (52) Theme and variations for piano
1898 (53) *Pelléas et Mélisande*, incidental music
Andante for violin and piano
Papillon, for cello and piano
Sicilienne, for cello and piano
Fantasia for flute and piano
1900 (55) *Promethée*, lyric tragedy
1901 (56) *La Voile du bonheur*, incidental music
1904 (59) Impromptu for harp
1906 (61) Piano Quintet in D minor
Le Chanson d'Eve, song cycle (1906–10)
1908 (63) *Sérénade*, for cello and piano
1910 (65) Nine Préludes
1913 (68) *Pénélope*, opera
1915–18 (70–73) *Le Jardin clos*, eight songs
1917 (72) Violin Sonata No. 2 in E minor and
E major
1918 (73) Cello Sonata No. 1 in D minor
Une Châtelaine et sa tour, for harp
1919 (74) Fantaisie for piano and orchestra
Mirages, four songs
1920 (75) *Masques et Bergamasques*, suite
1921 (76) Piano Quintet No. 2 in C minor
1922 (77) Cello Sonata No. 2 in G minor
L'Horizon chimerique, songs
1923 (78) Piano Trio in D minor
1924 (79) String Quartet

FELDMAN, Morton/b.1926/U.S.A.

1951 (25) *Projections* 1 and 2, for flute, trumpet,
violin and cello
Intersection I

1957 (31) Pieces for four pianos
1959 (33) *Atlantis,* for chamber orchestra
1960–61 (34) *Durations* I–V
1962 (36) *Last Pieces,* for piano
    The Swallows of Salangan, for chorus
     and sixteen instruments
1963 (37) *Christian Wolff in Cambridge*
1965 (39) *Journey to the End of Night,* for soprano
     and four wind instruments
    De Kooning, for piano trio, horn and
     percussion
    Four Instruments
1966–67 (40) *First Principles*
1967 (41) *Chorus and Instruments*
    In Search of an Orchestration
1968 (42) *Vertical Thoughts 2*
    *False Relationships and the Extended
     Ending,* for two chamber groups
1969 (43) *On Time and the Instrumental Factor,*
     for orchestra
1970 (44) *Madame Press Died Last Week at 90,*
     for instrumental ensemble
    The Viola in My Life I and II, for solo
     viola and instruments
    The Viola in My Life III, for viola and
     piano
1971 (45) *The Viola in My Life* IV, for viola and
     orchestra
    Chorus and Orchestra
    Three Clarinets, Cello and Piano
    Rothko Chapel, for solo viola, soprano,
     alto, chorus, percussion and celeste
    I Met Heine on the Rue Fürstenberg,
     for voice and chamber ensemble
1972 (46) *Cello and Orchestra*
    Voice and Instruments
    Chorus and Orchestra II
    Voices and Instruments
    Piano and Voices, for five pianos (pianists
     also hum)
    Pianos and Voices II, for five pianos and
     five voices

1973 (47) *String Quartet and Orchestra*
For Frank O'Hara, for instrumental
ensemble
Voices and Cello
1974 (48) *Instruments* I
Voice and Instruments II
1975 (49) *Piano and Orchestra*
Instruments II
Four Instruments II

FIELD, John/1782–1837/Great Britain

1814 (22) Three Nocturnes, for piano
1832 (50) *fp.* Piano Concerto No. 1 in E♭ major
Field also composed:
7 concertos
4 sonatas
20 nocturnes (invented the name and style of
Nocturne)
6 rondos
2 divertissements
2 fantasias
2 piano quintets
4 romances, etc.

FINE, Irving/1914–1962/U.S.A.

1942 (28) *Alice in Wonderland,* incidental music
1944 (30) *The Choral New Yorker,* cantata
1946 (32) *Fantasia,* for string trio
Violin Sonata
1948 (34) *Toccata Concertante,* for orchestra
Partita for wind quintet
1949 (35) *The Hour-glass,* choral cycle
1952 (38) String Quartet
Mutability, song cycle
1955 (41) *Serious Song and Lament,* for string
orchestra
1960 (46) *Diversion,* for orchestra
1961 (47) *Romanza,* for wind quintet
1962 (48) Symphony No. 2

1924 (23) *Severn Rhapsody*
1933 (32) *A Young Man's Exhortation,* song cycle
1934–37 (33–36) Seven Part-Songs (Bridges) for
                unaccompanied chorus
1935 (34) *Introit,* for violin and orchestra, revised
                1945
1936 (35) *Earth, Air and Rain,* song cycle
                Three Short Elegies, for unaccompanied
                  chorus
                Five Two-part Songs (Christina Rossetti)
                  and Five Unison Songs
                Two Sonnets by John Milton, for high
                  voice and small orchestra
                Interlude, for oboe and string quartet
1940 (39) *Dies Natalis,* cantata
1942 (41) *Let us Garlands Bring,* five songs
                Prelude and Fugue for violin, viola and
                  cello
1945 (44) *Farewell to Arms,* for tenor and small
                orchestra
                Five Bagatelles for clarinet and piano
1946 (45) "Lo, the full and final sacrifice", festival
                anthem
1947 (46) *Ode for St. Cecilia's Day* (possibly 1950)
1948 (47) *Love's Labours Lost,* incidental music
1949 (48) Clarinet Concerto
                Before and After Summer, song cycle
1950 (49) *Intimations of Immortality,* for tenor,
                chorus and orchestra
1952 (51) *Love's Labours Lost,* orchestral suite
1954 (53) *Grand Fantasia and Toccata,* for piano
                and orchestra
1955 (54) Cello Concerto
1956 (55) *In Terra Pax,* for chorus and orchestra
                Eclogue, for piano and string orchestra
1958 (posthumous) *p. The Fall of the Leaf,* for
                orchestra
1959 (posthumous) *p. To a Poet,* song cycle

FLOTOW, Friedrich/1812–1883/Germany

1847 (35) *Martha,* opera
Flotow composed a great many operas, only one of
which has survived.

FOSS, Lukas/b.1922/U.S.A. (b.Germany)

1938 (16) Four two-part Inventions for piano
Drei Goethe-Lieder
1940 (18) Music for *The Tempest*
Two Symphonic Pieces
Four Preludes, for flute, clarinet and
bassoon
1941 (19) *Allegro Concertante,* for orchestra
Dance Sketch, for orchestra
Duo for cello and piano
1942 (20) *The Prairie,* for chorus with soloists and
orchestra
Clarinet Concerto (later revised as Piano
Concerto No. 1)
1943 (21) *Paradigm,* for percussion
1944 (22) *The Heart Remembers,* ballet
Within These Walls, ballet
Symphony
Ode, for orchestra (revised 1958)
1945 (23) *Song of Anguish,* for voice and piano,
or orchestra
1946 (24) *Song of Songs,* for voice and orchestra
Composer's Holiday, for violin and piano
1947 (25) String Quartet
1948 (26) Oboe Concerto
Ricordare, for orchestra
Capriccio, for cello and piano
1949 (27) *The Jumping Frog of Calaveras County,*
opera
Piano Concerto No. 2
1952 (30) *Parable of Death,* for tenor, narrator and
orchestra
1955 (33) *Griffelkin,* opera
The Gift of the Magi, ballet

1956 (34) Psalms, for chorus and orchestra
1957 (35) *Behold! I Build an House,* for chorus
1958 (36) *Symphony of Chorales*
1959 (37) *Introductions and Goodbyes,* opera
1960 (38) *Time Cycle,* four songs with orchestra
1963 (41) *Echoi,* for clarinet, cello, piano and
        percussion
1964 (42) *Elytres,* for orchestra
1965 (43) *Fragments of Archilochos,* for chorus,
        speaker, soloists and chamber ensemble
1966 (44) *Discrepancy,* for twenty-four winds
1967 (45) Cello Concerto
        Phorion, for orchestra, electric organ,
        harpsichord and guitar
        Baroque Variations, for orchestra
1969 (47) *Geod,* for orchestra with optional voices
1972 (50) *Ni, bruit, ni vitesse,* for two pianos, two
        percussion and inside piano
        Cave of the Winds, for wind quintet
1973 (51) *MAP,* a musical game for an entire
        evening, any four musicians can play
1974 (52) *fp. Orpheus,* for viola, cello or guitar
        and orchestra

FRANCK, César/1822–1890/Belgium

1840 (18) Three Piano Trios, in F♯m: B♭: Bm
1842 (20) Piano Trio No. 4 in B major
1843 (21) Andante quietoso, for violin and piano,
        in A major
1846 (24) *Ruth*
        Ce qu'on entend sur la montagne,
        symphonic poem (*c.*1846)
1851–52 (29) *Le Valet de Ferme,* opera
1858 (36) Ave Maria, motet
1865 (43) *The Tower of Babel,* oratorio
1872 (50) *Panis Angelicus*
1874 (52) *Redemption,* cantata with symphonic
        interlude
1876 (54) *Les Éolides,* symphonic poem
1878 (56) Cantabile for organ

Fantasie in A major, for organ
Pièce héroïque, for organ
1879 (57) *Béatitudes,* cantata
Piano Quintet in F minor
1880 (58) *L'Organiste,* fifty-five pieces for
harmonium
1881 (59) *Rebecca*
1882 (60) *Le Chasseur maudit,* symphonic poem
Hulda, opera (1882–85)
1884 (62) *Les Djinns,* symphonic poem for piano
and orchestra
Prélude, Chorale et Fugue, for piano
Nocturne, vocal
1885 (63) *Symphonic Variations,* for piano and
orchestra
1886 (64) Violin Sonata in A major
1887 (65) Prélude, Aria et Finale, for piano
1888 (66) Symphony in D minor (1886–88)
Psyche, symphonic poem
Ghisele, opera (1888–90)
1889 (67) Quartet in D major
1890 (68) Chorales for organ

FRESCOBALDI, Girolamo/1583–1643/Italy

1615 (32) *p.* Toccate d'Involatura
p. Ricercare e canzone francesi
1624 (41) *p.* Capricci sopra diversi soggetti
1627 (44) *p.* Second Book of Toccate
1628 (45) *p.* Libro delle canzoni
1635 (52) *p.* Fiori musicali
Frescobaldi composed many toccatas, fugues, ricercari,
etc., for organ and harpsichord; also madrigals and
motets.

FRICKER, Peter Racine/b.1920/Great Britain

1941–44 (21–24) Three Preludes for piano
1946 (26) Four Fughettas for two pianos
1947 (27) Sonata for Organ
Two Madrigals

Wind Quintet
Three Sonnets of Cecco Angiolieri, for
tenor and seven instruments
String Quartet in one movement
1948 (28) Symphony No. 1 (1948–49)
Rondo Scherzoso, for orchestra
1949 (29) *Prelude, Elegy and Finale,* for string
orchestra
Concerto for Violin and small orchestra,
No. 1 (1949–50)
1950 (30) Violin Sonata
Concertante No. 1, for English horn and
strings
Symphony No. 2 (1950–51)
Four Impromptus, for piano
1951 (31) Concertante No. 2, for three pianos,
strings and timpani
Canterbury Prologue, ballet
Viola Concerto (1951–53)
1952 (32) String Quartet No. 2 (1952–53)
Concerto for piano and small orchestra
(1952–54)
1953–54 (33) Violin Concerto No. 2, *Rapsodia
Concertante*
1954 (34) *Dance Scene,* for orchestra
Nocturne and Scherzo for piano, four
hands
1955 (35) Horn Sonata
The Tomb of St. Eulalia, elegy for
counter-tenor, gamba and harpsichord
Litany, for double string orchestra
Musick's Empire, for chorus and small
orchestra
1956 (36) Cello Sonata
Suite for Harpsichord
1957–58 (37) *The Vision of Judgment,* oratorio
Octet for flute, clarinet, bassoon, horn,
violin, viola, cello and double-bass
Variations for piano
1958 (38) *Comedy Overture,* for orchestra
Toccata for piano and orchestra
(1958–59)

1959 (39)   Serenade No. 1, for flute, clarinet, bass-
             clarinet, viola, cello and harp
             Serenade No. 2, for flute, oboe and piano
1960 (40)   Symphony No. 3
1961 (41)   Cantata for tenor and chamber ensemble
             (1961–62)
             Twelve studies for piano
1963 (43)   *O Longs désirs,* five songs for soprano
             and orchestra
1964–66 (44–46)   Symphony No. 4
1965 (45)   Ricercare for organ
             Four *Dialogues,* for oboe and piano
             Four Songs for soprano and piano (also
             orchestrated)
1966 (46)   Fantasy for viola and piano
             Three Scenes, for orchestra
             The Day and the Spirits, for soprano
             and harp (1966–67)
1967 (47)   Seven Counterpoints for orchestra
             Ave Maris Stella, for male voices and
             piano
             Episodes I, for piano (1967–68)
             Cantilena and Cabaletta, for solo soprano
1968 (48)   *Refrains,* for solo oboe
             Magnificat, for solo voices, choir and
             orchestra
             Concertante No. 4, for flute, oboe, violin
             and strings
             Gladius Domini, toccata for organ
             Some Serious Nonsense, for tenor, flute,
             oboe, cello and harpsichord
1969 (49)   Saxophone Quartet
             Praeludium for organ
1970 (50)   *Paseo,* for guitar
             The Roofs, for coloratura soprano and
             percussion
1971 (51)   *Sarabande in memoriam Igor Stravinsky*
             Nocturne, for chamber orchestra
             Intrada, for organ
             A Bourrée for Sir Arthur Bliss, for cello
             Concertante No. 5 for piano and string
             quartet
1972 (52)   *Introitus,* for orchestra

Come Sleep, for contralto, alto flute and
    bass clarinet
Fanfare for Europe, for trumpet
Ballade, for flute and piano
Seven Little Songs for chorus
1973 (53) Gigue, for cello
The Groves of Dodona, for six flutes
1974 (54) *Spirit Puck,* for clarinet and percussion
Two Petrarch Madrigals
Trio-Sonata for organ
1975 (55) String Quartet No. 3
Symphony No. 5

GABRIELI, Andrea/*c.*1510–1586/Italy

1562–5 (52–55) *p.* Sacrae cantiones, a 5 v.v.
1576 (66) *p.* Cantiones ecclesiaticae, a 4 v.v.
1578 (68) *p.* Cantiones sacrae
1589 (posthumous) *p.* Madrigali e ricercare a 4
1605 (posthumous) *p.* Canzoni all francese et
    ricercare Arlosi

GABRIELI, Giovanni/1557–1612/Italy

1587 (30) *p.* Concerti a 6–16 voci
p. Madrigali e ricercare
1597 (40) *p.* Sacrae symphoniae, Book I
1608 (51) *p.* Canzona (La Spiritosa)
1615 (58) *p.* Canzoni e sonate
p. Sacrae Symphoniae, Book II

GADE, Niels Vilhelm/1817–1890/Denmark

1840 (23) *Faedrelandets Muser,* ballet
Echoes from Ossian, overture
Piano Sonata
1841 (24) Symphony No. 1 in C minor
1842 (25) *Napoli,* ballet
Violin Sonata No. 1 in A major
1844 (27) *In the Highlands,* overture

1846 (29) *p.* String Quintet in E minor
1847 (30) *Symphony No. 3 in A minor*
1849 (32) *p.* String Octet in F major
1850 (33) *Mariotta*, a play with music
           Symphony No. 4 in B♭ major
           p. Violin Sonata No. 2 in D minor
1852 (35) Symphony No. 5 in D minor
           Spring Fantasy, for voices and orchestra
1855 (38) *p. Novelleten*, for piano trio
*c.*1856 (*c.*39) Symphony No. 6 in G minor
1861 (44) *Hamlet*, concerto overture
           Michelangelo, overture
1864 (47) Symphony No. 2 in E major
           Symphony No. 7 in F major
           Fantasies for clarinet
           p. Piano Trio in F major
           p. Fantasiestücke for cello and piano
1865 (48) *p.* String Sextet in D minor
1871 (54) Symphony No. 8 in B minor
1874 (57) *Novelleten*, for string orchestra
1879 (62) *En Sommertag paa Landet,* five pieces
               for orchestra
1880 (63) Violin Concerto
1884 (67) *Holbergiana Suite*
1887 (70) *p.* Violin Sonata No. 3 in B♭ major
1888–90 (71–73) *Ulysses*, march
1890 (73) *p.* String Quartet in D major

GERHARD, Roberto/1896–1970/Spain

1918 (22) *L'Infantament Meravellos de Shahrazade,*
               for voice and piano
           Piano Trio
1922 (26) Seven Hai-Ku, for voice and five
               instruments
1928 (32) Wind Quintet
1934 (38) *Ariel*, ballet
1940–41 (44) *Don Quixote*, ballet
1941 (45) *Hommaje a Pedrell*, symphony
1942–45 (46–49) Violin Concerto
1944 (48) *Alegrias,* ballet suite
           Pandora, ballet (1944–45)

1945–47 (49–51) *The Duenna,* opera
1950 (54) Impromptus for piano
1951 (55) Concerto for piano and strings
1952–53 (56) Symphony No. 1
1955–56 (59) Concerto for harpsichord, strings and
                percussion
              String Quartet No. 1
1956 (60) Nonet for eight winds and accordion
1957 (61) *Don Quixote,* suite
1959 (63) Symphony No. 2
1960 (64) Symphony No. 3, *Collages,* for tape and
                orchestra
              String Quartet No. 2 (1960–62)
1962 (66) *Concert for Eight,* for flute, clarinet,
                guitar, mandolin, double-bass,
                accordion, piano and percussion
1963 (67) *Hymnody,* for eleven players
              The Plague, for speaker, chorus and
                orchestra (1963–64)
1965 (69) Concerto for orchestra
1966 (70) *Epithalium,* for orchestra
              Gemini, for violin and piano
1967 (71) Symphony No. 4, *New York*
1968 (72) *Libra,* for flute, clarinet, violin, guitar,
                piano and percussion
1969 (73) *Leo,* chamber symphony for ten players

GERMAN, Sir Edward/1862–1936/Great Britain

1886 (24) *The Rival Poets,* operetta
1889 (27) *Richard III,* incidental music
1890 (28) Symphony No. 1 in E minor
1891 (29) Funeral March
1892 (30) *Gipsy Suite*
              Henry VIII, incidental music
1893 (31) *The Tempter,* incidental music
              Romeo and Juliet, incidental music
              Symphony No. 2 in A minor
1895 (33) Symphonic Suite in D minor
1896 (34) *As You Like It,* incidental music
1897 (35) *In Commemoration,* fantasia
              Hamlet, symphonic poem

1899 (37) *The Seasons*, symphonic suite
1900 (38) *Nell Gwynne*, incidental music
1901 (39) *The Emerald Isle* (completion of
                  unfinished operetta by Sullivan, *q.v.*)
1902 (40) *Merrie England*, operetta
1903 (41) *A Princess of Kensington*, operetta
1904 (42) *Welsh Rhapsody*, for orchestra
1907 (45) *Tom Jones*, operetta
1909 (47) *Fallen Fairies*
1911 (49) Coronation March and Hymn (for the
                  coronation of George V)
1919 (57) Theme and Six Variations, for orchestra

GERSHWIN, George/1898–1937/U.S.A.

1924 (26) *Rhapsody in Blue*, for piano and
                  orchestra (orchestrated by Grofé, *q.v.*)
1925 (27) Piano Concerto
1928 (30) *An American in Paris*, for orchestra
1931 (33) Second Rhapsody
1934 (36) *Cuban Overture*
1935 (37) *Porgy and Bess*, opera
1936 (38) Three Preludes for piano
Gershwin also composed many popular songs.

GIBBONS, Orlando/1583–1625/Great Britain

1612 (29) *p.* Madrigals and Mottets of Five Parts:
                  Apt for viols and voyces
Gibbons' other works include about 40 anthems and
other church music, music for viols, keyboard pieces,
and expressive madrigals, such as "The Silver Swan".

GILLIS, Don/b.1912/U.S.A.

1936 (24) *Four Moods in Three Keys*, for chamber
                  orchestra
1937 (25) *The Woolyworm*, symphonic satire
           The Panhandle, suite for orchestra

> *Thoughts Provoked on Becoming a*
> *Prospective Papa,* suite for orchestra
> *The Crucifixion,* for solo voices, narrator,
> chorus and orchestra

1938 (26) *The Raven,* for narrator and orchestra

1939–40 (27) *An American Symphony,* Symphony
No. 1

1940 (28) *Portrait of a Frontier Town,* suite for
orchestra
Symphony Of Faith, Symphony No. 2
A Symphony of Free Men, Symphony
No. 3 (1940–41)

1941 (29) *The Night Before Christmas,* for narrator
and orchestra

1942 (30) Three Sketches for Strings

1943 (31) *Prairie Poem*
Symphony No. 4

1944 (32) *A Short Overture to an Unwritten Opera,*
for orchestra
The Alamo, symphonic poem
Symphony No. 5 (1944–45)

1945 (33) *To an Unknown Soldier,* symphonic poem

1946–47 (34) Symphony No. 5½ *(A Symphony
for Fun)*

1947 (35) Symphony No. 6
Dude Ranch
Three Short Pieces for Strings

1948 (36) *Saga of a Prairie School*

Gillis also composed:

Symphonies Nos. 7–12

A Short, short, symphony

Shindig, ballet

The Park Avenue Kids, opera

The Gift of the Magi, opera

Pep Rally, opera

The Legend of Star Valley Junction, opera

The Nazarene, opera

Behold the Man, opera

Atlanta, orchestral suite

Twinkletoes, suite for orchestra

Four Scenes from Yesterday, suite for orchestra

Tulsa—A symphonic Portrait in Oil, for orchestra

Amarillo—A Symphonic Celebration, for orchestra

119

The Man Who Invented Music, for narrator and
　　orchestra
Alice in Orchestralia, for narrator and orchestra
Thomas Wolfe, American, for narrator and orchestra
Toscanini: a portrait of a century, for narrator and
　　orchestra
A Ceremony of Allegiance, for narrator and orchestra
His Name Was John, for narrator and orchestra
The Answer, for narrator and orchestra
Piano Concertos Nos. 1 and 2
Chamber music
Choral music.

GIORDANO, Umberto/1867–1948/Italy

1889 (22)　*Marina,* opera
1892 (25)　*Mala Vita,* opera
1894 (27)　*Regina Diaz,* opera
1896 (29)　*Andrea Chénier,* opera
1898 (31)　*Fedora,* opera
1904 (37)　*Siberia,* opera
1907 (40)　*Marcella,* opera
1910 (43)　*Mese Mariano,* opera
1915 (48)　*Madame Sans-Gêne,* opera
1921 (54)　*Giove a Pompeii,* opera
1924 (57)　*La Cena delle Beffe,* opera
1929 (62)　*Il re,* opera

GLAZUNOV, Alexander/1865–1936/Russia

1881 (16)　Symphony No. 1 (first performed under
　　　　　　the baton of Balakirev, *q.v.*)
　　　　　　Overture on Greek Themes, No. 1
　　　　　　(1881–84)
1882 (17)　String Quartet in D major
　　　　　　Overture on Greek Themes, No. 2
　　　　　　(1883–85)
1883 (18)　Serenade No. 1
　　　　　　String Quartet in F major
1884 (19)　Serenade No. 2
1885 (20)　*Stenka Razin,* tone poem

1886 (21) Symphony No. 2
1887 (22) *Suite Caractéristique* (possibly 1884)
               Lyric Poem
1889 (24) *The Forest,* fantasia (possibly 1887)
1890 (25) *Wedding March*
               Un Fête Slav
               The Sea
1891 (26) *Oriental Rhapsody*
1892 (27) Symphony No. 3 (possibly 1890)
               The Kremlin (possibly 1890)
               Le Printemps
               String Quartet in A major
1893 (28) Symphony No. 4
1894 (29) *Carnival,* overture
               Chopiniana Suite
               String Quartet in A minor
1895 (30) Symphony No. 5
               Cortège Solenelle
1896 (31) Symphony No. 6
1899 (34) String Quartet in D minor
1900 (35) *Solenne Overture*
1901 (36) *The Seasons,* ballet (possibly earlier)
1902 (37) Symphony No. 7
               Ballade
1904 (39) Violin Concerto
1905 (40) *Scéne Dansante*
               Symphony No. 8
1907 (42) *Canto di destino,* overture
1909 (44) Symphony No. 9 (begun, left unfinished,
               first performed 1948)
1911 (46) Piano Concerto
1933 (68) *Epic Poem*
1936 (71) Saxophone Concerto

GLIÈRE, Reinhold Moritzovich/1875–1956/Russia

1899–1900 (24) Symphony No. 1
1900 (25) String Octet in D major
               String Sextet No. 1
               String Quartet No. 1 in A major
1902 (27) String Sextet No. 2
1904 (29) String Sextet No. 3 in C major

1905 (30) String Quartet No. 2 in G minor
1907 (32) Symphony No. 2
1908 (33) *The Sirens,* symphonic poem
1909–11 (34–36) Symphony No. 3, *Ilya Murometz*
1912 (37) *Chrysis,* ballet
1915 (40) *Trizna,* symphonic poem
1919 (44) *Imitation of Jezekiel,* symphonic poem
            for narrator and orchestra
1921 (46) *Cossacks of Zaporozh,* symphonic poem
1922, 1930 (47, 55) *Comedians,* ballet
1923–25 (48–50) *Shakh-Senem,* opera
1924 (49) Two Poems for soprano and orchestra
            For the Festival of the Comintern, fantasy
            for wind orchestra
            March of the Red Army, for wind
            orchestra
1925 (50) *Cleopatra,* ballet
1926–27 (51) *Red Poppy,* ballet
1928 (53) String Quartet No. 3
1938 (63) Harp Concerto in E♭ major
1942 (67) Concerto for coloratura soprano
Glière also composed many songs and piano pieces.

GLINKA, Michail/1804–1857/Russia

1822 (18) Variations on a Theme of Mozart, for
            piano
1826 (22) Memorial Cantata
            Pathétique Trio, for piano, clarinet and
            bassoon, or piano, violin and cello
            (1826–27)
1830 (26) String Quartet in F major
1833–34 (29) Sextet for piano and strings
1836 (32) *A Life for the Tsar,* opera (called *Ivan
            Sussanin* in Russia)
            The Moldavian Gipsy, incidental music
1839 (35) *Valse-fantaisie,* for orchestra (revised
            1856)
1840 (36) *Farewell to Petersburg,* song cycle
1842 (38) *Russlan and Ludmilla,* opera
1845 (41) Spanish Overture No. 1, *Jota Aragonesa*
1847 (43) *Greeting to the Fatherland,* for piano

1848 (44) *Wedding Song (Kamarinskaya)*, fantasia
for orchestra

Glinka also composed many piano pieces and songs.

GLUCK, Christoph Willibald (von)/1714–1787/
Bavaria (Germany)

1741 (27) *Artaserse*, opera
1742 (28) *Demetrio*, opera
1743 (29) *Il Tigrane*, opera
1745 (31) *Ippolito*, opera
1746 (32) *Artmene*, opera
 p. Six Sonatas for two violins and
continuo
1747 (33) *Le Nozze d'Ercole e d'Ebe*, opera
1750 (36) *Ezio*, opera
1752 (38) *Issipile*, opera
1753 (39) Nine Symphonies
1755 (41) *Les Amours champêtres*, opera
 Alessandro, ballet
1756 (42) *Antigono*, opera
 Le Chinois poli en France, opera
1758 (44) *L'Isle de Merlin, ou, le Monde renversé*,
opera
1759 (45) *L'Arbe enchanté*, opera
1761 (47) *La Cadi dupé*, opera
 Don Juan, ballet
1762 (48) *Orfeo ed Euridice*, opera
1764 (50) *Poro*, opera
 La Rencontre imprévue, opera
1765 (51) *Semiramide*, ballet
1766 (52) *L'Orfano della China*, ballet
1767 (53) *Alkestis*, opera
1770 (56) *Paride ed Elena*, opera
1774 (60) *Iphigénie en Aulide*, opera
1777 (63) *Armide*, opera
1779 (65) *Iphigénie en Tauride*, opera
?　　(?) Seven Sonatas for two violins and bass

GODARD, Benjamin/1849–1895/France

1876 (27) Violin Concerto No. 2, *Concerto
               romantique*
1878 (29) Piano Concerto
               La Tasse, dramatic symphony for solo
                   voices, chorus and orchestra
               Les Bijoux de Jeanette, one-act opera
1879 (30) *Scènes poétiques*
1880 (31) Symphony
               Diane: poème dramatique
1882 (33) *Symphonie,* ballet
1883 (34) *Symphonie Gothique*
1884 (35) *Symphonie Orientale*
               Pedro de Zalamea, four-act opera
1886 (37) *Symphonie Légendaire*
1888 (39) *Jocelyn,* opera
1890 (41) *Dante,* opera
Godard also composed:
3 string quartets
3 violin sonatas
1 piano trio
Suite de trois morceaux, for flute
Over 100 songs.

GOEHR, Alexander/b.1932/Germany

1951 (19) *Songs of Babel*
               Piano Sonata (1951–52)
1954 (22) Fantasias for clarinet and piano
               Fantasia for orchestra (revised 1958)
1956–57 (24) String Quartet No. 1
1957 (25) Capriccio for piano
               The Deluge, cantata for soprano,
                   contralto, flute, horn, trumpet, harp,
                   violin, viola, cello and double bass
1958 (26) *La Belle Dame sans merci,* ballet
1959 (27) Variations for flute and piano
               Four Songs from the Japanese, for high
                   voice with orchestra or piano

   Sutter's Gold, cantata for bass solo, chorus
    and orchestra (1959–60)
   Hecuba's Lament, for orchestra
    (1959–61)
1961 (29) Suite for flute, clarinet, horn, harp, violin
    (doubling viola) and cello
   Violin Concerto (1961–62)
1962 (30) A Little Cantata of Proverbs
   Two Choruses, for mixed chorus a
    cappella
1963 (31) *Virtutes,* cycle of songs and melodramas
    for chorus, piano duet and percussion
   Little Symphony (In memory of Walter
    Goehr), for small orchestra
   Little Music for Strings
1964 (32) Five Poems and an Epigram of William
    Blake, for mixed chorus
   Three Pieces for Piano
1965 (33) Pastorals for Orchestra
1966 (34) *Arden muss sterben,* opera
1967 (35) *Warngedichte,* for low voice and piano
   String Quartet No. 2
1968 (36) *Romanza,* for cello and orchestra
   Naboth's Vineyard, a dramatic madrigal
1969 (37) *Konzertstücke,* for piano and small
    orchestra
   Nonomiya, for piano
   Paraphrase on the Madrigal "Il
    combattimento de Tancredi e Clorinda"
    by Monteverdi, for solo clarinet
1970 (38) Symphony in one movement
   Shadowplay-2, music theater for tenor,
    alto flute, alto saxophone, horn, cello
    and piano
   Sonata about Jerusalem
   Concerto for eleven instruments

GOLDMARK, Karl/1830–1915/Hungary

1875 (45) *The Queen of Sheba,* opera
1876 (46) *Rustic Wedding,* symphony

1886 (56) *Merlin*
1896 (66) *The Cricket on the Hearth*
1908 (78) *A Winter's Tale*

GOSSEC, François Joseph/1734–1829/Belgium

1760 (26) Requiem Mass
1761 (27) *Le Tonnelier*, opera
1765 (31) *Le Faux Lord*, opera
1766 (32) *Les Pêcheurs*, opera
1767 (33) *Toinon et Toinette*, opera
Le Double déguisemente, opera
1774 (40) *Sabinus*, opera
La Nativité, oratorio
1775 (41) *Alexis et Daphné*, opera
1776 (42) *Hylas et Sylvie*, incidental music
1778 (44) *Le Fête du village*, opera
1779 (45) *Les Scythes enchaînes*, ballet
Mirsa, ballet
1781 (47) *L'Arche d'alliance*, oratorio
1782 (48) *Thesée*, opera
1786 (52) *Rosine*, opera
1796 (62) *La Reprise de Toulon*, opera
1803 (69) *Les Sabots et le Cerisier*, opera
1813 (79) *Dernière Messe des vivants*

GOULD, Morton/b.1913/U.S.A.

1932 (19) Chorale and Fugue in Jazz
1936 (23) Little Symphony
Symphonette No. 2
1937 (24) Piano Concerto
Spirituals for orchestra
1939 (26) Symphonette No. 3
Jericho, for concert band
1940 (27) *A Foster Gallery*
Latin-American Symphonette
1941 (28) *Lincoln Legend*
1943 (30) Symphony No. 1
Symphony No. 2 (on marching tunes)

Concertette for viola and orchestra
Viola Concerto
Interplay, for piano and orchestra
1944 (31) Concerto for orchestra
1945 (32) *Harvest*, for vibraphone, harp and strings
Ballade for band
1946 (33) *Minstrel Show*
Symphony No. 3
1947 (34) *Fall River Legend*, ballet
1948 (35) Serenade of Carols
1950 (37) *Family Album*
1951 (38) *Battle Hymn of the Republic*
1952 (39) *Dance Variations*, for two pianos and
orchestra
1953 (40) Inventions for four pianos and orchestra
1955 (42) *Jekyll & Hyde Variations*
Derivations, for clarinet and band
1956 (43) *Dialogue*, for piano and strings
Santa Fe Saga
1957 (44) *Declaration Suite*
1958 (45) *Rhythm Gallery*, for narrator and
orchestra
St. Lawrence Suite, for band
1964 (51) *Festive Music*, for off-stage trumpet and
orchestra
Marches: Formations
*World War I: Revolutionary Prelude,
Prologue* (1964–65)
1966 (53) *Venice*, audiograph for two orchestras
Columbia
1967 (54) *Vivaldi Gallery*, for string quartet and
divided orchestra
1968 (55) *Troubador Music*, for four guitars and
orchestra
1969 (56) *Soundings*
1971 (58) Suite for tuba and three horns

GOUNOD, Charles/1818–1893/France

1837 (19) Scherzo for orchestra
1840 (22) *Marche militaire suisse*, for orchestra
1851 (33) *Sappho*, opera

1852–54 (34–36) *La Nonne sanglante*, opera
1852–59 (34–41) *Faust*, opera
1855 (37) Symphony No. 1 in D major
 Symphony No. 2 in E♭ major
 Messe Solenelle à St. Cécile
1857 (39) *Le Médecin malgré lui*, opera
1860 (42) *Philémon et Baucis*, opera
1862 (44) *La Reine de Saba*, opera
1864 (46) *Mireille*, opera
1865 (47) Chant des Compagnons
1867 (49) *Roméo et Juliette*, opera
1871 (53) Saltarello for orchestra
1873 (55) *Funeral March of a Marionette*, for
 orchestra
1876–77 (58) *Cinq-Mars*, opera
1878 (60) *Marche Religieuse*, for orchestra
1879 (61) *The Redemption*, oratorio
1881 (63) *Le Tribut de Zamora*, opera
1884 (66) *fp. Mors et Vita*, oratorio
1888 (70) Petite Symphonie, for ten wind
 instruments

GRAINGER, Percy/1882–1961/Australia

1916 (34) *In a Nutshell*, suite for piano and
 orchestra
1918 (36) *Children's March*
1921 (39) *Molly on the Shore*
1922 (40) *Shepherd's Hey*
1925 (43) *Country Gardens*
1927 (45) *Shallow Brown*
 *Irish Tune from County Derry
 (Londonderry Air)*
1928 (46) Colonial Songs
 Over the Hills and Far Away
1929 (47) *English Dance*
1930 (48) *Lord Peter's Stable Boy*
 Spoon River
 To A Nordic Princess
1931 (49) *The Nightingale and the Two Sisters*
1932 (50) *Blithe Bells*

GRANDJANY, Marcel/1891–1975/U.S.A.
  (b. France)

(dates unknown) *Poème,* for harp, horn and orchestra
                  Aria in Classic Style, for harp and strings
                  Children's Hour Suite, for harp
                  Colorado Trail, for harp
                  Divertissement, for harp
                  Rhapsody, for harp
                  Fantasia on a Theme of Haydn
                  The Erie Canal

GRÉTRY, André Ernest Modeste/1742–1813/
  Belgium

1769 (27) *Le Tableau parlant,* opera-comique
1771 (29) *Zemire et Azor,* opera-comique
1778 (36) *L'Amant jaloux,* opera-comique
1784 (42) *L'Épreuve villageoise,* opera-comique
          Richard Coeur-de-Lion

GRIEG, Edvard Hagerup/1843–1907/Norway

1865 (22) *In Autumn,* concert overture
          Violin Sonata No. 1
1867 (24) Lyric Pieces for piano, Book I
          Violin Sonata No. 2
1869 (26) Piano Concerto in A minor
1872 (29) *Sigurd Jorsalfar,* incidental music
1875 (32) *Peer Gynt,* incidental music
1880 (37) Two Elegiac Melodies
1881 (38) Norwegian Dances
1883 (40) Lyric Pieces for piano, Book II
1884 (41) Lyric Pieces for piano, Book III
1885 (42) *Holberg Suite,* for strings
1887 (44) Violin Sonata No. 3
1888 (45) Lyric Pieces for piano, Book IV
1891 (48) Lyric Pieces for piano, Book V
1893 (50) Lyric Pieces for piano, Book VI
1895 (52) Lyric Pieces for piano, Book VII

1896 (53) Lyric Pieces for piano, Book VIII
1898 (55) Lyric Pieces for piano, Book IX
              Symphonic Dances
1901 (58) Lyric Pieces for piano, Book X
1906 (63) *Moods*

Grieg also composed other piano works and many songs.

GRIFFES, Charles Tomlinson/1884–1920/U.S.A.

1912 (28) *Tone Images,* for mezzo-soprano and piano
              The Pleasure Dome of Kubla Khan,
                  symphonic poem (1912–16)
1915 (31) Three Tone Pictures for piano:
                  The Lake at Evening
                  The Vale of Dreams
                  The Night Wind
              Fantasy Pieces for piano:
                  Barcarolle
                  Notturno
                  Scherzo
1916 (32) *The Kairn of Koridwen,* dance drama for
                  woodwinds, harp, celesta and piano
              Two Sketches on Indian Themes, for
                  string quartet
              Roman Sketches:
                  The White Peacock
                  Nightfall
                  The Fountain of Acqua Paolo
                  Clouds
1917 (33) *Sho-Jo,* pantomimic drama for four
                  woodwinds, four strings, harp and
                  percussion
1918 (34) *Poem,* for flute and orchestra
              Piano Sonata
1919 (35) Nocturnes for orchestra

Griffes also composed many choral works and songs.

GROFÉ, Ferde/1892–1972/U.S.A.

1931 (39) *Grand Canyon Suite,* for orchestra
1937 (45) *Broadway at Night*

> *Symphony in Steel* (uses four pairs of
> shoes, two brooms, locomotive bell,
> pneumatic drill and compressed air
> tank)

1964 (72) *World's Fair Suite*

Grofé also wrote: *Tabloid, Death Valley Suite,
Mississippi Suite, Mark Twain Suite, Hollywood Suite,
Milk, Wheels, Three Shades of Blue, New England
Suite, Metropolis, Aviation Suite.*

HAMILTON, Ian/b.1922/Great Britain

1948 (26) Quintet for clarinet and string quartet
            Symphonic Variations for string orchestra
1949 (27) Symphony No. 1
            String Quartet No. 1
1950 (28) Clarinet Concerto
1951 (29) Symphony No. 2
            Clerk Saunders, ballet
            Flute Quartet
            Piano Sonata (revised 1971)
1952 (30) Violin Concerto
            Bartholomew Fair, overture
1954 (32) String Octet
            Four Border Songs and the Fray of Suport
            Songs of Summer, for soprano and piano
1956 (34) Scottish Dances
            Sonata for chamber orchestra
1957 (35) Cantata for tenor and piano
            Five Love Songs, for tenor and orchestra
1958 (36) *Overture 1912*
            Concerto for jazz trumpet and orchestra
            Sonata for solo cello
1959 (37) Sinfonia for two orchestras
            Écossaise, for orchestra
1960 (38) Piano Concerto (revised 1967)
1962 (40) Arias for small orchestra
            Sextet
1963 (41) *Sonatas and Variants,* for ten wind
                instruments
            Nocturnes with Cadenza, for piano
1964 (42) Organ Concerto

        Cantos, for orchestra
        Jubilee, for orchestra
1965 (43) *Dialogues*, for soprano and five
                instruments
        Aubade, for solo organ
        String Quartet No. 2
1966 (44) *Threnos—In Time of War*, for solo organ
        Five Scenes, for trumpet and piano
        Flute Sonata
1967–69 (45–47) *Agamemnon*, opera
        The Royal Hunt of the Sun, opera
1968 (46) *Pharsalia*, opera
1969 (47) *Circus*, for two trumpets and orchestra
1970 (48) *Epitaph for This World and Time*, for
                three choruses and three organs
        Alastor, for orchestra
        Voyage, for horn and chamber orchestra
1971 (49) Violin Concerto No. 2, *Amphion*
1972 (50) *Commedia*, concerto for orchestra
        Descent of the Celestial City, for chorus
                and organ
        Palinodes, for solo piano
1974 (52) *The Cataline Conspiracy*, opera
        Piano Sonata No. 2
1975 (53) Te Deum
        Violin Sonata No. 1
        Cello Sonata No. 2
        Sea Music, for chorus and string quartet

HANDEL, George Frederick/1685–1759/Germany

1707 (22) "Laudate pueri Dominum", aria
        Rodrigo, opera (*c*.1707)
1708 (23) *La Resurrezione*, Easter oratorio
1711 (26) *Rinaldo*, opera
1712 (27) *Il Pastor fido*, opera (first version)
1713 (28) *Teseo*, opera
        Te Deum and Jubilate, for the Peace of
                Utrecht
1715 (30) *Amadigi de Gaule*, opera
        The *Water Music* (1715–17)
c.1720 (*c*.35) The *Chandos Anthems*

	Acis and Galatea, secular cantata
	Radamisto, opera
	Huit Suites de pièces, for harpsichord
1721 (36)	*Floridante,* opera
1723 (38)	*Ottone,* opera
1724 (39)	*Giulio Cesare,* opera
	Fifteen Chamber Sonatas
1725 (40)	*Rodelinda,* opera
	Trio Sonata in D minor
1727 (42)	*Zadok the Priest,* coronation anthem
	Admeto, opera
1728 (43)	*Tolomeo,* opera
*c.***1731** (*c.*46)	Nine sonatas for two violins and continuo
1732 (47)	*Esther,* English Biblical oratorio
	Sosarme, opera
	Ezio, opera
1733 (48)	*Orlando,* opera
	Huit Suites de pièces, for harpsichord
1734 (49)	*Persichore,* ballet
	Il Pastor fido (second and third versions)
	Arianna, opera
	p. Six concerti grossi
1735 (50)	*Alcina,* opera
1736 (51)	*Atalanta,* opera
	Alexander's Feast, secular cantata
	Six fugues for harpsichord
1737 (52)	*Berenice,* opera
	Concerto grosso in C major
1738 (53)	*Xerxes,* opera (which includes "Ombra mai fu", known as "Handel's Largo")
	Six organ concerti
1739 (54)	*Israel in Egypt,* oratorio
	Saul, oratorio (which includes the "Dead March")
	Ode for St. Cecilia's Day
	Twelve concerti grossi
	Seven trio sonatas
1740 (55)	*p.* Concerti for oboe and strings
	p. Six organ concerti
	Three double concerti (1740–50)
1741 (56)	*Messiah,* oratorio (composed in under four weeks)

Five concerti grossi
1742 (57) *Forest Music*
1743 (58) *Samson,* oratorio
The *Dettingen* Te Deum
1744 (59) *Semele,* secular oratorio
1745 (60) *Belshazzar,* oratorio
1746 (61) *Occasional Oratorio*
1747 (62) *Judas Maccabaeus,* oratorio
1748 (63) *Joshua,* oratorio
1749 (64) *Music for the Royal Fireworks*
Solomon, oratorio
Susanna, oratorio
1750 (65) *Theodora,* oratorio
1752 (67) *Jephtha,* oratorio
1760 (posthumous) *p.* Six organ concerti

HANSON, Howard/b.1896/U.S.A.

1915 (19) Prelude and Double Fugue, for two pianos
1916 (20) Symphonic Prelude
Piano Quintet
1917 (21) Symphonic Legend
Concerto da Camera, for piano and
string quartet
1919 (23) Symphonic Rhapsody
1920 (24) *Before the Dawn,* symphonic poem
Exaltation, symphonic poem with piano
obbligato
1921 (25) Concerto for organ, strings and harp
1922 (26) Symphony No. 1 in E minor, *Nordic*
1923 (27) *North and West,* symphonic poem
Lux Aeterna, symphonic poem with viola
obbligato
String Quartet
1925 (29) *The Lament of Beowulf,* for chorus
1926 (30) Organ Concerto
Pan and the Priest, symphonic poem
1927 (31) *Heroic Elegy,* for chorus and orchestra
1930 (34) Symphony No. 2, *Romantic*
1933 (37) *The Merry Mount,* opera
1935 (39) *Drum Taps,* for baritone, chorus and
orchestra

1938 (42) Symphony No. 3
1943 (47) Symphony No. 4, *Requiem* (in memory of his father)
1945 (49) *Serenade,* for flute, strings, harp and orchestra
1948 (52) Piano Concerto
1951 (55) *Fantasia on a Theme of Youth,* for piano and strings
1955 (59) Symphony No. 5, *Sinfonia sacrae*
1956 (60) *Elegy in memory of Serge Koussevitsky,* for orchestra
1958 (62) *Mosaics,* for orchestra
1959 (63) *Summer Seascapes*
1961 (65) *Bold Island Suite*
1963 (67) *For the First Time,* for orchestra
1967 (71) *Dies Natalis,* for orchestra
1968 (72) Symphony No. 6

HARRIS, Roy Ellsworth/b.1898/U.S.A.

1926 (28) *Impression of a rainy day,* for string quartet
1927 (29) Concerto for clarinet and string quartet
1928 (30) Piano Sonata
1929 (31) *American Portraits,* for orchestra
1930 (32) String Quartet No. 1
1931 (33) *Toccata,* for orchestra
1932 (34) *Chorale,* for strings
Fantasy, for piano and woodwind quintet
String Sextet
1933 (35) Symphony No. 1
String Quartet No. 2
1934 (36) Symphony No. 2
When Johnny comes marching home, overture
Songs for Occupations, for chorus
Piano Trio
1936 (38) *Symphony for Voices*
Time Suite, for orchestra
Prelude and fugue for string orchestra
Piano Quintet

1937 (39)	Symphony No. 3
	String Quartet No. 3
1938 (40)	*Soliloquy and Dance,* for viola and piano
1939 (41)	Symphony No. 4
	String Quartet
1940 (42)	*Western Landscape,* ballet
	Challenge, for baritone, chorus and orchestra
	American Creed, for orchestra
	Evening Piece, for orchestra
	Ode to Truth, for orchestra
	String Quintet
1941 (43)	*From This Earth,* ballet
	Acceleration, for orchestra
	Violin Sonata
1942 (44)	Piano Concerto, with band
	Symphony No. 5
	What so proudly we hail, ballet
1943 (45)	Cantata for chorus, organ and brass
	Mass, for male chorus and organ
1944 (46)	Symphony No. 6
1945 (47)	Piano Concerto No. 1
1946 (48)	Concerto for two pianos
	Accordion Concerto
1947 (49)	*Quest,* for orchestra
1948 (50)	*Elegy and Pæan,* for viola and orchestra
1949 (51)	*Kentucky Spring,* for orchestra
1951 (53)	*Cumberland Concerto,* for orchestra
	Symphony No. 7
1953 (55)	Piano Concerto No. 2
	Abraham Lincoln walks at midnight, chamber cantata
1954 (56)	*Fantasy,* for piano and orchestra
1956 (58)	*Folk Fantasy* for festivals, for piano and choir
1959 (61)	*Give me the splendid silent sun,* cantata for baritone and orchestra
1961 (63)	*Canticle to the sun,* cantata for soprano and chamber orchestra
1962 (64)	Symphony No. 8
	Symphony No. 9
1963 (65)	*Epilogue to Profiles in Courage: J.F.K.,* for orchestra

Salute to Death
1964 (66) Duo for cello and piano
            Horn of Plenty, for orchestra
1965 (67) Symphony No. 10
            Rhythm and Spaces, for string orchestra
1967 (69) Symphony No. 11
1968 (70) Concerto for amplified piano, brasses
                and percussion
            Piano Sextet
1969 (71) Symphony No. 12
?   ?   Symphony No. 13
1975 (77) Symphony No. 14

HAYDN, (Franz) Joseph/1732–1809/Austria

1755 (23) String Quartets Nos. 1–13
1756 (24) Organ Concerto No. 1 in C major
            Piano Concerto in C major
1759 (27) Symphony No. 1 in D major
1760 (28) Organ Concerto No. 2 in C major
            Symphony No. 2 in C major (*c.*1760)
*c.***1761** (*c.*29) Symphony No. 3 in G major
            Symphony No. 4 in D major
            Symphony No. 5 in A major
            Symphony No. 6 in D major, *Le matin*
            Symphony No. 7 in C major, *Le midi*
            Symphony No. 8 in G major, *Le soir,*
                ou la têmpete
            Symphony No. 19 in D major
1762 (30) Symphony No. 9 in C major
before **1763** Symphony No. 10 in D major
            Symphony No. 11 in E♭ major
            Piano Sonata No. 3 in A major
1763 (31) Symphony No. 12 in E major
            Symphony No. 13 in D major
before **1764** Symphonies Nos. 14 and 15
*c.***1764** (*c.*32) Symphonies Nos. 16–18
1764 (32) Symphony No. 22 in E♭ major,
                Der Philosoph
1765 (33) Symphony No. 30 in C major, *Alleluia*
            Symphony No. 31 in D major, *Horn Signal*
            String Quartets Nos. 14–19

Symphony No. 26 in D minor,
Lamentations (*c.*1765)
1766 (34) Mass No. 4, in E♭, *Great Organ*
Piano Sonatas Nos. 4–7
Piano Sonatas Nos. 8–12 (1766–67)
*c.***1767** (*c.*35) Piano Sonatas Nos. 13–16
1767 (35) Piano Sonata No. 17
before **1769** Violin Concerto in C major
Violin Concerto in G major
1769 (37) String Quartets Nos. 20–25
before **1770** Violin Concerto in D major
1770 (38) Mass No. 5 in B♭, *Little Organ* or *St. John*
after **1770** Piano Concerto in G major
before **1771** Piano Concerto in F major
Violin Concerto in A major
1771 (39) String Quartets Nos. 26–31
Piano Sonata No. 18 in C minor
before **1772** Symphony No. 43 in E♭ major, *Mercury*
Symphony No. 44 in E minor,
Trauersymphonie
1772 (40) Symphony No. 45 in F♯ minor, *Farewell*
Symphony No. 46 in B major
Symphony No. 48 in C major,
Maria Teresa
Mass No. 3, *St. Cecilia*
String Quartets Nos. 32–37, *Sun* or *Great*
Symphony No. 52 in C minor (1772–74)
before **1773** Symphony No. 49 in F minor,
The Passion
1773 (41) Violin Sonatas Nos. 2–4 (without violin,
Piano Sonatas Nos. 22–24)
Piano Sonatas Nos. 19–24
before **1774** Symphony No. 53 in D major, *The
Imperial*
1774 (42) Symphony No. 55 in E♭ major,
The Schoolmaster
before **1776** Symphony No. 59 in A major,
Feuersymphonie
1776 (44) Symphony No. 60 in C major, *Il Distratto*
Piano Sonatas Nos. 25–30
1777 (45) Symphony No. 63 in C major,
La Roxolane
Piano Sonatas Nos. 31 and 32 (1777–78)

1779 (47)   Symphony No. 69 in C major, *Laudon*
                Piano Sonatas Nos. 33–37 (1779–80)
1781 (49)   Symphony No. 73 in D major, *La Chasse*
                Concerto for horn and strings, No. 2
                String Quartets Nos. 38–43, *Russian* or
                    Jungfern
1783 (51)   Cello Concerto in D major
before **1784** Piano Sonatas Nos. 38–40
1784 (52)   *Armida,* opera
                String Quartets Nos. 44–50, dedicated to
                    the King of Prussia (1784–87)
*c.***1785** (*c.*53)   Piano Sonata No. 41 in A♭ major
1785 (53)   Piano Sonata No. 42 in G minor
                    (1785–86)
                Piano Sonata No. 44 in A♭ major
                    (1785–86)
                Symphony No. 87 in A major (with
                    Symphonies Nos. 82–86 comprise the
                    Paris symphonies)
1786 (54)   Symphony No. 82 in C major, *The Bear*
                Symphony No. 83 in G minor, *La Poule*
                Symphony No. 84 in E♭ major
                Symphony No. 85 in B♭ major, *La Reine*
                Symphony No. 86 in D major, *The Miracle*
1787 (55)   Symphony No. 88 in G major
                Symphony No. 89 in F major
                String Quartets Nos. 51–57, *The
                    Seven Words,* arranged for quartet
                Piano Sonata No. 45 in F major
                    (1787–88)
1788 (56)   Symphony No. 90 in C major
                Symphony No. 91 in E♭ major
                Symphony No. 92 in G major, *Oxford*
                Toy Symphony in C major, for two violins,
                    double-bass, keyboard and toy trumpet,
                    drum, rattle, triangle and bird-warblers
1789 (57)   String Quartets Nos. 58 and 59
                Piano Sonata No. 46 in C major
                Piano Sonata No. 47 in E♭ major
                    (1789–90)
before **1790** Violin Sonata No. 1
1790 (58)   Piano Sonata No. 48 in C major (*c.*1790)
                Seven Nocturnes for the King of Naples

1791 (59) Symphony No. 93 in D major
Symphony No. 94 in G major, *Surprise*
Symphony No. 95 in C minor
Symphony No. 96 in D major, *Miracle*
1792 (60) Symphony No. 97 in C major
Symphony No. 98 in B♭ major
The Storm, oratorio
before **1793** String Quartets Nos. 60–69
1793 (61) Symphony No. 99 in E♭ major
String Quartets Nos. 70–75, dedicated to
Count Apponyi
1794 (62) Symphony No. 100 in G major, *Military*
Symphony No. 101 in D major, *Clock*
before **1795** Piano Sonata No. 49 in D major
1795 (63) Symphony No. 102 in B♭ major
Symphony No. 103 in E♭ major,
Drum Roll
Symphony No. 104 in D major
1796 (64) Trumpet Concerto in E♭ major
Mass No. 9 in B♭, *Heiligenmesse*
Mass No. 10 in C major, *Paukenmesse*
1797–98 (65) *The Creation,* oratorio
String Quartets Nos. 76–81
1798 (66) Mass No. 11 in D minor, *Nelson* or
Imperial
Piano Sonata No. 50 in E♭ major
The Seasons, oratorio (1798–1801)
1799 (67) String Quartets Nos. 82–83
Mass No. 12 in B♭ major, *Theresienmesse*
1800 (68) Te Deum
1803 (71) String Quartet No. 84
Haydn's last 12 symphonies are known as the *Salomon*
symphonies. He also composed: 125 trios with bary-
tone, more than 20 Italian and German operas, many
songs, some in English.

HENZE, Hans Werner/b.1926/Germany

1946 (20) Chamber Concerto, for solo piano, solo
flute and strings
Violin Sonata
1947 (21) Symphony No. 1, first version

Violin Concerto No. 1
Concertino for piano and wind orchestra, with percussion
Five Madrigals for small mixed choir and eleven solo instruments
String Quartet No. 1

1948 (22) *Chorus of the Captured Trojans,* for mixed choir and large orchestra
The Reproach, concert aria for baritone, trumpet, trombone and string orchestra
Lullaby of the Blessed Virgin, for boys' choir and nine solo instruments
Whispers from Heavenly Death, cantata for high voice and eight solo instruments
The Magic Theater, one-act opera for actors (new version for singers, 1964)
Chamber Sonata, for piano, violin and cello (revised 1963)

1949 (23) *Jack Pudding,* ballet
Ballet Variations
Symphony No. 2
Symphony No. 3 (1949–50)
Apollo et Hyazinthus, improvisations for harpsichord, contralto and eight solo instruments
Variations for piano
Serenade, for solo cello

1950 (24) *Symphonic Variations,* for piano and orchestra
Piano Concerto No. 1
Rosa Silber, ballet

1951 (25) *Labyrinth,* Choreographic Fantasy
The Sleeping Princess, ballet
Boulevard Solitude, lyric drama
A Country Doctor, radio opera (stage version 1964)

1952 (26) *The Idiot,* ballet-pantomime
King Stag, opera (1952–55)
Quintet for wind instruments
String Quartet No. 2

1953 (27) *Ode to the Westwind,* for cello and orchestra
The End of a World, radio opera

1955 (29) Symphony No. 4 (in one movement)
Three Symphonic Studies for orchestra
(revised 1964)
Quattro Poemi, for orchestra
1956 (30) *Maratona*, ballet
Ondine, ballet (1956–57)
Concerto per il Marigny, for piano and
seven instruments
Five Neapolitan Songs, for medium voice
and chamber orchestra
1957 (31) *Nocturnes and Arias*, for soprano and
orchestra
Sonata per Archi (1957–58)
1858 (32) *Three Dithyrambs*, for chamber orchestra
Chamber Music
Der Prinz von Homburg, opera
Three Tentos, for guitar
1959 (33) *The Emperor's Nightingale*, ballet
Elegy for Young Lovers, opera (1959–61)
Piano Sonata
1960 (34) *Antifone*, for orchestra
1961 (35) *Six Absences pour le Clavecin*, for
harpsichord
1962 (36) Symphony No. 5
Les Caprices de Marianne, incidental
music
In re cervo (or *The Errantries of Truth*),
opera
Novae de Infinito Laudes, cantata
1963 (37) *Los Caprichos*, fantasia for orchestra
Ariosi, for soprano, violin and orchestra
Adagio, for clarinet, horn, bassoon and
string quintet
Lucy Escott Variations, for piano (also
for harpsichord)
Being Beauteous, cantata
Cantata della Fiaba Estrema
1964 (38) *Tancredi*, ballet
The Young Lord, comic opera
Choral Fantasy
Divertimenti for two pianos
1965 (39) *The Bassarids*, opera

> *In Memoriam: The White Rose,* for
> > chamber orchestra

1966 (40) Double Concerto for oboe, harp and
> strings
> Fantasia for strings
> *Muses of Sicily,* concerto for choir, two
> > pianos, wind instruments and timpani

1967 (41) Piano Concerto No. 2
> *Telemanniana,* for orchestra
> *Moralities,* three scenic cantatas for soli,
> > speaker, choir and small orchestra

1968 (42) *Essay on Pigs,* for voice and orchestra
> *The Raft of the "Medusa",* oratorio
> > vulgare e militare in due parti—per Che
> > Guevara, for soprano, baritone, speaker,
> > mixed choir with nine boys' voices and
> > orchestra

1969 (43) Symphony No. 6 for two chamber
> orchestras
> *Compases* (viola concerto) for viola and
> > twenty-two players (1969–70)
> *El Cimarrón,* recital for four musicians
> > (1969–70)

1971 (45) Violin Concerto No. 2
> *Heliogabalus Imperator,* for orchestra
> > (1971–72)

HINDEMITH, Paul/1895–1963/Germany

---

before **1917** Cello Concerto No. 1
1917 (22) Three pieces for cello and piano
1918 (23) Violin Sonata No. 1 in E♭ major
> Violin Sonata No. 2 in D major
> String Quartet No. 1 in F minor
1919 (24) Violin Sonata in F major
> Sonata for solo viola
> Cello Sonata
1921–22 (26) *Chamber Music,* No. 1
1922 (27) String Quartet No. 2 in C major
> String Quartet No. 3
> Suite for Klavier

	Sonata for solo viola
	Die Junge Magd, six songs
1923 (28)	String Quartet No. 4
	Kleine Sonata für viola d'amore und klavier
	Sonata for solo cello
1924 (29)	Piano Concerto
	Chamber Music, No. 2
	Sonata for solo violin
	Das Marienleben, song cycle
1925 (30)	Concerto for orchestra
	Chamber Music, Nos. 3 and 4
1926 (31)	*Cardillac,* opera
1927 (32)	*Chamber Music,* No. 5
1928 (33)	Concerto for organ and chamber orchestra
	Chamber Music, No. 6
1930 (35)	*Concert Music,* for piano, harps and brass
1931 (36)	*The Unceasing,* oratorio
1932 (37)	*Philharmonic Concerto*
1934 (39)	*Mathis der Maler,* opera, also symphony
1935 (40)	Viola Concerto, *Der Schwanendreher*
	Concerto for orchestra
1937 (42)	*Symphonic Dances,* for orchestra
	Organ Sonatas, Nos. 1 and 2
1938 (43)	*Nobilissima Visione,* ballet
1939 (44)	Violin Concerto
1940 (45)	Symphony in E♭ major
	Cello Concerto No. 2
	Theme and Variations for piano and strings, *The Four Temperaments*
	Harp Sonata
1943 (48)	*Symphonic Metamorphoses* on a Theme by Weber, for orchestra
	Cupid and Psyche, overture
	Ludus Tonalis, for piano
1944 (49)	*Hérodiade,* for speaker and chamber orchestra
1945 (50)	Piano Concerto
1946 (51)	*When Lilacs in the Dooryard Bloomed— an American Requiem* (for Walt Whitman)
1947 (52)	*Symphonia Serena* (possibly 1946)
	Clarinet Concerto

1948 (53) Concerto for trumpet, bassoon and strings
Septet for wind instruments
1949 (54) Horn Concerto
Concerto for woodwind, harp and
 orchestra
Organ Sonata No. 2
1950 (55) Sinfonietta
Requiem for Those We Love (possibly
 1946)
1951 (56) *Der Harmonie der Welt,* symphony
1952 (57) Symphony in E♭ for military band
Sonata for four horns
1958 (63) Octet

HODDINOTT, Alun/b.1929/Great Britain

1953 (24) *fp. Fugal Overture,* for orchestra
fp. Nocturne, for orchestra
1954 (25) *fp.* Concerto for clarinet and string
 orchestra
1955 (26) *fp.* Symphony No. 1
1956 (27) *fp.* Septet for wind, strings and piano
1957 (28) *Rondo Scherzoso,* for trumpet and piano
1958 (29) *fp.* Harp Concerto
fp. Serenade for string orchestra
fp. Concertino for viola and small
 orchestra
fp. Four Welsh Dances, for orchestra
1959 (30) *fp. Nocturne and Dance,* for harp and
 orchestra
fp. Piano Sonata No. 1
1960 (31) *fp.* Concerto No. 1 for piano, wind and
 percussion
fp. Sextet for flute, clarinet, bassoon,
 violin, viola and cello
1961 (32) *fp.* Concerto No. 2 for piano and
 orchestra
fp. Violin Concerto
1962 (33) *fp. Rebecca,* ballad for unaccompanied
 mixed voices
fp. Variations for flute, clarinet, harp and
 string quartet

fp. Symphony No. 2

1963 (34) fp. Divertimento for oboe, clarinet, horn and bassoon

fp. Sinfonia for string orchestra

1964 (35) fp. *Danegeld,* six episodes for unaccompanied mixed voices

fp. *Jack Straw,* overture

fp. Harp Sonata

fp. *Toccata all Giga,* for organ

fp. *Intrada,* for organ

fp. *Sarum Fanfare,* for organ

1965 (36) fp. *Dives and Lazarus,* cantata

fp. Concerto Grosso No. 1

fp. *Aubade and Scherzo,* for horn and strings

1966 (37) fp. String Quartet No. 1

fp. Concerto No. 3 for piano and orchestra

fp. *Pantomime,* overture

fp. Concerto Grosso No. 2

fp. *Variants,* for orchestra

fp. Piano Sonata No. 4

1967 (38) fp. *Night Music,* for orchestra

fp. Clarinet Sonata

fp. Organ Concerto

fp. Suite for harp

1968 (39) fp. Symphony No. 3

fp. *Nocturnes and Cadenzas,* for clarinet, violin and piano

fp. *Roman Dream,* scena for solo soprano and instrumental ensemble

fp. *An Apple Tree and a Pig,* scena for unaccompanied mixed voices

fp. Sinfonietta 1

fp. Piano Sonata No. 5

fp. Divertimenti for eight instruments

fp. *Fioriture,* for orchestra

1969 (40) fp. *Black Bart,* ballade for mixed voices and orchestra

fp. *Nocturnes and Cadenzas,* for cello and orchestra

fp. Violin Sonata No. 1

fp. Horn Concerto

	fp. Investiture Dances, for orchestra
	fp. Sinfonietta 2
	fp. Divertimento for orchestra
	fp. Symphony No. 4
1970 (41)	*fp.* Fantasy for harp
	fp. Sinfonietta 3
	fp. Violin Sonata No. 2
	fp. Cello Sonata
	fp. The Sun, the Great Luminary of the Universe, for orchestra
1971 (42)	*fp.* Concerto for oboe and strings
	fp. Concertino for trumpet, horn and orchestra
	fp. Out of the Deep, motet for unaccompanied mixed voices
	fp. Violin Sonata No. 3
	fp. Horn Sonata
	fp. The Tree of Life, for soprano and tenor, chorus, organ and orchestra
1972 (43)	*fp. Aubade,* for small orchestra
	fp. The Hawk is Set Free, for orchestra
	fp. Piano Sonata No. 6
1973 (44)	*fp. The Floore of Heav'n,* for orchestra
	fp. Symphony No. 5
1974 (45)	*fp. The Beach of Falesa,* opera
	fp. Ritornelli, for solo trombone, wind instruments and percussion
1975 (46)	*fp. Landscapes,* for orchestra

Hoddinott also composed *Welsh Dances,* Suite No. 2, for orchestra.

HOLST, Gustav (von)/1874–1934/Great Britain

1895 (21)	*The Revoke,* one-act opera
1896 (22)	*Fantasiestücke,* for oboe and string quartet
	Quintet for wind and piano
	Four songs
1897 (23)	*A Winter Idyll,* for orchestra
	Clear and Cool, for choir and orchestra
1898 (24)	*Ornulf's Drapa,* for baritone and orchestra

1899 (25) *Walt Whitman,* overture
            Five part-songs for mixed voices
              (1899–1900)
            Sita, opera (1899–1906)

1900 (26) *Cotswolds Symphony*
            Suite de Ballet, in E♭
            Ave Maria for eight-part female choir

1902 (28) *The Youth's Choice,* opera
            Four part-songs for mixed voices
            Six songs for baritone
            Six songs for soprano

1903 (29) *Indra,* symphonic poem
            King Estmere, for choir and orchestra
            Quintet for wind

1904 (30) *The Mystic Trumpeter,* for soprano and
              orchestra

1905 (31) *Song of the Night,* for violin and
              orchestra
            Four carols for mixed voices
            Song from "The Princess"

1906 (32) *Songs of the West,* for orchestra
            Two Songs Without Words, dedicated to
              Vaughan Williams *(q.v.)*

1907 (33) *Somerset Rhapsody,* for orchestra
            Nine Hymns from the Rìg-Veda
              (1907–08)

1908 (34) *Savitri,* opera
            Choral Hymns from the Rig-Veda,
              Group 1

1909 (35) *A Vision of Dame Christian,* incidental
              music
            First Suite for Military Band, in E♭ major
            Choral Hymns from the Rig-Veda,
              Group 2

1910 (36) *Beni Mora,* Oriental Suite
            The Cloud Messenger, ode
            Choral Hymns from the Rig-Veda,
              Group 3

1911 (37) *Invocations,* for cello and orchestra
            Oh England My Country, for choir and
              orchestra
            Hecuba's Lament, for choir and orchestra
            Second Suite for Military Band, in F major

1912 (38) *Choral Hymns from the Rig-Veda,*
        Group 4
1913 (39) *St. Paul's Suite,* for strings
        Hymn to Dionysus, for choir and
        orchestra
1914–16 (40–42) *The Planets,* orchestral suite in
        seven movements
1915 (41) *Japanese Suite*
1916 (42) Five part-songs
        Four songs for voice and violin
        Three festival choruses
1917 (43) *Hymn of Jesus,* for two choruses, semi-
        chorus and orchestra
        A Dream of Christmas
1919 (45) *Festival Te Deum*
        Ode to Death
1921 (47) *The Perfect Fool,* opera
        The Lure, ballet
1922 (48) Fugal Overture, No. 1
1923 (49) Fugal Overture, No. 2
        Choral Symphony (1923–24)
1924 (50) *At the Boar's Head,* opera
        Terzetto, for flute, oboe and viola
        Two Motets for mixed voices
1925–26 (51) Seven part-songs (Bridges)
1926 (52) *The Golden Goose,* choral ballet
        Chrissemas Day in the Morning, for piano
1927 (53) *Egdon Heath,* symphonic poem
        The Morning of the Year, choral ballet
        The Coming of Christ, mystery play
        Two folk song arrangements, for piano
1928 (54) *Moorside Suite,* for brass band
1929 (55) Concerto for two violins
        The Tale of the Wandering Scholar, opera
        Twelve songs
1930 (56) Choral Fantasia
        Hammersmith, Prelude and Scherzo, for
        orchestra
1933 (59) *Lyric Movement,* for viola and strings
        Brook Green Suite, for strings

1916–17 (24) String Quartet No. 1
1916–18 (24–26) Violin Sonata No. 1
1919 (27) Violin Sonata No. 2
               Dance of the Goat, for flute
1920 (28) *Pastorale d'été*
               Viola Sonata
               Cello Sonata
1921 (29) *King David,* oratorio with spoken
                   narration
               Horace Victorieux, "mimed symphony"
               Sonatina for clarinet and piano (1921–22)
1923 (31) *Chant de Joie*
1924 (32) *Pacific 231,* Mouvement Symphonique
                   No. 1, for orchestra
1925 (33) *Judith,* opera
               Concertino for piano and orchestra
1927 (35) *Antigone,* lyric drama
1928 (36) *Rugby,* Mouvement Symphonique No. 2,
                   for orchestra
1930 (38) Symphony No. 1
               Les Aventures du Roi Pausole, light opera
1931 (39) *Cries of the World,* choral-orchestral
               Amphion
               1001 Nights
1932 (40) Mouvement Symphonique No. 3, for
                   orchestra (1932–33)
               Sonatina for violin and cello
1934 (42) Cello Concerto
               Sémiramis, ballet, using voice and Ondes
                   Martenot
               String Quartet No. 2 (1934–36)
1936 (44) *Nocturne*
               String Quartet No. 3
1937 (45) *L'Aiglon,* opera (with Ibert, *q.v.*)
1938 (46) *La Famille Cardinal,* opera (with Ibert)
               Joan of Arc at the Stake, incidental music
               La Danse des Morts, for solo voices,
                   chorus and orchestra
1941 (49) Symphony No. 2, for strings and trumpet

1943 (51) *Jour de fête suisse,* suite
1946 (54) Symphony No. 3, *Liturgique*
           Symphony No. 4, *Deliciae Basiliensis*
1949 (57) Concerto da Camera
1951 (59) Symphony No. 5, *Di Tre Re*
           Monopartita, for orchestra; a suite whose
               movements are linked and intended to
               form a single musical structure
1952 (60) *Suite Archaïque*
1953 (61) *Christmas Cantata*

HUMPERDINCK, Engelbert/1854–1921/Germany

1880 (26) *Humoreske*
1893 (39) *Hänsel und Gretel,* opera
1895 (41) *Die Sieben Geislein,* opera
1898 (44) *Moorish Rhapsody,* for orchestra
1902 (48) *Dornroschen*
1905 (51) *Die Heirat wieder Willen*
1910 (56) *Koenigskinder,* opera
1911 (57) *The Miracle*
1914 (60) *Die Marketenderin*
1919 (65) *Gaudeamus*

IBERT, Jacques/1890–1962/France

1922 (32) *Ports of Call (Escales),* orchestral suite
           Ballad of Reading Gaol, ballet
1925 (35) *Scherzo féerique*
           Concerto for cello and wind instruments
1926 (36) *Jeux,* for orchestra
1927 (37) *Angélique,* opera
1929 (39) *Persée et Andromedée,* opera
1930 (40) *Le Roi d'Yvetot,* opera
           Divertissement, for chamber orchestra
1932 (42) *Donogoo,* for orchestra
           Paris, symphonic suite
1934 (44) *Diane de Poitiers,* ballet
           Concertino da Camera, for alto saxophone
               and small orchestra

151

1935 (45) *Gonzaque,* opera
1937 (47) *L'Aiglon,* opera (with Honegger, *q.v.*)
1938 (48) *La Famille Cardinal,* opera
(with Honegger)
Capriccio for ten instruments
1943 (53) String Quartet in C major
1944 (54) Trio for violin, cello and harp
Suite Elisabethaine, for orchestra
1949 (59) *Etude-Caprice, pour un Tombeau de
Chopin,* for solo cello
1951 (61) Sinfonia Concertante

d'INDY, Vincent/1851–1931/France

1874 (23) *Max et Thecla,* symphonic overture
(Part 2 of *Wallenstein Trilogy*)
Jean Hunyade, symphony (1874–75)
1876 (25) *Anthony and Cleopatra,* overture
Attendez-moi sous l'orme, opera
(1876–78)
1878 (27) *The Enchanted Forest,* ballad-symphony
Piano Quartet (1878–88)
1879–83 (28–32) *Le Chant de la cloche,* opera
1880 (29) *Le Camp de Wallenstein,* symphonic
overture (Part 1 of *Wallenstein Trilogy*)
1882 (31) *La Mort de Wallenstein,* symphonic
overture (Part 3 of *Wallenstein Trilogy*)
1884 (33) *Saugesfleure,* orchestral legend
Lied for cello (or viola) and orchestra
1886 (35) *Symphony on a French Mountain Air*
Suite in D major, for trumpet, two flutes
and string quartet
1887 (36) *Serenade and Valse,* for small orchestra
Trio for clarinet, cello and piano
1888 (37) *Fantasie,* for oboe and orchestra
1890 (39) *Karadec,* incidental music
String Quartet No. 1, in B♭
1891 (41) *Tableaux de voyage*
1896 (45) *Istar,* symphonic variations for orchestra
1897 (46) *Fervaal*
String Quartet No. 2, in E
1898 (47) *Medée,* incidental music

>>Chansons et danses,* for seven wind
>>>instruments, in B♭
>>*L'Étranger,* lyric drama (1898–1901)
1902–03 (51) Symphony No. 2 in B♭
1903 (52) *Choral Varié,* for saxophone and orchestra
1904 (53) Violin Sonata in C
1905 (54) *Jour d'été à la montagne*
1906 (55) *Souvenirs,* tone poem
1916–18 (65–67) Sinfonia brève de ballo Gallico
1918 (67) *Sarabande et Minuet,* for piano, flute,
>>>oboe, clarinet, horn and bassoon
1920 (69) *Légende de St. Christophe*
>>*Le Poème des Rivages* (1920–21)
1922–23 (71) *Le Rêve de Čynias*
1924 (73) Piano Quintet in G minor
1925 (74) Cello Sonata in D major
>>*Diptyque méditerranéen* (1925–26)
1927 (76) Concert for piano, flute, cello and string
>>>quartet
>>"Suites en parties", for harp, flute, viola,
>>>and cello
1929 (78) String Sextet in B♭
1930 (79) String Quartet No. 4 in D♭
>>Piano Trio No. 2, in the form of a suite
>>Suite for flute obbligato, violin, viola,
>>>cello and harp

IPPOLITOV-IVANOV, Mikhail/1859–1935/Russia

1882 (23) *Yar-Khmel,* for orchestra
1887 (28) *Ruth,* opera
>>*p.* Violin Sonata
1890 (31) *Asra,* opera
1894–95 (35) *Armenian Rhapsody*
1895 (36) *Caucasian Sketches,* suite for orchestra
1897 (38) *p.* String Quartet in A minor
1898 (39) *p.* Piano Quartet in A♭ major
1900 (41) *Assia*
1907 (48) Symphony
1909 (50) *Treachery*
1912 (53) *The Spy*
1916 (57) *Ole the Norseman*

1923–24 (64) *Mtzyry*
1928 (69) *Episodes from Schubert's Life*
1933–34 (74) *The Last Barricade*
1934 (75) *Catalan Suite*

IRELAND, John/1879–1962/Great Britain

1895 (16) Two pieces for piano
1905 (26) *Songs of a Wayfarer*
1906 (27) Piano Trio No. 1, *Phantasy Trio*
1909 (30) Violin Sonata No. 1
1912 (33) *Greater Love Hath No Man*, motet
1913 (34) *Forgotten Rite*, for orchestra
        Decorations, for piano:
            The Island Spell
            Moonglade
            Scarlet Ceremonies
        Three Dances for piano
        Sea Fever, song (words Masefield)
        Marigold, song
        Impressions, song
1915 (36) Preludes for piano
1917 (38) Piano Trio No. 2
        Violin Sonata No. 2
        The Cost, songs
1918 (39) *Leaves from a child's sketchbook*
1919 (40) *Summer Evening*
        The Holy Boy
1920 (41) Three *London Pieces*, for piano
        Piano Sonata
1921 (42) *Mai-Dun*, symphonic rhapsody
        Land of Lost Content, song cycle
1923 (44) Cello Sonata
1927 (48) *Sonatina*, for piano
1929 (50) *Ballade*, for piano
1930 (51) Piano Concerto in E♭ major
1931 (52) *Songs Sacred and Profane*
1932 (53) *A Downland Suite*, for brass band
1933 (54) *Legend*, for piano and orchestra
1934 (55) *A Comedy Overture*, for brass band
1936 (57) *London Overture*, for orchestra

1937 (58) *These Things Shall Be,* for baritone, choir and orchestra
      Green Ways, for piano
1938 (59) Piano Trio No. 3
1939 (60) *Concertino Pastorale,* for strings
1941 (62) *Sarnia,* for piano
      Three Pastels, for piano
      O Happy Land, song
1942 (63) *Epic March*
1943 (64) *Fantasy Sonata,* for clarinet and piano
1944 (65) *A Maritime Overture,* for military band
1946 (67) *fp. Satyricon Overture*
Ireland also composed:
Minuet and Elegy, for string orchestra
Equinox, for piano
Many songs and piano compositions.

IVES, Charles Edward/1874–1954/U.S.A.

1891 (17) Variations on "America", for organ
1896 (22) Quartet No. 1, *Revival Service*
      Symphony No. 1 in D minor (1896–98)
1897–1902 (23–28) Symphony No. 2
1898–1907 (24–33) *Calcium Light Night,* for chamber orchestra
      Central Park in the dark, for orchestra
1900–06 and **1914–15** *Children's Day at the Camp Meeting,* three pieces for violin and piano
1901–04 (27–30) Symphony No. 3
1902–10 (28–36) Violin Sonata No. 2
1903–08 (29–34) Violin Sonata No. 1
1903–14 (29–40) *Three Places in New England,* for orchestra
1904 (30) *Thanksgiving, and/or Father's Day* (Part 4 of *Holidays Symphony*)
1904–11 (30–37) Theater Orchestra Set No. 1:
      In the Cage
      In the Inn
      In the Night
1906 (32) *The Pond*
1908 (34) *The Unanswered Question*

1910–16 (36–42) Symphony No. 4
1911 (37) *Browning overture*
  Hallowe'en, for piano and strings
  The Gong on the Hook and Ladder
  Tone-Roads, No. 1 for chamber orchestra
  (1911–15)
1912 (38) *Decoration Day* (Part 2 of *Holidays
  Symphony*)
  Lincoln, the great commoner, for chorus
  and orchestra
1913 (39) *Washington's Birthday* (Part 1 of
  Holidays Symphony)
  Fourth of July (Part 3 of *Holidays
  Symphony*)
  Over the pavements, for chamber
  orchestra
1914 (40) *Protests,* piano sonata
1915 (41) *Concord,* piano sonata (1909–15)
  Orchestral Set No. 2
  Tone-Roads, No. 3 for chamber orchestra
1919–27 (45–53) Orchestral Set No. 3
Ives also composed:
11 volumes of chamber music
The celestial country, for chorus
3 Harvest home chorales
General Booth's entrance into heaven, with brass band
  and chorus
Many psalm settings and other choral works
About 200 songs
Many piano pieces.

JACOB, Gordon/b.1895/Great Britain

Up to and including
1936 (41) *The Jar in the Bush,* ballet
  Uncle Remus, ballet
  Symphony in C
  Oboe Concerto
  Piano Concerto
  Viola Concerto
  Violin Concerto

The Piper at the Gates of Dawn,
      tone poem
Variations on an Original Theme, for
      orchestra
Variations on an Air by Purcell, for string
      orchestra
Denbigh Suite, for strings
Donald Caird, for chorus and orchestra
William Byrd Suite, for military band
Serenäde, for five wind instruments
Quartets Nos. 1 and 2
1945 (50) Symphony No. 2
           Clarinet Concerto
1950 (55) Sinfonietta in D major
           A Goodly Heritage, cantata
1951 (56) Flute Concerto
           Fantasia on Songs of the British Isles
1956 (61) Piano Concerto No. 2
           Sextet
           Piano Trio
1958 (63) Suite for recorder and string quartet
           Diversions, for woodwind and strings
           Miniature String Quartet
           Old Wine in New Bottles, for wind
              instruments
1961 (66) Fantasia on Scottish Tunes
           Improvisations on a Scottish Tune, for
              orchestra
           Trombone Concerto
1962 (67) News from Newtown, cantata
1963 (68) Suite for brass band
1965 (70) Festival Te Deum, for chorus and
              orchestra
1966 (71) Oboe Sonata
           Variations on a Theme of Schubert
1967 (72) Concerto for Band
           Animal Magic, cantata for children
           Six miniatures
1968 (73) Suite for bassoon and string quartet
           Divertimento in E♭
1969 (74) Redbridge Variations
           Piano Quartet

157

1970 (75)   *A York Symphony*
              Pride of Youth, for brass band
              A Joyful Noise, for brass band
1971 (76)   *Rhapsody for Three Hands,* for piano
1972 (77)   Double-bass Concerto
              Tuba Suite, with orchestra or piano
              Psalm 103 for chorus
1973 (78)   Saxophone Quartet
1974 (79)   Quartet for Clarinets
              Sinfonia Brevis
              Havant Suite, for chamber orchestra
1975 (80)   Concerto for organ, strings and percussion
              Fantasy Sonata for organ
              Rhapsody, for piano

JANÁČEK, Leos/1854–1928/Czechoslovakia

1877 (23)   Suite for strings
1880 (26)   *Dumka,* for violin and piano
1887 (33)   *Sarka,* opera
1889 (35)   Six Lach Dances
1891 (37)   *The Beginning of a Romance,* opera
              Rákos Rákóczy, ballet
1894–1903 (40–49) *Jenufa,* opera
1904 (50)   *Osud (Fate),* opera
1908–17 (54–63) *Mr. Brouček's Excursion to the
                  Moon,* opera
1915–18 (61–64) *Taras Bulba,* rhapsody for
                  orchestra
1919 (65)   *Katya Kabanova,* opera (1919–21)
              Diary of a Young Man who disappeared,
                  song cycle
1920 (66)   *Ballad of Blanik,* symphonic poem
1921 (67)   Violin Sonata
1923 (69)   String Quartet No. 1 in E minor
1924 (70)   *The Cunning Little Vixen,* opera
              The Makropoulos Affair, opera
                  (1924–26)
              Miade (Youth), suite for wind
1925 (71)   Sinfonietta (1925–26)
              Concertino for piano, two violins, viola,
                  cello, bassoon and horn

1926 (72) *Capriccio,* for piano and wind instruments
Festliche Messe
1927 (73) *From the House of the Dead,* opera
(1927–28)
Glagolitic Mass
1928 (74) String Quartet No. 2, *Intimate Pages*

JONGEN, Joseph/1873–1953/Belgium

1893–1905 (20–32) Piano Trio in B minor
Violin Sonata No. 1 in D major
1894 (21) *p.* String Quartet No. 1 in C minor
1898 (25) *Fantaisie,* for violin and orchestra
1899 (26) Symphony
Violin Concerto
1902 (29) *Fantaisie sur deux Noëls wallons,* for
orchestra
Piano Quartet in E♭ major
1904 (31) *Lalla Rookh,* symphonic poem
1907 (34) *Félyane,* opera (unfinished)
after **1905** and
before **1909**   Piano Trio in F♯ minor
1909 (36) Violin Sonata No. 2 in E major
1911 (38) *S'Arka,* ballet
Cello Sonata (1911–12)
1912 (39) *Deux rondes wallons,* for orchestra
1913 (40) *Impressions d'Ardennes,* for orchestra
1915 (42) *Suites en deux parties,* for viola and
orchestra
1916 (43) String Quartet No. 2 in A major
1917 (44) *Tableaux pittoresques,* for orchestra
1918 (45) *p. Serenade Tendre* and *Serenade Triste,*
for string quartet
1919 (46) *Poème héroïque,* for violin and orchestra
1922 (49) *Rhapsody,* for piano, flute, oboe, clarinet,
horn and bassoon
1928 (55) *Pièce symphonique,* for piano and
orchestra
1929 (56) *Passacaille et Gigue,* for orchestra
Suite for viola and orchestra
1930 (57) *Sonata Eroica*

1933 (60) *La Légende de Saint-Nicholas,* for
children's choir and orchestra
Symphonie Concertante, for organ and
orchestra
1936 (63) *Triptyque,* three suites for orchestra
1938 (65) *Hymne à la Meuse,* for chorus and
orchestra
1939 (66) *Ouverture-Fanfare,* for orchestra
1941 (68) *La Cigale et le fourmi,* for children's
~chorus
Ouverture de fête, for orchestra
1943 (70) Piano Concerto
1944 (71) *Bourrée,* for orchestra
Jongen also composed:
Concerto for harp
Concerto for wind quintet.

KABALEVSKY, Dimitri/b.1904/Russia

1929 (25) Piano Concerto No. 1 in A minor
String Quartet in A minor
1930 (26) *Poem of Struggle,* for chorus and orchestra
1932 (28) Symphony No. 1, *Proletarians Unite!,*
for chorus and orchestra
Symphony No. 2 in E minor
1933 (29) Symphony No. 3, *Requiem for Lenin,*
for chorus and orchestra
1936 (32) Piano Concerto No. 2 in G minor
1938 (34) *Colas Breugnon,* opera, revised 1968–69
Vasilek, ballet
1939 (35) Symphony No. 4, *Shchors,* for chorus
and orchestra
1940 (36) *The Golden Spikes,* ballet
The Comedians, suite for small orchestra
1942 (38) *Peoples Avengers,* suite for chorus and
orchestra
Before Moscow, opera
Our Great Fatherland, cantata
*c.***1944** (*c.*40) *The Family of Taras,* opera
1948 (44) Violin Concerto
1949 (45) Cello Concerto

1952 (48)   Piano Concerto No. 3
           Cello Sonata
1955 (51)   *Nikita Vershinin,* opera
1956 (52)   Symphony No. 5
           Romeo and Juliet, symphonic suite
1960 (56)   *Overture Pathétique,* for orchestra
           The Spring, symphonic poem
           Camp of Friendship, six children's songs
              (begun 1935)
           Gasts in the kitchen-garden, play for
              children
           Major-minor études, for solo cello
           Three Dancing Songs for children
1961 (57)   Rondo for violin and piano
1962 (58)   *Requiem,* for two soloists, children's and
              mixed choirs and orchestra (1962–63)
           Cello Sonata
1963 (59)   Three Songs of Revolutionary Cuba
           Three Songs
           Five Songs (1963–64)
1964 (60)   Rhapsody for piano and orchestra, *School
              Years*
           Cello Concerto No. 2
1965 (61)   *Symphonic Prelude in memory of heroes
              of Gorlovka*
           Rondo for cello and piano
           Twenty easy pieces for violin and piano
           Spring Plays and Dances, for piano
1966 (62)   *The Motherland,* cantata for children's
              choir and orchestra
1967 (63)   *Recitative and Rondo,* for piano
1968–69 (64)   *Sisters,* lyric opera

KHACHATURIAN, Aram/b.1903/Armenia (Russia)

1927 (24)   *Poème,* for piano
1932 (29)   Violin Sonata
           String Quartet in C major
           Trio in G minor, for clarinet, violin and
              piano
1933 (30)   Symphony No. 1 (1933–34)
           Dance Suite

1936 (33) Piano Concerto
1937 (34) *Song of Stalin*, for chorus and orchestra
1939 (36) *Happiness*, ballet
              Masquerade, incidental music
1940 (37) Violin Concerto
1942 (39) *Gayane*, ballet
              Symphony No. 2
1944 (41) Concerto for violin and cello
              Masquerade suite
1945 (42) Solemn Overture *To the End of the War*
1947 (44) *Symphonie-Poème*
1950 (47) Cello Concerto
1954 (51) *Spartacus*, ballet
1955 (52) Three Suites for Orchestra
1956 (53) *Ode of Joy,* for soloist, chorus and
              orchestra
1957 (54) *Lermontov Suite*
1958 (55) Sonatina for piano
1960 (57) Rhapsody for violin and orchestra
              Ballade, for bass with orchestra
1961 (58) Piano Sonata
1962 (59) Cello Sonata
1965 (62) *Concerto-Rhapsody,* for cello and
              orchestra
1966 (63) Suite for Orchestra, No. 4

KODÁLY, Zoltán/1882–1967/Hungary

1897 (15) Overture for orchestra
1901 (19) Adagio for violin (or viola) and piano
1906 (24) *Summer Evening*
1908 (26) String Quartet No. 1 in C minor
1909–10 (27) Cello Sonata (Atonal)
1914 (32) Duo for violin and cello (Atonal)
1915 (33) Sonata for unaccompanied cello
1916–17 (34) String Quartet No. 2 in D major
1917–18 (35) Seven piano pieces
1919–20 (37) *Serenade,* for two violins and viola
1923 (41) *Psalmus Hungaricus,* for tenor, chorus
              and orchestra
1925 (43) *Meditation on a theme of Debussy,*
              for piano

1926 (44) *Háry János*, opera
1930 (48) *Dances of Marosszeck*, for piano
       (afterwards orchestrated)
1931 (49) *Theater Overture*
       The Spinning Room, lyric scenes
       (1931–32)
       Pange lingua, for mixed choir and organ
1933 (51) *Dances of Galanta*, orchestral suite
1934 (52) *Jesus and the Merchants*, for chorus and
       orchestra
1936 (54) Te Deum for chorus and orchestra
1938–39 (56) *Variations on a Hungarian Folk-song*,
       for orchestra
1939 (57) Concerto for orchestra
       The Peacock Variations
1945 (63) Missa Brevis
1947 (65) Viola Concerto
       String Quartet
1948 (66) *Czinka Panna*, opera
1954 (72) *Spartacus*, ballet
1960 (78) Symphony in C major
1965 (83) Variations for piano
1967 (85) *Laudes Organi*, fantasia on twelfth-
       century sequence, for mixed choir
       and organ

KORNGOLD, Erich Wolfgang/1897–1957/U.S.A.
  (b. Austria)

1910–13 (13–16) Piano Trio
1916 (19) *Der Ring des Polykrates*, opera buffe
1919 (22) *Much Ado About Nothing*, incidental
       music
1920 (23) *The Dead City*, opera
1939 (42) *Die Kathrin*, opera
1940 (43) *Songs of the Clown*
       Four Shakespeare Songs
1941 (44) *Psalm*, for solo, chorus and orchestra
1942 (45) *Prayer*, for tenor, chorus and orchestra
       Tomorrow, song
1945 (48) Violin Concerto
       String Quartet No. 3

1946 (49) *The silent serenade,* comedy with music
Cello Concerto
1947 (50) *Symphonic serenade,* for strings
Five songs for middle voice
1951 (54) Symphony in F♯ major
1952 (55) *Sonnet to Vienna,* song
1953 (56) Theme and Variations for orchestra
Straussiana, for orchestra

KORTE, Karl/b.1928/U.S.A.

1948 (20) String Quartet No. 1
1955 (27) *Concertato on a Choral Theme,* for
orchestra
1958 (30) *Story of the Flutes,* symphonic poem
1959 (31) *For a Young Audience,* for orchestra
Fantasy, for violin and piano
1960 (32) Quintet for oboe and strings
1961 (33) Symphony No. 2
Four Blake Songs, for women's voices
and piano
1962 (34) *Nocturne and March,* for band
Ceremonial Prelude and Passacaglia,
for band
1963 (35) *Southwest,* a dance overture
Prairie Song, for trumpet and band
Introductions, for brass quintet
Mass for Youth, with orchestra or
keyboard
1964 (36) *Diablerie,* for woodwind quintet
1965 (37) *Aspects of Love,* seven songs on various
texts
String Quartet No. 2
1968 (40) Symphony No. 3
Matrix, for woodwind quartet, piano,
percussion and saxophone
May the Sun Bless Us, four settings of
texts of Tagore, for male voices, brass
and percussion
1969 (41) *Facets,* for saxophone quartet
Dialogue, for saxophone and tape

1970 (42) *Gestures,* for electric brass, percussion, piano and band
Psalm XIII, for chorus and tape
1971 (43) *I Think You Would Have Understood,* for stage band, solo trumpet and two-channel tape
Remembrances, for flute and tape
1974 (46) Four Songs, *Libera me*

LALO, Édouard/1823–1892/France

1855 (32) String Quartet in E♭
1872 (49) *Deux Aubades,* for small orchestra
Violin Concerto in F major
Divertissement, for small orchestra
1873 (50) *Symphonie Espagnole,* for violin and orchestra, in five movements
1875 (52) *Allegro Symphonique*
1876 (53) Cello Concerto
1881 (58) *Rapsodie Norvégienne*
1882 (59) Ballet Suites Nos. 1 and 2, *Namouna*
1884 (61) Scherzo
1886 (63) Symphony in G minor
1888 (65) *Le Roi d'Ys,* opera
1889 (66) Piano Concerto in G minor

LAMBERT, Constant/1905–1951/Great Britain

1925–26 (20–21) *Romeo and Juliet,* ballet
1926 (21) *Pomona,* ballet
Poems by Li-Po
1927 (22) Music for Orchestra
Elegiac Blues
1928–29 (23) Piano Sonata
1929 (24) *The Rio Grande,* for chorus, orchestra and piano solo
1931 (26) Concerto for piano and nine instruments
1936 (31) *Summer's Last Will and Testament,* for chorus and orchestra
1937 (32) *Horoscope,* ballet
1940 (35) *Dirge,* for male voices and strings

1942 (37) *Aubade héroïque,* for orchestra
1950 (45) *Tiresias,* ballet

LECLAIR, Jean-Marie/1697–1764/France

1723 (26) *p.* Sonatas for Violin Alone, with a Bass,
              Book I
1728 (31) *p.* Sonatas for Violin Alone, with a Bass,
              Book II
1734 (37) *p.* Sonatas for Violin Alone, with a Bass,
              Book III
1737 (40) *p.* Six concertos for violin
1746 (49) *Scylla et Glaucus,* opera

LEHÁR, Franz (Ferencz)/1870–1948/Hungary

1905 (35) *The Merry Widow,* operetta
1909 (39) *Count of Luxemburg,* operetta
1928 (58) *Frederica,* operetta
1929 (59) *The Land of Smiles,* operetta
Lehár also composed many other operettas and a
violin concerto.

LEONCAVALLO, Ruggero/1858–1919/Italy

1892 (34) *I Pagliacci,* opera
1894 (36) *Serafita,* symphonic poem
1897 (39) *La Bohème,* opera (this failed whereas
              Puccini's on the same subject
              succeeded)
1900 (42) *Zaza,* opera

LIADOV, Anatol/1855–1914/Russia

1876 (21) *Birulki,* for piano
1879 (24) *Arabesque,* for piano
1887 (32) *Scherzo,* for orchestra
1888 (33) *Mazurka,* for orchestra
1890 (35) *Dal Tempo Antico,* for piano

1892 (37) *Kukalki,* for piano
1893 (38) *Une tabatière à musique,* for piano
1899 (44) *Slava,* for women's chorus, two harps and two pianos
1900 (45) *Polonaise,* for orchestra
1904 (49) *Baba Yaga,* symphonic poem
1906 (51) *Eight Popular Russian Songs,* for orchestra
1909 (54) *The Enchanted Lake,* symphonic poem
1910 (55) *Kikimora,* symphonic poem
Dance of the Amazons, for orchestra
1914 (59) *Naenia (Dirge)*

LIGETI, György/b.1923/Hungary

1953 (30) String Quartet
1958 (35) *Artikulation,* for tape
Apparitions, for large orchestra (1958–59)
1960 (37) *Atmospheres,* for large orchestra
1961 (38) *Fragment,* for eleven instruments
Volumina, for organ (1961–62)
1962 (39) *Poème Symphonique,* for one hundred metronomes
Aventures, for three singers and seven instruments
Nouvelles Aventures, for three singers and seven instruments (1962–65)
1963–65 (40–42) *Requiem*
1966 (43) Cello Concerto
Lux Aeterna
1967 (44) *Lontana,* for large orchestra
Two studies for organ (1967–69)
1968 (45) *Ramifications,* for string orchestra (1968–69)
Ten pieces for wind quintet
String Quartet No. 2
Continuum, for harpsichord
1969–70 (46) Chamber Concertato for thirteen instruments
1971 (48) *Melodien,* for orchestra
Horizont, for recorder

1972 (49) *Kylwiria,* opera
Double Concerto for flute, oboe and
orchestra

LISZT, Franz (Ferencz)/1811–1886/Hungary

1830–49 (19–38) Piano Concerto No. 1 in E♭ major
1831 (20) *Harmonies poétiques et religieuses,* for
piano and orchestra
1835–83 *Années de pèlerinage,* for piano
1839 (28) Piano Concerto No. 2 in A minor
*c.***1840** (*c.*29) *Malediction,* for piano and strings
1843 (32) *Valse Impromptu,* in A♭ major
1849–50 (38) *Héroïde funèbre,* for orchestra
1850 (39) *Consolations,* for piano
Prometheus, symphonic poem
Liebestraüme, nocturnes for piano
1852 (41) *Hungarian Rhapsodies,* Nos. 1–15
1854 (43) *Orpheus,* tone poem
Les préludes, symphonic poem
Hungaria, symphonic poem
*c.***1855** (*c.*44) *Totentanz,* for piano and orchestra
1856 (45) *Tasso,* symphonic poem
Die Hunnenschlacht, symphonic poem
1857 (46) *Mazeppa,* symphonic poem
Faust, symphony (possibly 1854–57)
Dante, symphony (possibly 1855–56)
1859 (48) *Hamlet,* symphonic poem
Die Ideale, for orchestra
*c.***1860** (*c.*49) *Fantasy on Hungarian Folktunes,* for
piano and orchestra
1863 (52) Two Concert Studies for piano
1866 (55) *Deux Légendes,* for piano
1867 (56) *Legend of St. Elizabeth* (possibly
1857–62)
1879 (68) *Via Crucis*
*c.***1880** (*c.*69) *Hungarian Rhapsodies,* Nos. 16–20
1881 (70) *Mephisto Waltz*

LOEFFLER, Charles/1861–1935/Alsace

1891 (30) *The Nights in the Ukraine,* for violin and
orchestra
1894 (33) *Fantasy Concerto,* for cello and orchestra
1895 (34) *Divertimento,* for violin and orchestra
1901 (40) *Divertissement Espagnol,* for saxophone
and orchestra
1902 (41) *Poem,* for orchestra
1905 (44) *La Mort de Tintagiles,* symphonic poem
for two viola d'amore and orchestra
La Villanelle du Diable, symphonic
fantasy for organ and orchestra
A Pagan Poem, for piano, English horn
and three trumpets
1916 (55) *Hora Mystica,* symphony with men's
chorus
1923 (62) "Avant que tu ne t'en ailles", poem
1925 (64) *Memories of my childhood,* for orchestra
1928 (67) *Clowns,* intermezzo

LULLY, Jean/1632–1687/Italy

1658 (26) *fp. Ballets d'Alcidiane*
1659 (27) *fp. Ballets de la raillerie*
1660 (28) *fp. Ballet de Xerxes*
1661 (29) *fp. Ballet de l'Impatience*
fp. Ballet des Saisons
fp. Ballet de l'Ercole amante
1663 (31) *fp. Ballets des Arts*
fp. Ballets des noces de village
1664 (32) *fp. Ballet des amours déguises*
fp. La Mariage forcé, comedy ballet
fp. La Princesse d'Elide, comedy ballet
fp. Entr'actes for Corneille's *Oedipe*
Miserere, concert setting of "Miserere
mei Deus", psalm
1665 (33) *fp. La Naissance de Venus,* ballet
fp. Ballet des Gardes
fp. L'Amour médecin, comedy ballet
1666 (34) *fp. Ballet des Muses*

              fp. Le Triomphe de Bacchus dans les
                   Indes, ballet
                   Versailles, ballet

1667 (35) *fp. Le Sicilien*, comedy ballet
1668 (36) *fp. Le Carnaval, ou Mascarade de*
               fp. Georges Dandin, comedy ballet
               fp. Plaude Laetare
1669 (37) *fp. Ballet de Flore*
               fp. Monsieur de Pourceaugnac,
                 comedy ballet
1670 (38) *fp. Les Amants magnifiques*, comedy ballet
               fp. Le Bourgeois gentilhomme, comedy
                 ballet
1671 (39) *fp. Ballet des Ballets*
               fp. Psyche, tragi-comedy
1673 (41) *fp. Cadmus et Hermione*, opera
1674 (42) *fp. Alceste*, opera
1675 (43) *fp. Thesée*, opera
1676 (44) *fp. Atys*, opera
1677 (45) *fp. Isis*, opera
               fp. Te Deum
1678 (46) *fp. Psyche*, opera
1679 (47) *fp. Bellérophon*, opera
1680 (48) *fp. Proserpine*, opera
1681 (49) *fp. Le Triomphe de l'amour*, ballet
1682 (50) *fp. Persée*, opera
1683 (51) *fp. Phaéton*, opera
               fp. De Profundis
1684 (52) *fp. Amadis de Gaule*, opera
               fp. Motets for two choirs
1685 (53) *fp. Roland*, opera
               fp. Le Temple de la Paix, ballet
1686 (54) *fp. Armide et Renaud*, opera
               fp. Acis et Galathée, opera

LUTOSLAWSKI, Witold/b.1913/Poland

1934 (21) Piano Sonata
1938 (25) *Symphonic Variations*, for orchestra
1941 (28) *Variations on a Theme of Paganini,*
               for two pianos
               Symphony No. 1 (1941–47)

1949 (36) *Overture for Strings*
1950–54 (37–41) *Concerto for Orchestra*
1951 (38) *Little Suite,* for orchestra
           Silesian Triptych, for soprano and
             orchestra
1954 (41) *Dance Preludes,* first version for clarinet
             and piano
1955 (42) *Dance Preludes,* second version for
             clarinet and instruments
1957 (44) Five Songs
1958 (45) *Funeral Music,* for strings
           Three Postludes for orchestra (1958–63)
1959 (46) *Dance Preludes,* third version, for
             instruments
1961 (48) *Jeux Vénitiens*
1962–63 (49) *Trois poèmes d'Henri Michaux,* for
             mixed chorus of twenty voices, wind
             instruments, two pianos, harp and
             percussion
1964 (51) String Quartet
1965 (52) *Paroles Tissées,* for voice and instruments
1967 (54) Symphony No. 2
1968 (55) *Livre pour orchestre*
1969–70 (56) Cello Concerto
1972 (59) *Preludes and fugue,* for thirteen solo
             strings

LUTYENS, Elisabeth/b.1906/Great Britain

1938 (32) String Quartets Nos. 1 and 2
           Partita for two violins
           Sonata for solo viola
1939 (33) *Three Pieces for Orchestra*
           String Trio
1940 (34) Chamber Concerto No. 1, for nine
             instruments
           Chamber Concerto No. 2, for clarinet,
             tenor saxophone, piano, concertante
             and string orchestra (1940–41)
           Midas, ballet for string quartet and piano
1941 (35) *Five Intermezzi for Piano*
1942 (36) Three Symphonic Preludes

Nine Bagatelles, for cello and piano
Two Songs (Auden) for voice and piano
1944 (38) *Suite Gauloise,* for small orchestra
1945 (39) Chamber Concerto No. 3, for bassoon,
string orchestra and percussion
Five Little Pieces for Clarinet and Piano
1947 (41) Viola Concerto
Chamber Concerto No. 4, for horn and
small orchestra
Chamber Concerto No. 5, for string
quartet and small orchestra
The Pit, dramatic scene for tenor and bass
soli, women's chorus and orchestra
1948 (42) Chamber Concerto No. 6, for oboe,
harp and string orchestra
Aptote, for solo viola
Three Improvisations for piano
Nine Songs, for voice and piano
1949 (43) String Quartet No. 3
1950 (44) *Concertante,* for five players
1951 (45) *Requiem for the Living*
Penelope, music drama for violin, cello
and piano soli, choir and orchestra
Nativity, for soprano and strings
1952 (46) String Quartets Nos. 4–6
1953 (47) Three songs and incidental music, for
Group Theater's *Homage to Dylan
Thomas*
1954 (48) *Infidelio,* seven scenes for soprano and
tenor soli and seven instruments
Valediction, for clarinet and piano
1955 (49) *Music for Orchestra I*
Capriccii, for two harps and percussion
Nocturnes, for violin, guitar and cello
Sinfonia for organ
1956 (50) *Chorale for Orchestra (Hômmage à
Stravinsky)*
In the Temple of a Bird's Wing, for
baritone and piano (also 1965)
1956–57 *Three Duos:*
1) Horn and piano
2) Cello and piano
3) Violin and piano

1957 (51) *Six Tempi for Ten Instruments,* for flute,
oboe, clarinet, bassoon, horn, trumpet,
violin, viola, cello and piano
De Amore, cantata for soprano and tenor
soli, choir and orchestra
Variations, for solo flute
1958 (52) *Piano e Forte,* for solo piano
1959–60 (53) *Quincunx,* for soprano and baritone
soli and orchestra
1960 (54) Wind Quintet
1961 (55) *Symphonies for solo piano, wind, harps
and percussion*
Catena, cantata for soprano and tenor soli
and twenty-one instruments
1962 (56) *Music for Orchestra II*
Five Bagatelles for piano
1963 (57) *Music for Orchestra III*
Encomion "Let us now praise famous
men . . .", for chorus, brass and
percussion
String Quintet
Wind Trio, for flute, clarinet and bassoon
Fantasie Trio, for flute, clarinet and piano
Présages, for solo oboe
The Country of the Stars, motet
1964 (58) *Music for Piano and Orchestra*
Music for Wind, for double wind quintet
Scena, for violin, cello and percussion
1965 (59) *The Numbered,* opera in prologue and
two acts (1965–67)
The Valley of Hatsu-Se, for soprano solo,
flute, clarinet, cello and piano
Magnificat and Nunc Dimittis, for
unaccompanied chorus
The Hymn of Man, motet for
unaccompanied male chorus (revised
for mixed chorus 1970)
1966 (60) *And Suddenly It's Evening,* for solo tenor
and eleven instruments
Akapotik Rose, for solo soprano, flute,
two clarinets, string trio and piano
The Fall of the Leafe, for solo oboe and
string quartet

Music for Three, for flute, oboe and piano
1967 (61) *Novenaria,* for orchestra
Time Off? Not a Ghost of a Chance,
    charade in four scenes and three inter-
    ruptions, for baritone, actor, vocal
    quartet, two mixed choruses and
    instruments
Scroll for Li-Ho, for violin and piano
Helix, for piano (four hands)
1968 (62) *Essence of Our Happiness,* for solo tenor,
    chorus and orchestra
Horai, for violin, horn and piano
Epithalanium, for organ (soprano solo
    optional)
A Phœnix, for solo soprano, violin,
    clarinet and piano
The Egocentric, for tenor or baritone
    and piano
The Tyme Doth Flete, for unaccompanied
    chorus, prelude and postlude for two
    trumpets and two trombones optional
1969 (63) *Isis and Osiris,* lyric drama for eight voices
    and small orchestra (1969–70)
Temenos, for organ
The Dying of the Sun, for solo guitar
Trois pièces brêve, for chamber organ
The Tides of Time, for double-bass and
    piano
String Trio
1970 (64) *Anerca* (Eskimo poetry), for speaker/
    actress, ten guitars and percussion
Visions of Youth, for soprano, three
    clarinets, piano and percussion
Oda a la Tormenta, for mezzo-soprano
    and piano
In the Direction of the Beginning, for
    bass and piano
Verses of Love, for mixed choir
    unaccompanied
1971 (65) *Islands,* for soprano, tenor, narrator
    and instrumental ensemble
The Tears of Night, for counter-tenor, six

sopranos and three instrumental
ensembles

Dirge for the Proud World, for soprano,
counter-tenor, harpsichord and cello

Requiescat (Igor Stravinsky 1971), for
soprano and string trio

Driving Out the Death, for oboe and
string trio

1972 (66) *The Linnet from the Leaf,* music/theater
for five singers and two instrumental
groups

Voice of Quiet Waters, for chorus and
orchestra

Counting Your Steps, for chorus, four
flutes and four percussion

Chimes and Cantos, for baritone solo,
two trumpets, two trombones, four
violins, two double-basses and
percussion

Plenum I, for piano solo

Dialogo, for tenor and lute

1973 (67) *One and the Same,* scena for soprano,
speaker, two female mimes, male mime
and instrumental ensemble

The Waiting Game, three scenes for
mezzo-soprano, baritone and small
orchestra

Roads, for two sopranos, counter-tenor,
baritone and bass

Rape of the Moone, for wind octet

Laudi, for soprano, three clarinets, piano
and percussion

Tre, for solo clarinet

Plenum II, for solo oboe

Plenum III, for string quartet

1974 (68) *The Winter of the World,* for orchestras

Kareniana (for Karen Phillips), for
instrumental ensemble

1975 (69) *Eos,* for small orchestra

Fanfare for a Festival, for three trumpets
and three trombones

Pietá, for harpsichord

Ring of Bone, for solo piano

MACDOWELL, Edward/1861–1908/U.S.A.

1882 (21) Piano Concerto No. 1 in A minor
1883 (22) *Modern Suite,* for piano, No. 1
1884 (23) *Forest Idylls,* four pieces for piano
1885 (24) *p. Hamlet and Ophelia,* symphonic poem
1887 (26) Six Idylls after Goethe, for piano
             Six Poems after Heine, for piano
1888 (27) *Lancelot and Elaine,* symphonic poem
             Marionettes, eight pieces for piano
             Romance, for cello
1889 (28) *Les Orientales,* after Hugo, for piano
             Lamia, symphonic poem
1890 (29) Piano Concerto No. 2 in D minor
             Twelve Studies for piano, Books I and II
1891 (30) Suite No. 1 for orchestra
             The Saracens, symphonic poem
             The Lovely Alda, symphonic poem
1893 (32) Piano Sonata No. 1, *Tragica*
1894 (33) Twelve Virtuoso Studies, for piano
1895 (34) Piano Sonata No. 2, *Eroica*
1896 (35) *Indian Suite* (Suite No. 2), for orchestra
             Woodland Sketches, for piano
1898 (37) *Sea Pieces*
1900 (39) Piano Sonata No. 3, *Norse* (dedicated to
             Grieg, *q.v.*)
1901 (40) Piano Sonata No. 4, *Keltic*
1902 (41) *Fireside tales*
             New England Idylls

MAHLER, Gustav/1860–1911/Austria (b. Bohemia)

1880 (20) Klagende Lieder
1882 (22) Lieder und Gesänge aus der Jugendzeit
1883 (23) Lieder eines fahrenden Gesellen, for
             voice and orchestra
1888 (28) Lieder aus des *Knaben Wunderhorn,*
             song cycle for voice and orchestra
             Symphony No. 1 in D major
1894 (34) Symphony No. 2 in C minor, *Resurrection,*

	with final movement for soprano and contralto soloists, choir and orchestra
1895 (35)	Symphony No. 3 in D minor, with final movement for contralto, boys' and female choruses and orchestra
1900 (40)	Symphony No. 4 in G major, with final movement for soprano and orchestra
1902 (42)	Symphony No. 5 in C♯ minor Five Rückert Songs
1904 (44)	Symphony No. 6 in A minor
1905 (45)	Symphony No. 7 in E minor *Kindertotenlieder,* song cycle for voice and orchestra
1907 (47)	Symphony No. 8 in E♭ major, *Symphony of a Thousand,* with eight vocal soloists, two choruses, boys' chorus, organ and orchestra
1908 (48)	*Das Lied von der Erde* (The Song of the Earth), song cycle of symphonic dimensions
1909 (49)	Symphony No. 9 in D major
1910 (50)	Symphony No. 10 begun, unfinished at Mahler's death (A completion was made in 1964 by Deryk Cooke which is now used as the performing version)

MALIPIERO, Gian Francesco/1882–1973/Italy

1906 (24)	*Sinfonia del Mare*
1908 (26)	Cello Sonata
1910 (28)	*Sinfonia del Silenzio e della Morte* *Impressioni dal Vero, I* (1910–11)
1914–15 (32)	*Impressioni dal Vero, II*
1917 (35)	*Ditirambo Tragico* *Armenia*
1918 (36)	*Grottesco,* for small orchestra *Pantea,* ballet *L'Orfeide,* opera (1918–21)
1919–21 (37–39)	*Tre Commedie Goldiane,* opera
1920 (38)	*Oriente Immaginario*
1921–22 (39)	*Impressioni dal Vero, III*
1925 (43)	*Filomela e l'Infatuato,* opera

177

                    Merlino maestro d'organi, opera
                        (1925–28)
                    Il Mistero di Venezia, opera (1925–28)
1926 (44) *L'Esilio dell'Eroe,* five symphonic
                        impressions
1929 (47) *Torneo Notturno,* opera
1930 (48) *La Bella e il Mostro,* opera
1931 (49) Concerto for Orchestra
1932 (50) Violin Concerto
                    Sette Invenzione
                    Inni
1933 (51) *La favola del figlio cambiato;* opera
1934 (52) Symphony No. 1
                    Piano Concerto No. 1
1936 (54) *Julius Caesar,* opera
                    Symphony No. 2, *Elegiaca*
1937 (55) Piano Concerto No. 2
                    Cello Concerto
1938 (56) *Anthony and Cleopatra,* opera
                    Triple Concerto, for violin, cello and piano
1939 (57) *Ecuba,* opera
1940 (58) *La Vita e'Sogno,* opera
1941–42 (59) *I Capriccio di Callot,* opera
1942 (60) *Minnie la Candida,* opera
1943 (61) *L' Allegra Brigata,* opera
1944 (62) Symphony No. 3, *delle Campane*
1946 (64) Symphony No. 4, *In Memoriam*
1947 (65) Symphony No. 5, *Concertante in eco,*
                        with two pianos
                    Symphony No. 6, *Degli archi,* for strings
1948 (66) Symphony No. 7, *delle Canzoni*
                    Piano Concerto No. 3
                    Mondi Celeste e Infernali, opera
                        (1948–49)
1950 (68) Symphony in one movement
                    Piano Concerto No. 4
1951 (69) *Sinfonia del Zodiaco*
1952 (70) Violin Concerto
1957 (75) Quintet for piano and strings
1959 (77) *Musica da Camera,* for wind quintet
                    Six poesie di Dylan Thomas, for soprano
                        and ten instruments
1960 (78) String Quartet No. 3

1964 (82) *In Time of Daffodils,* for soprano,
baritone, flute, clarinet, bass-clarinet,
viola, double-bass, guitar and percussion
Symphony No. 8
1965 (83) *Costellazioni,* for piano
1966 (84) Symphony No. 9
1967 (85) *Carnet de Notes,* for chamber orchestra
Cassazione, for string sextet
Symphony No. 10
1968 (86) *Gli Eroi di Bonaventura*
Flute Concerto
1970 (88) Symphony No. 11

MARTIN, Frank/1890–1974/Switzerland

1926 (36) *Rythmes,* three symphonic movements
1931 (41) Violin Sonata
Chaconne, for cello and piano
1933 (43) Four Short Pieces, for guitar
1934 (44) Piano Concerto No. 1
1935 (45) *Rhapsody,* for two violins, two violas and
double-bass, or string orchestra
1936 (46) Symphony for full orchestra (1936–37)
Danse de la peur, for two pianos and
small orchestra
String Trio
1938 (48) *Ballade,* for alto saxophone, string
orchestra, piano, timpani and percussion
Le Vin herbe, opera
Sonata da Chiesa, for viola d'amore and
organ
1939 (49) *Ballade,* for piano and orchestra
Ballade, for flute, string orchestra and
piano
Ballade, for flute and piano
1941 (51) Sonata da Chiesa, for flute and string
orchestra
1942–43 (52) *Die Weise von Liebe und Tod des
Cornets Christoph Rilke,* for high voice
and orchestra
1943 (53) *Sechs Monologe aus Jedermann,* for
baritone and piano

1944 (54) *Petite Symphonie Concertante* (1944–45)
In Terra Pax, oratorio
Passacaglia for organ
1945–48 (55–58) *Golgotha,* oratorio
1946 (56) Overture to Racine's *Athalie,* for orchestra
1947 (57) *Trois chants de Noël,* for high voice, flute
and piano
1948 (58) *Ballade,* for cello and piano
Eight Piano Preludes
1949 (59) Concerto for seven wind instruments
1950 (60) Violin Concerto (1950–51)
Five Ariel Songs, for mixed chamber choir
1951 (61) Concerto for cembalo and small orchestra
(1951–52)
1952–55 (62–65) *La Tempête,* opera
1955–56 (65) *Études,* for string orchestra
1956 (66) *Overture in Homage to Mozart,* for
orchestra
1957–59 (67–69) *La Mystère de la Nativité,* oratorio
1958 (68) *Overture in Rondo,* for orchestra
Pseaumes de Genève, for mixed choir,
children's voices, organ and orchestra
1960 (70) *Drey Minnelieder,* for soprano and piano
1961–62 (71) *Monsieur de Pourceaugnac,* opera
1963–64 (73) *Les Quatre élements,* symphonic
studies: Earth, Water, Air, Fire
1964 (74) *Pilate,* cantata
1965–66 (75) Cello Concerto
1967 (77) String Quartet
1968 (78) *Maria-Triptychon* (Ave Maria—Magnificat
—Stabat Mater), for soprano, solo
violin and orchestra
Piano Concerto No. 2
1969 (79) *Erasmi Monumentum,* for orchestra and
organ
Poèmes de la mort, for tenor, baritone,
bass and three electric guitars
(1969–71)
1970 (80) *Three Dances,* for oboe, harp, string
quintet and string orchestra
1971–72 (81) *Requiem,* for soprano, contralto, tenor
and bass soli, mixed choir, orchestra
and organ

1972 (82) *Ballade*, for viola, wind orchestra,
            cembalo, harp and timpani
1973 (83) *Polyptique*, for violin and two small string
            orchestras
            Fantasy on Flamenco rhythms, for piano
1974 (84) *Et la vie l'emporta*, chamber cantata

MARTINŮ, Bohuslav/1890–1959/Bohemia
(Czechoslovakia)

1918 (28) *Czech Rhapsody*, for chorus
1921 (31) *Istar*, ballet
1922 (32) *The Grove of the Satyrs*, symphonic poem
            Shadows, symphonic poem
            Vanishing Midnight, symphonic poem
1925 (35) *Half Time*, symphonic poem
            Piano Concerto No. 1
            On tourne, ballet
1927 (37) *La Bagarre*, symphonic poem
            La Revue de cuisine, ballet
            Le Raid merveilleux, ballet (1927–28)
1928 (38) *The Soldier and the Dancer*, opera
            Les Lames du Couteau, opera
            Échéc au roi, ballet
            La Rapsodie
            Entr'acte
            Concertino for piano (left hand) and
                chamber orchestra
1929 (39) *Journée de Bonte*, opera
            The Butterfly that Stamped, ballet
1930 (40) *Serenade*, for chamber orchestra
            Violin Sonata No. 1
1931 (41) Cello Concerto
            Partita (Suite No. 1)
            Spaliček, ballet
1932 (42) *Les Rondes*
            Sinfonia for two orchestras
            Overture for the Sokol Festival
1933 (43) *The Miracle of Our Lady*, opera
1934 (44) *Inventions*
1935 (45) *The Suburban Theater*, opera

               Le Jugement de Paris, ballet
               Concertino for piano, No. 2
1936–37 (46) *Juliette, or The Key to Dreams,* opera
1937 (47) *Alexandre bis,* opera
               Comedy on the Bridge, opera
1938 (48) Concerto for two string orchestras, piano
                 and timpani
               Concerto Grosso, for orchestra
               Tre Ricercare, for orchestra
               Quartet No. 5
               Madrigals for women's voices
1939 (49) Field Mass
1940 (50) Military March
1942 (52) Symphony No. 1
1943 (53) Symphony No. 2
               Concerto for two pianos
               Violin Concerto
               In Memory of Lidice
1944 (54) Symphony No. 3
               Cello Concerto (1944–45)
1945 (55) Symphony No. 4
               Thunderbolt P-47
1947 (57) Quartet No. 7
1948 (58) Piano Concerto No. 3
1953 (63) *The Marriage,* opera
1955 (65) *Three Frescoes*

MASCAGNI, Pietro/1863–1945/Italy

1879 (16) Symphony in C minor
1881 (18) Symphony in F major
               In Filanda, for voices and orchestra
1890 (27) *Cavalleria Rusticana,* opera
1891 (28) *L'Amico Fritz,* opera
               Solemn Mass
1892 (29) *I Rantzau,* opera
1895 (32) *Guglielmo Ratcliff,* opera
               Silvano, opera
1896 (33) *Zanetto,* opera
1898 (35) *Iris,* opera
1901 (38) *Le Maschera,* opera
1905 (42) *Amica,* opera

1911 (48) *Isabeau,* opera
1913 (50) *Parisina,* opera
1917 (54) *Lodoletta,* opera
            Satanic Rhapsody
1919 (56) *Si,* opera
1921 (58) *Il Piccolo Marat,* opera
1932 (69) *Pinotta,* opera
1935 (72) *Nero,* opera

MASSENET, Jules/1842–1912/France

1863 (21) Overture de Concert
            David Rizzio, cantata
1865 (23) Suite for Orchestra, No. 1
1871 (29) Suite for Orchestra, No. 2, *Scènes
                hongroises*
1873 (31) Suite for Orchestra, No. 3, *Scènes
                dramatiques*
            Phedre, concert overture
1874 (32) Suite for Orchestra, No. 4, *Scènes
                pittoresques*
1875 (33) *Eve,* oratorio
1876 (34) Suite for Orchestra, No. 5, *Scènes
                napolitaines*
1877 (35) *Le Roi de Lahore,* opera
            Narcisse, cantata
1879 (37) Suite for Orchestra, No. 6, *Scènes de féerie*
1880 (38) *La Vierge,* oratorio
1881 (39) Suite for Orchestra, No. 7, *Scènes
                alsaciennes Hérodiade,* opera
1884 (42) *Manon,* opera
1885 (43) *Le Cid,* opera
1887 (45) *Parade Militaire*
1890 (48) *Visions,* symphonic poem
1892 (50) *Werther,* opera
1894 (52) *Thaïs,* opera
            La Navarraise
1897 (55) *Marche Solenelle*
            Fantaisie, for cello and orchestra
            Sappho, lyric play
            Devant la Madone

1899 (57) *Brumaire*, overture
          Cendrillon, opera
1900 (58) *La Terre promisé*, oratorio
1902 (60) Piano Concerto
          Le Jongleur de Notre Dame
1910 (68) *Don Quixote*, opera

MAW, Nicholas/b.1935/Great Britain

1957 (22) *Sonatina,* for flute and piano
1958 (23) *Nocturne,* for mezzo-soprano and
          chamber orchestra
1960 (25) *Five Epigrams,* for mixed unaccompanied
          voices
1961 (26) *Essay,* for organ (revised 1963)
1962 (27) *Scenes and Arias,* for soprano, mezzo-
          soprano, contralto and orchestra
          (revised 1966)
          Chamber Music, for oboe, clarinet, horn,
          bassoon and piano
          Our Lady's Song, carol for unaccompanied
          mixed voices
1963 (28) *Round,* for children's chorus, mixed
          chorus and piano
          The Angel Gabriel, carol for
          unaccompanied mixed chorus
1964 (29) *One Man Show,* comic opera in two acts
          Balulalow, carol for unaccompanied mixed
          voices
          Corpus Christi Carol
1965 (30) String Quartet
1966 (31) *Sinfonia,* for small orchestra
          The Voice of Love, song cycle for mezzo-
          soprano and piano
1967 (32) Sonata for strings and two horns
          *Double Canon for Igor Stravinsky on his
          85th birthday,* for various instruments
1969–70 (34) *The Rising of the Moon,* opera
1971 (36) *Epitaph—Canon in memory of Igor
          Stravinsky,* for flute, clarinet and harp
1972 (37) *Concert Music for Orchestra* (derived
          from the opera, *Rising of the Moon*)

Five Irish Songs, for mixed chorus
1973 (38) *Serenade,* for chamber orchestra
Life Studies, for fifteen solo strings
Personae, for piano

MEDTNER, Nicholas/1880–1951/Russia

1904 (24) Nine Songs (Goethe)
1907 (27) Three Songs (Heine)
1908 (28) Twelve Songs (Goethe)
1910 (30) Three Songs (Nietzsche, etc.)
Violin Sonata
1912 (32) Three *Nocturnes,* for violin and piano
1916–18 (36–38) Piano Concerto No. 1 in C minor
1921 (41) Sonata-Vocalise No. 1
1924 (44) Violin Sonata
1926–27 (46) Piano Concerto No. 2 in C minor
1936 (56) Violin Sonata, *Sonata Epica*
1942–43 (62) Piano Concerto No. 3 in E minor,
Ballade

MENDELSSOHN (-Bartholdy), Felix/1809–1847/ Germany

1821 (12) Piano Sonata No. 2 in G minor
1822 (13) Piano Quartet No. 1 in C minor
1823 (14) Piano Quartet No. 2 in F minor
Violin Sonata in F minor
1824 (15) Piano Quartet No. 3 in B minor
Symphony No. 1 in C minor
1825 (16) *Wedding of the Camacho,* comic opera
Trumpet Overture, for orchestra
String Octet in E♭ major
Capriccio in F♯ minor, for piano
1826 (17) *A Midsummer Night's Dream,* overture
String Quintet in A major
Piano Sonata No. 1 in E major
Six Songs (1826–27)
1827 (18) String Quartet No. 2 in A minor
Fugue in E♭ major, for string quartet

Piano Sonata No. 3 in B♭ major
p. Seven pieces for piano
1829 (20) *Die Heimkehr aus der Fremde,* operetta
String Quartet No. 1 in E♭ major
Variations concertantes, for cello and
  piano, in D major
Three Fantasies for piano
Twelve Songs
1830 (21) Symphony No. 5, *Reformation*
Hebrides, concert overture
Twelve Songs
Six Songs
1831 (22) Piano Concerto No. 1 in G minor
Die erste Walpurgisnacht, for solo voices,
  chorus and orchestra
Song
1832 (23) *Meerstille (Calm Sea and Prosperous
  Voyage),* concert overture
Capriccio Brillant, in B minor, for piano
  and orchestra
Six Preludes and Fugues for piano
  (1832–37)
1833 (24) Symphony No. 4, *Italian*
Die Schöne Melusine, overture
Fantasy in F♯ minor, for piano
Three Capriccios for piano (1833–34)
1834 (25) *Rondo Brillant* in E♭, for piano and
  orchestra
p. Songs Without Words, Book I, for
  piano
Piano Sextet in D major
Three Studies for piano (1834–36)
Two Romances of Byron
Six Songs (1834–37)
Song
1835 (26) *p. Songs Without Words,* Book II, for
  piano
Two Sacred Songs
Two Songs after Eichendorff
1836 (27) *St. Paul,* oratorio
Étude in F minor, for piano
1837 (28) Piano Concerto No. 2 in D minor
Three Organ Preludes and Fugues

Capriccio in E major, for piano
Gondellied in A major, for piano
String Quartets Nos. 3–5 in D: Em: E♭
(1837–38)
Six Songs (1837–42)
1838 (29) Serenade and Allegro Gioioso in B minor,
for piano and orchestra
Cello Sonata No. 1 in B♭ major
Piano Trio No. 1 in D minor
Andante Cantabile, and Presto Agitato,
in B major, for piano
1839 (30) *Ruy Blas,* overture
Songs Without Words, Book III, for
piano
Six Songs
Song
1840 (31) *Lobegesang (Hymn of Praise),* symphony-
cantata (Symphony No. 2)
Festgesang, for male chorus and orchestra
1841 (32) *Cornelius March*
Songs Without Words, Books IV and VII,
for piano
Allegro Brillant in A major, for piano
Variations in B♭ major
Variations in E♭ major
Variations serieuses
Six Songs (1841–45)
1842 (33) Symphony No. 3, *Scotch*
Cello Sonata in D major (1842–43)
Songs Without Words, Book VIII, for
piano
Kinderstücke (Christmas Pieces), for
piano
1843 (34) *Athalie,* incidental music
Andante in E major, for string quartet
Scherzo in A minor, for string quartet
Capriccio in E minor, for string quartet
Songs Without Words, Books V and VI,
for piano
1844 (35) Violin Concerto in E minor
Hear My Prayer, for soprano, chorus and
organ
p. Six Organ Sonatas (1844–45)

187

1845 (36)   Piano Trio No. 2 in C minor
                 String Quintet in B♭ major
                 Songs Without Words, for cello and piano
1846 (37)   String Quartet No. 6, in F minor
                 fp. Elijah, oratorio
                 Lauda Sion, cantata
1847 (38)   *Lorely,* opera (unfinished)
1852 (posthumous) *fp.* Christus, oratorio
                 (unfinished)
Mendelssohn also composed:
1827–47   Four pieces for string quartet
1827–41   Prelude and Fugue in E minor, for piano

MENNIN, Peter/b.1923/U.S.A.

1945 (22)   Concertino for flute, strings and
                 percussion
1946 (23)   Symphony No. 3
1947 (24)   Fantasia for string orchestra
1949 (26)   Symphony No. 4, *The Cycle,* for choir
                 and orchestra
                 The Christmas Story, cantata
1950 (27)   Symphony No. 5
                 Violin Concerto
                 Canto and Toccata, for piano
                 Five pieces for piano
1951 (28)   *Canzona,* for band
1952 (29)   Concertato for orchestra, *Moby Dick*
                 Quartet No. 2
1953 (30)   Symphony No. 6
1956 (33)   Cello Concerto
                 Sonata Concertante for violin and piano
1958 (35)   Piano Concerto
1963 (40)   Symphony No. 7 (1963–64)
                 Canto, for orchestra
1967 (44)   Piano Sonata
1968–69 (45) *Cantata de Virtute,* for chorus and
                 orchestra, children's chorus, soloists
                 and narrator
1971 (48)   *Sinfonia for Orchestra*
1973 (50)   *fp.* Symphony No. 8

MENOTTI, Gian-Carlo/b.1911/U.S.A. (b.Italy)

1931 (20) *Variations on a theme of Schumann*, for
     piano
1936 (25) *Trio for a housewarming party*, for flute,
     cello and piano
1937 (26) *Amelia al Ballo*, opera (the only one
     Menotti wrote in Italian)
1939 (28) *The Old Maid and the Thief*, opera
1942 (31) *The Island God*, opera
1944 (33) *Sebastian*, ballet
1945 (34) Piano Concerto in A minor
1946 (35) *The Medium*, opera
1947 (36) *The Telephone*, opera
     Errand into the Maze, ballet
1950 (39) *The Consul*, opera
1951 (40) *Amahl and the Night Visitors*, opera
     Apocalypse, for orchestra
1952 (41) Violin Concerto
1954 (43) *The Saint of Bleecker Street*, opera
1956 (45) *The Unicorn, the Gorgon and the
     Manticore*, ballet
1958 (47) *Maria Golovin*, opera
1963 (52) *Labyrinth*, opera
     The Last Savage, opera
     Death of the Bishop of Brindisi, cantata
1964 (53) *Martin's Lie*, opera
1967 (56) *Canti della Lontananza*, song cycle
1968 (57) *Help, Help, the Globolinks*, children's
     opera
1970 (59) *The Leper*, drama
     Triplo Concerto a Tre, symphonic piece
1971 (60) *fp. The Most Important Man in the World*,
     opera
1973 (62) *fp.* Suite for two cellos and piano

MESSAGER, André Charles/1853–1929/France

1875 (22) Symphony
1877 (24) *Don Juan et Haydée*, cantata
1878 (25) *Fleur d'Oranger*, ballet

1885 (32) *Le Béarnaise*, operetta
1886 (33) *Les deux pigeons*, ballet
1888 (35) *Isoline*, opera
1890 (37) *La Basoche*, operetta
1893 (40) *Madame Chrysanthème*, operetta
1894 (41) *Mirette*, operetta
1896 (43) *Le Chevalier d'Harmenthal*, operetta
1897 (44) *Les P'tites Michu*, operetta
1898 (45) *Véronique*, operetta
1907 (54) *Fortuno*, operetta
1914 (61) *Béatrice*, operetta
1919 (66) *Monsieur Beaucaire*, operetta

MESSIAEN, Olivier/b.1908/France

1928 (20) Fugue in D minor, for orchestra
Le Banquet Eucharistique
Le Banquet Céleste, for organ
1929 (21) *Préludes*, for piano
1930 (22) *Simple chant d'une âme*
Les Offrandes oubliées
Diptyque, for organ
1931 (23) *Le Tombeau resplendissant*
1932 (24) *Hymne au Saint Sacrement*, for orchestra
Fantaisie Burlesque, for piano
Apparition de l'Eglise éternelle, for organ
1933 (25) *L'Ascension*, for organ
Mass, for eight sopranos and four violins
1935 (27) *La Nativité du Seigneur*, nine meditations
for organ
1937 (29) *Poèmes pour mi*, for voice and orchestra
1939 (31) *Les Corps glorieux*, for organ
1941 (33) *Quatuor pour la fin du temps*, for violin,
clarinet, cello and piano
1943 (35) *Visions de l'Amen*, for two pianos
Rondeau, for piano
1944 (36) *Vingt regards sur l'enfant Jésus*, for piano
1947 (39) *Turangalîla*, symphony for orchestra, piano
and Ondes Martenot
1950 (42) *Le Merle noir*, for piano and flute
Messe de la Pentecôte
1953 (45) *Reveil des oiseaux*, for piano and orchestra

1956 (48) *Oiseaux exotiques,* for piano, wind
                instruments and percussion
1960 (52) *Chronochromie*
1963 (55) *Sept Haï-Kaï*
1964 (56) *Couleurs de la cité céleste*
1965 (57) *La Transfiguration de notre Seigneur
                Jésus-Christ (1965–69)*

MEYERBEER, Giacomo/1791–1864/Germany

1831 (40) *Robert le diable,* opera
1836 (45) *Les Huguenots,* opera
1849 (58) *Le Prophète,* opera
1854 (63) *L'Étoile du nord,* opera
1859 (68) *Dinorah,* opera
1865 (posthumous) *fp. L'Africaine,* opera

MILHAUD, Darius/1892–1974/France

1910–15 (18–23) *La Brebis égàrée,* opera
1911 (19) Violin Sonata
1912 (20) String Quartet No. 1 in A minor
1913–14 (21) Suite Symphonique No. 1
1914 (22) Sonata for two violins and piano
           Printemps, for violin and piano
           String Quartet No. 2, (atonal) (1914–15)
1916 (24) String Quartet No. 3
1917 (25) Symphony for small orchestra, No. 1,
             Le Printemps
1918 (26) Symphony for small orchestra, No. 2,
             Pastorale
           Sonata for flute, oboe, clarinet and piano
           L'Homme et son desir, ballet
           String Quartet No. 4
1919 (27) Suite Symphonique No. 2, *Protée*
           Machines agricoles, six pastoral songs for
             middle voice and instruments
1920 (28) *Le Boeuf sur le toit,* ballet
           Ballade, for piano and orchestra
           Five Studies for piano and orchestra
           Sérénade (1920–21)

Printemps, six piano pieces
String Quartet No. 5
1921 (29) *Saudades de Brasil*, dance suite
Symphony for small orchestra, No. 3,
Sérénade
Symphony for strings, No. 4, *Ouverture,*
Choral, Étude
1922 (30) Symphony for small wind orchestra, No. 5
La Creation du monde, ballet, using
jazz idiom (1922–23)
Three *Rag-Caprices*
String Quartet No. 6
1923 (31) Symphony No. 6 for soprano, contralto,
tenor, bass, oboe and cello
1924 (32) *Les Malheurs d'Orphée,* opera
Esther de Carpentras (1924–25)
1925 (33) String Quartet No. 7
Deux Hymnes
1926 (34) *Le Pauvre matelot,* opera
1927 (35) Violin Concerto No. 1
Carnival of Aix, for piano and orchestra
1928 (36) *Christophe Columb,* opera (revised 1956)
Cantate pour louer le Seigneur
1929 (37) Viola Concerto
Concerto for percussion and small
orchestra
1930 (38) *Maximilien,* opera
1932 (40) String Quartet No. 8
1933 (41) Piano Concerto No. 1
1935 (43) Cello Concerto No. 1
String Quartet No. 9
1936 (44) *Suite provençale*
1937 (45) *Cantate de la paix*
1938 (46) *Medée,* opera
1939 (47) Symphony No. 1 for full orchestra
King Renée's chimney, for wind quartet
1940 (48) String Quartet No. 10, *Birthday Quartet*
1941 (49) Piano Concerto No. 2
Clarinet Concerto
Concerto for two pianos
Four Sketches
1942 (50) String Quartet No. 11
1943 (51) *Bolivar,* opera

1944 (52) Symphony No. 2 for full orchestra
Jeux de printemps
Suite Française
1945 (53) *The Bells,* ballet
Cello Concerto No. 2
String Quartet No. 12, *In memory of Fauré*
1946 (54) Symphony No. 3 for full orchestra and
chorus, *Hymnus Ambrosianus*
Piano Concerto No. 3
Violin Concerto No. 2
String Quartet No. 13
1947 (55) Symphony, *1848*
Concerto for marimba and vibraphone
1949 (57) Piano Concerto No. 4
String Quartets Nos. 14 and 15, to be
played together as octet, or separately
1951 (59) *The Seven-branched Candelabra*
1953 (61) *David,* opera
1954 (62) Harp Concerto
1955 (63) Symphonies Nos. 5 and 6
1956 (64) Symphony No. 7
1957 (65) Symphony No. 8, *Rhodanienne*
Oboe Concerto
Aspen Serenade
1958 (66) Violin Concerto No. 3, *Concerto royal*
1960 (68) Symphony No. 10
? ? Symphony No. 11
1962 (70) Symphony No. 12
1963 (71) *Pacem in terris,* for chorus and orchestra
1964 (72) *La Mère coupable,* opera
String Septet

MOERAN, Ernest/1894–1950/Great Britain

1919 (25) Three piano pieces
1920 (26) Theme and variations for piano
Piano Trio in E minor
Ludlow Town, song cycle
1921 (27) *In the Mountain Country,* symphonic
impression
On a May Morning, for piano

1922	(28)	Rhapsody No. 1 in F major
		Three Fancies, for piano
1924	(30)	Rhapsody No. 2 in E major
1925	(31)	*Summer Valley*, for piano
1926	(32)	*Irish Love Song*, for piano
1932	(38)	*Farrago*, suite for orchestra
1934	(40)	*Nocturne*, for baritone, chorus and
		orchestra
1937	(43)	Symphony in G minor
1942	(48)	Violin Concerto
1943	(49)	Rhapsody No. 3 in F♯ major, for piano
		and orchestra
1944	(50)	Sinfonietta
		Overture for a Masque
1945	(51)	Cello Concerto
1946	(52)	*Fantasy Quartet*, for oboe and strings
1948	(54)	*Serenade*, in G major

MONTEVERDI, Claudio/1567–1643/Italy

1584	(17)	p. Canzonettas for three voices
1587	(20)	p. Madrigals, for five voices, Book I
1590	(23)	p. Madrigals, for five voices, Book II
1592	(25)	p. Madrigals, for five voices, Book III
1603	(36)	p. Madrigals, for five voices, Book IV
1605	(38)	p. Madrigals, for five voices, Book V
1607	(40)	p. Scherzi Musicali for three voices
		fp. Orfeo, opera
1608	(41)	*Ballo delle Ingrate*
		fp. L'Arianna, opera
1610	(43)	Vespers
		p. Masses
1614	(47)	p. Madrigals, for five voices, Book VI
1615	(48)	*fp. Tirsi e Clori*, ballet
1617	(50)	*La Maddalena*, opera
1619	(52)	p. Madrigals, for one, two, three, four
		and six voices, Book VII
1627	(60)	*Armida*, opera
1628	(61)	*Mercurio e Marte*, opera
1632	(65)	p. Scherzi Musicali, for one or two voices
1638	(71)	p. Madrigals, of war and love (*Madrigali*
		guerrieri e amorosi) Book VIII

1640 (73) Selve Morale e Spirituale
1641 (74) *Il ritorno d'Ulisse in patria,* opera
1642 (75) *L'Incoronazione di Poppea,* opera
1650 (posthumous) *p.* Masses for four voices and
                         psalms
1651 (posthumous) *p.* Madrigals and Canzonettes,
                         for two or three voices, Book IX

MOORE, Douglas/b.1893/U.S.A.

1924 (31) *The Pageant of P.T. Barnum,* suite for
                 orchestra
1928 (35) *A Symphony of Autumn*
                 Moby Dick, for orchestra
1929 (36) Violin Sonata
1930 (37) *Overture on an American theme*
1933 (40) String Quartet
1935 (42) *White Wings,* opera (possibly 1948)
1936 (43) *The Headless Horseman,* opera
1938 (45) *Dedication,* for chorus
1939 (46) *The Devil and Daniel Webster,* opera
1941 (48) *Village Music,* suite for small orchestra
1942 (49) Quintet for woodwinds and horn
1943 (50) *In Memoriam,* symphonic poem
1944 (51) *Down East Suite,* for violin with piano or
                 orchestra
1945 (52) Symphony in A major
1946 (53) Quintet for clarinet and strings
1947 (54) *Farm Journal,* suite for chamber orchestra
1948 (55) *The Emperor's New Clothes,* opera for
                 children
1950 (57) *Giants in the Earth,* opera
1952 (59) *Cotillion,* suite for string orchestra
1953 (60) Piano Trio
1956 (63) *The Ballad of Baby Doe,* opera
1957 (64) *Gallantry,* a soap opera
1961 (68) *Wings of the Dove,* opera
1962 (69) *The Greenfield Christmas Tree,* a
                 Christmas entertainment
1966 (73) *Carry Nation,* opera

MORLEY, Thomas/1557–1603/Great Britain

1593 (36) *p.* Canzonets, or Little Short Songs to
                        Three Voyces
1594 (37) *p.* Madrigalls to Foure Voyces
1595 (38) *p.* The First Booke of Balletts to Fiue
                        Voyces
              p. The First Booke of Canzonets to Two
                        Voyces
1597 (40) *p.* Two songs in "Canzonets or Little Short
                        Songs to Foure Voyces. Celected out of
                        the best and approved Italian Authors"
              p. Canzonets or Little Short Aers to Fiue
                        and Sixe Voices
              p. A Plaine and Easie Introduction to
                        Practicall Musicke
1598 (41) *p.* Madrigalls to Fiue Voyces. Celected
                        out of the best approved Italian Authors
1599 (42) *p.* The First Booke of Consort Lessons,
                        made by diuerse exquisite Authors for
                        six Instruments
1600 (43) *p.* The First Booke of Ayres or Little Short
                        Songs; to sing and play to the Lute with
                        the Base Viole
1601 (44) *p.* Two madrigals in *"The Triumphs of
                        Oriana,* to five and six voices, composed
                        by diuerse seuerall authors"

MOZART, Wolfgang Amadeus/1756–1791/Austria

1762–64 (6–8) Sonata in C major for violin and
                        piano, K.6
1763–64 (7–8) Sonata in D major for violin and
                        piano, K.7
                    Sonata in B♭ major for violin and piano,
                    K.8
1764 (8)   Sonata in G major for violin and piano,
                    K.9
                    Sonata in B♭ major for violin and piano,
                    K.10

Sonata in G major for violin and piano, K.11

Sonata in A major for violin and piano, K.12

Sonata in F major for violin and piano, K.13

Sonata in C major for violin and piano, K.14

Sonata in B♭ major for violin and piano, K.15

Symphony No. 1 in E♭ major, K.16

Symphony No. 4 in D major, K.19

1765 (9) Piano Sonatas (four hands) in C major, K.19d (unpublished)

Three Sonatas by J.C. Bach arranged as Concertos with string orchestra, K.107

Symphony No. 5 in B♭ major, K.22

1766 (10) Sonata in E♭ major for violin and piano, K.26

Sonata in G major for violin and piano, K.27

Sonata in C major for violin and piano, K.28

Sonata in D major for violin and piano, K.29

Sonata in F major for violin and piano, K.30

Sonata in B♭ major for violin and piano, K.31

1767 (11) Piano Concerto in F major, K.37

Piano Concerto in B♭ major, K.39

Piano Concerto in D major, K.40

Piano Concerto in G major, K.41

Symphony No. 6 in F major, K.43

Sonata for Organ and Strings in E♭ major, K.62

Sonata for Organ and Strings in B♭ major, K.68

Sonata for Organ and Strings in D major, K.69

Symphony No. 43 in F major, K.76

1768 (12) *Bastien und Bastienne*, opera

Symphony No. 7 in D major, K.45

Symphony No. 8 in D major, K.48
1769 (13) Mass in C major, K.66
Symphony No. 9 in C major, K.73
Symphony No. 42 in F major, K.75
1770 (14) String Quartet in G major, K.80
Symphony No. 10 in G major, K.74
Symphony No. 11 in D major, K.80
Symphony No. 45 in D major, K.95
Symphony No. 47 in D major, K.97
Symphony No. 12 in G major, K.110
1771 (15) Symphony No. 46 in C major, K.96
Symphony No. 13 in F major, K.112
Symphony No. 14 in A major, K.114
Symphony No. 50 in D (finale only, to
the Overture of *Ascanio in Alba*), K.120
Overture of *La finta giardiniera*
1772 (16) Piano Sonata (four hands) in D major,
K.381
String Quartet in D major, K.155
String Quartet in G major, K.156
String Quartet in C major, K.157
String Quartet in F major, K.158
String Quartet in B♭ major, K.159
String Quartet in E♭ major, K.160
Sonata for organ and strings, in D major,
K.144
Sonata for organ and strings, in F major,
K.145
Mass in C minor and C major, K.139
Symphony No. 15 in G major, K.124
Symphony No. 16 in C major, K.128
Symphony No. 17 in G major, K.129
Symphony No. 19 in E♭ major, K.132
Symphony No. 20 in D major, K.133
Symphony No. 21 in A major, K.134
Symphony in D major (first two
movements identical with the overture
Il sogno di Scipiona, K.126), K.161
Symphony No. 22 in C major, K.162
Symphony No. 51 in D major (finale only,
to the overture of *Il sogno di Scipiona*),
K.163
Lucio Silla, opera

1773 (17) Piano Concerto in D major, K.175
Concertone in C major for two violins, K.190
String Quartet in F major, K.168
String Quartet in A major, K.169
String Quartet in C major, K.170
String Quartet in E♭ major, K.171
String Quartet in B♭ major, K.172
String Quartet in D minor, K.173
String Quintet in B♭ major, K.174
Symphony No. 23 in D major, K.181
Symphony No. 24 in B♭ major, K.182
Symphony No. 25 in G minor, K.183
Symphony No. 26 in E♭ major, K.184

1774 (18) Bassoon Concerto in B♭ major, K.191
Symphony No. 27 in G major, K.199
Symphony No. 28 in C major, K.200
Symphony No. 29 in A major, K.201
Symphony No. 30 in D major, K.202
Piano Sonata in C major, K.279
Piano Sonata in F major, K.280
Piano Sonata in B♭ major, K.281
Piano Sonata in E♭ major, K.282
Piano Sonata in G major, K.283
Piano Sonata in D major, K.284
Piano Sonata (four hands) in B♭ major, K.358

1775 (19) *La finta giardiniera,* opera
Il re pastore, opera
Symphony No. 49 in C major (finale only, to the overture of *Il re pastore*), K.102
Violin Concerto in B♭ major, K.207
Violin Concerto in D major, K.211
Violin Concerto in G major, K.216
Violin Concerto in D major, K.218
Violin Concerto in A major, K.219
Sonata for organ and strings, in B♭ major, K.212

1776 (20) Piano Concerto in B♭ major, K.238
Piano Concerto in F major, for three pianos, K.242
Piano Concerto in C major, K.246
Adagio to K.219 Violin Concerto, K.261

Rondo Concertante to K.207 Violin
    Concerto, K.269
Piano Trio in B♭ major, K.254
Sonata for organ and strings in F major,
    K.224
Sonata for organ and strings in A major,
    K.225
Sonata for organ and strings in G major,
    K.241
Sonata for organ and strings in F major,
    K.244
Sonata for organ and strings in D major,
    K.245
Mass in C major, K.257

1777 (21) Piano Concerto in E♭ major, K.271
Violin Concerto in D major, K.271a
Piano Sonata in C major, K.309
Sonata for organ and strings in G major,
    K.274

1778 (22) Concerto in C major for flute and harp,
    K.299
Concerto in G major for flute, K.313
Concerto in D major for flute, K.314
Andante in C major for flute, K.315
Sinfonia Concertante in E♭ for flute, oboe,
    horn and bassoon (app. K.9)
Piano Sonata in A minor, K.310
Piano Sonata in D major, K.311
Piano Sonata in C major, K.330
Piano Sonata in A major, K.331
Piano Sonata in F major, K.332
Piano Sonata in B♭ major, K.333
Violin Sonata in C major, K.296
Violin Sonata in G major, K.301
Violin Sonata in E♭ major, K.302
Violin Sonata in C major, K.303
Violin Sonata in E minor, K.304
Violin Sonata in A major, K.305
Violin Sonata in D major, K.306
Symphony No. 31 in D major, *Paris*,
    K.297

1779 (23) Sinfonia Concertante in E♭ for violin and
    viola, K.364

Sonata for organ and strings in C major, K.328
Concerto for two pianos, K.365
Mass in C major, K.317
Symphony No. 32 in G major, K.318
Symphony No. 33 in B♭ major, K.319

1780 (24) Violin Concerto in E♭ major, K.268 (1780–81) (authenticity doubtful)
Sonata for organ and strings in C major, K.336
String Quartet in B♭, K.46 (arrangement of K.361 Serenade, may be spurious)
Symphony No. 34 in C major, K.338
Six variations for violin and piano on *Hélas, j'ai perdu mon amant*, K.360

1781 (25) *Idomeneo,* opera
Rondo in C major, for violin, K.373
Concerto Rondo in E♭ for horn, K.371
Twelve variations on *La bergère Célimène,* for violin and piano, K.359
Violin Sonata in F major, K.376
Violin Sonata in F major, K.377
Violin Sonata in B♭ major, K.378
Violin Sonata in G minor and G major, K.379
Violin Sonata in E♭ major, K.380
Sonata for two pianos in D major, K.448

1782 (26) *Il Seraglio,* opera
Concerto Rondo in D minor to K.175 Piano Concerto, K.382
Concerto Rondo in A major, (discarded from K.414 Piano Concerto), K.386
Piano Concerto in F major, K.413
Piano Concerto in A major, K.414
Piano Concerto in C major, K.415
Horn Concerto in D major, K.412
Violin Sonata in A major and A minor (finished by Stadler), K.402
Violin Sonata in C major, unfinished, K.403
Violin Sonata in C major, unfinished, K.404

String Quartet in G major (Haydn Set,
    No. 1), K.387
Five fugues from Bach's *Well-Tempered
    Clavier,* for string quartet, K.405
Symphony No. 35 in D major, *Haffner,*
    K.385

1783 (27) Oboe Concerto in F major, fragment,
    K.293
Votive Mass
Horn Concerto in E♭ major, K.417
Horn Concerto in E♭ major, K.447
String Quartet in D minor (Haydn Set,
    No. 2), K.421
String Quartet in E♭ major (Haydn Set,
    No. 3), K.428
Piano Trio in D minor and D major
    (completed by Stadler), K.442
Symphony No. 36 in C major, *Linz,*
    K.425
Symphony No. 37 in G major, K.444
    (introduction only, the rest by M.
    Haydn)

1784 (28) Piano Concerto in E♭ major, K.449
Piano Concerto in B♭ major, K.450
Piano Concerto in D major, K.451
Piano Concerto in G major, K.453
Piano Concerto in B♭ major, K.456
Piano Concerto in F major, K.459
Violin Sonata in B♭ major, K.454
Piano Sonata in C minor, K.457
String Quartet in B♭ major (Haydn Set,
    No. 4), K.458

1785 (29) Piano Concerto in D minor, K.466
Piano Concerto in C major, K.467
Piano Concerto in E♭ major, K.482
Andante for a Violin Concerto, in
    A major, K.470
Violin Sonata in E♭ major, K.481
String Quartet in A major (Haydn Set,
    No. 5), K.464
String Quartet in C major (Haydn Set,
    No. 6), K.465
Piano Quartet in G minor, K.478

1786 (30)   *Impresario,* opera
            Marriage of Figaro, opera
            Piano Concerto in A major, K.488
            Piano Concerto in C minor, K.491
            Piano Concerto in C major, K.503
            Horn Concerto in E♭ major, K.495
            Piano Sonata (four hands) in G major, K.357
            Piano Sonata (four hands) in F major, K.497
            String Quartet in D major, K.499
            Piano Quartet in E♭ major, K.493
            Piano Trio in G major, K.496
            Piano Trio in B♭ major, for piano, clarinet and viola, K.498
            Piano Trio in B♭ major, K.502
            Symphony No. 38 in D major, *Prague,* K.504

1787 (31)   *Don Giovanni,* opera
            Piano Sonata (four hands) in C major, K.521
            Violin Sonata in A major, K.526
            String Quintet in C minor, K.406 (arrangement of *Serenade,* K.388)
            String Quintet in C major, K.515
            String Quintet in G minor, K.516
            Eine Kleine Nachtmusik, for strings

1788 (32)   Piano Concerto in D major, *Coronation,* K.537
            Piano Sonata (Sonatina) in C major, K.545
            Violin Sonata in F major, K.547
            String Quartet in D minor, Adagio and Fugue (fugue identical with K.426 for two pianos), K.546
            Piano Trio in E major, K.542
            Piano Trio in C major, K.548
            Piano Trio in G major, K.564
            Symphony No. 39 in E♭ major, K.543
            Symphony No. 40 in G minor, K.550
            Symphony No. 41 in C major, *Jupiter,* K.551

1789 (33)   Piano Sonata in B♭ major (better known

as a violin sonata, but the violin part
is not by Mozart), K.570
Piano Sonata in D major, K.576
String Quartet in D major (King of Prussia
Set, No. 1), K.575
1790 (34) *Così fan tutte,* opera
String Quartet in B♭ major (King of
Prussia Set, No. 2), K.589
String Quartet in F major (King of Prussia
Set, No. 3), K.590
String Quintet in D major, K.593
1791 (35) *Clemenza di Tito,* opera
The Magic Flute, opera
Piano Concerto in B♭ major, K.595
Clarinet Concerto in A major, K.622
String Quintet in E♭ major, K.614
Requiem in D minor, K.626. Unfinished,
completed by Süssmayr

MUSGRAVE, Thea/b.1928/Great Britain

1953 (25) *A Tale for Thieves,* ballet in one act
A Suite of Bairnsangs, for voice and piano
1954 (26) *Cantata for a Summer's Day*
1955 (27) *The Abbot of Drimock,* chamber opera
in one act
Five Love Songs, for soprano and guitar
1958 (30) *Obliques,* for orchestra
String Quartet
A Song for Christmas, for high voice and
piano
1959 (31) *Triptych,* for tenor and orchestra
1960 (32) *Colloquy,* for violin and piano
Trio for flute, oboe and piano
Monologue, for piano
1961 (33) *Serenade,* for flute, clarinet, harp, viola
and cello
Sir Patrick Spens, for tenor and guitar
1962 (34) Chamber Concerto No. 1
The Phoenix and the Turtle, for small
choir and orchestra

1963 (35) *The Five Ages of Man,* for chorus and
orchestra
1964–65 (36) *The Decision,* opera in three acts
1965 (37) *Festival Overture,* for orchestra
Excursions, for piano (four hands)
1966 (38) *Nocturnes and Arias,* for orchestra
Chamber Concerto No. 2, *In Homage to
Charles Ives*
Chamber Concerto No. 3
1967 (39) Concerto for Orchestra
Impromptu, for flute and oboe
Music for Horn and Piano
1968 (40) Concerto for Clarinet and Orchestra
Beauty and the Beast, ballet in two acts
for chamber orchestra and tape
(1968–69)
1969 (41) *Night Music,* for chamber orchestra
Soliloquy, for guitar and tape
*Memento Vitae (Concerto in Homage to
Beethoven),* for orchestra
1970 (42) *Elegy,* for viola and cello
Impromptu No. 2, for flute, oboe and
clarinet
From One to Another, for viola and tape
1971 (43) Concerto for Horn and Orchestra
Primavera, for soprano and flute
1972–73 (44) *The Voice of Ariadne,* chamber opera
in three acts
1973 (45) Viola Concerto
1974 (46) *Space Play,* a concerto for nine instruments
1975 (47) *Orfeo I,* an improvisation on a theme, for
flute and tape
Orfeo II, for solo flute and fifteen strings

MUSSORGSKY, Modeste/1839–1881/Russia

1857 (18) *Souvenir d'enfance,* for piano
1858 (19) Scherzo for orchestra
Edipo, for mixed chorus (1858–60)
1859 (20) *Marcia di Sciamie,* for soloists, choir and
orchestra

Impromptu passione, for piano
1861 (22) *Alla marcia notturna*, for orchestra
Scherzo and Finale, for a symphony in
D major (1861–62)
1867 (28) *St. John's Night on the Bare Mountain*
La disfatta di Sennacherib, first version
for choir and orchestra
Symphonic Intermezzo "in modo classico"
1868 (29) *fp. Zenitha* (The Marriage), opera
(private performance)
The Nursery, song cycle (1868–72)
1869 (30) *Boris Godunov*, opera, first version with
piano (rewritten 1872)
1872 (33) *Khovantschina*, opera
1874 (35) *Pictures from an Exhibition*, for piano
Sunless, song cycle
Sorochinsky Fair, opera (a passage from
this work was freely arranged and
orchestrated as *Night on the Bare
Mountain* by Rimsky-Korsakov, *q.v.*)
Jesus Navin, for contralto, bass, choir
and piano (1874–77)
1875–77 (36–38) *Songs and Dances of Death*, song
cycle
1879 (40) "Song of the Flea", setting of
Mephistopheles' song in Goethe's
Faust
1880 (41) Five Popular Russian Songs, for male
chorus
Turkish March, for orchestra
Meditation, for piano
Une larme, for piano
Au village, for piano

NICOLAI, Karl Otto/1810–1849/Germany

1831 (21) Symphony
1832 (22) Mass
1835 (25) Symphony
Funeral March (for the death of Bellini)
1838 (28) *Von Himmel Hoch*, overture
1839 (29) *Henry II*, opera

1840 (30) *Il Templario*, opera
Gildippe ed Odoardo, opera
1841 (31) *Il Proscritto*, opera
1844 (34) *Ein Feste Burg*, overture with chorus
1849 (39) *fp. The Merry Wives of Windsor*, opera

NIELSEN, Carl/1865–1931/Denmark

1888 (23) Little Suite in A minor, for strings
Quintet
1888–1907 String Quartet in F minor
String Quartet in G minor (1890)
String Quartet in E♭ major (1897)
String Quartet in F major
1889 (24) *Symphonic Rhapsody*
1891–92 (26) Symphony No. 1 in G minor
1894 (29) Symphonic Suite for piano
1902 (37) Symphony No. 2, *Four Temperaments*
Saul and David, opera
1903 (38) *Helios*, overture
1906 (41) *fp. Maskarade*, opera
1907–08 (42) *Saga-Drøm*
1910 (45) *At A Young Artist's Bier*
Symphony No. 3, *Espansiva* (1910–11)
1911 (46) Violin Concerto
1914 (49) *Serenate in vano*
1916 (51) Symphony No. 4, *Inextinguishable*
Chaconne, for piano
Theme and Variations for piano
1918 (53) *Pan and Syrinx*
1922 (57) Symphony No. 5
Quintet for Wind
1925 (60) Symphony No. 6, *Simple*
1926 (61) Flute Concerto
1927 (62) *En Fantasirejse til Faerøerne*, rhapsodic
overture
1928 (63) Clarinet Concerto
1931 (66) *Commotio*, for organ

NILSSON, Bo/b.1937/Sweden

---

c.1956 (c.19) *Frequenzen*, for eight players
207

1957 (20) *Kreutzungen*, for instrumental ensemble
Buch de Veränderungen
Mädchentotenlieder (1957–58)
1958 (21) *Quantitaten*, for piano
Zwanzig Gruppen für Blaser, for piccolo,
oboe, clarinet (1958–59)
Stunde eines Blocks, for soprano and six
players
1959 (22) *Und die Zeiger seiner Augen wurden*
langsam zurückgedreht, for solo voices,
chorus and mixed media
Ein irrender Sohn, for high voice and
instruments
1960 (23) *Szene I*
Reaktionen, for four percussionists
1961 (24) *Szene II*
1962 (25) *Szene III*
Entree, for large orchestra and tape
1963 (26) *Versuchungen*, for large orchestra
1964 (27) *La Bran*, for mixed choir and orchestra
1965 (28) *Litanei uber das verlorene Schlagzeug*
1967 (30) *Revue*, for orchestra
1970 (33) *Attraktionen*, for string quartet

OFFENBACH, Jacques/1819–1880/Germany

1853 (34) *Le Mariage aux lanternes*, operetta
1858 (39) *Orpheus in the Underworld*, operetta
1864 (45) *La Belle Hélène*, operetta
1866 (47) *Bluebeard*, operetta
La Vie parisienne, opera
1867 (48) *La Grande Duchesse de Gérolstein*,
operetta
1868 (49) *La Perichole*, operetta
1878 (59) *Madame Favart*, operetta
1881 (posthumous) *fp. The Tales of Hoffman*,
operetta

ORFF, Carl/b.1895/Germany

1925 (30) Prelude for Orchestra

1927 (32) *Concertino* for wind
1928 (33) *Entrata* (revised 1940)
1930 (35) *Catulli Carmina,* choral setting of poems
                of Catullus (revised 1943)
1934 (39) *Bayerische Musik*
1935 (40) *Carmina Burana,* scenic cantata on Latin
                texts
1936 (41) *Olympischer Reigen*
1937–38 (42) *Der Mond,* opera
1941–42 (46) *Die Kluge,* opera
1944 (49) *Die Bernauerin* (1944–45)
1945–46 (50) *Astutuli*
1947–48 (52) *Antigone,* opera
1950–51 (55) *Trionfo di Afrodite*
1955 (60) *Der Sänger der Vorwelt*
               Comoedia de Christi resurrectione
1956 (61) *Nanie und Dithyrambe,* choral work
1958 (63) *Oedipus, der Tyrann*
1960 (67) *Ludus de nato Infante mirificus*
1962 (67) *Ein Sommernachtstraum*
1969–71 (74–76) *De Temporum fine comoedia,*
               dramatic cantata
1973 (78) *Rota,* for chorus and instruments

PADEREWSKI, Ignacy/1860–1941/Poland

1880 (20) Violin Sonata
1884 (24) Polish Dances for Piano, Books I and II
1888 (28) Piano Concerto in A minor
1893 (33) *Polish Fantasy on Original Themes,* for
               piano and orchestra
1901 (41) *Manru,* opera
1903–07 (43–47) Symphony in B minor

PALESTRINA, Giovanni Pierluigi da/*c.*1525–1594/
Italy

1554 (*c.*29) *p.* First Book of Masses
1563 (*c.*38) *p.* First Book of Motets
1567 (*c.*42) *Missa Papae Marcelli*
1569 (*c.*44) *p.* Second Book of Masses

1570 (*c.*45) *p.* Third Book of Masses
  Missa Brevis
1584 (*c.*59) *p.* Settings of *The Song of Solomon*
1590 (*c.*65) *p. Aeterna Christi Munera,* mass
  Stabat Mater (*c.*1590)
Palestrina also composed many motets and madrigals.

PENDERECKI, Krzysztof/b.1933/Poland

1958 (25) *Epitaphium on the Death of Artur
  Malawski,* for string orchestra and
  timpani
  Emanations, for two string orchestras
  The Psalms of David, for mixed choir and
  instruments
1959 (26) *Strophes,* for soprano, narrator and ten
  instruments
1960 (27) *Anaklasis,* for strings and percussion
  groups
  String Quartet No. 1
1961 (28) *Fluorescences,* for orchestra
  Dimensions of Time and Silence, for choir
  and orchestra
  Threnody, for fifty-two stringed
  instruments
  Kanon, for strings and electronic tape
  Polymorphia
1962 (29) *Stabat Mater,* for three sixteen-part choirs
1964 (31) Sonata for cello and orchestra
1965 (32) *Capriccio,* for oboe and strings
1967 (34) *Dies Irae,* oratorio for soprano, tenor and
  bass soli, chorus and orchestra
  Pittsburgh Overture, for winds and
  percussion
1968 (35) *The Devils of Loudon,* opera (1968–69)
  String Quartet No. 2
  Capriccio for Siegfried Palm, for solo cello
1969–71 (36–38) *Utrenja,* for soprano, contralto,
  tenor, bass and basso profundo soli,
  two mixed choirs and orchestra
1970 (37) *Kosmogonia,* for soprano, tenor and bass
  soli, chorus and orchestra

1971 (38) *De Natura Sonoris II*, for wind, percussion and strings
Prélude (1971), for wind, percussion and contrabasses
Actions, for jazz ensemble
1972 (39) *Canticum Canticorum Salomonis (Song of Songs)*, for sixteen-voice chorus, chamber orchestra and dance pair
Partita, concerto for harpsichord, five solo instruments electronically amplified and orchestra
1973 (40) Symphony
1974 (41) *The Dream of Jacob*

PERGOLESI, Giovanni/1710–1736/Italy

1731 (21) *Salustia*, opera
1732 (22) *Lo Frate innamorato*, opera
La Serva padrona, opera
1733 (23) *Il Prigionier superbo*, opera
1734 (24) *Adriano in Siria*, opera
La Contadina astuta, opera
1735 (25) *L'Olimpiade*, opera
Flamincio, opera
1736 (26) *Stabat Mater*, for female voices
Pergolesi also composed: 8 other operas, 12 cantatas, over 30 sonatas, symphonies, concertos.

PIERNÉ, Gabriel/1863–1937/France

1882 (19) *Edith*, cantata
1883 (20) *Le Chemin de l'amour*, opera-comique
Trois pièces formant suite de concert, for orchestra
1885 (22) Symphonic Overture
Fantaisie-Ballet, for piano and orchestra
1886 (23) *Don Luis*, opera-comique
1887 (24) Piano Concerto in C minor
1889 (26) *Marche Solenelle*
Pantomime, for orchestra

1890 (27)	*Scherzo Caprice*, for piano and orchestra
1891 (28)	*Le Colliers de saphire*, ballet
1892 (29)	*Les Joyeuses commères de Paris*, ballet
1893 (30)	*Lizarda*, opera-comique (1893–94)
	Bouton d'or, ballet
	Le Docteur Blanc, ballet
1895 (32)	*La Coupe enchantée*, opera-comique
	Salomé, ballet
1897 (34)	*Vendée*, opera-comique
	L'An mil, symphonic poem with chorus
1900 (37)	Violin Sonata
1901 (38)	*La Fille de Tabarin*, opera-comique
	Poème Symphonique, for piano and orchestra
	Concertstücke, for harp
1902 (39)	*The Children's Crusade*, oratorio
1907 (44)	*Canzonetta*, for clarinet
1908 (45)	*The Children of Bethlehem*, oratorio
1919 (56)	Piano Quintet
	Cello Sonata
1920 (57)	*Paysages franciscains*, for orchestra
1923 (60)	*Cydalise and the Satyr*, ballet
1927 (64)	*Sophie Arnould*, opera-comique
1931 (68)	*Divertissement sur un thème pastorale*, for orchestra
	Fantaisie basque, for violin
1934 (71)	*Giration*, ballet
	Fragonard, ballet
1935 (72)	*Images*, ballet
1937 (74)	*Gulliver in Lilliput*

PISTON, Walter/b.1894/U.S.A.

1926 (32)	Three pieces for flute, clarinet and bassoon
	Piano Sonata
1927 (33)	Symphonic Piece
1929 (35)	Suite No. 1 for orchestra
1930 (36)	Flute Sonata
1931 (37)	Suite for oboe and piano
1933 (39)	Concerto for Orchestra
	String Quartet No. 1

1934	(40)	Prelude and Fugue for Orchestra
1935	(41)	String Quartet No. 2
		Piano Trio No. 1
1937	(43)	Symphony No. 1
		Concertino, for piano and chamber orchestra
1938	(44)	*The Incredible Flutist*, ballet
1939	(45)	Violin Concerto No. 1
		Violin Sonata
1940	(46)	Chromatic Study for Organ
1941	(47)	*Sinfonietta*, for orchestra
1942	(48)	*Fanfare for the Fighting French*
		Quintet for flute and strings
		Interlude, for viola and piano
1943	(49)	Symphony No. 2
		Prelude and Allegro, for organ and strings
		Passacaglia, for piano
1944	(50)	*Fugue on a Victory Tune*
		Partita, for violin, viola and organ
1945	(51)	Sonata for violin and harpsichord
1946	(52)	*Divertimento,* for nine instruments
1947	(53)	Symphony No. 3
		String Quartet No. 3
1948	(54)	Suite No. 2 for Orchestra
		Toccata, for orchestra
1949	(55)	Piano Quintet
		Duo for violin and cello
1950	(56)	Symphony No. 4
1951	(57)	String Quartet No. 4
1952	(58)	*Fantasy,* for English horn, harp and strings
1954	(60)	Symphony No. 5
1955	(61)	Symphony No. 6
1956	(62)	*Serenata*, for orchestra
		Quintet for Wind
1957	(63)	Viola Concerto
1958	(64)	*Psalm and Prayer of David*, for chorus and seven instruments
1959	(65)	*Three New England Sketches*, for orchestra
		Concerto for two pianos and orchestra
1960	(66)	Violin Concerto No. 2
		Symphony No. 7

1961 (67) Symphonic Prelude
1962 (68) *Lincoln Center*, Festival overture
   String Quartet No. 5
1963 (69) *Variations on a theme by Edward*
      Burlingame Hill, for orchestra
   Capriccio, for harp and string orchestra
1964 (70) Sextet for stringed instruments
   Piano Quartet
1965 (71) Symphony No. 8
   Pine Tree Fantasy, for orchestra
   Ricercare, for orchestra
1966 (72) Variations for cello and orchestra
   Piano Trio No. 2
1967 (73) Concerto for clarinet and orchestra

PIZZETTI, Ildebrando/1880–1968/Italy

1904 (24) Three Symphonic Preludes to *Oedipus Rex*
1906 (26) String Quartet in A major
1909–12 (29–32) *Phaedra*, opera
1914 (34) *Sinfonia del fuoco*
1915–21 (35–41) *Deborah and Jael*, opera
1918 (38) Violin Sonata in A minor and A major
1921 (41) Cello Sonata in F major
1922 (42) *La Straniero*, opera
   Requiem
1925–27 (45–47) *Fra Gherardo*, opera
1928 (48) *Concerto dell'estate*
1929 (49) *Rondo veneziano*, for orchestra
1930 (50) Piano Concerto
1931–35 (51–55) *Orseolo*, opera
1933–34 (53) Cello Concerto
1938–42 (58–62) *L'Oro*, opera
1940 (60) Symphony in A major
1942 (62) Piano Sonata
1944 (64) Violin Concerto
1949 (69) *Vanna Lupa*, opera
1950 (70) *Ifigenia*, opera
1953 (73) *Cagliostro*, opera
1958 (78) *Murder in the Cathedral*, opera (on T.S.
      Eliot's play)

PONCHIELLI, Amilcare/1834–1886/Italy

1861 (27) *La Savoiarda*, opera
1863 (29) *Roderico*, opera
1872 (38) *I Promessi Sposi*, opera
1873 (39) *Il Parlatore Eterno*, opera
            Le Due Gemelle, ballet
1874 (40) *I Lituani*, opera (revised as *Aldona*)
1875 (41) *A Gaetano Donizetti*, cantata
1876 (42) *La Gioconda*, opera (from which comes
            the *Dance of the Hours*)
1880 (46) *Il Figliuol Prodigo*, opera
1882 (48) *In Memoria di Garibaldi*, cantata
1885 (51) *Marion Delorme*, opera

PORPORA, Niccolò Antonio/1686–1766/Italy

1708 (22) *Agrippina*, opera
1711 (25) *Flavio Amicio Olibrio*, opera
            Il Martirio di S. Giovanni Nepomuceno,
            oratorio
1713 (27) *Basilio, re d'Oriente*, opera
1714 (28) *Arianna e Teseo*, opera
1718 (32) *Temistocle*, opera
1719 (33) *Faramondo*, opera
1721 (35) *Il Martirio di Santa Eugenia*, oratorio
1723 (37) *Adelaide*, opera
1724 (38) *Griselda*, opera
1726 (40) *Imeneo in Atene*, opera
1727 (41) *Ezio*, opera
1729 (43) *Semiramide riconosciuta*, opera
1730 (44) *Mitridate*, opera
1731 (45) *Poro*, opera
1732 (46) *Germanico in Germania*, opera
1733 (47) *Arianna in Nasso*, opera
1734 (48) *Enea nel Lazio*, opera
            Davide e Bersabea, oratorio
1735 (49) *Polifemo*, opera
            Ifigenia in Aulide, opera
1737 (51) *Lucio Papirio*, opera
1738 (52) *Carlo il Calvo*, opera

1739 (53) *Il Barone di Zampano*, opera
1740 (54) *Il Trionfo di Camilla*, opera
1742 (56) *Statira*, opera
1743 (57) *Temistocle*, opera
1747 (61) *Filandro*, opera
Porpora also wrote songs, chamber music, harpsichord music, etc.

POULENC, Francis/1899–1963/France

1917 (18) *Rapsodie nègre*, for cello, piano, flute and
                string quartet
1918 (19) Sonata for two clarinets
                Sonata for piano (four hands)
                Trois mouvements perpetuelles, for piano
                Toréador, songs (1918–32)
1919 (20) *Valse*, for piano
                Le Bestaire au cortège d'Orphée, songs
                Cocardes, songs
1920 (21) Cinq Impromptus, for piano
                Suite in C major, for piano
1921 (22) *La Baigneuse de Trouville* and *Discours
                du General:* two numbers of a group
                work composed by all members of "les
                Six" (except Louis Durey) for a play
                by Jean Cocteau
1922 (23) Sonata for trumpet, horn and trombone
                Sonata for clarinet and bassoon
                Chanson à boire, for a cappella male choir
1923 (24) *Les Biches*, ballet
1924 (25) *Promenade*, for piano
                Poèmes de Ronsard (1924–25)
1925 (26) *Napoli Suite*, for piano
1926 (27) Trio for oboe, bassoon and piano
                Chansons gaillardes
1927–28 (28) *Concert champêtre*, for harpsichord
                and orchestra
                Deux novelettes, for piano
                Airs chantés
1928 (29) *Trois pièces*, for piano
1929 (30) *Aubade*, for piano and eighteen
                instruments

Hommage à Roussel, for piano
Huit Nocturnes, for piano (1929–38)
1930 (31) Épitaphe, song
1931 (32) Bagatelle, for violin and piano
Trois poèmes de Louise Lalanne, songs
Four songs
Five songs
1932 (33) Concerto in D major, for two pianos and
orchestra
Sextet for piano and wind quintet
(1932–40)
Improvisations for piano (1932–43)
Intermezzo, in D minor, for piano
Le Bal masqué, cantata
1933 (34) Feuillets d'album, for piano (Ariette,
Rêve, Gigue)
Villageoises, children's piano pieces
1934 (35) Intermezzo, in D♭ major, for piano
Intermezzo, in C major, for piano
Presto, Badinage and Humoresque, for
piano
Huit chansons polonaises
Quatre chansons pour enfants (1934–35)
1935 (36) Suite française, for chamber orchestra
Cinq poèmes (Paul Eluard)
A sa guitare, song
Margot, incidental music (in collaboration
with Auric)
1936 (37) Sept chansons, for a cappella mixed choir
Litanies à la Vierge noire, for women's or
children's voices and organ
Petites voix, five choruses for three-part a
cappella children's choir
Les Soirées de Nazelles, for piano
1937 (38) Deux marches et un intermède, for
chamber orchestra
Mass in G major
Secheresses, cantata
Bourée d'Auvergne, for piano
Tel jour telle nuit, songs
1938 (39) Concerto in G major, for organ, strings
and timpani
Four penitential Motets (1938–39)

1939 (40) *Fiançailles pour rire*, songs
1940 (41) *Mélancolie*, for piano
　　　　　Banalities, songs
　　　　　Histoire de Babar le petit éléphant, for
　　　　　　　piano and narrator (1940–45)
　　　　　Cello Sonata (1940–48)
1941 (42) Salve regina, for four-part a cappella
　　　　　　　mixed choir
　　　　　Exultate Deo, for four-part a cappella
　　　　　　　mixed choir
　　　　　Les Animaux modèles, ballet
　　　　　La Fille du jardinier, incidental music
1942 (43) Violin Sonata (1942–43)
　　　　　Chansons villageoises, songs
1943 (44) *Figure humaine*, cantata
　　　　　Metamorphoses, songs
　　　　　Deux poèmes, songs
　　　　　Montparnasse, song
1944 (45) *Les Mamelles de Tiresias*, opera buffe
　　　　　Le Voyageur sans bagage, incidental
　　　　　　　music
　　　　　La Nuit de la Saint-Jean, incidental music
　　　　　Un Soir de neige, cantata
1945 (46) *Chansons françaises*, for a cappella mixed
　　　　　　　choir
　　　　　Le Soldat et la Sorcière, incidental music
1946 (47) Two songs
1947 (48) Flute Sonata
1948 (49) *Quatre petites prières (St. Francis)*, for a
　　　　　　　cappella male choir
1949 (50) Piano Concerto
1950 (51) *Stabat Mater*, for soprano, mixed choir
　　　　　　　and orchestra
1953 (54) Sonata for two pianos
　　　　　Dialogues des Carmelites, opera
　　　　　　　(1953–56)
1954 (55) *La Guirlande de Compra (Matelote
　　　　　　　provençale)*, for orchestra, in
　　　　　　　collaboration with other composers
　　　　　*Variations sur le nom de Marguerite Long
　　　　　　　(Bucolique)*, for orchestra, in
　　　　　　　collaboration with other composers

1956 (57) *Le Travail du peintre,* song cycle
          Deux mélodies, songs
1957 (58) *Elegy,* for horn and piano
1958 (59) *La Voix humaine,* lyric tragedy,
          monodrama for soprano
1959 (60) *Gloria,* for soprano, mixed choir and
          orchestra
1960 (61) *Elegy,* for two pianos
1961 (62) *La Dame de Monte Carlo,* monologue for
          soprano and orchestra .
1962 (63) *Sept Repons des ténèbres,* for soprano,
          choir and orchestra
          Oboe Sonata
          Clarinet Sonata

PREVIN, André/b.1929/U.S.A. (b. Germany)

1960 (31) *Overture to a Comedy,* for orchestra
Previn also composed:
Invitation to the Dance, ballet
Guitar Concerto
Portrait, for strings
String Quartet
Flute Quintet
Cello Sonata
Impressions, for piano.

PROKOFIEV, Sergei/1891–1953/Russia

1907–09 (16–18) Piano Sonata No. 1 in F minor
1907–11 (16–20) Four pieces for piano
1908–12 (17–21) Four pieces for piano
1909 (18) Four Études, for piano
          Sinfonietta in A major (final version
          · 1929) (1909–14)
          Two poems for female voices and
          orchestra (1909–10)
1910 (19) *Dreams,* symphonic poem
          Autumnal Sketch, for orchestra (revised
          1934)

>

        Deux Poèmes, for voice and piano
           (1910–11)
1911–12 (20) Piano Concerto No. 1 in D♭ major
1911–13 *Magdalene,* opera
1912 (21) Piano Concerto No. 2 in D minor
        Ballade, for cello and piano
        Piano Sonata No. 2 in D minor
        Toccata, in C major, for piano
        Sarcasms, for piano (1912–14)
1914 (23) Violin Concerto No. 1
        Scythian Suite (Ala et Lolly), for orchestra
           (1914–15)
        The Ugly Duckling, for voice and piano
1915 (24) *The Gambler,* opera (revised 1928)
        Chout, ballet (revised 1920)
        Visions fugitives, for piano
        Cinq Poésies, for voice and piano
1916 (25) Symphony No. 1, *Classical* (1916–17)
        Cinq Poésies d'Anna Akhmatova, for
           voice and piano
1917 (26) Piano Sonata No. 3 in A minor (begun
           in 1907)
        Piano Sonata No. 4 in C minor (begun in
           1908)
        Seven, they are seven, Akhadian
           Incantation for tenor, chorus and
           orchestra
        Piano Concerto No. 3 in C major
           (1917–21)
1919 (28) *The Love of Three Oranges,* opera
           (Symphonic Suite of the same name
           composed 1919–24)
        The Fiery Angel, opera (1919–27)
        Overture on Hebrew Themes, for piano,
           clarinet and string quartet
1920 (29) *Five Songs Without Words,* for voice and
           piano
1921 (30) Five Songs
1923 (32) Piano Sonata No. 5 in C major
1924 (33) Symphony No. 2 in D minor (1924–25)
        Quintet in G minor, for oboe, clarinet,
           violin, viola and double-bass

1925 (34) *Pas d'Acier,* ballet (1925–26)
Divertimento for orchestra (1925–29)

1928 (37) *The Prodigal Son,* ballet
Symphony No. 3 in C minor

1929–30 (38) Symphony No. 4 in C major (second
version 1947)

1930 (39) *Sur le Borysthène (On the Dnieper),*
ballet
Four Portraits, symphonic suite from the
opera *The Gambler* (1930–31)
String Quartet No. 1

1931 (40) Piano Concerto No. 4 in B♭ major, for the
left hand

1932 (41) Piano Concerto No. 5 in G major

1933 (42) *Chant Symphonique,* for orchestra
Cello Concerto in E minor (1933–38)

1934 (43) *Egyptian Night,* symphonic suite
Lieutenant Kijé, symphonic suite for
orchestra and baritone voice ad lib

1935 (44) *Romeo and Juliet,* ballet (1935–36)
Violin Concerto No. 2 in G minor
Musique d'enfants, for piano

1936 (45) *Peter and the Wolf,* for orchestra and
narrator
Russian Overture
Cantata for the Twentieth Anniversary of
the October Revolution, for double
chorus, military band, accordions and
orchestra (1936–37)

1938–39 (47) *Alexander Nevsky,* cantata for mezzo-
soprano, chorus and orchestra

1939 (48) *Simeon Kotko,* opera
Zdravitsa, cantata for chorus and orchestra
Piano Sonata No. 6 in A major (1939–40)
Piano Sonata No. 7 in B♭ major
(1939–42)
Piano Sonata No. 8 in B♭ major
(1939–44)

1940 (49) *The Duenna,* opera (1940–41)
Cinderella, ballet (1940–44)

1941 (50) *War and Peace,* opera (1941–42)
Symphonic March
Suite for Orchestra, *1941*

221

> A Summer's Day, suite for small
>   orchestra (transcribed from the
>   *Musique d'enfants* of 1935)
> String Quartet No. 2 in F major

1942–43 (51) Flute Sonata in D major
> *Ballad of an Unknown Boy*, cantata

1944 (53) Symphony No. 5 in B♭ major

1945–47 (54–56) Piano Sonata No. 9 in C major
> Symphony No. 6 in E♭ minor

1947–48 (56) *The Story of a Real Man*, opera

1948–53 (57–62) *The Stone Flower*, ballet

1949 (58) Cello Sonata in C major
> *Winter Bonfire*, suite for narrator, boys'
>   chorus and orchestra (1949–50)

1950–52 (59–61) *Sinfonia Concertante* in E minor,
>   for cello and orchestra (this is a
>   reworking of the 1933–38 cello
>   concerto

1951–52 (60–61) Symphony No. 7 in C♯ minor

1952 (61) Cello Concertino in G minor

Prokofiev left unfinished a Concerto for two pianos
and strings; a Cello Sonata in C♯ minor; a second
version of the Symphony No. 2; and sketches for a
10th and 11th piano sonata.

PUCCINI, Giacomo/1858–1924/Italy

1884 (26) *Le Villi*, opera

1889 (31) *Edgar*, opera

1893 (35) *Manon Lescaut*, opera

1896 (38) *La Bohème*, opera

1900 (42) *Tosca*, opera

1904 (46) *Madama Butterfly*, opera

1910 (52) *Girl of the Golden West (La Fanciulla del
>   West)*, opera

1917 (59) *La Rondine*, opera

1918 (60) *Il Trittico*, three contrasted one-act operas
>   to be produced in a single evening:
> > *Suor Angelica*
> > *Il Tabarro*
> > *Gianni Schicchi*

1926 (posthumous) *fp. Turandot*, opera

PURCELL, Henry/1659–1695/Great Britain

1680 (21) Nine fantasias of four parts
c.**1682** (*c*.23) Anthem: Hear my prayer
1683 (24) Twelve sonatas of three parts
1688 (29) *How pleasant is this flowery plain,* secular
            cantata
1689 (30) *Dido and Aeneas,* opera
          Musick's Handmaid, for harpsichord
1690 (31) *The Prophetess* or *The History of*
          Dioclesian, opera
1691 (32) *King Arthur* or *The British Worthy,* opera
          The Wives' Excuse, incidental music
1692 (33) *The Faery Queen,* opera
          The Libertine, incidental music
          Oedipus, incidental music
1693 (34) *Epsom Wells,* incidental music
1694 (35) *The Married Beau,* incidental music
1695 (36) *The Indian Queen,* opera
          The Tempest, or *The Enchanted Island,*
          opera
          Bonduca, incidental music
1696 (posthumous) *p.* A choice collection of Lessons
          for the Harpsichord or Spinet
          p. Harpsichord Suites Nos. 1–8
Purcell also composed much church music, stage
music, chamber music, complimentary odes to royalty,
harpsichord pieces, etc.

QUILTER, Roger/1877–1953/Great Britain

1906 (29) *To Julia,* song cycle
1907 (30) *Serenade,* for orchestra
1908 (31) *Songs of Sorrow*
1909 (32) Seven Elizabethan Lyrics
1910 (33) Three English Dances
          Four songs
1911 (34) *Where the Rainbow Ends,* incidental
          music
          Three Songs of the Sea

1914 (37) *A Children's Overture*
Four Child Songs
1916 (39) Three Songs of William Blake
1921 (44) Five Shakespeare Songs
Three Pastoral Songs
1922 (45) *As You Like It,* incidental music
1925 (48) *The Rake,* ballet suite
Five Jacobean Lyrics
1936 (59) *Julia,* opera
1946 (69) *Tulips,* for chorus and orchestra
1948 (71) *The Sailor and His Lass,* for soloist, choir
and orchestra
1949 (72) *Love at the Inn,* opera

RACHMANINOV, Sergei/1873–1943/Russia

1890–91 (17–18) Piano Concerto No. 1 in F♯ minor
1890–93 (17–20) Six songs
1891 (18) Scherzo for strings
1892 (19) *Prélude* and *Danse orientale,* for cello and
piano
Five *Morceaux de Fantaisie,* for piano
(includes the C♯ minor prélude)
Intermezzo
1893 (20) *Aleko,* opera
The Rock, fantasy
Trio élégiaque, in D minor
Romance and *Danse hongroise,* for violin
and piano
Suite No. 1, *Fantasy,* for two pianos
Six songs
1894 (21) *Caprice bohémien,* for orchestra
Seven piano pieces
Six piano duets
1895 (22) Symphony No. 1 in D minor
1896 (23) Six *Moments musicaux,* for piano
Twelve songs
Six songs for female, or boys', voices
1900–06 (27–33) Twelve songs
1901 (28) Piano Concerto No. 2 in C minor
Suite No. 2 for two pianos
Cello Sonata in G minor

1902 (29) *The Spring,* cantata
1903 (30) Variations on a theme by Chopin, for
              piano
              Ten preludes for piano
1906 (33) *Francesca da Rimini,* opera
              The Miserly Knight, opera
              Fifteen songs
1907 (34) Symphony No. 2 in E minor
              The Isle of the Dead, symphonic poem
              Piano Sonata No. 1 in D minor
1909 (36) Piano Concerto No. 3 in D minor
1910 (37) *The Bells,* choral symphony (after Poe)
              Thirteen piano preludes
              Liturgy of St. John Chrystostum
1911 (38) Six *Études-Tableaux,* for piano
1912 (39) Fourteen songs
1913 (40) Piano Sonata No. 2 in B♭ minor
1915 (42) Vesper Mass
1916 (43) Six songs
              Nine *Études-Tableaux,* for piano
              (1916–17)
1927 (54) Piano Concerto No. 4 in G minor
1930 (57) Three Russian Folk-songs, for chorus and
              orchestra (possibly 1927)
1932 (59) Variations on a theme by Corelli, for
              piano
1934 (61) *Rhapsody on a theme by Paganini,*
              variations for piano and orchestra
1936 (63) Symphony No. 3 in A minor
1941 (68) *Three Symphonic Dances,* for orchestra

RAMEAU, Jean/1683–1764/France

1706 (23) *p.* Harpsichord Works, Book I
1728 (45) *p.* Harpsichord Works, Book II
1733 (50) *Hippolyte et Aricie,* opera
1735 (52) *Les Indes galantes,* opera-ballet
1737 (54) *Castor et Pollux,* opera-ballet
1739 (56) *Dardanus,* opera
              Les Fêtes d'Hebe, ballet
1741 (57) *p.* Harpsichord Works, Book III

1745 (62) *Platée*, ballet
1748 (65) *Pigmalion*, ballet
Zais, ballet
1754 (71) *Zephyre*, ballet
1760 (78) *Les Paladins*, opera-ballet
Rameau composed more than 20 operas and opera-
ballets, church music, chamber music, cantatas, etc.

RAVEL, Maurice/1875–1937/France

1893 (18) *Sérénade grotesque*, for piano
1895 (20) *Menuet antique*
1896 (21) *Sainte*, song
1899 (24) *Pavane pour une Infante défunte*, for
piano
1901 (26) *Jeux d'eau*, for piano
Myrrha, cantata
1902 (27) *Alcyone*, cantata
1903 (28) *Shéhérazade*, three songs with orchestra
String Quartet in F major
Alyssa, cantata
1905 (30) *Miroirs*, for piano
Sonatina, for piano
1906 (31) Introduction and Allegro for harp, flute,
clarinet and string quartet
1907 (32) *Rapsodie espagnole*, for orchestra
Cinq Mélodies populaires greques
Piece en forme de Habanera
Sur le herbe, song
1908 (33) *Ma mère l'oye*, suite for piano
Gaspard de la nuit, for piano
1909 (34) *Menuet sur le nom d'Haydn*, for piano
1911 (36) *L'Heure espagnole*, opera
Valses nobles et sentimentales, for piano
or orchestra
1912 (37) *Daphnis et Chloé*, ballet with chorus
1914 (39) *Two Hebrew Songs*, for soprano and
orchestra
Piano Trio in A minor
1915 (40) Three songs for unaccompanied choir
1917 (42) *Le Tombeau de Couperin*, for piano

1920 (45) *La Valse,* choreographic poem for
orchestra
Sonata for violin and cello
1922 (47) *Berceuse sur le nom Fauré*
1924 (49) *Tzigane,* for violin and piano
1925 (50) *L'Enfant et les sortilèges,* opera
1926 (51) *Chansons madécasses,* for voice, flute, cello
and piano
1928 (53) *Bolero,* for orchestra
1931 (56) Piano Concerto in G major
Piano Concerto for the left hand

RAWSTHORNE, Alan/1905–1971/Great Britain

1935 (30) Viola Sonata (revised 1954)
1936 (31) Concerto for clarinet and string orchestra
1937 (32) Theme and variations, for two violins
1938 (33) Symphonic Studies, for orchestra
1939 (34) String Quartet No. 1, *Theme and
Variations*
1941 (36) *The Creel,* suite for piano duet
1942 (37) Piano Concerto No. 1
1944 (39) *Street Corner Overture*
1945 (40) *Cortèges,* fantasy overture
1946 (41) *Prisoner's March,* for orchestra
1947 (42) Concerto for oboe and strings
1948 (43) Violin Concerto No. 1
Clarinet Quartet
1949 (44) Concerto for string orchestra
Cello Sonata
1950 (45) Symphony No. 1
1951 (46) Piano Concerto No. 2
Concertante Pastorale, for flute, horn and
strings
1952 (47) *Canticle of Man,* chamber cantata for
baritone, mixed chorus, flute and strings
1954 (49) *Practical Cats,* for speaker and orchestra
String Quartet No. 2
1955 (50) *Madame Chrysanthème,* ballet
1956 (51) Violin Concerto No. 2
1957 (52) Violin Sonata
1958 (53) *Halle Overture*

1959 (54) Symphony No. 2, *A Pastoral Symphony*
1961 (56) *Improvisations on a theme by Constant Lambert,* for orchestra
Concerto for ten instruments
1962 (57) *Medieval Diptych,* for baritone and orchestra
Divertimento for chamber orchestra
Quintet for piano and wind
Piano Trio
1963 (58) *Carmen Vitale,* for soprano solo, mixed chorus and orchestra
1964 (59) Symphony No. 3
Elegiac Rhapsody, for strings
1965 (60) *Tankas of the Four Seasons,* for tenor and chamber ensemble
Concertante, for violin and piano
1966 (61) Cello Concerto
Sonatine, for flute, oboe and piano
String Quartet No. 3
1967 (62) *Overture for Farnham*
Theme, Variations and Finale, for orchestra
The God in the Cave, cantata for mixed chorus and orchestra
Scèna Rustica, for soprano and harp
1968 (63) Concerto for two pianos and orchestra
Trio for flute, viola and harp
1969 (64) *Triptych,* for orchestra
1970 (65) Oboe Quartet
1971 (66) Quintet for piano, clarinet, horn, violin and cello

---

REGER, Max/1873–1916/Germany

1891 (18) Piano Trio in B minor
Violin Sonata in D major
1892 (19) Cello Sonata in F minor
1897–98 (24) Piano Quintet in C minor
Cello Sonata in G minor
Violin Sonata in A major
1900 (27) Two *Romances,* for solo instruments and orchestra

Clarinet Sonata in A♭ major
Clarinet Sonata in F♯ minor
String Quartet in G minor (1900–01)
String Quartet in A major (1900–01)

1902 (29) Piano Quintet in C minor
Violin Sonata in C major

1903 (30) *Gesang der Verklarten,* for voice and orchestra

1904 (31) String Quartet in D minor
Serenade, for flute, violin and viola, or two violins and viola
String Trio in A minor
Cello Sonata in F major
Variations and Fugue on a theme of Beethoven, for two pianos
Violin Sonata in F♯ minor

1905 (32) *Sinfonietta,* for orchestra
Suite in the Old Style, for violin and piano, in F major

1906 (33) *Serenade*

1907 (34) Variations and Fugue on a theme of Hiller

1908 (35) *Symphonic Prologue to a Tragedy*
Violin Concerto
Sonata for clarinet (or viola) and piano
Piano Trio

1909 (36) *The 100th Psalm,* for voice and orchestra
Die Nonnen, for voice and orchestra
String Quartet in E♭ major

1910 (37) Piano Concerto
String Sextet in F major
Piano Quartet in D minor
Cello Sonata in A minor

1911 (38) *Die Weihe der Nacht,* for chorus and orchestra
Eine Lustspielouverture
String Quartet in F♯ minor
Violin Sonata in E minor

1912 (39) *Konzert im Alten Stil*
Romischer Triumphgesang, for voice and orchestra
A Romantic Suite

1913 (40) *Vier Tondichtunger nach A. Böcklin*
Eine Ballettsuite

1914 (41) *Eine Vaterländische Ouverture*
Three canons, duets and fugues in ancient style, for two violins
Variations and Fugue on a theme of Mozart
Piano Quartet in A minor
Piano Sonata in C minor
Cello Sonata in C minor
1915 (42) *Serenade*, for flute, violin and viola (or two violins and viola) in G major
String Trio in D minor
Der Einsiedler, for chorus and orchestra
1916 (43) Quintet in A major

RESPIGHI, Ottorino/1879–1936/Italy

1902 (23) Piano Concerto
1905 (26) *Re Enzo*, comic opera
Notturno, for orchestra
Burlesca
Suite in G major, for string orchestra and organ
1907 (28) *Fantasy*, for piano and orchestra
String Quartet in D major
String Quartet in D minor
1908 (29) *Concerto in the old style*, for violin and orchestra
1909 (30) *Chaconne* by Vitali, transcribed for violin, strings and organ
1910 (31) *Semirama*, lyric tragedy
1913 (34) *Carnival*, overture
1914 (35) Suite for strings and organ
1915 (36) *Sinfonia Drammatica*
1917 (38) *The Fountains of Rome*, symphonic poem
Old Airs and Dances for Lute, transcribed for orchestra, Series I
Violin Sonata in B minor
1918 (39) *Il Tramonto*, for mezzo-soprano and string quartet
1919 (40) *La Boutique Fantasque*, ballet music arranged from pieces by Rossini

1920 (41) *Scherzo Veneziano,* choreographic comedy
Dance of the Gnomes

1921 (42) *Adagio with Variations,* for cello and
orchestra

1922 (43) *The Sleeping Beauty,* musical fable in
three acts
Concerto Gregoriano, for violin and
orchestra

1923 (44) *Belfagor,* lyric comedy
La Primavera, lyric poem for soloists,
chorus and orchestra

1924 (45) *Concerto in the Mixo-Lydian Mode,* for
orchestra
The Pines of Rome, symphonic poem
Old Airs and Dances for Lute, Series II
Doric String Quartet

1927 (48) *The Sunken Bell,* opera
Three Botticelli Pictures, for orchestra:
Spring (Primavera)
The Adoration of the Magi
The Birth of Venus
The Birds, suite for small orchestra based
on seventeenth- and eighteenth-century
bird-pieces for lute and for harpsichord:
Prelude
Dove
Hen
Nightingale
Cuckoo
Church Windows, four symphonic
impressions for orchestra
Brazilian Impressions, for orchestra

1928 (49) *Toccata,* for piano and orchestra

1929 (50) *The Festivals of Rome,* orchestral suite

1930 (51) *Metamorphosen modi XII,* theme and
variations for orchestra
Bach's *Prelude and Fugue in D major,*
transcribed for orchestra

1932 (53) *Belkis, Queen of Sheba,* ballet
Mary of Egypt, mystery in one act and
three episodes
Old Airs and Dances for Lute, Series III

1934 (55) *La Fiamma,* melodrama in three acts

Concerto for oboe, horn, violin, double-
bass, piano and string orchestra
Passacaglia in C minor (Bach), orchestral
interpretation
1937 (posthumous) *fp. Lucrezia*

RIMSKY-KORSAKOV, Nikolas/1844–1908/Russia

1861–65 (17–21) Symphony No. 1 in E♭ major
1866 (22) Overture on Russian Themes
Symphony No. 3 in C major (1866–73)
1867 (23) *Sadko*, tone poem (later developed into a
ballet-opera)
Fantasia on Serbian Themes, for orchestra
1868–72 (24–28) *The Maid of Pskov (Ivan the
Terrible),* opera
1869 (25) *Antar,* symphonic suite (originally
Symphony No. 2)
1875 (31) Quartet No. 1
Three Pieces for piano
Six fugues
1876 (32) Sextet for strings
Quintet for piano and wind
1878 (34) *May Night,* opera
Variations on BACH, for piano
Four pieces for piano
1879 (35) *Sinfonietta on Russian Themes*
Legend, for orchestra (1879–80)
1880–81 (36) *The Snow Maiden,* opera
1882–83 (38) Piano Concerto in C♯ minor
1886 (42) *Fantasia Concertante on Russian Themes,*
for violin and orchestra
1887 (43) *Capriccio Espagnol,* for orchestra
1888 (44) *Russian Easter Festival Overture*
Schéhérezade, symphonic suite
1892 (48) *fp. Mlada,* opera
1895 (51) *Christmas Eve,* opera
1897 (53) Three song-cycles:
In Spring
To the Poet
By the Sea
Piano Trio

1898 (54)   *Mozart and Salieri*, opera
1899 (55)   *The Tsar's Bride*, opera
1900 (56)   *The Legend of Tsar Sultan*, opera
1902 (58)   *fp. Kaschey the Immortal*, opera
1903 (59)   *Souvenir de trois chants polonaise*, for
            violin and orchestra
            Serenade, for cello and piano
            The Invisible City of Kitezh, opera
            (1903–05)
1905 (61)   *fp.* Orchestral Variations on a Russian
            people's song
1906–07 (62)   *Coq d'Or,* opera
Rimsky-Korsakov also wrote a cantata, *Ballad of the Doom of Oleg.*

ROBERTSON, Leroy/1896–1971/U.S.A.

1923 (27)   *Endicott Overture*
1938 (42)   Piano Quintet
1940 (44)   Prelude, Scherzo and Ricercare for
            Orchestra
            String Quartet
1944 (48)   Rhapsody for Piano and Orchestra
            American Serenade, for string quartet
1945 (49)   *Punch and Judy Overture*
1947 (51)   *Trilogy*, for orchestra
1948 (52)   Violin Concerto
1953 (57)   *The Book of Mormon*, oratorio
1966 (70)   Piano Concerto
Robertson also composed:
Cello Concerto
Fantasia for Organ
Come, Come, Ye Saints, for chorus
Hatikva, for chorus
From the Crossroads, for chorus
The Lord's Prayer, for chorus
Passacaglia for Orchestra.

ROCHBERG, George/b.1918/U.S.A.

1949 (31)   *Night Music,* for chamber orchestra
            Symphony No. 1

1952 (34) Twelve Bagatelles for piano
String Quartet No. 1
1953 (35) Chamber Symphony for nine instruments
1954 (36) Three Psalms for Chorus
David the Psalmist, cantata
1955 (37) Duo Concertante for Violin and Cello
1956 (38) Sinfonia Fantasia
1958 (40) Symphony No. 2
Dialogues, for clarinet and piano
Cheltenham Concerto, for chamber
orchestra
1959 (41) *La Bocca della verita,* for oboe and piano
String Quartet No. 2
1960 (42) *Time-Span,* for orchestra (revised 1962)
1961 (43) *Songs of Innocence and Experience,* for
soprano and chamber orchestra
1963 (45) Piano Trio
1965 (47) Music for the Magic Theater
Zodiac, orchestral version of the twelve
Bagatelles
Contra mortem et tempus, for violin, flute,
clarinet and piano
Black Sounds, for winds and percussion
La bocca della verita, for violin and piano
1968 (50) *Tableaux,* for soprano and eleven players
Symphony No. 3, *A twentieth-century
Passion,* for orchestra, four solo voices,
eight-part chamber choir and double
chorus
1970 (52) *Songs of Krishna,* for soprano and piano
Mizmor L'Piyus, for bass-baritone and
small orchestra
1972 (54) *Electrikaleidoscope*
Ricordanza, for cello and piano
String Quartet No. 3
1974 (56) *Imago Mundi,* for orchestra
1975 (57) Violin Concerto
Rochberg also composed a Book of Songs (1937–69).

RODRIGO, Joaquín/b.1902/Spain

1934 (32) *Cantico de la Esposa,* for voice and piano

1939 (37) *Concierto de Aranjuez,* for guitar and
     orchestra
1942 (40) *Concierto Heroico,* for piano and
     orchestra
1943 (41) *Concierto de Estio,* for violin and
     orchestra
1947 (45) Four *Madrigales Amatorias,* for voice and
     piano (with orchestra, 1948)
1948 (46) *Ausencias de Dulcinea,* for bass, four
     sopranos and orchestra
1949 (47) *Concierto Galante,* for cello and orchestra
1952 (50) Four *Villancicos,* for voice and piano
     Four *Villancicos,* for chorus *(Canciones*
     de Navidad)
1954 (52) *Concert-Serenade,* for harp and orchestra
c.1955 (c.53) *Fantasia para un gentilhombre,* for
     guitar
1965 (63) *Sonata Pimpante,* for violin and piano
     (1965–66)
1967 (65) *Concierto Andaluz,* for four guitars and
     orchestra
1968 (66) *Concierto Madrigal,* for two guitars and
     orchestra
Rodrigo also composed:
Sones en la Giralda (Fantasia Sevillana), for harp
  and orchestra
Triptic de Mosen Cinto.

ROPARTZ, Guy (Joseph Marie Guy-Ropartz)/
1864–1955/France

1887 (23) *La Cloche des morts,* for orchestra
1888 (24) *Les Landes*
     Marche de fête
1889 (25) *Cinq pièces brève,* for orchestra
     Carnaval
1892 (28) *Serenade*
1893 (29) *Le Diable Couturier,* opera
     Dimanche breton
     String Quartet No. 1 in G minor
1900 (36) Five motets
1904 (40) Cello Sonata No. 1 in E major

1907 (43) Violin Sonata No. 1 in D minor
Pastorale and Dance, for oboe and
orchestra
1911–12 (47) String Quartet No. 2 in D minor
Serenade, for string quartet
1912 (48) *Le Pays,* opera
À Marie endormie
La Chasse du Prince Arthur
1913 (49) *Soir sur les Chaumes*
Dans l'ombre de la montagne
1915 (51) Divertissement No. 1
1917 (53) Violin Sonata No. 2 in E major
Musiques au jardin
1918 (54) Piano Trio in A minor
Cello Sonata No. 2 in A minor
1924–25 (60) String Quartet No. 3 in G major
1926 (62) Romance and Scherzino, for violin and
orchestra
1928 (64) *Rhapsody,* for cello and orchestra
1933 (69) *Sérénade champêtre*
1937 (73) *Requiem,* with orchestra
1942 (78) *De profundis,* with orchestra
1943 (79) *Indiscret,* ballet
Petit Symphonie
1947 (83) Divertissement, No. 2
Ropartz also composed 5 symphonies (1895–1945),
No. 3 with soloists and chorus.

ROSSINI, Gioacchino/1792–1868/Italy

1808 (16) Sonatas for two violins, cello and double-
bass
1809 (17) Variations for clarinet and orchestra, in
C major
1810 (18) *La cambiale di matrimonio,* opera
1812 (20) *La Scala di seta (The Silken Ladder),*
opera
1813 (21) *L'Italiana in Algeri,* opera
Tancredi, opera
1815 (23) *Elisabetta, Regina d'Inghilterra,* opera
1816 (24) *Otello,* opera
The Barber of Seville, opera

1817 (25) *La Cenerentola,* opera
La Gazza ladra (The Thieving Magpie),
opera
1818 (26) *Mosè,* opera
1820 (28) *Maometto* II, opera
Solemn Mass
1822 (30) *Zelmira,* opera
1823 (31) *Semiramide,* opera
1825 (33) *Il viaggio a Reims,* opera
1826 (34) *Le Siège de Corinthe,* opera (French-
language version of *Maometto II*)
1827 (35) *Moïse,* opera (French-language version
of *Mosè*)
1828 (36) *fp. Comte Ory,* comedy-opera
1829 (37) *William Tell,* opera
1863 (71) Petite Messe Solenelle
Rossini also composed:
Stabat Mater (1832–41)
Soirées musicales
Piano pieces, etc.

ROUSSEL, Albert/1869–1937/France

1902 (33) Piano Trio
1903 (34) *Resurrection,* for orchestra
Violin Sonata
1904–06 (35) Symphony No. 1, *La poème de la forêt*
1905 (36) *Divertissement,* for piano, flute, oboe,
clarinet, horn and bassoon
1910–11 (41) *Evocations*
1912 (43) *The Spider's Feast,* ballet
1919 (50) *Impromptu,* for harp
Symphony No. 2 in B♭ major
1925 (56) *Pour une fête de Printemps,* tone poem
Sérénade, for harp, flute, violin, viola and
cello
Violin Sonata
Joueurs de flûte, four pieces for flute and
piano
Segovia, for guitar
1927 (58) Piano Concerto in G major
1929–30 (60) Symphony No. 3 in G minor

1931 (62) *Bacchus and Ariadne,* ballet
1932 (63) Quartet
1934 (65) Symphony No. 4 in A major
　　　　　Sinfonietta for strings
1936 (67) Concertino for Cello
　　　　　Rhapsodie flamande
1937 (68) String Trio

RUBBRA, Edmund/b.1901/Great Britain

1921 (20) *The Secret Hymnody,* for mixed choir and
　　　　　orchestra
1924 (23) Double Fugue for orchestra
1925 (24) *La Belle Dame sans merci,* for mixed
　　　　　chorus and small orchestra
　　　　　Violin Sonata No. 1
1929 (28) Triple Fugue for orchestra
1931 (30) Piano Concerto
　　　　　Violin Sonata No. 2
1933 (32) *Bee-Bee-Bei,* one-act opera
1934 (33) *Sinfonia Concertante,* for piano and
　　　　　orchestra
　　　　　Rhapsody, for violin and orchestra
1936 (35) Symphony No. 1
1937 (36) Symphony No. 2
　　　　　String Quartet in F minor
1938 (37) *Prism,* ballet music
1939 (38) Symphony No. 3
1941 (40) Symphony No. 4
　　　　　The Morning Watch, for choir and
　　　　　orchestra
1944 (43) *Soliloquy,* for cello and orchestra
1946 (45) *Missa Cantuariensis,* for double choir
　　　　　unaccompanied except for organ in the
　　　　　Credo
1947 (46) *Festival Overture,* for orchestra
　　　　　Cello Sonata in G minor
　　　　　Symphony No. 5 in B♭ major
1948 (47) *The Buddha,* suite for flute, oboe, violin,
　　　　　viola and cello
1951 (50) *Festival Te Deum,* for soprano, chorus and
　　　　　orchestra

String Quartet No. 2 in E♭ major
1952 (51) Viola Concerto in A major
1954 (53) Symphony No. 6
1955 (54) Piano Concerto in G major
1956 (55) Symphony No. 7 in C major
1957 (56) *In Honoram Mariae Matris Dei,* cantata
1958 (57) Oboe Sonata in C major
               Pezzo Ostinato, for harp
1959 (58) Violin Concerto
1961 (60) *Cantata da Camera* (Crucifixus pro nobis)
1964 (63) String Quartet No. 3
               Improvisation, for solo cello
1965 (64) *Inscape,* suite for chorus, strings and harp
1966 (65) Eight Preludes for Piano
1968 (67) Symphony No. 8
               Advent Cantata (Natum Maria Virgine),
                   for baritone, chorus and small orchestra
               Violin Sonata No. 3
1969 (68) Missa Brevis, for treble voices and organ
1970 (69) Piano Trio No. 2
Rubbra also composed:
Sinfonia Sacra (The Resurrection) for soprano,
   contralto, baritone, mixed chorus and orchestra
Transformations, for solo harp
Chamber Symphony (No. 10)
Resurgam, overture
String Quartet No. 4
Much music for unaccompanied choir, anthems, part-
songs and liturgical choral works.

SAINT-SAËNS, Camille/1835–1921/France

1855 (20) Symphony No. 1 in E♭ major
               Piano Quintet in A major, with double-
                   bass ad lib
1857 (22) Organ Fantasia No. 1
1858 (23) Piano Concerto No. 1 in D major
1859 (24) Violin Concerto No. 1 in A minor
1863 (28) Piano Trio No. 1 in F major
1866 (31) Suite in D minor, for piano, cello (violin
                   or viola)
1868 (33) Piano Concerto No. 2 in G minor

1869 (34) Piano Concerto No. 3 in E♭ major
1870 (35) *Introduction and Rondo Capriccioso,* for
            violin and orchestra
            Mélodies persanes, six songs
1871 (36) *Omphale's Spinning-Wheel,* symphonic
            poem
            Marche heroïque, for orchestra
1872 (37) *La Princesse jaune,* opera
1873 (38) Cello Concerto No. 1 in A minor
            Phaeton, symphonic poem
1874 (39) *Danse macabre,* symphonic poem
1875 (40) Piano Concerto No. 4 in C minor
1876 (41) *The Deluge,* oratorio
1877 (42) *Samson et Delilah,* opera
            La Jeunesse d'Hercule, symphonic poem
            Suite for Orchestra
1878 (43) Symphony No. 2 in A minor
1879 (44) Violin Concerto No. 2 in C major
            Suite algérienne
1880 (45) Violin Concerto No. 3 in B minor
1885 (50) Violin Sonata No. 1 in D minor
1886 (51) *Le Carnaval des animaux,* for piano and
            orchestra
            Symphony No. 3 in C minor, with organ
            and two pianos
1892 (57) Piano Trio No. 2 in E minor
1894 (59) Preludes and fugues for organ
1895 (60) Piano Concerto No. 5 in F major
1896 (61) Violin Sonata No. 2 in E♭ major
1897 (62) Seven Improvisations for Grand Organ
1898 (63) Preludes and fugues for organ
1900 (65) String Quartet in E minor
1902 (67) Cello Concerto No. 2 in D minor
            Coronation March
1913 (78) *fp. The Promised Land,* oratorio
1915 (80) *La Cendre Rouge,* ten songs
1918 (83) *Fantasia* No. 3, for organ
Saint-Saëns also composed:
Serenade, for piano, organ, violin, and viola (or cello)
Cello Sonata No. 1 in C minor
Piano Quartet in B♭ major
Septet in E♭ major for piano, trumpet, oboe and string
    quartet

240

Caprice on Danish and Russian Airs
Cello Sonata No. 2 in F major
Fantaisie, for harp and violin
La Muse et le poète, piano trio
String Quartet in G major
Clarinet Sonata in E♭ major
Bassoon Sonata in G major.

SARASATE, Pablo/1844–1908/Spain

1878 (34) *Zigeunerweisen,* orchestra fantasy
Sarasate also composed:
Danses espagnoles: *Malaguena*
Danses espagnoles: *Habanera*
Romanza Andaluza
Jota Navarra
Playera
Zapateado
Caprice basque
Introduction and Tarantella, for violin and orchestra
Many works for violin.

SATIE, Erik/1866–1925/France

1886 (20) *Ogives,* for piano
1887 (21) Trois sarabandes, for piano
1888 (22) *Trois Gymnopédies,* for piano
1890 (24) *Trois Gnossiennes,* for piano
1891 (25) Trois Préludes from *Les Fils des étoiles,*
        for piano
1892 (26) *Uspud,* ballet
        Sonneries de la Rose-Croix, for piano
1893 (27) *Danses gothiques,* for piano
        Quatre Préludes, for piano
1894 (28) *Prélude de la porte héroïque du ciel,*
        for piano
1895 (29) Messe des Pauvres
1897 (31) *Deux pièces froides,* for piano
1899 (33) *Généviève de Brabant,* puppet opera
        Jack-in-the-Box, ballet

1903 (37)   *Trois morceaux en forme de poire*, for piano duet

1905 (39)   *Pousse l'amour*, operetta

1906 (40)   *Prélude en tapisserie*, for piano
                 Passacaille, for piano

1908 (42)   *Aperçus désagréables*, for piano duet

1911 (45)   *En Habit de cheval*, two chorales and two fugues, for orchestra

1912 (46)   *Choses vues à droite et à gauche (sans lunette)*, for violin and piano

1913 (47)   *Le Piège de Medusa*, operetta
                 Descriptions automatiques, for piano
                 Embryons desséchés, for piano
                 Croquis et agarceries d'un gros bonhomme en bois, for piano
                 Chapitres tournés en tous sens, for piano
                 Enfantines, three sets of children's pieces for piano

1914 (48)   *Cinq Grimaces pour le songe d'une nuit d'été*, for orchestra
                 Vieux Sequins et vieilles cuirasses, for piano
                 Heures séculaires et instantées, for piano
                 Trois Valses du précieux dégoûte, for piano
                 Sports et divertissements, for piano
                 Les Pantins dansent, for piano
                 Trois Poèmes d'amour, songs

1915 (49)   *Avant-dernières pensées*, for piano

1916 (50)   *Parade*, ballet
                 Trois mélodies, songs

1918 (52)   *Socrates*, symphonic drama for four sopranos and chamber orchestra

1919 (53)   *Quatre petites pièces montées*, for small orchestra
                 Nocturnes, for piano

1920 (54)   *La Belle Excentrique*, for orchestra
                 Premier minuet, for piano
                 Trois petites mélodies, songs

1923 (57)   *Ludions*, songs

1924 (58)   *Mercure*, ballet
                 Relâche, ballet

SCARLATTI, Alessandro/1660–1725/Italy

1679 (19)   *fp. Gli equivoci nel sembiante,* opera
1683 (23)   *fp. Pompeo,* opera
             fp. Psiche, opera
1690 (30)   *fp. Gli equivoci in amore,* opera
1694 (34)   *fp. Pirro e Demetrio,* opera
1698 (38)   *fp. Flavio cuniberto,* opera
             fp. La donna ancora e'fedele, opera
1699 (39)   Two Sonatas for flute and continuo
1706 (46)   *Il sedecia, re di Gerusalemme,* oratorio
1707 (47)   *fp. Mitridate eupatore,* opera
             fp. Il trionfo della libertà, opera
*c.***1710** (*c.*50)   Motet: Est dies tropael
             Informata vulnerate, cantata
1715 (55)   *fp. Tigrone,* opera
             Twelve sinfonias
             Four quartets for two violins, viola and
                cello, without harpsichord
1718 (58)   *fp. Telemaco,* opera
1719 (59)   *fp. Marco Attilo Regolo,* opera
1720 (60)   *fp. Tito o sempronio gracco,* opera
1721 (61)   *fp. Griselda,* opera
Scarlatti also composed:
101 more operas
500 chamber cantatas
200 masses
14 oratorios

SCARLATTI, Domenico/1685–1757/Italy

1703 (18)   *fp. Ottavia ristituta al trono,* opera
             fp. Giustina, opera
1704 (19)   *fp. Irene,* opera
1710 (25)   *fp. La Sylvia,* opera
1711 (26)   *fp. Orlando,* opera
             fp. Tolomeo e Alessandro, opera
1712 (27)   *fp. Tetide in sciro,* opera
1713 (28)   *fp. Ifigenie in Aulide,* opera
             fp. Ifigenie in Tauride, opera
1714 (29)   *fp. Amor d'un ombra,* opera

1715 (30) *fp. Ambleto,* opera
1718 (33) *fp. Berenice,* opera
1738 (53) *p.* Essercizi per Gravicembalo
1739 (54) *p.* XLII Suites de pièces pour le Clavecin
Scarlatti also wrote over 550 single-movement
harpsichord sonatas.

SCHOECK, Othmar/1886–1957/Switzerland

1906–07 (20) *Serenade,* for small orchestra
1911 (25) *Dithyrambe,* for double chorus and
orchestra
Violin Concerto (1911–12)
Erwin und Elmire, incidental music
(1911–16)
1915 (29) *Trommelschlage*
1917–18 (31) *Don Ranudo de Colibrados*
1918 (32) *Das Wandbild*
1919–20 (33) *Venus,* opera
1922–23 (36) *Élégie,* song cycle for voice and
chamber orchestra
1924–25 (38) *Penthesiles*
1928–30 (42–44) *Vom Fischer und syner Fru,*
dramatic cantata
1932 (46) *Praeludium*
1937 (51) *Massimilla Doni,* opera
1938–39 (52) *Das Schloss Durande,* opera
1945 (59) *Sommernacht*
Suite in A major, for strings
1947 (61) Cello Concerto
1951 (65) Horn Concerto
Festlichen Hymnus
1952 (66) *Befreite Sehnsucht,* song cycle for voice
and orchestra
Schoeck also composed many songs.

SCHOENBERG, Arnold/1874–1951/Austria

1899 (25) *Verklaerte Nacht,* for string sextet
(arranged for string orchestra 1917;
revised 1943)

1900–13 (26–39) *Gurre-Lieder,* for four solo singers, three male choruses, one mixed chorus, large orchestra including eight flutes and a set of iron chains

1903 (29) *Pelleas und Melisande,* suite for orchestra

1905 (31) String Quartet No. 1 in D minor

1906 (32) Chamber Symphonies Nos. 1 and 2

1907 (33) String Quartet No. 2 (transcribed for string orchestra 1917)
Friede auf Erden, for choir

1908 (34) *Buch der hängenden Gärten,* setting of fifteen poems by Stefan George for solo voice and piano

1909 (35) *Erwartung,* monodrama, for soprano and orchestra
Five pieces for orchestra (revised 1949)

1910–13 (36–39) *Die Glückliche Hand,* music drama

1911 (37) *Herzgewächse,* for coloratura soprano, celesta, harmonium and harp

1912 (38) *Pierrot Lunaire,* song cycle of twenty-one poems

1923 (49) *Serenade,* for septet and baritone

1924 (50) Quintet for wind instruments

1927 (53) String Quartet No. 3

1928 (54) Variations for orchestra

1929 (55) *Von Heute auf Morgen,* opera

1932 (58) *Moses und Aron,* two-act opera

1934 (60) Suite in G major for strings

1936 (62) Violin Concerto

1937 (63) String Quartet No. 4

1939 (65) *Kol Nidrei*

1941 (67) Variations and Recitative for organ

1942 (68) Piano Concerto

1943 (69) *Ode to Napoleon,* for speaker, strings and piano

1945 (71) Prelude to a *Genesis* Suite

1947 (73) *A Survivor from Warsaw,* cantata, for speaker, men's chorus and orchestra

1949 (75) *Fantasia,* for violin and piano

1951 (77) *De profundis,* for a cappella choir

1811 (14) Quintet-overture
1812 (15) *Eine Kleine Trauermusik,* nonet
Quartet-overture
String Quartet Nos. 1–3 in B♭: C: B♭
Sonata movement for piano trio, in B♭
major
1813 (16) Symphony No. 1 in D major
Minuet and Finale of a wind octet, in
F major
String Quartets Nos. 4–6, in C: B♭: D
Three Sonatinas for violin and piano, in
D: Am: Gm
Five German Dances, with coda and
seven trios
Five minuets with six trios
Des Teufels Lustschloss, opera
1814 (17) Quartet for flute, guitar, violin and cello,
in G major
String Quartets Nos. 7 and 8, in D: B♭
"Gretchen at the Spinning-wheel", song
1815 (18) Symphony No. 2 in E♭ major
Symphony No. 3 in D major
String Quartet No. 9 in G minor
Piano Sonatas Nos. 1 and 2, in E: C
"Der Erlkönig", song
1816 (19) Symphony No. 4 in C minor, *Tragic*
Symphony No. 5 in B♭ major
Concertstücke, for violin and orchestra
Rondo for violin and string quartet
String Trio (one movement) in B♭ major
Piano Sonata No. 3 in E major, five
movements
Adagio and Rondo Concertante, for piano
quartet
1817 (20) String Quartet No. 10 in E♭ major
(possibly 1813)
String Quartet No. 11 in E major
Violin Sonata in A major
Piano Sonata No. 4 in A♭, with finale
in E♭

Piano Sonata No. 5 in E minor, two
    movements
Piano Sonata No. 6 in E♭ major
Piano Sonata No. 7 in F♯ minor
Piano Sonata No. 8 in B major
Piano Sonata No. 9 in E minor
"An die Musik" and "Tod und das
    Mädchen", songs

1818 (21) Symphony No. 6 in C major
Piano Sonatas Nos. 10 and 11, in C: Fm
    (unfinished)

1819 (22) Piano Quintet in A major, *Trout*
Piano Sonata No. 12 in C♯ minor
    (fragmentary)
Piano Sonata No. 13 in A major

1820 (23) *Die Zauberharfe,* melodrama
String Quartet No. 12 in C minor

1821 (24) Variation on a theme by Diabelli
Symphony No. 7 in E major (sketched
    only)
Alfonso und Estrella, opera (1821–22)

1822 (25) Symphony No. 8 in B minor, *Unfinished*

1823 (26) *Fierrabras,* opera
Die häusliche Krieg, opera
Rosamunde, incidental music
Piano Sonata No. 14 in A minor
Die Schöne Mullerin, song cycle

1824 (27) Octet in F major, for strings and wind
    instruments
String Quartet No. 13 in A minor
String Quartet No. 14 in D minor, *Death
    and the Maiden*
Cello Sonata in A minor, *Arpeggione*
Introduction and Variations for flute and
    piano, in E minor

1825 (28) Piano Sonata No. 15 in C major
Piano Sonata No. 16 in A minor
Piano Sonata No. 17 in D major

1826 (29) String Quartet No. 15
Piano Trio in B♭ major
Rondo Brillant, for violin and piano, in
    B minor
Piano Sonata No. 18 in G major

1827 (30) Piano Trio in E♭ major
Phantasie, for violin and piano, in C major
Die Winterreise, song cycle
1828 (31) Symphony No. 9, *The Great C major*
String Quintet in C major
Piano Sonata No. 19 in C minor
Piano Sonata No. 20 in A major
Piano Sonata No. 21 in B♭ major
Schwanengesang, song cycle
Schubert also composed more than 600 songs.

SCHUMAN, William/b.1910/U.S.A.

1934 (24) *Choreographic Poem,* for seven
instruments
1935 (25) Symphony No. 1, for eighteen
instruments
1936 (26) String Quartet No. 1
1937 (27) Symphony No. 2
String Quartet No. 2
Choral étude
1939 (29) *American Festival Overture*
Quartettino, for four bassoons
String Quartet No. 3
Prelude for Voices
1940 (30) Secular Cantata No. 1, *This is our time*
1941 (31) Symphony No. 3
Symphony No. 4
Newsreel Suite, for orchestra
1942 (32) Piano Concerto
Secular Cantata No. 2, *A free song*
Requiescat
1943 (33) *William Billings Overture*
Symphony No. 5, for strings
A prayer in time of war, for orchestra
1944 (34) *Circus Overture*
Te Deum
1945 (35) *Undertow,* ballet
1947 (37) *Night Journey,* ballet
Violin Concerto
1948 (38) Symphony No. 6
1949 (39) *Judith,* ballet

1950 (40) String Quartet No. 4
1953 (43) *The Mighty Casey,* baseball opera
               Voyage, for piano
1955 (45) *Credendum,* for orchestra
1956 (46) *New England Triptych,* for orchestra
1957 (47) *Prologues,* for chorus and orchestra
1959 (49) *Three Moods,* for piano
1960 (50) Symphony No. 7
1962 (52) *Song of Orpheus,* fantasy for cello and
               orchestra
1963 (53) Symphony No. 8
1964 (54) Symphony No. 9
               String Trio
1969 (59) *In Praise of Shahn,* canticle for orchestra
1973 (63) *Concerto on Old English rounds,* for solo
               viola, women's chorus and orchestra

SCHUMANN, Robert/1810–1856/Germany

1829–31 (19–21) *Papillons,* twelve pieces for piano
1830 (20) *Theme and Variations on the name Abegg,*
               for piano
1832 (22) Six Concert Studies on Caprices by
               Paganini, Set I
1833 (23) Six Concert Studies on Caprices by
               Paganini, Set II
1834–35 (24) *Carnaval* (Scènes mignonnes), twenty-
               one piano pieces
1836 (26) *Phantasie* in C major, for piano
1837 (27) *Fantasiestücke,* for piano, Books I and II
               p. *Études symphoniques,* twelve
               symphonic studies for piano
               Davidsbündler-Tänze, eighteen piano
               pieces (revised 1850)
1838 (28) *Kinderscenen,* thirteen short piano pieces
               Kreisleriana, for piano (dedicated to
               Chopin)
               Novelleten, eight piano pieces
1839 (29) *Nachtstücke,* for piano
1840 (30) *Dichterliebe* (Poet's Love), song cycle
               Frauenliebe und -leben, song cycle
               Liederkreis, nine songs (Heine)

249

1841 (31) Symphony No. 1, *Spring,* in B♭ major
Symphony No. 4 in D minor (withdrawn
and revised in 1851)
Overture, Scherzo and Finale, for orchestra
(*Finale* revised 1845)
Piano Concerto in A minor (1841–45)

1842 (32) Piano Quintet in E♭ major
Piano Quartet in E♭ major
Four *Fantasiestücke* for piano trio, in Am:
F: Fm: Am
Andante and Variations, for two pianos,
two cellos and horn (best known as
duet for two pianos) (1842?)
Three String Quartets, in Am: F: A
Liederkreis, twelve songs (Eichendorff)

1843 (33) *Das Paradies und die Peri,* cantata

1845–46 (35) Symphony No. 2 in C major

1847 (37) *Genoveva,* opera (1847–48)
Piano Trio No. 1 in D minor and D major
Piano Trio No. 2 in F major

1849 (39) *Manfred,* dramatic poem
Three *Fantasiestücke,* for piano and
clarinet with violin or cello ad lib, in
Am: A: A
Adagio and Allegro, for piano and horn,
in A♭ major

1850 (40) Symphony No. 3 in E♭ major, *Rhenish*
Cello Concerto in A minor

1851 (41) Piano Trio No. 3 in G minor and G major
Violin Sonata in A minor
Violin Sonata in D minor
Four *Marchenbilder,* for piano and viola
(or violin)

1853 (43) Violin Concerto
Märchenerzählungen, four pieces for
piano, clarinet (or violin), and viola
Introduction and Allegro, for piano
Fantasy, for violin

1854 (44) p. *Albumblätter,* twenty pieces for piano

SCHÜTZ, Heinrich/1585–1672/Germany

1611 (26) *p.* Italian Madrigals
1619 (34) *p.* Psalms and Motets
          p. Psalmen Davids, for two, three or four
                choirs of voices and instruments
1623 (38) *Resurrection Oratorio*
          Easter Oratorio
          p. Historia der Auferstehung Jesu Christi,
                for voices and instruments
1625 (40) *p. Cantiones sacrae,* for four voices
1627 (42) *fp. Dafne,* opera
1629 (44) *p. Symphoniae sacrae,* Part I
1636 (51) *Musicalische exequien* (Funeral music)
          Kleine Geistliche Concerte, Book I
1638 (53) *fp. Orpheus and Euridice,* ballet
1639 (54) *Kleine Geistliche Concerte,* Book II
1645 (60) *The Seven Words from the Cross,* choral
1647 (62) *p. Symphoniae sacrae,* Part II
1648 (63) *p.* Musicali ad chorum sacrum
1650 (65) *p. Symphoniae sacrae,* Part III
1664 (79) *Christmas Oratorio*
1665–66 (80) Four Passions *(Matthew, Mark, Luke*
                and John)
1671 (86) *Deutsches Magnificat*

SEIBER, Mátyás/1905–1960/Hungary

1924 (19) String Quartet No. 1
          Sarabande and Gigue, for cello and piano
          Missa Brevis, for unaccompanied chorus
1925 (20) *Serenade,* for six wind instruments
          Sonata da Camera, for cello and violin
1926–28 (21–23) *Divertimento,* for clarinet and
                string quartet
1934 (29) *Eva spielt mit Puppen,* opera
          String Quartet No. 2 (1934–35)
1940 (35) *Besardo Suite* No. 1
1941 (36) *Besardo Suite No. 2,* for strings
          Transylvanian Rhapsody
          Fantasy, for cello and piano

251

> *Pastorale and Burlesque,* for flute and
> strings (1941–42)
1942 (37) *Balaton,* opera
> *La Blanchisseuse,* ballet music
1943–44 (38) *Fantasia Concertante,* for violin and
> strings
1944 (39) *Notturno,* for horn and strings
1945 (40) *Phantasy,* for flute, horn and strings
1948 (43) *Johnny Miner,* radio opera
> String Quartet No. 3, *Quartetto lyrico*
> (1948–51)
1949 (44) *Ulysses,* cantata (possibly 1946–47)
> *Andantino and Pastorale,* for clarinet and
> piano
1951 (46) *The Seasons*
> *Concertino,* for clarinet and strings
1953 (48) Three pieces for cello and orchestra
1954 (49) *Elegy,* for violin and small orchestra
> *To Poetry,* song cycle
1958 (53) *Permutazione a cinque,* for flute, oboe,
> clarinet, horn and bassoon
> *Portrait of the Artist as a Young Man,*
> chamber cantata
1959 (54) *Improvisation for Jazz Band and
> Symphony Orchestra* (with Dankworth)
1960 (55) *Invitation,* ballet
> *A Three-cornered Fanfare*
1962 (posthumous) *p.* Violin Sonata

SESSIONS, Roger/b.1896/U.S.A.

1923 (27) *The Black Maskers,* incidental music
1927 (31) Symphony No. 1
1930 (34) Piano Sonata No. 1
1935 (39) Violin Concerto, with orchestra which
> includes five clarinets but no violins
1936 (40) String Quartet No. 1
1938 (42) *Scherzino and March,* for orchestra
1939 (43) *Pages from a Diary* (From My Diary),
> for piano
1942 (46) Duo for violin and piano
1944–46 (48–50) Symphony No. 2

1946 (50) Piano Sonata No. 2
1947 (51) *fp. The Trial of Lucullus,* opera
1951 (55) String Quartet No. 2
1953 (57) Sonata for solo violin
1954 (58) *The Idyll of Theocritus,* for soprano and
orchestra
1955 (59) Mass, for unison male voices and organ
1956 (60) Piano Concerto
1957 (61) Symphony No. 3
1958 (62) Symphony No. 4
String Quintet
1960 (64) *Divertimento,* for orchestra
1963 (67) *Psalm 140,* for soprano with organ or
orchestra
1964 (68) Symphony No. 5
1965 (69) Piano Sonata No. 3
1966 (70) Symphony No. 6
Six pieces for cello
1967 (71) Symphony No. 7
1968 (72) Symphony No. 8
1970 (74) *Rhapsody,* for orchestra
*When Lilacs Last in the Dooryard
Bloom'd,* cantata
1971 (75) Concerto for viola and cello
1975 (79) Three choruses on Biblical texts
Sessions also composed *Montezuma,* an opera.

SHAPERO, Harold Samuel/b.1920/U.S.A.

1938 (18) *Three Pieces for Three Pieces,* for
woodwind trio
1939 (19) Trumpet Sonata
1940 (20) String Quartet
1941 (21) *Nine-minute Overture*
Piano Sonata (four hands)
1942 (22) Violin Sonata
1944 (24) *Three amateur sonatas,* for piano
1945 (25) *Serenade* in D major, for string orchestra
1947 (27) Piano Sonata No. 1
1948 (28) *Symphony for classical orchestra*
The Travellers, for orchestra
1951–58 (31–38) Concerto for orchestra

1955 (35) *Credo*, for orchestra
1958 (38) *On Green Mountain*, for jazz combo
1960 (40) *Partita*, for piano and orchestra
Shapero also composed:
Pocahontas, ballet
The Minotaurs, ballet
The Defence of Corinth, for men's voices and piano
  (four hands)
Emblems, for men's voices
Hebrew Cantata
Sinfonia in C major
Variations in C major, for piano.

SHAPEY, Ralph/b.1921/U.S.A.

1946 (25) String Quartet No. 1
          Piano Sonata
1947 (26) Piano Quintet
1949 (28) String Quartet No. 2
          Three Essays on Thomas Wolfe, for piano
1950 (29) Violin Sonata
1951 (30) *Fantasy*, for orchestra
          String Quartet No. 3
          Cantata, for soprano, tenor, bass, narrator,
              chamber orchestra and percussion
1952 (31) Symphony No. 1
          Quartet for oboe and string trio
          Oboe Sonata
          Suite for piano
1953 (32) String Quartet No. 4
          Cello Sonata
1954 (33) Concerto for clarinet, with violin, cello,
              piano, horn, tom-tom and bass drum
          Sonata-Variations, for piano
1955 (34) *Challenge—The Family of Man*, for
              orchestra
          Piano Trio
1956 (35) *Mutations No. 1*, for piano
1957 (36) String Quartet No. 5, with female voices
              (1957–58)
          Rhapsodie, for oboe and piano
          Duo for viola and piano

1958 (37)   *Ontogeny,* for orchestra
          Walking Upright, eight songs for female
            voice and violin
1959 (38) Violin Concerto
          Rituals, for orchestra
          Soliloquy, for narrator, string quartet and
            percussion
          Evocation, for violin, piano and percussion
          Form, for piano
1960 (39) *Dimensions,* for soprano and twenty-three
            instruments
          De Profundis, for solo contrabass and
            instruments
          Movements, for woodwind quartet
          Five, for violin and piano
          This Day, for female voice and piano
1961 (40) *Incantations,* for soprano and ten
            instruments
          Discourse, for flute, clarinet, violin and
            piano
1962 (41) *Chamber Symphony,* for ten solo players
          Convocation, for chamber group
          Piece, for violin and instruments
          Birthday Piece, for piano
1963 (42) Brass Quintet
          String Quartet No. 6
          Seven, for piano (four hands)
1965 (44) String Trio
          Configurations, for flute and piano
1966 (45) *Partita,* for violin and thirteen players
          Poème, for violin and piano
          Mutations No. 2, for piano
          Partita, for solo violin
1967 (46) *Partita-Fantasy,* for cello and sixteen
            players
          Reyem, for flute, violin and piano
          Deux, for two pianos
          For Solo Trumpet
          Songs of Ecstasy, for soprano, piano,
            percussion and tape

1919 (13) Scherzo in F♯ minor, for orchestra
Eight Preludes for piano
1920–21 (14–15) Five Preludes for piano
1921–22 (15–16) Theme with Variations, in B major,
for orchestra
1922 (16) *Two Fables of Krilov*, for mezzo-soprano
and orchestra
Three Fantastic Dances, for piano
Suite in F♯ minor, for two pianos
1923 (17) Piano Trio No. 1
1924 (18) Symphony No. 1 in F minor (1924–25)
Scherzo in E♭, for orchestra
Prelude and Scherzo, for string octet
(double string quartet) or string
orchestra (1924–25)
1926 (20) Piano Sonata No. 1
1927 (21) *The Nose*, opera (1927–28)
The Age of Gold, ballet (1927–30)
Symphony No. 2 in B major, *October*,
with chorus
Aphorisms, ten pieces for piano
1928 (22) *New Babylon*, for orchestra (film music)
Six Romances on words by Japanese poets,
for tenor and orchestra (1928–32)
1929 (23) Symphony No. 3 in E♭ major, *The First of
May*, with chorus
1930 (24) *The Bolt*, choreographic spectacle
(1930–31)
Alone, film music (1930–31)
Lady Macbeth of the Mtsensk District,
opera (1930–32)
1931–32 (25) *Hamlet*, incidental music
1932 (26) *From Karl Marx to our own days*,
symphonic poem for solo voices, chorus
and orchestra
Encounter, film music
Twenty-four Preludes for piano
(1932–33)
1933 (27) Piano Concerto No. 1 in C minor, for
piano, string orchestra and trumpet

                    The Human Comedy, incidental music
                         (1933–34)
1934 (28) *Bright Stream*, comedy ballet (1934–35)
                    Suite for Jazz Orchestra, No. 1
                    Cello Sonata in D minor
                    Girl Companions, film music (1934–35)
                    Love and Hate, film music
                    Maxim's Youth (The Bolshevik), film
                         music (1934–35)
1935 (29) Symphony No. 4 in C minor
                    Five Fragments, for small orchestra
1936 (30) *Salute to Spain*, incidental music
                    Four Romances on Verses of Pushkin, for
                         bass and piano
                    Maxim's Return, film music
                    Volochayevka Days, film music
1937 (31) Symphony No. 5 in D minor
1938 (32) Suite for Jazz Orchestra, No. 2
                    String Quartet No. 1 in C major
                    Friends, film music
                    The Great Citizen, film music
                    Man at Arms, film music
                    Vyborg District, film music
1939 (33) Symphony No. 6 in B minor
                    The Great Citizen, Part II, film music
1940 (34) Piano Quintet in G minor
                    Three pieces for solo violin
                    King Lear, incidental music
1941 (35) Symphony No. 7 in C major, *Leningrad*
                    The Gamblers, opera
1942 (36) *Native Leningrad*, suite included in the
                         theater show "Motherland"
                    Piano Sonata No. 2
                    Six Romances on verses of English poets,
                         for bass and piano
1943 (37) Symphony No. 8 in C minor
1944 (38) *Russian River*, suite
                    String Quartet No. 2, in A major
                    Piano Trio No. 2
                    Children's Notebook, six pieces for piano
                    Eight English and American Folk-songs,
                         for low voice and orchestra
                    Zoya, film music

1945 (39) Symphony No. 9 in E♭ major
Two Songs
Simple Folk, film music
1946 (40) String Quartet No. 3, in F major
1947 (41) Violin Concerto No. 1 (1947–48)
Poem of the Motherland, cantata
Pirogov, film music
Young Guards, film music
1948 (42) *From Jewish Folk poetry,* song cycle for
soprano, contralto, tenor and piano
Meeting on the Elbe, film music
Michurin, film music
1949 (43) Ballet Suite No. 1, for orchestra
String Quartet No. 4 in D major
The Song of the Forests, oratorio
The Fall of Berlin, film music
1950 (44) Twenty-Four Preludes and Fugues, for
piano (1950–51)
Two Romances on verses by Mikhail
Lermontov, for male voice and piano
Byelinski, film music
1951 (45) Ballet Suite No. 2, for orchestra
Ten poems on texts by Revolutionary
poets, for chorus a cappella
The Memorable Year 1919, film music
1952 (46) Ballet Suite No. 3, for orchestra
String Quartet No. 5 in B♭ major
Four Monologues on verses of Pushkin,
for bass and piano
The Sun shines over our Motherland,
cantata
1953 (47) Symphony No. 10 in E minor
Ballet Suite No. 4, for orchestra
Concertino, for two pianos
1954 (48) *Festival Overture.* for orchestra
Five Romances (Songs of our Days), for
bass and piano
1955 (49) *The Gadfly,* film music
1956 (50) *Katerina Ismailova,* opera (new version
of *Lady Macbeth of Mtensk*)
String Quartet No. 6 in G major
Spanish Songs, for soprano and piano
The First Echelon, film music

1957 (51) Piano Concerto No. 2 in F major
Symphony No. 11 in G minor, *The Year 1905*
1958 (52) *Moscow, Cheremushki,* musical comedy
1959 (53) Cello Concerto No. 1 in E♭ major
1960 (54) *Novorossiysk Chimes* (The Fire of Eternal Glory), for orchestra
String Quartet No. 7 in F♯ minor
String Quartet No. 8 in C minor
Satires (Pictures of the Past), for soprano and piano
Five Days—Five Nights, film music
1961 (55) Symphony No. 12 in D minor, *1917*
1962 (56) Symphony No. 13 in B♭ minor, *Babi-Yar,* for bass solo, bass choir and orchestra
1963 (57) Overture on Russian and Kirghiz Folk Themes, for orchestra
Hamlet, film music
1964 (58) String Quartet No. 9, in E♭ major
String Quartet No. 10 in A♭ major
The Execution of Stepan Razin, cantata
1965 (59) Five Romances on texts from *Krokodil* magazine, for bass and piano
1966 (60) Cello Concerto No. 2 in G major
String Quartet No. 11 in F minor
Preface to the Complete Collection of my Works, and Brief Reflections apropos this Preface, for bass and grand piano
1967 (61) Violin Concerto No. 2 in C♯ minor
Funeral-Triumphal Prelude, for orchestra
October, symphonic poem
Spring, Spring, for bass and grand piano
Sofya Perovoskaya, film music
Seven Romances on poems of Alexander Blok, for soprano and piano trio
1968 (62) String Quartet No. 12 in D♭ major
Sonata, for violin and grand piano
1969 (63) Symphony No. 14, for soprano, bass, string orchestra and percussion
1970 (64) *March of the Soviet Militia,* for wind orchestra
String Quartet No. 13 in B♭ minor

    Loyalty, eight ballads for male chorus
    King Lear, film music
1971 (65) Symphony No. 15 in A major
1972–73 (66) String Quartet No. 14 in F♯ major
1973 (67) Six poems of Marina Tsvetaeva, suite for
     contralto and piano
1974 (68) String Quartet No. 15, in E♭ minor
    Suite on verses of Michelangelo
     Buonarroti, for bass and piano
    Four verses of Capitan Lebjadkin, for bass
     and piano
1975 (69) Sonata for viola and grand piano
    The Dreamers, ballet (largely drawn from
     The Age of Gold and *The Bolt,* with
     some new material)
It is believed that Shostakovich had completed two
movements of Symphony No. 16 just before his death,
but this has not so far been confirmed by the Soviet
authorities.

SIBELIUS, Jean/1865–1957/Finland

1881–82 (16–17) Piano Trio in F minor
    Piano Quartet in E minor
1885 (20) Quartet in E♭ major
1888 (23) Theme and Variations for quartet, in C♯
     minor
1889 (24) Piano Quintet
    Quartet in B♭ major
    Suite for violin, viola and cello
    Violin Sonata in F major
1890–91 (25) Overture in A minor
    Overture in E major
1891 (26) *Scène de ballet*
    Piano Quartet in C major
1892 (27) *En Saga,* symphonic poem (revised 1901)
    Kullervo, symphonic poem
1893 (28) *Karelia,* overture
    Karelia, suite, for orchestra
    The Swan of Tuonela, for orchestra (No. 3
     of *Four Legends from Kalevala*)
1894 (29) *Spring Song,* symphonic poem

1895 (30) *Cassazione*
              Lemminkäinen and the Maidens (No. 1 of
                the *Four Legends from Kalevala*)
              Lemminkäinen in Tuonela (No. 2 of the
                Four Legends from Kalevala)
              Lemminkäinen's Homecoming (No. 4 of
                the *Four Legends from Kalevala*)

1896 (31) *The Girl in the Tower*, opera (unpublished)

1898 (33) *King Christian II*, incidental music
              Symphony No. 1 in E minor (1898–99)

1899 (34) *Scènes historiques*, Suite No. 1, three
                orchestral pieces

1900 (35) *Finlandia*, symphonic poem

1901 (36) Symphony No. 2 in D major
              Cortège
              Portraits, for strings

1903 (38) Violin Concerto in D minor (revised
                1905)
              Romance, for strings

1904 (39) *Kuolema*, incidental music, includes "Valse
                Triste"
              Symphony No. 3 in C major (1904–07)

1905 (40) *Pelléas et Mélisande*, incidental music

1906 (41) *Pohjola's Daughter*, symphonic fantasia

1908 (43) String Quartet in five movements, *Voces
                Intimae*

1909 (44) *Night-ride and Sunrise*, tone poem

1911 (46) Symphony No. 4 in A minor
              Rakastava Suite
              Valse Romantique
              Canzonetta, for strings

1912 (47) *Scènes historiques*, Suite No. 2, three
                orchestral pieces
              Two *Serenades*, for violin

1913 (48) *Scaramouche*, pantomime
              Il Bardo, symphonic poem

1914 (49) *Oceanides*, symphonic poem
              Symphony No. 5 in E♭ major (1914–15)

1916 (51) *Everyman*, incidental music

1922 (57) *Suite caractéristique* (Vivo, Lento,
              Commodo)

1923 (58) Symphony No. 6 in D minor

1924 (59) Symphony No. 7 in C major, in one
movement
1925 (60) *Tapiola*, symphonic poem
1926 (61) *The Tempest*, incidental music

SKRIABIN, Alexander/1872–1915/Russia

1894 (22) Piano Concerto
Réverie, for orchestra
1895 (23) Symphony No. 1 in E major
1901 (29) Symphony No. 2 in C minor
1903 (31) Symphony No. 3 in C major, *The Divine
Poem*
1908 (36) *Poem of Ecstasy*, for orchestra
1909–10 (38) *Poem of Fire—Prometheus*, for
orchestra, piano, chorus "ad lib", organ
and colour keyboard
Skriabin also composed:
10 piano sonatas (1892–1913)
84 preludes for piano
21 mazurkas for piano
8 impromptus for piano
23 studies for piano
15 "poems" for piano

SMETANA, Bedřich/1824–1884/Bohemia
(Czechoslovakia)

1848–49 (24) *Festive Overture*, in D major
1853–54 (29) *Festive Symphony*, in E major
1855 (31) Piano Trio in G minor
1858 (34) *Richard III*, symphonic poem
Wallenstein's Camp, symphonic poem
(1858–59)
1860–61 (36) *Haakon Jarl*, symphonic poem
1862 (38) *On the Sea-shore*, for piano
1863 (39) *The Brandenburgers in Bohemia*, opera
1866 (42) *The Bartered Bride*, opera
1868 (44) *fp. Dalibor*, opera
Solemn Prelude in C major, for orchestra
1874 (50) *The Two Widows*, opera

262

                    Ma Vlast, six symphonic poems:
                        Vyšehrad (The High Castle)
                        Vltava
                        Sàrka
                        From Bohemia's Woods and Fields
                        Tabor
                        Blanik
1876 (52)   *The Kiss*, opera
            String Quartet No. 1, *From My Life*, in
                E minor
1878 (54)   *The Secret*, opera ·
            Czech Dances
1881 (57)   *fp. Libuse*, opera
1882 (58)   String Quartet No. 2 in D minor
1883 (59)   *The Prague Carnival*
            String Quartet No. 2

SMYTH, Ethel/1858–1944/Great Britain

1887 (29)   Violin Sonata in A minor
1890 (32)   *Anthony and Cleopatra*, overture
            Serenade in D major, for orchestra
1891 (33)   Suite for strings
1893 (35)   Mass in D major
1898 (40)   *Fantastic*, opera
1901 (43)   *The Forest*, opera
1902 (44)   String Quartet in E minor (completed
                c.1912)
1906 (48)   *The Wreckers*, opera
1911 (53)   *March of the Women*, for orchestra
            Three Songs of Sunrise, for unaccompanied
                chorus
1916 (58)   *The Boatswain's Mate*, opera
1920 (62)   *Dreamings*
1923 (65)   *Fête galante*, opera
            Soul's Joy, for unaccompanied chorus
1926 (68)   *Entente Cordial*, opera
            A Spring Canticle, for chorus and
                orchestra
            Sleepless Dreams, for chorus and
                orchestra

1927 (69) Concerto for Violin and Horn (also
            known as Horn Concerto)
1930 (72) *The Prison*, for unaccompanied chorus

SOWERBY, Leo/1895–1968/U.S.A.

1916 (21) Woodwind Quintet
1917 (22) Piano Concerto No. 1 (revised 1919)
            Serenade, for string quartet
            Comes Autumn Time, for organ
1919 (24) Trio for flute, viola and piano
1920 (25) Cello Sonata
            The Edge of Dreams, song cycle
1921 (26) Symphony No. 1
            Violin Sonata No. 1
1922 (27) *From the Northland*, for piano
            Ballad of King Estmere, for two pianos
            and orchestra
1924 (29) *Synconata*, for jazz orchestra
1925 (30) *From the Northland*, for orchestra
            The Vision of Sir Launfal, for chorus and
            orchestra
            Monotony, for jazz orchestra
1926 (31) *Mediaeval Poem*, for organ and orchestra
1928 (33) Symphony No. 2
1929 (34) Cello Concerto (1929–34)
            Prairie, symphonic poem
            Florida Suite, for piano
1930 (35) Organ Symphony
1931 (36) *Passacaglia, Interlude and Fugue*, for
            orchestra
1932 (37) Piano Concerto No. 2
1936 (41) Organ Concerto No. 1
1938 (43) *Theme in Yellow*, for orchestra
            Clarinet Sonata
1939 (44) *Forsaken of Man*, cantata
1940 (45) Symphony No. 3
1941 (46) *Poem*, for viola with organ or orchestra
1944 (49) *Classic Concerto*, for organ and strings
            Violin Sonata No. 2
            Canticle of the Sun, cantata
1945 (50) Trumpet Sonata

1947 (52) Symphony No. 4
1949 (54) *Ballade,* for English horn and strings
1950 (55) *Christ Reborn,* cantata
1951 (56) *Concert Piece,* for organ and orchestra
1952 (57) String Trio
1954 (59) *All on a Summer's Day,* for orchestra
           Fantasy, for trumpet and organ
1957 (62) *The Throne of God,* for chorus and
           orchestra
1959 (64) *Ask of the Covenant,* cantata
1964 (69) Symphony No. 5
           Piano Sonata
1965 (70) *Solomon's Garden,* for chorus and
           orchestra
1966 (71) *Symphonia Brevis,* for organ
1967 (72) *Dialogue,* for organ and piano
           Organ Concerto No. 2
           Organ Passacaglia
Sowerby also composed over 300 songs.

SPONTINI, Gasparo/1774–1851/Italy

1807 (33) *La Vestale,* opera
1809 (35) *Ferdinand Cortez,* opera
1819 (45) *Olympie,* opera
1821 (47) *Nurmahal,* opera
1829 (55) *Agnes von Hohenstaufen,* opera

STANFORD, Charles Villiers/1852–1924/
  Great Britain

1876 (24) Symphony in B♭ major
1877 (25) *Festival Overture*
1881 (29) *The Veiled Prophet,* opera
1882 (30) *Elegiac Symphony,* in D minor
           Serenade, in G major, for orchestra
1884 (32) *Canterbury Pilgrims,* opera
           Savonarola, opera
1886 (34) *The Revenge,* choral-ballad
1887 (35) *Queen of the Seas,* overture

265

　　　　　　　Irish Symphony in F minor
　　　　　　　Prelude *Oedipus Rex*
1888 (36)　Symphony in F major
1891 (39)　*Eden,* oratorio
1894 (42)　Symphony in D major, *L'Allegro ed il*
　　　　　　　　Pensiero
1895 (43)　Piano Concerto No. 1 in G major
　　　　　　　Suite of Ancient Dances
1896 (44)　*Shamus O'Brien,* opera
1898 (46)　Te Deum
1899 (47)　Evening Service in C major
1901 (49)　*Much Ado About Nothing,* opera
　　　　　　　Irish Rhapsody No. 1 in D minor
1904 (52)　Violin Concerto No. 1 in D major
　　　　　　　Evening Service in G major
1907 (55)　Stabat Mater
1911 (59)　Symphony No. 7 in D minor
1914 (62)　*Irish Rhapsody* No. 4 in A minor
1915 (63)　Piano Concerto No. 2 in C minor
1916 (64)　*The Critic,* opera
1925 (posthumous)　*fp. The Travelling Companion,*
　　　　　　　　opera

STOCKHAUSEN, Karlheinz/b.1928/Germany

1950 (22)　*Chöre für Doris,* three movements for
　　　　　　　　mixed choir a cappella
　　　　　　　Three Lieder, for voice and chamber
　　　　　　　　orchestra: 1) Der Rebell, 2) Frei,
　　　　　　　　3) Der Saitenmann
　　　　　　　Choral, for mixed choir a cappella
1951 (23)　*Sonatine,* for violin and piano
　　　　　　　Kreuzspiel, for oboe, bass-clarinet, piano
　　　　　　　　and percussion
　　　　　　　Formel, for orchestra
1952 (24)　*Étude,* musique concrète
　　　　　　　Spiel, for orchestra
　　　　　　　Schlagtrio, for piano and timpani
　　　　　　　Punkte, for orchestra
　　　　　　　Kontra-punkte, for ten instruments
　　　　　　　　(1952–53)
　　　　　　　Klavierstücke I–IV (1952–53)

1953 (25) *Elektronische Studie I,* electronic music
1954 (26) *Elektronische Studie II,* electronic music
    Klavierstücke V–VIII (1954–55)
    Klavierstücke IX–X (revised 1961)
1955–56 (27) *Gruppen,* for three orchestras
    (1955–57)
    Zeitmasze, for oboe, flute, English horn,
    clarinet and bassoon
    Gesang der Jünglinge, electronic music
1956 (28) *Klavierstücke XI*
1959 (31) *Carré,* for four orchestras and four choirs
    (1959–60)
    Refrain, for piano, celesta and percussion
    Zyklus, for one percussionist
    Kontakte, for electronic sound (1959–60)
1962–64 (34–36) *Momente,* for soprano solo, four
    choral groups and thirteen
    instrumentalists
1963 (35) *Plus Minus,* 2 x 7 pages "for working out"
1964 (36) *Mikrophonie I,* for mixed media
    Mixtur, for five orchestral groups and
    electronics
1965 (37) *Mikrophonie II,* for choir, Hammond
    organ, electronic instruments and tape
    Stop, for orchestra
    Solo (1965–66)
1966 (38) *Telemusik,* electronic music
    Adieu, for flute, oboe, clarinet, horn and
    bassoon
    Hymnen, for electronics and music
    concrète (4-channel tape)
1967 (39) *Prozession,* for Tam-tam, viola,
    elektronium, piano and electronics
1968 (40) *Stimmung,* for six vocalists
    Kurzwellen, for piano, amplified
    instruments and electronics
    Aus den Sieben Tagen, fifteen
    compositions for ensemble
    Spiral, for one soloist with short-wave
    receiver
    Für Kommende Zeiten, seventeen texts
    for intuitive music

1969 (41) *For Dr. K.,* for flute, bass clarinet,
　　　　　　　　percussion, piano, viola and cello
　　　　　　Fresco, for four orchestral groups
　　　　　　Pole für 2 (1969–70)
　　　　　　Expo für 3 (1969–70)
1970 (42) *Mantra,* for two pianists
　　　　　　Sternklang, for five groups
　　　　　　Trans, for orchestra
1972 (44) *Alphabet für Liège*
　　　　　　Am Himmel Wandre Ich . . . ,
　　　　　　　　Indianerlieder
　　　　　　Ylem, for nineteen players/singers
1973–74 (45) *Inori,* for soloist and orchestra
1974 (46) *Atmen gibt das leben . . . ,* for mixed choir
　　　　　　Herbstmusik
　　　　　　Vortrag uber Hu, for solo voice
1975 (47) *Musik im Bauch*
　　　　　　Tierkreis (Zodiac)

STRAUSS (Jr), Johann/1825–1899/Austria

1867 (42) *Blue Danube Waltz*
1868 (43) *Tales from the Vienna Woods*
1871 (46) *Indigo und die vierzig Rauber,* operetta
1874 (49) *Die Fledermaus,* operetta
1883 (58) *Eine Nacht in Venedig,* operetta
1885 (60) *Zigeunerbaron,* operetta
1887 (62) *Simplizius,* operetta
1895 (70) *Waldmeister,* operetta

STRAUSS, Richard/1864–1949/Germany

1876 (12) *Festmarch,* for orchestra
1879 (15) Overture in A minor
1880 (16) Symphony in D minor
　　　　　　String Quartet in A major
1881–82 (17) Violin Concerto in D minor
1882–83 (18) Horn Concerto No. 1 in E♭ major
1883 (19) *Concert Overture* in C minor
　　　　　　Piano Quartet in C minor (1883–84)

1884 (20)   Symphony in F minor
        p. Serenade for Wind
        p. Cello Sonata in F major
1886 (22)   *Aus Italien*, symphonic fantasia
        Macbeth, symphonic poem (1886–90)
1888 (24)   *Don Juan*, symphonic poem
        p. Violin Sonata in E♭ major
1889 (25)   *Tod und Verklaerung*, symphonic poem
1892–93 (28)   *Guntram*, opera (new version, 1940)
1894 (30)   *Also sprach Zarathustra*, symphonic poem
1895 (31)   *Till Eulenspiegel*, symphonic poem
1896 (32)   *Don Quixote*, fantasy variations for cello
        and orchestra
1898 (34)   *Ein Heldenleben*, symphonic poem
1901 (37)   *Feuersnot*, opera
1904 (40)   *Symphonia Domestica*
1905 (41)   *Salome*, opera
1906–08 (42–44)   *Elektra*, opera
1909–10 (45)   *Der Rosenkavalier*, opera
1912 (48)   *Ariadne auf Naxos*, opera
1913 (49)   *Alpine Symphony*
1914 (50)   *Josephs-Legend*, ballet
        Die Frau ohne Schatten, opera (1914–17)
1921 (57)   *Schlagobers*, ballet
1922–23 (58)   *Intermezzo*, opera
1924–27 (60–63)   *The Egyptian Helen*, opera
1930–32 (66–68)   *Arabella*, opera
1934 (70)   Symphony for wind instruments
1935 (71)   *The Silent Woman*, opera
        Der Friedenstag, opera (1935–36)
1936–37 (72)   *Daphne*, opera
1938–40 (74–76)   *The Love of Danae*, opera
        (*fp.*1952)
1940–41 (76)   *Capriccio*, opera
1942 (78)   Horn Concerto No. 2 in E♭ major
1945 (81)   *Metamorphoses*, for twenty-three solo
        instruments
        Oboe Concerto
1948 (84)   *Duet Concertino*, for clarinet, bassoon
        and strings
1950 (posthumous)   *fp.* Four Last Songs
Strauss also composed many songs.

1905–07 (23–25) Symphony in E♭ major
1908 (26) *Scherzo fantastique*
           Fireworks, for orchestra
           Lament on the Death of Rimsky-Korsakov,
              for chorus and orchestra
1910 (28) *The Firebird*, ballet
           Petrouchka, ballet (1910–11, revised
              1946–47)
1911 (29) *The King of the Stars*, cantata
1913 (31) *The Rite of Spring*, ballet
1914 (32) *Le Rossignol* (The Nightingale), lyric tale
              in three acts (1908–14, revised 1962)
           Chansons plaisants, for voice and small
              orchestra
           Three pieces for string quartet
1915 (33) *Rénard*, a burlesque
1916 (34) *Berceuse du Chat*, for voice and three
              clarinets
1917 (35) *Les Noces*, cantata-ballet (1917–23)
           Song of the Nightingale, symphonic poem
           The Soldier's Tale, opera-ballet
1918 (36) *Ragtime*, for eleven instruments
           Four Russian Songs
1920 (38) *Pulcinella*, ballet suite, after Pergolesi
           Symphonies for Wind Instruments
           Concertino, for string quartet
1921–22 (39) *Mavra*, opera buffe in one act
1922–23 (40) *Octet for Wind Instruments* (revised
                 1952)
1924 (42) Concerto for piano and wind instruments
           Piano Sonata
1925 (43) *Serenade* in A major, for piano
1927 (45) *Oedipus Rex*, opera-oratorio
1928 (46) *Apollo Musagetes*, ballet
           Le Baiser de la Fée, ballet
1929 (47) *Capriccio*, for piano and orchestra
1930 (48) *Symphony of Psalms*, for chorus and
              orchestra
1931 (49) Violin Concerto in D major
1932 (50) *Duo Concertante*, for violin and piano

1933 (51) *Suite Italienne,* for cello and piano
1934 (52) *Persephone,* melodrama for narrator,
           tenor, chorus, children's choir and
           orchestra
1935 (53) Concerto for two pianos
1937 (55) *Jeu des Cartes,* ballet
1938 (56) *Dumbarton Oaks,* concerto for sixteen
           instruments, in E♭ major
1940 (58) Symphony in C major
1942 (60) *Danses concertantes*
           Norwegian Moods
           Polka for Circus Elephants
1944 (62) *Élégie,* for solo viola
           Sonata for two pianos
1945 (63) *Symphony in Three Movements*
1946 (64) *Ebony Concerto,* for clarinet and orchestra
           Concerto in D major for strings
1947 (65) *Orpheus,* ballet
1948 (66) *Mass,* for chorus and double wind quintet
1951 (69) *The Rake's Progress,* opera
           Mass, for horns and orchestra
1952 (70) Cantata on Old English Texts
1953 (71) Septet
           Three Songs from Shakespeare, for mezzo-
           soprano and piano
1954 (72) *In Memoriam Dylan Thomas,* for tenor,
           two tenor trombones, two bass
           trombones and string quartet
1955 (73) *Canticum sacrum*
1957 (75) *Agon,* ballet
           Threni (Lamentations of Jeremiah), for
           soloists, chorus and orchestra
1959 (77) *Movements,* for piano and orchestra
           Epitaphium, for flute, clarinet and harp
           Double Canon for string quartet
1960 (78) *Monumentus Pro Gesualdo,* for orchestra
1962 (80) *The Flood,* opera
           Abraham and Isaac, for baritone and
           orchestra
1963–64 (81) *In Memoriam Aldous Huxley,*
           variations for orchestra
1964 (82) *Elegy for J.F.K.,* for baritone or mezzo-
           soprano and three clarinets

> > *Fanfare for a new theater,* for two
> > trumpets
> **1966** (84) *Requiem Canticles,* for contralto and bass
> > soli, chorus and orchestra

SUK, Josef/1874–1935/Czechoslovakia

1888 (14) Mass in B♭ major
1889 (15) *Fantasy,* for strings
> Piano Trio in C minor (1889–90)
1891 (17) *Dramatic Overture*
> Piano Quartet in A minor
1892 (18) *Serenade for Strings*
1893 (19) Piano Quintet in B minor
1896 (22) String Quartet No. 1 in B♭ major
1899 (25) Symphony No. 1 in E major
1903 (29) *Fantasy,* for violin and orchestra
1904 (30) *Prague,* symphonic poem
> Symphony No. 2 in C minor, *Asrael*
> (1904–06)
1907 (33) *A Summer Tale,* symphonic poem
1910–11 (36) String Quartet No. 2
1914 (40) *Meditation on a theme of an old Bohemian
> chorale,* for string quartet
1917 (43) *Harvestide,* symphonic poem
1919 (45) *Legend of Dead Victors*
> *Towards a New Life*
1931 (57) Mass in B♭ major

SULLIVAN, Sir Arthur/1842–1900/Great Britain

1862 (20) *The Tempest,* incidental music
1864 (22) *L'Ile enchantée,* ballet music
> *Kenilworth,* cantata
1866 (24) Cello Concerto
> *Irish Symphony*
> *In Memoriam Overture*
1867 (25) *Cox and Box,* operetta (libretto, Burnand)
1869 (27) *The Prodigal Son,* oratorio
1870 (28) *Overture di Ballo,* concert overture
1873 (31) *The Light of the World,* oratorio

1875 (33)   *The Zoo,* operetta (libretto, Stephenson)
                Trial by Jury, operetta (libretto, Gilbert)
1877 (35)   *The Sorcerer,* operetta (libretto, Gilbert)
                "The Lost Chord", song
1878 (36)   *H.M.S. Pinafore,* operetta (libretto, Gilbert)
                Henry VIII, incidental music
                The Martyr of Antioch, oratorio
1880 (38)   *The Pirates of Penzance,* operetta (libretto, Gilbert)
1881 (39)   *Patience,* operetta (libretto, Gilbert)
1882 (40)   *Iolanthe,* operetta (libretto, Gilbert)
1884 (42)   *Princess Ida,* operetta (libretto, Gilbert)
1885 (43)   *The Mikado,* operetta (libretto, Gilbert)
1886 (44)   *The Golden Legend,* cantata
1887 (45)   *Ruddigore,* operetta (libretto, Gilbert)
1888 (46)   *The Yeomen of the Guard,* operetta (libretto, Gilbert)
1889 (47)   *The Gondoliers,* operetta (libretto, Gilbert)
1891 (49)   *Ivanhoe,* opera (libretto, Sturgis)
1892 (50)   *Haddon Hall,* opera (libretto, Grundy)
1893 (51)   *Utopia, Ltd.,* operetta (libretto, Gilbert)
1895 (53)   *The Chieftain,* operetta (libretto, Burnand)
1896 (54)   *The Grand Duke,* operetta (libretto, Gilbert)
1897 (55)   Te Deum
1898 (56)   *The Beauty Stone,* opera (libretto, Pinero and Conyers Carr)
1899 (57)   *The Rose of Persia,* operetta (libretto, Hood)
1901 (posthumous)   *The Emerald Isle,* operetta (libretto, Hood), completed by German *(q.v.)*

SWEELINCK, Jan/1562–1621/Holland

1592–94 (30–32)   *p. Chansons françaises,* in three parts
1612 (50)   *p. Rimes françoises et italiennes*
1619 (57)   *p. Cantiones sacrae*
Sweelinck also composed:

Psaeumes mis en musique
Many organ, harpsichord and choral (sacred and
  secular) works.

SZYMANOWSKI, Karol/1883–1937/Poland

1905 (22) *Concert Overture*
1907 (24) Symphony No. 1 in F minor
1909 (26) Symphony No. 2 in B♭ major
1912–13 (29) *Hagith,* opera
1915–16 (32) Symphony No. 3, *Song of the Night,*
                  with tenor and chorus
1917 (34) Violin Concerto No. 1
               String Quartet in C major
1920–24 (37–41) *King Roger,* opera
1924 (41) *Prince Potemkin,* incidental music
1926 (43) *Harnasie,* ballet
               Stabat Mater
1931–32 (48) *Symphonie Concertante,* for piano
1932–33 (49) Violin Concerto No. 2
Szymanowski also composed symphonic poems, piano
music, choral music and songs.

TALLIS, Thomas/*c.*1505–1585/Great Britain

1567 (*c.*62) *p.* Psalms tunes in "Archbishop Parker's
                   Psalter"
Tallis composed many Latin masses, lamentations,
motets (including *Spem in alium,* for forty-part choir),
pieces for keyboard, viols, etc.

TANSMAN, Alexandre/b.1897/Poland

1916 (19) Symphony No. 1
1922 (25) *Sextuor,* ballet
1924 (27) Sinfonietta
1925 (28) Symphony No. 2
               La Nuit Kurde, opera (1925–27)
1926 (29) Piano Concerto No. 1
1927 (30) Piano Concerto No. 2

1928 (31) *Lumières*
1929 (32) *Le cercle éternel*, ballet
1930 (33) *Triptych*, for string orchestra
1931 (34) Symphony No. 3, *Symphony Concertante* (1931–32)
  Concertino, for piano
1932 (35) *La Grande Ville*, ballet
  Two symphonic movements
1933 (36) *Partita*, for string orchestra
1936 (39) Viola Concerto
  Two Intermezzi
1937 (40) *Bric-a-Brac*
  Fantasy for violin
  Fantasy for cello
1938 (41) *Le toison d'or*
  Symphony No. 4
1942 (45) Symphony No. 5
1943 (46) Symphony No. 6, *In Memoriam*
  Symphonic études
1944 (47) Symphony No. 7
  Le roi qui jouait le fou
  Partita, for piano and orchestra
1945 (48) *Concertino*, for guitar and orchestra
1947 (50) *Isiah the Prophet*
  Music for Orchestra
1948 (51) *Music for Strings*
1949 (52) *Ricercari*
  Tombeau de Chopin, for strings
1950 (53) *Phèdre*, ballet
1951 (54) Symphony No. 8
1955 (58) *Le Sermant*, opera
  Capriccio
  Concerto for orchestra
1961 (64) *Psalms*, for tenor, chorus and orchestra
1962 (65) *Resurrection*, for orchestra
  Six symphonic studies, for orchestra
1963 (66) Six Movements for string orchestra
1964 (67) *Il Usignolo di Boboli*, opera
1966 (69) *Concertino*, for oboe and chamber orchestra
1968 (71) Four Movements for orchestra
1969 (72) *Concertino*, for flute and chamber orchestra

Hommage à Erasme de Rotherdam, for
orchestra

TAVENER, John/b.1944/Great Britain

1962 (18) Piano Concerto (1962–63)
Three Holy Sonnets, for voice and
orchestra
1963–64 (19) *Three Sections,* from T.S. Eliot's "The
Four Quartets", for tenor and piano
1964 (20) *The Cappemakers,* for two narrators, two
soloists, male chorus and instruments
1965 (21) Chamber Concerto (revised 1968)
Cain and Abel, dramatic cantata
The Whale, for choir and orchestra
(1965–66)
1967–68 (23) *Grandma's Footsteps,* for chamber
orchestra
Three surrealist songs, for mezzo-soprano,
tape and piano doubling bongoes
1968 (24) *In Alium,* for high soprano and orchestra
1969 (25) *Celtic Requiem,* for voices and orchestra
1970 (26) *Nomine Jesu,* for voices and orchestra
Coplas, for voices and tape
1971 (27) *In Memoriam Igor Stravinsky,* for two alto
flutes, organ and bells
*Responsorium in Memory of Annon Lee
Silver,* for two soprano soli, mixed
chorus and two flutes
1972 (28) *Variations on "Three Blind Mice",* for
orchestra
Ma fin est mon commencement, for voices
and instruments
Little Requiem for Father Malachy Lynch,
for voices and instruments
Ultimos Ritos, for voices and orchestra,
including amplified instruments
Canciones espanolas, for voices and
instruments
1973 (29) *Requiem for Father Malachy,* for choir
and instruments
Thérèse, opera (1973–76)

TAYLOR, (Joseph) Deems/1885–1966/U.S.A.

1912 (27) *The Siren Song,* for orchestra
1914 (29) *The Highwayman,* for baritone, women's
         voices and orchestra
         The Chambered Nautilus, for chorus and
         orchestra
1918 (33) *The Portrait of a Lady,* for eleven
         instruments
1919 (34) *Through the Looking-glass,* suite for
         chamber orchestra (version for full
         orchestra, 1922)
1923 (38) *A Kiss in Xanadu,* pantomime in two
         scenes, for two pianos
1925 (40) *Jurgen,* for orchestra
         Fantasy on Two Themes, for orchestra
         Circus Days, for jazz orchestra (version
         for full orchestra, 1933)
1926 (41) *The King's Henchman,* opera
1930 (45) *Peter Ibbetson,* opera
1936 (51) *Lucrece,* for string quartet
1937 (52) *Ramuntcho,* opera
         Casanova, ballet
1941 (56) *Processional,* for orchestra
1943 (58) *Christmas Overture,* for orchestra
1945 (60) *Elegy,* for orchestra
1950 (65) *Restoration Suite,* for orchestra
1954 (69) *The Dragon,* opera

TCHAIKOVSKY, Peter Ilych/1840–1893/Russia

1866 (26) Symphony No. 1 in G minor, *Winter
         Daydreams*
1868 (28) *Fate,* symphonic poem
1869 (29) *Romeo and Juliet,* overture (final version
         1880)
1871 (31) String Quartet in D major
1872 (32) Symphony No. 2 in C minor, *Little
         Russian*
1873 (33) *The Tempest,* symphonic fantasia

1874–75 (34) Piano Concerto No. 1 in B♭ minor
String Quartet in F major
1875 (35) *Swan Lake,* ballet (*fp.* 1895)
Symphony No. 3 in D major, *Polish*
String Quartet in E♭ minor
1876 (36) *Variations on a Rococo theme,* for cello
and orchestra
Slavonic March, for orchestra
1877 (37) Symphony No. 4 in F minor
Francesca da Rimini, symphonic fantasy
Waltz-Scherzo, for violin and orchestra
1878 (38) Violin Concerto in D major
1879 (39) *Eugene Onegin,* opera
Capriccio Italien, for orchestra
Piano Concerto No. 2 in G major
(1879–80)
1880 (40) *Serenade for Strings*
1881 (41) *Joan of Arc,* opera
1882 (42) *1812 Overture*
Piano Trio in A minor
1884 (44) *Mazeppa,* opera
Concert-Fantasy, for piano and orchestra
1885 (45) *Manfred Symphony*
1888 (48) *The Sleeping Beauty,* ballet
Hamlet, overture
Symphony No. 5 in E minor
1890 (50) *The Queen of Spades,* opera
1892 (52) *Iolanthe,* opera
Casse Noisette (The Nutcracker), ballet
p. String Sextet in D minor
1893 (53) Symphony No. 6 in B minor, *Pathétique*
Piano Concerto No. 3

TELEMANN, Georg/1681–1767/Germany

1708–12 (27–31) Trio Sonata in E♭ major
1715–20 (34–39) Concerto in A major
Suite in D minor
1716 (35) *Die Kleine Kammermusik*
Six suites for violin, querflute and piano
1718 (37) Six trios for two violins and cello, with
bass continuo

1723 (42) *Hamburger Ebb und Fluht*, overture in
            C major
1725 (44) *Pimpinone*, opera
1728 (47) *Der getreuer Musikmeister*, cantata
1759 (78) St. Mark Passion
Telemann also composed:
40 operas
600 overtures
44 liturgical passions
Several oratorios
Innumerable cantatas and psalms.

THOMAS, Ambroise/1811–1896/France

1832 (21) *Hermann et Ketty*, cantata
1837 (26) *La Double échelle*, opera
1838 (27) *Le Perruquier de la Regence*, opera
1839 (28) *La Panier fleuri*, opera
            La Gipsy, ballet
1840 (29) *Carlino*, opera
1841 (30) *Le Comte de Carmagnola*, opera
1842 (31) *Le Guerillero*, opera
1843 (32) *Angélique et Medor*, opera
            Mina, opera
1846 (35) *Betty*, ballet
1849 (38) *Le Caïd*, opera
1850 (39) *Le Songe d'une nuit d'été*, opera
1851 (40) *Raymond*, opera
1853 (42) *La Tonelli*, opera
1855 (44) *La Cour de Célimène*, opera
1857 (46) *Psyché*, opera
            Le Carnaval de Venise, opera
            Messe solenelle
1860 (49) *Le Roman d'Elvire*, opera
1865 (54) *Marche religieuse*, for orchestra
1866 (55) *Mignon*, opera
1868 (57) *Hamlet*, grand opera
1874 (63) *Gille et Gillotin*, opera
1882 (71) *Francoise de Rimini*, opera
1889 (78) *La Tempête*, ballet

1923 (27) *Two Sentimental Tangoes*
1926 (30) *Sonata da Chiesa,* for five instruments
1928 (32) *Symphony on a Hymn Tune*
1929 (33) *Five Portraits,* for four clarinets
1930 (34) Violin Sonata
1931 (35) Quartet No. 1
    Serenade, for flute and violin
    Four Portraits, for violin and piano
    Stabat Mater
1932 (36) Quartet No. 2
1934 (38) *Four Saints in Three Acts,* opera
1937 (41) *Filling Station,* ballet
1941 (45) Symphony No. 2
1942 (46) *Canon for Dorothy Thomson*
    The Mayor La Guardia Waltzes
1943 (47) Flute Sonata
1944 (48) Suite No. 1, *Portraits*
    Suite No. 2
1947 (51) *The Mother of Us All,* opera
    The Seine at Night, for orchestra
1948 (52) *Wheatfield at Noon,* for orchestra
    Acadian Songs and Dances
1949 (53) Cello Concerto
1951 (55) *Five Songs of William Blake,* for baritone
    and orchestra
1952 (56) *Sea Piece with Birds,* for orchestra
1954 (58) Concerto for flute, strings and percussion
1957 (61) *The Lively Arts,* fugue
1959 (63) *Fugues and Cantilenas,* for orchestra
    Collected Poems
1960 (64) Mass, for solo voice and piano (version
    with orchestra, 1962)
    Missa pro defunctis (Requiem Mass), for
    men's chorus, women's chorus and
    orchestra
1961 (65) *A Solemn Music,* for orchestra
    (transcribed from original band score)
1962 (66) *A Joyful Fugue,* to follow *A Solemn Music*
    Pange lingua, for organ

1964 (68) *The Feast of Love,* for baritone and
orchestra
Autumn Concertino, for harp, strings and
percussion
1966 (70) *Lord Byron,* opera (1966–68)
Fantasy in Homage to an Earlier England,
for orchestra
The Nativity, for mixed chorus, soloists
and orchestra (1966–67)
Étude, for cello and piano
1967 (71) *Shipwreck and Love Scene,* from Byron's
"Don Juan", for orchestra and tenor
soloist
1973 (77) *Cantata based on Nonsense Rhymes*
Thomson also composed 4 piano sonatas.

TIPPETT, Sir Michael/b.1905/Great Britain

1934–35 (29) String Quartet No. 1 in A major
(revised 1943)
1936–37 (31) Piano Sonata (revised 1942)
1937 (32) *A Song of Liberty*
1938–39 (33) Concerto for double string orchestra
1939–41 (34) *A Child of Our Time,* oratorio
Fantasia on a Theme by Handel, for piano
and orchestra
1941–42 (36) String Quartet No. 2
1942 (37) *The Source* and *The Windhover,* madrigals
1943 (38) *Boyhood's End,* song cycle
Plebs angelica, motet for double chorus
1944 (39) Symphony No. 1 (1944–45)
The Weeping Babe, motet for soprano solo
and chorus
1945–46 (40) String Quartet No. 3
1946 (41) *Little Music,* for strings
1947–52 (42–47) *The Midsummer Marriage,* opera
1948 (43) Suite in D major
1950–51 (45) *Heart's Assurance,* song cycle for
high voice and piano
1952 (47) *Dance Clarion Air,* madrigal
1953 (48) *Fantasia Concertante on a Theme by
Corelli,* for strings

                    Divertimento for chamber orchestra
                        "Sellingers Round" (1953–54)
                    Piano Concerto (1953–55)
1955 (50) Sonata for four horns
1956–57 (51) Symphony No. 2
1958 (53) *King Priam*, opera (1958–61)
                    Crown of the Year, for chorus and
                        orchestra
                    Prelude, Recitative and Aria, for flute,
                        oboe and harpsichord
1961 (56) *Three songs for Achilles*, for voice and
                        guitar
                    Magnificat and Nunc Dimittis
1962 (57) Concerto for orchestra (1962–63)
                    Praeludium, for brass, bells and percussion
                    Piano Sonata No. 2, in one movement
                    Songs for Ariel
1964 (59) *Prologue and Epilogue*, for choir and
                        orchestra
1965 (60) *Vision of St. Augustine*, for baritone, choir
                        and orchestra
                    The Shires Suite, for choir and orchestra
                        (1965–70)
1966–70 (61–65) *The Knot Garden*, opera
1970 (65) Symphony No. 3, with soprano soloist
                        (1970–72)
                    Songs for Dov, for tenor solo and small
                        orchestra
1972–73 (67) Piano Sonata No. 3

TURINA, Joaquín/1882–1949/Spain

1907 (25) Piano Quintet
1911 (29) Quartet
1912 (30) *La Procesion del Rocio*, symphonic poem
1914 (32) *Margot*, lyric comedy
1915 (33) *Evangelio*, symphonic poem
1916 (34) *Navidad*, incidental music
1917 (35) *La Adultera penitente*, incidental music
1918 (36) *Poema en forma de canciones*
1920 (38) *Sinfonia Sevillana*
                    Danzas fantasticas

1921 (39) *Canto a Sevillana*, song cycle
1923 (41) *Jardin de Oriente*
1926 (44) *La oracion del torero*, for quartet
Piano Trio
1928 (46) *Ritmos*, choreographic fantasy
1929 (47) *Triptico*
1931 (49) *Rapsodia sinfonica*, for piano and strings
Piano Quartet
1933 (51) Piano Trio
1935 (53) *Serenade*, for quartet

VAUGHAN WILLIAMS, Ralph/1872–1958/
Great Britain

1888 (16) Piano Trio
1900 (28) *Bucolic Suite,* for orchestra
1903 (31) *The House of Life,* song cycle (No. 2 is
"Silent Noon")
1904 (32) Songs of Travel
1906 (34) *Norfolk Rhapsodies* Nos. 1–3, for orchestra
(Nos. 2 and 3 are lost)
1907 (35) *In the Fen country*, symphonic impression
Towards the Unknown Region, song for
chorus and orchestra
1908 (36) String Quartet in G minor
1909 (37) *A Sea Symphony* (Symphony No. 1),
words by Walt Whitman, for soprano,
baritone, chorus and orchestra
The Wasps, incidental music
On Wenlock Edge, song cycle
1910 (38) *Fantasia on a Theme by Thomas Tallis*,
for strings (No. 9 in Archbishop
Parker's Psalter, *p.* 1567)
1911 (39) *Five Mystical Songs*, for baritone, mixed
chorus and orchestra
1912 (40) Fantasia on Christmas Carols
Phantasy Quintet, for strings
1913 (41) *A London Symphony* (Symphony No. 2)
1920 (48) *Shepherd of the Delectable Mountains*,
one-act opera (now also forms Act IV
of *The Pilgrim's Progress*) (1920–21)

	The Lark Ascending, for violin and small orchestra
	Suite de Ballet, for flute and piano
	Mass in G minor (1920–21)
	Three Preludes for organ
1921 (49)	*A Pastoral Symphony* (Symphony No. 3)
1923 (51)	*Old King Cole,* ballet
1924 (52)	*Hugh the Drover,* opera
1925 (53)	*Concerto Accademico,* for violin and string orchestra
	Flos Campi, suite for viola, small wordless choir and small orchestra
	Sancta civitas, oratorio
1927 (55)	*Along the Field,* eight songs (Housman) for voice and violin
1928 (56)	*Sir John in Love,* opera
	Te Deum, in G major
1929 (57)	*Benedicite,* for soprano, mixed choir and orchestra
1930 (58)	*Job, a Masque for Dancing,* for orchestra
	Prelude and Fugue in C minor, for orchestra
1931 (59)	Symphony No. 4 in F minor (1931–34)
	Piano Concerto in C major
	In Windsor Forest, cantata
1932 (60)	*Magnificat,* for contralto, women's chorus, solo flute and orchestra
1933 (61)	*The Running Set,* for medium orchestra
1934 (62)	*Fantasia on Greensleeves,* for orchestra
	Suite for viola and small orchestra
1935 (63)	*Five Tudor Portraits,* choral suite in five movements
1936 (64)	*Riders to the Sea,* opera in one act
	The Poisoned Kiss, romantic extravaganza with spoken dialogue, for thirteen soloists, mixed chorus and orchestra
	Dona nobis pacem, cantata
1937 (65)	Festival Te Deum, in F major
1938 (66)	*The Bridal Day,* masque
	Serenade to Music, for sixteen solo voices and orchestra
1939 (67)	*Five Variants of Dives and Lazurus,* for strings and harp

1940 (68) *Six Choral Songs—to be sung in time of war*
Valiant for Truth, motet

1941 (69) *England, My England*, for baritone, double chorus, unison voices and orchestra

1942 (70) *Coastal Command*, orchestral suite from the film

1943 (71) Symphony No. 5 in D major

1944 (72) Symphony No. 6 in E minor (1944–47)
Concerto for oboe and strings
A Song of Thanksgiving, for soprano, speaker, mixed choir and orchestra
String Quartet No. 2, in A minor

1945 (75) *Story of a Flemish Farm*, orchestral suite from the film

1946–48 (74–76) *Partita*, for double string orchestra
Introduction and fugue, for two pianos

1949 (77) *Fantasia (quasi variazione) on the "Old 104th" Psalm Tune*, for piano, chorus, organ (optional) and orchestra
An Oxford Elegy, for speaker, chorus and small orchestra
Folk-songs of the Four Seasons, cantata

1950 (78) Concerto Grosso, for string orchestra
The Sons of Light, cantata
Sun, Moon, Stars and Man, song cycle

1951 (79) *The Pilgrim's Progress*, a Morality in a Prologue, Four Acts, and an Epilogue, for thirty-four soloists, chorus and orchestra
Romance in D♭ major, for harmonica, strings and piano

1952 (80) *Sinfonia Antartica* (Symphony No. 7), in five movements

1954 (82) Concerto for Bass Tuba and Orchestra, in F minor
This Day (Hodie), a Christmas cantata
Violin Sonata in A minor

1955 (83) Symphony No. 8 in D minor (this was the first of the symphonies which Vaughan Williams allowed to be given a number)

1956 (84) *A Vision of Aeroplanes*, motet

Symphony No. 9 in E minor (revised 1958)

Two Organ Preludes, *Romanza* and *Toccata*

Epithalamion, cantata (1956–57)

Ten Blake Songs, for tenor and oboe

1958 (86) *The First Nowell*, nativity play for soloist, mixed chorus and small orchestra

Vocalises, for soprano and B♭ clarinet

Four Last Songs, for voice and piano

Thomas the Rhymer, opera in three acts (uncompleted at Vaughan Williams' death; exists in short score only)

VERDI, Giuseppe/1813–1901/Italy

1839 (26) *fp. Oberto*, opera
1842 (29) *fp. Nabucco*, opera
1843 (30) *fp. I Lombardi*, opera
1844 (31) *fp. Ernani*, opera
            fp. I Due Foscari, opera
1845 (32) *fp. Alzira*, opera
            fp. Giovanna d'Arco, opera
1846 (33) *fp. Attila*, opera
1847 (34) *fp. Macbeth*, opera
            fp. I Masnadieri, opera
1849 (36) *fp. Luisa Miller*, opera
1851 (38) *fp. Rigoletto*, opera
1853 (40) *fp. La Traviata*, opera
            fp. Il Trovatore, opera
1855 (42) *fp. I Vespri Siciliani*, opera
1857 (44) *fp. Aroldo*, opera
            fp. Simon Boccanegra, opera
1859 (46) *fp. Un Ballo in Maschera*, opera
1862 (49) *fp. La Forza del Destino*, opera
            fp. Inno delle Nazioni, for chorus
1867 (54) *fp. Don Carlos*, opera
1871 (58) *fp. Aida*, opera
1873 (60) String Quartet in E minor
1874 (61) Requiem Mass
1887 (74) *fp. Otello*, opera

1889–98 (76–85) Four sacred pieces
1893 (80) *fp. Falstaff*, opera

VILLA-LOBOS, Heitor/1887–1959/Brazil

1908 (21) *Recouli*, for small orchestra
1910 (23) *Suite dos canticos sertanejos,* for small
      orchestra
1912 (25) *Aglaia*, opera
1913 (26) *Suite da terra*, for small orchestra
      Suite for piano
1914 (27) *Izaht*, opera
      Suite popular Brasiliera
      Ibericarabé, symphonic poem
      Dansas dos Indios Mesticos, for orchestra
      Suite for strings
1915 (28) String Quartets Nos. 1 and 2
1916 (29) Symphony No. 1, *The Unforseen*
      Centauro de Ouro, symphonic poem
      Miremis, symphonic poem
      Naufragio de Kleonica, symphonic poem
      Marcha religiosa No. 1, for orchestra
      Sinfonietta on a theme by Mozart
      Cello Concerto
      String Quartet No. 3
1917 (30) *Uirapurú*, ballet
      Amazonas, ballet for orchestra
      Symphony No. 2, *The Ascension*
      Fantasia, symphonic poem
      Iara, symphonic poem
      Lobishome, symphonic poem
      Saci Pererê, symphonic poem
      Tédio de alvorado, symphonic poem
      Sexteto mistico, for flute, clarinet,
        saxophone, harp, celesta and double-
        bass
      String Quartet No. 4
1918 (31) *Jesus*, opera
      Marcha religiosa No. 3, for orchestra
      Marcha religiosa No. 7, for orchestra
      Vidapura, oratorio

1919 (32)	*Zoé*, opera
	Symphony No. 3, *The War*
	Symphony No. 4, *The Victory*
	Dansa frenetica, for orchestra
1920 (33)	Symphony No. 5, *The Peace*
	Dansa diabolica, for orchestra
	Chôros No. 1, for guitar
1921 (34)	*Malazarte*, opera
	Quartet for harp, celesta, flute and saxophone, with women's voices
1923 (36)	Suite for voice and viola
1924 (37)	*Chôros No. 2*, for flute and clarinet
	Chôros No. 7, for flute, oboe, clarinet, saxophone, bassoon, violin and cello
1925 (38)	*Chôros No. 3*, for clarinet, saxophone, bassoon, three horns and trombones, with male voice choir
	Chôros No. 8, for two pianos and orchestra
	Chôros No. 10, for choir and orchestra
1926 (39)	*Chôros No. 4*, for three horns and trombones
	Chôros No. 5, for piano
	Chôros No. 6, for orchestra
	Chôros No. 6 bis, for violin and cello
1928 (41)	*Chôros No. 11*, for piano and orchestra
	Chôros No. 14, for orchestra, band and choir
1929 (42)	*Suite sugestiva*, for voice and orchestra
	Chôros No. 9, for orchestra
	Chôros No. 12, for orchestra
	Chôros No. 13, for two orchestras and band
	Introdução aos Chôros, for orchestra
	Twelve Studies for guitar
1930 (43)	*Bachianas Brasilieras No. 1*, for orchestra: Preludio, Aria, Fuga
	Bachianas Brasilieras No. 2, for orchestra: Preludio, Aria, Dansa, Tocata
1931 (44)	String Quartet No. 5
1932 (45)	*Caixinha de Bôas Festas,* ballet (also an orchestral suite)
1933 (46)	*Pedra Bonita,* ballet

1936 (49) *Bachiánas Brasilieras No. 4*, for piano:
        Preludio, Aria, Coral Dansa (1930–36)
1937 (50) *Currupira*, ballet
        Sebastiao
        Descobrimento do Brasil, four suites
        for chorus and orchestra
1938 (51) *Bachianas Brasilieras No. 3*, for piano
        and orchestra: Preludio, Aria, Tocata
        Bachianas Brasilieras No. 6, for flute and
        bassoon: Aria, Fantasia
        String Quartet No. 6
1939 (52) *New York Skyline,* for orchestra (Villa-
        Lobos "drew" the melody by following
        the outline of skyscrapers on graph
        paper. He then harmonized the resultant
        melodic line and scored it for orchestra.)
1940 (53) *Saudades da juventude,* Suite I
        Preludes for guitar
1942 (55) *Bachianas Brasilieras No. 7,* for orchestra:
        Preludio, Giga, Tocata, Fuga
        String Quartet No. 7
1944 (57) *Bachianas Brasilieras No. 8,* for orchestra:
        Preludio, Aria, Tocata, Fuga
        String Quartet No. 8
1945 (58) *Bachianas Brasilieras No. 5,* for voice
        and orchestra of cellos: Aria, Dansa
        (1938–45)
        Bachianas Brasilieras No. 9, for vocal
        orchestra
        Piano Concerto No. 1
        Fantasia for cello
Villa-Lobos also composed much chamber music and
many songs.

VIVALDI, Antonio/*c.*1675–1741/Italy

1705 (*c.*30) *p.* Suonate da camera a tre, Op. 1
1709 (*c.*34) *p.* Sonate a violino e basso per il
        cambala, Op. 2
*c.***1712** (*c.*37) *p.* Twelve concerti, *L'Estro armonico,*
        Op. 3

p. Twelve concerti, *La Stravaganza*, Op. 4
(*c*.1712–13)

1713 (*c*.38) *fp. Ottone in Villa*, opera
1714 (*c*.39) *fp. Orlando finto pazzo*, opera
Moyses deus Pharaonis, oratorio
1715 (*c*.40) *fp. Nerone fatto Cesare*, opera
1716 (*c*.41) *fp. Arsilda Regine di Ponto*, opera
Juditha triumphans, oratorio
p. Six sonate; four for violin solo and bass,
two for two violins and basso continuo,
Op. 5
p. Sei concerti a cinque, Op. 6
(1716–*c*.1717)
p. Sette concerti a cinque, Books I and II,
Op. 7 (1716–*c*.1717)
1717 (*c*.42) *fp. Tieteberga*, opera
1718 (*c*.43) *fp. Scanderbeg*, opera
1720 (*c*.45) *fp. La Verità in cimento*, opera
1721 (*c*.46) *fp. Silvia*, opera
1722 (*c*.47) *L' Adorazione delli tre Re Magi*, oratorio
1724 (*c*.49) *fp. Giustino*, opera
*c***.1725** (*c*.50) p. *Il cimento dell'Armonia e
dell'Inventione*, twelve concerti of which
four are known as *The Four Seasons*,
Op. 8
1726 (*c*.51) *Cunegonda*, opera
1727 (*c*.52) *Ipermestra*, opera
1728 (*c*.53) *Rosilena ed Oronta*, opera
p. Twelve concerti, *Le Cetra*, Op. 9
1729–30 (*c*.54) p. Sei concerti a flauto traverso, due
violini, alto (viola), organo e
violoncello, Op. 10
p. Sei concerti a violino principale, Op. 11
p. Sei concerti a violino principale, Op. 12
1732 (*c*.57) *fp. La fida ninfa*, opera
1733 (*c*.58) *fp. Motezuma*, opera
1734 (*c*.59) *fp. L'Olimpiade*, opera
1735 (*c*.60) *fp. Griselda*, opera
fp. Aristide, opera
1736 (*c*.61) *fp. Ginevra, Principessa di Scozia*, opera
1737 (*c*.62) *fp. Catone in Utica*, opera
p. *Il pastor fido*, sonates pour la musette,

viele, flute, hautbois, violon avec la
Basso continuo, Op. 13 (*c*.1737)
1738 (*c*.63) *fp. L'Oracolo in Messenia,* opera
1739 (*c*.64) *fp. Feraspe,* opera
c.1740 (*c*.65) *p.* Six sonates a violincelle et basse,
Op. 14

Vivaldi's total output in the concerto genre numbers
over 400, including 220 solo concerti, some 60 concerti
ripieni, 48 bassoon concerti, 25 cello concerti, plus
many works for various instruments. There are about
46 known operas of the 100 that Vivaldi claimed to
have written.

WAGNER, Richard/1813–1883/Germany

1832 (19) Symphony in C major
1840 (27) *Faust,* overture
1842 (29) *fp. Rienzi,* opera
1843 (30) *fp. The Flying Dutchman,* opera
1845 (32) *fp. Tannhäuser,* opera
1851 (38) *fp. Lohengrin,* opera
1857–58 (44) The *Wesendonck Lieder,* five songs
with orchestra
1865 (52) *fp. Tristan und Isolde,* music drama
1868 (55) *fp. Die Meistersinger von Nürnberg,* opera
1869 (56) *fp. Das Rheingold* (No. 1 of *Der Ring
des Nibelungen*)
1870 (57) *fp. Die Walküre* (No. 2 of *Der Ring des
Nibelungen*)
Siegfried Idyll, for orchestra
1876 (63) *fp. Siegfried* (No. 3 of *Der Ring des
Nibelungen*)
fp. Götterdämmerung (No. 4 of *Der Ring
des Nibelungen*)
1882 (69) *fp. Parsifal,* religious music drama

WALTON, Sir William/b.1902/Great Britain

1916 (14) Piano Quartet
1922 (20) *fp.* (privately) *Façade—An Entertainment,*
for reciter and chamber ensemble

1925 (23) *Portsmouth Point*, overture
1926 (24) *Siesta*, for orchestra
1927 (25) Viola Concerto (soloist at *fp.* was
                Hindemith, *q.v.*)
            Sinfonia Concertante, for piano and
                orchestra
1931 (29) *fp. Belshazzar's Feast,* for baritone,
                chorus and orchestra
1934 (32) *fp.* Symphony.No. 1 (first three movements
                only, performed in full 1935)
            Escape Me Never, ballet from the film
1937 (35) *Crown Imperial,* coronation march for
                orchestra
            In Honour of the City, for chorus and
                orchestra
1939 (37) Violin Concerto
1940 (38) *The Wise Virgins,* ballet (arranged from
                the music of J.S. Bach)
1941 (39) *Scapino,* overture
1942 (40) *Prelude and Fugue (The Spitfire),* for
                orchestra
1943 (41) *Henry V,* incidental music for the film
            The Quest, ballet
1947 (45) *Hamlet,* incidental music for the film
            String Quartet in A minor
1949 (47) Violin Sonata
1953 (51) *Orb and Sceptre,* coronation march for
                orchestra
            Coronation Te Deum
1954 (52) *Troilus and Cressida,* opera
1955 (53) *Richard III,* incidental music for the film
            Johannesburg Festival Overture
1956 (54) Cello Concerto
1957 (55) *Partita,* for orchestra
1960 (58) Symphony No. 2
            fp. Anon. in Love, six songs for tenor and
                guitar
1961 (59) *Gloria,* for contralto, tenor and bass soli,
                mixed choir and orchestra
1962 (60) *fp. A Song for the Lord Mayor's Table,*
                cycle of six songs for soprano and piano
1963 (61) *Variations on a Theme of Hindemith,* for

orchestra (theme from Hindemith's
Nobilissima Visione)
1965 (63) *The Twelve,* for choir and orchestra, or
organ
1966 (64) Missa Brevis
1967 (65) *The Bear,* one-act opera for three solo
voices and chamber orchestra
1968 (66) *Capriccio Burlesca,* for orchestra
1970 (68) *Improvisations on an Impromptu of
Benjamin Britten,* for orchestra
1972 (70) *Jubilate Deo,* for double mixed chorus and
organ
Sonata for string orchestra, arranged from
the String Quartet
Five bagatelles for guitar
1974 (72) *Cantico del Sole*
Magnificat and *Nunc Dimittis*

WARLOCK, Peter (Philip Heseltine)/1894–1930/
Great Britain

1917 (23) *An Old Song,* for small orchestra
1922 (28) *Serenade for Frederick Delius,* for
orchestra
1923 (29) *The Curlew,* song cycle for voice, flute,
English horn and string quartet
1926 (32) *Capriol Suite,* for strings (also arranged
for full orchestra)

WEBER, Carl Maria von/1786–1826/Germany

1800 (14) *Das Waldmädchen,* opera
1801 (15) *Peter Schmoll und seine Nachbarn,* opera
1806–07 (20) Symphony No. 1 in C major
1807 (21) Symphony No. 2 in C major
1810 (24) Piano Concerto No. 1 in C major
1811 (25) *Abu Hassan,* opera
Bassoon Concerto
Clarinet Concerto No. 1 in F minor
Clarinet Concerto No. 2 in E♭ major

        Concertino for clarinet, in C minor and
           Eb major
1812 (26) Piano Concerto No. 2 in Eb major
           Piano Sonata No. 1 in C major
1815 (29) Concertino for horn, in E minor
           Quintet for clarinet and strings, in Eb
             major
1816 (30) Piano Sonata No. 2 in Ab major
           Piano Sonata No. 3 in D minor
1819 (33) *Invitation to the Dance,* for piano
           (orchestrated by Berlioz, 1841)
1821 (35) *fp. Der Freischütz,* opera
           Concertstücke, for piano and orchestra,
             in E minor
1822 (36) Piano Sonata No. 4, in E minor
1823 (37) *fp. Euryanthe,* opera
1826 (40) *fp. Oberon,* opera

WEBERN, Anton von/1883–1945/Austria

1908 (25) *Passacaglia,* for orchestra, Op. 1
           Entflieht auf Leichten Kahnan, for chorus,
             Op. 2
           Five Lieder, Op. 3
           Five Lieder, Op. 4 (1908–09)
1909 (26) Five Movements for string quartet, Op. 5
1910 (27) Six pieces for large orchestra, Op. 6
           Four pieces for violin and piano, Op. 7
             (1910–15)
1911–12 (28) Two Lieder, Op. 8
1913 (30) Six Bagatelles for string quartet, Op. 9
           Five pieces for orchestra, Op. 10
             (1911–13)
1914 (31) Three little pieces for cello and piano,
             Op. 11
1915–17 (32–34) Four Lieder, Op. 12
1914–18 (31–35) Four Lieder, with thirteen
             instruments, Op. 13
1917–21 (34–38) Six Lieder, with violin, clarinet,
             bass clarinet, viola and cello, Op. 14
1917–21 (34–39) Five Geistliche Lieder, Op. 15

1924 (41) Five canons, for voice, clarinet and bass
            clarinet, Op. 16
          Six Volkstexte, Op. 17
1925 (42) Three Lieder, Op. 18
1926 (43) Two Lieder, Op. 19
1927 (44) String Trio, Op. 20
1928 (45) Symphony for small orchestra, Op. 21
1930 (47) Quartet for violin, clarinet, saxophone
            and piano, Op. 22
1934 (51) Three Gesänge from *Viae invaie,* Op. 23
          Concerto for flute, oboe, clarinet, horn,
            trumpet, trombone, violin, viola and
            piano, Op. 24
1935 (52) Three Lieder, Op. 25
          Das Augenlicht, for mixed chorus and
            orchestra, Op. 26
1936 (53) Variations for piano, Op. 27
1938 (55) String Quartet, Op. 28
1939 (56) Cantata No. 1, *Jone,* Op. 29
1940 (57) Variations for orchestra, Op. 30
1941–43 (58–60) Cantata No. 2, *Jone,* Op. 31

WEINBERGER, Jaromir/1896–1967/Bohemia
(Czechoslovakia)

1927 (31) *Schwanda the Bagpiper,* opera
1929 (33) *Christmas,* for orchestra
1930 (34) *The Beloved Voice,* opera
          Bohemian Songs and Dances, for orchestra
1931 (35) *Passacaglia,* for orchestra
1932 (36) *The Outcasts of Poker Flat,* opera
1934 (38) *A Bed of Roses,* opera
1937 (41) *Wallenstein,* opera
1938 (42) Variations on *Under the Spreading
            Chestnut Tree,* for orchestra
1940 (44) *Song of the High Seas,* for orchestra
          Saxophone Concerto
1941 (45) *Lincoln Symphony
          Czech Rhapsody,* for orchestra
          The Bird's Opera, for orchestra
1957 (61) *Préludes Religieuses et Profanes,* for organ
1960 (64) *Aus Tirol*

1961 (65) *Eine Walserouverture*
Weinberger also composed:
Overture to a Puppet Show, for orchestra
Overture to a Cavalier's Play, for orchestra
The Legend of Sleepy Hollow, for orchestra
Mississippi Rhapsody, for band
Prelude to the Festival, for band
Homage to the Pioneers, for band
Chamber music, choral works and songs.

WILLIAMSON, Malcolm/b.1931/Australia

1957 (26) First Piano Sonata
1958 (27) *Santiago de Espada,* overture
 Piano Concerto No. 1
1961 (30) Organ Concerto
1963 (32) *Our Man in Havana,* opera
 Elevamini Symphony
1964 (33) *Sinfonia Concertante,* for piano, three
 trumpets and string orchestra
 Piano Concerto No. 3
 Variations for Cello and Piano
 The Display, a dance symphony in four
 movements
 The Merry Wives of Windsor, incidental
 music
 Elegy J.F.K., for organ
 Three Shakespeare Songs, for high voice
 and guitar (or piano)
1965 (34) *The Happy Prince,* one-act opera
 Sinfonietta
 Symphonic Variations, for orchestra
 Concerto Grosso, for orchestra
 Violin Concerto
 Four North-Country Songs, for voice and
 orchestra
 Concerto for two pianos (eight hands)
 and wind quintet
1966 (35) *The Violins of St. Jacques,* opera
 Julius Caesar Jones, opera
 Sun Into Darkness, ballet
 Five Preludes for Piano

Two Organ Epitaphs for Edith Sitwell
Six English Lyrics, for low voice and piano

1967 (36) *Dunstan and the Devil,* one-act opera

Pas de Quatre, music to the ballet *Nonet,* for flute, oboe, clarinet, bassoon and piano

Spectrum, ballet (music identical with the *Variations* for cello and piano, 1964)

The Moonrakers, cassation for audience and orchestra

Serenade, for flute, piano, violin, viola and cello

Sonata for two pianos

1968 (37) *The Growing Castle,* chamber opera for four singers

Knights in Shining Armour, cassation for audience and piano

The Snow Wolf, cassation for audience and piano

Piano Quintet

From a Child's Garden, settings of twelve poems, for high voice and piano

1969 (38) *Lucky-Peter's Journey,* a comedy with music

Symphony No. 2

The Brilliant and the Dark, choral-operatic sequence for women's voices

1971 (40) *Genesis,* cassation for audience and instruments

The Stone Wall, cassation for audience and orchestra

Peace Pieces, six organ pieces in two volumes

Death of Cuchulain, for five male voices and percussion instruments

In Place of Belief, setting of ten poems by Per Lagerqvist for voices and piano duet

1972 (41) *The Red Sea,* one-act children's opera

Symphony No. 3, *The Icy Mirror,* for soprano, mezzo-soprano, two baritones, chorus and orchestra

Partita for Viola, on themes of Walton

The Musicians of Bremen, for six male
    voices

Love the Sentinel, for unaccompanied
    choir

1973 (42) The Winter Star, cassation for audience
    and instruments

Concerto for two pianos and strings

Ode to Music, for chorus, echo chorus
    and orchestra

Pietà, four poems for soprano, oboe,
    bassoon and piano

Little Carols of the Saints, five organ
    pieces

The World at the Manger, Christmas
    cantata

Canticle of Fire, for chorus and organ

1974 (43) The Glitter Gang, cassation for audience
    and orchestra

WOLF, Hugo/1860–1903/Austria

1877–78 (17+) Lieder aus der Jugenzeit
1877–97 (17+) Lieder nach verscheidenen Dichten
1879–80 (19) String Quartet in D minor
1880–88 (20–28) Eichendorff-Lieder
1883–85 (23–25) Penthesilea, symphonic poem
1887 (27) Italian Serenade, for string quartet
    (arranged for small orchestra in 1892)
1888 (28) Mörike-Lieder, fifty-three songs
Goethe-Lieder, fifty-one songs (1888–89)
1890 (30) Spanish Song-Book, song settings of forty-
    four Spanish poems
1891 (31) Italian Song-Book, Book I, twenty-two
    songs
The Feast of Sulhaug, incidental music
1896 (36) fp. Der Corregidor, opera
Italian Song-Book, Book II, twenty-four
    songs

1895 (19) Violin Sonata in G minor, Op. 1
1901 (25) *p.* Piano Quintet in D♭ major, Op. 6
. *p.* Piano Trio in F♯ major, Op. 7
1902 (26) *p.* Piano Trio in D major, Op. 5
  p. Violin Sonata in A minor, Op. 10
1903 (27) *p.* Chamber Symphony in B♭ major, Op. 8
  fp. Donne curiose, opera
  La Vita nuova, oratorio
1906 (30) *fp. School for Fathers,* opera
  fp. I quatro (sic) rusteghi, comedy-opera
1909 (33) *fp. Susanna's Secret,* opera
1911 (35) *fp. The Jewels of the Madonna,* opera
1936 (60) *fp. Il Campiello,* opera
1939 (63) *fp. Dama Boba,* opera

This chronologically arranged survey of compositions begins in 1554 and continues through 1975. Before 1554, four major composers were born: Tallis (*c*.1505), A. Gabrieli (1510), Palestrina (*c*.1525), and Byrd (1543).

Which composers were born, which died, and what music was written (or first performed or published) in any given year can be seen under the heading for that year. Within each year composers are listed chronologically, the oldest first. As in Part One, composers' ages are given beside each entry.

The entries in this section are sometimes condensed; for fuller details, cross-reference should be made to Part One.

1554

PALESTRINA (*c*.29)   *p*. First Book of Masses

1557   MORLEY and GABRIELI, G. were born

1560   FARNABY was born

1562   CAMPIAN and SWEELINCK were born

GABRIELI, A. (52)   *p*. Sacrae cantiones a 5
                            v.v., motets (1562–65)

1563   BULL and DOWLAND were born

PALESTRINA (*c*.38)
p. First Book of Motets

1567   MONTEVERDI was born

TALLIS (*c*.62)   **PALESTRINA** (*c*.42)
p. Psalm Tunes printed in   *Missa Papae Marcelli*
   Archbishop Parker's
   Psalter

1569

PALESTRINA (*c*.44)   *p*. Second Book of Masses

1570

PALESTRINA (*c.*45)   *p.* Third Book of Masses
Missa Brevis

1575

BYRD (32)   *p.* Seventeen Motets

1576

GABRIELI, A. (66)   *p.* Cantiones ecclesiasticae
a 4 v.v., motets

1578

GABRIELI, A. (68)   *p.* Cantiones sacrae,
motets

1583   FRESCOBALDI and GIBBONS were born

1584

PALESTRINA (*c.*59)   **MONTEVERDI** (17)
p. Settings of the *Song of*   Canzonettas for three
Solomon   voices

1585   SCHÜTZ was born; TALLIS died

1586   GABRIELI, A. died

BYRD (43)   *p.* A Printed Broadside
for six voices

1587

GABRIELI, G. (30)
p. Concerti for six to
    sixteen voices
p. Madrigali e ricercare

MONTEVERDI (20)
p. Madrigals, for five
    voices, Book I

1588

BYRD (45)

p. Psalmes, Songs and
    Sonnets

1589

GABRIELI, A.
    (posthumous)
p. Madrigali e ricercare
BYRD (46)
p. Cantiones sacrae, Book

I, twenty-nine motets
    for five voices
p. Songs of sundrie
    natures

1590

PALESTRINA (*c.*65)
p. Aeterne Christe
    Munera, mass
Stabat Mater (*c.*1590)

MONTEVERDI (23)
p. Madrigals, for five
    voices, Book II

1591

BYRD (48)

p. Cantiones sacrae, Book
    II, thirty-two motets

1592

MONTEVERDI (25)
p. Madrigals, for five
    voices, Book III

SWEELINCK (30)
p. Chansons françaises, in
    three parts (1592–94)

1593

MORLEY (36)
p. Canzonets, or Little

Short Songs to Three
Voyces

1594   PALESTRINA died

MORLEY (37)

p. Madrigalls to Foure
Voyces

1595

MORLEY (38)
p. The First Booke of
Ballets to fiue voyces

p. The First Booke of
Canzonets to two
voyces

1597

MORLEY (40)
p. Two songs in
"Canzonets or Little
Short Songs to foure
voyces"
p. Canzonets or Little
Short Aers to fiue and
sixe voices

p. A Plaine and Easie
Introduction to
Practicall Musicke
GABRIELI, G. (40)
p. Sacrae Symphoniae,
Book I
DOWLAND (34)
p. First Book of Songes or
Ayres

1598

MORLEY (41)
p. Madrigalls to fiue
Voyces

FARNABY (38)
p. Canzonets to Foure
Voyces

1599

MORLEY (42)

p. The Firste Booke of
Consort Lessons

1600   FARNABY died

MORLEY (43)
p. The First Book of
Ayres or Little Short
Songs to sing and play
to the Lute with the
Base Viole
DOWLAND (37)
p. Second Book of Songes

1601

MORLEY (44)
p. Two madrigals in *The
Triumphs of Oriana*
CAMPIAN (39)
p. A Book of Airs to be
Sung to the Lute

1603   MORLEY died

MONTEVERDI (36)
p. Madrigals, for Five
Voices, Book IV
DOWLAND (40)
p. Third Book of Songes
or Ayres

1604

DOWLAND (41)   *p. Lachrymae*

1605

GABRIELI, A.
(posthumous)
*p. Canzoni alla francese et
Ricercare Arlosi*
BYRD (62)
p. Gradualia, Book I
MONTEVERDI (38)
p. Madrigals, for five
voices, Book V

1607

BYRD (64)
p. Gradualia, Book II
MONTEVERDI (40)
Scherzi Musicali for three
voices
fp. Orfeo, opera
CAMPIAN (45)
p. Songs for a Masque

306

1608

GABRIELI, G. (51)
p. Canzona *La Spiritosa*

MONTEVERDI (41)
fp. L'Arianna, opera
Il Ballo delle ingrate,
   ballet

1610

MONTEVERDI (43)
p. Masses
p. Vespers

1611

BYRD (68)
p. Psalmes, Songs and
   Sonnets

SCHÜTZ (26)
p. Italian Madrigals

1612   GABRIELI, G. died

SWEELINCK (50)
*Rimes françoises et
   italiennes*
DOWLAND (49)
p. Fourth Book of Songes,
   A Pilgrimes Solace

GIBBONS (29)
p. Madrigals and Mottets
   of five parts: Apt for
   Viols and Voyces

1613

BULL (49)
p. Anthem for the
   marriage of Princess
   Elizabeth

CAMPIAN (51)
p. Songs for a Masque

1614

MONTEVERDI (47)

p. Madrigals, Book VI

1615

GABRIELI, G.
(posthumous)
p. Canzoni e sonate
p. Sacrae Symphoniae,
 Book II

MONTEVERDI (48)
fp. Tirsi e Clori, ballet
FRESCOBALDI (32)
p. Toccate d'Involatura
*p. Ricercare e canzone
 francesi*

1617

MONTEVERDI (50)   *La Maddalena,* opera

1619

MONTEVERDI (52)
p. Madrigals, Book VII

SWEELINCK (57)
p. Cantiones sacrae
SCHÜTZ (34)
p. Psalms and Motets

1620   CAMPIAN died

1621   SWEELINCK died

1623   BYRD died

SCHÜTZ (38)   *Resurrection Oratorio
 Easter Oratorio*

1624

FRESCOBALDI (41)   *Capricci sopra diversi
 soggetti*

1625	GIBBONS died

SCHÜTZ (40)	*Cantiones sacrae,* for four voices

1626	DOWLAND died

1627	

MONTEVERDI (60)	SCHÜTZ (42)
Armida, opera	*fp. Dafne,* opera
FRESCOBALDI (44)	
Second Book of Toccate	

1628	BULL died

MONTEVERDI (61)	FRESCOBALDI (45)
fp. Mercurio e Marte, opera	*Libro delle canzoni*

1629	

SCHÜTZ (44)	*p. Symphoniae sacrae,* Part I

1632	LULLY was born

MONTEVERDI (65)	*p.* Scherzi musicali, for one or two voices

1635	

FRESCOBALDI (52)	*p. Fiori musicali*

1636

SCHÜTZ (51)
Musicalische exequien
  (Funeral music)

*Kleine Geistliche
Concerte*, Book I

1637 BUXTEHUDE was born

1638

MONTEVERDI (71)
*p. Madrigali guerrieri e
  amorosi*, Book VIII

SCHÜTZ (53)
fp. Orpheus and Euridice,
  ballet

1639

SCHÜTZ (54)

*Kleine Geistliche
Concerte*, Book II

1640

MONTEVERDI (73)

Selva morale e spirituale

1641

MONTEVERDI (74)

*Il ritorno d'Ulisse in
  patria*, opera

1642

MONTEVERDI (75)

*L'Incoronazione di
  Poppea*, opera

1643 MONTEVERDI and FRESCOBALDI died

1645

SCHÜTZ (60)   *The Seven Words from
                            the Cross,* choral work

1647

SCHÜTZ (62)   *p. Symphoniae sacrae,*
                            Part II

1648

SCHÜTZ (63)   *p. Musicali ad chorum
                            sacrum*

1649 BLOW was born

1650

SCHÜTZ (65)   MONTEVERDI
p. Symphoniae sacrae,   (posthumous)
 Part III   *p.* Masses for four voices,
                            and psalms

1651

MONTEVERDI   *p.* Madrigals and
 (posthumous)   Canzonettes, Book IX

1653 CORELLI was born

1658

LULLY (26)   *fp. Ballets d'Alcidiane*

1659   PURCELL was born

LULLY (27)   *fp. Ballet de la raillerie*

1660   SCARLATTI, A. was born

LULLY (28)   *fp. Ballet de Xerxes*

1661

LULLY (29)   *fp. Ballet de l'Ercole*
fp. Ballet de l'impatience   *amante*
fp. Ballet des saisons

1663

LULLY (31)   *fp. Ballet des noces de*
fp. Ballet des arts   *village*

1664

SCHÜTZ (79)   *fp. Miserere,* concert
Christmas Oratorio   setting of "Miserere
LULLY (32)   mei Deus"
fp. Ballet des amours   *fp. La mariage forcé,*
   déguises   comedy ballet
fp. Entr'actes for   *fp. La Princesse d'Elide,*
   Corneille's *Oedipe*   comedy ballet

1665

LULLY (33)
fp. L'Amour médecin,
comedy ballet
fp. La Naissance de
Venus, ballet

fp. Ballet des Gardes
SCHÜTZ (80)
Four passions

1666

LULLY (34)
fp. Le triomphe de

Bacchus dans les Indes,
ballet
fp. Ballet des Muses

1667

LULLY (35)

fp. Le Sicilien, comedy
ballet

1668   COUPERIN was born

LULLY (36)
fp. Georges Dandin,
comedy ballet

fp. Le Carnaval, ou
Mascarade de
Versailles, ballet

1669

LULLY (37)
fp. Monsieur de

Pourceaugnac,
comedy ballet
fp. Ballet de Flore

1670

LULLY (38)
fp. Les amants
magnifiques, comedy
ballet

fp. Le Bourgeois
gentilhomme, comedy
ballet

1671   ALBINONI was born

SCHÜTZ (86)	**LULLY** (39)
Deutsches Magnificat	*fp. Psyche*, tragi-comedy
BUXTEHUDE (34)	*fp. Ballet des Ballets*
Wedding Arias	

1672   SCHÜTZ died

1673

LULLY (41)	*fp. Cadmus et Hermione*, opera

1674

LULLY (42)	*Triomphe d'Alcide*,
fp. Alceste, ou Le	opera

1675   VIVALDI was born (*c.*1675)

LULLY (43)	*fp. Thésée*, opera

1676

LULLY (44)	*fp. Atys*, opera

1677

LULLY (45)	*fp. Isis*, opera
	fp. Te Deum

1678

LULLY (46)
fp. Psyche, opera

BUXTEHUDE (41)
Wedding Arias

1679

LULLY (47)
fp. Bellérophon, opera

SCARLATTI, A. (19)
*fp. Gli equivoci nel
    sembiante,* opera

1680

LULLY (48)
fp. Proserpine, opera

PURCELL (21)
Nine fantasias of four
parts

1681   TELEMANN was born

LULLY (49)
*fp. Le Triomphe de
    l'Amour,* ballet

CORELLI (28)
p. Sonatas in three parts
(twelve sonatas da
chiesa)

1682

LULLY (50)
fp. Persée, opera

PURCELL (23)
Hear My Prayer, anthem
(*c*.1682)

1683   RAMEAU was born

LULLY (51)
fp. Phaéton, opera
De profundis
PURCELL (24)

Twelve sonatas of three
parts
SCARLATTI, A. (23)
fp. Pompeo, opera
fp. Psiche, opera

1684

LULLY (52)
fp. Amadis de Gaule,
   opera
Motets for two choirs

BLOW (35)
Venus and Adonis,
   masque
Ode for St. Cecilia's Day
   "Begin the Song"

1685   BACH, J.S., HANDEL and SCARLATTI, D.
   were born

LULLY (53)
fp. Roland, opera
fp. Le Temple de la Paix,
   ballet

CORELLI (32)
p. Sonatas in three parts
   (twelve sonatas da
   camera)

1686   PORPORA was born

LULLY (54)
fp. Armide et Renaud,
   opera

fp. Acis de Galathée,
   opera

1687   LULLY died

1688

PURCELL (29)
How pleasant is this

flowery plain, secular
cantata

1689

CORELLI (36)
p. Sonatas in three parts
   (twelve sonatas da
   chiesa)

PURCELL (30)
fp. Dido and Aeneas,
   opera
Musick's Handmaid, for
   harpsichord

1690

PURCELL (31)
The Prophetess or *The History of Dioclesian*, opera
SCARLATTI, A. (30)
fp. Gli equivoci in amore, opera

COUPERIN (22)
Pièces d'orgue en deux messes: *Messe pour les couvents*, twenty-one organ pieces
Messe pour les Paroisses, twenty-one organ pieces
Messe solenelle

1691

PURCELL (32)
King Arthur or *The British Worthy*, opera

The Wives' Excuse, incidental music

1692   TARTINI was born

BUXTEHUDE (55)
Sonata in D major, for viola da gamba, cello and harpsichord
PURCELL (33)
The Faery Queen, opera

The Libertine, incidental music
Oedipus, incidental music
COUPERIN (24)
Trio Sonata, *La Steinkerque*

1693

PURCELL (34)

Epsom Wells, incidental music

1694

PURCELL (35)
The Married Beau, incidental music

SCARLATTI, A. (34)
fp. Pirro e Demetrio, opera

CONTINUED

317

ALBINONI (23)
*Zenobia, regina de
    Palmireni,* opera

CORELLI (41)
p. Sonatas in three parts
    (twelve sonatas da
    camera)

1695   PURCELL died

PURCELL (36)
The Indian Queen,
    opera

The Tempest or *The
    Enchanted Island,*
    opera
Bonduca, incidental music

1696

BUXTEHUDE (59)
Seven Trio Sonatas, for
    violin, gamba and basso
    continuo, Op. 1
Seven Trio Sonatas, for
    violin, gamba and basso
    continuo, Op. 2

PURCELL (posthumous)
p. A choice collection of
    Lessons for the
    Harpsichord or Spinet
p. Harpsichord Suites,
    1–8

1697   LECLAIR was born

BLOW (48)

"My God, my God, look
    upon me", anthem

1698

SCARLATTI, A. (38)
fp. Flavio Cuniberto,
    opera

*fp. La donna ancore e'
    fedele,* opera

1699

SCARLATTI, A. (39)

Two sonatas for flute and
    continuo

1700

BLOW (51)
p. Amphion Anglicus,
collection of songs and
vocal chamber music

CORELLI (47)
p. Sonatas for violin and
violone or harpsichord
(six 'da chiesa'; five 'da
camera'; one Variations
on "La Folia")

1703

SCARLATTI, D. (18)
*fp. Ottavia ristituta al
trono,* opera
fp. Giustina, opera
*c.*1703–07

BACH, J.S. (18–22)
Prelude and Fugue in C
minor, for clavier
Toccata and Fugue in C
major, for clavier
Sonata in D major, for
clavier (*c.*1704)

1704

SCARLATTI, D. (19)

fp. Irene, opera

1705

BUXTEHUDE (68)
Wedding Arias

VIVALDI (*c.*30)
p. Suonate da Camera,
Op. 1

1706

SCARLATTI, A. (46)
*Il sedecia, re di
Gerusalemme,*
oratorio

RAMEAU (23)
p. Harpsichord Works,
Book I

pre **1707**

HANDEL   Sonata for viola da gamba

1707 BUXTEHUDE died

SCARLATTI, A. (47)   **ALBINONI** (36)
fp. Il trionfo della libertà,   *Sinfonie e concerti a 5*
  opera   **HANDEL** (22)
fp. Mitridate eupatore,   "Laudate pueri
  opera   Dominum", aria
                                Rodrigo, opera (*c.*1707)

1708 BLOW died

TELEMANN (27)   Most of the "Great"
Trio Sonata in E♭ major   Preludes and Fugues
  (1708–12)   (*c.*1708–17)
BACH, J.S. (23)   The Toccatas (*c.*1708–17)
Passacaglia and Fugue in   **HANDEL** (23)
  C minor for organ   *La Resurrezione,* Easter
  (*c.*1708–17)   oratorio
                                PORPORA (22)
                                Agrippina, opera

1709

COUPERIN (41)   **VIVALDI** (*c.*34)
Messe à l'usage des   *p.* Sonata a violini e bassi,
  Couvents   Op. 2

1710 ARNE, BACH, W.F., BOYCE, PARADIES
          and PERGOLESI were born

SCARLATTI, A. (50)   *Informata vulnerate,*
Est dies tropael, motet   *cantata* (*c.*1710)
  (*c.*1710)

ALBINONI (39)
Concerti a 5

SCARLATTI, D. (25)
fp. La Sylvia, opera

1711

SCARLATTI, D. (26)
fp. Tolomeo e Alessandro,
opera
HANDEL (26)
Rinaldo, opera

PORPORA (25)
Flavio Anicio Olibrio,
opera
*Il martirio di S. Giovanni
Nepomucéno,* oratorio

1712

VIVALDI (*c.*37)
p. L'Estro harmonico,
Op. 3, concertos
(*c.*1712)
p. La stravaganza, Op. 4,
concertos (1712–13)

SCARLATTI, D. (27)
fp. Tetide in sciro, opera
HANDEL (27)
Il Pastor Fido, opera
(first version)

1713   CORELLI died

COUPERIN (45)
Harpsichord Works, Book
I
VIVALDI (*c.*38)
fp. Ottone in Villa, opera
HANDEL (28)
Teseo, opera
Te Deum and Jubilate, for
the Peace of Utrecht

SCARLATTI, D. (28)
fp. Ifigenia in Aulide,
opera
fp. Ifigenia in Tauride,
opera
PORPORA (27)
Basilio, re d'oriente, opera

1714   BACH, C.P.E. and GLUCK were born

CORELLI (posthumous)
p. Concerti Grossi
VIVALDI (*c.*39)
fp. Orlando finto pazzo,
opera

Moyses deus Pharaonis,
oratorio
SCARLATTI, D. (29)
fp. Amor d'un ombra,
opera

CONTINUED

PORPORA (28)
Arianna e Teseo, opera

TARTINI (23)
Violin Sonata in G minor,
"Devil's Trill"

1715

SCARLATTI, A. (55)
fp. Tigrone, opera
Twelve sinfonias
Four string quartets
(without harpsichord)
COUPERIN (47)
Leçons de ténèbres, for
one and two voices
VIVALDI (c.40)
fp. Nerone fatto Cesare,
opera

TELEMANN (34)
Concerto in A major
(1715–20)
Suite in D minor
(1715–20)
HANDEL (30)
Amadigi di Gaula, opera
Water Music (1715–17)
SCARLATTI, D. (30)
fp. Ambleto, opera

1716

ALBINONI (45)
Twelve concerti a 5
(c.1716)
VIVALDI (c.41)
*fp. Arsilda Regina di
Ponto,* opera
Juditha, oratorio
p. Six sonate, Op. 5
(c.1716)

p. Six concerti a cinque,
Op. 6 (1716–c.17)
p. Seven concerti a cinque,
Op. 7 (1716–c.17)
TELEMANN (35)
Die Kleine Kammermusik
Six Suites for violin,
querflute and piano

1717

COUPERIN (49)
Harpsichord Works, Book
II
VIVALDI (c.42)
fp. Tieteberga, opera
BACH, J.S. (32–38)
English Suites (c.1717–23)

The Inventions, Little
Preludes and Sym-
phonies (c.1717–23)
The *Brandenburg* Concerti
(c.1717–23)
The Suites (Overtures)
for orchestra
(c.1717–23)

The Violin Concerti
(*c*.1717–23)
The Sonatas (Suites)

for violin, flute, cello
and viola da gamba
(*c*.1717–23)

1718

SCARLATTI, A. (58)
fp. Telemaco, opera
VIVALDI (*c*.43)
fp. Scanderbeg, opera
TELEMANN (37)

Six Trios for two violins,
cello and bass continuo
SCARLATTI, D. (33)
fp. Berenice, opera
PORPORA (32)
Temistocle, opera

1719

SCARLATTI, A. (59)
fp. Marco Attilo Regolo,
opera

PORPORA (33)
Faramondo, opera

1720

SCARLATTI, A. (60)
*fp. Tito o sempronio
gracco,* opera (com-
pleted version for
Rome production)
VIVALDI (*c*.45)
fp. La verità in cimento,
opera
BACH, J.S. (35)
Chromatic Fantasia and

Fugue, for clavier
(1720–23)
HANDEL (35)
Chandos Anthems
(*c*.1720)
Huit Suites de pièces, for
harpsichord (*c*.1720)
Acis and Galatea, secular
cantata (*c*.1720)
Radamisto, opera (*c*.1720)

1721

SCARLATTI, A. (61)
fp. Griselda, opera
VIVALDI (*c*.46)
fp. Silvia, opera

HANDEL (36)
Floridante, opera
PORPORA (35)
*Il martirio di Santa
Eugenia,* oratorio

1722

COUPERIN (54)
Harpsichord Works, Book
  III
Four *Concerts Royaux*
ALBINONI (51)
Twelve concerti a cinque
  (*c*.1722)

VIVALDI (*c*.47)
*L'adorazione delle tre Re
  Magi,* oratorio
BACH, J.S. (37)
*The Well-Tempered
  Clavier,* Part I
French Suites

1723

TELEMANN (42)
*Hamburger Ebb und
  Fluht,* overture
BACH, J.S. (38)
St. John Passion
HANDEL (38)
Ottone, opera

PORPORA (37)
Adelaide, opera
LECLAIR (26)
p. Sonatas for Violin
  alone, with a Bass,
  Book I

1724

COUPERIN (56)
Les Goûts-Réunis, ten
  "concerts" for various
  instruments
VIVALDI (*c*.49)
fp. Giustino, opera

HANDEL (39)
Giulio Cesare, opera
Fifteen Chamber Sonatas
PORPORA (38)
Griselda, opera

1725 SCARLATTI, A. died

VIVALDI (*c*.50)
p. Concerto *The Seasons*
  (from Op. 8)
TELEMANN (44)
Pimpinone, opera

HANDEL (40)
Rodelinda, opera
Trio Sonata in D minor

1726

VIVALDI (c.51)
Cunegonda, opera

PORPORA (40)
Imeneo in Atene, opera

1727

VIVALDI (c.52)
Ipermestra, opera
HANDEL (42)
Zadok, the Priest,
  coronation anthem
Admeto, opera

PORPORA (41)
Ezio, opera

1728

VIVALDI (c.53)
Rosilena ed Oronta, opera
p. La Cetra concerti,
  Op. 9
TELEMANN (47)
*Der getreuer Musik-
  meister*, cantata

RAMEAU (45)
p. Harpsichord Works,
  Book II
HANDEL (43)
Tolomeo, opera
LECLAIR (31)
p. Sonatas for violin alone,
  with a Bass, Book II

1729

VIVALDI (c.54)
Concerti, Op. 10, 11 and
  12 (1729–30)
BACH, J.S. (44)
St. Matthew Passion

The Clavier Concerti
  (1729–36)
PORPORA (43)
Semiramide riconosciuta,
  opera

1730

COUPERIN (62)
p. Harpsichord Works,
  Book IV

PORPORA (44)
Mitridate, opera

1731

BACH, J.S. (46)
St. Mark Passion
HANDEL (46)
Nine sonatas for two
  violins and continuo
  (*c.*1731)

PORPORA (45)
Poro, opera
PERGOLESI (21)
Salustia, opera
BACH, C.P.E. (17)
Trio in B minor

1732   HAYDN was born

VIVALDI (*c.*57)
fp. La fida ninfa, opera
HANDEL (47)
Ezio, opera
Sosarme, opera
Esther, oratorio

PORPORA (46)
Germanico in Germania,
  opera
PERGOLESI (22)
Lo frate innamorato,
  opera
La serva padrona, opera

1733   COUPERIN died

VIVALDI (*c.*58)
fp. Motezuma, opera
RAMEAU (50)
Hippolyte et Aricie,
  opera
BACH, J.S. (48)
Mass in B minor
Christmas Oratorio
HANDEL (48)
Orlando, opera
Huit Suites de Pièces, for
  harpsichord

PORPORA (47)
Arianna in Nasso, opera
ARNE (23)
Dido and Aenas, opera
The Opera of Operas,
  opera
Rosamund, opera
PERGOLESI (23)
Il Prigionier superbo,
  opera

1734

VIVALDI (*c.*59)
fp. L'Olimpiade, opera

HANDEL (49)
Persichore, ballet

Arianna, opera
Il Pastor fido, opera
  (second and third
  versions)
p. Six concerti grossi
PORPORA (48)
Enea nel Lazio, opera
Davide e Bersabea,
  oratorio

LECLAIR (37)
p. Sonatas for violin
  alone, with a Bass,
  Book III
PERGOLESI (24)
Adriano in Siria, opera
La Contadina astuta,
  opera

1735

VIVALDI (*c.*60)
fp. Griselda, opera
fp. Aristide, opera
RAMEAU (52)
Les Indes galantes,
  opera-ballet
BACH, J.S. (50)
Italian Concerto
Partita in B minor, for
  clavier

Ascension Oratorio
  (1735–36)
HANDEL (50)
Alcina, opera
PORPORA (49)
Ifigenia in Aulide, opera
Polifemo, opera
PERGOLESI (25)
L'Olimpiade, opera
Flamincio, opera

1736

VIVALDI (*c.*61)
*fp. Ginevra, Principessa di
  Scozia,* opera
BACH, J.S. (51)
Easter Oratorio
HANDEL (51)
Atalanta, opera
Alexander's Feast,
  secular cantata

Six Fugues for
  Harpsichord
ARNE (26)
Zara, incidental music
PERGOLESI (26)
Stabat Mater, for female
  voices

1737

VIVALDI (*c.*62)
fp. Catone in Utica, opera

p. Il Pastor Fido, sonatas
  (*c.*1737)
CONTINUED

BACH, J.S. (52)
Masses, in F: A: Gm and
    G major (1737–40)
HANDEL (52)
Berenice, opera

Concerto grosso
PORPORA (51)
Lucio Papirio, opera
LECLAIR (40)
p. Six concertos for violin

1738

VIVALDI (*c*.63)
fp. L'Oracolo in Messenia,
    opera
HANDEL (53)
Xerxes, opera
Six organ concerti
SCARLATTI, D. (53)
p. Essercizi per
    Gravicembalo

PORPORA (52)
Carlo il Calvo, opera
ARNE (28)
Comus, masque
PARADIES (28)
Alessandro in Persia,
    opera

1739   DITTERSDORF was born

VIVALDI (*c*.64)
fp. Feraspe, opera
RAMEAU (56)
Dardanus, opera
Les Fêtes d'Hebe, ballet
HANDEL (54)
Israel in Egypt, oratorio
Saul, oratorio
Ode for Saint Cecilia's
    Day

Twelve Concerti Grossi
Seven Trio Sonatas
SCARLATTI, D. (54)
*p. XLII Suites de pièces
    pour la Clavecin*
PORPORA (53)
Il Barone di Zampano,
    opera

1740

VIVALDI (*c*.65)
p. Six sonate a cello e
    basse, Op. 14 (*c*.1740)
HANDEL (55)
p. Concerti for oboe and
    strings

p. Six organ concerti
Three Double Concerti
    (1740–50)
PORPORA (54)
Il trionfo di Camilla,
    opera

ARNE (30)
Alfred, masque

The Judgment of Paris,
   opera

1741   VIVALDI died

RAMEAU (58)
p. Harpsichord Works,
   Book III
BACH, J.S. (56)
Six partitas for clavier

HANDEL (56)
Messiah, oratorio
Five concerti grossi
GLUCK (27)
Artaserse, opera

1742   GRÉTRY was born

BACH, J.S. (57)
The "Goldberg" Varia-
   tions for clavier
HANDEL (57)
Forest Music

PORPORA (56)
Statira, opera
BACH, C.P.E. (28)
"Prussian" Sonata
GLUCK (28)
Demetrio, opera

1743   BOCCHERINI was born

HANDEL (58)
Samson, oratorio
The *Dettingen* Te Deum
PORPORA (57)
Temistocle, opera
ARNE (33)
Britannia, masque
Eliza, opera

BACH, C.P.E. (29)
Sonata for clavier,
   Wurtemburgian
GLUCK (29)
Il Tigrane, opera

1744

BACH, J.S. (59)
*The Well-Tempered
   Clavier*, Part II
HANDEL (59)
Semele, secular oratorio

ARNE (34)
Abel, oratorio
BACH, W.F. (34)
Clavier sonata No. 2, in
   A major (*c*.1744)

1745

RAMEAU (62)
Platée, ballet
HANDEL (60)
Balshazzar, oratorio

GLUCK (31)
Ippolito, opera

1746

HANDEL (61)
Occasional Oratorio
LECLAIR (49)
Scylla et Glaucus, opera

GLUCK (32)
Artamene, opera
p. Six sonatas for two
  violins and continuo

1747

BACH, J.S. (62)
A Musical Offering, for
  flute, violin and clavier
HANDEL (62)
Judas Maccabeus,
  oratorio

PORPORA (61)
Filandro, opera
BACH, C.P.E. (33)
Sonata in D major
GLUCK (33)
Le nozze d'Ercole e d'Ebe,
  opera

1748

RAMEAU (65)
Pigmalion, ballet
Zais, ballet

HANDEL (63)
Joshua, oratorio

1749 CIMAROSA was born

BACH, J.S. (64)
The Art of Fugue
HANDEL (64)

Music for the Royal
  Fireworks
Solomon, oratorio
Susanna, oratorio

1750   BACH. J.S. and ALBINONI died

HANDEL (65)
Theodora, oratorio
ARNE (40)
Seven trio-sonatas for two
   violins with figured bass

BOYCE (40)
p. Eight Symphonies in
   Eight Parts . . . Opera
   seconda (*c.*1750)
GLUCK (38)
Ezio, opera

1752   CLEMENTI was born

HANDEL (67)
Jephtha, oratorio

GLUCK (38)
Issipile, opera

1753

GLUCK (39)

Nine Symphonies

1754

RAMEAU (71)

Zephyre, ballet

1755

GLUCK (41)
Les Amours champêtres,
   opera
Alessandro, ballet

HAYDN (23)
String Quartets Nos. 1–13

1756   MOZART was born

GLUCK (42)
Antigono, opera
Le Chinois poli en France,
   opera

HAYDN (24)
Organ Concerto No. 1 in
   C major
Piano Concerto in C
   major

1757   SCARLATTI, D. died

1758

GLUCK (44)   *L'Isle de Merlin, ou Le*
                            Monde renversé, opera

1759   HANDEL died

TELEMANN (78)   HAYDN (27)
St. Mark Passion   Symphony No. 1 in D
GLUCK (45)   major
L'Arbre enchanté, opera

1760   CHERUBINI was born

RAMEAU (78)   HAYDN (28)
Les Paladins, opera-ballet   Organ Concerto No. 2 in
HANDEL (posthumous)   C major
p. Six Organ Concerti   Symphony No. 2 in C
                              major (*c.*1760)
                            GOSSEC (26)
                            Requiem Mass

1761

GLUCK (47)   Symphony No. 7 in C
Le Cadi dupé, opera   major, *Le Midi*
Don Juan, ballet   Symphony No. 8 in G
HAYDN (29)   major, *Le Soir, ou La*
Symphony No. 3 in G   *Tempête*
  major   Symphony No. 19 in D
Symphony No. 4 in D   major
  major   GOSSEC (27)
Symphony No. 5 in A   *Le Tonnelier,* opera
  major   BACH, J.C. (26)
Symphony No. 6 in D   *Artaserse,* opera
  major, *Le Matin*   *Catone in Utica,* opera

1762

ARNE (52)
Artaxerxes, opera
Love in a Village,
  pasticcio
BACH, C.P.E. (48)
Harp Sonata in B minor
GLUCK (48)
Orfeo ed Euridice, opera

HAYDN (30)
Symphony No. 9 in C
  major
BACH, J.C. (27)
Alessandro nell'Indie,
  opera
MOZART (6)
Sonata in C major, for
  violin and piano, K.6
  (1762–64)

pre 1763

HAYDN
Symphony No. 10 in D
  major

Symphony No. 11 in E♭
  major
Piano Sonata No. 3 in A
  major

1763

HAYDN (31)
Symphony No. 12 in E
  major
Symphony No. 13 in D
  major

BACH, J.C. (28)
Orione, opera
Zanaida, opera
MOZART (7)
Violin Sonata in D major,
  K.7
Violin Sonata in B♭ major,
  K.8

pre 1764

HAYDN

Symphonies Nos. 14 and
  15

1764   RAMEAU and LECLAIR died

ARNE (54)
Judith, oratorio
L'Olimpiade, opera
GLUCK (50)
Poro, opera
La Rencontre imprévue,
  opera
HAYDN (32)
Symphonies No. 16–18
  (c.1764)
Symphony No. 22 in Eb
  major, *Der Philosoph*

MOZART (8)
Symphony No. 1 in Eb
  major, K.16
Symphony No. 4 in D
  major, K.19
Seven Violin Sonatas, K.9
  in G: K.10 in Bb: K.11
  in G: K.12 in A: K.13
  in F: K.14 in C: K.15
  in Bb

1765

GLUCK (51)
Semiramide, ballet
HAYDN (33)
Symphony No. 26 in D
  minor, *Lamentations*
  (c.1765)
Symphony No. 30 in C
  major, *Alleluia*
Symphony No. 31 in D
  major, *Horn Signal*
String Quartets Nos.
  14–19
GOSSEC (31)
Le Faux Lord, opera

BACH, J.C. (30)
Adriano in Siria, opera
BOCCHERINI (22)
La confedarazione, opera
MOZART (9)
Symphony No. 5 in Bb
  major, K.22
Piano Sonata in C major
  (four hands), K.19d
Three Sonatas by J.C.
  Bach arranged as
  concertos with string
  orchestra, K.107

1766

GLUCK (52)
L'Orfano della China,
  ballet
HAYDN (34)
Piano Sonatas Nos. 4–7

Piano Sonatas Nos. 8–12
  (1766–67)
Mass No. 4, *Great Organ*
GOSSEC (32)
Les Pêcheurs, opera

334

MOZART (10)
Six Violin Sonatas, K.26
  in E♭: K.27 in G: K.28
in D: K.29 in D: K.30
in F: K.31 in B♭

1767

GLUCK (53)
Alkestis, opera
HAYDN (35)
Piano Sonatas Nos. 13–16
  (*c*.1767)
Piano Sonata No. 17
GOSSEC (33)
Le Double déguisemente,
  opera
Toinon et Toinette, opera
BACH, J.C. (32)
Carattaco, opera
DITTERSDORF (28)
Amore in musica, opera

MOZART (11)
Symphony No. 6 in F
  major, K.43
Symphony No. 43 in F
  major, K.76
Four Piano Concertos,
  K.37 in F: K.39 in B♭:
  K.40 in D: K.41 in G
Three Sonatas for organ
  and strings, K.62 in
  E♭: K.68 in B♭: K.69
  in D

1768 PORPORA died

MOZART (12)
Bastien und Bastienne,
  operetta

Symphony No. 7 in D,
  K.45
Symphony No. 8 in D,
  K.48

---

pre **1769**

HAYDN

Two Violin Concerti in C
  and G

1769 TELEMANN died

HAYDN (37)
String Quartets Nos.
  20–25

GRÉTRY (27)
Le Tableau parlant, opera

CONTINUED

335

MOZART (13)
Symphony No. 9 in C
   major, K.73

Symphony No. 42 in F
   major, K.75
Mass in C major, K.66

1770   BEETHOVEN was born; TARTINI died

BACH, C.P.E. (56)
Passion Cantata
Duo in E minor
Solfeggio in C minor
GLUCK (56)
Paride ed Elena, opera
HAYDN (38)
Violin Concerto in D
   major (pre 1770)
Mass No. 5, *Little Organ,*
   or *St. John* (1770–80)
BACH, J.C. (35)
Gioas Re di Giuda,
   oratorio

DITTERSDORF (31)
Il Viaggatore americano,
   opera
MOZART (14)
Five Symphonies, No. 10
   in G, K.74: No. 11 in
   D, K.80: No. 45 in D,
   K.95: No. 47 in D,
   K.97: No. 12 in G,
   K.110
String Quartet in G major,
   K.80

---

after **1770**

HAYDN

Piano Concerto in G
   major

---

pre **1771**

HAYDN
Piano Concerto in F
   major

Violin Concerto in A
   major

1771

HAYDN (39)
Piano Sonata No. 18 in
   C minor
String Quartets Nos.
   26–31

DITTERSDORF (32)
L'amore disprezzato,
   opera
GRÉTRY (29)
Zémire et Azor, opera

MOZART (15)
Five Symphonies, No. 46 in C, K.96: No. 13 in F, K.112: No. 14 in A, K.114: No: 50 in D, finale only, to the overture of *Ascanio in Alba*, K.120: Symphony in D, finale only, to the overture of *La finta giardiniera*, K.121

---

pre **1772**

HAYDN
Symphony No. 43, *Mercury*

Symphony No. 44, *Trauersymphonie*

1772

HAYDN (40)
Symphony No. 45, *Farewell*
Symphony No. 46
Symphony No. 48, *Maria Teresa*
Symphony No. 52 (1772–74)
Mass No. 3, *St. Cecilia*
String Quartets Nos. 32–37, *Sun* or *Great* Quartets
BACH, J.C. (37)
Endimione, cantata
Temistocle, opera

CIMAROSA (23)
Le stravaganze del conte, opera
MOZART (16)
Lucio Silla, opera
Nine Symphonies, No. 15 in G, K.124: No. 16 in C, K.128: No. 17 in G, K.129: No. 19 in E♭, K.132: No. 20 in D, K.133: No. 21 in A, K.134: Symphony in D, K.161: No. 22 in C, K.162: No. 51 in D, K.163

---

pre **1773**

HAYDN

Symphony No. 49, *The Passion*

1773

BACH, C.P.E. (59)
Fantasia in C minor
HAYDN (41)
Piano Sonatas Nos. 19–24
   (Nos. 22–24 with violin
   parts are Violin Sonatas
   No. 2–4)
DITTERSDORF (34)
Il Tutore e la Pupilla,
   opera
MOZART (17)
Four Symphonies, No. 23
   in D, K. 181: No. 24 in
   B♭, K.182: No. 25 in

Gm, K. 183: No. 26 in
   E♭, K.184
Piano Concerto in D
   major, K.175
"Concertone" in C major,
   for two violins, K.190
Six String Quartets, K.168
   in F: K.169 in A:
   K.170 in C: K.171 in
   E♭: K.172 in B♭:
   K.173 in Dm
String Quintet in B♭,
   K.174

---

pre **1774**

HAYDN

Symphony No. 53, *The
   Imperial*

1774   SPONTINI was born

GLUCK (60)
Iphigénie en Aulide,
   opera
HAYDN (42)
Symphony No. 55, *The
   Schoolmaster*
GOSSEC (40)
Sabinus, opera
La Nativité, oratorio
DITTERSDORF (35)
Il tribunale di Giove,
   opera

MOZART (18)
Four Symphonies, No. 27
   in G, K.199: No. 28 in
   C, K.200: No. 29 in A,
   K.201: No. 30 in D,
   K.202
Bassoon Concerto in B♭,
   K.191
Six Piano Sonatas, K.279
   in C: K.280 in F:
   K.281 in B♭: K.282
   in E♭: K.283 in G:
   K.284 in D
Piano Sonata in B♭ (four
   hands), K.358

ARNE (65)
Caractacus, incidental
   music
BACH, C.P.E. (61)
*The Israelites in the
   Wilderness*, oratorio
GOSSEC (41)
Alexis et Daphné, opera
DITTERSDORF (36)
Il finto pazzo per amore,
   opera
Il maniscalco, opera
Lo sposo burlato, opera

MOZART (19)
La finta giardiniera,
   opera
Il re pastore, dramatic
   festival play
Symphony No. 49 in C,
   K.102
Five Violin Concerti,
   K.207 in B♭: K.211 in
   D: K.216 in G: K.218
   in D: K.219 in A
Sonata in B♭, for organ
   and strings, K.212

---

pre **1776**

HAYDN

Symphony No. 59,
   Feuersymphonie

1776

GLUCK (62)
Alceste, opera
HAYDN (44)
Symphony No. 60 in C,
   Il distratto
Piano Sonatas, Nos.
   25–30
GOSSEC (42)
Hylas et Sylvie, incidental
   music
BACH, J.C. (41)
Lucio Silla, opera
DITTERSDORF (37)
La contadina felice, opera
La moda, opera

Il barone di Rocco Antica,
   opera
MOZART (20)
Three Piano Concerti,
   K.238 in B♭: K.242 in
   F, for three pianos:
   K.246 in C
Piano Trio in B♭, K.254
Five Sonatas for organ
   and strings, K.224 in
   F: K.225 in A: K.241
   in G: K.244 in F:
   K.245 in D
Mass in C major, K.257

GLUCK (63)
Armide, opera
HAYDN (45)
Symphony No. 63, *La Roxolane*
Piano Sonatas Nos. 31 and 32 (1777–78)
DITTERSDORF (38)
L'Arcifanfano, re de' matti, opera

MOZART (21)
Piano Concerto in E♭, K.271
Violin Concerto in D, K.271a
Piano Sonata in C, K.309
Sonata for organ and strings in G, K.274

1778   ARNE died

GOSSEC (44)
La Fête du village, opera
GRÉTRY (36)
L'amant jaloux, opera
CIMAROSA (29)
L'Italiana in Londra, opera
MOZART (22)
Symphony No. 31 in D, *Paris,* K.297
Concerto in C, for flute and harp, K.299
Two Flute Concerti, K.313 in G: K.314 in D

Sinfonia Concertante for wind instruments, app. K.9
Six Piano Sonatas, K.310 in Am: K.311 in D: K.330 in C: K.331 in A: K.332 in F: K.333 in B♭
Seven Violin Sonatas, K.296 in C: K.301 in G: K.302 in E♭: K.303 in C: K.304 in Em: K.305 in A: K.306 in D
CHERUBINI (18)
Demophon, opera

1779   BOYCE died

GLUCK (65)
Iphigénie en Tauride, opera
HAYDN (47)
Symphony No. 69, *Laudon*

Piano Sonatas Nos. 33–37 (1779–80)
GOSSEC (45)
Les Scythes enchaînés, divertissement
Mirsa, ballet

BACH, J.C. (44)
Amadis des Gaules,
  opera
MOZART (23)
Symphony No. 32 in G,
  K.318
Symphony No. 33 in B♭,
  K.319

Sinfonia Concertante in
  E♭, for violin and viola,
  K.364
Sonata for organ and
  strings in C, K.328
Mass in C major, K.317
Concerto for two pianos,
  K.365

1780

BACH, C.P.E. (66)
Symphony in F major
CIMAROSA (31)
Giuditta, oratorio
MOZART (24)
Symphony No. 34 in C
  major, K.338
Six Variations for violin

and piano on "Hélas,
  j'ai perdu mon amant",
  K.360
Sonata for organ and
  strings in C, K.336
BEETHOVEN (10)
Nine variations on a
  March by Dressler

1781

HAYDN (49)
Symphony No. 73, *La
  Chasse*
Concerto No. 2 for Horn
  and Strings
String Quartets Nos.
  38–43, *Russian* or
  Jungfern Quartets
GOSSEC (47)
L'Arche d'Alliance,
  oratorio
CIMAROSA (32)
Il convito, opera
Il pittore parigino,
  opera
MOZART (25)
Idomeneo, opera

Rondo for violin and
  orchestra in C, K.373
Concerto Rondo in E♭
  for horn, K.371
Twelve Variations on "La
  bergère Célimène" for
  violin and piano, K.359
Sonata for two pianos,
  K.448
Five Violin Sonatas,
  K.376 in F: K.377 in
  F: K.378 in B♭: K.379
  in Gm and G: K.380
  in E♭
BEETHOVEN (11)
"Schilderung eines
  Mädchen", song

1782   AUBER, FIELD and PAGANINI were born

GOSSEC (48)
Thésée, opera
CIMAROSA (33)
La ballerina amante,
    opera
Absalon, oratorio
MOZART (26)
Il Seraglio, opera
Symphony No. 35 in D,
    Haffner, K.385

Three Piano Concerti,
    K.413 in F: K.414 in
    A: K.415 in C
Horn Concerto, K.412
Three unfinished violin
    sonatas, K.402–404
String Quartet, K.387
BEETHOVEN (12–32)
Bagatelles for piano
    (1782–1802)

1783

HAYDN (51)
Cello Concerto in D
    major
MOZART (27)
Symphony No. 36 in C,
    Linz, K.425
Two Horn Concerti,
    K.417 in E♭: K.447
    in E♭

Two String Quartets,
    K.421 in D: K.428
    in E♭
BEETHOVEN (13)
p. Three Piano Sonatas
    (composed very early)
Minuet for piano

pre 1784

HAYDN   Piano Sonatas Nos. 38–40

1784   BACH, W.F. died

HAYDN (52)
Armida, opera
String Quartets Nos.
    44–50 (1784–87)
GRÉTRY (42)
L'Épreuve villageoise,
    opera

Richard Coeur de Lion,
    opera
CIMAROSA (35)
L'Olimpiade, opera
Artaserse, opera
MOZART (28)
Six Piano Concerti, K.449
    in E♭: K.450 in B♭:

K.451 in D: K.453 in
G: K.456 in B♭: K.459
in F
Violin Sonata in B♭,
K.454
Piano Sonata in Cm,
K.457

String Quartet in B♭,
K.458
BEETHOVEN (14)
p. Rondo, allegretto for
piano
p. "An einem Saugling",
song

1785

HAYDN (53)
Symphony No. 87 in A
major
Piano Sonata No. 41 in
A♭ (*c.*1785)
Piano Sonata No. 42 in
G minor (1785–86)
Piano Sonata No. 44 in
A♭ (1785–86)
MOZART (29)
Three Piano Concerti,
K.466 in Dm: K.467
in C: K.482 in E♭

Two String Quartets,
K.464 in A: K.465
in C
Piano Quartet in Gm,
K.478
Violin Sonata in E♭,
K.481
BEETHOVEN (15)
Piano Quartets Nos. 1–3
Piano Trio No. 9
Prelude in F minor
for piano

1786   WEBER was born

HAYDN (54)
Symphony No. 82, *The
Bear*
Symphony No. 83, *La
Poule*
Symphony No. 84
Symphony No. 85, *La
Reine* (*c.*1786)
Symphony No. 86, *The
Miracle* (*c.*1786)
GOSSEC (52)
Rosine, opera

DITTERSDORF (47)
Doktor und Apotheker,
opera
*Betrug durch Aber-
glauben,* opera
BOCCHERINI (43)
La Clementina, opera
CIMAROSA (37)
L'impresario in Angustie,
opera
MOZART (30)
The Impresario, opera

CONTINUED

The Marriage of Figaro,
  opera
Symphony No. 38 in D,
  Prague, K.504
Three Piano Concerti,
  K.488 in A: K.491 in
  Cm: K.503 in C
Horn Concerto in E♭,
  K.495
Two Piano Sonatas
  (four hands), K.357
  in G: K.497 in F

String Quartet in D,
  K.499
Piano Quartet in E♭,
  K.493
Three Piano Trios, K.496
  in G: K.498 in B♭, for
  clarinet, viola and
  piano: K.502 in B♭
BEETHOVEN (16)
Trio for piano, flute and
  bassoon

1787   GLUCK died

BACH, C.P.E. (73)
*The Resurrection and
  Ascension of Jesus,*
  oratorio
HAYDN (55)
Symphonies Nos. 88 and
  89
String Quartets Nos.
  51–57, *Seven Words*
Piano Sonata No. 45
  (1787–88)

DITTERSDORF (48)
Die Liebe in Narrenhaus,
  opera
Democrito coretto, opera
MOZART (31)
Don Giovanni, opera
Eine Kleine Nachtmusik,
  for strings
Three String Quartets,
  K.406 in Cm: K.515
  in C: K.516 in Gm
Piano Sonata in C (four
  hands), K.521
Violin Sonata in A, K.526

1788   BACH, C.P.E. died

BACH, C.P.E. (74)
Concerto for harpsichord,
  fortepiano and strings
Quartet in G major
HAYDN (56)
Symphonies Nos. 90 and
  91
Symphony No. 92,
  Oxford

Toy Symphony
MOZART (32)
Symphony No. 39 in E♭
  major, K.543
Symphony No. 40 in G
  minor, K.550
Symphony No. 41 in C
  major, *Jupiter,* K.551
Piano Concerto in D

344

major, *Coronation*,
K.537
String Quartet in D minor,
K.546
Three piano trios, K.542
in E: K.548 in C:

K.564 in G
Piano Sonata in C
(Sonatina), K.545
Violin Sonata in F, K.547
CHERUBINI (28)
Ifigenia in Aulide, opera

1789

HAYDN (57)
String Quartets Nos.
58–59
Piano Sonata No. 46
Piano Sonata No. 47
(1789–90)
DITTERSDORF (50)
Hieronimus Knicker,
opera
CIMAROSA (40)
Cleopatra, opera

MOZART (33)
String Quartet in D,
K.575
Two Piano Sonatas, K.570
in B♭: K.576 in D
BEETHOVEN (19)
Two Preludes through all
twelve major keys, for
piano or organ

---

pre 1790

HAYDN

Violin Sonata No. 1

1790

HAYDN (58)
Piano Sonata No. 48
(c.1790)
Seven Nocturnes for the
King of Naples
DITTERSDORF (51)
Das rote Käppchen, opera
MOZART (34)
Così fan tutte, opera
String Quintet in D,
K.593

Two String Quartets,
K.589 in B♭: K.590
in F
BEETHOVEN (20)
"Musik zu einem Ritter-
ballett", for orchestra
Twenty-four Variations on
"Venni Amore", for
piano
Two Cantatas

1791   MEYERBEER was born: MOZART died

HAYDN (59)
Symphony No. 93
Symphony No. 94,
  Surprise
Symphony No. 95
Symphony No. 96,
  Miracle
DITTERSDORF (52)
Hokus Pokus, opera
MOZART (35)
The Magic Flute, opera
La Clemenza di Tito,
  opera

Piano Concerto in B♭,
  K.595
Clarinet Concerto in A,
  K.622
String Quartet in E♭,
  K.614
Requiem in D minor,
  K.626. Unfinished,
  completed by Süssmayr
BEETHOVEN (21)
Variations on "Es was
  einmal", for piano

1792   ROSSINI was born; PARADIES died

HAYDN (60)
Symphonies Nos. 97 and
  98
The Storm, oratorio

CIMAROSA (43)
Il matrimonio segreto,
  opera
BEETHOVEN (22)
Allegro and menuetto for
  two flutes

1793

HAYDN (61)
Symphony No. 99
String Quartets Nos.
  60–69 (probably
  before 1793)
String Quartets Nos.
  70–75
CIMAROSA (44)
I Traci amanti, opera

Concerto for two flutes
  and orchestra
BEETHOVEN (23)
p. Variations on "Se vuol
  ballare", for violin and
  piano
BOÏELDIEU (18)
La Fille coupable, opera

HAYDN (62)
Symphony No. 100, *Military*
Symphony No. 101, *The Clock*
DITTERSDORF (55)
Das Gespeust mit der Trommel, opera
CIMAROSA (45)
Penelope, opera

BEETHOVEN (24)
Trio for two oboes and English horn
Rondo allegro for violin and piano
p. Variations on a Waldstein theme for piano (four hands)

---

pre 1795

HAYDN   Piano Sonata No. 49

1795

HAYDN (63)
Symphony No. 102
Symphony No. 103, *Drum Roll*
Symphony No. 104
DITTERSDORF (56)
Don Quixote der Zweite, opera
Gott Mars, opera
Schach vom Schiras, opera
BEETHOVEN (25)
p. Twelve *Deutsche Tänze*, for orchestra

Piano Concerto No. 2
Six allemandes for violin and piano
Six minuets for piano
p. Variations on "Quant' è più bello", for piano
Variations on minuet from *Le Nozze Disturbate*, for piano
"Die Flamme Iodert", opferlied
Four Songs
BOÏELDIEU (20)
Harp Concerto

1796   BERWALD was born

HAYDN (64)
Trumpet Concerto

Mass No. 9, *Heiligenmesse*

CONTINUED

Mass No. 10,
Paukenmesse
GOSSEC (62)
La Reprise de Toulon,
opera
DITTERSDORF (57)
Der Durchmarsch, opera
*Die Lustigen Weiber von
Windsor,* opera
Ugolino, opera

CIMAROSA (47)
Gli Orazi e Curiazi,
opera
BEETHOVEN (26)
"Ah, perfido", scena and
aria for soprano and
orchestra
p. Variations on "Nel cor
più", for piano
"Farewell to Vienna's
citizens", song

1797   SCHUBERT was born

HAYDN (65)
The Creation, oratorio
(1797–98)
String Quartets Nos.
76–81 (1797–98)
DITTERSDORF (58)
Der Terno secco, opera
Der Mädchenmarkt,
opera
CHERUBINI (37)
Médée, opera
BEETHOVEN (27)
Symphony in C, *Jena*
(authenticity doubtful)
Quintet for piano and
wind

p. String Quintet
p. String Trio
p. Serenade for string trio
p. Piano Sonatas Nos. 1–4
p. Sonatas Nos. 1 and 2
for cello and piano
p. Variations on "See, the
conquering hero
comes", for piano and
cello
p. Sonata for piano (four
hands)
p. Rondo, for piano
War Song of the Austrians,
for voices and piano

1798   DONIZETTI was born

HAYDN (66)
Mass No. 11, *Nelson*
The Seasons, oratorio
(1798–1801)
Piano Sonata No. 50
BEETHOVEN (28)
p. Three String Trios

p. Trio for clarinet (or
violin), cello and piano
p. Variations on "Ein
Mädchen", for piano
and cello
p. Six variations on a
Swiss Air, for piano or
harp

p. Piano Sonatas Nos. 5–7
p. Twelve minuets

p. Variations on "Une
fièvre brûlante", for
piano

1799   DITTERSDORF died

HAYDN (67)
String Quartets Nos. 82
and 83
Mass No. 12,
Theresienmesse
BEETHOVEN (29)
p. Violin Sonatas Nos.
1–3
p. Piano Sonata No. 8,
Pathétique
p. Piano Sonatas Nos. 9
and 10

p. Seven Ländler Dances
for piano
p. Variations on "Kind
willst du", for piano
Variations on "La stessa,
la Stessissima", for
piano
Variation on "Tandeln
und Scherzen"
"Der Wachtelschlag",
song

1800

HAYDN (68)
Te Deum
CHERUBINI (40)
Les Deux journeés, opera
BEETHOVEN (30)
Symphony No. 1 in C
major
Mount of Olives, oratorio
Piano Concerto No. 3
Septet for strings and
wind
String Quartets Nos. 1–6
Sonata for piano, violin
and viola

Sonata for piano and
horn (or violin)
Piano Sonata No. 11
Air with six variations on
"Ich denke dein", for
piano (four hands)
Six very easy variations on
an original theme, for
piano
BOÏELDIEU (25)
Le Calife de Bagdad,
opera
WEBER (14)
Das Waldmädchen, opera

1801   BELLINI was born; CIMAROSA died ·

BOCCHERINI (58)
Stabat Mater
BEETHOVEN (31)
*fp. The Creatures of
Prometheus*, ballet
p. Piano Concerto No. 1

String Quintet
p. Violin Sonata No. 5,
Spring
WEBER (15)
*Peter Schmoll und seine
Nachbarn*, opera

1802

BEETHOVEN (32)
Symphony No. 2
p. Serenade for flute,
violin and viola
p. Variations on "Bei
mannern", for cello and
piano
p. Piano Sonatas Nos. 12
and 13
p. Piano Sonata No. 14,
Moonlight
p. Piano Sonata No. 15,
Pastoral

Piano Sonatas Nos. 16–20
Violin Sonatas Nos. 6–8
Violin Sonata No. 9,
Kreutzer
p. Rondo, for piano
Variations on an original
theme, for piano
Variations and Fugue on
a theme from "Prome-
theus", for piano
Terzetto, *Tremate*
p. Six Ländler Dances
Opferlied

1803   ADAM and BERLIOZ were born

HAYDN (71)
String Quartet No. 84
GOSSEC (69)
Les Sabots et le Cerisier,
opera
CHERUBINI (43)
Anacréon, opera
BEETHOVEN (33)
Fidelio, opera, begun (last
revision 1814)

Romance in G, for violin
and orchestra
p. Twelve *Kontretänze*,
for orchestra
p. Nine songs
Six songs (1803–10)
BOÏELDIEU (28)
Ma Tante Aurore, opera

1804   GLINKA and STRAUSS, J. (Sr.) were born

BEETHOVEN (34)
Symphony No. 3, *Eroica*
Triple Concerto in C
  major, for violin, cello,
  piano and orchestra
p. Fourteen variations in
  E♭, for violin, cello and
  piano
p. Three Grand Marches,
  for piano (four hands)

Piano Sonata No. 21,
  Waldstein
Piano Sonata No. 23,
  Appassionata
Andante favori, for piano
p. Seven Variations on
  "God Save the King",
  for piano
p. Five Variations on
  "Rule, Britannia", for
  piano

1805   BOCCHERINI died

BEETHOVEN (35)
Symphony No. 5
Piano Concerto No. 4

p. Romance in F, for
  violin and orchestra
p. Nine songs

1806

BEETHOVEN (36)
Symphony No. 4
Violin Concerto in D
  major
p. Piano Sonata No. 22

Thirty-two Variations in C
  minor, for piano
  (1806–07)
WEBER (20)
Symphony No. 1
  (1806–07)

1807

BEETHOVEN (37)
Coriolanus, overture
Leonora No. 1, overture
String Quartets Nos. 7–9,
  Rasumovsky
Mass in C major

"In questa tomba oscura",
  arietta
SPONTINI (33)
La Vestale, opera
WEBER (21)
Symphony No. 2

1808   BALFE was born

BEETHOVEN (38)
p. "Sehnsucht", songs
    with piano

ROSSINI (16)
Sonata for two violins,
    cello and double-bass

1809   MENDELSSOHN was born; HAYDN died

BEETHOVEN (39)
p. Symphony No. 6,
    Pastoral
Piano Concerto No. 5,
    Emperor
String Quartet No. 10,
    Harp
p. Trios Nos. 4 and 5, for
    violin, cello and piano

p. Cello Sonata No. 3
Military March in F
Three songs
SPONTINI (35)
Ferdinand Cortez, opera
ROSSINI (17)
Variations for clarinet
    and orchestra

1810   CHOPIN, NICOLAI and SCHUMANN
    were born

BEETHOVEN (40)
Egmont, incidental music
p. Sextet in E♭ for strings
    and horns
String Quartet No. 11,
    Quartett Serioso
p. Piano Sonatas Nos. 24
    and 25
p. Fantasy in G minor,
    for piano

p. Six variations in D, for
    piano
p. Three songs for
    soprano
WEBER (24)
Piano Concerto No. 1
ROSSINI (18)
*La cambiale di
    matrimonio,* opera

1811   LISZT and THOMAS were born

BEETHOVEN (41)
The Ruins of Athens,
    overture and eight
    numbers

King Stephen, overture
    and nine numbers
p. Choral Fantasia, for
    chorus, piano and
    orchestra

Piano Trio No. 6, *The Archduke*
p. Piano Sonata No. 26, *Les Adieux*
p. Four ariettas and duet, for soprano, tenor and piano
Song

WEBER (25)
Abu Hassan, opera
Bassoon Concerto
Clarinet Concertos Nos. 1 and 2
Concertino for clarinet
SCHUBERT (14)
Quintet-overture

1812   FLOTOW and WALLACE were born

BEETHOVEN (42)
Symphonies Nos. 7 and 8
Piano Trio No. 10
Violin Sonata No. 10
BOÏELDIEU (37)
Jean de Paris, opera
WEBER (26)
Piano Concerto No. 2
Piano Sonata No. 1

ROSSINI (20)
La Scala di seta (The Silken Ladder), opera
SCHUBERT (15)
Quartet-Overture
String Quartets Nos. 1–3
Eine Kleine Trauermusik, nonet

1813   DARGOMIZHSKY, VERDI and WAGNER were born; GRÉTRY died

GOSSEC (79)
Dernière Messe des vivants
BEETHOVEN (43)
Wellington's Victory, for orchestra
Triumphal March, for orchestra
Song
ROSSINI (21)
L'Italiana in Algeri, opera
Tancredi, opera

SCHUBERT (16)
Des Teufels Lustschloss, opera (1813–14)
Symphony No. 1
String Quartets Nos. 4–6
Three Sonatinas, for violin and piano
Five Minuets
Five German Dances

1814

CHERUBINI (54)
String Quartet No. 1
BEETHOVEN (44)
Leonore Prohaska,
  incidental music
Der Glorreiche
  Augenblick, cantata
Overture in C,
  Namensfeier
Piano Sonata No. 27
Polonaise in C, for piano
Markenstein, duet
p. Three books of Irish
  songs

p. "Germania", bass solo
Elegiac song
FIELD (22)
Three Nocturnes for piano
SCHUBERT (17)
String Quartets Nos. 7
  and 8
Quartet for flute, guitar,
  viola and cello
"Gretchen am Spinnrade"
  (Gretchen at the
  Spinning Wheel), song

1815

CHERUBINI (55)
String Quartets Nos. 2
  and 3 (1815–29)
BEETHOVEN (45)
Calm Sea and Prosperous
  Voyage, for chorus and
  orchestra
Cello Sonatas Nos. 4 and
  5
Three Duos, for clarinet
  and bassoon
Twenty-five Scotch songs
Twelve songs of varied
  nationality
Song

WEBER (29)
Quintet for clarinet and
  string quartet
Concertino for horn and
  orchestra
ROSSINI (23)
Elisabetta, Regina
  d'Inghelterra, opera
SCHUBERT (18)
Symphonies Nos. 2 and 3
String Quartet No. 9
Piano Sonatas Nos. 1
  and 2
"Der Erlkönig", song

1816

BEETHOVEN (46)
An die ferne Geliebte,
  song cycle

Military March
Three songs
WEBER (30)

Piano Sonatas Nos. 2
   and 3
ROSSINI (24)
Otello, opera
The Barber of Seville,
   opera
BERWALD (20)
Theme and Variations for
   violin and orchestra
SCHUBERT (19)
Symphony No. 4, *Tragic*

Symphony No. 5
Concertstücke, for violin
   and orchestra
Rondo, for violin and
   orchestra
*Adagio and Rondo
   Concertante,* for piano
   quartet
String Trio
Piano Sonata No. 3

1817   GADE was born

BEETHOVEN (47)
Symphony No. 9, *Choral*
   (1817–23)
String Quintet
p. Piano Sonata No. 28
ROSSINI (25)
La Cenerentola, opera
*La Gazza Ladra (The
   Thieving Magpie),*
   opera
BERWALD (21)
Double Concerto for two
   violins and orchestra
   (lost)

Septet for violin, viola,
   cello, clarinet, bassoon,
   horn and double-bass
SCHUBERT (20)
String Quartets Nos. 10
   and 11
Piano Sonatas Nos. 4–9
Violin Sonata in A major
"An die Musik", song
"Tod und das Mädchen",
   song
CHOPIN (7)
Polonaises Nos. 13 and 24

1818   GOUNOD was born

BEETHOVEN (48)
Six Themes Varied for
   piano, flute or violin
   (1818–19)
Ten National Themes with
   variations, for flute, or
   violin and piano
Piano Sonata No. 29,
   Hammerklavier
   (1818–19)

"Ziemlich lebhaft", for
   piano
Missa Solemnis in D
   major
ROSSINI (26)
Mosè, opera
SCHUBERT (21)
Symphony No. 6
Piano Sonatas Nos. 10
   and 11

SPONTINI (45)
Olympie, opera
WEBER (33)
Invitation to the Dance,
  for piano

BERWALD (23)
Quartet for piano,
  clarinet, horn and
  bassoon
SCHUBERT (22)
Piano Quintet, *The Trout*
Piano Sonatas Nos. 12
  and 13

1820

BEETHOVEN (50)
Allegro con Brio, for
  violin and orchestra
Piano Sonata No. 30
Song
WEBER (34)
Der Freischütz, opera
ROSSINI (28)
Maometto II, opera
Solemn Mass

BERWALD (24)
Symphony No. 1
Violin Concerto
SCHUBERT (23)
Die Zauberharfe,
  melodrama
String Quartet No. 12

1821

BEETHOVEN (51)
Piano Sonata No. 31
p. Bagatelles for piano
SPONTINI (47)
Nurmahal, opera
WEBER (35)
Concertstücke, for piano
  and orchestra

SCHUBERT (24)
Alfonso und Estrella,
  opera (1821–22)
Symphony No. 7
  (sketched)
Variation on a Theme by
  Diabelli
MENDELSSOHN (12)
Piano Sonata No. 2
CHOPIN (11)
Polonaise No. 15

1822   FRANCK and RAFF were born

BEETHOVEN (52)
*Consecration of the
    House,* overture
Bundeslied (1822–23)
"The Kiss", arietta
WEBER (36)
Piano Sonata No. 4
ROSSINI (30)
Zelmira, opera

SCHUBERT (25)
Symphony No. 8,
    Unfinished
GLINKA (18)
Variations on a Theme of
    Mozart, for piano
MENDELSSOHN (13)
Piano Quartet No. 1,
    Op. 1
CHOPIN (12)
Polonaise No. 16

1823   LALO was born

BEETHOVEN (53)
Piano Sonata No. 32
p. Bagatelles for piano
Variations on a Waltz by
    Diabelli
"Minuet of
    Congratulation"
Cantata E♭
WEBER (37)
fp. Euryanthe, opera
ROSSINI (31)
Semiramide, opera

SCHUBERT (26)
Fierrebras, opera
Der häusliche Krieg,
    opera
Rosamunde, incidental
    music
Piano Sonata No. 14
Die Schöne Mullerin,
    song cycle
MENDELSSOHN (14)
Piano Quartet No. 2
Violin Sonata

1824   BRUCKNER and SMETANA were born

BEETHOVEN (54)
String Quartet No. 12
p. The Ruins of Athens,
    March and Chorus
p. Variations on "Ich bin
    der Schneider Kakadu"
SCHUBERT (27)
Octet in F major, for
    strings and wind
String Quartet No. 13

String Quartet No. 14,
    Death and the Maiden
Introduction and
    Variations for flute and
    piano
Arpeggione Sonata, for
    cello and piano
MENDELSSOHN (15)
Symphony No. 1
Piano Quartet No. 3

357

1825   STRAUSS, J. (Jr.) was born

BEETHOVEN (55)
Great Fugue in B♭, for
   strings
String Quartet No. 13,
   Scherzoso (1825–26)
Rondo a capriccio, for
   piano (1825–26)
BOÏELDIEU (50)
La Dame blanche, opera
ROSSINI (33)
Il viaggio a Rheims, opera
BERWALD (29)
Serenade for tenor and six
   instruments

SCHUBERT (28)
Piano Sonatas Nos. 15–17
BELLINI (24)
Adelson e Salvina, opera
Bianca e Cernando, opera
MENDELSSOHN (16)
Wedding of the Camacho,
   comic opera
Trumpet Overture, for
   orchestra
String Octet
Capriccio, for piano
CHOPIN (15)
Polonaise No. 8

1826   WEBER died

BEETHOVEN (56)
String Quartets Nos.
   14–16
Andante maestoso in C
   major, for piano
WEBER (40)
fp. Oberon, opera
ROSSINI (34)
Siège de Corinthe, opera
SCHUBERT (29)
String Quartet No. 15
Piano Trio
Rondo Brillant, for violin
   and piano
Piano Sonata No. 18

GLINKA (22)
Memorial Cantata
Trio for piano, clarinet
   and bassoon, or piano,
   violin and cello,
   Pathétique
MENDELSSOHN (17)
*A Midsummer Night's
   Dream,* overture
String Quintet
Piano Sonata No. 1
Six songs (1826–27)
CHOPIN (16)
Polonaise No. 11
Three écossaises
Introduction and
   Variations on "Der
   Schweizerbub"

1827   BEETHOVEN died

ROSSINI (35)
Moïse, opera (French
    version of *Mosè*)
BERWALD (31)
Gustav Wasa, opera
Concertstücke, for
    bassoon and orchestra
SCHUBERT (30)
Piano Trio
Phantasie, for violin and
    piano
Die Winterreise, song
    cycle

BELLINI (26)
Il Pirata, opera
BERLIOZ (24)
Les Francs-Juges,
    overture
Waverley, overture
La Mort d'Orphée,
    cantata
MENDELSSOHN (18)
String Quartet No. 2
Fugue for String Quartet
Piano Sonata No. 3
p. Seven pieces for piano
CHOPIN (17)
Nocturne No. 19

1828   SCHUBERT died

AUBER (46)
La Muette de Portici,
    opera
ROSSINI (36)
fp. Comte Ory, comedy-
    opera
SCHUBERT (31)
Symphony No. 9 in C
    major, *The Great*
String Quintet in C major
Piano Sonatas Nos. 19–21
Schwanengesang, song
    cycle

BERLIOZ (25)
Herminie, cantata
CHOPIN (18)
Krakowiak, concert rondo
    for orchestra
Fantasia on Polish airs,
    for piano and orchestra
Rondo for two pianos
Piano Sonata No. 1
Polonaises Nos. 9 and 10

1829   RUBINSTEIN was born; GOSSEC died

SPONTINI (55)
Agnes von Hohenstaufen,
    opera

ROSSINI (37)
William Tell, opera

CONTINUED

BELLINI (28)
La Straniera, opera
Zaira, opera
BERLIOZ (26)
Cleopâtre, cantata
Huit Scènes de Faust,
    cantata
Irlande, five songs with
    piano (1829–39)
BALFE (21)
I rivali di se stesso, opera
SCHUMANN (19)
Papillons, twelve pieces
    for piano (1829–31)
MENDELSSOHN (20)
*Die Heimkehr aus der
    Fremde,* operetta
String Quartet No. 1

Variations Concertantes,
    for cello and piano
Three fantasies, for piano
Twelve songs
CHOPIN (19)
Piano Concerto No. 2
Introduction and
    Polonaise for cello and
    piano
Twelve Grand Studies for
    piano (1829–32); No.
    5 "Black Keys", No. 12
    "Revolutionary"
Polonaise No. 12
Waltzes Nos. 10 and 13
Variations on a Theme by
    Paganini

1830   GOLDMARK was born

AUBER (48)
Fra Diavolo, opera
DONIZETTI (33)
Anna Bolena, opera
BELLINI (29)
I Capuletti ed i Montecchi,
    opera
BERLIOZ (27)
Symphonie Fantastique
    (revised 1831)
Sardanapale, cantata
GLINKA (26)
String Quartet
BALFE (22)
Un avvertimento ai gelosi,
    opera

MENDELSSOHN (21)
Hebrides, concert overture
Symphony No. 5,
    Reformation
Eighteen songs
CHOPIN (20)
Piano Concerto No. 1
Nine Mazurkas for piano
    (1830–31)
Nocturnes Nos. 4–6 for
    piano (1830–31)
SCHUMANN (20)
*Theme and Variations on
    the name "Abegg",* for
    piano
LISZT (19–38)
Piano Concerto No. 1
    (1830–49)

1831

MEYERBEER (41)
Robert le diable, opera
BELLINI (30)
La Sonnambula, opera
Norma, opera
BERLIOZ (28)
Le Corsaire, concert-
   overture (revised 1855)
King Lear, overture
MENDELSSOHN (22)
Piano Concerto No. 1
Die erste Walpurgisnacht,
   for solo voices, chorus
   and orchestra

CHOPIN (21)
Waltzes Nos. 1 and 3
Andante Spianoto, and
   Grand Polonaise
   Brillant (1831–34)
NICOLAI (21)
Symphony
LISZT (20)
*Harmonies poétiques et
   religieuses,* for piano
   and orchestra

1832   CLEMENTI died

FIELD (50)
fp. Piano Concerto No. 1
ROSSINI (40)
Stabat Mater (1832–41)
DONIZETTI (35)
L'Elisir d'Amore, opera
ADAM (29)
Faust, ballet
BERLIOZ (29)
Le Cinq Mai, cantata
MENDELSSOHN (23)
Meeresstille (Calm Sea
   and Prosperous
   Voyage), concert-
   overture
Capriccio Brillant, for
   piano and orchestra

Six Preludes and Fugues
   for piano
CHOPIN (22–26)
Allegro de Concert
Scherzo No. 1
NICOLAI (22)
Mass
SCHUMANN (22)
Six Concert Studies on
   Caprices by Paganini,
   Set I
THOMAS (21)
Hermann et Ketty,
   cantata
WAGNER (19)
Symphony in C major

1833 BORODIN and BRAHMS were born

CHERUBINI (76)
Ali Baba, opera
DONIZETTI (36)
Lucrezia Borgia, opera
BELLINI (32)
Beatrice di Tenda, opera
GLINKA (29)
Sextet for piano and
   strings (1833–34)
BALFE (25)
*Enrico IV al passo della
   Marna,* opera
MENDELSSOHN (24)
Symphony No. 4, *Italian*
Die schöne Melusine,
   overture

Fantasy in F♯ minor, for
   piano
Three capriccios for piano
CHOPIN (23)
Bolero in C major
Introduction and
   Variations on a theme
   by Hérold
SCHUMANN (23)
Six Concert Studies on
   Caprices by Paganini,
   Set II
Sonata No. 2 in G minor,
   Op. 22

1834 PONCHIELLI was born; BOÏELDIEU died

DONIZETTI (37)
Rosmonda d'Inghilterra,
   opera
ADAM (31)
Le Châlet, opera
BERLIOZ (31)
Harold in Italy,
   symphony with solo
   viola
Les Nuits d'été, song cycle
   for soprano and
   orchestra
Sara la baigneuse, choral
   ballad
MENDELSSOHN (25)
Rondo Brillant, for piano
   and orchestra
Piano sextet

p. Songs Without Words,
   Book I, for piano
Three Studies for piano
   (1834–37)
Seven songs
CHOPIN (24)
Études Nos. 13–24
   (1834–36)
Fantaisie Impromptu in
   C♯ minor
Polonaises Nos. 1–2
   (1834–35)
Prelude No. 26
SCHUMANN (24)
Carnaval, twenty-one
   pieces for piano
   (1834–35)

1835   CUI and SAINT-SAËNS were born; BELLINI
          died

CHERUBINI (78)
String Quartets Nos.
   4–6
AUBER (53)
The Bronze Horse, opera
   (revised 1857)
DONIZETTI (38)
Lucia di Lammermoor,
   opera
BELLINI (34)
I Puritani, opera
BALFE (27)
The Siege of Rochelle,
   opera

MENDELSSOHN (26)
p. Songs Without Words,
   Book II, for piano
CHOPIN (25)
Ballade
Nocturnes, Nos. 7 and 8
Waltzes Nos. 2, 9 and 11
NICOLAI (25)
Symphony
Funeral March (for the
   death of Bellini)
LISZT (24)
Années de pèlerinage,
   for piano begun
   (completed 1883)

1836   DELIBES was born

CHERUBINI (79)
Requiem Mass
MEYERBEER (45)
Les Huguenots, opera
ADAM (33)
*Le Postillon de
   Longjumeau,* opera
GLINKA (32)
A Life for the Tzar,
   opera
The Moldavian Gipsy,
   incidental music

BALFE (28)
The Maid of Artois,
   opera
MENDELSSOHN (27)
St. Paul, oratorio
CHOPIN (26)
Ballade (1836–39)
Nocturnes Nos. 9 and 10
   (1836–37)
Twenty-four Preludes
   for piano (1836–39)
SCHUMANN (26)
Phantasie, for piano

1837   BALAKÍREV and WALDTEUFEL were
          born; FIELD died

CHERUBINI (80)
String Quintet

AUBER (55)
Le Domino noir, opera
CONTINUED

BERLIOZ (34)
Grande Messe des Morts
BALFE (29)
Catherine Grey, opera
Joan of Arc, opera
MENDELSSOHN (28)
Piano Concerto No. 2
String Quartets Nos. 3–5
  (1837–38)
CHOPIN (27)
Impromptu, Op. 29
Nocturne in C minor, Op.
  20
Scherzo, No. 2

SCHUMANN (27)
Davidsbündler-Tänze,
  eighteen piano pieces
  (revised 1850)
p. *Études symphoniques*,
  twelve symphonic
  studies for piano
Fantasiestücke for piano,
  Books I and II
THOMAS (26)
La Double échelle,
  opera
GOUNOD (19)
Scherzo for orchestra

1838   BIZET and BRUCH were born

BERLIOZ (35)
Benvenuto Cellini, opera
Roméo and Juliet,
  dramatic symphony
  (1838–39)
BALFE (30)
Falstaff, opera
Diadeste, opera
MENDELSSOHN (29)
Serenade and Allegro
  gioioso, for piano and
  orchestra
Cello Sonata
Piano Trio No. 1
CHOPIN (28)
Nocturnes, Nos. 11 and
  12 (1838–39)

Polonaises Nos. 3 and 4
  (1838–39)
Waltz No. 4
NICOLAI (28)
Von Himmel Hoch,
  overture
SCHUMANN (28)
Kinderscenen, thirteen
  short piano pieces
Kreisleriana, for piano
Novelleten, eight piano
  pieces
THOMAS (27)
*Le Perruquier de la
  Régence*, opera

1839   MUSSORGSKY was born

ADAM (36)
La Jolie Fille de Gand,
  ballet

BERLIOZ (36)
Rêverie and Caprice, for
  violin and orchestra

GLINKA (35)
Valse-fantasie, for
  orchestra
MENDELSSOHN (30)
Ruy Blas, overture
p. *Songs Without Words*,
  Book III, for piano
CHOPIN (29)
Études, Nos. 25–27
Impromptu, Op. 36
Scherzo, No. 3
Piano Sonata No. 2

SCHUMANN (29)
Nachtstücke, for piano
NICOLAI (29)
Henry II, opera
LISZT (28)
Piano Concerto No. 2
THOMAS (28)
Le Panier fleuri, opera
La Gipsy, ballet
VERDI (26)
Oberto, opera

1840   TCHAIKOVSKY was born; PAGANINI died

DONIZETTI (43)
La Favorita, opera
La Fille du régiment,
  opera
BERLIOZ (37)
*Symphonie Funèbre et
  Triomphale*, for chorus,
  strings and military
  band
GLINKA (36)
Farewell to Petersburg,
  song cycle
MENDELSSOHN (31)
Lobgesang (Hymn of
  Praise), symphony-
  cantata (Symphony
  No. 2)
CHOPIN (30)
Ballade, Op. 47
  (1840–41)
Fantasia in F minor
Waltz No. 5
NICOLAI (30)
Gildippe ed Odoardo,
  opera
Il Templario, opera

SCHUMANN (30)
Dichterliebe, song cycle
Frauenliebe und Leben,
  song cycle
Liederkreis, nine songs
  (Heine)
LISZT (29)
Malediction, for piano
  and strings (c.1840)
THOMAS (29)
Carlino, opera
WAGNER (27)
Faust, overture
GADE (23)
Faedrelandets Muser,
  ballet
Echoes from Ossian,
  overture
Piano Sonata
GOUNOD (22)
Marche militaire suisse,
  for orchestra
FRANCK (18)
Three Piano Trios, Op. 1

1841 CHABRIER and DVOŘÁK were born

AUBER (59)
*Les Diamants de la
    couronne*, opera
ADAM (38)
Giselle, ballet
BALFE (33)
Keolanthe, opera
MENDELSSOHN (32)
Songs Without Words,
    Books IV and VII, for
    piano
CHOPIN (31)
Nocturnes Nos. 13 and 14
Polonaise No. 5
Prelude No. 25
Waltz No. 12

NICOLAI (31)
Il Proscritto, opera
SCHUMANN (31)
Symphony No. 1, *Spring*
Symphony No. 4 (revised
    1851)
*Overture, Scherzo and
    Finale* for orchestra
    (*Finale* revised 1845)
Piano Concerto
    (1841–45)
THOMAS (30)
Le Comte de Carmagnola,
    opera
GADE (24)
Symphony No. 1

1842 MASSENET and SULLIVAN were born; CHERUBINI died

BERWALD (46)
Symphony No. 2,
    Sérieuse
Symphony No. 3
DONIZETTI (45)
Linda de Chamounix,
    opera
GLINKA (38)
Russlan and Ludmilla,
    opera
MENDELSSOHN (33)
Symphony No. 3, *Scottish*
Cello Sonata (1842–43)
Songs Without Words,
    Book VIII, for piano
    (1842–45)
CHOPIN (32)
Ballade, Op. 52
Impromptu, Op. 51

Polonaise No. 6
Scherzo No. 4
SCHUMANN (32)
Piano Quintet
Piano Quartet
Three String Quartets
Andante and Variations
    for two pianos, two
    cellos and horn (1842?)
Four *Fantasiestücke,* for
    piano trio
Liederkreis, twelve songs
    (Eichendorf)
THOMAS (31)
Le Guerillero, opera
VERDI (29)
Nabucco, opera
WAGNER (29)
fp. Rienzi, opera

GADE (25)
Napoli, ballet
Violin Sonata No. **1**

FRANCK (20)
Piano Trio No. 4

1843   GRIEG was born

DONIZETTI (46)
Maria de Rohan, opera
Don Pasquale, opera
Dom Sébastien, opera
BALFE (35)
The Bohemian Girl, opera
Geraldine, opera
MENDELSSOHN (34)
Athalie, incidental music
String Quartet Pieces, Op. 81
Songs Without Words, Books V and VI, for piano
CHOPIN (33)
Berceuse, Op. 57
Nocturnes Nos. 15 and 16

SCHUMANN (33)
Das Paradies und die Peri, cantata
LISZT (32)
Valse Impromptu in A♭ major
THOMAS (32)
Angélique et Médor, opera
Mina, opera
VERDI (30)
I Lombardi, opera
WAGNER (30)
fp. *The Flying Dutchman*, opera
FRANCK (21)
Andante quietoso, for violin and piano

1844   RIMSKY-KORSAKOV and SARASATE were born

BERWALD (48)
A Country Wedding, for organ (four hands)
BERLIOZ (41)
Roman Carnival Overture
BALFE (36)
The Castle of Aymon, opera
The Daughter of St. Mark, opera
MENDELSSOHN (35)
Violin Concerto

CHOPIN (34)
Piano Sonata No. **3**
NICOLAI (34)
Ein Feste Burg, overture with chorus
VERDI (31)
Ernani, opera
I due Foscari, opera
GADE (27)
In the Highlands, overture

1845   FAURÉ was born

BERWALD (49)
Symphony No. 5,
  Singulière
Symphony No. 6
Five Piano Trios
GLINKA (41)
Spanish Overture No. 1,
  Jota Aragonesa
BALFE (37)
The Enchantress, opera
SCHUMANN (35)
Symphony No. 2
  (1845–46)
MENDELSSOHN (36)
Piano Trio No. 2

String Quintet
Songs Without Words, for
  cello and piano
CHOPIN (35)
Cello Sonata, Op. 65
Barcarolle, Op. 60
Polonaise, No. 7
WALLACE (33)
fp. Maritana, opera
VERDI (32)
Alzira, opera
Giovanna d'Arco, opera
WAGNER (32)
fp. Tannhäuser, opera

1846

AUBER (74)
Manon Lescaut, opera
BERLIOZ (43)
The Damnation of Faust,
  dramatic cantata
BALFE (38)
The Bondman, opera
MENDELSSOHN (37)
fp. Elijah, oratorio
String Quartet No. 6
CHOPIN (36)
Nocturnes Nos. 17 and 18
Waltzes Nos. 6–8. Op. 64
  (1846–47)

THOMAS (35)
Betty, ballet
VERDI (33)
Attila, opera
GADE (28)
p. String Quintet
FRANCK (24)
Ruth, oratorio
*Ce qu'on entend sur la
  montagne*, symphonic
  poem

1847   MENDELSSOHN died

GLINKA (43)
*Greeting to the Father-
  land*, for piano

BALFE (39)
The Maid of Honour,
  opera

MENDELSSOHN (38)
Lorely, opera (unfinished)
SCHUMANN (37)
Genoveva, opera
  (1847–48)
Piano Trios Nos. 1 and 2
FLOTOW (35)
Martha, opera
DARGOMIZHSKY (34)
Esmeralda, opera
  (possibly *c.*1839)

VERDI (34)
Macbeth, opera
I masnadieri, opera
GADE (30)
Symphony No. 3
BORODIN (14)
Flute Concerto (with
  piano)

1848   DONIZETTI died

BERLIOZ (45)
La Mort d'Ophelie, for
  two-part female chorus
  (also for voice and
  piano)
GLINKA (44)
Wedding Song

(Kamarinskaya),
  fantasia for
  orchestra
SMETANA (24)
Festive Overture
  (1848–49)

1849   GODARD was born; STRAUSS, J. (Sr.),
         CHOPIN and NICOLAI died

MEYERBEER (58)
Le Prophète, opera
ADAM (46)
Le Toréador, opera
NICOLAI (39)
*The Merry Wives of
  Windsor,* opera
SCHUMANN (39)
Manfred, dramatic poem
Three *Fantasiestücke,* for
  piano and clarinet with
  violin or cello

Adagio and Allegro, for
  piano and horn
LISZT (38)
Héroïde funèbre, for
  orchestra (1849–50)
THOMAS (38)
Le Caïd, opera
VERDI (36)
Luisa Miller, opera
GADE (32)
p. String Octet
BRUCKNER (25)
Requiem in D minor

1850

SCHUMANN (40)
Symphony No. 3, *Rhenish*
Cello Concerto in A
  minor
LISZT (39)
Prometheus, symphonic
  poem
Consolations, for piano

Liebestraüme, nocturnes
  for piano
THOMAS (39)
Le Songe d'une nuit d'été,
  opera
GADE (33)
Mariotta, incidental music
Symphony No. 4
p. Violin Sonata No. 2

1851   d'INDY was born; SPONTINI died

SCHUMANN (41)
Piano Trio No. 3
Four *Marchenbilder*, for
  piano and viola (or
  violin)
Two Violin Sonatas
THOMAS (40)
Raymond, opera
VERDI (38)
Rigoletto, opera

WAGNER (38)
fp. Lohengrin, opera
GOUNOD (33)
Sapho, opera
FRANCK (29)
Le Valet de ferme, opera
BRAHMS (18)
Scherzo in E♭ minor
The first three sets of
  songs (1851-53)

1852   STANFORD was born

BERWALD (56)
Three piano trios
  (1852–54)
ADAM (49)
Si j'étais Roi, opera
BALFE (44)
The Devil's in It, opera
The Sicilian Bride, opera
MENDELSSOHN
  (posthumous)
fp. Christus, oratorio
  (unfinished)

LISZT (41)
Hungarian Rhapsodies,
  Nos. 1–15
GADE (35)
Symphony No. 5
Spring Fantasy, for voices
  and orchestra
GOUNOD (34)
Faust, opera (1852–59)
La Nonne sanglante,
  opera (1852–54)

BRAHMS (19)
Piano Sonata No. 1
   (1852–53)
Piano Sonata No. 2

BALAKIREV (15)
*Grande Fantaisie on
   Russian Folksongs,* for
   piano and orchestra
Septet for flute, cello,
   strings and piano

1853   MESSAGER was born

SCHUMANN (43)
Violin Concerto
Märchenerzählungen,
   four pieces for piano,
   clarinet (or violin) and
   viola
Introduction and Allegro,
   for piano
Fantasy, for violin
THOMAS (42)
La Tonelli, opera
VERDI (40)
La Traviata, opera
Il Trovatore, opera

OFFENBACH (34)
*Le mariage aux
   lanternes,* opera
SMETANA (29)
Festive Symphony
   (1853–54)
RUBINSTEIN (24)
Melody in F
BRAHMS (20)
Piano Trio No. 1
   (1853–54)
Piano Sonata No. 3

**1854   CATALANI, HUMPERDINCK, JANÁČEK
   and MOSKOWSKI were born**

MEYERBEER (63)
L'Étoile du nord, opera
BERLIOZ (51)
L'Enfance du Christ,
   oratorio
SCHUMANN (44)
p. *Albumblätter,* twenty
   pieces for piano
LISZT (43)
Hungaria, symphonic
   poem
Orpheus, symphonic
   poem
Les préludes, symphonic
   poem

BRUCKNER (30)
Solemn Mass in B♭ major
BRAHMS (21)
Piano Concerto No. 1
   (1854–58)
Four Ballads for piano
Variations on a Theme by
   Schumann, for piano
BALAKIREV (17)
String Quartet, *Quatuor
   original russe*
   (1854–55)
BIZET (16)
La Prêtresse, one-act
   opera

BERWALD (59)
Piano Concerto
LISZT (44)
Totentanz, for piano and
orchestra
THOMAS (44)
La Cour de Célimène,
opera
VERDI (42)
I Vespri siciliani, opera
GADE (38)
p. Novelleten, for piano
trio
GOUNOD (37)
Symphonies Nos. 1 and 2
Messe solenelle à St.
Cecile
LALO (32)
String Quartet
SMETANA (31)
Piano Trio

BRAHMS (22)
Symphony No. 1 begun
(completed 1876)
Piano Quartet No. 3
begun (completed
1875)
SAINT-SAËNS (20)
Symphony No. 1
Piano Quintet
BALAKIREV (18)
Piano Concerto No. 1
(*c.*1855)
Octet for flute, oboe, horn,
piano and strings
(1855–56)
"Three Forgotten Songs"
BIZET (17)
Symphony in C major
DVOŘÁK (14)
"Forget-Me-Not Polka"
(1855–56)

1856 CHAUSSON and LIADOV were born; ADAM
and SCHUMANN died

BERWALD (60)
Two piano quintets
(1856–58, possibly
1853–54)
ADAM (53)
Le Corsaire, ballet
BERLIOZ (53)
The Trojans, opera
(1856–59)
LISZT (45)
Hunnenschlacht,
symphonic poem
Tasso, symphonic poem

DARGOMIZHSKY (43)
fp. Russalka, opera
GADE (39)
Symphony No. 6
(*c.*1856)
BRAHMS (23)
Variations on a Hungarian
theme, for piano
Variations on an original
theme, for piano
BRUCH (18)
String Quartet

1857 CHAMINADE and ELGAR were born;
GLINKA died

BALFE (49)
The Rose of Castille,
  opera
LISZT (46)
Dante Symphony
  (possibly 1855–56)
Faust Symphony
  (possibly 1854–57)
Mazeppa, tone poem
THOMAS (46)
Le Carnaval de Venise,
  opera
Psyche, opera
Messe Solenelle
VERDI (44)
Aroldo, opera
Simon Boccanegra,
  opera
WAGNER (44)
Wesendonck Lieder
  (1857–58)
GOUNOD (39)
Le Médecin malgré lui,
  opera

BRAHMS (24)
Serenade for Orchestra in
  D major (1857–58)
Serenade for Orchestra in
  A major (1857–60)
German Requiem
  (1857–68)
CUI (22)
Scherzo for Orchestra,
  Nos. 1 and 2
SAINT-SAËNS (22)
Organ Fantasia No. 1
BIZET (19)
Clovis et Clothilde,
  cantata
Le Docteur Miracle,
  operetta
BRUCH (19)
Piano Trio
MUSSORGSKY (18)
Souvenir d'enfance, for
  piano
DVOŘÁK (16)
Mass in B♭ major
  (1857–59)

1858 LEONCAVALLO, PUCCINI and SMYTH
were born

OFFENBACH (39)
Orpheus in the Under-
  world, operetta
FRANCK (36)
Ave Maria, motet
SMETANA (34)
Richard III, symphonic
  poem

Wallenstein's Camp,
  symphonic poem
  (1858–59)
CUI (23)
The Caucasian Prisoner,
  opera
SAINT-SAËNS (23)
Piano Concerto No. 1
CONTINUED

BALAKIREV (21)
Overture on Russian
    Themes
BRUCH (20)
Scherz, List und Rache,
    opera

MUSSORGSKY (19)
Scherzo for Orchestra
"Edipo" for mixed chorus
    (1858–60)

1859   IPPOLITOV-IVANOV was born

MEYERBEER (68)
Dinorah, opera
BERWALD (63)
p. Cello sonata
LISZT (48)
Hamlet, symphonic poem
Die Ideale, for orchestra
VERDI (46)
Un ballo in maschera,
    opera
BRAHMS (26)
Marienlieder, for
    four-part mixed choir
String Quartets Nos. 1 and
    2 (1859–73)

CUI (24)
The Mandarin's Son,
    opera
Tarantella
SAINT-SAËNS (24)
Violin Concerto No. 1
BIZET (21)
Don Procopio, opera
MUSSORGSKY (20)
Marcia di Sciamie, for
    soloist, choir and
    orchestra
Impromptu Passione,
    for piano

1860   ALBÉNIZ, CHARPENTIER, WOLF and
          MAHLER were born; PADEREWSKI was
          born (or possibly in 1866)

BALFE (52)
Bianca, opera
LISZT (49)
*Fantasy on Hungarian
    Folk Tunes,* for piano
    and orchestra
    (*c.*1860)
THOMAS (49)
Le Roman d'Elvire, opera
GOUNOD (42)
Philémon et Baucis, opera

SMETANA (36)
Haakon Jarl, symphonic
    poem (1860–61)
BRAHMS (27)
String Sextet No. 1, in B♭
    major
BRUCH (22)
String Quartet
CHABRIER (19)
Impromptu for piano

1861   ARENSKY, LOEFFLER and MACDOWELL
were born

BALFE (53)
The Puritan's Daughter,
opera
DARGOMIZHSKY (48)
Baba-Yaga, fantasy for
orchestra
GADE (44)
Hamlet, concert overture
Michelangelo, overture
BRAHMS (28)
Piano Quartets Nos. 1 and
2
Variations and Fugue on
a Theme by Handel,
for piano
Soldaten Lieder
Fifteen songs from
Magalone (1861–68)

PONCHIELLI (27)
La Savoiarda, opera
BALAKIREV (24)
Piano Concerto No. 2
begun (resumed 1909)
MUSSORGSKY (22)
Alla marcia notturna, for
orchestra
Scherzo and finale, for
a symphony in D major
DVOŘÁK (20)
String Quintet
RIMSKY-KORSAKOV
(17)
Symphony No. 1
(1861–65)

1862   BOËLLMANN, DEBUSSY, DELIUS and
GERMAN were born

BERWALD (66)
Estrella de Soria, opera
BERLIOZ (59)
Beatrice et Bénédict,
opera
VERDI (49)
La Forza del destino,
opera
Inno delle nazioni, for
chorus
GOUNOD (44)
La Reine de Saba, opera
SMETANA (38)
On the Seashore, for
piano

BORODIN (29)
Symphony No. 1
(1862–67)
BRAHMS (29)
Cello Sonata No. 1
(1862–65)
Piano Studies (Variations
on a Theme by
Paganini), Books I and
II (1862–63)
DVOŘÁK (21)
String Quartet No. 1
SULLIVAN (20)
The Tempest, incidental
music

1863   MASCAGNI and PIERNÉ were born

ROSSINI (71)
Petite Messe Solenelle
BALFE (55)
The Armourer of Nantes,
   opera
Blanche de Nevers, opéra
LISZT (52)
Two Concert Studies for
   piano
BRUCKNER (39)
Symphony in F minor
   (unnumbered)
Overture in G minor
Germanenzug, for chorus
   and brass

SMETANA (39)
*The Brandenburgers in
   Bohemia,* opera
BRAHMS (30)
Rinaldo, cantata
   (1863–68)
PONCHIELLI (29)
Roderico, opera
SAINT-SAËNS (28)
Piano Trio No. 1
BIZET (25)
The Pearl Fishers, opera
BRUCH (25)
Die Lorely, opera
MASSENET (21)
Overture de Concert
David Rizzio, cantata

1864   STRAUSS, R. and ROPARTZ were born;
       MEYERBEER died

BALFE (56)
The Sleeping Queen,
   opera
GADE (47)
Symphonies Nos. 2 and 7
p. Piano Trio in F major
p. Fantasiestücke, for
   cello and piano
Fantasies for clarinet
GOUNOD (46)
Mireille, opera
OFFENBACH (45)
La Belle Hélène, operetta
BRUCKNER (40)
Mass No. 1 in D minor
Symphony in D minor
   (revised 1869, known
   as No. 0)

"Um Mitternacht", for
   male-voice chorus
BRAHMS (31)
String Sextet No. 2
   (1864–65)
Piano Quintet
BRUCH (26)
Frithjof-Scenen, for solo
   voices, chorus and
   orchestra (*c.*1864)
SULLIVAN (22)
L'Ile enchantée, ballet
   music
Kenilworth, cantata
GRIEG (21)
Album Leaves, for piano
   (1864–78)

MEYERBEER
  (posthumous)
fp. L'Africaine, opera
THOMAS (54)
Marche religieuse, for
  orchestra
WAGNER (52)
fp. Tristan und Isolde,
  music drama
GADE (48)
p. String sextet
GOUNOD (47)
Chant des Compagnons
FRANCK (43)
The Tower of Babel,
  oratorio
BRAHMS (32)
Trio for piano, violin and
  horn

BIZET (27)
Ivan the Terrible, opera
Chasse fantastique, for
  piano
DVOŘÁK (24)
Symphonies Nos. 1 and 2
Cello Concerto in A
  major
The Cypresses, originally
  for string quartet, later
  for voice and piano
Clarinet Quintet
MASSENET (23)
Suite for Orchestra, No. 1
GRIEG (22)
In Autumn, concert
  overture
Violin Sonata No. 1

LISZT (55)
Deux Légendes, for piano
THOMAS (55)
Mignon, opera
DARGOMIZHSKY (53)
The Stone Guest, opera
  (unfinished)
OFFENBACH (47)
Bluebeard, operetta
La Vie parisienne,
  operetta
BRUCKNER (42)
Symphony No. 1 (revised
  1891)
Mass No. 2 in E minor

SMETANA (42)
The Bartered Bride,
  opera
SAINT-SAËNS (31)
Suite in D minor, for
  piano and cello (or
  violin, or viola)
DELIBES (30)
La Source, ballet
BALAKIREV (29)
Symphony No. 1 begun
  (completed 1898)
BIZET (28)
Trois esquisses musicales,
  for piano

CONTINUED

TCHAIKOVSKY (26)
Symphony No. 1, *Winter Daydreams*
SULLIVAN (24)
In Memoriam Overture
Irish Symphony
Cello Concerto

RIMSKY-KORSAKOV (22)
Overture on Russian Themes
Symphony No. 3 (1866–73)

1867   GIORDANO was born

LISZT (56)
Legend of St. Elizabeth (possibly 1857–62)
DARGOMIZHSKY (54)
The Triumph of Bacchus, opera-ballet
VERDI (54)
Don Carlos, opera
GOUNOD (49)
Roméo et Juliette, opera
OFFENBACH (48)
La Grande Duchesse de Gérolstein, operetta
STRAUSS, J. (Jr.) (42)
The Blue Danube Waltz
BORODIN (34)
The Bogatirs, opera-farce
BALAKIREV (30)
Overture on Czech Themes
Thamar, symphonic poem (1867–82)

BIZET (29)
The Fair Maid of Perth, opera
MUSSORGSKY (28)
La Disfatta di Sennacherib, for chorus and orchestra, first version
Symphonic Intermezzo "in modo classico"
SULLIVAN (25)
Cox and Box, operetta
GRIEG (24)
Violin Sonata No. 2
Lyric Pieces for piano, Book I
RIMSKY-KORSAKOV (23)
Fantasia on Serbian Themes, for orchestra
Sadko, symphonic poem

1868   BANTOCK was born; ROSSINI and BERWALD died

THOMAS (57)
Hamlet, grand opera
WAGNER (55)
fp. *Die Meistersinger von Nürnberg*, opera

OFFENBACH (49)
La Périchole, operetta
BRUCKNER (44)
Mass No. 3, *Grosse Messe*

(revised 1871 and
1890)
SMETANA (44)
fp. Dalibor, opera
Solemn Prelude for
orchestra
STRAUSS, J. (Jr.) (43)
"Tales from the Vienna
Woods"
SAINT-SAËNS (33)
Piano Concerto No. 2
BIZET (30)
Symphony in C major,
Roma
Marche funèbre, for
orchestra
Marine, for piano

Variations chromatiques,
for piano
BRUCH (30)
Violin Concerto No. 1
MUSSORGSKY (29)
fp. (privately) *Zenitha
(The Marriage),* opera
The Nursery, song cycle
(1868–72)
TCHAIKOVSKY (28)
Fate, symphonic poem
RIMSKY-KORSAKOV
(24)
*The Maid of Pskov (Ivan
the Terrible),* opera
(1868–72)

1869 ROUSSEL was born: BERLIOZ and
DARGOMIZHSKY died

WAGNER (56)
fp. Das Rheingold, music
drama
BRUCKNER (45)
Locus iste, motet
BORODIN (36)
Prince Igor, opera begun
(left unfinished)
Symphony No. 2 begun
(completed 1876)
BRAHMS (36)
p. Books I and II, of
piano studies in five
books
Eighteen Liebeslieder
Waltzes
CUI (34)
William Ratcliffe, opera
SAINT-SAËNS (34)
Piano Concerto No. 3
BALAKIREV (32)

fp. Islamey, piano fantasy
BIZET (31)
Vasco da Gama,
symphonic ode with
chorus
MUSSORGSKY (30)
Boris Godunov, opera
(first version with
piano)
TCHAIKOVSKY (29)
Romeo and Juliet, fantasy
overture (final version
1880)
SULLIVAN (27)
The Prodigal Son,
oratorio
RIMSKY-KORSAKOV
(25)
Antar, symphonic suite
GRIEG (24)
Piano Concerto

1870 LEHÁR was born; BALFE died

WAGNER (57)
fp. Die Walküre, music
   drama
Siegfried Idyll, for
   orchestra
BRAHMS (37)
Alto Rhapsody, for
   contralto, chorus and
   orchestra
Triumphlied, for chorus
   and orchestra
SAINT-SAËNS (35)
*Introduction and Rondo
   Capriccioso,* for violin
   and orchestra

Mélodies persanes, six
   songs
DELIBES (34)
Coppélia, ballet
BRUCH (32)
Symphonies Nos. 1 and 2
DVOŘÁK (29)
*Dramatic (Tragic)
   Overture*
Three String Quartets
Notturno, for strings
SULLIVAN (28)
Di Ballo, concert overture
FAURÉ (25)
Two vocal duets

1871

VERDI (58)
Aida, opera
GADE (54)
Symphony No. 8
GOUNOD (53)
Saltarello for orchestra
BRUCKNER (47)
Os uisti, motet
STRAUSS, J. (Jr.) (46)
*Indigo und die vierzig
   Rauber,* operetta
BRAHMS (38)
*Schicksalied (Song of
   Destiny)*
SAINT-SAËNS (36)
Marche héroïque, for
   orchestra
Omphale's Spinning

Wheel, symphonic
   poem
BIZET (33)
Jeux d'enfants, for piano
   duet
Petite Suite d'Orchestre
TCHAIKOVSKY (31)
String Quartet
DVOŘÁK (30)
*King and Charcoal
   Burner,* opera (first
   version)
Overture in F major
Piano Trios Nos. 1 and 2
Cello Sonata
MASSENET (29)
Suite for Orchestra No. 2,
   Scènes hongroises

1872 ALFVÉN, SKRIABIN and VAUGHAN WILLIAMS were born

DARGOMIZHSKY
(posthumous)
fp. The Stone Guest,
opera
FRANCK (50)
Panis Angelicus
LALO (49)
Deux Aubades, for small
orchestra
Divertissement, for small
orchestra
Violin Concerto
BRUCKNER (48)
Symphony No. 2, revised
1891
PONCHIELLI (38)
I Promessi Sposi, opera
SAINT-SAËNS (37)
La Princesse jaune, opera

BIZET (34)
L'Arlésienne, incidental
music
Djarmileh, opera
BRUCH (34)
Hermione, opera
Odysseus, cantata
MUSSORGSKY (33)
Khovantschina, opera
TCHAIKOVSKY (32)
Symphony No. 2, *Little
Russian*
DVOŘÁK (31)
May Night, nocturne
for orchestra
Piano Quintet in A major
GRIEG (29)
Sigurd Jorsalfar,
incidental music

1873 RACHMANINOV, REGER and JONGEN were born

VERDI (60)
String Quartet
GOUNOD (55)
*Funeral March of a
Marionette,* for
orchestra
LALO (50)
Symphonie Espagnole,
for violin and orchestra
BRUCKNER (49)
Symphony No. 3, *Wagner*
(revised 1877 and
1888)

BRAHMS (40)
Variations on a Theme by
Haydn, *St. Anthony,*
for orchestra
PONCHIELLI (39)
Il Parlatore Eterno, opera
Le Due Gemelle, ballet
SAINT-SAËNS (38)
Phaeton, symphonic poem
Cello Concerto No. 1
BIZET (35)
Patrie, overture

CONTINUED

TCHAIKOVSKY (33)
The Tempest, symphonic
   fantasia
DVOŘÁK (32)
Symphony No. 3
Romance, for violin and
   orchestra
Octet, *Serenade*
String Quartet in A minor
String Quartet in F minor

Violin Sonata
MASSENET (31)
Phèdre, concert overture
Suite for Orchestra No. 3,
   Scènes dramatiques
SULLIVAN (31)
The Light of the World,
   oratorio
FAURÉ (28)
Cantique de Jean Racine

1874 HOLST, SCHOENBERG and SUK were born

THOMAS (63)
Gille et Gillotin, opera
VERDI (61)
Requiem Mass
GADE (57)
Novelleten, for string
   orchestra
FRANCK (52)
Redemption, for soprano,
   chorus and orchestra
   (second edition with
   one orchestral number
   and male chorus added)
BRUCKNER (50)
Symphony No. 4,
   Romantic (revised
   1880)
SMETANA (50)
The Two Widows, opera
Má Vlast, cycle of six
   symphonic poems
   (1874–79)
STRAUSS, J. (Jr.) (49)
Die Fledermaus, operetta
PONCHIELLI (40)
I Lituani, opera, revised
   as *Aldona*
SAINT-SAËNS (39)
Danse macabre,
   symphonic poem

MUSSORGSKY (35)
Sorochintsky Fair, opera
*Night on the Bare
   Mountain,* arrangement
   by Rimsky-Korsakov
   of a passage in
   Sorochintsky Fair
Jesus Navin, for contralto,
   bass, chorus and piano
*Pictures from an
   Exhibition,* for piano
Sunless, song cycle
TCHAIKOVSKY (34)
Piano Concerto No. 1
   (1874–75)
String Quartet
DVOŘÁK (33)
Symphony No. 4
Rhapsody for orchestra,
   in A minor
String Quartet
MASSENET (32)
Suite for Orchestra No. 4,
   Scènes pittoresques
d'INDY (23)
Max et Thecla, symphonic
   overture, Part 2 of
   Wallenstein Trilogy
Jean Hunyade,
   symphony

1875 COLERIDGE-TAYLOR and RAVEL were
born; BIZET died

LALO (52)
Allegro Symphonique
GOLDMARK (45)
The Queen of Sheba, opera
BORODIN (42–46)
String Quartet No. 1
  (1875–79)
BRAHMS (42)
Fifteen new Liebeslieder
  for piano duet
String Quartet No. 3
SAINT-SAËNS (40)
Piano Concerto No. 4
BIZET (37)
fp. Carmen, opera
MUSSORGSKY (36–38)
*Songs and Dances of
  Death,* song cycle
  (1875–77)
CUI (41)
Angelo, opera
PONCHIELLI (41)
A Gaetano Donizetti,
  cantata
TCHAIKOVSKY (35)
Symphony No. 3, *Polish*
Swan Lake, ballet
String Quartet

DVOŘÁK (34)
Symphony No. 5
Serenade for Strings
String Quintet, with
  double-bass
Piano Quartet
Piano Trio
Moravian duets, for voices
  and piano
MASSENET (33)
Eve, oratorio
SULLIVAN (33)
Trial by Jury, operetta
The Zoo, operetta
GRIEG (32)
Peer Gynt, incidental
  music
RIMSKY-KORSAKOV
  (31)
Quartet No. 1
FAURÉ (30)
Allegro Symphonique, for
  orchestra
Suite for Orchestra
Les Djinns, for chorus and
  orchestra
MESSAGER (22)
Symphony

1876 FALLA, WOLF-FERRARI and CARPENTER
were born

WAGNER (63)
fp. Siegfried, music drama
fp. Götterdämmerung,
  music drama

GOUNOD (58)
Cinq-Mars, opera
  (1876–77)
FRANCK (54)
Les Éolides, symphonic
  poem

CONTINUED

383

LALO (53)
Cello Concerto
SMETANA (52)
The Kiss, opera
String Quartet No. 1,
From My Life
GOLDMARK (46)
Rustic Wedding,
symphony
BRAHMS (43)
Symphony No. 1
(completed)
PONCHIELLI (42)
La Gioconda, opera
SAINT-SAËNS (41)
The Deluge, oratorio
DELIBES (40)
Silvia, ballet
TCHAIKOVSKY (36)
Slavonic March, for
orchestra
*Variations on a Rococo
Theme*, for cello and
orchestra
DVOŘÁK (35)
Piano Concerto in G
minor
String Quartet in E major
Piano Trio
Stabat Mater

MASSENET (34)
Suite for Orchestra, No. 5,
Scènes napolitaines
RIMSKY-KORSAKOV
(32)
String Sextet
Quintet for piano and
wind
FAURÉ (31)
Violin Sonata in A major
GODARD (27)
Violin Concerto No. 2,
Concerto romantique
d'INDY (25)
Attendez-moi sous l'orme,
opera (1876–78)
Anthony and Cleopatra,
overture
STANFORD (24)
Symphony
LIADOV (21)
Birulki, for piano
WOLF (16–30)
Nachgelassene Werke
(1876–90)
DEBUSSY (14–17)
Trio in G minor
(1876–79)
STRAUSS, R. (12)
Festmarch, for orchestra,
Op. 1

1877 AUBERT, DOHNÁNYI and QUILTER were
born

BRUCKNER (53)
Symphony No. 5
(revised 1878)
BRAHMS (44)
Symphony No. 2
SAINT-SAËNS (42)
Samson and Delilah,
opera

Suite for Orchestra
La Jeunesse d'Hercule,
symphonic poem
TCHAIKOVSKY (37)
Symphony No. 4
Francesca da Rimini,
symphonic fantasy

Waltz-Scherzo, for violin
 and orchestra
CHABRIER (36)
L'Étoile, opera
DVOŘÁK (36)
The Cunning Peasant,
 opera
Symphonic Variations for
 orchestra
String Quartet in D minor
MASSENET (35)
Le Roi de Lahore, opera
Narcisse, cantata

SULLIVAN (35)
The Sorcerer, operetta
"The Lost Chord", song
STANFORD (25)
Festival Overture
MESSAGER (24)
Don Juan et Haydée,
 cantata
JANÁČEK (23)
Suite for strings
WOLF (17)
*Lieder aus der
 Jugendzeit* (1877–78)
*Lieder nach verschiedenen
 Dichtern* (1877–97)

1878   BOUGHTON was born

GOUNOD (60)
Marche religieuse, for
 orchestra
OFFENBACH (59)
Madame Favart, operetta
FRANCK (56)
Cantabile for organ
Fantaisie for organ
Pièce héroïque, for organ
BRUCKNER (54)
Abendzauber, for baritone
 and male chorus
SMETANA (54)
The Secret, opera
Czech Dances
BRAHMS (45)
Piano Concerto No. 2
 (1878–81)
Violin Concerto
Violin Sonata No. 1
 (1878–79)
SAINT-SAËNS (43)
Symphony No. 2

BRUCH (40)
Violin Concerto No. 2
TCHAIKOVSKY (38)
Violin Concerto
DVOŘÁK (37)
Serenade in D minor, for
 orchestra
Slavonic Dances, for
 orchestra, first series
Slavonic Rhapsodies, for
 orchestra
String Sextet
SULLIVAN (36)
Henry VIII, incidental
 music
H.M.S. Pinafore, operetta
The Martyr of Antioch,
 oratorio
RIMSKY-KORSAKOV
 (34)
May Night, opera

CONTINUED

SARASATE (34)
Zigeunerweisen, orchestral
  fantasy
FAURÉ (33)
Violin Concerto
GODARD (29)
Les Bijoux de Jeanette,
  opera
La Tasse, dramatic
  symphony, for solo
  voices, chorus and
  orchestra
Piano Concerto

d'INDY (27)
The Enchanted Forest,
  ballad-symphony
Quartet in A major for
  piano and strings
  (1878–88)
MESSAGER (25)
Fleur d'Oranger, ballet
ELGAR (21)
Romance, for violin and
  piano (or orchestra)
Promenades, for wind

1879   IRELAND, RESPIGHI and BRIDGE were
       born

LISZT (68)
Via Crucis
GADE (62)
*En Sommertag paa
  Landet,* for orchestra
GOUNOD (61)
The Redemption, oratorio
FRANCK (57)
Béatitudes, cantata
Piano Quintet in F minor
BRUCKNER (55)
String Quartet
BRAHMS (46)
Rhapsody in G minor, for
  piano
Rhapsody in B minor, for
  piano
p. Piano Studies,
  Books III–V
SAINT-SAËNS (44)
Suite Algerienne
Violin Concerto No. 2
MUSSORGSKY (40)
"Song of the Flea", song

TCHAIKOVSKY (39)
Eugene Onegin, opera
Capriccio Italien
Piano Concerto No. 2
  (1879–80)
CHABRIER (38)
Une Éducation manquée
DVOŘÁK (38)
Czech Suite for orchestra
Festival March
Polonaise in E♭, for
  orchestra
Mazurka, for violin and
  orchestra
Violin Concerto, in A
  minor (1879–80)
String Quartet in E♭
  major
MASSENET (37)
Suite for Orchestra No. 6,
  Scènes de féerie
RIMSKY-KORSAKOV
  (35)
Legend, for orchestra
  (1879–80)

Sinfonietta on Russian Themes
FAURÉ (34)
Piano Quartet No. 1
GODARD (30)
Scènes poétiques
d'INDY (28)
Le Chant de la Cloche, opera (1879–83)
LIADOV (24)
Arabesque, for piano

ELGAR (22)
Harmony Music, for wind instruments
Intermezzos, for wind instruments
WOLF (19)
String Quartet (1879–80)
MASCAGNI (16)
Symphony in C minor
STRAUSS, R. (15)
Overture in A minor

1880   BLOCH, INGHELBRECHT, MEDTNER, PIZZETTI were born; OFFENBACH died

---

LISZT (69)
The remaining five Hungarian Rhapsodies (*c.* 1880)
GADE (63)
Violin Concerto
FRANCK (58)
L'Organiste, fifty-five pieces for harmonium
BORODIN (47)
In the Steppes of Central Asia, orchestral "picture"
BRAHMS (47)
Academic Festival Overture
Tragic Overture
Piano Trio No. 2 (1880–82)
PONCHIELLI (46)
Il Figliuol Prodigo, opera
SAINT-SAËNS (45)
Violin Concerto No. 3
MUSSORGSKY (41)
Turkish March, for orchestra

Piano Pieces
Five Popular Russian Songs, for male chorus
TCHAIKOVSKY (40)
Romeo and Juliet, overture (final revision)
Serenade for Strings
CHABRIER (39)
Dix pièces pittoresques, for piano
DVOŘÁK (39)
Symphony No. 6
Violin Sonata
Seven Gipsy Songs
MASSENET (38)
La Vierge, oratorio
SULLIVAN (38)
The Pirates of Penzance, operetta
GRIEG (37)
Two Elegiac Melodies
RIMSKY-KORSAKOV.. (36)
The Snow Maiden, opera (1880–81)

CONTINUED

387

FAURÉ (35)
Berceuse, for violin and
    piano
GODARD (31)
Symphony
Diane: poème dramatique
d'INDY (29)
Le Camp de Wallenstein,
    symphonic overture,
    Part 1 of Wallenstein
    Trilogy
JANÁČEK (26)
Dumka, for violin and
    piano
HUMPERDINCK (26)
Humoreske
CHAUSSON (25)
Les Caprices de Marianne,
    opera
Joan of Arc, choral

MAHLER (20)
Klagende Lieder
PADEREWSKI (*c.*20)
Violin Sonata
WOLF (20–28)
Eichendorf-Lieder
    (1880–88)
DEBUSSY (18)
Andante, for piano
Danse bohémienne, for
    piano
"La Belle au bois
    dormant", song
    (1880–83)
STRAUSS, R. (16)
Symphony in D minor
String Quartet
BUSONI (14)
String Quartet No. 1
    (1880–81)

1881   BARTÓK and ENESCO were born;
        MUSSORGSKY died

LISZT (70)
Mephisto Waltz
GOUNOD (63)
Le Tribut de Zamora,
    opera
OFFENBACH
    (posthumous)
fp. The Tales of Hoffman,
    operetta
FRANCK (59)
Rebecca
LALO (58)
Rhapsodie Norvégienne
BRUCKNER (57)
Symphony No. 6
SMETANA (57)
fp. Libuse, opera

BORODIN (48)
String Quartet No. 2
CUI (46)
Marche solenelle
BRUCH (43)
p. Kol Nidrei, for cello
    and piano (or
    orchestra)
DVOŘÁK (40)
Legends, for orchestra
String Quartet
MASSENET (39)
Suite No. 7 for orchestra,
    Scènes alsaciennes
Hérodiade, opera
SULLIVAN (39)
Patience, operetta

GRIEG (38)
Norwegian Dances
FAURÉ (36)
Le Ruisseau
Ballade, for piano and
  orchestra
STANFORD (29)
The Veiled Prophet,
  opera
DEBUSSY (19)
Fugue for piano
MASCAGNI (18)
Symphony in F major

In Filanda, for voices and
  orchestra
STRAUSS, R. (17)
Violin Concerto in D
  minor (1881–82)
GLAZUNOV (16)
Overture on Greek
  Themes, No. 1
  (1881–84)
Symphony No. 1
SIBELIUS (16)
Piano Quartet
Piano Trio

1882 GRAINGER, KODÁLY, MALIPIERO,
       STRAVINSKY and TURINA were born;
       RAFF died

THOMAS (71)
Francoise de Rimini
WAGNER (69)
fp. Parsifal, music drama
FRANCK (60)
Hulda, opera (1882–85)
Le Chasseur maudit,
  symphonic poem
LALO (59)
Ballet Suites Nos. 1 and 2,
  Namouna
SMETANA (58)
String Quartet No. 2
BRAHMS (49)
String Quintet No. 1
PONCHIELLI (48)
In Memoria di Garibaldi,
  cantata
DELIBES (46)
Le Roi s'amuse, incidental
  music
TCHAIKOVSKY (42)
1812, overture

Piano Trio
DVOŘÁK (41)
My Home, overture
SULLIVAN (40)
Iolanthe, operetta
RIMSKY-KORSAKOV
  (38)
Piano Concerto
  (1882–83)
FAURÉ (37)
Romance, for violin and
  orchestra
La Naissance de Venus
GODARD (33)
Symphonie, ballet
d'INDY (31)
La Mort de Wallenstein,
  symphonic overture,
  Part 3 of Wallenstein
  Trilogy
STANFORD (30)
Serenade in G, for
  orchestra

CONTINUED

Elegiac symphony
CHAUSSON (27)
Viviane, symphonic poem
*Poème de l'amour et de
la mer,* for voice and
piano (1882–92)
Piano Trio
IPPOLITOV-IVANOV
(23)
Yar-Khmel, for orchestra
MAHLER (22)
Lieder und Gesänge aus
der Jugendzeit
MACDOWELL (21)
Piano Concerto No. 1
DEBUSSY (20)
Intermezzo, for orchestra
Printemps, for women's
choir and orchestra
Triomphe de Bacchus, for
piano duet

Two four-part Fugues, for
piano
PIERNÉ (19)
Edith, Cantata
STRAUSS, R. (18)
Horn Concerto No. 1
(1882–83)
GLAZUNOV (17)
Overture on Greek
Themes, No. 2
(1882–85)
String Quartet
BUSONI (16)
*Spring, Summer, Autumn,
Winter,* for male voice
and orchestra
Il Sabato del villagio, for
solo voice, chorus and
orchestra
Serenata, for cello and
piano

1883 BAX, CASELLA, SZYMANOWSKI and
WEBERN were born; FLOTOW and
WAGNER died

BRUCKNER (59)
Symphony No. 7
SMETANA (59)
The Prague Carnival
String Quartet No. 2
STRAUSS, J. (Jr.) (58)
Eine Nacht in Venedig,
operetta
BRAHMS (50)
Symphony No. 3
DELIBES (47)
Lakmé, opera
CUI (48)
Suite Concertante, for
violin and orchestra

CHABRIER (42)
fp. España, orchestral
rhapsody
Three *Valses romantiques,*
for piano duo
DVOŘÁK (42)
Husitská, overture
Scherzo capriccioso, for
orchestra
Piano Trio
GRIEG (40)
Lyric Pieces for piano,
Book II
FAURÉ (38)
Élégie, in C minor

GODARD (34)
Symphonie Gothique
CATALANI (29)
Dejanire, opera
ELGAR (26)
Une Idyll, for violin and
  piano
Fugue, for oboe and
  violin
MAHLER (23)
*Lieder eines fahrenden
  Gesellen*, song cycle
  for voice and orchestra
WOLF (23)
Penthesilea, symphonic
  poem
MACDOWELL (22)
Modern Suite, for piano

DEBUSSY (21)
Invocation, for men's
  chorus and orchestra
Le Gladiateur, cantata
PIERNÉ (20)
Le Chemin de l'amour,
  opera-comique
*Trois pièces formant suite
  de concert*, for
  orchestra
STRAUSS, R. (19)
Concert Overture
Piano Quartet (1833–84)
GLAZUNOV (18)
Serenade No. 1
String Quartet
BUSONI (17)
Piano Sonata in F minor

1884   GRIFFES was born; SMETANA died

GADE (67)
Holbergiana Suite
GOUNOD (66)
fp. Mors et Vita, oratorio
FRANCK (62)
Les Djinns, symphonic
  poem for piano and
  orchestra
Prelude, Chorale et Fugue,
  for piano
"Nocturne", song
LALO (61)
Scherzo
BRUCKNER (60)
Symphony No. 8,
  Apocalyptic (possibly
  1887, revised 1890)
Te Deum

BRAHMS (51)
Symphony No. 4
  (1884–85)
BALAKIREV (47)
Russia, symphonic poem
TCHAIKOVSKY (44)
Mazeppa, opera
Concert-fantasy, for piano
  and orchestra
MASSENET (42)
Manon, opera
SULLIVAN (42)
Princess Ida, operetta
GRIEG (41)
Lyric Pieces for piano,
  Book III
FAURÉ (39)
Symphony in D minor
  (unpublished)
                    CONTINUED

391

GODARD (35)
Pedro de Zalamea, opera
Symphonie Orientale
d'INDY (33)
Lied for cello (or viola)
  and orchestra
Saugefleure, orchestral
  legend
STANFORD (32)
Canterbury Pilgrims,
  opera
Savonarola, opera
CHAUSSON (29)
Hélène, opera
  (1884–85)
PUCCINI (26)
Le Villi, opera

PADEREWSKI (*c.*24)
Polish Dances for piano,
  Books I and II
MACDOWELL (23)
Forest Idylls, for piano
DEBUSSY (22)
Suite for Orchestra
Divertissement No. 1 for
  orchestra
Diane au bois, for chorus
L'Enfant prodigue,
  cantata
STRAUSS, R. (20)
Symphony in F minor
p. Serenade for wind
p. Cello Sonata
GLAZUNOV (19)
Serenade No. 2

1885   BERG, BUTTERWORTH and TAYLOR
          were born

FRANCK (63)
Symphonic Variations,
  for piano and orchestra
STRAUSS, J. (Jr.) (60)
Zigeunerbaron, operetta
BORODIN (52)
Petite Suite, for piano
Scherzo in A♭, for piano
PONCHIELLI (51)
Marion Delorme, opera
SAINT-SAËNS (50)
Violin Sonata No. 1
TCHAIKOVSKY (45)
Manfred Symphony
CHABRIER (44)
Habanèra, for piano
DVOŘÁK (44)
Symphony No. 7

The Spectre's Bride,
  cantata
MASSENET (43)
Le Cid, opera
SULLIVAN (43)
The Mikado, operetta
GRIEG (42)
Holberg Suite, for piano
  or strings
MESSAGER (32)
La Béarnaise, operetta
MACDOWELL (24)
p. Hamlet and Ophelia,
  symphonic poem
DEBUSSY (23)
Almanzor, for chorus
PIERNÉ (22)
Symphonic Overture

Fantaisie-Ballet, for piano
and orchestra
GLAZUNOV (20)
Stenka Razin, tone poem

SIBELIUS (20)
String Quartet

1886 SCHOECK was born; LISZT and
PONCHIELLI died

FRANCK (64)
Violin Sonata in A major
LALO (63)
Symphony in G minor
GOLDMARK (56)
Merlin
BORODIN (53)
Serenata alla Spagnola
(Movement in String
Quartet "B-La-F")
BRAHMS (53)
Cello Sonata No. 2
Violin Sonatas Nos. 2
and 3
CUI (51)
Deux Morceaux, for
cello and orchestra
SAINT-SAËNS (51)
Le Carnaval des animaux,
for piano and orchestra
Symphony No. 3 with
organ and two pianos
CHABRIER (45)
Gwendoline, opera
DVOŘÁK (45)
Slavonic Dances, for
orchestra, second series
St. Ludmila, oratorio
SULLIVAN (44)
The Golden Legend,
cantata

RIMSKY-KORSAKOV
(42)
*Fantasia Concertante on
Russian Themes,* for
violin and orchestra
FAURÉ (41)
Piano Quartet No. 2
GODARD (37)
Symphony Légendaire
d'INDY (35)
*Symphony on a French
Mountain Air*
Suite in D, for trumpet,
two flutes and string
quartet
STANFORD (34)
The Revenge, choral-
ballad
MESSAGER (33)
Les deux pigeons, ballet
CATALANI (32)
Edmea, opera
CHAUSSON (31)
Hymne Védique, for
chorus and orchestra
Solitude dans les bois,
for orchestra
DELIUS (24)
Florida Suite, for
orchestra
GERMAN (24)
The Rival Poets, operetta
CONTINUED

PIERNÉ (23)
Don Luis, opera-comique
STRAUSS, R. (22)
Aus Italien, symphonic
  fantasia
Macbeth, symphonic
  poem (1886–90)
GLAZUNOV (21)
Symphony No. 2

BUSONI (20)
String Quartet in C minor
Little Suite, for cello and
  piano
CILEA (20)
Piano Trio
SATIE (20)
Ogives, for piano

**1887 GRANADOS and VILLA-LOBOS were born;
      BORODIN died**

VERDI (74)
fp. Otello, opera
GADE (70)
p. Violin Sonata No. 3
FRANCK (65)
Prelude, aria et finale, for
  piano
STRAUSS, J. (Jr.) (62)
Simplizius, operetta
BRAHMS (54)
Double Concerto, for
  violin, cello and
  orchestra
Zigeunerliede
BRUCH (49)
Symphony No. 3
CHABRIER (46)
Le Roi malgré lui, opera
DVOŘÁK (46)
Piano Quintet
Piano Quartet
Terzetto, for two violins
  and viola
MASSENET (45)
Parade Militaire
SULLIVAN (45)
Ruddigore, operetta
GRIEG (44)
Violin Sonata No. 3

RIMSKY-KORSAKOV
  (43)
Capriccio Espagnole, for
  orchestra
FAURÉ (42)
Pavane, with chorus ad lib
Requiem
d'INDY (36)
Serenade and Valse, for
  small orchestra
Trio for clarinet, cello
  and piano
STANFORD (35)
Irish symphony
Prelude *Oedipus Rex*
Queen of the Seas,
  overture
JANÁČEK (33)
Sarka, opera
CHAUSSON (32)
Chant Nuptial
LIADOV (32)
Scherzo, for orchestra
SMYTH (29)
Violin Sonata
IPPOLITOV-IVANOV
  (28)
Ruth, opera
p. Violin Sonata

WOLF (27)
Italian Serenade, for
   string quartet, later for
   orchestra
p. Violin Sonata
MACDOWELL (26)
Six Idylls after Goethe,
   for piano
Six Poems after Heine, for
   piano
DEBUSSY (25)
*The Blessed Damozel
   (La Damoiselle élue),*
   cantata (1887–88)
Cinq Poèmes de
Baudelaire, songs
   (1887–89)
PIERNÉ (24)
Piano Concerto
ROPARTZ (23)
La Cloche de morts, for
   orchestra
GLAZUNOV (22)
Suite Caractèristique
   (possibly 1884)
Lyric Poem, for orchestra
CILÈA (21)
Suite for Orchestra
SATIE (21)
Trois sarabandes, for
   piano

1888

GADE (71–73)
Ulysses, march (1888–90)
GOUNOD (70)
Petite Symphonie, for ten
   wind instruments
FRANCK (66)
Ghisele, opera
Symphony in D minor
   (1886–88)
Psyche, symphonic poem
LALO (65)
Le Roi d'Ys, opera
CUI (53)
Le Filibustier, opera
   (1888–89)
TCHAIKOVSKY (48)
Sleeping Beauty, ballet
Hamlet, overture
Symphony No. 5
CHABRIER (47)
Marche joyeuse, for
   orchestra

SULLIVAN (46)
*The Yeoman of the
   Guard,* operetta
GRIEG (45)
Lyric Pieces for piano,
   Book IV
RIMSKY-KORSAKOV
   (44)
*Russian Easter Festival
   Overture*
Schéhérazade, symphonic
   suite
FAURÉ (43)
Caligula, incidental music
GODARD (39)
Jocelyn, opera
d'INDY (37)
Fantasie, for oboe and
   orchestra
STANFORD (36)
Symphony in F major

CONTINUED

MESSAGER (35)
Isoline, opera
LIADOV (33)
Mazurka, for orchestra
CHAMINADE (31)
Callirhoe, ballet
MAHLER (28)
Symphony No. 1
Des Knaben Wunderhorn,
  song cycle for voice and
  orchestra
PADEREWSKI (*c.*28)
Piano Concerto
WOLF (28)
Mörike-Lieder
Goethe-Lieder
MACDOWELL (27)
Lancelot and Elaine,
  symphonic poem
Romance, for cello
Marionettes, for piano
DEBUSSY (26)
Petite Suite, for piano
  duet
Arabesques 1 and 2, for
  piano
Ariettes oubliées, songs
DELIUS (26)
Marche caprice, for
  orchestra
Sleigh Ride, for orchestra

ROPARTZ (24)
Les Landes
Marche de fête
STRAUSS, R. (24)
Don Juan, symphonic
  poem
p. Violin Sonata
NIELSEN (23)
Little Suite in A minor,
  for strings
Quintet
Four String Quartets
  (1888–1907)
SIBELIUS (23)
Theme and Variations for
  quartet
BUSONI (22)
Symphonic Suite
Konzert-Fantasie
  (Symphonisches
  Tongedicht), for piano
  and orchestra
SATIE (22)
Three *Gymnopédies*, for
  piano
VAUGHAN WILLIAMS
  (16)
Piano Trio
SUK (14)
Mass in B♭ major

1889

THOMAS (78)
La Tempête, ballet
VERDI (76–85)
Four Sacred Pieces
  (1889–98)
FRANCK (67)
String Quartet

LALO (66)
Piano Concerto
DVOŘÁK (48)
Symphony No. 8
SULLIVAN (47)
The Gondoliers, operetta
FAURÉ (44)
Shylock, incidental music

396

Petite pièce, for cello and
  piano
JANÁČEK (35)
Six Lach Dances
PUCCINI (31)
Edgar, opera
MACDOWELL (28)
Lamia, symphonic
  poem
Les Orientales, for piano
DEBUSSY (27)
Fantaisie, for piano and
  orchestra (1889–90)
GERMAN (27)
Richard III, incidental
  music
PIERNÉ (26)
Marche solenelle
Pantomime, for orchestra
ROPARTZ (25)
Carnaval
Cinq pièces brève, for
  orchestra

STRAUSS, R. (25)
Tod und Verklaerung,
  symphonic poem
GLAZUNOV (24)
Fantasia, *The Forest*
  (possibly 1887)
NIELSEN (24)
Symphonic Rhapsody
SIBELIUS (24)
Piano Quintet
Suite for String Trio
String Quartet
Violin Sonata
BUSONI (23)
String Quartet No. 2
CILÈA (23)
Gina, opera
GIORDANO (22)
Marina, opera
SUK (15)
Fantasy, for strings
Piano Trio (1889–90)

1890 MARTINŮ, IBERT and MARTIN were
       born; GADE and FRANCK died

GADE (73)
p. String Quartet
FRANCK (68)
Chorales for organ
BRAHMS (57)
String Quintet No. 2
CUI (55–68)
Three String Quartets in
  Cm: D: E♭
  (1890–1913)
TCHAIKOVSKY (50)
The Queen of Spades,
  opera

DVOŘÁK (49)
Dumka, for piano trio
  (1890–91)
MASSENET (48)
Visions, symphonic poem
FAURÉ (45)
Cinq mélodies de
  Verlaine, songs
GODARD (41)
Dante, opera
d'INDY (39)
Karadec, incidental music
String Quartet No. 1
CONTINUED

MESSAGER (37)
La Basoche, operetta
CATALANI (36)
Lorely, opera
CHAUSSON (35)
Symphony in B♭ major
LIADOV (35)
Dal tempo antico, for
   piano
ELGAR (33)
Froissart, concert overture
SMYTH (32)
Anthony and Cleopatra,
   overture
Serenade in D, for
   orchestra
IPPOLITOV-IVANOV
   (31)
Asra, opera
CHARPENTIER (30)
Impressions d'Italie,
   orchestra suite
WOLF (30)
Spanish Song Book
ARENSKY (29)
A Dream on the Volga,
   opera
MACDOWELL (29)
Piano Concerto No. 2
Twelve Studies for Piano,
   Books I and II
DEBUSSY (28)
Ballade, for piano

Rêverie, for piano
Suite Bergamasque, for
   piano (1890–1905)
Tarantelle styrienne
   (*Danse*), for piano
Valse romantique, for
   piano
GERMAN (28)
Symphony No. 1
MASCAGNI (27)
Cavalleria Rusticana,
   opera
PIERNÉ (27)
Scherzo Caprice, for
   piano and orchestra
GLAZUNOV (25)
The Sea
Wedding March
Une fête Slav
SIBELIUS (25)
Two Overtures
   (1890–91)
BUSONI (24)
Konzertstücke for piano
Violin Sonata No. 1
SATIE (24)
Three *Gnossiennes*, for
   piano
RACHMANINOV (17)
Piano Concerto No. 1
   (1890–91)
Six songs (1890–93)

1891   BLISS, PROKOFIEV and GRANDJANY
       were born; DELIBES died

BRAHMS (58)
Clarinet Quintet
Piano Trio
BRUCH (53)
Violin Concerto No. 3

DVOŘÁK (50)
Nature, Life and Love,
   cycle of overtures:
   "Amid Nature"
   "Carnaval"

"Othello"
Forest Calm, for cello and orchestra
Rondo, for cello and orchestra
SULLIVAN (49)
Ivanhoe, opera
GRIEG (48)
Lyric Pieces for piano, Book V
FAURÉ (46)
La Bonne chanson, song cycle (1891–92)
d'INDY (41)
Tableaux de voyage
STANFORD (39)
Eden, oratario
JANÁČEK (37)
The Beginning of a Romance, opera
Rákos Rákóczy, ballet
CHAUSSON (36)
Concerto for piano, violin and string quartet
ELGAR (34)
La Capriceuse, for violin and piano
SMYTH (33)
Suite for Strings
WOLF (31)
The Feast of Suhaug, incidental music
Italian Song Book, Book I
LOEFFLER (30)
The Nights in the Ukraine, for violin and orchestra
MACDOWELL (30)
Suite No. 1 for orchestra
The Lovely Alda, symphonic poem

The Saracens, symphonic poem
DEBUSSY (29)
Rodrigue et Chimène, opera (1891–92, unfinished)
Marche écossaise
Mazurka, for piano
Trois mélodies de Verlaine, songs
Deux Romances, songs
GERMAN (29)
Funeral March
MASCAGNI (28)
Solemn Mass
L'Amico Fritz, opera
PIERNÉ (28)
Le Colliers de saphire, ballet
GLAZUNOV (26)
Oriental Rhapsody
NIELSEN (26)
Symphony No. 1
SIBELIUS (26)
Scène de ballet
Piano Quartet
SATIE (25)
Three Préludes from *Les fils des étoiles,* for piano
RACHMANINOV (18)
Scherzo for strings
REGER (18)
Piano Trio
Violin Sonata
IVES (17)
Variations on "America", for organ
SUK (17)
Dramatic Overture
Piano Quartet

BRAHMS (59)
Fantasien, for piano
SAINT-SAËNS (57)
Piano Trio No. 2
DVOŘÁK (52)
Te Deum
TCHAIKOVSKY (52)
Iolanthe, opera
*Casse Noisette
(Nutcracker)*, ballet
p. String sextet
MASSENET (50)
Werther, opera
SULLIVAN (50)
Haddon Hall, opera
RIMSKY-KORSAKOV
(48)
fp. Mlada, opera
CATALANI (38)
La Wally, opera
LIADOV (37)
Kukalki, for piano
ELGAR (35)
Serenade for Strings
The Black Knight,
cantata
LEONCAVALLO (34)
I Pagliacci, opera
CHARPENTIER (32)
La Vie du poète,
cantata
DEBUSSY (30)
Fêtes galantes, songs,
first series
DELIUS (30)
Irmelin, opera
GERMAN (30)
Gipsy Suite

Henry VIII, incidental
music
MASCAGNI (29)
I Rantzau, opera
PIERNÉ (29)
*Les Joyeuses commères
de Paris*, ballet
ROPARTZ (28)
Serenade
STRAUSS, R. (28)
Guntram, opera
DUKAS (27)
Polyeucte, overture
GLAZUNOV (27)
Symphony No. 3
(possibly 1890)
The Kremlin (possibly
1890)
Le Printemps
String Quintet
SIBELIUS (27)
En Saga, symphonic
poem
Kullervo, symphonic
poem
CILEA (26)
La Tilda, opera
SATIE (26)
Uspud, ballet
*Sonneries de la Rose-
Croix*, for piano
GIORDANO (25)
Mala Vita, opera
BANTOCK (24)
Aegypt, ballet
Fire Worshippers
RACHMANINOV (19)
Prélude and *Danse*

400

Orientale, for cello and
    piano
Five pieces for piano
Intermezzo
REGER (19)
Cello Sonata

SUK (18)
Serenade for Strings
AUBERT (17)
Sous bois, song

1893 BENJAMIN and MOORE were born;
        GOUNOD, TCHAIKOVSKY and CATALANI
        died

VERDI (80)
fp. Falstaff, opera
TCHAIKOVSKY (53)
Symphony No. 6,
    Pathétique
Piano Concerto No. 3
DVOŘÁK (52)
Symphony No. 9, *From
    the New World*
String Quintet
American String Quartet
SULLIVAN (51)
Utopia, Ltd., operetta
GRIEG (50)
Lyric pieces for piano,
    Book VI
FAURÉ (48)
Dolly Suite, for piano
    duet
MESSAGER (40)
Madame Chrysanthème,
    operetta
HUMPERDINCK (39)
Hänsel und Gretel, opera
LIADOV (38)
Une Tabatière à musique,
    for piano
PUCCINI (35)
Manon Lescaut, opera

SMYTH (35)
Mass in D
ALBÉNIZ (33)
The Magic Opal, opera
PADEREWSKI (*c.*33)
Polish Fantasy on
    Original Themes, for
    piano and orchestra
MACDOWELL (32)
Piano Sonata No. 1,
    Tragica
DEBUSSY (31)
String Quartet in G minor
Proses lyriques, songs
GERMAN (31)
Symphony No. 2
Romeo and Juliet,
    incidental music
The Tempter, incidental
    music
PIERNÉ (30)
Lizarda, opera-comique
    (1893–94)
Bouton d'or, ballet
Le Docteur Blanc, ballet
ROPARTZ (29)
Le Diable couturier,
    opera
Dimanche breton
                    CONTINUED

401

String Quartet No. 1
GLAZUNOV (28)
Symphony No. 4
SIBELIUS (28)
Karelia, overture and
    orchestral suite
The Swan of Tuonela,
    symphonic legend
SATIE (27)
Danses gothiques, for
    piano
Four Préludes for piano
RACHMANINOV (20)
Aleko, opera

The Rock, fantasy for
    orchestra
Trio elégiaque
Romance and *Danse
    hongroise*, for violin
    and piano
Suite No. 1 *Fantasy*, for
    two pianos
Six songs
SUK (19)
Piano Quintet
RAVEL (18)
Sérénade grotesque, for
    piano

1894 MOERAN, PISTON, WARLOCK were born;
        RUBINSTEIN and CHABRIER died

BRUCKNER (70)
Symphony No. 9
    (unfinished, *fp*. 1903)
BRAHMS (61)
Two sonatas for clarinet
    or viola and piano
SAINT-SAËNS (59)
Preludes and Fugues for
    organ
MASSENET (52)
La Navarraise, opera
Thaïs, opera
STANFORD (42)
Symphony in D major,
    L'Allegro ed il pensiero
MESSAGER (41)
Mirette, operetta
JANÁČEK (40–49)
Jenufa, opera
    (1894–1903)
ELGAR (37–39)
King Olaf, cantata
    (1894–96)

LEONCAVALLO (36)
Serafita, symphonic poem
IPPOLITOV-IVANOV
    (35)
Armenian Rhapsody
    (1894–95)
ALBÉNIZ (34)
San Antonio de la Florida
CHARPENTIER (34)
Poèmes chantées, for
    voice and piano or
    orchestra
MAHLER (34)
Symphony No. 2,
    Resurrection
ARENSKY (33)
Raphael, opera
LOEFFLER (33)
Fantasy Concerto, for
    cello and orchestra
MACDOWELL (33)
Twelve Virtuoso Studies,
    for piano

DEBUSSY (32)
Prélude à l'après-midi d'un faune, for orchestra
STRAUSS, R. (30)
Also sprach Zarathustra, symphonic poem
GLAZUNOV (29)
Carnival Overture
"Chopiniana" Suite
String Quartet
NIELSEN (29)
Symphonic Suite for piano
SIBELIUS (29)
Spring Song, symphonic poem
CILÈA (28)
Cello Sonata

SATIE (28)
Prélude de la porte héroïque du ciel, for piano
GIORDANO (27)
Regina Diaz, opera
SKRIABIN (22)
Piano Concerto
Rêverie, for orchestra
JONGEN (21)
p. String Quartet No. 1
RACHMANINOV (21)
Caprice bohémien, for orchestra
Six piano duets
Seven piano pieces
AUBERT (17)
"Vieille chanson espagnole"

1895 HINDEMITH, ORFF, JACOB, CASTELNUOVO-TEDESCO and SOWERBY were born; GODARD died

---

STRAUSS, J. (Jr.) (70)
Waldmeister, operetta
SAINT-SAËNS (60)
Piano Concerto No. 5
BALAKIREV (58)
Ten songs (1895–96)
DVOŘÁK (54)
Suite for orchestra
Cello Concerto
Two String Quartets
SULLIVAN (53)
The Chieftain, operetta
GRIEG (52)
Lyric Pieces for piano, Book VII

RIMSKY-KORSAKOV (51)
Christmas Eve, opera
FAURÉ (50)
Romance, for cello and piano
STANFORD (43)
Suite of Ancient Dances
Piano Concerto No. 1
HUMPERDINCK (41)
Die Sieben Geislein, opera
ELGAR (38)
Organ Sonata in G major
IPPOLITOV-IVANOV (36)
Caucasian Sketches, orchestral suite
CONTINUED

ALBÉNIZ (35)
Enrico Clifford, opera
CHARPENTIER (35)
Impressions fausses, for
    voice and orchestra
MAHLER (35)
Symphony No. 3
LOEFFLER (34)
Divertimento, for violin
    and orchestra
MACDOWELL (34)
Piano Sonata No. 2,
    Eroica
DELIUS (33)
*Over the Hills and Far
    Away,* tone poem
GERMAN (33)
Symphonic Suite in D
    minor
MASCAGNI (32)
Guglielmo Ratcliff, opera
Silvano, opera
PIERNÉ (32)
La Coupe enchantée,
    opera-comique
Salome, ballet
STRAUSS, R. (31)
Till Eulenspiegel,
    symphonic poem
GLAZUNOV (30)
Cortège solenelle
Symphony No. 5

SIBELIUS (30)
Cassazione
*Lemminkäinen and the
    Maidens,* symphonic
    poem
Lemminkäinen in Tuonela,
    symphonic poem
*Lemminkäinen's Home-
    coming,* symphonic
    poem
BUSONI (29)
Suite for Orchestra, No. 2
SATIE (29)
Messe des pauvres
SKRIABIN (23)
Symphony No. 1
RACHMANINOV (22)
Symphony No. 1
HOLST (21)
The Revoke, opera
RAVEL (20)
Menuet antique
WOLF-FERRARI (19)
Violin Sonata
DOHNÁNYI (18)
fp. Piano Quintet
IRELAND (16)
Two pieces for piano
ENESCO (14)
*Ouverture tragica e
    ouverture trionfale*
Four *Sinfonie Scolastiche*
    (1895–96)

1896   HANSON, THOMSON, WEINBERGER,
        ROBERTSON, GERHARD and SESSIONS
        were born; THOMAS and BRUCKNER died

GOLDMARK (66)
The Cricket on the Hearth

BRAHMS (63)
Four Serious Songs

SAINT-SAËNS (61)
Violin Sonata No. 2
DVOŘÁK (55)
Four symphonic poems:
The Watersprite
The Noonday Witch
The Golden Spinning-wheel
The Wood Dove
SULLIVAN (54)
The Grand Duke, operetta
GRIEG (53)
Lyric Pieces for piano,
Book VIII
d'INDY (45)
Istar, symphonic variations
for orchestra
STANFORD (44)
Shamus O'Brien, opera
MESSAGER (43)
*Le Chevalier
d'Harmenthal,*
operetta
CHAUSSON (41)
Poème, for violin and
orchestra
ELGAR (39)
*The Light of Life (Lux
Christi),* oratorio
PUCCINI (38)
La Bohème, opera
ALBÉNIZ (36)
Pepita Jiménez, opera
CHARPENTIER (36)
Sérénade à Watteau, for
voice and orchestra
WOLF (36)
fp. Der Corregidor, opera
Italian Song Book, Book
II

MACDOWELL (35)
Indian Suite (Suite No.
2), for orchestra
Woodland Sketches, for
piano
GERMAN (34)
As You Like It, incidental
music
MASCAGNI (33)
Zanetto, opera
STRAUSS, R. (32)
Don Quixote, fantasy
variations for cello and
orchestra
DUKAS (31)
Symphony in C major
GLAZUNOV (31)
Symphony No. 6
BUSONI (30)
Violin Concerto
(1896–97)
GIORDANO (29)
Andrea Chénier, opera
ALFVÉN (24)
"Sonata" and "Romance",
for violin and piano
RACHMANINOV (23)
Six *Moments musicaux,*
for piano
Six songs for female or
boys' voices
Twelve songs
HOLST (22)
Fantasiestücke, for oboe
and string quartet
Quintet for wind and
piano
Four songs
IVES (22)
Symphony No. 1
(1896–98)

Quartet No. 1, *Revival
Service*
SUK (22)
String Quartet No. 1
COLERIDGE-TAYLOR
(21)
Symphony in A minor

RAVEL (21)
"Sainte", song
AUBERT (19)
Rimes tendres, song cycle
DOHNÁNYI (19)
Zrinyi, overture

1897   TANSMAN and KORNGOLD were born;
BRAHMS and BOËLLMANN died

CUI (62)
p. Five Little Duets, for
flute and violin with
piano
SAINT-SAËNS (62)
Seven Improvisations for
Grand Organ
DVOŘÁK (56)
"Heroic Song"
MASSENET (55)
Sappho, lyric play
Fantaisie, for cello and
orchestra
Marche solenelle
Devant la Madone
SULLIVAN (55)
Te Deum
RIMSKY-KORSAKOV
(53)
Three Song Cycles:
    In Spring
    To the Poet
    By the Sea
Piano Trio
FAURÉ (52)
Theme and Variations, for
piano
d'INDY (46)
Fervaal, music drama
String Quartet No. 2

MESSAGER (44)
Les P'tites Michu,
operetta
CHAUSSON (42)
Chant funèbre
Ballata
Piano Quartet
ELGAR (40)
Imperial March
The Banner of St. George,
ballad for soprano,
chorus and orchestra
Sea Pictures, for contralto
and orchestra
LEONCAVALLO (39)
La Bohème, opera
IPPOLITOV-IVANOV
(38)
p. String Quartet
DEBUSSY (35)
Chansons de Bilitis, songs
GERMAN (35)
Hamlet, symphonic poem
Fantasia *In
    Commemoration*
PIERNÉ (34)
Vendée, opera-comique
L'An Mil, symphonic
poem with chorus

DUKAS (32)
The Sorcerer's Apprentice,
  symphonic poem
BUSONI (31)
Comedy Overture
CILÈA (31)
L'Arlesiania, opera
SATIE (31)
Deux pièces froids, for
  piano
ALFVÉN (25)
Symphony No. 1
REGER (24)
Piano Quintet
Cello Sonata
Violin Sonata (1897–98)

HOLST (23)
A Winter Idyll, for
  orchestra
Clear and Cool, for
  chorus and orchestra
IVES (23–28)
Symphony No. 2
  (1897–1902)
AUBERT (20)
*Les Noces d'Apollon et
  d'Uranie,* cantata
DOHNÁNYI (20)
Symphony No. 1
ENESCO (16)
Rumainian Poem
KODÁLY (15)
Overture for orchestra

1898 GERSHWIN and HARRIS were born

SAINT-SAËNS (63)
Preludes and Fugues for
  organ
SULLIVAN (56)
The Beauty Stone, opera
GRIEG (55)
Symphonic Dances, for
  orchestra
Lyric Pieces for piano,
  Book IX
RIMSKY-KORSAKOV
  (54)
Mozart and Salieri, opera
FAURÉ (53)
Pelléas et Mélisande,
  incidental music
Papillon, for cello and
  piano
Sicilienne, for cello and
  piano

Fantaisie, for flute and
  piano
Andante, for violin and
  piano
d'INDY (47)
L'Étranger, lyric drama
Medée, incidental music
Chansons et danses, for
  seven wind instruments
STANFORD (46)
Te deum
MESSAGER (45)
Véronique, operetta
HUMPERDINCK (44)
Moorish Rhapsody, for
  orchestra
CHAUSSON (43)
Soir de fête
ELGAR (41)
Caractacus, cantata
CONTINUED

Variations on an original
  theme, *Enigma,* for
  orchestra (1898–99)
SMYTH (40)
Fantastic, opera
IPPOLITOV-IVANOV
  (39)
p. Piano Quartet
MACDOWELL (37)
Sea Pieces
MASCAGNI (35)
Iris, opera
STRAUSS, R. (34)
Ein Heldenleben,
  symphonic poem
SIBELIUS (33)
Symphony No. 1
  (1898–99)
King Christian II,
  incidental music
BUSONI (32)
Violin Sonata No. 2
GIORDANO (31)
Fedora, opera

ALFVÉN (26)
Symphony No. 2
  (1898–99)
Elegy, for horn and organ
JONGEN (25)
Fantaisie, for violin and
  orchestra
HOLST (24)
Ornulf's Drapa, for
  baritone and orchestra
IVES (24–33)
Calcium Light Night, for
  chamber orchestra
  (1898–1907)
Central Park in the Dark,
  for orchestra
  (1898–1907)
COLERIDGE-TAYLOR
  (23)
Ballade, for orchestra
*Hiawatha's Wedding
  Feast,* cantata
ENESCO (17)
p. Violin Sonata No. 1

1899 CHÁVEZ and POULENC were born;
  STRAUSS, J. (Jr.) and CHAUSSON died

CUI (64)
The Saracen, opera
MASSENET (57)
Cendrillon, opera
Brumaire, overture
SULLIVAN (57)
The Rose of Persia, opera
RIMSKY-KORSAKOV
  (55)
The Tsar's Bride, opera
CHAUSSON (44)
String Quartet (unfinished)

LIADOV (44)
Slava, for voices, harps
  and pianos
ELGAR (42)
In the South (Alassio),
  concert overture
  (1899–1904)
Sérénade lyrique, for
  orchestra
ALBÉNIZ (39)
p. Catalonia, for orchestra
ARENSKY (38)
Nal and Damayanti

DELIUS (37)
Paris—The Song of a Great City, nocturne for orchestra
GERMAN (37)
The Seasons, symphonic suite
GLAZUNOV (34)
String Quartet
SIBELIUS (34)
Scènes historiques, Suite No. 1
SATIE (33)
Généviève de Brabant, puppet opera
Jack in the Box, ballet
BANTOCK (31)
String Quartet
JONGEN (26)
Symphony
Violin Concerto
HOLST (25)
Sita, opera (1899–1906)
Walt Whitman, overture

SCHOENBERG (25)
Verklaerte Nacht, for string sextet (arranged for string orchestra 1917)
SUK (25)
Symphony No. 1 in E major
COLERIDGE-TAYLOR (24)
Solemn Prelude
Death of Minnehaha, cantata
GLIÈRE (24)
Symphony No. 1 (1899–1900)
RAVEL (24)
Pavane pour une Infante défunte, for piano
AUBERT (22)
Fantaisie, for piano and orchestra
ENESCO (18)
Fantaisie Pastorale

1900 COPLAND and ANTHEIL were born; SULLIVAN died

SAINT-SAËNS (65)
String Quartet
MASSENET (58)
La Terre promisé, oratorio
RIMSKY-KORSAKOV (56)
Legend of Tsar Sultan, opera
FAURÉ (55)
Promethée, lyric tragedy
LIADOV (45)
Polonaise, for orchestra

ELGAR (43)
The Dream of Gerontius, oratorio
LEONCAVALLO (42)
Zaza, opera
PUCCINI (42)
Tosca, opera
IPPOLITOV-IVANOV (41)
Assia
CHARPENTIER (40)
Louise, opera

CONTINUED

MAHLER (40)
Symphony No. 4
MACDOWELL (39)
Piano Sonata No. 3,
  Norse
DEBUSSY (38)
Nocturnes, for orchestra
  and chorus
GERMAN (38)
Nell Gwynne, incidental
  music
PIERNÉ (37)
Violin Sonata
ROPARTZ (36)
Five motets
GLAZUNOV (35)
Solenne Overture
SIBELIUS (35)
Finlandia, symphonic
  poem
BANTOCK (32)
Tone Poem No. 1,
  Thalaba the Destroyer
VAUGHAN WILLIAMS
  (28)
Bucolic Suite, for
  orchestra
RACHMANINOV
  (27–33)
Twelve songs (1900–06)
REGER (27)
Two *Romances,* for solo

instruments and
  orchestra
Two String Quartets
Two Clarinet Sonatas
HOLST (26)
Cotswolds Symphony
Suite de Ballet
Ave Maria, for eight-part
  female choir
SCHOENBERG (26–39)
Gurre-Lieder, for solo
  voices, chorus and
  orchestra (1900–13)
COLERIDGE-TAYLOR
  (25)
Hiawatha's Departure,
  cantata
GLIÈRE (25)
String Octet
String Sextet No. 1
String Quartet No. 1
AUBERT (23)
"Suite Brève", for two
  pianos
"Trois esquisses", for
  piano
"La Lettre", vocal
BLOCH (20–49)
Helvetia, symphonic
  fresco for orchestra
  (1900–29)

1901   FINZI and RUBBRA were born; VERDI died

DVOŘÁK (60)
fp. Rusalka, opera
GRIEG (58)
Lyric pieces for piano,
  Book X
FAURÉ (56)
La Voile du bonheur,
  incidental music

STANFORD (49)
*Much Ado About
  Nothing,* opera
Irish Rhapsody No. 1
ELGAR (44)
Cockaigne, overture
Introduction and Allegro,
  for strings (1901–05)

410

Pomp and Circumstance
  Marches Nos. 1–4
Concert Allegro, for piano
SMYTH (43)
The Forest, opera
PADEREWSKI (*c*.41)
Manru, opera
LOEFFLER (40)
Divertissement Espagnol,
  for saxophone and
  orchestra
MACDOWELL (40)
Piano Sonata No. 4,
  Keltic
DEBUSSY (39)
Pour le Piano (possibly
  1896)
GERMAN (39) /
  SULLIVAN
  (posthumous)
The Emerald Isle
  (completed by
  German after Sullivan's
  death)
MASCAGNI (38)
Le Maschera, opera
PIERNÉ (38)
La Fille de Tabarin,
  opera-comique
Poème symphonique, for
  piano and orchestra
Concertstücke, for harp
STRAUSS, R. (37)
Feuersnot, opera
DUKAS (36)
Piano Sonata in E♭ minor
GLAZUNOV (36)
The Seasons, ballet
  (possibly earlier)
Symphony No. 2
Cortège, for orchestra
Portraits, for strings

BANTOCK (33)
Tone Poem No. 2, *Dante*
Tone Poem No. 3, *Fifine
  at the Fair*
SKRIABIN (29)
Symphony No. 2
RACHMANINOV (28)
Piano Concerto No. 2
Cello Sonata
Suite No. 2, for two
  pianos
IVES (27–30)
Symphony No. 3
  (1901–04)
COLERIDGE-TAYLOR
  (26)
*The Blind Girl of
  Castel-Cuille*
Toussaint l'Ouverture,
  concert overture
Idyll
RAVEL (26)
Jeux d'eau, for piano
Myrrha, cantata
WOLF-FERRARI (25)
p. Piano Quintet
p. Piano Trio
BLOCH (21)
Symphony in C♯ minor
  (1901–02)
ENESCO (20)
Rumainian Rhapsody,
  No. 1
Symphonie concertante,
  for cello and orchestra
p. Violin Sonata No. 2
KODÁLY (19)
Adagio, for violin (or
  viola) and piano
CASELLA (18)
Pavana, for piano

1902 DURUFLÉ, RODRIGO and WALTON were
born

SAINT-SAËNS (67)
Coronation March
Cello Concerto No. 2
MASSENET (61)
*Le Jongleur de Notre
Dame*, opera
Piano Concerto
RIMSKY-KORSAKOV
(58)
fp. Kaschey the Immortal,
opera
d'INDY (51)
Symphony No. 2
(1902–03)
HUMPERDINCK (51)
Dornroschen
ELGAR (45)
Coronation Ode
Falstaff, symphonic study
(1902–13)
Dream Children, for
piano, or small
orchestra
MAHLER (42)
Symphony No. 5
Five Rückert Songs
LOEFFLER (41)
Poème, for orchestra
MACDOWELL (41)
Fireside Tales
New England Idylls
DEBUSSY (40)
Pelléas at Mélisande,
opera
DELIUS (40)
Appalachia, for orchestra
and chorus
GERMAN (40)
Merrie England, operetta

PIERNÉ (39)
The Children's Crusade,
oratorio
GLAZUNOV (37)
Symphony No. 7
Ballade
NIELSEN (37)
Saul and David, opera
Symphony No. 2, *The
Four Temperaments*
CILÈA (36)
Adriana Lecouvreur,
opera
BANTOCK (34)
Tone Poem No. 4,
Hudibras
Tone Poem No. 5,
Witch of Atlas
Tone Poem No. 6,
Lalla Rookh
The Time Spirit
ROUSSEL (33)
Piano Trio
JONGEN (29)
*Fantaisie sur deux Noëls
wallons*, for orchestra
Piano Quartet
RACHMANINOV (29)
The Spring, cantata
REGER (29)
Piano Quintet
Violin Sonata
HOLST (28)
The Youth's Choice,
opera
IVES (28–36)
Violin Sonata No. 2
(1902–10)

412

COLERIDGE-TAYLOR
(27)
Meg Blane
GLIÈRE (27)
String Sextet No. 2
RAVEL (27)
Alcyone, cantata
WOLF-FERRARI (26)
p. Piano Trio
p. Violin Sonata
AUBERT (25)
La Légende du Sang

BRIDGE (25)
Berceuse, for violin and
small orchestra
RESPIGHI (23)
Piano Concerto
BARTÓK (21)
Scherzo for orchestra
ENESCO (21)
Rumainian Rhapsody,
No. 2

1903 BERKELEY and KHACHATURIAN were
born: WOLF died

CUI (68)
Mlle. Fifi, opera
RIMSKY-KORSAKOV
(59–61)
*The Invisible City of
Kitezh,* opera
(1903–05)
Serenade, for cello and
piano
d'INDY (52)
Choral Varié, for
saxophone and
orchestra
CHAUSSON
(posthumous)
fp. Le Roi Arthus
ELGAR (46)
Symphony No. 2
(*c.*1903–10)
The Apostles, oratorio
PADEREWSKI (*c.*42)
Symphony (1903–07)
DEBUSSY (41)
La Diable dans le beffroi,
libretto and musical
sketches

Rhapsody, for saxophone,
contralto and orchestra
*Danse sacré et danse
profane,* for harp and
strings
D'un cahier d'esquisses,
for piano
Estampes, for piano
DELIUS (41)
Sea Drift, for baritone,
chorus and orchestra
GERMAN (41)
A Princess of Kensington,
operetta
DUKAS (38)
Variations, Interlude et
Finale, on a Theme by
Rameau, for piano
NIELSEN (38)
Helios, overture
SIBELIUS (38)
Violin Concerto
Romance, for strings
BUSONI (37)
Piano Concerto, with
male chorus (1903–04)
CONTINUED

413

SATIE (37)
*Trois morceaux en forme
de poire,* for piano duet
BANTOCK (35)
Serenade, for four horns
ROUSSEL (34)
Resurrection, for
orchestra
Violin Sonata
SKRIABIN (31)
Symphony No. 3, *Divine
Poem*
VAUGHAN WILLIAMS
(31)
The House of Life, song
cycle
RACHMANINOV (30)
Variations on a Theme by
Chopin, for piano
Ten Preludes for piano
REGER (30)
Gesang der Verklarten,
for voice and orchestra
HOLST (29)
Indra, symphonic poem
King Estmere, for chorus
and orchestra
Quintet for wind
IVES (29–34)
*Three Places in New
England,* for orchestra
(1903–14)
Violin Sonata No. 1
(1903–08)

SCHOENBERG (29)
Pelleas und Melisande,
suite for orchestra
SUK (29)
Fantasy, for violin and
orchestra
COLERIDGE-TAYLOR
(28)
The Atonement, oratorio
RAVEL (28)
Shéhérazade, song cycle
with orchestra
Alyssa, cantata
String Quartet in F major
WOLF-FERRARI (27)
fp. Le Donne curiose,
opera
p. Chamber Symphony
La Vita nuova, oratorio
AUBERT (26)
La Momie, ballet
DOHNÁNYI (26)
p. String Quartet
p. Cello Sonata
BARTÓK (22)
Kossuth, tone poem
Violin Sonata
ENESCO (22)
Suite for orchestra
CASELLA (20)
*Variations sur une
chaconne,* for piano

1904 DALLAPICCOLA and KABALEVSKY
were born; DVOŘÁK died

FAURÉ (59)
Impromptu, for harp
d'INDY (53)
Violin Sonata

STANFORD (52)
Violin Concerto
JANÁČEK (50)
Osud (Fate), opera

414

LIADOV (49)
Baba Yaga, symphonic
poem
PUCCINI (46)
Madama Butterfly, opera
MAHLER (44)
Symphony No. 6
DEBUSSY (42)
La Mer, three symphonic
sketches
L'Isle joyeuse, for piano
Masques, for piano
Fêtes galantes, songs
(second series)
Trois Chansons de France
DELIUS (42)
Koanga, opera
GERMAN (42)
Welsh Rhapsody, for
orchestra
ROPARTZ (40)
Cello Sonata No. 1
STRAUSS, R. (40)
Symphonia Domestica
GLAZUNOV (39)
Violin Concerto
SIBELIUS (39)
Symphony No. 3
(1904–07)
Kuolema, incidental music
(includes "Valse
Triste")
GIORDANO (37)
Siberia, opera
ROUSSEL (35–37)
Symphony No. 1, *La
poème de la forêt*
(1904–06)
ALFVÉN (32)
Swedish Rhapsody No. 1,
Midsommervaka

VAUGHAN WILLIAMS
(32)
Songs of Travel
JONGEN (31)
Lalla Rookh, symphonic
poem
REGER (31)
String Quartet
Serenade, for flute, violin
and viola
Variations and Fugue on
a Theme of Beethoven,
for two pianos
String Trio
Cello Sonata
Violin Sonata
HOLST (30)
The Mystic Trumpeter,
for soprano and
orchestra
IVES (30)
Orchestra Set No. 1
(1904–11)
*Thanksgiving and/or
Father's Day,* Part 4 of
Holidays Symphony
SUK (30)
Symphony in C minor,
Asrael (1904–06)
Prague, symphonic poem
GLIÈRE (29)
String Sextet No. 3
CARPENTER (28)
Improving Songs for
Anxious Children
AUBERT (27)
The Blue Forest, opera
(1904–10)
Chrysothemis, ballet
DOHNÁNYI (27)
p. Serenade, for string trio
CONTINUED

415

BRIDGE (25)
Novelleten, for string
quartet
Violin Sonata
BLOCH (24)
Hiver, symphonic poem
(1904–05)
Printemps, symphonic
poem (1904–05)
MEDTNER (24)
Nine songs (Goethe)

PIZZETTI (24)
Three Symphonic
Preludes to *Oedipus
Rex*
BARTÓK (23)
Rhapsody, for piano and
orchestra
Burlesca
Piano Quintet
CASELLA (21)
Toccata, for piano

1905 ALWYN, LAMBERT, RAWSTHORNE,
SIEBER and TIPPETT were born

BALAKIREV (68)
Piano Sonata in B minor
BRUCH (67)
Suite on a popular
Russian melody
d'INDY (54)
Jour d'été a la montagne
HUMPERDINCK (51)
Die Heirat wieder Willen
MAHLER (45)
Symphony No. 7 in E
minor
Kindertotenlieder, song
cycle for voice and
orchestra
LOEFFLER (44)
La Mort de Tintagiles,
symphonic poem for
two viole d'amore and
orchestra
La Villanelle du diable,
symphonic fantasy for
organ and orchestra
A Pagan poem, for piano,
English horn and three
trumpets

DEBUSSY (43)
Images, for piano, Book I
DELIUS (43)
A Mass of Life, for solo
voices, chorus and
orchestra
MASCAGNI (42)
Amica, opera
STRAUSS, R. (41)
Salome, opera
GLAZUNOV (40)
Symphony No. 8
Scène dansante
SIBELIUS (40)
Pelléas et Mélisande,
incidental music
SATIE (39)
Pousse l'amour, operetta
ROUSSEL (36)
Divertissement, for piano
and wind quartet
LEHÁR (35)
The Merry Widow,
operetta
ALFVÉN (33)
Symphony No. 3

En Skargardssagen,
symphonic poem
REGER (32)
Sinfonietta, for orchestra
Suite in the Old Style, for
violin and piano
HOLST (31)
Song of the Night, for
violin and orchestra
SCHOENBERG (31)
String Quartet No. 1
COLERIDGE-TAYLOR
(30)
Five Choral Ballads
GLIÈRE (30)
String Quartet No. 2
RAVEL (30)
Miroirs, for piano
Sonatina, for piano
BRIDGE (26)
Piano Quintet
Phantasie Quartet
Norse Legend, for violin
and piano
IRELAND (26)
Songs of a Wayfarer
RESPIGHI (26)

Re Enzo, comic opera
Notturno, for orchestra
Suite in G major, for
string orchestra and
organ
Burlesca
BARTÓK (24)
Suite No. 1, for orchestra
Suite No. 2, for orchestra
(revised 1943)
ENESCO (24)
Symphony No. 1
p. String Octet
STRAVINSKY (23)
Symphony in E♭ major
(1905–07)
CASELLA (22)
Symphony No. 1
(1905–06)
SZYMANOWSKI (22)
Concert Overture
WEBERN (22)
Quartet
BERG (20–23)
Seven "Frühe Lieder", for
soprano and piano
(1905–08)

1906   LUTYENS was born; ARENSKY died

GRIEG (63)
Moods
RIMSKY-KORSAKOV
(62)
Le Coq d'Or, opera
(1906–07)
FAURÉ (61)
Piano Quintet
La Chanson d'Eve,
song cycle (1906–10)
d'INDY (55)
Souvenirs, tone poem

LIADOV (51)
Eight Popular Russian
Songs, for orchestra
ELGAR (49)
The Wand of Youth,
suites for orchestra
(final versions,
1906–07)
The Kingdom, oratorio
SMYTH (48)
The Wreckers, opera

CONTINUED

ALBÉNIZ (46–49)
Ibéria, piano cycle
  (1906–09)
DELIUS (44)
Piano Concerto
STRAUSS, R. (42)
Elektra, opera (1906–08)
DUKAS (41)
Villanelle, for horn and
  piano
NIELSEN (41)
fp. Maskarade, opera
SIBELIUS (41)
Pohjola's Daughter,
  symphonic fantasy
SATIE (40)
Passacaille, for piano
Prélude en tapisserie,
  for piano
BANTOCK (38)
Omar Khayyam
VAUGHAN WILLIAMS
  (34)
Norfolk Rhapsodies
RACHMANINOV (33)
Francesca da Rimini,
  opera
The Miserly Knight, opera
Fifteen songs
REGER (33)
Serenade
HOLST (32)
Songs of the West, for
  orchestra
Two *Songs Without
  Words*
SCHOENBERG (32)
Chamber Symphonies
  Nos. 1 and 2
IVES (32)
The Pond, for flute, harp,
  piano and string quartet

COLERIDGE-TAYLOR
  (31)
Kubla Khan
RAVEL (31)
Introduction and Allegro,
  for harp, flute, clarinet
  and string quartet
WOLF-FERRARI (30)
fp. School for Fathers,
  opera
fp. I quatro (sic) rusteghi,
  comedy-opera
QUILTER (29)
To Julia, song cycle
BRIDGE (27)
Three Idylls for string
  orchestra
String Quartet in E minor
Nine Miniatures for cello
  and piano
IRELAND (27)
Piano Trio No. 1
  (Phantasy Trio)
BLOCH (26)
Poèmes d'Automne, for
  voice and orchestra
PIZZETTI (26)
String Quartet
KODÁLY (24)
Summer Evening, for
  orchestra
MALIPIERO (24)
Sinfonia del Mare
BAX (23)
Piano Trio
BERG (21–23)
Piano Sonata (1906–08)
SCHOECK (20)
Serenade, for small
  orchestra (1906–07)

418

CUI (72)
Matteo Falcone, opera
BALAKIREV (70)
Symphony No. 2
 (1906–07)
STANFORD (55)
Stabat Mater
MESSAGER (54)
Fortuno, operetta
ELGAR (50)
Symphony No. 1
 (1907–08)
IPPOLITOV-IVANOV
 (48)
Symphony
MAHLER (47)
Symphony No. 8,
 *Symphony of a
 Thousand*
DEBUSSY (45)
Images, for piano,
 Book II
DELIUS (45)
*A Village Romeo and
 Juliet,* opera
Brigg Fair, orchestral
 rhapsody
Songs of Sunset
GERMAN (45)
Tom Jones, operetta
PIERNÉ (44)
Canzonetta, for clarinet
ROPARTZ (43)
Pastoral and Dance, for
 oboe and orchestra
Violin Sonata No. 1
DUKAS (42)
Ariadne and Bluebeard,
 opera

GLAZUNOV (42)
Canto di Destino,
 overture
NIELSEN (42)
Saga-Drøm, for
 orchestra (1907–08)
BUSONI (41)
Elégien, for piano
CILEA (41)
Gloria, opera
GIORDANO (40)
Marcella, opera
ALFVÉN (35)
Swedish Rhapsody No. 2,
 Uppsalarapsodi
VAUGHAN WILLIAMS
 (35)
*Towards the Unknown
 Region,* for chorus and
 orchestra
In the Fen Country,
 symphonic impression
JONGEN (34)
Félyane, opera
 (unfinished)
RACHMANINOV (34)
Symphony No. 2
The Isle of the Dead,
 symphonic poem
Piano Sonata No. 1
REGER (34)
Variations and Fugue on
 a Theme of Hiller
HOLST (33)
Somerset Rhapsody, for
 orchestra
Nine Hymns from the
 Rig-Veda

CONTINUED

SCHOENBERG (33)
String Quartet No. 2
Friede auf Erden, for
  choir
SUK (33)
A Summer Tale,
  symphonic poem
GLIÈRE (32)
Symphony No. 2
RAVEL (32)
Rapsodie espagnole,
  for orchestra
*Pièce en forme de
  habanera*
*Cinq mélodies populaires
  greques,* for voice and
  piano
DOHNÁNYI (30)
p. String Quartet in D
  major
QUILTER (30)
Serenade, for orchestra
BRIDGE (28)
Isabella, symphonic poem
Trio No. 1, *Phantasie*

RESPIGHI (28)
Fantasy, for piano and
  orchestra
String Quartet in D major
String Quartet in D minor
MEDTNER (27)
Three Songs (Heine)
BARTÓK (26)
Hungarian Folksongs, for
  piano
TURINA (25)
Piano Quintet
BAX (24)
Fatherland, for two
  sopranos, chorus and
  orchestra
CASELLA (24)
Cello sonata
SZYMANOWSKY (24)
Symphony No. 1
PROKOFIEV (16)
Piano Sonata No. 1
  (1907–09)
Four Pieces for piano
  (1907–11)

1908 MESSIAEN was born; RIMSKY-KORSAKOV,
  SARASATE and MACDOWELL died

GOLDMARK (78)
A Winter's Tale
FAURÉ (63)
Serenade, for cello and
  piano
JANÁČEK (54–63)
*Mr. Brouček's Excursion
  to the Moon,* opera
  (1908–17)
MAHLER (48)
Das Lied von der Erde
  (The Song of the

Earth), song cycle
  with orchestra
DEBUSSY (46)
Ibéria, from *Images* for
  orchestra
*The Fall of the House of
  Usher* (sketched,
  uncompleted 1908–10)
Children's Corner, for
  piano
Trois chansons de Charles

d'Orléans, for
unaccompanied choir
DELIUS (46)
Dance Rhapsody No. 1,
for orchestra
In a Summer Garden,
for orchestra
PIERNÉ (45)
*The Children of
Bethlehem,* oratorio
SIBELIUS (43)
String Quartet in five
movements, *Voces
Intimae*
BUSONI (42–45)
The Bridal Choice
(1908–11)
SATIE (42)
Aperçus désagréables, for
piano duet
SKRIABIN (36)
Poem of Ecstasy, for
orchestra
VAUGHAN WILLIAMS
(36)
String Quartet in G minor
REGER (35)
*Symphonic Prologue to a
Tragedy*
Violin Concerto
Piano Trio
Sonata for clarinet, or
viola, and piano
IVES (34)
*The Unanswered
Question,* for orchestra
HOLST (34)
Savitri, opera
Choral Hymns from the
Rig-Veda, Group I
SCHOENBERG (34)
Buch der hängenden

Gärten, setting of
fifteen poems for voice
and piano
GLIÈRE (33)
The Sirens, symphonic
poem
RAVEL (33)
Gaspard de la nuit, for
piano
Ma Mère l'Oye, for piano
FALLA (32)
Pièces espagnoles, for
piano
AUBERT (31)
Crépuscules d'Automne,
song cycle
QUILTER (31)
Songs of Sorrow
BRIDGE (29)
Dance Rhapsody, for
orchestra
Suite for Strings
RESPIGHI (29)
Concerto in the old style,
for violin and orchestra
MEDTNER (28)
Twelve songs (Goethe)
BARTÓK (27)
Portraits, for orchestra
(1907–08)
Violin Concerto No. 1
String Quartet No. 1
KODÁLY (26)
String Quartet No. 1
MALIPIERO (26)
Cello Sonata
STRAVINSKY (26)
Fireworks, for orchestra
Scherzo fantastique
*Lament on the Death of
Rimsky-Korsakov,* for
chorus and orchestra
CONTINUED

BAX (25)
Lyrical Interlude, for
   string quintet
CASELLA (25)
Symphony No. 2
   (1908–09)
Sarabande, for piano or
   harp
WEBERN (25)
Passacaglia, for orchestra

*Entflieht auf Leichten
   Kahnan,* for chorus
Ten Lieder
BERG (23)
An Leukon
VILLA-LOBOS (21)
Recouli, for small
   orchestra
PROKOFIEV (17–21)
Four pieces for piano
   (1908–12)

1909   ALBÉNIZ died

LIADOV (54)
The Enchanted Lake,
   symphonic poem
ELGAR (52)
Elegy, for string orchestra
Violin Concerto
   (*c.*1909–10)
IPPOLITOV-IVANOV
   (50)
Treachery
MAHLER (49)
Symphony No. 9
DEBUSSY (47)
Rondes de Printemps,
   from *Images* for
   orchestra
Rhapsody, for clarinet and
   orchestra (1909–10)
Petite pièce, for clarinet
   and piano, in B♭ major
Préludes for piano, Book I
   (1909–10)
Homage à Haydn, for
   piano
La plus que lente, for
   piano
Trois ballades de François

Villon, songs
   (1909–10)
*Le Promenoir des deux
   amants,* songs
   (1904–10)
GERMAN (47)
Fallen Fairies
STRAUSS, R. (45)
Der Rosenkavalier, opera
   (1909–10)
DUKAS (44)
Prélude élégiaque, for
   piano
Vocalise
GLAZUNOV (44)
Symphony No. 9 begun
SIBELIUS (44)
Night-ride and Sunrise,
   tone poem
BUSONI (43)
Berceuse élégiaque
LEHÁR (39)
The Count of Luxemburg,
   operetta
SKRIABIN (38)
*Poem of Fire—
   Prometheus,* for

orchestra, piano and chorus
VAUGHAN WILLIAMS (37)
A Sea Symphony (Symphony No. 1), for soloists, chorus and orchestra
The Wasps, incidental music
On Wenlock Edge, song cycle
JONGEN (36)
Violin Sonata No. 2
RACHMANINOV (36)
Piano Concerto No. 3
REGER (36)
The 100th Psalm, for voice and orchestra
Die Nonnen, for voice and orchestra
String Quartet
HOLST (35)
First Suite for Military Band
A Vision of Dame Christian, incidental music
Choral Hymns from the Rig-Veda, Group II
SCHOENBERG (35)
Five Pieces for Orchestra (revised 1949)
Erwartung, monodrama, for voice and orchestra
COLERIDGE-TAYLOR (34)
Bon-Bon Suite
GLIÈRE (34–36)
Symphony No. 3, *Ilya Murometz*

RAVEL (34)
Menuet sur le nom d'Haydn, for piano
FALLA (33–39)
Nights in the gardens of Spain, for piano and orchestra (1909–15)
WOLF-FERRARI (33)
Susanna's Secret, operetta
QUILTER (32)
Seven Elizabethan Lyrics
BRIDGE (30)
Dance Poem, for orchestra
IRELAND (30)
Violin Sonata No. 1
PIZZETTI (29–32)
Phaedra, opera
BARTÓK (28)
For Children, for piano
KODÁLY (27)
Cello Sonata (1909–10)
BAX (26)
Enchanted Summer, for tenor, chorus and orchestra
Christmas Carol
CASELLA (26)
Italia, orchestral rhapsody
Orchestral Suite in G major
Notturnino, for piano, or harp
Berceuse triste, for piano
SZYMANOWSKI (26)
Symphony No. 2
WEBERN (26)
Five movements for string quartet
BERG (24)
Four songs (1909–10)

CONTINUED

BUTTERWORTH (24)
"I Fear Thy Kisses", song
PROKOFIEV (18)
Sinfonietta (1909–14)

Two Poems, for female
voices and orchestra
(1909–10)
Four Études, for piano

1910   BARBER and SCHUMAN were born;
        BALAKIREV died

BALAKIREV (73)
Suite on pieces by Chopin
MASSENET (68)
Don Quixote, opera
FAURÉ (65)
Nine preludes
HUMPERDINCK (56)
Koenigskinder, opera
LIADOV (55)
Dance of the Amazons,
  for orchestra
Kikimora, symphonic
  poem
ELGAR (53)
Romance, for bassoon and
  orchestra
PUCCINI (52)
Girl of the Golden West,
  opera
MAHLER (50)
Symphony No. 10 begun
  (left unfinished)
NIELSEN (45)
Symphony No. 3,
  Espansiva (1910–11)
At a Young Artist's Bier
GIORDANO (43)
Mese Mariano, opera
ROUSSEL (41)
Evocations (1910–11)
VAUGHAN WILLIAMS
  (38)
*Fantasia on a Theme by
  Thomas Tallis,* for
  strings

RACHMANINOV (37)
The Bells, choral
  symphony
Thirteen Piano Preludes
Liturgy of St. John
  Chrysostom
REGER (37)
Piano Concerto
Piano Quartet
Cello Sonata
String Sextet
HOLST (36)
*Beni Mora—Oriental
  Suite,* for orchestra
The Cloud Messenger,
  ode
Choral Hymns for the
  Rig-Veda, Group III
IVES (36–42)
Symphony No. 4
  (1910–16)
SCHOENBERG (36–39)
Die Glückliche Hand,
  music drama (1910–13)
SUK (36)
String Quartet No. 2
  (1910–11)
COLERIDGE-TAYLOR
  (35)
Endymion's Dream, for
  chorus
DOHNÁNYI (33)
Der Schlier der Pierette,
  ballet
p. Piano Quartet

QUILTER (33)
Three English Dances
Four Songs
RESPIGHI (31)
Semirama, lyric tragedy
BLOCH (30)
fp. Macbeth, opera
MEDTNER (30)
Three songs (Nietzsche)
Violin Sonata
BARTÓK (29)
Four Dirges, for piano
Deux Images, for
  orchestra
MALIPIERO (28)
*Sinfonia del Silenzio e
  della Morte*
Impressioni dal vero, I
  (1910–11)
STRAVINSKY (28)
The Firebird, ballet
Petrouchka, ballet
  (1910–11,
  revised 1946–47)
BAX (27)
In the Faery Hills,
  symphonic poem

Violin Sonata No. 1
  (1910–15)
CASELLA (27)
Barcarola, for piano
WEBERN (27)
Six pieces for large
  orchestra
Four pieces for violin and
  piano (1910–15)
BERG (25)
String Quartet
VILLA-LOBOS (23)
*Suite dos canticos
  sertanejos*, for small
  orchestra
PROKOFIEV (19)
Dreams, symphonic poem
Autumnal Sketch, for
  orchestra (revised
  1934)
Deux poèmes, for voice
  and piano (1910–11)
MILHAUD (18–23)
La Brebis égarée, opera
  (1910–15)
KORNGOLD (13)
Piano Trio (1910–13)

1911   MENOTTI was born; MAHLER died

CUI (76)
The Captain's Daughter,
  opera
p. Violin Sonata
BRUCH (73)
Concertstücke, for violin
STANFORD (59)
Symphony No. 7
HUMPERDINCK (57)
The Miracle

SMYTH (53)
March of the Women, for
  orchestra
Three Songs of Sunrise,
  for unaccompanied
  chorus
DEBUSSY (49)
*The Martyrdom of St.
  Sebastian*, incidental
  music

CONTINUED

GERMAN (49)
Coronation March and
 Hymn
MASCAGNI (48)
Isabeau, opera
ROPARTZ (47)
Serenade, for string
 quartet (1911–12)
String Quartet No. 2
GLAZUNOV (46)
Piano Concerto
NIELSEN (46)
Violin Concerto
SIBELIUS (46)
Symphony No. 4
Rakastava Suite, for
 orchestra
Canzonetta, for strings
Valse romantique, for
 orchestra
SATIE (45)
En habit de cheval, for
 orchestra
VAUGHAN WILLIAMS
 (39)
Five Mystical Songs, for
 baritone, chorus and
 orchestra
JONGEN (38)
S'Arka, ballet
Cello Sonata (1911–12)
RACHMANINOV (38)
Six Études-Tableaux, for
 piano
REGER (38)
Eine Lustspielouverture
Die Weihe der Nacht, for
 chorus and orchestra
String Quartet
Violin Sonata
HOLST (37)
Invocations, for cello and
 orchestra

Hecuba's Lament, for
 chorus and orchestra
Second Suite for Military
 Band
IVES (37)
Browning Overture
*The Gong on the Hook
 and Ladder*
Tone-roads No. 1, for
 chamber orchestra
 (1911–15)
Hallowe'en, for piano and
 strings
SCHOENBERG (37)
Herzewächse, for soprano,
 celesta, harmonium and
 harp
COLERIDGE-TAYLOR
 (36)
Bamboula, rhapsodic
 dance
Violin Concerto
A Tale of Old Japan,
 cantata
RAVEL (36)
L'Heure espagnole, opera
*Valses nobles et
 sentimentales,* for
 piano, or orchestra
WOLF-FERRARI (35)
*fp. The Jewels of the
 Madonna,* operetta
AUBERT (34)
Nuit Mauresque
 (possibly 1907)
QUILTER (34)
Where the Rainbow Ends,
 incidental music
Three Songs of the Sea
BRIDGE (32)
The Sea, for orchestra

BARTÓK (30)
Duke Bluebeard's Castle,
  opera
Allegro barbaro, for piano
Three *Burlesques,* for
  piano
ENESCO (30)
Symphony No. 2
STRAVINSKY (29)
The King of the Stars,
  cantata
TURINA (29)
Quartet
WEBERN (28)
Five pieces for orchestra
  (1911–13)
Two lieder
BUTTERWORTH (26)
Two English Idylls, for
  small orchestra

Six songs from Housman's
  A Shropshire Lad
SCHOECK (25)
Violin Concerto
  (1911–12)
Dithyrambe, for double
  chorus and orchestra
Erwin und Elmire,
  incidental music
  (1911–16)
PROKOFIEV (20)
Magdalene, opera
  (1911–13)
Piano Concerto No. 1
  (1911–12)
MILHAUD (19)
Violin Sonata

1912   CAGE and GILLIS were born;
         COLERIDGE-TAYLOR and MASSENET
         died

ELGAR (55)
The Music Makers, for
  contralto, chorus and
  orchestra
IPPOLITOV-IVANOV
  (53)
The Spy
DEBUSSY (50)
Jeux, poème dansé
Khamma, ballet
Gigues, from *Images* for
  orchestra
Syrinx, for solo flute
DELIUS (50)
On Hearing the First

Cuckoo in Spring, for
  orchestra
Song of the High Hills,
  for wordless chorus and
  orchestra
*Summer Night on the
  River,* for orchestra
ROPARTZ (48)
La Pays, opera
À Marie endormé
*La Chasse du Prince
  Arthur*
STRAUSS, R. (48)
Ariadne auf Naxos, opera,
  first version
                    CONTINUED

427

DUKAS (47)
La Péri, poème dansé
SIBELIUS (47)
Scènes historiques,
Suite No. 2 for
orchestra
Two *Serenades*, for violin
(1912–13)
BUSONI (46)
Nocturne symphonique
SATIE (46)
Choses vues à droit et à
gauche (sans lunettes),
for violin and piano
ROUSSEL (43)
The Spider's Feast, ballet
ALFVÉN (40)
Sten Sture, cantata for
male voices
VAUGHAN WILLIAMS
(40)
Fantasia on Christmas
Carols
Phantasy Quintet, for
strings
JONGEN (39)
Deux rondes wallons, for
orchestra
RACHMANINOV (39)
Fourteen songs
REGER (39)
A Romantic Suite
Konzert im Alten Stil
Romischer
Triumphgesang, for
voice and orchestra
HOLST (38)
Choral Hymns from the
Rig-Veda, Group IV
IVES (38)
Decoration Day, Part 2 of
Holidays Symphony
Lincoln, the Great

Commoner, for chorus
and orchestra
SCHOENBERG (38)
Pierrot Lunaire, song
cycle
GLIÈRE (37)
Chrysis, ballet
RAVEL (37)
Daphnis et Chloé, ballet
with chorus
CARPENTER (36)
Violin Sonata
BRIDGE (33)
String Sextet
IRELAND (33)
Greater love hath no man,
motet
BLOCH (32)
Israel Symphony, for
voices and orchestra
(1912–16)
Prelude and two psalms
for high voice
(1912–14)
MEDTNER (32)
Three *Nocturnes* for piano
and violin
BARTÓK (31)
Four Pieces for Orchestra
TURINA (30)
La Procesion del Rocio,
symphonic poem
BAX (29)
Christmas Eve on the
Mountains, for
orchestra
Nympholept, for
orchestra
CASELLA (29)
Le Couvent sur l'eau,
ballet (1912–13)
GRIFFES (28)
The Pleasure Dome of

Kubla Khan,
symphonic poem
(1912–16)
Tone Images, for
mezzo-soprano and
piano
BERG (27)
Five Orchestral Songs
BUTTERWORTH (27)
A Shropshire Lad,
rhapsody for orchestra
Eleven Folk Songs from
Sussex
"Bredon Hill" and other
songs

TAYLOR (27)
The Siren Song, for
orchestra
VILLA-LOBOS (25)
Aglaia, opera
PROKOFIEV (21)
Piano Concerto No. 2
Ballade, for cello and
piano
Piano Sonata No. 2
Sarcasms, for piano
(1912–14)
Toccata in C major, for
piano
MILHAUD (20)
String Quartet No. 1

1913 BRITTEN, GOULD and LUTOSLAWSKI
were born

SAINT-SAËNS (78)
fp. The Promised Land,
oratorio
FAURÉ (68)
Pénélope, opera
CHARPENTIER (53)
Julien, opera
DEBUSSY (51)
La Boîte à Joujoux, ballet
music for piano
Preludes for piano,
Book 2
Trois poèmes de
Mallarmé, songs
MASCAGNI (50)
Parisina, opera
ROPARTZ (49)
*Dans l'ombre de la
montagne*
Soir sur les Chaumes

STRAUSS, R. (49)
Alpine Symphony
SIBELIUS (48)
Scaramouche, pantomime
Il Bardo, symphonic poem
BUSONI (47)
Indian Fantasy, for
piano and orchestra
CILÈA (47)
Il Canto della vita, for
voice, chorus and
orchestra
SATIE (47)
Le piège de Medusa,
operetta
*Chapitres tournés en tous
sens,* for piano
*Croques et agarceries
d'un gros bonhomme
en bois,* for piano
CONTINUED

Descriptions automatiques, for piano
Embryons desséchés, for piano
Enfantines, children's piano pieces

VAUGHAN WILLIAMS (41)
A London Symphony (Symphony No. 2)

JONGEN (40)
Impressions d'Ardennes, for orchestra

RACHMANINOV (40)
Piano Sonata No. 2

REGER (40)
Vier Tondichtunger nach Böcklin
Eine Ballettsuite

HOLST (39)
St. Paul's Suite, for strings
Hymn to Dionysus, for choir and orchestra

IVES (39)
The Fourth of July, Part 3 of *Holidays Symphony*
Washington's Birthday, Part 1 of *Holidays Symphony*
Over the Pavements, for chamber orchestra

FALLA (38)
fp. *La Vida brève,* opera

CARPENTER (37)
Gitanjali, song cycle

AUBERT (36)
Sillages, three pieces for piano

DOHNÁNYI (36)
Tante Simone, opera
p. Violin Sonata

IRELAND (34)
The Forgotten Rite, for orchestra
Decorations, for piano
Three Dances for piano
Three songs

RESPIGHI (34)
Carnival, overture

BLOCH (33)
Trois poèmes juifs, for orchestra

STRAVINSKY (31)
The Rite of Spring, ballet

BAX (30)
Scherzo for orchestra

CASELLA (30)
Notte di Maggio, for voice and orchestra

WEBERN (30)
Six Bagatelles, for string quartet

BERG (28)
Three Orchestral Pieces (1913–14)
Four Pieces for clarinet and piano

VILLA-LOBOS (26)
Suite da terra, for small orchestra
Suite for piano

MILHAUD (21)
Suite symphonique No. 1 (1913–14)

STANFORD (62)
Irish Rhapsody No. 4
MESSAGER (61)
Béatrice, operetta
HUMPERDINCK (60)
Die Marketenderin
LIADOV (59)
Naenia—Dirge
ELGAR (57)
p. Sospiri, for orchestra
Carillon, recitation with
 orchestra
DEBUSSY (52)
Berceuse héroïque, for
 piano
DELIUS (52)
North Country Sketches,
 for orchestra
STRAUSS, R. (50)
Die Frau ohne Schatten,
 opera (1914–17)
Josephs-Legende, ballet
NIELSEN (49)
Serenato in vano
SIBELIUS (49)
Symphony No. 5
 (1914–15)
Oceanides, symphonic
 poem
BUSONI (48–50)
Arlecchino, opera
 (1914–16)
SATIE (48)
*Cinq grimaces pour le
 "Songe d'une nuit
 d'été"*, for orchestra
*Heures séculaires et
 instantées*, for piano

Les Pantins dansent, for
 piano
Sports et divertissements,
 for piano
*Trois valses du précieux
 dégoûte*, for piano
*Vieux sequins et vieilles
 cuirasses*, for piano
REGER (41)
*Eine Vaterländische
 Overture*
Piano Quartet
Piano Sonata
Variations and fugue on a
 theme of Mozart, for
 piano
Cello Sonata
HOLST (40)
The Planets, suite for
 orchestra (1914–16)
IVES (40)
Protests, piano sonata
SUK (40)
*Meditation on a Theme of
 an old Bohemian
 Chorale*, for string
 quartet
RAVEL (39)
Two Hebrew Songs, for
 soprano and orchestra
Piano Trio
QUILTER (37)
A Children's Overture
Four Child Songs
BRIDGE (35)
Summer, tone poem
RESPIGHI (35)
Suite for strings and organ
CONTINUED

431

PIZZETTI (34)
Sinfonia del Fuoco
BARTÓK (33)
The Wooden Prince,
   ballet (1914–16)
Fifteen Hungarian
   Peasant Songs
   (1914–17)
KODÁLY (32)
Duo for violin and cello
MALIPIERO (32)
Impressioni dal vero, II
   (1914–15)
STRAVINSKY (32)
Le Rossignol (The
   Nightingale), lyric tale
   in three acts
Chansons plaisants, for
   voice and small
   orchestra
Three pieces for string
   quartet
TURINA (32)
Margot, lyric comedy
BAX (31)
Quintet for piano and
   strings (1914–15)
CASELLA (31–34)
Siciliana and *Burlesca,*
   for piano trio
   (1914–17)

WEBERN (31)
Three Little Pieces, for
   cello and piano
Four Lieder (1914–18)
TAYLOR (29)
The Chambered Nautilus,
   for chorus and
   orchestra
The Highwayman, for
   baritone, women's
   voices and orchestra
VILLA-LOBOS (27)
Izaht, opera
Ibericarabé, symphonic
   poem
*Dansas dos Indios
   Mesticos,* for orchestra
Suite for strings
Suite popular brasiliera,
   for guitar
PROKOFIEV (23)
Violin Concerto
Scythian Suite, for
   orchestra (1914–15)
The Ugly Duckling, for
   voice and piano
MILHAUD (22)
String Quartet No. 2
   (1914–15)
Sonata for two violins and
   piano
Printemps, for violin and
   piano

1915   DIAMOND was born; GOLDMARK and
            SKRIABIN died

SAINT-SAËNS (80)
La Cendre rouge, ten
   songs
FAURÉ (70–73)
Le Jardin clos, songs
   (1915–18)

STANFORD (63)
Piano Concerto No. 2
JANÁČEK (61)
Taras Bulba, rhapsody for
   orchestra (1915–18)

ELGAR (58)
Polonia
Une Voix dans le desert,
  recitation with
  orchestra
DEBUSSY (53)
Cello Sonata
En blanc et noir, for two
  pianos
Six épigraphes antiques,
  for piano
Douze études, for piano
ROPARTZ (51)
Divertissement No. 1
BUSONI (49)
Indian Diary
SATIE (49)
Avant-dernières pensées,
  for piano
GIORDANO (48)
Madame Sans-gêne, opera
BANTOCK (47)
Hebridean Symphony
JONGEN (42)
Suites en deux parties, for
  viola and orchestra
RACHMANINOV (42)
Vesper Mass
REGER (42)
Der Einsiedler, for chorus
  and orchestra
Serenade, for flute, violin,
  viola, or two violins
  and viola
String Trio
HOLST (41)
Japanese Suite, for
  orchestra
IVES (41)
Orchestral Set No. 2
Tone-Roads No. 3, for
  chamber orchestra

Concord, piano sonata
GLIÈRE (40)
Trizna, symphonic poem
RAVEL (40)
Three songs for
  unaccompanied choir
CARPENTER (39)
Adventures in a
  Perambulator, for
  orchestra
Concertino for piano and
  orchestra
FALLA (39)
fp. El Amor Brujo, ballet
DOHNÁNYI (38)
Violin Concerto No. 1
BRIDGE (36)
The Open Air and *The*
  Story of My Heart, for
  orchestra
Lament, for strings
String Quartet in G minor
IRELAND (36)
Preludes for piano
RESPIGHI (36)
Sinfonia drammatica
BLOCH (35)
Schelomo, for cello and
  orchestra (1915–16)
PIZZETTI (35–41)
Deborah and Jael, opera
  (1915–21)
BARTÓK (34)
Rumanian Christmas
  Songs, for piano
Rumanian Folk Dances,
  for piano
String Quartet No. 2
  (1915–17)
ENESCO (34)
Suite for orchestra

CONTINUED

KODÁLY (33)
Sonata for unaccompanied
    cello
STRAVINSKY (33)
Rénard, burlesque
TURINA (33)
Evangelio, symphonic
    poem
BAX (32)
Violin Sonata No. 2
Légende, for violin and
    piano
Maiden with the Daffodils,
    for piano
Winter Waters, for piano
SZYMANOWSKI (32)
Symphony No. 3, *Song of
    the Night* (1915–16)
WEBERN (32–34)
Four Lieder (1915–17)
GRIFFES (31)
Fantasy Pieces, for piano
Three Tone Pictures, for
    piano

SCHOECK (29)
Trommelschlage
VILLA-LOBOS (28)
String Quartets Nos. 1
    and 2
BLISS (24)
Piano Quartet (*c.*1915)
String Quartet (*c.*1915)
PROKOFIEV (24)
Chout, ballet, revised
    1920
The Gambler, opera,
    revised 1928
Cinq poésies, for voice
    and piano
Visions fugitives, for
    piano (1915–17)
**CASTELNUOVO-
    TEDESCO** (20)
Copias
HANSON (19)
Prelude and Double
    Fugue, for two pianos

1916   BUTTERWORTH killed in action,
        GRANADOS drowned when the "Sussex"
        was torpedoed, REGER died

---

d'INDY (65–67)
*Sinfonia brève de ballo
    gallico*
STANFORD (64)
The Critic, opera
SMYTH (58)
The Boatswain's Mate,
    opera
IPPOLITOV-IVANOV
    (57)
Ole the Norseman

LOEFFLER (55)
Hora Mystica, symphony
    with men's voices
DEBUSSY (54)
Ode à la France, for
    chorus (1916–17)
Sonata for flute, viola and
    harp
DELIUS (54)
Dance Rhapsody No. 2,
    for orchestra

Violin Concerto
NIELSEN (51)
Symphony No. 4,
   Inextinguishable
Chaconne, for piano
Theme and Variations, for
   piano
SIBELIUS (51)
Everyman, incidental
   music
BUSONI (50–58)
Doktor Faust, opera
   (1916–24)
SATIE (50)
Parade, ballet
JONGEN (43)
String Quartet No. 2
RACHMANINOV (43)
Nine *Études-Tableaux,*
   for piano (1916–17)
Six songs
REGER (43)
Quintet in A major
DOHNÁNYI (39)
*Variations on a Nursery
   Song,* for piano and
   orchestra
QUILTER (39)
Three songs of William
   Blake
BRIDGE (37)
"A Prayer", for chorus
BLOCH (36)
String Quartet No. 1
MEDTNER (36–38)
Piano Concerto No. 1
   (1916–18)
BARTÓK (35)
Suite for piano
GRAINGER (34)
In a Nutshell, for piano
   and orchestra

KODÁLY (34)
String Quartet No. 2
   (1916–17)
STRAVINSKY (34)
Berceuse du chat, for
   voice and three
   clarinets
TURINA (34)
Navidad, incidental music
BAX (33)
Elegy Trio, for flute, viola
   and harp
Ballade, for violin and
   piano
Dream in Exile, for piano
CASELLA (33)
Elegia Eroica
Pagine di Guerra
Pupazzetti
GRIFFES (32)
The Kairn of Koridwen,
   dance drama
Roman Sketches, for
   orchestra
*Two Sketches on Indian
   Themes,* for string
   quartet
VILLA-LOBOS (29)
Symphony No. 1, *The
   Unforseen*
Three Symphonic poems
   Centauro de Ouro
   Miremis
   Naufragio de Kleonica
*Sinfonietta on a Theme
   by Mozart*
Marcha religiosa No. 1,
   for orchestra
Cello Concerto
String Quartet No. 3

CONTINUED

BLISS (25)
Two pieces for clarinet
  and piano
PROKOFIEV (25)
Symphony No. 1, *Classical*
  (1916–17)
HONEGGER (24)
String Quartet No. 1
  (1916–18)
Violin Sonata (1916–18)
MILHAUD (24)
String Quartet No. 3

SOWERBY (21)
Woodwind Quintet
HANSON (20)
Symphonic Prelude
Piano Quintet
KORNGOLD (19)
Der Ring des Polykrates,
  opera buffe
TANSMAN (19)
Symphony No. 1
WALTON (14)
Piano Quartet

---

pre **1917**

HINDEMITH   Cello Concerto No. 1

1917   ARNELL was born: CUI died

FAURÉ (72)
Violin Sonata No. 2
ELGAR (60)
fp. The Spirit of England,
  for voices and orchestra
Le Drapeau Belge,
  recitation with
  orchestra
Fringes of the Fleet, song
  cycle
PUCCINI (59)
La Rondine, opera
DEBUSSY (55)
Violin Sonata
DELIUS (55)
Eventyr, for chorus and
  orchestra
MASCAGNI (54)
Lodoletta, opera
Satanic Rhapsody

ROPARTZ (53)
Musiques au jardin
Violin Sonata No. 2
BUSONI (51)
Turandot, opera
Die Brautwahl, orchestral
  suite
JONGEN (44)
Tableaux pittoresques,
  for orchestra
HOLST (43)
Hymn of Jesus, for chorus
  and orchestra
A Dream of Christmas
SUK (43)
Harvestide, symphonic
  poem
RAVEL (42)
Le Tombeau de Couperin,
  for piano

CARPENTER (41)
Symphony No. 1
AUBERT (40)
Tu es Patrus, for chorus
and organ
Six poèmes arabes
(possibly 1907)
BRIDGE (38)
Cello Sonata
IRELAND (38)
Violin Sonata No. 2
Piano Trio No. 2
The Cost, songs
RESPIGHI (38)
The Fountains of Rome,
symphonic poem
*Old Airs and Dances for
Lute,* transcribed for
orchestra, Series I
Violin Sonata in B minor
KODÁLY (35)
Seven piano pieces
(1917–18)
MALIPIERO (35)
Armenia
Ditirambo Tragico
STRAVINSKY (35)
The Soldier's Tale,
opera-ballet
Les Noces, cantata-ballet
(1917–23)
Song of the Nightingale,
symphonic poem
*Song of the Haulers on
the Volga*
TURINA (35)
La Adultera penitente,
incidental music
BAX (34)
Between Dusk and Dawn,
ballet

Symphonic Variations,
for piano and orchestra
November Woods,
symphonic poem
*Moy Well (An Irish Tone
Poem),* for two pianos
Tintagel, symphonic poem
An Irish Elegy, for
English horn, harp
and strings
SZYMANOWSKI (34)
Violin Concerto No. 1
String Quartet
WEBERN (34)
Six Lieder, with
instruments (1917–21)
Five Lieder (1917–22)
GRIFFES (33)
Sho-Jo, pantomimic
drama
BERG (32)
Wozzeck, opera
(1917–21)
SCHOECK (31)
*Don Ranudo de
Colibrados* (1917–18)
VILLA-LOBOS (30)
Amazonas, ballet for
orchestra
Uirapurú, ballet
Symphony No. 2, *The
Ascension*
Five symphonic poems:
Fantasma
Lobishome
Iara
Saci Perêrê
Tedio de alvorada
Sexteto mistico, for flute,
clarinet, saxophone,
harp, celesta and
double-bass

CONTINUED

437

String Quartet No. 4
PROKOFIEV (26)
Piano Concerto No. 3
  (1917–21)
Piano Sonatas Nos. 3
  and 4
Seven, they are seven, for
  voices and orchestra
MILHAUD (25)
Symphony for small
  orchestra, No. 1,
  Le Printemps
WARLOCK (23)
An Old Song, for small
  orchestra
HINDEMITH (22)
Three Pieces for cello and
  piano

SOWERBY (22)
Piano Concerto No. 1
  (revised 1919)
Serenade, for string
  quartet
Comes Autumn Time,
  for organ
HANSON (21)
Symphonic Legend
Concerto da camera, for
  piano and string quartet
POULENC (18)
Rapsodie nègre, for cello,
  piano, flute and string
  quartet

1918 BERNSTEIN and ROCHBERG were born;
        DEBUSSY died

SAINT-SAËNS (83)
Fantasia No. 3, for organ
FAURÉ (73)
Cello Sonata No. 1
Une Châtelaine et sa tour,
  for harp
d'INDY (67)
Sarabande et Minuet, for
  piano and instruments
ELGAR (61)
Piano Quintet in A minor
  (1918–19)
String Quartet in E minor
Violin Sonata
PUCCINI (60)
Il Trittico, three one-act
  operas:
  Suor Angelica
  Il Tabarro
  Gianni Schicchi

DELIUS (56)
A Song Before Sunset
ROPARTZ (54)
Piano Trio
Cello Sonata No. 2
  (1918–19)
NIELSEN (53)
Pan and Syrinx, for
  orchestra
SATIE (52)
Socrates, symphonic
  drama for four
  sopranos and chamber
  orchestra
BANTOCK (50)
Pibroch, for cello and
  piano, or harp
ALFVÉN (46)
Symphony No. 4
  (1918–19)

JONGEN (45)
p. *Serenade tendre,* for
    string quartet
p. *Serenade triste,* for
    string quartet
CARPENTER (42)
Four Negro Songs
IRELAND (39)
*Leaves from a Child's
    Sketchbook*
RESPIGHI (39)
Il Tramonto, for
    mezzo-soprano and
    string quartet
BLOCH (38)
Suite for Viola (1918–19)
Suite for Viola and Piano
    (1918–19)
PIZZETTI (38)
Violin Sonata
BARTÓK (37)
The Miraculous Mandarin,
    ballet (1918–19)
GRAINGER (36)
Children's March
MALIPIERO (36)
Pantea, ballet
L'Orfeide, opera
    (1918–21)
Grottesco, for small
    orchestra
STRAVINSKY (36)
Ragtime, for eleven
    instruments
Four Russian songs
TURINA (36)
*Poema en forma de
    canciones,* for voice
    and piano
BAX (35)
String Quartet No. 1

Folk Tale, for cello and
    piano
GRIFFES (34)
Poem, for flute and
    orchestra
Piano Sonata
TAYLOR (33)
Portrait of a Lady, for
    eleven instruments
SCHOECK (32)
Das Wandbild
VILLA-LOBOS (31)
Jesus, opera
Vidapura, oratorio
Marcha religiosa, Nos. 3
    and 7
MARTINŮ (28)
Czech Rhapsody
BLISS (27)
Madame Noy, for soprano
    and instruments
MILHAUD (26)
L'Homme et son desir,
    ballet
Symphony for small
    orchestra, No. 2,
    Pastorale
Sonata for flute, oboe,
    clarinet and piano
String Quartet No. 4
HINDEMITH (23)
String Quartet No. 1
Violin Sonatas Nos. 1
    and 2
GERHARD (22)
Piano Trio
*L'Infantament Meravellos
    de Shahrazade,* for
    voice and piano
POULENC (19)
*Trois mouvements
    perpetuelles,* for piano

CONTINUED

Sonata for piano (four
hands)
Sonata for two clarinets

Toréador, songs
(1918–32)

1919 LEONCAVALLO died

FAURÉ (74)
Fantaisie, for piano and
orchestra
Mirages, songs
MESSAGER (66)
Monsieur Beaucaire,
opera
HUMPERDINCK (65)
Gaudeamus
JANÁČEK (65)
Katya Kabanova, opera
(1919–21)
*The Diary of a Young
Man Who Disappeared,*
song cycle
ELGAR (62)
Cello Concerto
DELIUS (57)
Fennimore and Gerda,
opera
GERMAN (57)
Theme and Six Variations
for orchestra
PIERNÉ (56)
Piano Quintet
Cello Sonata
MASCAGNI (56)
Si, opera
BUSONI (53)
Concertino for clarinet
and small orchestra
SATIE (53)
Four *Petites pièces
montées,* for small
orchestra
Nocturnes, for piano

BANTOCK (51)
Colleen, viola sonata
ROUSSEL (50)
Symphony No. 2
(1919–21)
Impromptu for harp
JONGEN (46)
Poème héroïque, for
violin and orchestra
HOLST (45)
Ode to Death
Festival Te Deum
IVES (45–53)
Orchestral Set No. 3
(1919–27)
SUK (45)
Legend of Dead Victors
Towards a New Life
GLIÈRE (44)
Imitation of Jezekiel,
symphonic poem
CARPENTER (43)
Birthday of the Infanta,
ballet
FALLA (43)
*fp. The Three-Cornered
Hat,* ballet
Fantasia bética, piano solo
AUBERT (42)
La Habanera, symphonic
poem
DOHNÁNYI (42)
Suite in F♯ minor
BRIDGE (40–50)
The Christmas Rose,
opera (1919–29)

IRELAND (40)
The Holy Boy, prelude for piano, later orchestrated
Summer Evening, for piano
RESPIGHI (40)
La Boutique fantasque, ballet
ENESCO (38)
Symphony No. 3, with organ and chorus
KODÁLY (37)
Serenade, for two violins and viola
MALIPIERO (37–39)
Tre Commedie Goldiane, opera (1919–21)
BAX (36)
Harp Quintet
Piano Sonatas Nos. 1 and 2
What the Minstrel Told Us, for piano
GRIFFES (35)
Nocturnes, for orchestra
TAYLOR (34)
Through the Looking-Glass, Suite for chamber orchestra
SCHOECK (33)
Venus, opera (1919–20)
VILLA-LOBOS (32)
Zoé, opera
Symphony No. 3, *The War*
Symphony No. 4, *The Victory*
Dansa frenetica, for orchestra
BLISS (28)
As You Like It, incidental music

Rhapsody, for solo voices and instruments
Piano Quintet
PROKOFIEV (28)
The Love of Three Oranges, opera
The Fiery Angel, opera
Overture on Hebrew Themes, for piano, clarinet and string quartet
HONEGGER (27)
Violin Sonata, No. 2
Dance of the Goat, for flute
MILHAUD (27)
Suite symphonique No. 2, *Protée*
Machines agricoles, songs
MOERAN (25)
Three piano pieces
HINDEMITH (24)
Cello Sonata
Viola Sonata
Sonata for Solo Viola
SOWERBY (24)
Trio for flute, viola and piano
HANSON (23)
Symphonic Rhapsody
KORNGOLD (22)
Much Ado About Nothing, incidental music
POULENC (20)
Le Bestaire, song cycle
Cocardes, songs
SHOSTAKOVICH (13)
Scherzo for orchestra
Eight preludes for piano

FAURÉ (75)
Masques et Bergamasques,
  suite for orchestra
d'INDY (69)
Le Poème de rivages
  (1920–21)
Légende de St. Christophe
JANÁČEK (66)
Ballad of Blaník,
  symphonic poem
SYMTH (62)
Dreamings
DELIUS (58)
Hassan, incidental music
PIERNÉ (57)
Paysages franciscains
BUSONI (54)
Divertimento, for flute
  and orchestra
Sonatina No. 6, for piano
SATIE (54)
La Belle excentrique,
  for orchestra
VAUGHAN WILLIAMS
  (48)
*Shepherd of the
  Delectable Mountains,*
  opera
The Lark Ascending, for
  violin and orchestra
Three preludes for organ
Suite de ballet, for flute
  and piano
Mass in G minor
  (1920–21)
RAVEL (45)
La Valse, choreographic
  poem for orchestra

Sonata for violin and
  cello (1920–22)
CARPENTER (44)
A Pilgrim Vision, for
  orchestra
DOHNÁNYI (43)
Hitvallás, for tenor,
  chorus and orchestra
IRELAND (41)
Piano Sonata
Three London pieces,
  for piano
RESPIGHI (41)
Scherzo Veneziano,
  choreographic comedy
Dance of the Gnomes
BLOCH (40)
Violin Sonata No. 1
BARTÓK (39)
Eight Improvisations on
  Peasant Songs
MALIPIERO (38)
Oriente immaginario
STRAVINSKY (38)
Pulcinella, ballet suite
*Symphonies for Wind
  Instruments*
Concertino for string
  quartet
TURINA (38)
Sinfonia Sevillana
Danzas fantasticas
BAX (37)
*The Truth About Russian
  Dancers,* ballet
The Garden of Fand,
  symphonic poem
Summer Music, for
  orchestra

Four pieces for piano
BERG (35)
Das Wein, concert aria
(possibly 1929)
VILLA-LOBOS (33)
Symphony No. 5, *The
Peace*
Dansa diabolica, for
orchestra
Chôros No. 1
BLISS (29)
The Tempest, overture
and interludes
(1920–21)
Two Studies for Orchestra
Concerto for piano,
tenor voice, strings and
percussion (revised as
Concerto for two
pianos and orchestra,
1924)
Conversations, for
chamber orchestra
Rout, for soprano and
chamber orchestra,
revised for full
orchestra 1921
PROKOFIEV (29)
Five *Songs Without
Words,* for voice and
piano
HONEGGER (28)
Pastorale d'été, for
orchestra
Viola Sonata
Cello Sonata
MILHAUD (28)
Le Boeuf sur le toit,
ballet
Ballade, for piano and
orchestra

Five *Études,* for piano
and orchestra
Serenade (1920–21)
String Quartet No. 5
Printemps, six pieces for
piano
BENJAMIN (27)
Three Impressions, for
voice and string quartet
MOERAN (26)
Theme and Variations
for piano
Piano Trio in E minor
Ludlow Town, song cycle
**CASTELNUOVO-
TEDESCO** (25)
La Mandragola, opera
(1920–23)
Cipressi
SOWERBY (25)
Cello Sonata
The Edge of Dreams,
song cycle
HANSON (24)
Before the Dawn,
symphonic poem
Exaltation, symphonic
poem
KORNGOLD (23)
The Dead City, opera
CHÁVEZ (21)
Symphony
Piano Sonata No. 1
POULENC (21)
Five Impromptus for
piano
Suite in C major, for
piano
SHOSTAKOVICH (14)
Five Preludes for piano

FAURÉ (76)
Piano Quintet No. 2
JANÁČEK (67)
Violin Sonata
MASCAGNI (58)
Il Piccolo Marat, opera
STRAUSS, R. (57)
Schlagobers, ballet
DUKAS (56)
*La Plainte, au loin, du
    faune*, for piano
BUSONI (55)
Elegy, for clarinet and
    piano
Romance and Scherzo
    for piano
GIORDANO (54)
Giove a Pompeii
VAUGHAN WILLIAMS
    (49)
A Pastoral Symphony
    (Symphony No. 3)
HOLST (47)
The Perfect Fool, opera
The Lure, ballet
GLIÈRE (46)
Cossacks of Zaporozh,
    symphonic poem
CARPENTER (45)
Krazy Kat, ballet
FALLA (45)
*Homage pour la tombeau
    de Debussy*, for guitar
AUBERT (44)
Dryade, symphonic poem
QUILTER (44)
Three Pastoral Songs
Five Shakespeare Songs

IRELAND (42)
Mai-Dun, symphonic
    rhapsody
Land of Lost Content,
    song cycle
RESPIGHI (42)
Adagio with Variations,
    for cello and orchestra
BLOCH (41–43)
Piano Quintet (1921–23)
MEDTNER (41)
Sonata-Vocalise No. 1
PIZZETTI (41)
Cello Sonata
BARTÓK (40)
Violin Sonata No. 1
ENESCO (40)
Oedipus, opera (begun
    c.1921)
Violin Concerto
GRAINGER (39)
Molly on the Shore, for
    solo piano
MALIPIERO (39)
Impressioni dal vero, III
    (1921–22)
STRAVINSKY (39)
Mavra, opera buffe
    (1921–22)
TURINA (39)
Canto a Sevilla, song
    cycle
BAX (38)
Symphony No. 1
    (1921–22)
Of a Rose I sing, for
    small chorus, harp,
    cello and double-bass

Viola Sonata
Mater Ora Filium, for
  unaccompanied chorus
CASELLA (38)
A Notte Alta
VILLA-LOBOS (34)
Malazarte, opera
Quartet for harp, celesta,
  flute and saxophone,
  with women's voices
MARTINŮ (31)
Istar, ballet
BLISS (30)
A Colour Symphony
  (1921–22, revised
  1932)
Mêlée fantasque, for
  orchestra (revised
  1965)
PROKOFIEV (30)
Five Songs
HONEGGER (29)
Horace Victorieux,
  "mimed symphony"
Sonatina for clarinet and
  piano (1921–22)
King David, oratorio
MILHAUD (29)
Symphony No. 3 for small
  orchestra, *Sérénade*
Symphony No. 4 for

strings, *Ouverture,*
  Chorale, Étude
Saudades de Brasil, dance
  suite for orchestra
MOERAN (27)
In the Mountain Country,
  symphonic impression
On a May Morning, for
  piano
HINDEMITH (26)
Chamber Music No. 1
  (1921–22)
SOWERBY (26)
Symphony No. 1
Violin Sonata No. 1
**CASTELNUOVO-
  TEDESCO** (25)
Thirty-three Shakespeare
  Songs
HANSON (25)
Concerto for organ,
  strings and harp
CHÁVEZ (22)
El Fuego nuevo, ballet
String Quartet No. 1
RUBBRA (20)
The Secret Hymnody,
  for chorus and
  orchestra
SHOSTAKOVICH (15)
Theme with Variations,
  for orchestra

1922   FOSS and HAMILTON were born

FAURÉ (77)
Cello Sonata No. 2
L'Horizon chimerique,
  songs

d'INDY (71)
Le rêve de Cynias
  (1922–23)

CONTINUED

DELIUS (60)
Pagan Requiem (possibly 1914–16)
STRAUSS, R. (58)
Intermezzo, opera (1922–23)
NIELSEN (57)
Symphony No. 5
Quintet for wind
SIBELIUS (57)
Suite caractéristique
BANTOCK (54)
Song of Songs
JONGEN (49)
Rhapsody, for piano and instruments
HOLST (48)
Fugal Overture No. 1
GLIÈRE (47)
Comedians, ballet (also in 1930)
RAVEL (47)
Berceuse sur le nom Fauré
FALLA (46)
El Retablo de Maese Pedro, opera
Seven Spanish Popular Songs
DOHNÁNYI (45)
The Tower of the Voivod
QUILTER (45)
As You Like It, incidental music
BRIDGE (43)
Sir Roger de Coverley, for string quartet, or orchestra
Piano Sonata (1922–25)
RESPIGHI (43)
The Sleeping Beauty, musical fable

Concerto Gregoriano, for violin and orchestra
BLOCH (42)
In the Night; for piano
Poems of the Sea, for piano (1922–24)
PIZZETTI (42)
Lo Straniero, opera
Requiem
BARTÓK (41)
Violin Sonata No. 2
GRAINGER (40)
Shepherd's Hey, for solo piano
STRAVINSKY (40)
Octet for wind (1922–23)
BAX (39)
The Happy Forest, symphonic poem
SCHOECK (36)
Élégie, song cycle (1922–23)
IBERT (32)
Ballad of Reading Gaol, ballet
Ports of Call (Escales), orchestral suite
MARTINŮ (32)
Three Symphonic poems:
The Grove of Satyrs
Shadows
Vanishing Midnight
MILHAUD (30)
La Création du monde, ballet (1922–23)
Symphony No. 5, for small wind orchestra
Three *Rag-Caprices*
String Quartet No. 6
MOERAN (28)
Rhapsody No. 1
Three Fancies, for piano

WARLOCK (28)
*Serenade for Frederick
 Delius,* for orchestra
HINDEMITH (27)
String Quartets Nos. 2
 and 3
Suite for Klavier
Sonata for Solo Viola
Die Junge Magd, song
 cycle
SOWERBY (27)
Ballad of King Estmere,
 for two pianos and
 orchestra
From the Northlands,
 for piano
GERHARD (26)
Seven Haï-Ku, for voice
 and five instruments
HANSON (26)
Symphony No. 1, *Nordic*
TANSMAN (25)
Sextour, ballet

POULENC (23)
Sonata for clarinet and
 bassoon
Sonata for trumpet, horn
 and trombone
Chanson à boire, for a
 cappella male choir
ANTHEIL (22)
Symphony No. 1
Airplane Sonata, for
 piano
Sonata Sauvage, for piano
WALTON (20)
fp. (privately) *Façade,*
 for reciter and chamber
 ensemble
SHOSTAKOVICH (16)
Two Fables of Krilov,
 for mezzo-soprano and
 orchestra
Suite in F♯ minor, for
 two pianos
Three Fantastic Dances,
 for piano

1923   LIGETI and MENNIN were born

FAURÉ (78)
Piano Trio
JANÁČEK (69)
Quartet No. 1
ELGAR (66)
fp. King Arthur,
 incidental music
SMYTH (65)
Fête galante, opera
Soul's Joy, for
 unaccompanied chorus
IPPOLITOV-IVANOV
 (64)
Mtzyry (1923–24)

LOEFFLER (62)
*Avant que tu ne t'en
 ailles,* poem
PIERNÉ (60)
Cydalise and the Satyr,
 ballet
SIBELIUS (58)
Symphony No. 6
SATIE (57)
Ludions, songs
BUSONI (56)
Ten Variations on a
 Chopin prelude

CONTINUED

447

BANTOCK (55)
Pagan Symphony
ALFVÉN (51)
Bergakungen,
pantomime drama
VAUGHAN WILLIAMS
(51)
Old King Cole, ballet
HOLST (49)
Choral Symphony
(1923-24)
Fugal Overture No. 2
SCHOENBERG (49)
Serenade, for septet and
baritone
GLIÈRE (48–50)
Shahk-Senem, opera
(1923-25)
FALLA (47–50)
Concerto for harpsichord,
flute, oboe, clarinet,
violin and cello
(1923–26)
AUBERT (46)
La Nuit ensorcelée, ballet
IRELAND (44)
Cello Sonata
RESPIGHI (44)
Belfagor, lyric comedy
La Primavera, lyric poem
for soloists, chorus and
orchestra
BLOCH (43)
Baal Shem, for violin and
piano
Melody, for violin and
piano
Enfantines, for piano
Five Sketches in Sepia,
for piano
Nirvana, for piano
BARTÓK (42)
Dance Suite, for orchestra

KODÁLY (41)
Psalmus Hungaricus, for
tenor, chorus and
orchestra
TURINA (41)
Jardin de oriente
BAX (40)
Romantic Overture, for
small orchestra
Saga Fragment, for piano,
strings, trumpet and
cymbals
Piano Quartet
Oboe Quintet
Cello Sonata
CASELLA (40)
Concerto for string
quartet (1923–24)
BERG (38–40)
Chamber Concerto
(1923–25)
TAYLOR (38)
A Kiss in Xanadu,
pantomime for two
pianos
VILLA-LOBOS (36)
Suite for voice and viola
BLISS (32)
String Quartet (1923-24)
*Ballads of the Four
Seasons,* song cycle
The Women of Yueh,
song cycle
PROKOFIEV (32)
Piano Sonata No. 5
HONEGGER (31)
Chant de joie
MILHAUD (31)
Symphony No. 6, for
soprano, contralto,
tenor and bass soli,
oboe and cello

WARLOCK (29)
The Curlew, song cycle
HINDEMITH (28)
String Quartet No. 4
Kleine Sonata for viola
    d'amore and klavier
Sonata for solo cello
HANSON (27)
North and West,
    symphonic poem
Lux Aeterna, symphonic
    poem with viola
    obbligato
String Quartet
ROBERTSON (27)
Overture
SESSIONS (27)
The Black Maskers,
    incidental music

THOMSON (27)
Two sentimental tangoes
CHÁVEZ (24)
Piano Sonata No. 2
POULENC (24)
Les Biches, ballet
ANTHEIL (23)
Violin Sonata No. 1
Ballet mécanique
    (1923–24, revised
    1953)
COPLAND (23)
As it fell upon a day, for
    soprano, flute and
    clarinet
SHOSTAKOVICH (17)
Piano Trio No. 1

1924   BUSONI, FAURÉ, PUCCINI and STANFORD
         died

FAURÉ (79)
String Quartet
d'INDY (73)
Piano Quintet
JANÁČEK (70)
The Cunning Little Vixen,
    opera
The Makropoulos Affair,
    opera (1924–26)
Miade, Suite for wind
ELGAR (67)
fp. *Pageant of Empire*
ROPARTZ (60)
String Quartet No. 3
    (1924–25)
STRAUSS, R. (60–63)
The Egyptian Helen,
    opera (1924–27)

DUKAS (59)
Sonnet de Ronsard, for
    voice and piano
SIBELIUS (59)
Symphony No. 7
SATIE (58)
Mercure, ballet
Relâche, ballet
GIORDANO (57)
Le Cena delle beffe,
    opera
BANTOCK (56)
The Seal-Woman, opera
VAUGHAN WILLIAMS
    (52)
Hugh the Drover, opera

CONTINUED

HOLST (50)
At The Boar's Head,
  opera
Terzetto, for flute, oboe
  and viola
SCHOENBERG (50)
Quintet for Wind
GLIÈRE (49)
Two Poems for soprano
  and orchestra
*For the Festival of the
  Comintern,* fantasy for
  wind orchestra
March of the Red Army,
  for wind orchestra
RAVEL (49)
Tzigane, for violin and
  piano
RESPIGHI (45)
*Concerto in the Mixo-
  Lydian mode,* for
  orchestra
The Pines of Rome,
  symphonic poem
*Old Airs and Dances for
  Lute,* second series
Doric, String Quartet
BLOCH (44)
Concerto Grosso for
  strings with piano
  obbligato (1924–25)
*In The Mountains (Haute
  Savoie),* for string
  quartet
Night, for string quartet
Three Landscapes, for
  string quartet
Three Nocturnes, for
  piano trio
Violin Sonata No. 2,
  Poème mystique
Exotic Night, for violin
  and piano

From Jewish Life, for
  cello and piano
Méditation hébraïque, for
  cello and piano
MEDTNER (44)
Violin Sonata
BARTÓK (43)
Five Village Scenes, for
  female voice and piano
STRAVINSKY (42)
Concerto for piano and
  wind
Piano Sonata
BAX (41)
Symphony No. 2
  (1924–25)
Cortège, for orchestra
String Quartet No. 2
  (1924–25)
CASELLA (41)
La Giara, ballet
Partita, for piano
  (1924–25)
SZYMANOWSKI (41)
Prince Potemkin,
  incidental music
WEBERN (41)
Five canons for voice,
  clarinet and
  bass-clarinet
Six "Volkstexte"
SCHOECK (38)
Penthesiles (1924–25)
VILLA-LOBOS (37)
Chôros, Nos. 2 and 7
BLISS (33)
Masks I–IV, for piano
PROKOFIEV (33)
Symphony No. 2
  (1924–25)
Quintet for oboe, clarinet,
  violin, viola and
  double-bass

HONEGGER (32)
Mouvement symphonique
No. 1, *Pacific 231*
MILHAUD (32)
Les Malheurs d'Orphée,
opera
Esther de Carpentras
(1924–25)
BENJAMIN (31)
Pastoral Fantasy for string
quartet
Sonatina for violin and
piano
MOORE (31)
*The Pageant of P.T.
Barnum,* suite for
orchestra
MOERAN (30)
Rhapsody No. 2
HINDEMITH (29)
Piano Concerto
Chamber Music No. 2
Sonata for solo violin
Das Marienleben, song
cycle
SOWERBY (29)
Synconata, for jazz
orchestra
TANSMAN (27)
Sinfonietta

GERSHWIN (26)
Rhapsody in Blue, for
piano and orchestra
CHÁVEZ (25)
Sonatina for violin and
piano
Sonatina for cello and
piano
POULENC (25)
Promenade, for piano
Poèmes de Ronsard
(1924–25)
COPLAND (24)
Symphony for organ and
orchestra
FINZI (23)
Severn Rhapsody
RUBBRA (23)
Double Fugue for
orchestra
SEIBER (19)
String Quartet No. 1
Sarabande and Gigue,
for cello and piano
Missa Brevis, for
unaccompanied chorus
SHOSTAKOVICH (18)
Symphony No. 1
(1924–25)
Scherzo, for orchestra
Prelude and Scherzo, for
string octet (1924–25)

1925 BERIO and BOULEZ were born; SATIE died

---

d'INDY (74)
Diptyque méditerranéen
(1925–26)
Cello Sonata
JANÁČEK (71)
Sinfonietta (1925–26)

Concertino for seven
instruments
STANFORD
(posthumous)
*fp. The Travelling
Companion,* opera
CONTINUED

LOEFFLER (64)
*Memories of my
Childhood*, for
orchestra
DELIUS (63)
Caprice and Elegy, for
cello and orchestra
NIELSEN (60)
Symphony No. 6, *Simple*
SIBELIUS (60)
Tapiola, symphonic poem
ROUSSEL (56)
*Pour une fête de
printemps*, tone poem
Serenade, for harp, flute,
violin, viola and cello
Jouers de flûte, for flute
and piano
Violin Sonata
Segovia, for guitar
VAUGHAN WILLIAMS
(53)
Concerto accademico, for
violin and string
orchestra
Flos Campi, suite for
viola, chorus and small
orchestra
Sancta Civitas, oratorio
GLIÈRE (50)
Cleopatra, ballet
RAVEL (50)
L'Enfant et les sortilèges,
opera
CARPENTER (49)
Skyscrapers, ballet
AUBERT (48)
Capriccio, for violin and
orchestra
QUILTER (48)
The Rake, ballet suite
Five Jacobean Lyrics

BLOCH (45)
Prélude (Recueillement),
for string quartet
PIZZETTI (45–47)
Fra Gherado, opera
(1925–27)
GRAINGER (43)
Country Gardens, for
orchestra
KODÁLY (43)
*Meditations on a theme of
Debussy*, for piano
MALIPIERO (43)
Filomela a l'infatuato,
opera
Merlino maestro d'organi,
opera (1925–28)
Il Mistero de Venezia,
opera (1925–28)
STRAVINSKY (43)
Serenade in A major, for
piano
BAX (42)
Piano Sonata No. 3
WEBERN (42)
Three Lieder
TAYLOR (40)
Fantasy on Two Themes,
for orchestra
Jurgen, for orchestra
Circus Days, for jazz
orchestra
BERG (40)
Lyric Suite, for string
quartet (1925–26)
VILLA-LOBOS (38)
Chôros Nos. 3, 8 and 10
IBERT (35)
Concerto for cello and
wind instruments
Scherzo féerique
MARTINŮ (35)
On Tourne, ballet

Half-Time, symphonic
poem
Piano Concerto No. 1
PROKOFIEV (34)
Pas d'acier, ballet
(1925–26)
Divertimento for orchestra
(1925–29)
HONEGGER (33)
Judith, opera
Concertino for piano and
orchestra
MILHAUD (33)
String Quartet No. 7
Deux Hymnes
BENJAMIN (32)
Three Mystical Songs, for
unaccompanied chorus
MOERAN (31)
Summer Valley, for piano
HINDEMITH (30)
Concerto for orchestra
Chamber Music Nos. 3
and 4
ORFF (30)
Prelude for orchestra
SOWERBY (30)
From the Northland,
for orchestra
Monotony, for jazz
orchestra
The Vision of Sir Launfal,
for chorus and
orchestra
**CASTELNUOVO-
TEDESCO** (29)
Le danze del re David,
for piano

HANSON (29)
The Lament of Beowulf,
for chorus
TANSMAN (28)
La Nuit Kurde, opera
(1925–27)
Symphony No. 2
GERSHWIN (27)
Piano Concerto
CHÁVEZ (26)
Energia, for nine
instruments
POULENC (26)
Napoli Suite, for piano
COPLAND (25)
Grogh, ballet
Dance Symphony
Music for the Theater,
suite for small orchestra
RUBBRA (24)
La Belle Dame sans merci,
for orchestra and
chorus
Violin Sonata No. 1
WALTON (23)
Portsmouth Point,
overture
BERKELEY (22)
"The Thresher", for voice
and piano
LAMBERT (20)
Romeo and Juliet, ballet
(1925–26)
SEIBER (20)
Serenade, for six wind
instruments
Sonata da Camera, for
violin and cello

PUCCINI (posthumous)
fp. Turandot, opera
JANÁČEK (72)
Capriccio, for piano and
    wind
Festliche Messe
SMYTH (68)
Entente Cordiale, opera
Sleepless Dreams, for
    chorus and orchestra
A Spring Canticle, for
    chorus and orchestra
ROPARTZ (62)
Romance and Scherzino,
    for violin and orchestra
NIELSEN (61)
Flute Concerto
SIBELIUS (61)
The Tempest, incidental
    music
HOLST (52)
The Golden Goose,
    choral ballet
GLIÈRE (51)
Red Poppy, ballet
    (1926–27)
RAVEL (51)
Chansons madécasses, for
    voice, flute, cello and
    piano
BRIDGE (47)
String Quartet No. 3
BLOCH (46)
*America: An Epic
    Rhapsody,* for orchestra
Four Episodes for
    chamber orchestra
MEDTNER (46)
Piano Concerto No. 2
    (1926–27)

BARTÓK (45)
Piano Concerto No. 1
Three Village Scenes, for
    chorus and orchestra
Cantata Profana, for tenor
    and baritone soli,
    chorus and orchestra
Out of Doors, suite for
    piano
Mikrokosmos, for piano
    (1926–37)
Nine Little Pieces for
    piano
Piano Sonata
KODÁLY (44)
Háry János, opera
MALIPIERO (44)
L'esilio dell' eroe, five
    symphonic impressions
TURINA (44)
La oracion del torero,
    for string quartet
Piano Trio
CASELLA (43)
*Introduction, Aria and
    Toccata,* for orchestra
Concerto Romano, for
    organ and orchestra
Adieu à la vie, for voice
    and orchestra
Scarlattiana
SZYMANOWSKI (43)
Harnasie, ballet
Stabat Mater
WEBERN (43)
Two Lieder
TAYLOR (41)
The King's Henchman,
    opera

VILLA-LOBOS (39)
Chôros Nos. 4, 5, 6
and 6bis.
IBERT (36)
Jeux, for orchestra
MARTIN (36)
Rythmes, three symphonic
movements
BLISS (35)
Hymn to Apollo, for
orchestra (revised
1965)
Introduction and Allegro
for orchestra (revised
1937)
MILHAUD (34)
Le Pauvre matelot, opera
MOERAN (32)
Irish Love Song, for piano
PISTON (32)
Three Pieces for flute,
clarinet and bassoon
Piano Sonata
WARLOCK (32)
Capriol Suite, for strings
HINDEMITH (31)
Cardillac, opera
SOWERBY (31)
Mediaeval Poem, for
organ and orchestra
HANSON (30)
Pan and the Priest,
symphonic poem

Organ Concerto
THOMSON (30)
Sonata da Chiesa, for five
instruments
TANSMAN (29)
Piano Concerto No. 1
HARRIS (28)
*Impressions of a rainy
day,* for string quartet
CHÁVEZ (27)
Los cuatro soles, ballet
POULENC (27)
Trio for oboe, bassoon
and piano
Chansons gaillardes
ANTHEIL (26)
Jazz Symphonietta, for
twenty-two instruments
COPLAND (26)
Piano Concerto
DURUFLÉ (24)
Scherzo for organ
WALTON (24)
Siesta, for orchestra
LAMBERT (21)
Pomona, ballet
Poems by Li-Po
SEIBER (21–23)
Divertimento, for clarinet
and string quartet
(1926–28)
SHOSTAKOVICH (20)
Piano Sonata No. 1

1927

---

d'INDY (76)
Concerto for piano, flute,
cello and string quartet
"Suites en parties", for

harp, flute, viola and
cello
JANÁČEK (73)
From the House of the
CONTINUED

Dead, opera
(1927–28)
Glagolitic Mass
SMYTH (69)
Concerto for violin and
horn
PIERNÉ (64)
Sophie Arnould,
opera-comique
NIELSEN (62)
*En Fantasirejse til
Faerøerne,* rhapsodic
overture
ROUSSEL (58)
Piano Concerto
VAUGHAN WILLIAMS
(55)
Along the Field, eight
songs for voice and
violin
RACHMANINOV (54)
Piano Concerto No. 4
HOLST (53)
The Morning of the Year,
choral ballet
Egdon Heath, symphonic
poem
The Coming of Christ,
mystery play
SCHOENBERG (53)
String Quartet No. 3
AUBERT (50)
p. *Noël pastoral,* for
piano and orchestra
p. Violin Sonata
BRIDGE (48)
Enter Spring, for
orchestra
IRELAND (48)
Sonatina, for piano
RESPIGHI (48)
The Sunken Bell, opera

Church Windows,
symphonic impressions
The Birds, suite for small
orchestra
Three Botticelli Pictures,
for orchestra
Brazilian Impressions,
for orchestra
BARTÓK (46)
String Quartet No. 3
GRAINGER (45)
Shallow Brown
*Irish Tune from County
Derry*
STRAVINSKY (45)
Oedipus Rex,
opera-oratorio
BAX (44)
Violin Sonata No. 3
CASELLA (44)
Concerto for Strings
Cello Sonata No. 2
WEBERN (44)
String Trio
IBERT (37)
Angélique, opera
MARTINU (37)
Le Raid merveilleux,
ballet (1927–28)
La Revue de cuisine,
ballet
La Bagarre, symphonic
poem
BLISS (36)
Oboe Quintet
Four Songs, for high
voice and violin
HONEGGER (35)
Antigone, lyric drama
MILHAUD (35)
Violin Concerto No. 1
Carnival of Aix, for
piano and orchestra

PISTON (33)
Symphonic Piece
CASTELNUOVO-
TEDESCO (32)
Piano Concerto No. 1
HINDEMITH (32)
Chamber Music, No. 5
ORFF (32)
Concertino for wind
HANSON (31)
Heroic Elegy, for chorus
and orchestra
SESSIONS (31)
Symphony No. 1
WEINBERGER (31)
Schwanda the Bagpiper,
opera
TANSMAN (30)
Piano Concerto No. 2
HARRIS (29)
Concerto for clarinet,
piano and string quartet
CHÁVEZ (28)
"HP", ballet
POULENC (28)
Concert champêtre, for

harpsichord and
orchestra (1927–28)
Deux novelettes, for piano
(1927–28)
Airs chantés (1927–28)
DURUFLÉ (25)
Triptyque, for piano
WALTON (25)
Viola Concerto
Sinfonia concertante,
for piano and orchestra
KHACHATURIAN (24)
Poème, for piano
ALWYN (22)
Five Preludes for
Orchestra
LAMBERT (22)
Music for Orchestra
Elegiac Blues
SHOSTAKOVICH (21)
The Nose, opera
(1927–28)
The Age of Gold, ballet
(1927–30)
Symphony No. 2, *October*
Aphorisms, for piano

1928   KORTE, MUSGRAVE and STOCKHAUSEN
were born; JANÁČEK died

JANÁČEK (74)
String Quartet No. 2,
Intimate Pages
ELGAR (71)
fp. Beau Brummell,
incidental music
IPPOLITOV-IVANOV
(69)
*Episodes from Schubert's
Life*

LOEFFLER (67)
Intermezzo, *Clowns*
ROPARTZ (64)
Rhapsody, for cello and
orchestra
NIELSEN (63)
Clarinet Concerto
BANTOCK (60)
Pilgrim's Progress
LEHÁR (58)
Frederica, operetta
CONTINUED

457

ALFVÉN (56)
Manhem, cantata for male
  voices
VAUGHAN WILLIAMS
  (56)
Sir John in Love, opera
Te Deum, in G major
JONGEN (55)
Pièce symphonique, for
  piano and orchestra
HOLST (54)
Moorside Suite, for brass
  band
SCHOENBERG (54)
Variations for orchestra
GLIÈRE (53)
String Quartet No. 3
RAVEL (53)
Bolero, for orchestra
CARPENTER (52)
String Quartet
BRIDGE (49)
Rhapsody, for two violins
  and viola
RESPIGHI (49)
Toccata, for piano and
  orchestra
PIZZETTI (48)
Concerto dell'estate
BARTÓK (47)
Rhapsodies Nos. 1 and 2,
  for violin and orchestra
Rhapsody No. 1 for cello
  and piano
String Quartet No. 4
GRAINGER (46)
Colonial Songs
*Over the Hills and Far
  Away*
STRAVINSKY (46)
Apollo Musagetes, ballet
Le Baiser de la fée, ballet

TURINA (46)
Ritmos, choreographic
  fantasy
BAX (45)
Symphony No. 3
  (1928–29)
Sonata for two pianos
Sonata for violin and harp
CASELLA (45)
La Donna serpente, opera
  (1928–31)
Violin Concerto
WEBERN (45)
Symphony for small
  orchestra
BERG (43–49)
Lulu, opera (1928–34)
SCHOECK (42–44)
*Vom Fischer und syner
  Fru,* dramatic cantata
  (1928–30)
VILLA-LOBOS (41)
Chôros, Nos. 11 and 14
MARTINŮ (38)
Les Lames de Couteau,
  opera
*The Soldier and the
  Dancer,* opera
Échec au roi, ballet
Concertino for piano (left
  hand) and chamber
  orchestra
Entr'acte
La Rapsodie
BLISS (37)
*Pastoral: Lie strewn the
  white flocks,* for mezzo-
  soprano, chorus, flute,
  drums and string
  orchestra
PROKOFIEV (37)
The Prodigal Son, ballet
Symphony No. 3

HONEGGER (36)
Mouvement symphonique
   No. 2, *Rugby*
MILHAUD (36)
Christophe Columb, opera
   (revised 1956)
*Cantate pour louer le
   Seigneur*
MOORE (35)
A Symphony of Autumn
Moby Dick, for orchestra
HINDEMITH (33)
Concerto for organ and
   chamber orchestra
Chamber Music, No. 6
ORFF (33)
Entrata (revised 1940)
SOWERBY (33)
Symphony No. 2
GERHARD (32)
Wind Quintet
THOMSON (32)
*Symphony on a Hymn
   Tune*
TANSMAN (31)
Lumières
GERSHWIN (30)
An American in Paris, for
   orchestra

HARRIS (30)
Piano Sonata
POULENC (29)
Trois pièces, for piano
ANTHEIL (28)
Transatlantic, opera
   (1928–29)
COPLAND (28)
Symphony No. 1
DURUFLÉ (26)
*Prélude, recitatif et
   variations,* for flute,
   viola and piano
LAMBERT (23)
Piano Sonata (1928–29)
SHOSTAKOVICH (22)
*Six romances on words
   by Japanese poets,* for
   tenor and orchestra
   (1928–32)
Film music
MESSIAEN (20)
Fugue in D minor for
   orchestra
La Banquet céleste, for
   organ
Le Banquet eucharistique

1929   HODDINOTT and PREVIN were born

---

d'INDY (78)
String Sextet
GIORDANO (62)
Il Re, opera
ROUSSEL (60)
Symphony No. 3
   (1929–30)
LEHÁR (59)
The Land of Smiles,
   operetta

VAUGHAN WILLIAMS
   (57)
Benedicite, for soprano,
   chorus and orchestra
JONGEN (56)
Passacaille et Gigue, for
   orchestra
Suite for viola and
   orchestra

CONTINUED

HOLST (55)
*The Tale of the
    Wandering Scholar,*
  opera
Concerto for two violins
Twelve songs
SCHOENBERG (55)
Von Heute auf Morgen,
  opera
DOHNÁNYI (52)
A Tenor, opera
BRIDGE (50)
Trio No. 2
IRELAND (50)
Ballade, for piano
RESPIGHI (50)
The Festivals of Rome,
  orchestral suite
BLOCH (49)
Abodah, for violin and
  piano
PIZZETTI (49)
Rondo veneziano, for
  orchestra
GRAINGER (47)
English Dance
MALIPIERO (47)
Torneo notturno, opera
STRAVINSKY (47)
Capriccio, for piano and
  orchestra
TURINA (47)
Triptico
BAX (46)
Overture, Elegy and
  Rondo, for orchestra
Legend, for viola and
  piano
BERG (44)
Three Pieces for Orchestra
VILLA-LOBOS (42)
Introdução aos Chôros,
  for orchestra

Chôros Nos. 9, 12 and 13
Suite sugestiva, for voice
  and orchestra
Twelve studies for guitar
IBERT (39)
Persée et Andromédée,
  opera
MARTINŮ (39)
Journée de bonté, opera
*The Butterfly that
  stamped,* ballet
BLISS (38)
Serenade, for baritone and
  orchestra
PROKOFIEV (38)
Symphony No. 4
  (1929–30, revised
  1947)
MILHAUD (37)
Viola Concerto
Concerto for percussion
  and small orchestra
BENJAMIN (36)
Concerto quasi una
  fantasia, for piano and
  orchestra
MOORE (36)
Violin Sonata
PISTON (35)
Suite No. 1 for orchestra
SOWERBY (34)
Cello Concerto
  (1929–34)
Prairie, symphonic poem
Florida Suite, for piano
THOMSON (33)
Five Portraits, for four
  clarinets
WEINBERGER (33)
Christmas, for orchestra
TANSMAN (32)
Le cercle éternel, ballet

HARRIS (31)
American Portraits, for
orchestra
POULENC (30)
Aubade, for piano and
instruments
Hommage à Roussel, for
piano
Eight piano Nocturnes
(1929–38)
COPLAND (29)
Symphonic Ode (revised
1955)
Vitebsk, for piano trio
RUBBRA (28)
Triple Fugue, for
orchestra

DURUFLÉ (27)
Prélude, Adagio and
Chorale, for organ
KABALEVSKY (25)
Piano Concerto No. 1
String Quartet in A minor
LAMBERT (24)
The Rio Grande, for
chorus, piano and
orchestra
SHOSTAKOVICH (23)
Symphony No. 3,
The 1st of May
MESSIAEN (21)
Préludes, for piano
BARBER (19)
Serenade for string
orchestra, or string
quartet

1930   WARLOCK died

---

d'INDY (79)
String Quartet No. 4
Suite for flute obbligato,
violin, viola, cello and
harp
Piano Trio No. 2, in the
form of a suite
ELGAR (73)
*Pomp and Circumstance
March,* No. 5
Severn Suite, for brass
band, or orchestra
SMYTH (72)
The Prison, for
unaccompanied chorus
DELIUS (68)
A Song of Summer
STRAUSS, R. (66–68)
Arabella, opera
(1930–32)

VAUGHAN WILLIAMS
(58)
Prelude and Fugue for
orchestra
*Job, a Masque for
Dancing,* for orchestra
JONGEN (57)
Sonata Eroica
RACHMANINOV (57)
Three Russian Folksongs,
for chorus and
orchestra (possibly
1927)
HOLST (56)
Choral Fantasia
Hammersmith, prelude
and scherzo for
orchestra
AUBERT (53) -
Feuilles d'images
CONTINUED

BRIDGE (51)
Oration, "concert
   elegiaco" for cello
IRELAND (51)
Piano Concerto
RESPIGHI (51)
*Metamorphosen modi
   XII,* theme and
   variations for orchestra
PIZZETTI (50)
Piano Concerto
BARTÓK (49)
Piano Concerto No. 2
   (1930–31)
GRAINGER (48)
*Lord Peter's Stable-boy
Spoon River
To a Nordic Princess*
KODÁLY (48)
Dances of Marosszek,
   for piano
MALIPIERO (48)
La Bella ed il mostro,
   opera
STRAVINSKY (48)
Symphony of Psalms, for
   chorus and orchestra
BAX (47)
Symphony No. 4
*Overture to a picaresque
   comedy,* for orchestra
Winter Legends, for piano
   and orchestra
CASELLA (47)
Serenade for small
   orchestra
WEBERN (47)
Quartet for violin, clarinet,
   saxophone and piano
TAYLOR (45)
Peter Ibbetson, opera

VILLA-LOBOS (43)
Bachianas Brasileiras,
   Nos. 1 and 2
IBERT (40)
Le Roi d'Yvetot, opera
Divertissement, for
   chamber orchestra
MARTINŮ (40)
Serenade, for chamber
   orchestra
Violin Sonata No. 1
BLISS (39)
Morning Heroes,
   symphony for orator,
   chorus and orchestra
PROKOFIEV (39)
*Sur le Borythène (On the
   Dnieper),* ballet
Four Portraits, symphonic
   suite (1930–31)
String Quartet No. 1
HONEGGER (38)
*Les aventures du roi
   pausole,* light opera
Symphony No. 1
MILHAUD (38)
Maximilien, opera
MOORE (37)
*Overture on an American
   theme*
PISTON (36)
Flute Sonata
HINDEMITH (35)
Concert music, for piano,
   brass and harps
ORFF (35)
Catulli Carmina, for
   chorus and orchestra
   (revised 1943)
SOWERBY (35)
Organ Symphony

HANSON (34)
Symphony No. 2,
    Romantic
SESSIONS (34)
Piano Sonata No. 1
THOMSON (34)
Violin Sonata
WEINBERGER (34)
The Beloved Voice, opera
*Bohemian Songs and
    Dances*, for orchestra
TANSMAN (33)
Triptyque, for string
    orchestra
HARRIS (32)
String Quartet No. 1
CHÁVEZ (31)
Sonata for horns
POULENC (31)
Épitaphe, song
COPLAND (30)
Piano Variations

DURUFLÉ (28)
Suite for organ
KABALEVSKY (26)
Poem of Struggle, for
    chorus and orchestra
ALWYN (25)
Piano Concerto
SHOSTAKOVICH (24)
*Lady Macbeth of the
    Mtsensk District*, opera
The Bolt, choreographic
    spectacle (1930–31)
Film music
MESSIAEN (22)
Les Offrandes oubliées,
    for orchestra
Simple chant d'une âme
Diptyque, for organ
BRITTEN (17)
Hymn to the Virgin

1931   WILLIAMSON was born; d'INDY and
            NIELSEN died

ELGAR (74)
p. Nursery Suite, for
    orchestra
NIELSEN (66)
Commotio, for organ
PIERNÉ (68)
*Divertissement sur un
    thème pastorale*, for
    orchestra
Fantaisie basque, for
    violin
CILÈA (65)
Suite for orchestra

ROUSSEL (62)
Bacchus and Ariadne,
    ballet
VAUGHAN WILLIAMS
    (59)
Symphony No. 4
    (1931–34)
Piano Concerto
In Windsor Forest,
    cantata
SUK (57)
Mass in B♭ major

CONTINUED

RAVEL (56)
Piano Concerto in G major
Piano Concerto for the left hand
BRIDGE (52)
Phantasm, rhapsody for piano and orchestra
IRELAND (52)
Songs Sacred and Profane
PIZZETTI (51–55)
Oreseolo, opera (1931–35)
BARTÓK (50)
Forty-four duos for two violins
GRAINGER (49)
The Nightingale and the Two Sisters
KODÁLY (49)
The Spinning Room, lyric scenes (1931–32)
Theater Overture
Pange lingua, for chorus and organ
MALIPIERO (49)
Concerto for Orchestra
STRAVINSKY (49)
Violin Concerto
TURINA (49)
Rapsodia sinfonica, for piano and strings
Piano Quartet
BAX (48)
Symphony No. 5 (1931–32)
The Tale the Pine Trees Knew, symphonic poem
Nonet for flute, oboe, clarinet, harp and strings
String Quintet

CASELLA (48–52)
Introduction, corale e marcia, for woodwind (1931–35)
SZYMANOWSKI (48)
Symphonie concertante, for piano (1931–32)
VILLA-LOBOS (44)
String Quartet No. 5
MARTIN (41)
Chaconne, for cello and piano
Violin Sonata
MARTINŮ (41)
Spaliček, ballet
Partita (Suite No. 1)
Cello Concerto
BLISS (40)
Clarinet Quintet
PROKOFIEV (40)
Piano Concerto No. 4 for the left hand
GROFÉ (39)
Grand Canyon Suite, for orchestra
HONEGGER (39)
Cries of the World, choral-orchestral
Amphion
1001 Nights
BENJAMIN (38)
The Devil Take Her, comic opera
PISTON (37)
Suite for oboe and piano
HINDEMITH (36)
The Unceasing, oratorio
SOWERBY (36)
Passacaglia, Interlude and Fugue, for orchestra

THOMSON (35)
Four Portraits, for violin
and piano
Serenade, for flute and
violin
Quartet No. 1
Stabat Mater
WEINBERGER (35)
Passacaglia, for orchestra
TANSMAN (34)
Symphony No. 3,
Symphony concertante
Concertino, for piano
GERSHWIN (33)
Second Rhapsody
HARRIS (33)
Toccata, for orchestra
POULENC (32)
Bagatelle, for violin and
piano
*Troi poèmes de Louise
Lalanne,* songs
Nine songs

ANTHEIL (31)
Helen Retires, opera
RUBBRA (30)
Piano Concerto
Violin Sonata No. 2
WALTON (29)
fp. Belshazzar's Feast,
for baritone, chorus
and orchestra
LAMBERT (26)
Concerto for piano and
nine instruments
SHOSTAKOVICH (25)
Hamlet, incidental music
MESSIAEN (23)
*Le Tombeau
resplendissant*
BARBER (21)
School for Scandal,
overture
Dover Beach, for voice
and string quartet
MENOTTI (20)
*Variations on a Theme of
Schumann,* for piano

1932   GOEHR was born

DELIUS (70)
Prelude to Irmelin
MASCAGNI (69)
Pinotta, opera
ROUSSEL (63)
Quartet
ALFVÉN (60)
Spamannen, incidental
music
Vi, incidental music
VAUGHAN WILLIAMS
(60)
Magnificat

RACHMANINOV (59)
Variations on a Theme by
Corelli, for piano
SCHOENBERG (58)
Moses und Aron, opera
CARPENTER (56)
Patterns, for piano and
orchestra
Song of Faith, for chorus
and orchestra
IRELAND (53)
A Downland Suite, for
brass band

CONTINUED

RESPIGHI (53)
Belkis, Queen of Sheba,
    ballet
Mary of Egypt, mystery
    play
Airs and Dances for Lute,
    3rd series
GRAINGER (50)
Blithe Bells
MALIPIERO (50)
Violin Concerto
Sette Invenzione
Inni
STRAVINSKY (50)
Duo concertante, for viola
    and piano
BAX (49)
Cello Concerto
Sinfonietta
A Northern Ballad, for
    orchestra (1932–33)
Piano Sonata No. 4
CASELLA (49)
La Favola d'Orfeo, opera
Sinfonia for clarinet,
    trumpet and piano
SZYMANOWSKI (49)
Violin Concerto No. 2
    (1932–33)
SCHOECK (46)
Praeludium
VILLA-LOBOS (45)
Caixinha de Bôas Festas,
    ballet
IBERT (42)
Donogoo, for orchestra
Paris, symphonic suite
MARTINŮ (42)
Sinfonia for two
    orchestras
Les Rondes
PROKOFIEV (41)
Piano Concerto No. 5

HONEGGER (40)
Mouvement symphonique
    No. 3 (1932–33)
Sonatina for violin and
    cello
MILHAUD (40)
String Quartet No. 8
BENJAMIN (39)
Violin Concerto
MOERAN (38)
Farrago, suite for
    orchestra
HINDEMITH (37)
Philharmonic Concerto
SOWERBY (37)
Piano Concerto No. 2
THOMSON (36)
Quartet No. 2
WEINBERGER (36)
*The Outcasts of Poker
    Flat,* opera
TANSMAN (35)
La Grand Ville, ballet
Two Symphonic
    Movements
HARRIS (34)
Chorale for strings
Fantasy, for piano and
    woodwind quintet
String Sextet
CHÁVEZ (33)
String Quartet No. 2
POULENC (33)
Concerto for two pianos
    and orchestra
Sextet for piano and wind
    (1932–40)
Intermezzo, in D minor
    for piano
Improvisations for piano
    (1932–43)
Le bal masqué, cantata

KHACHATURIAN (29)
String Quartet
Trio for clarinet, violin
  and piano
Violin Sonata
KABALEVSKY (28)
Symphonies Nos. 1 and 2
SHOSTAKOVICH (26)
*From Karl Marx to our
  own days,* symphonic
  poem with voices
Twenty-four Preludes
  for piano (1932–33)
Film music
MESSIAEN (24)
Hymne au Saint

Sacrement, for
  orchestra
*Apparition de l'Église
  Éternelle,* for organ
Fantaisie burlesque, for
  piano
BARBER (22)
Cello Sonata
BRITTEN (19)
Sinfonietta for chamber
  orchestra
Phantasy Quartet, for
  oboe and strings
GOULD (19)
Chorale and Fugue in Jazz

1933   PENDERECKI was born

IPPOLITOV-IVANOV
  (74)
The Last Barricade
  (1933–34)
ROPARTZ (69)
Sérénade champêtre
GLAZUNOV (68)
Epic Poem
VAUGHAN WILLIAMS
  (61)
The Running Set, for
  orchestra
JONGEN (60)
Symphonie concertante,
  for organ and orchestra
*La légende de Saint-
  Nicholas,* for children's
  chorus and orchestra
HOLST (59)
Brook Green, suite for
  strings

Lyric Movement for viola
  and strings
CARPENTER (57)
Sea Drift, symphonic
  poem
IRELAND (54)
Legend, for piano and
  orchestra
BLOCH (53)
Avodath Hakodesh,
  sacred service for
  baritone, chorus and
  orchestra
PIZZETTI (53)
Cello Concerto
  (1933–34)
KODÁLY (51)
Dances of Galantá, for
  orchestra
MALIPIERO (51)
*La favola del figlio
  cambiato,* opera
CONTINUED

STRAVINSKY (51)
Suite italienne, for cello
  and piano
TURINA (51)
Piano Trio
BAX (50)
Sonatina for cello and
  piano
CASELLA (50)
Concerto for violin, cello,
  piano and orchestra
VILLA-LOBOS (46)
Pedra Bonita, ballet
MARTIN (43)
Four Short Pieces for
  guitar
MARTINŮ (43)
The Miracle of Our Lady,
  opera
BLISS (42)
Viola Sonata
PROKOFIEV (42)
Cello Concerto
  (1933–38)
Chant symphonique,
  for orchestra
MILHAUD (41)
Piano Concerto No. 1
BENJAMIN (40)
Prima Donna, comic
  opera
MOORE (40)
String Quartet
PISTON (39)
Concerto for Orchestra
String Quartet No. 1
**CASTELNUOVO-
  TEDESCO** (38)
Sonata for guitar,
  Homage to Boccherini
HANSON (37)
The Merry Mount, opera

TANSMAN (36)
Partita, for string
  orchestra
HARRIS (35)
Symphony No. 1
String Quartet No. 2
CHÁVEZ (34)
Symphony No. 1,
  Sinfonia de Antigona
Soli, No. 1 for oboe,
  clarinet, trumpet and
  bassoon
Cantos de Mexico
POULENC (34)
Feuillets d'album, for
  piano
Villageoises, for piano
COPLAND (33)
Symphony No. 2, *Short
  Symphony*
FINZI (32)
*A Young Man's
  Exhortation*, song cycle
RUBBRA (32)
Bee-Bee-Bei, opera
BERKELEY (30)
Violin Sonata No. 2
  (*c.*1933)
KHACHATURIAN (30)
Symphony No. 1
  (1933–34)
Dance Suite
KABALEVSKY (29)
Symphony No. 3
SHOSTAKOVICH (27)
Concerto No. 1 for piano,
  string orchestra and
  trumpet
The Human Comedy,
  incidental music
  (1933–34)

MESSIAEN (25)
L'Ascension, for organ
Mass for eight sopranos
  and four violins
BARBER (23)
*Music for a Scene from
  Shelley*
CAGE (21)
Sonata for solo clarinet

BRITTEN (20)
A Boy was Born, for
  unaccompanied voices
Friday Afternoons, twelve
  children's songs with
  piano (1933–35)
Two Part-songs for chorus
  and piano

1934 BIRTWISTLE and (MAXWELL) DAVIES
  were born; DELIUS, ELGAR and HOLST
  died

IPPOLITOV-IVANOV
  (75)
Catalan Suite
DELIUS (72)
Songs of Farewell, for
  chorus and orchestra
PIERNÉ (71)
Fragonard, ballet
Giration, ballet
STRAUSS, R. (70)
Symphony for wind
  instruments
ROUSSEL (65)
Symphony No. 4
Sinfonietta for Strings
VAUGHAN WILLIAMS
  (62)
*Fantasia on "Green-
  sleeves"*, for orchestra
Suite for viola and small
  orchestra
SCHOENBERG (60)
Suite in G for strings
RACHMANINOV (61)
*Rhapsody on a Theme by
  Paganini*, for piano and
  orchestra

CARPENTER (58)
Piano Quintet
FALLA (58)
Fanfare for wind and
  percussion
IRELAND (55)
A Comedy Overture, for
  brass band
RESPIGHI (55)
La Fiamma, melodrama
Concerto for oboe, horn,
  violin, double-bass,
  piano and string
  orchestra
BLOCH (54–56)
*A Voice in the
  Wilderness*, symphonic
  poem for cello and
  orchestra (1934–36)
BARTÓK (53)
String Quartet No. 5
KODÁLY (52)
Jesus and the Merchants,
  for chorus and
  orchestra
MALIPIERO (52)
Symphony No. 1
CONTINUED

469

Piano Concerto No. 1
STRAVINSKY (52)
Persephone, for speaker,
  singers, and orchestra
BAX (51)
Symphony No. 6
Concerto for flute, oboe,
  harp and string quartet
Octet for horn, strings
  and piano
Clarinet Sonata
CASELLA (51)
Cello Concerto
  (1934–35)
Notturno e Tarentella,
  for cello
WEBERN (50)
Concerto for nine
  instruments
IBERT (44)
Diane de Poitiers, ballet
Concertino da camera,
  for alto saxophone and
  small orchestra
MARTIN (44)
Piano Concerto No. 1
MARTINŮ (44)
Inventions
BLISS (43)
Things to Come, suite for
  orchestra, from music
  for the film
PROKOFIEV (43)
Lieutenant Kijé,
  symphonic suite with
  baritone ad lib
Egyptian Night,
  symphonic suite
HONEGGER (42)
Sémiramis, ballet
Cello Concerto
String Quartet No. 2
  (1934–36)

MOERAN (40)
Nocturne, for baritone,
  chorus and orchestra
PISTON (40)
Prelude and Fugue for
  organ
HINDEMITH (39)
Mathis der Maler, opera,
  also symphony
ORFF (39)
Bayerische Musik
GERHARD (38)
Ariel, ballet
THOMSON (38)
Four Saints in Three Acts,
  opera
WEINBERGER (38)
A Bed of Roses, opera
GERSHWIN (36)
Cuban Overture
HARRIS (36)
Symphony No. 2
*When Johnny Comes
  Marching Home,*
  overture
Songs for Occupations,
  for chorus
Piano Trio
POULENC (35)
Two Intermezzi for piano
*Presto, Badinage,
  Humoresque,* for piano
Eight *Chansons polonaises*
Four *Chansons pour
  enfants* (1934–35)
COPLAND (34)
Hear Ye! Hear Ye!,
  ballet
Statements, for orchestra
RUBBRA (33)
Sinfonia concertante, for
  piano and orchestra
Rhapsody, for violin

RODRIGO (32)
Cantico de la Esposa, for
   voice and piano
WALTON (32)
Escape Me Never, ballet
   from the film
fp. Symphony No. 1. (first
   three movements only)
BERKELEY (31)
Three pieces for two
   pianos (1934–38)
Polka for piano
SEIBER (29)
Eva Spielt mit Puppen,
   opera
String Quartet No. 2
   (1934–35)
TIPPETT (29)
String Quartet No. 1

SHOSTAKOVICH (28)
Bright Stream, comedy
   ballet
Suite for Jazz Orchestra,
   No. 1
Cello Sonata
Film music
SCHUMAN (24)
Choreographic Poem, for
   seven instruments
CAGE (22)
Six short Inventions for
   seven instruments
BRITTEN (21)
Simple Symphony, for
   string orchestra
Suite for violin and piano
Holiday Diary, for piano
Te Deum
LUTOSLAWSKI (21)
Piano Sonata

1935   MAW was born; BERG, DUKAS,
         IPPOLITOV-IVANOV, LOEFFLER and
         SUK died

PIERNÉ (72)
Images, ballet
MASCAGNI (72)
Nero, opera
STRAUSS, R. (71)
The Silent Woman, opera
Der Friedenstag, opera
   (1935–36)
VAUGHAN WILLIAMS
   (63)
Five Tudor Portraits,
   choral suite
CARPENTER (59)
Danza, for orchestra

FALLA (59)
*Pour le tombeau de Paul
   Dukas,* for piano
BLOCH (55)
Piano Sonata
STRAVINSKY (53)
Concerto for two pianos
TURINA (53)
Serenade, for quartet
BAX (52)
The Morning Watch, for
   chorus and orchestra
Overture to Adventure,
   for orchestra
CONTINUED

WEBERN (52)
Das Augenlicht, for
    chorus and orchestra
Three Lieder
BERG (50)
Violin Concerto
IBERT (45)
Gonzaque, opera
MARTIN (45)
Rhapsody for strings
MARTINŮ (45)
The Suburban Theatre,
    opera
Le Jugement de Paris,
    ballet
Concertino No. 2, for
    piano
BLISS (44)
Music for Strings
PROKOFIEV (44)
Romeo and Juliet, ballet
    (1935–36)
Violin Concerto No. 2
Musiques d'enfants, for
    piano
MILHAUD (43)
Cello Concerto No. 1
String Quartet No. 9
BENJAMIN (42)
Heritage, for orchestra
Romantic Phantasy, for
    violin, viola and
    orchestra
MOORE (42)
White Wings, opera
PISTON (41)
String Quartet No. 2
Piano Trio No. 1
HINDEMITH (40)
Concerto for Orchestra
Viola Concerto, *Der
    Schwanendreher*

ORFF (40)
Carmina Burana, scenic
    cantata (1935–36)
HANSON (39)
Drum Taps, for baritone,
    chorus and orchestra
SESSIONS (39)
Violin Concerto
GERSHWIN (37)
Porgy and Bess, opera
CHÁVEZ (36)
Symphony No. 2,
    Sinfonia India
Obertura Republicana
POULENC (36)
Margot, incidental music
Suite française, for
    chamber orchestra
Cinq poèmes (Eluard)
"A sa guitare" (Ronsard)
ANTHEIL (35)
Dreams, ballet
FINZI (34)
Introit, for violin and
    orchestra (revised
    1945)
DURUFLÉ (33)
Three Dances for
    Orchestra
BERKELEY (32)
Overture for Orchestra
Jonah, oratorio
String Quartet No. 1
*Etude, Berceuse,
    Capriccio,* for piano
How Love Came In, for
    voice and piano
RAWSTHORNE (30)
Viola Sonata (revised
    1954)
SHOSTAKOVICH (29)
Symphony No. 4
    (1935–36)

Five fragments for small
orchestra
MESSIAEN (27)
La nativité du Seigneur,
nine meditations for
organ

SCHUMAN (25)
Symphony No. 1 for
eighteen instruments
DIAMOND (20)
Partita for oboe, bassoon
and piano

1936   BENNETT was born; GERMAN,
GLAZUNOV and RESPIGHI died

STRAUSS, R. (72)
Daphne, opera
GLAZUNOV (71)
Saxophone Concerto
ROUSSEL (67)
Rhapsodie flamande
Concertino for Cello
VAUGHAN WILLIAMS
(64)
Riders to the Sea, one-act
opera
The Poisoned Kiss,
romantic extravaganza,
for voices and orchestra
Dona nobis pacem,
cantata
JONGEN (63)
Triptyque, three suites
for orchestra
RACHMANINOV (63)
Symphony No. 3
SCHOENBERG (62)
Violin Concerto
CARPENTER (60)
Violin Concerto
WOLF-FERRARI (60)
Il campiello, opera
QUILTER (59)
Julia, opera
IRELAND (57)
London Overture, for
orchestra

MEDTNER (56)
Violin Sonata, *Sonata
Epica*
BARTÓK (55)
*Music for Strings,
Percussion and Celesta*
Petite Suite for piano
KODÁLY (54)
Te Deum
MALIPIERO (54)
Julius Caesar, opera
Symphony No. 2,
Elegiaca
BAX (53)
Concerto for bassoon,
harp and string sextet
String Quartet No. 3
WEBERN (53)
Variations for Piano
TAYLOR (51)
Lucrece, for string quartet
VILLA-LOBOS (49)
Bachianas brasilieras,
No. 4, for piano
MARTIN (46)
Symphony for Full
Orchestra (1936–37)
Danse de la peur, for two
pianos and small
orchestra
String Trio

CONTINUED

MARTINŮ (46)
*Juliette: or The Key to
Dreams*, opera
(1936–37)
BLISS (45)
Kenilworth Suite, for
brass
PROKOFIEV (45)
Peter and the Wolf, for
narrator and orchestra
Russian Overture
Cantata for the twentieth
anniversary of the
October Revolution
(1936–37)
HONEGGER (44)
Nocturne
String Quartet No. 3
MILHAUD (44)
Suite provençale
MOORE (43)
The Headless Horseman,
opera
**CASTELNUOVO-
TEDESCO** (41)
Concerto for two guitars
and orchestra
Concertino, for harp and
chamber orchestra
Tarantella
ORFF (41)
Olympischer Reigen
SOWERBY (41)
Organ Concerto No. 1
SESSIONS (40)
String Quartet No. 1
TANSMAN (39)
Viola Concerto
Two Intermezzi
GERSHWIN (38)
Three Preludes for piano
HARRIS (38)
Symphony for Voices

Time Suite, for orchestra
Prelude and Fugue for
string orchestra
Piano Quintet
POULENC (37)
Litanies à la Vierge noire,
for voices and organ
Petites voix, for children's
choir
Seven songs for a cappella
choir
Les soirées de Nazelles,
for piano
ANTHEIL (36)
Course, dance score
COPLAND (36)
El salon Mexico, for
orchestra
FINZI (35)
Interlude, for oboe and
string quartet
Earth, Air and Rain, song
cycle
RUBBRA (35)
Symphony No. 1
BERKELEY (33)
Five short pieces for
piano
KHACHATURIAN (33)
Piano Concerto
KABALEVSKY (32)
Piano Concerto No. 2
ALWYN (31)
*Marriage of Heaven and
Hell*, choral work
LAMBERT (31)
*Summer's Last Will and
Testament*, for chorus
and orchestra
RAWSTHORNE (31)
Concerto for clarinet and
string orchestra

TIPPETT (31)
Piano Sonata (1936-37, revised 1942)
SHOSTAKOVICH (30)
Salute to Spain, incidental music
Four Romances on verses of Pushkin, for bass and piano
Film music
BARBER (26)
Symphony No. 1
Adagio for strings (arranged from String Quartet No. 1)
String Quartet No. 1
SCHUMAN (26)
String Quartet No. 1
MENOTTI (25)
Trio for a Housewarming

Party, for flute, cello and piano
GILLIS (24)
Four Moods in Three Keys, for chamber orchestra
BRITTEN (23)
Our Hunting Fathers, song cycle
Soirées musicales, suite
GOULD (23)
Little Symphony
Symphonette No. 2
DIAMOND (21)
TOM, ballet
Violin Concerto No. 1
Psalm, for orchestra
Concerto for string quartet
Cello Sonata
BERIO (11)
Pastorale

1937   BEDFORD and NILSSON were born; GERSHWIN, PIERNÉ, RAVEL, ROUSSEL and SZYMANOWSKI died

---

PIERNÉ (74)
Gulliver in Lilliput
ROPARTZ (73)
Requiem, with orchestra
BANTOCK (69)
King Solomon
ROUSSEL (68)
String Trio
ALFVÉN (65)
Swedish Rhapsody No. 3, *Dalarapsodi*
VAUGHAN WILLIAMS (65)
Festival Te Deum

SCHOENBERG (63)
String Quartet No. 4
AUBERT (60)
Les fêtes d'été
RESPIGHI (posthumous)
fp. Lucrezia, opera
BRIDGE (58)
String Quartet No. 4
IRELAND (58)
These Things Shall Be, for baritone, chorus and orchestra
Green Ways, for piano

CONTINUED

BLOCH (57)
Violin Concerto (1937–38)
Evocations, symphonic
  suite
ENESCO (56)
Suite villageoise, for
  orchestra
MALIPIERO (55)
Piano Concerto No. 2
Cello Concerto
STRAVINSKY (55)
Jeu de cartes, ballet
BAX (54)
Violin Concerto
A London Pageant, for
  orchestra
Northern Ballad, No. 2
  for orchestra
CASELLA (54)
Concerto for Orchestra
Il deserto tentato,
  oratorio
TAYLOR (52)
Ramuntcho, opera
Casanova, ballet
SCHOECK (51)
Massimilla Doni, opera
VILLA-LOBOS (50)
Currupira, ballet
Sabastiao
*Descobrimento do
  Brasil*, four suites for
  chorus and orchestra
MARTINŮ (47)
Alexandra bis, opera
Comedy on the Bridge,
  opera
IBERT/HONEGGER
  (47/45)
L'Aiglon, opera
BLISS (46)
Checkmate, ballet

GROFÉ (45)
Broadway at Night
Symphony in Steel
MILHAUD (45)
Cantate de la paix
BENJAMIN (44)
*Overture to an Italian
  comedy*, for orchestra
Nightingale Lane, for two
  voices and piano
MOERAN (43)
Symphony in G minor
PISTON (43)
Symphony No. 1
Concertino, for piano and
  chamber orchestra
HINDEMITH (42)
Symphonic Dances, for
  orchestra
Organ Sonatas Nos. 1
  and 2
ORFF (42)
Der Mond, opera
  (1937–38)
THOMSON (41)
Filling Station, ballet
WEINBERGER (41)
Wallenstein, opera
TANSMAN (40)
Bric-a-Brac
Fantasy, for cello
Fantasy, for violin
HARRIS (39)
Symphony No. 3
String Quartet No. 3
POULENC (38)
*Deux marches et un
  intermède*, for chamber
  orchestra
Mass in G major
Sécheresses, cantata
Bourée d'Auvergne, for
  piano

Tel jour telle nuit, songs
RUBBRA (36)
Symphony No. 2
String Quartet
WALTON (35)
Crown Imperial,
 coronation march
In Honour of the City,
 for chorus and
 orchestra
BERKELEY (34)
Domini est terra, for
 chorus and orchestra
Mont Juic, suite of
 Catalan dances for
 orchestra (with Britten)
KHACHATURIAN (34)
Song of Stalin, for chorus
 and orchestra
DALLAPICCOLA (33)
Volo di Notte, opera
 (1937–38)
LAMBERT (32)
Horoscope, ballet
RAWSTHORNE (32)
Theme and Variations,
 for two violins
TIPPETT (32)
A Song of Liberty
SHOSTAKOVICH (31)
Symphony No. 5
MESSIAEN (29)
Poèmes pour Mi, for
 voice and orchestra

BARBER (27)
First Essay for Orchestra
SCHUMAN (27)
Symphony No. 2
String Quartet No. 2
Choral étude
MENOTTI (26)
Amelia al Ballo, opera
GILLIS (25)
The Woolyworm,
 symphonic satire
The Crucifixion, for solo
 voices, narrator, chorus
 and orchestra
The Panhandle, suite
*Thoughts Provoked on
 Becoming a Prospective
 Papa,* suite
BRITTEN (24)
Mont Juic, suite of
 Catalan dances for
 orchestra (with
 Berkeley)
Variations on a Theme
 of Frank Bridge, for
 strings
On This Island, song cycle
GOULD (24)
Piano Concerto
Spirituals for orchestra
DIAMOND (22)
Variations for small
 orchestra
Quintet for flute, string
 trio and piano

1938

STRAUSS, R. (74–76)
The Love of Danae,
 opera (1938–40)

BANTOCK (70)
Aphrodite in Cyprus,
 symphonic ode
 CONTINUED

VAUGHAN WILLIAMS (66)
The Bridal Day, masque
Serenade to Music, for
  sixteen solo voices
  and orchestra
JONGEN (65)
Hymne à la Meuse, for
  chorus and orchestra
GLIÈRE (63)
Harp Concerto
IRELAND (59)
Piano Trio No. 3
PIZZETTI (58–62)
L'Oro, opera (1938–42)
BARTÓK (57)
Violin Concerto No. 2
Sonata for two pianos and
  percussion
Contrasts, for clarinet,
  violin and piano
KODÁLY (56)
Variations on a Hungarian
  Folksong, for orchestra
  (1938–39)
MALIPIERO (56)
Anthony and Cleopatra,
  opera
Triple concerto for violin,
  cello and piano
STRAVINSKY (56)
Dumbarton Oaks,
  concerto for sixteen
  instruments
WEBERN (55)
String Quartet
SCHOECK (52)
Das Schloss Durande,
  opera (1938–39)
VILLA-LOBOS (51)
Bachianas brasilieras Nos.
  3 and 6
String Quartet No. 6

IBERT (48)
La Famille cardinal,
  opera (with Honegger)
Capriccio, for ten
  instruments
MARTIN (48)
*Le Vin herbe (Der
  Zaubertrank),* opera
  (1938–41)
Ballade, for saxophone,
  strings, piano and
  percussion
Sonata da chiesa
MARTINŮ (48)
Concerto for two string
  orchestras, piano and
  timpani
Concerto grosso for
  orchestra
Tre ricercare, for
  orchestra
Quartet No. 5
Madrigals for women's
  voices
BLISS (47)
Piano Concerto
PROKOFIEV (47)
Alexander Nevsky,
  cantata (1938–39)
HONEGGER (46)
La Famille cardinal, opera
  (with Ibert)
La Danse des morts, for
  solo voices, chorus
  and orchestra
Joan of Arc at the stake,
  incidental music
MILHAUD (46)
Medée, opera
BENJAMIN (45)
Two Jamaican pieces for
  orchestra:

CONTINUED

CAGE (26)
Metamorphosis, for piano
GILLIS (26)
The Raven
BRITTEN (25)
Piano Concerto No. 1
   in D major
LUTOSLAWSKI (25)
Symphonic Variations
DIAMOND (23)
Cello Concerto
Music for double string
   orchestra, brass and
   timpani

Heroic Piece, for small
   orchestra
*Elegy in memory of
   Ravel,* for brass, harps
   and percussion
Piano Quartet
SHAPERO (18)
*Three Pieces for Three
   Pieces,* for woodwind
   trio
FOSS (16)
Four two-voice Inventions
   for piano
Three Goethe-Lieder

1939

VAUGHAN WILLIAMS
   (67)
*Five Variants of Dives
   and Lazarus,* for strings
   and harp
JONGEN (66)
Ouverture-Fanfare, for
   orchestra
SCHOENBERG (65)
Kol Nidrei
WOLF-FERRARI (63)
Dama Boba, opera
IRELAND (60)
Concertino pastorale,
   for strings
BARTÓK (58)
Divertimento for Strings
String Quartet No. 6
KODÁLY (57)
Concerto for Orchestra
The Peacock Variations,
   for orchestra
MALIPIERO (57)
Ecuba, opera

BAX (56)
Symphony No. 7
CASELLA (56)
Sinfonia (1939–40)
WEBERN (56)
First Cantata (Jone)
VILLA-LOBOS (52)
New York Skyline, for
   orchestra
MARTIN (49)
Three Ballades, for
   instruments
MARTINŮ (49)
Field Mass
PROKOFIEV (48)
Simeon Kotko, opera
Zdravitsa, cantata
Piano Sonata No. 6
   (1939–40)
Piano Sonata No. 7
   (1939–42)
Piano Sonata No. 8
   (1939–44)

MILHAUD (47)
Symphony No. 1 for full
　orchestra
King René's Chimney,
　for wind quartet
MOORE (46)
*The Devil and Daniel
　Webster*, opera
PISTON (45)
Violin Concerto No. 1
Violin Sonata
**CASTELNUOVO-
　TEDESCO** (44)
Guitar Concerto
Violin Concerto No. 2,
　The Prophets
HINDEMITH (44)
Violin Concerto
SOWERBY (44)
Forsaken of Man, cantata
SESSIONS (43)
Pages from a Diary, for
　piano
KORNGOLD (42)
Die Kathrin, opera
HARRIS (41)
Symphony No. 4
String Quartet
CHÁVEZ (40)
Four nocturnes for voice
　and orchestra
POULENC (40)
Fiançailles pour rire,
　songs
RUBBRA (38)
Symphony No. 3
RODRIGO (37)
Concierto de Aranjuez,
　for guitar and orchestra
WALTON (37)
Violin Concerto
BERKELEY (36)

Serenade for string
　orchestra
Five songs (1939–40)
KHACHATURIAN (36)
Happiness, ballet
Masquerade, incidental
　music
KABALEVSKY (35)
Symphony No. 4
ALWYN (34)
Violin Concerto
Rhapsody, for piano
　quartet
Sonata-Impromptu, for
　violin and viola
RAWSTHORNE (34)
String Quartet No. 1
TIPPETT (34)
*Fantasia on a Theme by
　Handel*, for piano and
　orchestra (1939–41)
A Child of Our Time,
　oratorio (1939–41)
LUTYENS (33)
Three pieces for orchestra
String Trio
SHOSTAKOVICH (33)
Symphony No. 6
Film music
MESSIAEN (31)
Les corps glorieux, for
　organ
BARBER (29)
Violin Concerto
SCHUMAN (29)
*American Festival
　Overture*
Prelude for Voices
String Quartet No. 3
Quartettino, for four
　bassoons

CONTINUED

MENOTTI (28)
The Old Maid and the Thief, opera
CAGE (27)
Imaginary Landscape, No. 1
First Construction (In metal), for percussion sextet
GILLIS (27)
An American Symphony (Symphony No. 1) (1939–40)
BRITTEN (26)
Violin Concerto in D minor (revised 1958)

Canadian Carnival, for orchestra (1939–40)
Ballad of Heroes, for voices and orchestra
Les Illuminations, song cycle
GOULD (26)
Symphonette No. 3
Jericho, for concert band
ARNELL (22)
String Quartet No. 1
SHAPERO (19)
Trumpet Sonata

1940

STRAUSS, R. (76)
Capriccio, opera (1940–41)
VAUGHAN WILLIAMS (68)
Six Choral Songs—to be sung in time of war
Valiant for truth, motet
CARPENTER (64)
Symphony No. 2
FALLA (64)
Homenajes, for orchestra
BRIDGE (61)
Rebus, for orchestra
Vignettes de danse, for small orchestra
Divertimento for flute, oboe, clarinet and bassoon
PIZZETTI (60)
Symphony in A major
MALIPIERO (58)
La vita e'sogno, opera

STRAVINSKY (58)
Symphony in C
WEBERN (57)
Variations for Orchestra
VILLA-LOBOS (53)
Preludes for guitar
Saudades da juventude, Suite I
MARTINŮ (50)
Military March
BLISS (49)
Seven American Poems, for low voice and piano
PROKOFIEV (49)
The Duenna, opera (1940–41)
Cinderella, ballet (1940–44)
MILHAUD (48)
String Quartet No. 10, *Birthday*

BENJAMIN (47)
Sonatina for chamber
  orchestra
PISTON (46)
Chromatic Study for
  Organ
HINDEMITH (45)
Symphony in E♭ major
Cello Concerto No. 2
The Four Temperaments,
  for piano and strings
Harp Sonata
SOWERBY (45)
Symphony No. 3
GERHARD (44)
Don Quixote, ballet
  (1940–41)
ROBERTSON (44)
*Prelude, Scherzo and
  Ricercare,* for orchestra
String Quartet
WEINBERGER (44)
Saxophone Concerto
Song of the High Seas,
  for orchestra
KORNGOLD (43)
Songs of the Clown
Four Shakespeare Songs
HARRIS (42)
Western Landscape, ballet
American Creed, for
  orchestra
Ode to Truth, for
  orchestra
Challenge, for baritone,
  chorus and orchestra
Evening Piece, for
  orchestra
String Quintet
CHÁVEZ (41)
Antigona, ballet
Piano Concerto

Xochipili-Macuilxochitl,
  for Mexican orchestra
POULENC (41)
*Histoire de Babar le
  petit éléphant,* for piano
  and narrator (1940–45)
Mélancolie, for piano
Cello Sonata
Banalities, songs
COPLAND (40)
Quiet City, suite for
  trumpet, English horn
  and strings
FINZI (39)
Dies natalis, cantata
DURUFLÉ (38)
Andante and Scherzo for
  orchestra
WALTON (38)
The Wise Virgins, ballet
BERKELEY (37)
Symphony No. 1
Sonatina for recorder
  and piano
Four Concert Studies,
  Set I, for piano
Five Housman songs, for
  tenor and piano
KHACHATURIAN (37)
Violin Concerto
KABALEVSKY (36)
The Golden Spikes, ballet
The Comedians Suite,
  for small orchestra
ALWYN (35)
Masquerade, overture
Divertimento for solo
  flute
LAMBERT (35)
Dirge, for voices and
  strings

CONTINUED

SEIBER (35)
Besardo Suite No. 1
LUTYENS (34)
Midas, ballet, for string
    quartet and piano
Chamber Concertos Nos.
    1 and 2 (1940–41)
SHOSTAKOVICH (34)
King Lear, incidental
    music
Piano Quintet in G minor
Three pieces for solo
    violin
BARBER (30)
*A Stop-watch and an
    Ordnance Map,* for
    male chorus and
    orchestra
SCHUMAN (30)
Secular Cantata No. 1,
    This is our time
GILLIS (28)
A Symphony of Faith
    (Symphony No. 2)
A Symphony of Free Men
    (Symphony No. 3)
    (1940–41)
*Portrait of a Frontier
    Town*

BRITTEN (27)
Paul Bunyan, operetta
    (1940–41, revised
    1974)
Sinfonia da requiem
Diversions on a Theme,
    for piano (left hand)
    and orchestra
*Seven Sonnets of
    Michelangelo,* for tenor
    and piano
GOULD (27)
*Latin-American
    Symphonette*
A Foster Gallery, for
    orchestra
DIAMOND (25)
Symphony No. 1
Concerto for small
    orchestra
Quartet No. 1
ARNELL (23)
Violin Concerto
SHAPERO (20)
String Quartet
FOSS (18)
Music for *The Tempest*
Two Symphonic Pieces
Four Preludes for flute,
    clarinet and bassoon

1941   BRIDGE and PADEREWSKI died

VAUGHAN WILLIAMS
    (69)
England, My England, for
    baritone, chorus and
    orchestra
JONGEN (68)
Ouverture de fête, for
    orchestra

La Cigale et le fourmi,
    for children's choir
RACHMANINOV (68)
Three Symphonic Dances,
    for orchestra
SCHOENBERG (67)
Variations and Recitative,
    for organ

CARPENTER (65)
Song of Freedom, for
chorus and orchestra
IRELAND (62)
Sarnia, for piano
Three Pastels, for piano
O Happy Land, song
BARTÓK (60)
Concerto for two pianos
and percussion
MALIPIERO (59)
I Capriccio di Callot,
opera (1941–42)
WEBERN (58–60)
Second Cantata (Jone)
(1941–43)
TAYLOR (56)
Processional, for orchestra
MARTIN (51)
Sonata da chiesa, for
flute and string
orchestra
BLISS (50)
String Quartet
PROKOFIEV (50)
War and Peace, opera
(1941–42)
Suite for Orchestra, *1941*
A Summer's Day, suite
for small orchestra
Symphonic March
String Quartet No. 2
HONEGGER (49)
Symphony No. 2 for
strings and trumpet
MILHAUD (49)
Clarinet Concerto
Piano Concerto No. 2
Concerto for two pianos
Four Sketches

MOORE (48)
Village Music, suite for
small orchestra
PISTON (47)
Sinfonietta, for orchestra
ORFF (46)
Die Kluge, opera
(1941–42)
SOWERBY (46)
Poem, for viola with
organ or orchestra
GERHARD (45)
Hommaje a Pedrell,
symphony
SESSIONS (45)
Montezuma, opera
(1941–62)
THOMSON (45)
Symphony No. 2
WEINBERGER (45)
Lincoln Symphony
Czech Rhapsody, for
orchestra
The Bird's Opera, for
orchestra
KORNGOLD (44)
Psalm, for voices and
orchestra
HARRIS (43)
From this Earth, ballet
Acceleration, for
orchestra
Violin Sonata
POULENC (42)
Les animaux modèles,
ballet
La Fille du jardinier,
incidental music
Exultate Deo, for voices
Salve Regina, for voices

CONTINUED

COPLAND (41)
Piano Sonata
RUBBRA (40)
Symphony No. 4
The Morning Watch, for
choir and orchestra
WALTON (39)
Scapino, overture
RAWSTHORNE (36)
The Creel Suite, for piano
duet
SEIBER (36)
Besardo Suite No. 2, for
strings
Pastorale and Burlesque,
for flute and strings
(1941–42)
Transylvanian Rhapsody
Fantasy, for cello and
piano
TIPPETT (36)
String Quartet No. 2
(1941–42)
LUTYENS (35)
Five Intermezzi for Piano
SHOSTAKOVICH (35)
The Gamblers, opera
Symphony No. 7,
Leningrad
MESSIAEN (33)
*Quatuor pour la fin du
temps,* for violin,
clarinet, cello and
piano
SCHUMAN (31)
Symphonies Nos. 3 and 4
Newsreel, suite for
orchestra
CAGE (29)
Double Music, for
percussion

GILLIS (29)
*The Night Before
Christmas,* for narrator
and orchestra
BRITTEN (28)
Scottish Ballad, for two
pianos and orchestra
Matinées musicales, for
orchestra
String Quartet
GOULD (28)
Lincoln Legend
LUTOSLAWSKI (28)
Symphony No. 1
(1941–47)
*Variations on a Theme of
Paganini,* for two
pianos
DIAMOND (26)
The Dream of Audubon,
ballet
ARNELL (24)
String Quartet No. 2
BERNSTEIN (23)
Symphony No. 1,
Jeremiah (1941–44)
Clarinet Sonata
(1941–42)
FRICKER (21)
Three Piano Preludes
(1941–44)
SHAPERO (21)
Nine-minute Overture
Piano Sonata (four
hands)
FOSS (19)
Allegro concertante
Dance Sketch
Duo for cello and piano

ROPARTZ (78)
De Profundis, with
  orchestra
STRAUSS, R. (78)
Horn Concerto No. 2
ALFVÉN (70)
Symphony No. 5
VAUGHAN WILLIAMS
  (70)
Coastal Command,
  orchestral suite
SCHOENBERG (68)
Piano Concerto
GLIÈRE (67)
Concerto for coloratura
  soprano
CARPENTER (66)
Symphony No. 3
IRELAND (63)
Epic March
MEDTNER (62)
Piano Concerto No. 3,
  Ballade (1942–43)
PIZZETTI (62)
Piano Sonata
MALIPIERO (60)
Minnie la candida, opera
STRAVINSKY (60)
Danses concertantes
Norwegian Moods
Polka for Circus
  Elephants
CASELLA (59)
Paganiniana
VILLA-LOBOS (55)
Bachianas brasileiras, No.
  7, for orchestra
String Quartet No. 7

PROKOFIEV (51)
Flute Sonata
Ballad of an Unknown
  Boy, cantata
MARTIN (52)
Die Weise von Liebe und
  Tod des Cornets, for
  voice and orchestra
  (1942–43)
MARTINŮ (52)
Symphony No. 1
MILHAUD (50)
String Quartet No. 11
BENJAMIN (49)
Concerto for oboe and
  strings
MOORE (49)
Quintet for woodwinds
  and horn
MOERAN (48)
Violin Concerto
PISTON (48)
Fanfare for the Fighting
  French
Flute Quintet
Interlude, for viola and
  piano
GERHARD (46)
Violin Concerto
  (1942–45)
SESSIONS (46)
Duo for violin and piano
THOMSON (46)
Canon for Dorothy
  Thomson
The Mayor La Guardia
  Waltzes

CONTINUED

KORNGOLD (45)
Prayer, for tenor, chorus
and orchestra
Tomorrow, song
TANSMAN (45)
Symphony No. 2
HARRIS (44)
What so proudly we hail,
ballet
Symphony No. 5
Piano Concerto, with
band
CHÁVEZ (43)
Toccata for percussion
instruments
POULENC (43)
Violin Sonata (1942–43)
Chansons villageoises
ANTHEIL (42)
Symphony No. 4
COPLAND (42)
Rodeo, ballet
fp. A Lincoln Portrait, for
narrator and orchestra
Danzon Cubano
FINZI (41)
Prelude and Fugue for
string trio
Let us Garlands Bring,
songs
DURUFLÉ (40)
*Prélude et Fugue sur
l'nom Alain,* for organ
RODRIGO (40)
Concierto Heroico, for
piano and orchestra
WALTON (40)
*Prelude and Fugue (The
Spitfire),* for orchestra
BERKELEY (39)
String Quartet No. 2
Sonatina for violin and
piano

KHACHATURIAN (39)
Gayane, ballet
Symphony No. 2
DALLAPICCOLA (38)
Marsia, ballet (1942–43)
Five *Frammente de Saffo*
KABALEVSKY (38)
Before Moscow, opera
People's Avengers, suite
for chorus and
orchestra
Our Great Fatherland,
cantata
ALWYN (37)
Concerto Grosso No. 1
LAMBERT (37)
Aubade héroïque, for
orchestra
RAWSTHORNE (37)
Piano Concerto No. 1
SEIBER (37)
Balaton, opera
La Blanchisseuse, ballet
music
TIPPETT (37)
Two madrigals: *The
Source,* and *The
Windhover*
LUTYENS (36)
Three symphonic preludes
Nine bagatelles for cello
and piano
Two songs (Auden)
SHOSTAKOVICH (36)
Native Leningrad, suite
Piano Sonata No. 2
*Six Romances on verses
of English poets,* for
bass and piano
BARBER (32)
Second Essay for
Orchestra

SCHUMAN (32)
Piano Concerto
Requiescat
Secular Cantata No. 2,
   A Free Song
MENOTTI (31)
The Island God, opera
CAGE (30)
*Wonderful Widow of 18
   Springs,* for voice and
   closed piano
GILLIS (30)
Three Sketches for strings
BRITTEN (29)
A Ceremony of Carols,
   for treble voices and
   harp
Hymn to St. Cecilia, for
   unaccompanied voices

FINE (28)
Music for *Alice in
   Wonderland*
DIAMOND (27)
Symphony No. 2
Concerto for two solo
   pianos
ARNELL (25)
Symphony No. 2
BERNSTEIN (24)
Seven Anniversaries, for
   piano (1942–43)
SHAPERO (22)
Violin Sonata
FOSS (20)
The Prairie, for soloists,
   chorus and orchestra
Clarinet Concerto (later
   arranged as Piano
   Concerto No. 1)

1943   RACHMANINOV died

ROPARTZ (79)
Indiscret, ballet
Petit Symphonie
VAUGHAN WILLIAMS
   (71)
Symphony No. 5
JONGEN (70)
Piano Concerto
SCHOENBERG (69)
Ode to Napoleon, for
   speaker, strings and
   piano
CARPENTER (67)
The Anxious Bugler, for
   orchestra
IRELAND (64)
Fantasy Sonata, for
   clarinet and piano

BARTÓK (62)
Concerto for Orchestra
MALIPIERO (61)
L'allegra brigata, opera
BAX (60)
Work in Progress,
   overture
CASELLA (60)
Concerto for strings,
   piano and percussion
Harp Sonata
TAYLOR (58)
Christmas Overture
MARTIN (53)
*Sechs Monologe aus
   Jedermann,* for voice
   and piano

CONTINUED

MARTINŮ (53)
Symphony No. 2
In Memory of Lidice,
for orchestra
Concerto for two pianos
Violin Concerto
IBERT (53)
String Quartet in C
HONEGGER (51)
Jour de fête suisse, suite
MILHAUD (51)
Bolivar, opera
MOORE (50)
In Memoriam, symphonic
poem
MOERAN (49)
Rhapsody No. 3, for
piano and orchestra
PISTON (49)
Symphony No. 2
Prelude and Allegro, for
organ and strings
Passacaglia, for piano
HINDEMITH (48)
Cupid and Psyche,
overture
*Symphonic
Metamorphoses on
a theme by Weber*
Ludus Tonalis, for
piano
ORFF (48)
Catulli Carmina (revised
version)
HANSON (47)
Symphony No. 4,
Requiem
THOMSON (47)
Flute Sonata
TANSMAN (46)
Symphony No. 6,
In Memoriam
Symphonic études

HARRIS (45)
Cantata for chorus, organ
and brass
Mass for male chorus and
organ
POULENC (44)
Figure humaine, cantata
Metamorphoses, songs
Deux poèmes, songs
Montparnasse, song
COPLAND (43)
Violin Sonata
RODRIGO (41)
Concierto de estio, for
violin and orchestra
WALTON (41)
The Quest, ballet
Henry V, incidental music
BERKELEY (40)
Divertimento for orchestra
String Trio
DALLAPICCOLA (39)
Sex Carmina Alcaei, for
soprano and
instruments
ALWYN (38)
Pastoral Fantasia, for
viola and strings
SEIBER (38)
Fantasia concertante, for
violin and strings
(1943–44)
TIPPETT (38)
Boyhood's End, song
cycle
Plebs angelica, motet for
double chorus
SHOSTAKOVICH (37)
Symphony No. 8
MESSIAEN (35)
Visions de l'Amen, for
two pianos
Rondeau, for piano

SCHUMAN (33)
Symphony No. 5, for
  strings
William Billings, overture
Prayer in Time of War,
  for orchestra
CAGE (31)
She is Asleep, for
  percussion, voice and
  prepared piano
Amores, for prepared
  piano and percussion
Perilous Night, for
  prepared piano
  (1943–44)
GILLIS (31)
Symphony No. 4
Prairie Poem
BRITTEN (30)
Prelude and Fugue for
  strings
Rejoice in the Lamb,
  festival cantata

Serenade, song cycle
GOULD (30)
Symphonies Nos. 1 and 2
Viola Concerto
Interplay, for piano and
  orchestra
Concertette, for viola and
  orchestra
DIAMOND (28)
Quartet No. 2
ARNELL (26)
Symphony No. 1
BERNSTEIN (25)
I Hate Music, five songs
  for soprano
ARNOLD (22)
Beckus the Dandipratt,
  overture
Larch Trees, symphonic
  poem
FOSS (21)
Paradigm, for percussion

1944   TAVENER was born; CHAMINADE and
       SMYTH died

VAUGHAN WILLIAMS
  (72)
Symphony No. 6
  (1944–47)
Concerto for oboe and
  strings
A Song of Thanksgiving,
  for soprano, chorus and
  orchestra
String Quartet No. 2
JONGEN (71)
Bourrée, for orchestra

IRELAND (65)
A Maritime Overture, for
  military band
BLOCH (64)
Suite symphonique
PIZZETTI (64)
Violin Concerto
BARTÓK (63)
Sonata for unaccompanied
  violin
MALIPIERO (62)
Symphony No. 3, *delle
  campane*

CONTINUED

STRAVINSKY (62)
Élégie, for solo viola
Sonata for two pianos
CASELLA (61)
Missa Solemnis, *Pro pace*
BAX (60)
Legend, for orchestra
VILLA-LOBOS (57)
Bachianas brasilieras,
   No. 8, for orchestra
String Quartet No. 8
IBERT (54)
Suite elisabethaine, for
   orchestra
Trio for violin, cello and
   harp
MARTIN (54)
*Petite symphonie
   concertante* (1944–45)
Passacaglia, for organ
In terra pax, oratorio
MARTINŮ (54)
Symphony No. 3
Cello Concerto (1944–45)
BLISS (53)
Miracle in the Gorbals,
   ballet
The Phoenix, march
"Auvergnat" for voice
   and piano
PROKOFIEV (53)
Symphony No. 5
MILHAUD (52)
Symphony No. 2 for full
   orchestra
Suite française
Jeux de printemps
BENJAMIN (51)
Symphony No. 1
   (1944–45)
MOORE (51)
Down East Suite, for

violin with piano or
   orchestra
MOERAN (50)
Overture for a Masque
Sinfonietta
PISTON (50)
Fugue on a Victory Tune
Partita, for violin, viola
   and organ
HINDEMITH (49)
Hérodiade, for speaker
   and chamber orchestra
ORFF (49)
Die Bernauerin (1944–45)
SOWERBY (49)
Classic Concerto, for
   organ and strings
Violin Sonata No. 2
Canticle of the Sun,
   cantata
GERHARD (48)
Alegrias, ballet suite
Pandora, ballet (1944–45)
ROBERTSON (48)
Rhapsody, for piano and
   orchestra
American Serenade, for
   string quartet
SESSIONS (48)
Symphony No. 2
   (1944–45)
THOMSON (48)
Suite No. 1, *Portraits*
Suite No. 2
TANSMAN (47)
Symphony No. 7
Partita, for piano and
   orchestra
Le roi qui jouait le fou
HARRIS (46)
Symphony No. 6
CHÁVEZ (45)
Hija de Colquide, ballet

String Quartet No. 3
POULENC (45)
Les Mamelles de Tiresias,
  opera buffe
La Nuit de la Saint-Jean,
  incidental music
Le Voyageur sans
  baggage, incidental
  music
Un Soir de neige, cantata
COPLAND (44)
Appalachian Spring, ballet
RUBBRA (43)
Soliloquy, for cello and
  orchestra
BERKELEY (41)
"Lord, when the sense of
  Thy sweet grace," for
  mixed chorus and
  orchestra
KHACHATURIAN (41)
Concerto for violin and
  cello
Masquerade Suite
DALLAPICCOLA (40)
Il Prigioniero, opera
  (1944–48)
Due liriche de Anacreonte
  (1944–45)
KABALEVSKY (40)
The Family of Taras,
  opera (*c.*1944)
RAWSTHORNE (39)
Street Corner Overture
SEIBER (39)
Notturno, for horn and
  strings
TIPPETT (39)
Symphony No. 1
  (1944–45)
"The Weeping Babe",
  motet

LUTYENS (38)
Suite gauloise, for small
  orchestra
SHOSTAKOVICH (38)
Russian River, suite
Eight English and
  American Folksongs,
  for low voice and
  orchestra
Piano Trio No. 2
String Quartet No. 2
Children's Notebook, for
  piano
Film music
MESSIAEN (36)
Vingt regards sur l'enfant
  Jésus, for piano
BARBER (34)
Symphony No. 2 (revised
  1947)
Capricorn Concerto, for
  flute, oboe, trumpet and
  strings
Excursions, for piano
SCHUMAN (34)
Circus, overture
Te Deum
MENOTTI (33)
Sebastian, ballet
CAGE (32)
A Book of Music, for two
  prepared pianos
Three Dances for two
  amplified prepared
  pianos (1944–45)
GILLIS (32)
Symphony No. 5
  (1944–45)
A Short Overture to an
  Unwritten Opera
The Alamo, symphonic
  poem

CONTINUED

BRITTEN (31)
Festival Te Deum
GOULD (31)
Concerto for Orchestra
FINE (30)
The Choral New Yorker,
  cantata
DIAMOND (29)
The Tempest, incidental
  music
Rounds, for string
  orchestra
ARNELL (27)
Symphony No. 3
BERNSTEIN (26)
Fancy Free, ballet
On the Town, dance
  episodes

FRICKER (24)
Piano Prelude
SHAPERO (24)
Three amateur sonatas,
  for piano
ARNOLD (23)
Horn Concerto
*Variations on a Ukrainian
  Folksong*, for piano
FOSS (22)
The Heart Remembers,
  ballet
Within These Walls,
  ballet
Symphony
Ode

1945 BARTÓK and MASCAGNI died, WEBERN
  was accidentally shot dead

STRAUSS, R. (81)
Metamorphoses, for
  twenty-three solo
  instruments
Oboe Concerto
VAUGHAN WILLIAMS
  (75)
Story of a Flemish Farm,
  orchestral suite
SCHOENBERG (71)
Prelude to a *Genesis* suite
CARPENTER (69)
The Seven Ages, for
  orchestra
BLOCH (65)
String Quartet No. 2
BARTÓK (64)
Piano Concerto No. 3
Viola Concerto

KODÁLY (63)
Missa Brevis
STRAVINSKY (63)
*Symphony in Three
  Movements*
BAX (62)
Legend-Sonata, for cello
  and piano
TAYLOR (60)
Elegy, for orchestra
SCHOECK (59)
Sommernacht
Suite in A for strings
VILLA-LOBOS (58)
Piano Concerto No. 1
Bachianas brasilieras,
  Nos. 5 and 9
Fantasia for cello

MARTIN (55)
Golgotha, oratorio
(1945–48)
MARTINŮ (55)
Symphony No. 4
Thunderbolt P-47
BLISS (54)
Baraza, concert piece for
piano and orchestra,
with men's voices ad lib
PROKOFIEV (54)
Symphony No. 6
(1945–47)
Piano Sonata No. 9
(1945–47)
MILHAUD (53)
The Bells, ballet
Cello Concerto No. 2
String Quartet No. 12,
In memory of Fauré
BENJAMIN (52)
From San Domingo, for
orchestra
Red River Jig, for
orchestra
Elegy, Waltz and Toccata,
for viola and orchestra
MOORE (52)
Symphony in A major
MOERAN (51)
Cello Concerto
PISTON (51)
Sonata for violin and
harpsichord
HINDEMITH (50)
Piano Concerto
JACOB (50)
Symphony No. 2
Clarinet Concerto
ORFF (50)
Astutuli (1945–46)

SOWERBY (50)
Trumpet Sonata
GERHARD (49)
The Duenna, opera
(1945–47)
HANSON (49)
Serenade for flute, strings,
harp and orchestra
ROBERTSON (49)
Punch and Judy, overture
KORNGOLD (48)
Violin Concerto
String Quartet No. 3
TANSMAN (48)
Concertino, for guitar and
orchestra
HARRIS (47)
Piano Concerto No. 1
CHÁVEZ (46)
Piramide
POULENC (46)
Le Soldat et la sorcière,
incidental music
Chansons françaises, for
choir
FINZI (44)
Farewell to Arms, for
tenor and small
orchestra
BERKELEY (42)
Piano Sonata
Violin Sonata
Six piano preludes
Festival Anthem, for
mixed choir and organ
KHACHATURIAN (42)
Solemn Overture *To the
End of the War*
DALLAPICCOLA (41)
Ciaccona, Intermezzo e
Adagio, for cello
CONTINUED

ALWYN (40)
Concerto for oboe, harp
 and strings
RAWSTHORNE (40)
Cortèges, fantasy overture
SEIBER (40)
Phantasy, for flute, horn
 and strings
TIPPETT (40)
String Quartet No. 3
 (1945–46)
LUTYENS (39)
Chamber Concerto No. 3
Five Little Pieces for
 Clarinet and Piano
SHOSTAKOVICH (39)
Symphony No. 9
Two songs
Film music
BARBER (35)
Cello Concerto
SCHUMAN (35)
Undertow, ballet
MENOTTI (34)
Piano Concerto in A
 minor
GILLIS (33)
To an Unknown Sailor,
 symphonic poem

BRITTEN (32)
Peter Grimes, opera
String Quartet No. 2
*The Holy Sonnets of
 John Donne,* for voice
 and piano
GOULD (32)
Harvest, for vibraphone,
 harp and strings
Ballad, for band
DIAMOND (30)
Symphonies Nos. 3 and 4
ARNELL (28)
String Quartet No. 3
BERNSTEIN (27)
Hashkivenu, for voices
 and organ
SHAPERO (25)
Serenade, for string
 orchestra
FOSS (23)
Song of Anguish, for
 voice and piano, or
 orchestra
MENNIN (22)
Concertino for flute,
 strings and percussion

1946 FALLA died

VAUGHAN WILLIAMS
 (74)
Partita, for double string
 orchestra (1946–48)
Introduction and Fugue
 for two pianos
DOHNÁNYI (69)
Piano Concerto No. 2

QUILTER (69)
Tulips, for chorus and
 orchestra
IRELAND (67)
fp. Satyricon Overture
BLOCH (66–68)
Concerto symphonique,
 for piano

MALIPIERO (64)
Symphony No. 4,
In Memoriam
STRAVINSKY (64)
Ebony Concerto, for
clarinet and orchestra
Concerto in D for strings
BAX (63)
Te Deum
Gloria
MARTIN (56)
Overture to Racine's
Athalie
BLISS (55)
Adam Zero, ballet
HONEGGER (54)
Symphony No. 3,
Liturgique
Symphony No. 4,
Deliciae basiliensis
MILHAUD (54)
Symphony No. 3, *Hymnus
ambrosianus*
Piano Concerto No. 3
Violin Concerto No. 2
String Quartet No. 13
BENJAMIN (53)
Caribbean Dance, for
orchestra
MOORE (53)
Quintet for clarinet and
strings
MOERAN (52)
Fantasy Quartet for oboe
and strings
PISTON (52)
Divertimento, for nine
instruments
HINDEMITH (51)
*When Lilacs in the
Dooryard Bloomed*,
requiem

SESSIONS (50)
Piano Sonata No. 2
KORNGOLD (49)
The silent serenade,
comedy with music
Cello Concerto
HARRIS (48)
Accordion Concerto
Concerto for two pianos
POULENC (47)
Two songs
COPLAND (46)
Symphony No. 3
BERKELEY (43)
Nocturne for orchestra
Introduction and Allegro
for solo violin
Five songs
RUBBRA (43)
Missa cantauriensis, for
double choir
DALLAPICCOLA (42)
Two pieces for orchestra
(1946–47)
ALWYN (41)
Suite of Scottish Dances
RAWSTHORNE (41)
Prisoner's March, for
orchestra
TIPPETT (41)
Little Music, for strings
SHOSTAKOVICH (40)
String Quartet No. 3
BARBER (36)
*Medea: the Cave of the
Heart,* ballet
MENOTTI (35)
The Medium, opera
CAGE (34)
Sonatas and Interludes for
Prepared Pianos
(1946–48)

CONTINUED

GILLIS (34)
Symphony No. 5½,
  Symphony for Fun
  (1946–47)
BRITTEN (33)
The Rape of Lucretia,
  opera
Variations and Fugue on
  a Theme of Purcell
  *(A Young Person's
  Guide to the Orchestra)*
GOULD (33)
Minstrel Show, for
  orchestra
Symphony No. 3
FINE (32)
Fantasia, for string trio
Violin Sonata
DIAMOND (31)
Quartet No. 3
Violin Sonata
ARNELL (29)
Piano Concerto
Piano Trio
BERNSTEIN (28)
Facsimile, ballet
FRICKER (26)
Four Fughettas for two
  pianos

ARNOLD (25)
Symphony for strings
SHAPEY (25)
String Quartet No. 1
Piano Sonata
FOSS (24)
Song of Songs, for voice
  and orchestra
Composer's Holiday, for
  violin and piano
MENNIN (23)
Symphony No. 3
BOULEZ (21)
Piano Sonata No. 1
Sonatina for flute and
  piano
Le Visage nuptial, for
  voices and chamber
  orchestra
BERIO (21)
Four Popular Songs
  (1946–47)
HENZE (20)
Chamber concerto, for
  solo piano, solo flute
  and strings
Sonata for violin and
  piano

1947 CASELLA died

ROPARTZ (83)
Divertissement No. 2
SCHOENBERG (73)
A Survivor from Warsaw,
  cantata
AUBERT (70)
Offrande
KODÁLY (65)
Viola Concerto
String Quartet

MALIPIERO (65)
Symphony No. 5,
  Concertante in eco
Symphony No. 6, *degli
  archi*
STRAVINSKY (65)
Orpheus, ballet
BAX (64)
Two Fanfares for the
  Wedding of Princess

Elizabeth and Prince Philip
Morning Song, for piano and small orchestra
Epithalamium, for chorus and organ
SCHOECK (61)
Cello Concerto
MARTIN (57)
Trois chants de Noël, for voice, flute and piano
MARTINŮ (57)
Quartet No. 7
PROKOFIEV (56)
The Story of a Real Man, opera (1947–48)
MILHAUD (55)
Symphony, *1848*
Concerto for marimba and vibraphone
BENJAMIN (54)
Ballade for strings
MOORE (54)
Farm Journal, suite for chamber orchestra
PISTON (53)
Symphony No. 3
String Quartet No. 3
HINDEMITH (52)
Symphonia serena (possibly 1946)
Clarinet Concerto
ORFF (52)
Antigone, opera (1947–48)
SOWERBY (52)
Symphony No. 4
ROBERTSON (51)
Trilogy, for orchestra
SESSIONS (51)
fp. The Trial of Lucullus, opera

THOMSON (51)
The Seine at Night, for orchestra
The Mother of us all, opera
KORNGOLD (50)
Symphonic Serenade, for strings
Five songs for middle voice
TANSMAN (50)
Music for Orchestra
Isaiah the Prophet
HARRIS (49)
Quest, for orchestra
POULENC (48)
Flute Sonata
ANTHEIL (47)
Symphony No. 5 (1947–48)
FINZI (46)
Ode for St. Cecilia's Day (possibly 1950)
RUBBRA (46)
Festival Overture
Symphony No. 5 (1947–48)
Cello Sonata
DURUFLÉ (45)
Requiem, for solo voices, chorus, organ and orchestra
RODRIGO (45)
Four *Madrigales amatorias,* for voice and piano
WALTON (45)
Hamlet, incidental music
String Quartet in A minor
BERKELEY (44)
Piano Concerto
Four Poems of St. Teresa
CONTINUED

499

of Avila, for contralto
and orchestra
Stabat Mater
"The Lowlands of
Holland", for voice and
piano
KHACHATURIAN (44)
Symphonie-Poème
ALWYN (42)
Manchester Suite, for
orchestra
Piano Sonata
Three songs (Louis
MacNiece)
RAWSTHORNE (42)
Concerto for oboe and
string orchestra
TIPPETT (42)
*The Midsummer
Marriage,* opera
LUTYENS (41)
The Pit, dramatic scene
for voices and orchestra
Viola Concerto
Chamber Concertos Nos.
4 and 5
SHOSTAKOVICH (41)
Violin Concerto No. 1
(1947–48)
Poem of the Motherland,
cantata
Film music
MESSIAEN (39)
Turangalîla, symphony
BARBER (37)
*Knoxville: Summer of
1915,* ballet suite for
voice and orchestra
SCHUMAN (37)
Night Journey, ballet
Violin Concerto
MENOTTI (36)
The Telephone, opera

Errand into the Maze,
ballet
GILLIS (35)
Symphony No. 6
Dude Ranch
Three Short Pieces, for
strings
BRITTEN (34)
Albert Herring, opera
Canticle No. 1, "My
beloved is mine"
Prelude and Fugue for
organ
GOULD (34)
Fall River Legend, ballet
DIAMOND (32)
Romeo and Juliet,
incidental music
Violin Concerto No. 2
Piano Sonata
ARNELL (30)
Punch and the Child,
ballet
Harpsichord Concerto
BERNSTEIN (29)
Symphony No. 2, *The
Age of Anxiety,* for
piano and orchestra
(1947–49)
Five Pieces for Piano
(1947–48)
FRICKER (27)
Wind Quintet
String Quartet in one
movement
Sonata for Organ
*Three Sonnets of Cecco
Angiolier,* for tenor
and seven instruments
Two Madrigals
SHAPERO (27)
Piano Sonata No. 1

ARNOLD (26)
Violin Sonata
Viola Sonata
Children's Suite, for piano
SHAPEY (26)
Piano Quintet
FOSS (25)
String Quartet
MENNIN (24)
Fantasia for String
  Orchestra
BERIO (22)
Petite Suite for piano
BOULEZ (22)
Soleil des eaux, for voices
  and orchestra

Piano Sonata No. 2
  (1947–48)
HENZE (21)
Symphony No. 1 (first
  version)
Violin Concerto No. 1
Concertino for piano and
  wind orchestra with
  percussion
String Quartet No. 1
Five Madrigals for small
  mixed choir and eleven
  solo instruments

1948 GIORDANO, LEHÁR and WOLF-FERRARI
       died

STRAUSS, R. (84)
Duet concertino, for
  clarinet, bassoon and
  strings
CARPENTER (72)
Carmel Concerto
AUBERT (71)
*Le Tombeau de
  Chateaubriande*
QUILTER (71)
The Sailor and His Lass,
  for soloist, chorus and
  orchestra
KODÁLY (66)
Czinka Panna, opera
MALIPIERO (66)
Mondi celeste e infernali,
  opera (1948–49)
Symphony No. 7, *delle
  canzoni*
Piano Concerto No. 3

STRAVINSKY (66)
Mass, for chorus and
  double wind quintet
MARTIN (58)
Ballade, for cello and
  piano
Eight piano preludes
MARTINŮ (58)
Piano Concerto No. 3
BLISS (57)
The Olympians, opera
  (1948–49)
PROKOFIEV (57)
The Stone Flower, ballet
  (1948–53)
MOORE (55)
*The Emperor's New
  Clothes,* opera for
  children
MOERAN (54)
Serenade in G major
CONTINUED

PISTON (54)
Toccata, for orchestra
Suite No. 2 for orchestra
HINDEMITH (53)
Concerto for trumpet,
  bassoon and strings
Septet for wind
  instruments
HANSON (52)
Piano Concerto
ROBERTSON (52)
Violin Concerto
THOMSON (52)
Wheatfield at Noon, for
  orchestra
*Acadian Songs and
  Dances*
TANSMAN (51)
Music for Strings
HARRIS (50)
Elegy and Paean, for
  viola and orchestra
CHÁVEZ (49–51)
Violin Concerto
  (1948–50, revised
  1962)
POULENC (49)
*Quatre petites prières
  (St. Francis),* for choir
ANTHEIL (48)
McKonkey's Ferry,
  overture
Symphony No. 6
Serenade, for string
  orchestra
Piano Sonata No. 4
Songs of Experience, for
  voice and piano
COPLAND (48)
Concerto for clarinet and
  strings, with harp and
  piano

RUBBRA (47)
The Buddha, suite for
  flute, oboe, violin, viola
  and cello
RODRIGO (46)
Ausencias de Dulcinea,
  for bass, four sopranos
  and orchestra
BERKELEY (45)
Concerto for two pianos
  and orchestra
DALLAPICCOLA (44)
*Quattro liriche di
  Antonio Machado,* for
  soprano and piano
KABALEVSKY (44)
Violin Concerto
ALWYN (43)
Three Winter Poems, for
  string quartet
RAWSTHORNE (43)
Violin Concerto No. 1
Clarinet Quartet
SEIBER (43)
Johnny Miner, radio
  opera
String Quartet No. 3,
  Quartetto lyrico
  (1948–51)
TIPPETT (43)
Suite in D major
LUTYENS (42)
Chamber Concerto No. 6
Three Improvisations,
  for piano
Aptote, for solo violin
Nine songs
SHOSTAKOVICH (42)
From Jewish Folk Poetry,
  song cycle
Film music
BARBER (38)
String Quartet No. 2

Piano Sonata
SCHUMAN (38)
Symphony No. 6
GILLIS (36)
Saga of a Prairie School
BRITTEN (35)
St. Nicholas, for voices
   and instruments
GOULD (35)
Serenade of Carols
FINE (34)
Toccata concertante
Partita for wind quintet
DIAMOND (33)
Chaconne, for violin and
   piano
ARNELL (31)
Symphony No. 4
BERNSTEIN (30)
Four Anniversaries, for
   piano
FRICKER (28)
Symphony No. 1
Rondo Scherzoso, for
   orchestra
SHAPERO (28)
*Symphony for Classical
   Orchestra*
The Travellers, for
   orchestra
ARNOLD (27)
Festival Overture
The Smoke, overture

Symphonic Suite
Sonatina for flute and
   piano
FOSS (26)
Oboe Concerto
Ricordare, for orchestra
Capriccio, for cello and
   piano
HAMILTON (26)
Symphonic Variations for
   string orchestra
Quintet for clarinet and
   string quartet
HENZE (22)
The Magic Theatre,
   opera
*Chorus of the Captured
   Trojans,* for chorus and
   orchestra
Chamber Sonata, for
   piano, violin and cello
   (revised 1963)
*Lullaby of the Blessed
   Virgin,* for boys' choir
   and instruments
The Reproach, concert
   aria for voice and
   instruments
*Whispers from the
   Heavenly Death,*
   cantata
KORTE (20)
String Quartet No. 1

1949 STRAUSS, R. and TURINA died

VAUGHAN WILLIAMS
   (77)
Fantasia (quasi

*variazione) on "Old
   104th",* for piano,
   chorus and orchestra

CONTINUED

An Oxford Elegy, for
  speaker, chorus and
  small orchestra
*Folksongs of the Four
  Seasons,* cantata
SCHOENBERG (75)
Fantasia, for violin and
  piano
QUILTER (72)
Love at the Inn, opera
BLOCH (69)
Scherzo fantasque, for
  piano
PIZZETTI (69)
Vanna Lupa, opera
IBERT (59)
*Étude-Caprice, pour un
  Tombeau de Chopin,*
  for solo cello
MARTIN (59)
Concerto for seven wind
  instruments
PROKOFIEV (58)
Winter Bonfire, suite for
  narrator, boys' chorus
  and orchestra
  (1949–50)
Cello Sonata
HONEGGER (57)
Concerto da camera
MILHAUD (57)
Piano Concerto No. 4
String Quartets Nos. 14
  and 15 (can be played
  together as octet)
BENJAMIN (56)
The Tale of Two Cities,
  opera (1949–50)
Valses Caprices, for
  clarinet and piano
PISTON (55)
Piano Quintet
Duo for violin and cello

HINDEMITH (54)
Horn Concerto
Concerto for woodwind,
  harp and orchestra
Organ Sonata No. 2
SOWERBY (54)
Ballade, for English horn
  and strings
THOMSON (53)
Cello Concerto
TANSMAN (52)
Ricercari
Tombeau de Chopin, for
  strings
HARRIS (51)
Kentucky Spring, for
  orchestra
POULENC (50)
Piano Concerto
FINZI (48)
Clarinet Concerto
Before and After Summer,
  song cycle
RODRIGO (47)
Concierto galante, for
  cello and orchestra
WALTON (47)
Violin Sonata
BERKELEY (46)
Colonus' Praise, for
  chorus and orchestra
Three Mazurkas for piano
Scherzo for piano
DALLAPICCOLA (45)
Job, mystery play
  (1949–50)
Tre poemi, for soprano
  and chamber orchestra
KABALEVSKY (45)
Cello Concerto
ALWYN (44)
Symphony No. 1

RAWSTHORNE (44)
Concerto for string
  orchestra
Cello Sonata
SEIBER (44)
Andantino and pastorale,
  for clarinet and piano
Ulysses, cantata
  (possibly 1946–47)
LUTYENS (43)
String Quartet No. 3
SHOSTAKOVICH (43)
Ballet Suite No. 1, for
  orchestra
String Quartet No. 4
The Song of the Forests,
  oratorio
Film music
SCHUMAN (39)
Judith, ballet
BRITTEN (36)
*The Little Sweep (Let's
  Make an Opera)*
Spring Symphony, for
  voices and orchestra
A Wedding Anthem, for
  voices and organ
LUTOSLAWSKI (36)
Overture for Strings
FINE (35)
The Hourglass, choral
  cycle
DIAMOND (34)
Timon of Athens,
  symphonic portrait
L'âme de Debussy, song
  cycle
BERNSTEIN (31)
La bonne cuisine, song
  cycle
Two love songs

ROCHBERG (31)
Symphony No. 1
Night Music, for chamber
  orchestra
FRICKER (29)
Concerto for violin and
  small orchestra, No. 1
  (1949–50)
Prelude, Elegy and Finale,
  for string orchestra
ARNOLD (28)
Clarinet Concerto
SHAPEY (28)
String Quartet No. 2
*Three Essays on Thomas
  Wolfe,* for piano
FOSS (27)
*The Jumping Frog of
  Calaveras County*
  opera
Piano Concerto No. 2
HAMILTON (27)
Symphony No. 1
String Quartet No. 1
MENNIN (26)
Symphony No. 4, *The
  Cycle,* for choir and
  orchestra
The Christmas Story,
  cantata
BERIO (24)
Magnificat
BOULEZ (24)
Livre pour cordes, for
  string orchestra
Livre pour quatuor, for
  string quartet
HENZE (23)
Ballet Variations
Jack Pudding, ballet
Symphony No. 2

Symphony No. 3
  (1949–50)
Apollo et Hyazinthus, for
  harpsichord, contralto
and eight solo
  instruments
Variations for piano
Serenade, for solo cello

1950   CILÈA and MOERAN died

STRAUSS, R.
  (posthumous)
Four Last Songs
VAUGHAN WILLIAMS
  (78)
Concerto grosso, for
  string orchestra
The Sons of Light, cantata
*Sun, Moon, Stars and
  Man,* song cycle
DOHNÁNYI (73)
Twelve studies for piano
BLOCH (70)
Concertino for viola, flute
  and strings
PIZZETTI (70)
Ifigenia, opera
ENESCO (69)
Vox Maris, symphonic
  poem
MALIPIERO (68)
Symphony in one
  movement
Piano Concerto No. 4
BAX (67)
Concertante for orchestra
  with piano (left hand)
TAYLOR (65)
Restoration Suite, for
  orchestra
MARTIN (60)
Violin Concerto
  (1950–51)
Five Ariel Songs, for
  chamber choir

BLISS (59)
String Quartet No. 2
PROKOFIEV (59)
Sinfonia concertante, for
  cello and orchestra
  (reworking of the
  1933–38 cello
  concerto)
MOORE (57)
Giants in the Earth, opera
PISTON (56)
Symphony No. 4
HINDEMITH (55)
Sinfonietta
*Requiem for Those we
  Love* (possibly 1946)
JACOB (55)
Sinfonietta in D major
A Goodly Heritage,
  cantata
ORFF (55)
Trionfo di Afrodite
SOWERBY (55)
Christ Reborn, cantata
GERHARD (54)
Impromptus for piano
TANSMAN (53)
Phèdre, ballet
POULENC (51)
Stabat Mater
ANTHEIL (50)
Volpone, opera
COPLAND (50)
Piano Quartet
Twelve Poems of Emily

Dickinson, for voice
and piano
FINZI (49)
*Intimations of
Immortality,* for tenor,
chorus and orchestra
BERKELEY (47)
Sinfonietta for orchestra
Elegy for violin and piano
Toccata for violin and
piano
Theme and Variations for
solo violin
KHACHATURIAN (47)
Cello Concerto
LAMBERT (45)
Tiresias, ballet
RAWSTHORNE (45)
Symphony No. 1
TIPPETT (45)
Heart's Assurance, song
cycle
LUTYENS (44)
Concertante, for five
players
SHOSTAKOVICH (44)
Two Romances on verse
by Mikhail Lermontov,
for voice and piano
Twenty-four Preludes and
Fugues for piano
Film music
MESSIAEN (42)
Le merle noir, for piano
and flute
Messe de la Pentecôte
SCHUMAN (40)
String Quartet No. 4
MENOTTI (39)
The Consul, opera

CAGE (38)
String Quartet in Four
Parts
BRITTEN (37)
Lachrymae, for viola and
piano
Five Flower Songs, for
unaccompanied chorus
GOULD (37)
Family Album, for
orchestra
LUTOSLAWSKI (37)
Concerto for Orchestra
(1950–54)
DIAMOND (35)
Piano Concerto
Chorale, for chorus
Quintet for two violas,
two cellos, and clarinet
ARNELL (33)
Symphony No. 5
String Quintet
BERNSTEIN (32)
Prelude, Fugue and Riffs,
for jazz combo and
orchestra
FRICKER (30)
Symphony No. 2
(1950–51)
Concertante No. 1, for
English horn and
strings
Violin Sonata
Four Impromptus
(1950–52)
ARNOLD (29)
Symphony No. 1
Serenade for small
orchestra
Eight English Dances

CONTINUED

String Quartet No. 1
  (possibly 1946)
SHAPEY (29)
Violin Sonata
HAMILTON (28)
Clarinet Concerto
MENNIN (27)
Symphony No. 5
Violin Concerto
Canto and Toccata, for
  piano
Five Pieces for Piano
BERIO (25)
Concertino for solo
  clarinet, solo violin,
  harp, celeste and strings

Opus Number Zoo, for
  woodwind quintet and
  narrator (revised
  1970)
HENZE (24)
Rosa Silber, ballet
Piano Concerto No. 1
Symphonic Variations,
  for piano and orchestra
STOCKHAUSEN (22)
Chore für Doris, for choir
Choral, for choir
Three Lieder, for voice
  and chamber orchestra

1951 LAMBERT, MEDTNER and SCHOENBERG
       died

VAUGHAN WILLIAMS
  (79)
Pilgrim's Progress, for
  soloists, chorus and
  orchestra
Romance in Db, for
  harmonica
SCHOENBERG (77)
De Profundis, for
  a cappella choir
BLOCH (71)
Cinq Pièces hébraïques
String Quartet No. 3
  (1951–52)
MALIPIERO (69)
Sinfonia del zodiaco
STRAVINSKY (69)
The Rake's Progress,
  opera
Mass, for horns and
  orchestra

SCHOECK (65)
Horn Concerto
Festlichen Hymnus
IBERT (61)
Sinfonia concertante
MARTIN (61)
Concerto for cembalo
  and small orchestra
  (1951–52)
PROKOFIEV (60)
Symphony No. 7
  (1951–52)
HONEGGER (59)
Symphony No. 5, *Di
  Tre Re*
Monopartita, for orchestra
MILHAUD (59)
*The Seven-branched
  candelabra*
BENJAMIN (58)
Orlando's Silver Wedding,
  ballet

PISTON (57)
String Quartet No. 4
HINDEMITH (56)
Die Harmonie der Welt,
  symphony
JACOB (56)
Concerto for Flute
Fantasia on Songs of the
  British Isles
SOWERBY (56)
Concert Piece, for organ
  and orchestra
GERHARD (55)
Concerto for piano and
  strings
HANSON (55)
*Fantasia on a Theme of
  youth,* for piano and
  strings
SESSIONS (55)
String Quartet No. 2
THOMSON (55)
*Five Songs of William
  Blake,* for baritone
  and orchestra
KORNGOLD (54)
Symphony in F♯ major
TANSMAN (54)
Symphony No. 8
HARRIS (53)
Cumberland Concerto,
  for orchestra
Symphony No. 7
CHÁVEZ (52)
Symphony No. 3
ANTHEIL (51)
*Eight Fragments from
  Shelley,* for chorus
COPLAND (51)
Pied Piper, ballet
RUBBRA (50)
Festival Te Deum

String Quartet No. 2
BERKELEY (48)
Gibbons Variations, for
  voices, strings and
  organ
Three Greek songs, for
  voice and piano
DALLAPICCOLA (47)
Canti di Liberazione,
  for chorus and
  orchestra (1951–55)
ALWYN (46)
Concerto Grosso No. 2
Festival March
RAWSTHORNE (46)
Piano Concerto No. 2
Concertante pastorale,
  for flute, horn and
  strings
SEIBER (46)
Concertino for clarinet
  and strings
The Seasons
LUTYENS (45)
Penelope, music drama
Requiem for the Living
Nativity, for soprano and
  strings, or organ
SHOSTAKOVICH (45)
Ballet Suite No. 2, for
  orchestra
Ten poems on texts by
  revolutionary poets,
  for chorus
Film music
MENOTTI (40)
*Amahl and the Night
  Visitors,* opera
Apocalypse, for orchestra
CAGE (39)
Concerto for prepared

CONTINUED

piano and chamber
orchestra
Imaginary Landscape,
No. 4
Music of Changes, for
piano
BRITTEN (38)
Billy Budd, opera
*Six Metamorphoses after
Ovid,* for solo oboe
GOULD (38)
*The Battle Hymn of the
Republic*
LUTOSLAWSKI (38)
Little Suite, for
orchestra
Silesian Triptych, for
voice and orchestra
DIAMOND (36)
Symphony No. 6
Quartet No. 4
Piano Trio
Mizmor L'David, for
voices, organ and
orchestra
The Midnight Meditation,
song cycle
ARNELL (34)
Harlequin in April, ballet
String Quartet No. 4
BERNSTEIN (33)
"Afterthought", song
FRICKER (31)
Canterbury Prologue,
ballet
Viola Concerto
Concertante No. 2, for
three pianos, strings
and timpani
SHAPERO (31–38)
Concerto for Orchestra
(1951-58)

ARNOLD (30)
Sussex, overture
Concerto for piano duet
and strings
Sonatina for clarinet and
piano
Sonatina for oboe and
piano
SHAPEY (30)
Fantasy, for orchestra
String Quartet No. 3
Cantata
HAMILTON (29)
Clerk Saunders, ballet
Symphony No. 2
Flute Quartet
Piano Sonata (revised
1971)
MENNIN (28)
Canzona, for band
BERIO (26)
Two Pieces for Violin and
Piano
BOULEZ (26)
fp. Polyphonie X, for
eighteen instruments
HENZE (25)
Boulevard Solitude, lyric
drama
A Country Doctor, radio
opera
Labyrinth, choreographic
fantasy
The Sleeping Princess,
ballet
FELDMAN (25)
Intersection I
Projections I and II
STOCKHAUSEN (23)
Formel, for orchestra
Kreuzspiel, for
instrumental ensemble

Sonatine, for violin and
   piano

GOEHR (19)
Piano Sonata (1951–52)
Songs of Babel

1952

VAUGHAN WILLIAMS
   (80)
Sinfonia Antarctica
   (Symphony No. 7)
AUBERT (76)
Cinéma
DOHNÁNYI (75)
Violin Concerto No. 2
Harp Concerto
BLOCH (72)
Sinfonia brève
Concerto Grosso, for
   string quartet and string
   orchestra
STRAVINSKY (70)
Cantata on old English
   texts
MALIPIERO (70)
Violin Concerto
SCHOECK (66)
Befreite Sehnsucht, song
   cycle
MARTIN (62)
La Tempête, opera
   (1952-55)
HONEGGER (60)
Suite archaïque
PROKOFIEV (61)
Cello Concertino
BLISS (61)
The Enchantress, scena
   for contralto and
   orchestra
Piano Sonata

MOORE (59)
Cotillion Suite, for string
   orchestra
PISTON (58)
Fantasy, for English horn,
   harp and strings
HINDEMITH (57)
Symphony in B♭ for
   military band
Sonata for four horns
SOWERBY (57)
String Trio
GERHARD (56)
Symphony No. 1
   (1952–53)
THOMSON (56)
Sea Piece with Birds, for
   orchestra
KORNGOLD (55)
Sonnet to Vienna, song
RUBBRA (51)
Viola Concerto
FINZI (51)
Love's Labour Lost, suite
RODRIGO (50)
Four *Villancicos,* for
   voice and piano
Four *Villancicos,* for
   chorus "Canciones de
   Navidad"
BERKELEY (49)
Flute Concerto
Four Ronsard Sonnets,
   Set I, for two tenors
   and piano

CONTINUED

DALLAPICCOLA (48)
Quaderno musicale di Annalibera, for piano
Goethe-Lieder
KABALEVSKY (48)
Piano Concerto No. 3
Cello Sonata
RAWSTHORNE (47)
Canticle of Man, chamber cantata
TIPPETT (47)
"Dance Clarion Air", madrigal
LUTYENS (46)
String Quartets Nos. 4–6
SHOSTAKOVICH (46)
Ballet Suite No. 3, for orchestra
String Quartet No. 5
Four Monologues on verses of Pushkin, for bass and piano
The Sun Shines Over Our Motherland, cantata
MENOTTI (41)
Violin Concerto
CAGE (40)
Water Music
Williams Mix
4' 33" (tacet) for piano, in four movements
BRITTEN (39)
Canticle No. 2, "Abraham and Isaac", for contralto, tenor and piano
GOULD (39)
Dance Variations, for two pianos and orchestra
FINE (38)
String Quartet
Mutability, song cycle

BERNSTEIN (35)
Trouble in Tahiti, opera
Wonderful Town
ROCHBERG (34)
String Quartet No. 1
Twelve bagatelles, for piano
FRICKER (32)
Concerto for piano and small orchestra (1952–54)
String Quartet No. 2
ARNOLD (31)
Curtain Up
Three Shanties, for wind quintet
SHAPEY (31)
Symphony No. 1
Quartet for oboe and string trio
Oboe Sonata
Suite for piano
FOSS (30)
Parable of Death, for narrator, tenor and orchestra
HAMILTON (30)
Bartholomew Fair, overture
Violin Concerto
MENNIN (29)
Concertato for orchestra, *Moby Dick*
Quartet No. 2
BERIO (27)
Allez Hop, for voice, mime and dance
Five Variations, for piano (1952–53)
BOULEZ (27)
fp. Structures, for two pianos, Book I

BROWN (26)
Folio and Four Systems,
  for piano and orchestra
*Music for Violin, Cello
  and Piano*
HENZE (26)
King Stag, opera
  (1952–55)
The Idiot, ballet-
  pantomime
Quintet for wind
  instruments

String Quartet No. 2
STOCKHAUSEN (24)
Spiel, for orchestra
Punkte, for orchestra
  (1952–53)
Kontrapunkte, for ten
  instruments (1952–53)
Schlagtrio, for piano and
  timpani
Klavierstücke I–IV
Étude, musique concrete

1953   BAX, JONGEN, QUILTER and
         PROKOFIEV died

DOHNÁNYI (76)
Stabat Mater
PIZZETTI (73)
Cagliostro, opera
STRAVINSKY (71)
Septet
Three songs from
  Shakespeare, for mezzo-
  soprano and piano
BAX (70)
Coronation March
MARTINŮ (63)
The Marriage, opera
BLISS (62)
Processional, for
  orchestra and organ
HONEGGER (61)
Christmas Cantata
MILHAUD (61)
David, opera
MOORE (60)
Piano Trio
ROBERTSON (57)
The Book of Mormon,
  oratorio

SESSIONS (57)
Sonata for solo violin
KORNGOLD (56)
Straussiana, for orchestra
Theme and Variations for
  orchestra
HARRIS (55)
Piano Concerto No. 2
*Abraham Lincoln walks
  at midnight,* chamber
  cantata
CHÁVEZ (54)
Symphony No. 4, *Sinfonia
  romantica*
Symphony No. 5,
  Symphony for Strings
POULENC (54)
Dialogues des Carmelites,
  opera
Sonata for two pianos
ANTHEIL (53)
Capital of the World,
  ballet
WALTON (51)
Coronation Te Deum
                    CONTINUED

Orb and Sceptre,
  coronation march for
  orchestra
BERKELEY (50)
Suite for orchestra
ALWYN (48)
Symphony No. 2
The Magic Island,
  symphonic prelude
SEIBER (48)
Three pieces for cello and
  orchestra
TIPPETT (48)
Piano Concerto
  (1953–55)
Divertimento for chamber
  orchestra, *Sellinger's
  Round* (1953–55)
*Fantasia concertante on a
  Theme by Corelli,* for
  strings
LUTYENS (47)
Three songs and
  incidental music for
  Group Theater's
  *Homage to Dylan
  Thomas*
SHOSTAKOVICH (47)
Ballet Suite No. 4
Symphony No. 10
Concertino, for two
  pianos
MESSIAEN (45)
Reveil des oiseaux, for
  piano and orchestra
BARBER (43)
Souvenirs, ballet suite
SCHUMAN (43)
The Mighty Casey,
  baseball opera
Voyage, for piano
CAGE (41)
Music for piano—"4–84

for 1–84 Pianists"
  (1953–56)
BRITTEN (40)
Gloriana, opera
Winter Words, songs
GOULD (40)
Inventions for four pianos
  and orchestra
ARNELL (36)
The Great Detective,
  ballet
Lord Byron, symphonic
  portrait
ROCHBERG (35)
Chamber Symphony, for
  nine instruments
FRICKER (33)
Violin Concerto No. 2,
  Rapsodie concertante
ARNOLD (32)
Homage to the Queen,
  ballet
Symphony No. 2
Oboe Concerto
Violin Sonata No. 2
SHAPEY (32)
String Quartet No. 4
Cello Sonata
LIGETI (30)
String Quartet
MENNIN (30)
Symphony No. 6
BERIO (28)
Chamber Music, for
  female voice, clarinet,
  cello and harp
BROWN (27)
"25 Pages—from 1 to 25
  pianos"
HENZE (27)
The End of a World,
  radio opera

Ode to the Westwind, for
cello and orchestra
MUSGRAVE (25)
A Tale for Thieves, ballet
A Suite of Bairnsangs,
for voice and piano

STOCKHAUSEN (25)
Elektronische Studie, I
HODDINOTT (24)
fp. Fugal Overture, for
orchestra
fp. Nocturne, for
orchestra

1954

VAUGHAN WILLIAMS
(82)
Concerto for bass tuba
and orchestra
Violin Sonata in A minor
This Day (Hodie),
cantata
DOHNÁNYI (77)
American Rhapsody
KODÁLY (72)
Spartacus, ballet
STRAVINSKY (72)
*In Memoriam Dylan
Thomas*, for voice,
trombones and string
quartet
TAYLOR (69)
The Dragon, opera
BLISS (63)
A Song of Welcome, for
solo voices, chorus and
orchestra
MILHAUD (62)
Harp Concerto
PISTON (60)
Symphony No. 5
SOWERBY (59)
All on a Summer's Day,
for orchestra
Fantasy, for trumpet and
organ

SESSIONS (58)
The Idyll of Theocritus,
for soprano and
orchestra
THOMSON (58)
Concerto for flute, strings
and percussion
HARRIS (56)
Fantasy, for piano and
orchestra
POULENC (55)
Bucolique, for orchestra
Matelote provençale, for
orchestra
COPLAND (54)
The Tender Land, opera
FINZI (53)
*Grand Fantasia and
Toccata*, for piano and
orchestra
RUBBRA (53)
Symphony No. 6
RODRIGO (52)
Concert-Serenade, for
harp and orchestra
WALTON (52)
Troilus and Cressida,
opera
BERKELEY (51)
A Dinner Engagement,
opera

CONTINUED

Nelson, opera
Trio for violin, horn and piano
Sonatina for piano duet
KHACHATURIAN (51)
Spartacus, ballet
DALLAPICCOLA (50)
Piccola musica notturna, for orchestra
ALWYN (49)
Lyra angelica, for harp and strings
RAWSTHORNE (49)
Practical Cats, for speaker and orchestra
String Quartet No. 2
SEIBER (49)
Elegy, for solo violin and small orchestra
To Poetry, song cycle
LUTYENS (48)
Infidelio, seven scenes for voices and instruments
Valediction, for clarinet and piano
SHOSTAKOVICH (48)
Festival Overture
Five Romances (Songs of Our Days), for bass and piano
Film music
BARBER (44)
Prayers of Kierkegaard, for soprano, chorus and orchestra
MENOTTI (43)
The Saint of Bleecker Street, opera
CAGE (42)
34' 46.776" for a pianist, for prepared piano

BRITTEN (41)
The Turn of the Screw, opera
Canticle No. 3, "Still Falls the Rain", for tenor, chorus and piano
LUTOSLAWSKI (41)
Dance Preludes, first version for clarinet and piano
DIAMOND (40)
Sinfonia concertante
Sonata for solo violin
BERNSTEIN (36)
Serenade for violin, strings and percussion
Five Anniversaries, for piano
On the Waterfront, film score
ROCHBERG (36)
David the Psalmist, cantata
Three psalms, for chorus
FRICKER (34)
Dance Scene, for orchestra
Nocturne and Scherzo, for piano (four hands)
ARNOLD (33)
Sinfonietta No. 1
Concerto for flute and strings
Harmonica Concerto
Organ Concerto
The Tempest, incidental music
SHAPEY (33)
Concerto for clarinet with six instruments
Sonata Variations, for piano

HAMILTON (32)
String Octet
*Four Border Songs and
the Fray of Suport*
Songs of Summer, for
soprano and piano
BERIO (29)
Nones, for orchestra
Variations for chamber
orchestra
Mutations, electronic
music
BOULEZ (29)
Le marteau sans maître,
for alto voice and six
instruments

MUSGRAVE (26)
*Cantata for a Summer's
Day*
STOCKHAUSEN (26)
Elektronische Studie, II
Klavierstücke V–X
HODDINOTT (23)
fp. Concerto for clarinet
and string orchestra
GOEHR (22)
Fantasia for orchestra
(revised 1958)
Fantasias for clarinet and
piano
BENNETT (18)
Piano Sonata
Sonatina for flute

1955   ENESCO, HONEGGER and ROPARTZ died

VAUGHAN WILLIAMS
(83)
Symphony No. 8
MARTIN (65)
Études, for string
orchestra (1955–56)
MARTINŮ (65)
Three frescoes
BLISS (64)
Violin Concerto
*Meditations on a Theme
of John Blow,* for
orchestra
Elegiac Sonnet, for tenor,
string quartet and piano
MILHAUD (63)
Symphonies Nos. 5 and 6
PISTON (61)
Symphony No. 6
ORFF (60)
Der Sänger der Vorwelt

*Comoedia de Christi
resurrectione*
GERHARD (59)
Concerto for harpsichord,
strings and percussion
(1955–56)
String Quartet No. 1
(1955–56)
HANSON (59)
Symphony No. 5,
Sinfonia sacrae
SESSIONS (59)
Mass, for unison male
voices and organ
TANSMAN (58)
Capriccio
Le Sermant, opera
Concerto for Orchestra
ANTHEIL (55)
Cabezza de Vacca,
cantata (1955–56)

CONTINUED

COPLAND (55)
Symphonic Ode
A Canticle of Freedom,
  for chorus and
  orchestra (revised
  1965)
FINZI (55)
Cello Concerto
RUBBRA (54)
Piano Concerto
RODRIGO (53)
*Fantasia para un
  Gentilhombre,* for
  guitar (*c.*1955)
WALTON (53)
*Johannesburg Festival
  Overture*
Richard III, incidental
  music
BERKELEY (52)
Suite from *Nelson,* for
  orchestra
Concerto for flute, violin,
  cello and harpsichord
  (or piano)
Sextet, for clarinet, horn
  and string quartet
Concert Study in E♭, for
  piano
Crux fidelis, for solo tenor
  and mixed chorus
Look up sweet Babe, for
  soprano and mixed
  chorus
Salve Regina, for voices
  and organ
KHACHATURIAN (52)
Three Suites for Orchestra
DALLAPICCOLA (51)
An Mathilde, cantata
KABALEVSKY (51)
Nikita Vershinin, opera

ALWYN (50)
Autumn Legend, for
  English horn and
  strings
RAWSTHORNE (50)
Madame Chrysanthème,
  ballet
TIPPETT (50)
Sonata for four horns
LUTYENS (49)
Music for Orchestra, I
Capriccii, for two harps
  and percussion
Nocturnes, for violin,
  guitar and cello
Sinfonia for organ
SHOSTAKOVICH (49)
Film music
SCHUMAN (45)
Credendum, for orchestra
CAGE (43)
*26′ 1.499″ for a string
  player*
BRITTEN (42)
Hymn to St. Peter
Alpine Suite, for recorder
  trio
GOULD (42)
*Jekyll and Hyde Vari-
  ations,* for orchestra
Derivations, for clarinet
  and band
LUTOSLAWSKI (42)
Dance Preludes, second
  version for clarinet and
  instruments
FINE (41)
Serious Song and Lament,
  for string orchestra
ARNELL (38)
Love in Transit, opera

518

ROCHBERG (37)
Duo concertante, for
violin and cello
FRICKER (35)
Litany, for double string
orchestra
Musick's Empire, for
chorus and small
orchestra
The Tomb of St. Eulalia,
for counter-tenor,
gamba and harpsichord
Horn sonata
SHAPERO (35)
Credo, for orchestra
ARNOLD (34)
Tam O'Shanter, overture
Little Suite for Orchestra,
No. 1
Serenade, for guitar and
strings
John Clare, cantata
FOSS (34)
Griffelkin, opera
The Gift of the Magi,
ballet
SHAPEY (34)
*Challenge—the Family of
Man,* for orchestra
Piano Trio

BOULEZ (30)
Symphonie mecanique
HENZE (29)
Symphony No. 4
Quattro Poemi, for
orchestra
Three Symphonic Studies
(revised 1964)
KORTE (27)
*Concertato on a Choral
theme,* for orchestra
MUSGRAVE (27)
The Abbot of Drimock,
chamber opera
Five Love Songs, for
soprano and guitar
STOCKHAUSEN (27)
Gruppen, for three
orchestras
Zeitmasze, for oboe, flute,
English horn, clarinet
and bassoon
Gesang de Jünglinge,
electronic music
HODDINOTT (26)
fp. Symphony No. 1
DAVIES (21)
Stedman Doubles, for
clarinet and percussion
Trumpet Sonata

1956 CHARPENTIER and FINZI died

VAUGHAN WILLIAMS
(84)
Symphony No. 9 (revised
1958)
Two organ preludes,
Romanza and *Toccata*
Epithalamion, cantata
(1956–57)

Ten Blake Songs, for
tenor and oboe
A Vision of Aeroplanes,
motet
STRAVINSKY (74)
Canticum sacrum

CONTINUED

MARTIN (66)
*Overture in Homage to
    Mozart*
BLISS (65)
Edinburgh Overture
MILHAUD (64)
Symphony No. 7
MOORE (63)
The Ballad of Baby Doe,
    opera
PISTON (62)
Serenata, for orchestra
Quintet for wind
**CASTELNUOVO-
    TEDESCO** (61)
All's Well that Ends Well,
    opera
JACOB (61)
Piano Concerto No. 2
Sextet
Piano Trio
ORFF (61)
Nanie and Dithyrambe,
    with choir
GERHARD (60)
Nonet for eight winds and
    accordion
HANSON (60)
*Elegy in Memory of Serge
    Koussevitsky,* for
    orchestra
SESSIONS (60)
Piano Concerto
HARRIS (58)
Folk Fantasy for
    Festivals, for piano and
    choir
POULENC (57)
Le travail du peintre,
    song cycle
"Deux mélodies", songs

FINZI (55)
In Terra Pax, for chorus
    and orchestra
Eclogue, for piano and
    strings
RUBBRA (55)
Symphony No. 7
WALTON (54)
Cello Concerto
BERKELEY (53)
Ruth, opera
KHACHATURIAN (53)
Ode of Joy, for voices
    and orchestra
DALLAPICCOLA (52)
*Concerto per la notte di
    natale dell'anno*
Cinque canti, for baritone
    and eight instruments
KABALEVSKY (52)
Symphony No. 5
Romeo and Juliet,
    symphonic suite
ALWYN (51)
Symphony No. 3
RAWSTHORNE (51)
Violin Concerto No. 2
TIPPETT (51)
Symphony No. 2
    (1956–57)
LUTYENS (50)
*Chorale for Orchestra
    (Hommage à Stravinsky)*
Three Duos (horn and
    piano; cello and piano;
    violin and piano)
    (1956–57)
*In the Temple of a Bird's
    Wing,* for baritone and
    piano
SHOSTAKOVICH (50)
Katerina Ismailova, opera
String Quartet No. 6

Spanish Songs, for
   soprano and piano
Film music
MESSIAEN (48)
Oiseaux exotiques, for
   piano, wind and
   percussion
BARBER (46)
Summer Music, for
   woodwind quintet
SCHUMAN (46)
New England Triptych,
   for orchestra
MENOTTI (45)
*The Unicorn, the Gorgon
   and the Manticore,*
   ballet
GOULD (43)
Santa Fé Saga, for band
Dialogue, for piano and
   strings
BRITTEN (43)
*The Prince of the
   Pagodas,* ballet
Antiphon, for choir and
   organ
DIAMOND (41)
Sonata for solo cello
ARNELL (39)
Landscape and Figures,
   for orchestra
BERNSTEIN (38)
Candide
ROCHBERG (38)
Sinfonia fantasia
FRICKER (36)
Suite for harpsichord
Cello sonata
ARNOLD (35)
The Dancing Master,
   opera
The Open Window, opera

Solitaire, ballet suite
A Grand Overture
SHAPEY (35)
Mutations No. 1, for
   piano
FOSS (34)
Psalms, with orchestra
HAMILTON (34)
Scottish Dances
Sonata for chamber
   orchestra
MENNIN (33)
Cello Concerto
Sonata concertante, for
   violin and piano
BERIO (31)
Allelujah, I and II, for
   orchestra
String Quartet
Perspectives, electronic
   music
HENZE (30)
Maratona, ballet
Ondine, ballet (1956–57)
Concerto per il Marigny,
   for piano and seven
   instruments
Five Neapolitan Songs,
   for voice and chamber
   orchestra
STOCKHAUSEN (28)
Klavierstücke XI
HODDINOTT (27)
fp. Septet for wind, strings
   and piano
GOEHR (24)
String Quartet No. 1
   (1956–57)
DAVIES (21)
Five pieces for piano
NILSSON (19)
Frequenzen, for eight
   players (*c.*1956)

MALIPIERO (75)
Piano Quintet
STRAVINSKY (75)
Agon, ballet
*Threni (Lamentations of
Jeremiah)*, for soloists,
chorus and orchestra
(1957–58)
MARTIN (67)
La mystère de la Nativité,
oratorio (1957–59)
BLISS (66)
Discourse, for orchestra,
first version
(recomposed 1965)
MILHAUD (65)
Symphony No. 8,
Rhodanienne
Oboe Concerto
Aspen Serenade
MOORE (64)
Gallantry, a soap opera
PISTON (63)
Viola Concerto
SOWERBY (62)
The Throne of God, for
chorus and orchestra
GERHARD (61)
Don Quixote, ballet suite
SESSIONS (61)
Symphony No. 3
THOMSON (61)
The Lively Arts, Fugue
WEINBERGER (61)
*Préludes religieuses et
profanes*, for organ
POULENC (58)
Elegy, for horn and piano
COPLAND (57)
Orchestral Variations

Piano Fantasy
RUBBRA (56)
*In Memoriam Mariae
matris Dei*, cantata
WALTON (55)
Partita, for orchestra
BERKELEY (54)
"Sweet was the Song", for
voices and organ
Sonatina for guitar
KHACHATURIAN (54)
Lermontov Suite
DALLAPICCOLA (53)
Requiescat, for chorus
and orchestra
(1957–58)
ALWYN (52)
Elizabethan Dances, for
orchestra
RAWSTHORNE (52)
Violin Sonata
LUTYENS (51)
*Six Tempi for Ten
Instruments*
Variations for solo flute
De Amore, cantata
SHOSTAKOVICH (51)
Symphony No. 11, *The
Year 1905*
Piano Concerto No. 2
SCHUMAN (47)
Prologues, for chorus and
orchestra
CAGE (45)
Piano Concerto
(1957–58)
*Winter Music: for 1–20
Pianists*

BRITTEN (44)
Noye's Fludde, mystery
play
Songs from the Chinese,
for high voice and
guitar
GOULD (44)
Declaration Suite
LUTOSLAWSKI (44)
Five songs
DIAMOND (42)
The World of Paul Klee,
for orchestra
ARNELL (40)
The Angels, ballet
BERNSTEIN (39)
West Side Story, film score
FRICKER (37)
Octet, for flute, clarinet,
bassoon, horn, violin,
viola, cello and
double-bass
Piano Variations
A Vision of Judgment,
oratorio
ARNOLD (36)
Symphony No. 3
Toy Symphony
Four Scottish Dances, for
orchestra
SHAPEY (36)
String Quartet No. 5, with
female voices
(1957–58)
Rhapsodie, for oboe and
piano
Duo for viola and piano
FOSS (35)
Behold! I built an house
HAMILTON (35)
Five Love Songs, for
tenor and orchestra

Cantata for tenor and
piano
BERIO (32)
Divertimento for
Orchestra
Serenata, for flute and
fourteen instruments
El mar la mar, for voices
and instruments
Momenti, electronic
sound
BOULEZ (32)
Doubles, for orchestra
Poésie pour pouvoir, for
reciter, orchestra and
tape
*Deux improvisations sur
Mallarmé,* for soprano
and instrumental
ensemble
Piano Sonata No. 3
FELDMAN (31)
Pieces for four pianos
HENZE (31)
Nocturnes and arias, for
soprano and orchestra
Sonata per archi
(1957–58)
HODDINOTT (28)
fp. Rondo Scherzoso, for
trumpet and piano
WILLIAMSON (26)
Piano Sonata No. 1
GOEHR (25)
The Deluge, cantata
Capriccio, for piano
BIRTWISTLE (23)
Refrains and Choruses,
for flute, oboe, clarinet,
bassoon and horn
DAVIES (23)
St. Michael, sonata for
CONTINUED

523

seventeen wind
instruments
Alma redemptoris mater,
for six wind instruments
MAW (22)
Sonatina, for flute and
piano
BENNETT (21)
Five Pieces for Orchestra
String Quartet No. 3
Violin Sonata

Sonata for solo violin
Sonata for solo cello
Four improvisations for
violin
NILSSON (20)
Kreutzungen, for
instrumental ensemble
Buch der Veränderungen
Mädchentotenlieder
(1957–58)

1958   VAUGHAN WILLIAMS died

VAUGHAN WILLIAMS
(86)
The First Nowell, for
soloist, chorus and
orchestra
Four last songs, for voice
and piano
Vocalises, for soprano
and clarinet
PIZZETTI (78)
Murder in the Cathedral,
opera
MARTIN (68)
Overture in Rondo
Pseaumes de Genève, for
mixed choir, children's
voices, organ and
orchestra
BLISS (67)
The Lady of Shalott,
ballet
MILHAUD (66)
Violin Concerto No. 3,
Concerto royal
PISTON (64)
*Psalm and Prayer of
David*, for chorus and
seven instruments

**CASTELNUOVO-
TEDESCO** (63)
The Merchant of Venice,
opera
Saul
HINDEMITH (63)
Octet
JACOB (63)
Diversions, for woodwind
and strings
Old Wine in New Bottles,
for wind instruments
Suite for recorder and
string quartet
Miniature string quartet
ORFF (63)
Oedipus, der Tyrann
HANSON (62)
Mosaics, for orchestra
SESSIONS (62)
Symphony No. 4
String Quintet
CHÁVEZ (59)
Inventions, No. 1 for
piano
POULENC (59)
La voix humaine, lyric
tragedy (monodrama
for soprano)

RUBBRA (57)
Oboe Sonata
Pezzo ostinato, for solo
  harp
BERKELEY (55)
Concerto for piano and
  double string orchestra
Five Poems by W.H.
  Auden, for voice and
  piano
KHACHATURIAN (55)
Sonatina for piano
RAWSTHORNE (53)
Halle Overture
SEIBER (53)
Permutazione a cinque,
  for flute, oboe, clarinet,
  horn and bassoon
*Portrait of the Artist as a
  Young Man,* chamber
  cantata
TIPPETT (53)
King Priam, opera
  (1958–61)
Crown of the Year, for
  chorus and orchestra
*Prelude, Recitative and
  Aria,* for flute, oboe and
  harpsichord
LUTYENS (52)
Piano e Forte, for piano
SHOSTAKOVICH (52)
Moscow, Cheremushki,
  musical comedy
BARBER (48)
Vanessa, opera
MENOTTI (47)
Maria Golovin, opera
CAGE (46)
Fontana Mix
Variations I

BRITTEN (45)
Nocturne, for tenor, seven
  obbligato instruments
  and strings
*Sechs Hölderlin-
  Fragmente,* song cycle
GOULD (45)
Rhythm Gallery, for
  narrator and orchestra
St. Lawrence Suite, for
  band
LUTOSLAWSKI (45)
Funeral Music, for strings
Three Postludes
  (1958–63)
DIAMOND (43)
Woodwind Quintet
ARNELL (41)
Moonflowers, opera
ROCHBERG (40)
Symphony No. 2
Cheltenham Concerto, for
  chamber orchestra
Dialogues, for clarinet and
  piano
FRICKER (38)
Comedy Overture
Toccata for piano and
  orchestra (1958–59)
SHAPERO (38)
On Green Mountain, for
  jazz combo
ARNOLD (37)
Sinfonietta No. 2
SHAPEY (37)
Ontogeny, for orchestra
Walking Upright, song
  cycle
FOSS (36)
Symphony of Chorales
HAMILTON (36)
Overture 1912

CONTINUED

Concerto for jazz trumpet
and orchestra
Sonata for solo cello
LIGETI (35)
Apparitions, for orchestra
(1958–59)
Artikulation, for tape
MENNIN (35)
Piano Concerto
BERIO (33)
Tempi concertati, for
flute, violin, two pianos
and other instruments
(1958–59)
Differences, for five
instruments and tape
Sequence I, for flute
*Theme (Homage to
Joyce)*, electronic music
HENZE (32)
Der Prinz von Homburg,
opera
Three Dithyrambs, for
chamber orchestra
Chamber Music
Three Tentos, for guitar
KORTE (30)
The Story of the Flutes,
tone poem
MUSGRAVE (30)
Obliques, for orchestra
String Quartet
A Song for Christmas,
for voice and piano
HODDINOTT (29)
fp. Harp Concerto
fp. Four Welsh Dances,
for orchestra

fp. Concertino for viola
and small orchestra
fp. Serenade, for string
orchestra
WILLIAMSON (27)
Santiago de Espada,
overture
Piano Concerto No. 1
GOEHR (26)
*La Belle Dame sans
merci*, ballet
PENDERECKI (25)
Emanations, for two string
orchestras
*Epithaphiom on the death
of Artur Malawski*, for
string orchestra and
timpani
The Psalms of David, for
chorus and instruments
DAVIES (24)
Stedman Caters (revised
1968)
Sextet
MAW (23)
Nocturne, for mezzo-
soprano and chamber
orchestra
NILSSON (21)
Stunde eines Blocks, for
soprano and six players
*Zwanzig Gruppen für
Blaser*, for piccolo,
oboe and clarinet
(1958–59)
Quantitaten, for piano

MALIPIERO (77)
Sei poesie di Dylan Thomas, for soprano and ten instruments
Musica da Camera, for wind quintet

STRAVINSKY (77)
Movements, for piano and orchestra
Double Canon for string quartet
Epitaphium, for flute, clarinet and harp

PISTON (65)
Concerto for two pianos and orchestra
Three New England Sketches, for orchestra

SOWERBY (64)
Ask of the Covenant, cantata

GERHARD (63)
Symphony No. 2

HANSON (63)
Summer Seascapes

THOMSON (63)
Collected Poems
Fugues and Cantilenas, for orchestra

HARRIS (61)
Give me the splendid silent sun, cantata

POULENC (60)
Gloria, for voices and orchestra

COPLAND (59)
Dance Panels, ballet

RUBBRA (58)
Violin Concerto

BERKELEY (56)
Overture for Light Orchestra
Sonatina for two pianos
"So sweet love seemed", for voice and piano

DALLAPICCOLA (55)
Dialoghi, for cello and orchestra

ALWYN (54)
Symphony No. 4

RAWSTHORNE (54)
Symphony No. 2, *A pastoral symphony*

SEIBER (54)
Improvisation for Jazz Band and Symphony Orchestra

LUTYENS (53)
Quincunx, for solo voices and orchestra

SHOSTAKOVICH (53)
Cello Concerto No. 1

BARBER (49)
A Hand of Bridge, opera, for four solo voices and chamber orchestra

SCHUMAN (49)
Three Moods, for piano

BRITTEN (46)
Cantata Academica, *Carmen basiliense,* for solo voices, chorus and orchestra
Missa brevis

CONTINUED

527

LUTOSLAWSKI (46)
Dance Preludes, third
   version for instruments
DIAMOND (44)
Symphony No. 7
ARNELL (42)
Paralyzed Princess,
   operetta
ROCHBERG (41)
La bocca della verita, for
   oboe and piano
String Quartet No. 2
FRICKER (39)
Serenade No. 1, for
   flute, clarinet, bass-
   clarinet, viola, cello
   and harp
Serenade No. 2, for flute,
   oboe and piano
ARNOLD (38)
Guitar Concerto
Oboe Quartet
Six Songs of William
   Blake, for voice and
   strings
SHAPEY (38)
Violin Concerto
Rituals, for orchestra
Soliloquy, for narrator,
   string quartet and
   percussion
Evocation, for violin,
   piano and percussion
Form, for piano
FOSS (37)
*Introductions and
   Goodbyes,* opera
HAMILTON (37)
Sinfonia for two
   orchestras
Écossaise, for orchestra
BERIO (34)
Quaderni I, II and III

from *Epifanie* for
   orchestra (1959–63)
BOULEZ (34)
fp. Tombeau, for
   orchestra
FELDMAN (33)
Atlantis, for chamber
   orchestra
HENZE (33)
Elegy for Young Lovers,
   opera (1959–61)
*The Emperor's
   Nightingale,* ballet
Piano Sonata
KORTE (31)
For a Young Audience,
   for orchestra
Fantasy, for violin and
   piano
MUSGRAVE (31)
Triptych, for tenor and
   orchestra
STOCKHAUSEN (31)
Carré, for four orchestras
   and four choirs
Refrain, for piano, celesta
   and percussion
Zyklus, for one
   percussionist
Kontakte, electronic
   sound
HODDINOTT (30)
fp. Nocturne and Dance,
   for harp and orchestra
fp. Piano Sonata No. 1
GOEHR (27)
Hecuba's Lament, for
   orchestra (1959–61)
Variations for flute and
   piano
Four songs from the
   Japanese

Sutter's Gold, cantata
  (1959–60)
PENDERECKI (26)
Strophes, for soprano,
  narrator and ten
  instruments
BIRTWISTLE (25)
*Monody for Corpus
  Christi*, for soprano,
  flute, horn and violin
Précis, for piano
DAVIES (25)
Prolation, for orchestra

Ricercare and doubles
  on "To many a well"
Five motets
BENNETT (23)
The Approaches of Sleep
NILSSON (22)
*Und die Zieger seiner
  Augen wurden langsam
  züruckgedreht*, for solo
  voices, chorus and
  mixed media
Ein irrender Sohn, for
  voice and instruments

1960   ALFVÉN, BENJAMIN, DOHNÁNYI and
           SEIBER died

KODÁLY (78)
Symphony in C
MALIPIERO (78)
String Quartet No. 3
STRAVINSKY (78)
*Monumentum pro
  Gesualdo*, for orchestra
MARTIN (70)
Drey minnelieder, for
  soprano and piano
BLISS (69)
Tobias and the Angel,
  opera
MILHAUD (68)
Symphony No. 10
PISTON (66)
Symphony No. 7
Violin Concerto No. 2
ORFF (65)
*Ludus de nato Infante
  mirificus*
GERHARD (64)
Symphony No. 3, *Collages*

String Quartet No. 2
  (1960–62)
SESSIONS (64)
Divertimento, for orchestra
THOMSON (64)
Requiem Mass
Mass for solo voice and
  piano (with orchestra
  1962)
WEINBERGER (64)
Aus Tirol
CHÁVEZ (61)
Love Propitiated, opera
POULENC (61)
Elegy, for two pianos
COPLAND (60)
Nonet for strings
DURUFLÉ (58)
Four motets on Gregorian
  themes, for a cappella
  choir
WALTON (58)
Symphony No. 2
CONTINUED

fp. Anon. in Love, six songs for tenor and guitar

BERKELEY (57)

A Winter's Tale, suite for orchestra

Prelude and Fugue for clavichord

Improvisation on a Theme of Falla, for piano

Missa brevis

KHACHATURIAN (57)

Rhapsody, for violin and orchestra

Ballade, for bass with orchestra

DALLAPICCOLA (56)

Ulisse, opera (1960–68)

KABALEVSKY (56)

Overture pathétique, for orchestra

The Spring, symphonic poem

Major-minor études, for cello

Camp of Friendship, songs

SEIBER (55)

Invitation, ballet

A Three-cornered fanfare

LUTYENS (54)

Wind Quintet

SHOSTAKOVICH (54)

Novorossiysk Chimes (The Fire of Eternal Glory), for orchestra

String Quartets Nos. 7 and 8

Satires (Pictures of the Past), for soprano and piano

Film music

MESSIAEN (52)

Chronochromie

BARBER (50)

Toccata festiva, for organ and orchestra

SCHUMAN (50)

Symphony No. 7

CAGE (48)

Cartridge Music

Theater Piece, for 1–8 Performers

BRITTEN (47)

A Midsummer Night's Dream, opera

FINE (46)

Diversion, for orchestra

DIAMOND (45)

Symphony No. 8

Quartet No. 5

ROCHBERG (42)

Time-Span, for orchestra

FRICKER (40)

Symphony No. 3

SHAPERO (40)

Partita, for piano and orchestra

ARNOLD (39)

Rinaldo and Armida, ballet

Symphony No. 4

Song of Simeon, nativity play

SHAPEY (39)

Dimensions, for soprano and twenty-three instruments

De profundis, for solo double-bass and instruments

Movements, for woodwind quartet

Five, for violin and piano

This Day, for voice and
    piano
FOSS (38)
Time Cycle, four songs
    with orchestra
HAMILTON (38)
Piano Concerto
LIGETI (37)
Atmospheres, for
    orchestra
BERIO (35)
Circles, for voice, harp
    and two percussion
BOULEZ (35)
fp. Pli selon pli, for
    soprano and orchestra
FELDMAN (34)
Durations I–V (1960–61)
HENZE (34)
Antifone, for orchestra
KORTE (32)
Quintet for oboe and
    strings
MUSGRAVE (32)
Trio for flute, oboe and
    piano
Colloquy, for violin and
    piano
Monologue, for piano
HODDINOTT (31)
fp. Concerto No. 1 for
    piano, wind and
    percussion

Sextet for flute, clarinet,
    bassoon, violin, viola
    and cello
PREVIN (31)
Overture to a Comedy,
    for orchestra
PENDERECKI (27)
Anaklasis, for strings and
    percussion groups
String Quartet No. 1
BIRTWISTLE (26)
The World is Discovered,
    for instrumental
    ensemble
DAVIES (26)
O Magnum Mysterium,
    for chorus, instruments
    and organ
MAW (25)
Five Epigrams, for
    unaccompanied chorus
BENNETT (24)
Journal, for orchestra
Calendar, for chamber
    ensemble
Winter Music, for flute
    and piano (or orchestra)
NILSSON (23)
Szene I
Reaktionen, for four
    percussionists

1961   GRAINGER died

MARTIN (71)
*Monsieur de
    Pourceaugnac,*
    opera (1961–62)

MOORE (68)
Wings of the Dove, opera
PISTON (67)
Symphonic Prelude
CONTINUED

JACOB (66)
Trombone Concerto
Fantasia on Scottish
  Tunes
HANSON (65)
Bold Island, suite
THOMSON (65)
A Solemn Music, for
  orchestra
WEINBERGER (65)
Eine walserouverture
TANSMAN (64)
Psalms, for tenor, chorus
  and orchestra
HARRIS (63)
Canticle to the Sun,
  cantata
CHÁVEZ (62)
Symphony No. 6
Soli No. 2, for wind
  quintet
POULENC (62)
La dame de Monte Carlo,
  monologue for soprano
  and orchestra
RUBBRA (60)
Cantata da camera
  (Crucifixus pro nobis)
WALTON (59)
Gloria, for solo voices,
  chorus and orchestra
BERKELEY (58)
Concerto for violin and
  chamber orchestra
Five pieces for violin and
  orchestra
KHACHATURIAN (58)
Piano Sonata
KABALEVSKY (57)
Rondo for violin and
  piano

RAWSTHORNE (56)
Concerto for ten
  instruments
*Improvisations on a theme
  by Constant Lambert,*
  for orchestra
TIPPETT (56)
Magnificat and Nunc
  Dimittis
Three songs for Achilles,
  for voice and guitar
LUTYENS (55)
Symphonies for solo
  piano, winds, harps
  and percussion
Catena, cantata
SHOSTAKOVICH (55)
Symphony No. 12, *1917*
BARBER (51)
Dies Natalis, choral
  preludes
CAGE (49)
Atlas eclipticalis, for
  orchestra (1961–62)
Variations II
Music for Carillon No. 4
BRITTEN (48)
Cello Sonata
War Requiem
LUTOSLAWSKI (48)
Jeux vénitiens
FINE (47)
Romanza, for wind
  quintet
DIAMOND (46)
Nonet, for three violins,
  three violas and three
  cellos
ARNELL (44)
Brass Quintet

ROCHBERG (43)
Songs of Innocence and Experience, for soprano and chamber orchestra
FRICKER (41)
Twelve studies for piano
Cantata for tenor and chamber ensemble (1961–62)
ARNOLD (40)
Symphony No. 5
Divertimento No. 2, for full orchestra
SHAPEY (40)
Incantations, for soprano and ten instruments
Discourse, for flute, clarinet, violin and piano
FOSS (39)
Echoi, for clarinet, cello, piano and percussion (1961–63)
LIGETI (38)
Fragment, for eleven instruments
Volumina, for organ (1961–62)
BERIO (36)
Visage, electronic music with voice
BOULEZ (36)
Structures, for two pianos, Book II
BROWN (35)
Available Forms II
HENZE (35)
Six absences, pour le clavecin
KORTE (33)
Symphony No. 2

Four Blake Songs, for voices and piano
MUSGRAVE (33)
Serenade, for five instruments
Sir Patrick Spens, for tenor and guitar
HODDINOTT (32)
fp. Piano Concerto No. 2
fp. Violin Concerto
WILLIAMSON (30)
Organ Concerto
GOEHR (29)
Violin Concerto (1961–62)
Suite for six instruments
PENDERECKI (28)
Fluorescences, for orchestra
Dimensions of Time and Silence, for choir and orchestra
Polymorphia
Threnody, for fifty-two stringed instruments
Kanon, for strings and tape
DAVIES (27)
String Quartet
Te Lucis Ante Terminius, for choir and chamber orchestra
MAW (26)
Essay, for organ (revised 1963)
BENNETT (25)
The Ledges, opera
Suite française, for small orchestra
Oboe sonata
NILSSON (24)
Szene II

533

STRAVINSKY (80)
The Flood, opera
Abraham and Isaac, for
  baritone and orchestra
BLISS (71)
The Beatitudes, cantata
MILHAUD (70)
Symphony No. 12
MOORE (69)
*The Greenfield Christmas
  Tree,* a Christmas
  entertainment
PISTON (68)
Lincoln Center, Festival
  overture
String Quartet No. 5
JACOB (67)
News from Newtown,
  cantata
ORFF (67)
Ein Sommernachtstraum
GERHARD (66)
Concert for Eight
THOMSON (66)
A Joyful Fugue, to
  follow *A Solemn Music*
Pange lingua, for organ
TANSMAN (65)
Resurrection, for
  orchestra
Six symphonic studies
  for orchestra
HARRIS (64)
Symphonies Nos. 8 and 9
POULENC (63)
Sept répons des ténèbres,
  for soprano, chorus
  and orchestra
Clarinet Sonata
Oboe Sonata

COPLAND (62)
Connotations, for
  orchestra
Down a Country Lane,
  for orchestra
WALTON (60)
*fp. A Song for the Lord
  Mayor's Table,* song
  cycle
BERKELEY (59)
Batter My Heart, for
  soprano, chorus, organ
  and chamber orchestra
Sonatina, for oboe and
  piano
"Autumn's Legacy", for
  voice and piano
KHACHATURIAN (59)
Cello Sonata
DALLAPICCOLA (58)
Preghiere, for baritone
  and chamber orchestra
KABALEVSKY (58)
Cello Sonata
Requiem (1962–63)
RAWSTHORNE (57)
Medieval Diptych, for
  baritone and orchestra
Divertimento for chamber
  orchestra
Quintet for piano and
  wind
Piano trio
SEIBER (posthumous)
p. Violin Sonata
TIPPETT (57)
Concerto for orchestra
  (1962–63)
Praeludium, for brass,
  bells and percussion

Piano Sonata No. 2
Songs for Ariel
LUTYENS (56)
Music for Orchestra II
Five bagatelles for piano
SHOSTAKOVICH (56)
Symphony No. 13,
   Babi-Yar
BARBER (52)
Piano Concerto
Andromache's Farewell,
   for soprano and
   orchestra
SCHUMAN (52)
Song of Orpheus, fantasy
   for cello and orchestra
LUTOSLAWSKI (49)
*Trois poèmes d'Henri
   Michaux,* for chorus
   and orchestra
   (1962–63)
FINE (48)
Symphony No. 2
DIAMOND (47)
This Sacred Ground, for
   baritone, choruses and
   orchestra
Quartet No. 6
ARNELL (45)
String Quartet No. 5
ARNOLD (41)
Concerto for two violins
   and strings
SHAPEY (41)
Convocation, for chamber
   group
Chamber Symphony for
   ten solo players
Piece for violin and
   instruments
Birthday Piece, for piano

HAMILTON (40)
Arias for small orchestra
Sextet
LIGETI (39)
Poème symphonique,
   for one hundred
   metronomes
Aventures, for three
   singers and seven
   instruments
Nouvelles aventures, for
   three singers and seven
   instruments (1962–63)
BERIO (37)
Passaggio, messa in scena
   for soprano, two choirs
   and instruments
BROWN (36)
Novara, for instrumental
   ensemble
FELDMAN (36)
*The Swallows of
   Salangan,* for chorus
   and instruments
Last Pieces, for piano
HENZE (36)
In re cervo, opera
Les Caprices de Marianne,
   incidental music
Symphony No. 5
Novae de Infinito laudes,
   cantata
KORTE (34)
*Ceremonial Prelude and
   Passacaglia,* for band
Nocturne and March, for
   band
MUSGRAVE (34)
Chamber Concerto No. 1
*The Phoenix and the
   Turtle,* for small chorus
   and orchestra

CONTINUED

STOCKHAUSEN (34)
Momente, for voices and
   instruments (1962–64)
HODDINOTT (33)
fp. Symphony No. 2
fp. Variations for flute,
   clarinet, harp and
   string quartet
fp. Rebecca, for
   unaccompanied voices
GOEHR (30)
A Little Cantata of
   Proverbs
Two Choruses, for mixed
   choir a cappella
PENDERECKI (29)
Stabat Mater
BIRTWISTLE (28)
Chorales for Orchestra
   (1962–63)
DAVIES (28)
First fantasia on an "In
   Nomine" of John
   Taverner, for orchestra
Sinfonia for chamber
   orchestra

Leopardi Fragments, for
   voices and instruments
MAW (27)
Chamber Music for five
   instruments
Scenes and Arias, for
   voices and instruments
Our Lady's Song, for
   unaccompanied voices
BENNETT (26)
London Pastoral Fantasy,
   for tenor and chamber
   orchestra
Sonata No. 2 for solo
   violin
Fantasy, for piano
Three Elegies, for choir
NILSSON (25)
Entree, for orchestra and
   tape
Szene III
TAVENER (18)
Piano Concerto
   (1962–63)
Three Holy Sonnets, for
   voice and orchestra

1963   HINDEMITH and POULENC died

STRAVINSKY (81)
*In Memoriam Aldous
   Huxley,* variations for
   orchestra (1963–64)
MARTIN (73)
Le quatre éléments,
   symphonic studies
   (1963–64)
BLISS (72)
Belmont Variations, for
   brass band
A Knot of Riddles, for

baritone and eleven
   instruments
Mary of Magdala, cantata
MILHAUD (71)
Pacem in terris, for choir
   and orchestra
PISTON (69)
*Variations on a theme of
   Edward Burlinghame
   Hill,* for orchestra
Capriccio, for harp and
   string orchestra

CASTELNUOVO-TEDESCO (68)
Song of Songs
JACOB (68)
Suite for brass band
GERHARD (67)
The Plague, for speaker, chorus and orchestra
Hymnody, for eleven players
HANSON (67)
For the First Time, for orchestra
SESSIONS (67)
Psalm 140, for soprano and organ, or orchestra
TANSMAN (66)
Six movements for string orchestra
HARRIS (65)
Epilogue to Profiles in Courage: J.F.K., for orchestra
Salute to Death
WALTON (61)
Variations on a theme of Hindemith, for orchestra
BERKELEY (60)
Four Ronsard Sonnets, for tenor and orchestra
KABALEVSKY (59)
Three Songs of Revolutionary Cuba
Three Songs
Five songs (1963–64)
RAWSTHORNE (58)
Carmen Vitale, for soprano, chorus and orchestra
LUTYENS (57)
Music for Orchestra III

Encomion, for chorus, brass and percussion
String Quintet
Fantasie Trio, for flute, clarinet and piano
Wind Trio
Présages, for solo oboe
The Country of the Stars, motet
SHOSTAKOVICH (57)
Overture on Russian and Kirghiz Folk Themes
Film music
MESSIAEN (55)
Sept Haï-Kaï
SCHUMAN (53)
Symphony No. 8
MENOTTI (52)
Labyrinth, opera
The Last Savage, opera
Death of the Bishop of Brindisi, cantata
CAGE (51)
Variations III and IV
BRITTEN (50)
Symphony for cello and orchestra
Cantata misericordium, for tenor, baritone, string quartet, string orchestra, piano, harp and timpani
DIAMOND (48)
Quartet No. 7
ARNELL (46)
Musica pacifica
BERNSTEIN (45)
Symphony No. 3, *Kaddish*
ROCHBERG (45)
Piano Trio

CONTINUED

FRICKER (43)
O longs désirs, songs for soprano and orchestra
ARNOLD (42)
Little Suite for Orchestra No. 2
SHAPEY (42)
Brass Quintet
String Quartet No. 6
Seven, for piano (four hands)
HAMILTON (41)
Sonatas and Variants, for ten wind instruments
Nocturnes with Cadenza, for piano
LIGETI (40)
Requiem (1963–65)
MENNIN (40)
Symphony No. 7 (1963–64)
Canto, for orchestra
BERIO (38)
Sincronie, for string quartet (1963–64)
Sequence II, for harp
BROWN (37)
Times Five, for orchestra
From Here, for chorus and orchestra
FELDMAN (37)
Christian Wolff in Cambridge
HENZE (37)
Adagio, for clarinet, horn, bassoon and string quintet
Ariosi, for soprano, violin and orchestra
Los Caprichos, for orchestra
Lucy Escott Variations,

for piano or harpsichord
Being Beauteous, cantata
Cantata della fiaba estrema
KORTE (35)
Southwest, dance overture
Prairie Song, for trumpet and band
Introductions, for brass quintet
Mass for Youth, with orchestra or keyboard
MUSGRAVE (35)
The Five Ages of Man, for chorus and orchestra
STOCKHAUSEN (35)
Plus Minus
HODDINOTT (34)
fp. Sinfonia for string orchestra
fp. Divertimento for oboe, clarinet, horn and bassoon
WILLIAMSON (32)
Our Man in Havana, opera
Elevamini Symphony
GOEHR (31)
Little Symphony
Little Music for Strings
Virtutes, cycle of songs and melodies for chorus, piano duet, and percussion
DAVIES (29)
Veni Sancte Spiritus, for soloists, chorus and small orchestra
Seven *"In Nomine",* for instruments (1963–65)

MAW (28)
Round, for children's choir, mixed choir and piano
The Angel Gabriel, for unaccompanied voices
BEDFORD (26)
Piece for Mo, for instrumental ensemble

Two Poems, for chorus
NILSSON (26)
Versuchungen, for orchestra
TAVENER (19)
Three Sections, from T.S. Eliot's "The Four Quartets" for tenor and piano (1963–64)

1964

MALIPIERO (82)
Symphony No. 8
In Time of Daffodils, for solo voices and instruments
STRAVINSKY (82)
Elegy for J.F.K., for baritone (or mezzo-soprano) and three clarinets
Fanfare for a new theater, for two trumpets
MARTIN (74)
Pilate, cantata
BLISS (73)
Homage to a Great Man (Winston Churchill), march for orchestra
The Golden Cantata
GROFÉ (72)
World's Fair Suite
MILHAUD (72)
La mère coupable, opera (1964–65)
String Septet
PISTON (70)
Sextet for stringed instruments
Piano Quartet

SOWERBY (69)
Symphony No. 5
Piano Sonata
SESSIONS (68)
Symphony No. 5
THOMSON (68)
Autumn Concertino, for harp, strings and percussion
The Feast of Love, for baritone and orchestra
TANSMAN (67)
Il usignolo di Boboli, opera
HARRIS (66)
Horn of Plenty, for orchestra
Duo for cello and piano
CHÁVEZ (65)
Resonancias, for orchestra
Tambuco, for percussion
COPLAND (64)
Emblems for a symphonic band
Music for a Great City, for orchestra
RUBBRA (63)
String Quartet No. 3

CONTINUED

Improvisation for solo
    cello
BERKELEY (61)
Diversions, for eight
    instruments
"Songs of the Half-light",
    for high voice and
    guitar
Mass for five voices
DALLAPICCOLA (60)
*Quattro liriche di Antonio
    Machado,* for soprano
    and orchestra
Parole di San Paolo, for
    voice and instruments
KABALEVSKY (60)
Cello Concerto No. 2
Rhapsody for piano and
    orchestra
ALWYN (59)
Concerto Grosso, No. 3
RAWSTHORNE (59)
Symphony No. 3
Elegiac Rhapsody, for
    strings
TIPPETT (59)
Prologue and Epilogue,
    for choir and orchestra
LUTYENS (58)
*Music for Piano and
    Orchestra*
Music for Wind
Scena, for violin, cello
    and percussion
SHOSTAKOVICH (58)
String Quartets Nos. 9
    and 10
*The Execution of Stepan
    Razin,* cantata
MESSIAEN (56)
*Couleurs de la cité
    céleste*

SCHUMAN (54)
Symphony No. 9
String Trio
MENOTTI (53)
Martin's Lie, opera
BRITTEN (51)
Cello Suite No. 1
Curlew River, parable for
    church performance
GOULD (51)
*World War I:
    Revolutionary Prelude,
    Prologue* (1964–65)
Marches: Formations, for
    band
Festive Music, for
    off-stage trumpet and
    orchestra
LUTOSLAWSKI (51)
String Quartet
DIAMOND (49)
Quartet No. 8
We Two, song cycle
FRICKER (44)
Symphony No. 4
    (1964–66)
ARNOLD (43)
Sinfonietta No. 3
Water Music
FOSS (42)
Elytres, for orchestra
HAMILTON (42)
Organ Concerto
Cantos, for orchestra
Jubilee, for orchestra
BOULEZ (39)
*fp. Figures—Doubles—
    Prismes,* for orchestra
Éclat, for fifteen
    instruments
BROWN (38)
Corroborree, for two or
    three pianos

HENZE (38)

The Young Lord, comic opera

Tancredi, ballet

Divertimenti for two pianos

Choral Fantasy

KORTE (36)

Diablerie, for woodwind quintet

MUSGRAVE (36)

The Decision, opera (1964–65)

STOCKHAUSEN (36)

Mikrophonie I

Mixtur, for five orchestral groups and electronics

HODDINOTT (35)

fp. Jack Straw, overture

fp. Harp Sonata

fp. Intrada, for organ

fp. Sarum Fanfare, for organ

fp. Toccata all Giga, for organ

fp. Dangegeld, for unaccompanied voices

WILLIAMSON (33)

The Display, dance symphony

The Merry Wives of Windsor, incidental music

Piano Concerto No. 3

Sinfonia concertante, for piano, trumpets and orchestra

Variations for cello and piano

Elegy J.F.K., for organ

Three Shakespeare Songs,

for voice and guitar (or piano)

GOEHR (32)

Five poems and an Epigram of William Blake, for chorus

PENDERECKI (31)

Sonata for cello and orchestra

BIRTWISTLE (30)

Three Movements with Fanfares, for orchestra

Entr'actes and Sappho Fragments, for soprano and instruments

Description of the Passing of a Year, narration for mixed choir a cappella

DAVIES (30)

Second Fantasia on John Taverner's "In Nomine", for orchestra

Shakespeare Music

MAW (29)

One Man Show, comic opera

Corpus Christi Carol

Balulalow, for unaccompanied voices

BENNETT (28)

The Mines of Sulphur, opera

Jazz Calendar, ballet

Aubade, for orchestra

String Quartet No. 4

Nocturnes, for piano

BEDFORD (27)

A Dream of Seven Lost Stars, for choir and

CONTINUED

chamber orchestra
(1964–65)
NILSSON (27)
La Bran, for choir and
orchestra

TAVENER (20)
The Cappemakers, for
narrators, solo voices,
chorus and instruments

1965

KODÁLY (83)
Variations for piano
MALIPIERO (83)
Costellazioni, for piano
MARTIN (75)
Cello Concerto
(1965–66)
PISTON (71)
Symphony No. 8
Pine Tree Fantasy, for
orchestra
Ricercare, for orchestra
JACOB (70)
Festival Te Deum
SOWERBY (70)
Solomon's Garden, for
chorus and orchestra
GERHARD (69)
Concerto for orchestra
SESSIONS (69)
Piano Sonata No. 3
HARRIS (67)
Symphony No. 10
Rhythm and Spaces, for
string orchestra
CHÁVEZ (66)
Violin Concerto No. 2
Soli No. 3, for bassoon,
trumpet, viola, timpani
and orchestra
Inventions No. 2, for
violin, viola and cello

RUBBRA (64)
Inscape, suite for chorus,
strings and harp
RODRIGO (63)
Sonata Pimpante, for
violin and piano
(1965–66)
WALTON (63)
The Twelve, for chorus
and orchestra
BERKELEY (62)
Partita, for chamber
orchestra
Three songs for four male
voices
KHACHATURIAN (62)
Concerto-Rhapsody, for
cello and orchestra
KABALEVSKY (61)
Symphonic Prelude
Rondo for cello and piano
RAWSTHORNE (60)
*Tankas of the Four
Seasons,* for tenor and
chamber ensemble
Concertante, for violin
and piano
TIPPETT (60)
Vision of St. Augustine,
for baritone, chorus
and orchestra
The Shires Suite, for

chorus and orchestra
(1965–70)
LUTYENS (59)
The Numbered, opera
The Valley of Hatsu-Se,
for solo voice and
instruments
SHOSTAKOVICH (59)
Five Romances on texts
from *Krokodil*
magazine, for bass
and piano
MESSIAEN (57)
*La Transfiguration de
notre Seigneur
Jésus-Christ* (1965–69)
CAGE (53)
Variations V
BRITTEN (52)
Gemini Variations, for
flute, violin and piano
(four hands)
*Songs and Proverbs of
William Blake,* for
voice and piano
The Poet's Echo, for
voice and piano
Voices for Today, for
chorus
LUTOSLAWSKI (62)
Paroles tissées, for voice
and instruments
BERNSTEIN (47)
Chichester Psalms, for
chorus and orchestra
ROCHBERG (47)
*Music for the Magic
Theater*
Zodiac, for orchestra
Black Sounds, for winds
and percussion
Contra Mortem et

Tempus, for violin,
flute, clarinet and piano
La bocca della verita,
for violin and piano
FRICKER (45)
Four *Dialogues,* for
oboe and piano
Ricercare for organ
Four songs for soprano
and piano (or
orchestra)
ARNOLD (44)
Five *Fantasies,* for
bassoon: clarinet: flute:
horn: oboe
SHAPEY (44)
String Trio
Configurations, for flute
and piano
FOSS (43)
Fragments of Archilochos,
for chorus, speaker,
soloists and chamber
ensemble
HAMILTON (43)
String Quartet No. 2
Dialogues, for soprano
and instruments
Aubade, for solo organ
BERIO (40)
Laborintus II, for voices,
instruments and tape
Rounds, for cembalo
Sequence III, for solo
voice
BROWN (39)
String Quartet
Nine Rarebits, for one or
two harpsichords
FELDMAN (39)
De Kooning, for piano

CONTINUED

543

trio, horn and
percussion
*Journey to the End of
Night,* for soprano and
four wind instruments
Four Instruments
HENZE (38)
The Bassarids, opera
*In Memoriam: The White
Rose,* for chamber
orchestra
KORTE (37)
String Quartet No. 2
Aspects of Love, songs
MUSGRAVE (37)
Festival Overture
Excursions, for piano
(four hands)
STOCKHAUSEN (37)
Stop, for orchestra
Mikrophonie II
Solo (1965–66)
HODDINOTT (36)
fp. Concerto grosso No. 1
fp. Aubade and Scherzo,
for horn and strings
fp. Dives and Lazarus,
cantata
WILLIAMSON (34)
The Happy Prince, opera
Violin Concerto
Concerto grosso, for
orchestra
Sinfonietta
Symphonic Variations,
for orchestra
Concerto for two pianos
and wind quintet
*Four North-Country
Songs,* for voice and
orchestra
GOEHR (33)
Pastorals, for orchestra

PENDERECKI (32)
Capriccio, for oboe and
strings
BIRTWISTLE (31)
Tragoedia, for
instrumental ensemble
Ring a Dumb Carillon,
for soprano, clarinet
and percussion
Carmen Paschale, motet
for mixed chorus and
organ
DAVIES (31)
Revelation and Fall, for
soprano and
instruments
The Shepherd's Calendar,
for singer and
instruments
*Shall I die for mannes
sake,* for soprano and
alto voices and piano
Ecce manus tradentis, for
mixed choir and
instruments
MAW (30)
String Quartet
BENNETT (29)
Symphony No. 1
Trio for oboe, flute and
clarinet
Diversions, for piano
BEDFORD (28)
This One for You, for
orchestra
*Music for Albion
Moonlight,* for soprano
and instruments
"O now the drenched
land awakes", for
baritone and piano duet

NILSSON (28)
Litanei uber das verlorene Schlagzeug
TAVENER (21)
Chamber Concerto
(revised 1968)

The Whale, for chorus and orchestra
(1965–66)
Cain and Abel, cantata

1966   TAYLOR died

MALIPIERO (84)
Symphony No. 9
STRAVINSKY (84)
Requiem Canticles, for solo voices, chorus and orchestra
MOORE (73)
Carry Nation, opera
PISTON (72)
Variations for cello and orchestra
Piano Trio No. 2
CASTELNUOVO-TEDESCO (71)
Sonata for cello and harp
JACOB (71)
Oboe Sonata
Variations on a theme of Schubert
SOWERBY (71)
Symphonia brevis, for organ
GERHARD (70)
Epithalium, for orchestra
Gemini, for violin and piano
HANSON (70)
Summer Seascape
ROBERTSON (70)
Piano Concerto
SESSIONS (70)
Symphony No. 6

Six Pieces for Cello
THOMSON (70)
Lord Byron, opera
(1966–68)
Fantasy in Homage to an Earlier England, for orchestra
The Nativity, for soloists, chorus and orchestra
(1966–67)
Étude, for cello and piano
TANSMAN (69)
Concertino, for oboe and chamber orchestra
CHÁVEZ (67)
Soli No. 4, for brass trio
WALTON (64)
Missa brevis
KHACHATURIAN (63)
Suite for Orchestra, No. 4
KABALEVSKY (62)
The Motherland, cantata
ALWYN (61)
Derby Day, overture
RAWSTHORNE (61)
Cello Concerto
Sonatine, for flute, oboe and piano
String Quartet No. 3
TIPPETT (61)
The Knot Garden, opera
(1966–70)

CONTINUED

545

546

MUSGRAVE (38)
Nocturnes and Arias, for
  orchestra
Chamber Concertos Nos.
  2 and 3
STOCKHAUSEN (38)
Adieu, for wind quintet
Hymnen, for mixed media
Telemusik, electronic
  music
HODDINOTT (37)
fp. Pantomime, overture
fp. Piano Concerto No. 3
fp. Varlants, for
  orchestra
fp. Concerto grosso, No. 2
fp. String Quartet No. 1
fp. Piano Sonata No. 4
WILLIAMSON (35)
Julius Caesar Jones, opera
The Violins of St. Jacques,
  opera
Sun Into Darkness, ballet
Five Preludes for piano
Two Organ Epitaphs for
  Edith Sitwell
Six English Lyrics, for
  voice and piano

GOEHR (34)
Arden Muss Sterben
  (Arden Must Die),
  opera
BIRTWISTLE (32)
Punch and Judy, opera
  (1966–67)
Verses, for clarinet and
  piano
DAVIES (32)
Notre Dame des fleurs,
  for solo voices and
  instruments
Five carols
MAW (31)
Sinfonia for small
  orchestra
The Voice of Love, song
  cycle
BENNETT (30)
Epithalamion, for voices
  and orchestra
Childe Rolande, for voice
  and piano
BEDFORD (29)
*That White and Radiant
  Legend,* for soprano,
  speaker and instruments
Piano Piece I

1967 AUBERT and KODÁLY died

KODÁLY (85)
Laudes Organi, for chorus
  and organ
MALIPIERO (85)
Symphony No. 10
Carnet de Notes, for
  chamber orchestra
Cassazione, for string
  sextet

MARTIN (77)
String Quartet
BLISS (76)
River Music, for
  unaccompanied choir
PISTON (73)
Clarinet Concerto
JACOB (72)
Concerto for Band
CONTINUED

Six miniatures
Animal Magic, cantata
SOWERBY (72)
Organ Concerto No. 2
Dialogue, for organ and
  piano
Organ Passacaglia
GERHARD (71)
Symphony No. 4,
  New York
HANSON (71)
Dies Natalis, for
  orchestra
SESSIONS (71)
Symphony No. 7
THOMSON (71)
*Shipwreck and Love
  Scene,* from "Don
  Juan", for tenor and
  orchestra
HARRIS (69)
Symphony No. 11
CHÁVEZ (68)
Inventions No. 3, for harp
COPLAND (67)
Inscape, for orchestra
DURUFLÉ (65)
Mass *Cum jubilo,* for
  baritone, choir, organ
  and orchestra
RODRIGO (65)
Concierto andaluz, for
  four guitars and
  orchestra
WALTON (65)
The Bear, opera
BERKELEY (64)
Castaway, opera
Oboe Quartet
Nocturne for harp
Signs in the Dark, for
  voices and strings

KABALEVSKY (63)
Recitative and Rondo, for
  piano
RAWSTHORNE (62)
Overture for Farnham
*Theme, Variations and
  Finale,* for orchestra
Scena rustica, for soprano
  and harp
The God in the Cave,
  cantata
LUTYENS (61)
*Time Off? Not the ghost
  of a chance,* charade
Novenaria, for orchestra
Scroll for Li-Ho, for
  violin and piano
Helix, for piano (four
  hands)
SHOSTAKOVICH (61)
Violin Concerto No. 2
*Funeral—Triumphal
  Prelude,* for orchestra
October, symphonic poem
Seven Romances on
  poems of Alexander
  Blok, for soprano and
  piano trio
Spring, Spring, for bass
  and piano
Film music
MENOTTI (56)
Canti della lontananza,
  song cycle
CAGE (55)
H P S C H D (1967–69)
BRITTEN (54)
*The Building of the
  House,* overture
Cello Suite No. 2
GOULD (54)
Vivaldi Gallery, for string

quartet or divided orchestra

LUTOSLAWSKI (54)
Symphony No. 2

DIAMOND (52)
Choral Symphony, *To Music*
Violin Concerto No. 3
Hebrew Melodies, song cycle

ARNELL (50)
Sections, for piano and orchestra

FRICKER (47)
Seven Counterpoints for Orchestra
Episodes I, for piano (1967–68)
Ave Maris Stella, for male voices and piano
Cantilena and Cabaletta, for solo soprano (1967–68)

ARNOLD (46)
Symphony No. 6
Peterloo, for orchestra
Concert Piece, for piano and percussion
Trevelyan Suite, for wind band

SHAPEY (46)
Partita-Fantasy, for cello and sixteen players
Reyem, for flute, violin and piano
Deux, for two pianos
For Solo Trumpet
Songs of Ecstasy, for soprano, tape and instruments

FOSS (45)
Cello Concerto

Baroque Variations, for orchestra
Phorion, for orchestra, electronic organ, harpsichord and guitar

HAMILTON (45)
Agamemnon, opera (1967–69)
Royal Hunt of the Sun, opera (1967–69)

LIGETI (44)
Lontana, for orchestra
Two Studies for Organ (1967–69)

MENNIN (44)
Piano Sonata

BERIO (42)
Rounds, for piano
Sequence VI, for viola
O King, for voice and five players

BROWN (41)
Event—Synergy II (1967–68)

FELDMAN (41)
Chorus and Instruments
In Search of an Orchestration

HENZE (40)
Piano Concerto No. 2
Telemanniana, for orchestra
Moralities, three scenic cantatas

MUSGRAVE (39)
Concerto for Orchestra
Music for horn and piano
Impromptu, for flute and oboe

STOCKHAUSEN (39)
Prozession, for mixed media

CONTINUED

549

HODDINOTT (37)
fp. Organ Concerto
fp. Night Music, for
  orchestra
fp. Clarinet Sonata
fp. Suite for harp
WILLIAMSON (36)
Dunstan and the Devil,
  opera
Pas de Quatre, ballet
The Moonrakers,
  cassation
Serenade, for instruments
Sonata for two pianos
GOEHR (35)
String Quartet No. 2
Warngedichte, for voice
  and piano
PENDERECKI (34)
Pittsburgh Overture, for
  wind and percussion
Dies Irae, oratorio
DAVIES (33)
Antechrist, for chamber
  ensemble
Hymnos, for clarinet and
  piano

MAW (32)
Sonata for strings and
  two horns
*Double Canon for Igor
  Stravinsky*
BENNETT (31)
A Penny for a Song, opera
Symphony No. 2
Wind Quintet
*The Music That Her Echo
  Is,* song cycle
BEDFORD (30)
Trona for Twelve,
  instrumental ensemble
Five, for five strings
*18 Bricks Left on April
  21st,* for two electric
  guitars
NILSSON (30)
Revue, for orchestra
TAVENER (23)
Grandma's Footsteps, for
  chamber orchestra
Three Surrealist Songs
  (1967–68)

1968 CASTELNUOVO-TEDESCO and SOWERBY
        died

MALIPIERO (86)
Gli eroi di Bonaventura
Flute Concerto
MARTIN (78)
Piano Concerto No. 2
Maria-Triptychon, for
  soprano, solo violin and
  orchestra
JACOB (73)
Divertimento

Suite for bassoon and
  string quartet
GERHARD (72)
Libra, for flute, clarinet,
  violin, guitar, piano and
  percussion
HANSON (72)
Symphony No. 6
SESSIONS (72)
Symphony No. 8

TANSMAN (71)
Four Movements for
  orchestra
HARRIS (70)
Concerto for amplified
  piano, brasses and
  percussion
Piano Sextet
RUBBRA (67)
Symphony No. 8
Violin Sonata No. 3
Advent Cantata
RODRIGO (66)
Concierto madrigal, for
  two guitars and
  orchestra
WALTON (66)
Capriccio burlesca, for
  orchestra
BERKELEY (65)
Theme and variations for
  piano duet
The Windhover, for mixed
  choir
KABALEVSKY (64)
Sisters, opera
Colas Breugnon, revised
  version
RAWSTHORNE (63)
Concerto for two pianos
  and orchestra
Trio for flute, viola and
  harp
LUTYENS (62)
Essence of Our Happiness,
  for voices and orchestra
A Phoenix, for soprano
  and instruments
Horai, for violin, horn and
  piano
Epithalamium, for organ
  (soprano solo optional)

The Egocentric, for voice
  and piano
The Tyme Doth Flete, for
  unaccompanied voices
SHOSTAKOVICH (62)
String Quartet No. 12
Sonata, for violin and
  grand piano
MENOTTI (57)
*Help, help, the
  Globolinks*, children's
  opera
BRITTEN (55)
The Children's Crusade,
  for children's voices
  and orchestra
The Prodigal Son,
  parable for church
  performance
GOULD (55)
Troubador Music, for
  four guitars and
  orchestra
LUTOSLAWSKI (55)
Livre pour orchestre
ARNELL (51)
The Food of Love,
  overture
Nocturne: Prague 1968,
  for mixed media
ROCHBERG (50)
Symphony No. 3, *A
  20th-century Passion*
Tableaux, for soprano and
  eleven players
FRICKER (48)
Concertante No. 4, for
  flute, oboe, violin and
  strings
Refrains, for solo oboe
Gladius Domini, toccata
  for organ

CONTINUED

Six Pieces for organ

Magnificat, for solo
  voices, choir and
  orchestra

Some Serious Nonsense,
  for tenor and
  instruments

HAMILTON (46)

Pharsalia, opera

LIGETI (45)

Ramifications, for string
  orchestra (1968–69)

Ten Pieces for wind
  quintet

String Quartet No. 2

Continuum, for
  harpsichord

MENNIN (45)

Cantata de virtute
  (1968–69)

BERIO (43)

Sinfonia

Queste vuol dire che, for
  three female voices,
  small choir and tape

BOULEZ (43)

fp. Domaines, for clarinet
  and twenty-one
  instruments

FELDMAN (42)

*False Relationships and
  the Extended Ending*,
  for two chamber groups

Vertical Thoughts 2

HENZE (41)

Essay on Pigs, for voice
  and orchestra

*The Raft of the
  "Medusa"*, oratorio

KORTE (40)

Symphony No. 3

Matrix, for instruments

May the Sun Bless Us,
  for male voices, brass
  and percussion

MUSGRAVE (40)

Beauty and the Beast,
  ballet (1968–69)

Clarinet Concerto

STOCKHAUSEN (40)

Aus den Sieben Tagen,
  fifteen compositions for
  ensemble

Für Kommende Zeiten,
  for ensemble

Kurzwellen, for piano and
  amplified instruments

Spiral, for mixed media

Stimmung, for six
  vocalists

HODDINOTT (39)

fp. Symphony No. 3

fp. Sinfonietta 1

fp. Fioriture, for
  orchestra

fp. Divertimenti for eight
  instruments

*fp. Nocturnes and
  Cadenzas*, for clarinet,
  violin and piano

fp. Piano Sonata No. 5

fp. Roman Dream, for
  soprano and
  instruments

*fp. An Apple Tree and a
  Pig*, for unaccompanied
  voices

WILLIAMSON (37)

The Growing Castle,
  opera

*Knights in Shining
  Armour*, cassation

The Snow Wolf, cassation

Piano Quintet

From a Child's Garden,
   twelve poems for voice
   and piano
GOEHR (36)
Naboth's Vineyard,
   dramatic madrigal
Romanza, for cello and
   orchestra
PENDERECKI (35)
The Devils of Loudon,
   opera
String Quartet No. 2
*Capriccio for Siegfried
   Palm,* for solo cello
BIRTWISTLE (34)
Nomos, for four amplified
   wind instruments and
   orchestra
Linoi, for clarinet and
   piano

DAVIES (34)
L'Homme Armé, for
   speaker (or singer) and
   chamber ensemble
BENNETT (32)
All the King's Men,
   children's opera
Piano Concerto
Crazy Jane, for soprano
   and instruments
BEDFORD (31)
Gastrula, for orchestra
Pentomino, for wind
   quintet
Piano Piece II
"Come in here, child", for
   soprano and amplified
   piano
TAVENER (24)
In Alium, for soprano and
   orchestra

1969

MARTIN (79)
Erasme Monumentum,
   for orchestra and organ
Poèmes de la mort, for
   solo male voices and
   three electric guitars
BLISS (78)
*The World is Charged
   with the Grandeur of
   God,* for chorus and
   wind
Miniature Scherzo for
   piano
Angels of the Mind, song
   cycle
JACOB (74)
Redbridge Variations

Piano Quartet
ORFF (74)
*De Temporum fine
   comoedia,* cantata
   (1969–71)
GERHARD (73)
Leo, chamber symphony
TANSMAN (72)
*Hommage à Erasme de
   Rotherdam,* for
   orchestra
Concertino, for flute and
   chamber orchestra
HARRIS (71)
Symphony No. 12
CHÁVEZ (70)
Clio, Symphonic ode

CONTINUED

553

Soliloquy, for guitar and
tape

STOCKHAUSEN (41)

Fresco, for four orchestral
groups

For Dr. K., for
instruments

Pole für 2 (1969–70)

Expo für 3 (1969–70)

HODDINOTT (40)

fp. Symphony No. 4

fp. Divertimento, for
orchestra

fp. Sinfonietta 2

fp. Horn Concerto

*fp. Nocturnes and
Cadenzas,* for cello and
orchestra

fp. Investiture Dances,
for orchestra

fp. Black Bart, for voices
and orchestra

fp. Violin Sonata No. 1

WILLIAMSON (38)

Lucky Peter's Journey,
comedy with music

*The Brilliant and the
Dark,* choral-operatic
sequence

Symphony No. 2

GOEHR (37)

Konzertstücke, for piano
and small orchestra

Nonomiya, for piano

Paraphrase on a
Monteverdi madrigal,
for solo clarinet

PENDERECKI (36)

Utrenja, for solo voices,
choirs, and orchestra
(1969–71)

BIRTWISTLE (35)

*Down by the Greenwood
Side,* dramatic pastoral

Verses for ensemble, for
instrumental ensemble

Medusa, for instrumental
ensemble (1969–70)

Ut Heremita Solus,
arrangement of
instrumental motet

*Hoquetus David (Double
Hoquet),* arrangement
of instrumental motet

Cantata for soprano and
instrumental ensemble

DAVIES (35)

St. Thomas Wake, for
orchestra

Worldes Bliss, for
orchestra

*Eight Songs for a Mad
King,* for male singer
and chamber ensemble

Vesalii icones, for dancer,
solo cello and ensemble

Eram quasi Agnus,
instrumental motet

MAW (34)

The Rising of the Moon,
opera (1969–70)

BENNETT (33)

*A Garland for Marjory
Fleming,* for soprano
and piano

BEDFORD (32)

*The Tentacles of the Dark
Nebula,* for tenor and
instruments

TAVENER (25)

Celtic Requiem, for voices
and orchestra

MALIPIERO (88)
Symphony No. 11
MARTIN (80)
Three Dances, for oboe,
  harp, string quintet and
  string orchestra
BLISS (79)
Cello Concerto
JACOB (75)
A York Symphony, for
  orchestra
A Joyful Noise, for brass
  band
The Pride of Youth, for
  brass band
SESSIONS (74)
Rhapsody, for orchestra
*When Lilacs Last in the
  Dooryard Bloom'd,*
  cantata
RUBBRA (69)
Piano Trio No. 2
WALTON (68)
*Improvisations on an
  Impromptu of Britten,*
  for orchestra
BERKELEY (67)
Dialogues, for cello and
  chamber orchestra
String Quartet No. 3
Theme and Variations, for
  guitar
DALLAPICCOLA (66)
Sicut umbra
Tempus aedificandi
ALWYN (65)
Sinfonietta for strings
RAWSTHORNE (65)
Oboe Quartet

TIPPETT (65)
Symphony No. 3
  (1970–72)
Songs for Dov, for voice
  and orchestra
LUTYENS (64)
Anerca, for narrator,
  guitars and percussion
Vision of Youth, for
  soprano and
  instruments
*In the Direction of the
  Beginning,* for voice
  and piano
Oda a la Tormenta, for
  mezzo-soprano and
  piano
Verses of Love, for
  unaccompanied voices
SHOSTAKOVICH (64)
*March of the Soviet
  Militia,* for wind
  orchestra
String Quartet No. 13
Loyalty, for male chorus
Film music
MENOTTI (59)
The Leper, drama
Triplo concerto a tre,
  symphonic piece
BRITTEN (57)
Owen Wingrave, opera
ROCHBERG (52)
Mizmor L'Piyus, for
  bass-baritone and small
  orchestra
Songs of Krishna, for
  soprano and piano

FRICKER (50)
Paseo, for guitar
The Roofs, for soprano and percussion
HAMILTON (48)
Alastor, for orchestra
Voyage, for horn and chamber orchestra
Epitaph for this world and time, for three choirs and three organs
BERIO (45)
Memory, for electric piano and electric cembalo
BOULEZ (45)
Multiples, for orchestra
fp. Cummings ist der Dichter, for voices and instruments
FELDMAN (44)
Madam Press died last week at 90
The Viola in My Life, I, II and III
BROWN (43)
Syntagm II, for instrumental ensemble
KORTE (42)
Gestures, for electric brass, percussion, piano and band
Psalm XIII, for chorus and tape
MUSGRAVE (42)
Elegy, for viola and cello
From one to another, for viola and tape
Impromptu No. 2 for flute, oboe and clarinet
STOCKHAUSEN (42)
Mantra, for two pianists

HODDINOTT (41)
fp. The Sun, the Great Luminary of the Universe, for orchestra
fp. Sinfonietta 3
fp. Violin Sonata No. 2
fp. Cello Sonata
fp. Fantasy for harp
GOEHR (38)
Symphony in one movement
Concerto for eleven instruments
Sonata about Jerusalem
Shadowplay 2, music theater for tenor and instruments
PENDERECKI (37)
Kosmogonia, for solo voices, chorus and orchestra
BIRTWISTLE (36)
Four Interludes from a Tragedy, for clarinet and tape
Nenia on the Death of Orpheus, for soprano and instruments
Prologue, for tenor and instruments
DAVIES (36)
Taverner, opera
BENNETT (34)
Guitar Concerto
BEDFORD (33)
The Garden of Love, for instrumental ensemble
The Sword of Orion, for instrumental ensemble
NILSSON (33)
Attraktionen, for string quartet

CONTINUED

TAVENER (26)
Nomine Jesu, for voices
  and orchestra

Coplas, for voices and
  tape

1971   RAWSTHORNE, ROBERTSON and
         STRAVINSKY died

MARTIN (81)
Requiem (1971–72)
BLISS (80)
Two Ballads for women's
  chorus and small
  orchestra
Triptych, for piano
JACOB (76)
Rhapsody for three hands
  (piano)
SESSIONS (75)
Concerto for viola and
  cello
COPLAND (71)
Duo for flute and piano
BERKELEY (68)
"Palm Court Waltz", for
  orchestra, or piano duet
*In Memoriam Igor
  Stravinsky,* for string
  quartet
"Duo" for cello and piano
Introduction and Allegro,
  for double-bass and
  piano
Chinese Songs, for voice
  and piano
DALLAPICCOLA (67)
Tempus destruendi
RAWSTHORNE (66)
Quintet for piano, clarinet,
  horn, violin and cello
LUTYENS (65)
*Dirge for the Proud
  World,* for soprano,

  counter-tenor,
  harpsichord and cello
Driving Out the Death,
  for oboe and string trio
Islands, for narrator, solo
  voices and instrumental
  ensemble
*Requiescat (Igor
  Stravinsky 1971),* for
  soprano and string trio
The Tears of Night, for
  voices and instruments
SHOSTAKOVICH (65)
Symphony No. 15
BARBER (61)
The Lovers, for baritone,
  chorus and orchestra
MENOTTI (60)
*fp. The Most Important
  Man in the World,*
  opera
BRITTEN (58)
Cello Suite No. 3
Canticle IV, "Journey of
  the Magi"
GOULD (58)
Suite for tuba and three
  horns
ARNELL (54)
I think of all soft limbs,
  for mixed media
BERNSTEIN (53)
Mass, theater piece for
  singers, players and
  dancers

FRICKER (51)

Sarabande in memoriam Igor Stravinsky

Nocturne, for chamber orchestra

Concertante No. 5, for piano and string quartet

A Bourrée for Sir Arthur Bliss, for cello

Intrada, for organ

HAMILTON (49)

Violin Concerto No. 2, *Amphion*

LIGETI (48)

Melodien, for orchestra

Horizont, for recorder

MENNIN (48)

Sinfonia for Orchestra

BERIO (46)

Bewegung I and II, for orchestra

Ora, for voice, instruments and small orchestra

Autre fois, for flute, clarinet and harp

Agnus, for two sopranos and three clarinets

Amores, for voices and instruments

FELDMAN (45)

Chorus and Orchestra I

The Viola in My Life IV

Three clarinets, cello and piano

Rothko Chapel

I Met Heine . . .

HENZE (44)

Violin Concerto No. 2

Heliogabalus imperator, for orchestra (1971–72)

KORTE (43)

I think you would have understood, for mixed media

Remembrances, for flute and tape

MUSGRAVE (43)

Horn Concerto

Primavera, for soprano and flute

STOCKHAUSEN (43)

Sternklang, for five groups

Trans, for orchestra

HODDINOTT (42)

fp. *The Tree of Life,* for solo voices, chorus, organ and orchestra

fp. Concertino, for trumpet, horn and orchestra

fp. Oboe Concerto

fp. Horn Sonata

fp. Violin Sonata No. 3

fp. Out of the Deep, motet

WILLIAMSON (40)

Genesis, cassation

The Stone Wall, cassation

Death of Cuchulain, for five male voices and percussion

Peace Pieces, for organ

In Place of Belief, settings of ten poems, for voices and piano duet

PENDERECKI (38)

Actions, for jazz ensemble

De Natura Sonoris, II, for winds, percussion and strings

Prélude (1971), for winds, percussion and double-basses

CONTINUED

559

BIRTWISTLE (37)
An Imaginary Landscape,
  for orchestra
The Fields of Sorrow, for
  voices and instruments
Meridian, for voices and
  instruments
Chronometer, for eight-
  track electronic tape
DAVIES (37)
From Stone to Thorn, for
  mezzo-soprano and
  instruments
MAW (36)
*Epitaph—Canon in
  memory of Igor
  Stravinsky,* for flute,
  clarinet and harp
BEDFORD (34)
Nurse's Song with

Elephants, for singer
  and ten acoustic guitars
*Star Clusters, Nebulae
  and Places in Devon,*
  for mixed double
  chorus and brass
*With One Hundred
  Kazoos,* for
  instrumental ensemble
  and kazoos
"Some Stars Above
  Magnitude 2.9", for
  soprano and piano
TAVENER (27)
*In memoriam Igor
  Stravinsky,* for two
  alto flutes, organ and
  bells
Responsorium, for voices
  and flutes

1972 GROFÉ died

MARTIN (82)
Ballade, for viola, wind
  orchestra, cembalo,
  harp and timpani
BLISS (81)
Metamorphic Variations,
  for orchestra
Three songs
JACOB (77)
Double-bass Concerto
Tuba Suite
Psalm 103
COPLAND (72)
Three Latin-American
  Sketches
WALTON (70)
Sonata for string orchestra
Jubilate Deo, for double
  chorus and organ

Five bagatelles for guitar
BERKELEY (69)
Four Concert Studies
  for piano, set 2
"Hymn for Shakespeare's
  Birthday", for mixed
  choir and organ
Three Latin motets, for
  five-part choir
TIPPETT (67)
Piano Sonata No. 3
  (1972–73)
LUTYENS (66)
*The Linnet from the
  Leaf,* for voices and
  instrumental groups
Voice of Quiet Waters,
  for chorus and
  orchestra

Counting Your Steps, for
chorus, flutes and
percussion
Chimes and Cantos, for
voice and instruments
Dialogo, for tenor and
lute
Plenum I, for piano
SHOSTAKOVICH (66)
String Quartet No. 14
LUTOSLAWSKI (59)
Preludes and Fugue, for
thirteen solo strings
ROCHBERG (54)
String Quartet No. 3
Electrikaleidoscope
Ricordanza, for cello and
piano
FRICKER (52)
Introitus, for orchestra
Ballade, for flute and
piano
Fanfare for Europe, for
trumpet
Come Sleep, for contralto,
alto flute and bass-
clarinet
Seven Little Songs for
Chorus
FOSS (50)
Ni bruit, ni vitesse, for
pianos and percussion
Cave of the Winds, for
wind quintet
HAMILTON (50)
Commedia, concerto for
orchestra
Palinodes, for solo piano
*Descent of the Celestial
City,* for chorus and
organ

LIGETI (49)
Kylwyria, opera
Double Concerto for flute,
oboe and orchestra
BERIO (47)
Concerto for two pianos
and orchestra
(1972–73)
E Vó, for soprano and
instruments
Recital I (for Cathy), for
mezzo-soprano and
instruments
BOULEZ (47)
. . . Explosante-fixe . . . ,
for ensemble and live
electronics (1972–74)
FELDMAN (46)
Cello and Orchestra
Chorus and Orchestra II
Voice and Instruments
Voices and Instruments
*Pianos and Voices I
and II*
BROWN (45)
Time Spans, for orchestra
New Piece: Loops, for
chorus and/or
orchestra
Sign Sounds, for
instrumental ensemble
MUSGRAVE (44)
The Voice of Ariadne,
chamber opera
(1972–73)
STOCKHAUSEN (44)
Alphabet für Liege
*Am Himmel Wander
Ich . . . ,* Indianerlieder
Ylem, for nineteen
players/singers
CONTINUED

HODDINOTT (43)

fp. Aubade, for small
orchestra

fp. Piano Sonata No. 6

fp. The Hawk is Set Free,
for orchestra

WILLIAMSON (41)

The Red Sea, opera

Symphony No. 3, *The
Icy Mirror,* for solo
voices, chorus and
orchestra

Partita for Viola, on
themes of Walton

The Musicians of Bremen,
for six male voices

Love the Sentinel, for
unaccompanied voices

PENDERECKI (39)

Partita, for harpsichord,
five solo instruments
(amplified) and
orchestra

Canticum canticorum
Salomonis (Song of
Songs), for sixteen-
voice chorus, chamber
orchestra and dance
pair

BIRTWISTLE (38)

The Triumph of Time,
for orchestra

*Tombeau—In memoriam
Igor Stravinsky,* for
flute, clarinet, harp and
string quartet

*Dinah and Nick's Love
Song,* for instruments

La Plage, for soprano
and instruments

*Epilogue—Full Fathom
Five,* for baritone and
instruments

DAVIES (38)

Blind Man's Buff,
masque

*Canon in memory
of Igor Stravinsky,*
for instrumental
ensemble

Fool's Fanfare, for
speaker and instruments

Hymn to St. Magnus,
for soprano and
chamber ensemble

Tenebrae super Gesualdo,
for mezzo-soprano,
guitar and chamber
ensemble

MAW (37)

*Concert Music for
Orchestra*

Five Irish Songs, for
chorus

BENNETT (36)

Commedia II, for flute,
cello and piano

BEDFORD (35)

An Easy Decision, for
soprano and piano

*Holy Thursday with
Squeakers,* for soprano
and instruments

Spillihpnerak, for viola

*When I Heard the
Learned Astronomer,*
for tenor and
instruments

TAVENER (28)

Variations on "Three
Blind Mice", for
orchestra

Ultimos ritos, for voices
and orchestra with
amplified instruments

Ma fin est mon

commencement,
for voices and
instruments

Canciones espanolas, for
voices and instruments
*Little Requiem for Father
Malachy Lynch*

1973 MALIPIERO died

MARTIN (83)
Polyptyque, for violin
and two small string
orchestras
*Fantasy on Flamenco
rhythms,* for piano
JACOB (78)
Saxophone Quartet
ORFF (78)
Rota, for chorus and
instruments
THOMSON (77)
Cantata based on
Nonsense Rhymes
BERKELEY (71)
Antiphon, for string
orchestra
Voices of the Night, for
orchestra
Sinfonia concertante, for
oboe and orchestra
ALWYN (68)
Symphony No. 5,
Hydriotaphia
LUTYENS (67)
One and the Same, scena
for soprano, speaker,
two female mimes,
male mime and
instrumental ensemble
The Waiting Game, three
scenes for mezzo-
soprano, baritone and
small orchestra

Rape of the Moone, for
wind octet
Laudi, for soprano and
instruments
Roads, for two sopranos,
counter-tenor, baritone
and bass
Plenum II, for solo oboe
Plenum III, for string
quartet
Tre, for solo clarinet
SHOSTAKOVICH (67)
Six poems of Maria
Tsvetaeva, suite for
contralto and piano
BARBER (63)
fp. String Quartet
SCHUMAN (63)
*Concerto on Old English
Rounds,* for solo viola,
women's chorus and
orchestra
MENOTTI (62)
fp. Suite for two cellos
and piano
BRITTEN (60)
Death in Venice, opera
ARNELL (56)
Astronaut One, for mixed
media
FRICKER (53)
Gigue for cello
The Grove of Dodona,
for six flutes

CONTINUED

563

ARNOLD (52)
Symphony No. 7
FOSS (51)
MAP, a musical game
MENNIN (50)
fp. Symphony No. 8
BERIO (48)
Eindrücke, for orchestra
  (1973–74)
Still, for orchestra
*. . . Points on the Curve
  to Find . . .* , for piano
  and twenty-two
  instruments
Linea, for two pianos,
  vibraphone and
  marimba
FELDMAN (47)
*String Quartet and
  orchestra*
Voices and cello
For Frank O'Hara
BROWN (46)
Centering, for solo violin
  and ten instruments
MUSGRAVE (45)
Viola Concerto
STOCKHAUSEN (45)
Inori, for soloist and
  orchestra (1973–74)
HODDINOTT (44)
fp. Symphony No. 5
fp. The Floore of Heav'n,
  for orchestra
WILLIAMSON (42)
The Winter Star, cassation
Concerto for two pianos
  and strings
Ode to Music, for chorus,
  echo chorus and
  orchestra
Pietà, for soprano, oboe,
  bassoon and piano

Canticle of Fire, for
  chorus and organ
*Little Carols of the
  Saints*, five organ pieces
The World at the Manger,
  cantata
PENDERECKI (40)
Symphony
BIRTWISTLE (39)
Grimethorpe Aria, for
  brass band
Five Choral Preludes
  arranged from Bach,
  for soprano and
  instrumental ensemble
Chanson de geste, for
  solo sustaining
  instrument and tape
DAVIES (39)
Fiddlers at the Wedding,
  for mezzo-soprano and
  chamber orchestra
  (1973–74)
Stone Litany, for mezzo-
  soprano and orchestra
Scottish Dances, for
  instrumental ensemble
MAW (38)
Serenade, for chamber
  orchestra
Life Studies, for fifteen
  solo strings
Personae, for piano
BENNETT (37)
Concerto for Orchestra
Viola Concerto
Commedia III and IV
Scena I and II
Alba, for organ
BEDFORD (36)
*A Horse, His Name was
  Hunry Fencewaver
  Walkins*, for

instrumental ensemble
Jack of Shadows, for solo
 viola and instruments.
Pancakes . . ., for wind
 quintet
Variations on a Rhythm

by Mike Oldfield, for
 percussion
TAVENER (29)
Thérèse, opera (1973–76)
*Requiem for Father
 Malachy*

1974   MARTIN and MILHAUD died

BLISS (84)
Orchestral prelude
 Lancaster
MARTIN (84)
Et la vie l'emporta,
 chamber cantata
JACOB (79)
Sinfonia brevis
Havant Suite, for chamber
 orchestra
Quartet for clarinets
BERKELEY (72)
Guitar Concerto
Suite for Strings
Herrick Songs, for voices
 and harp
WALTON (72)
Cantico del Sole
Magnificat and Nunc
 Dimittis
LUTYENS (68)
The Winter of the World,
 for orchestras
Kareniana, for
 instrumental ensemble
SHOSTAKOVICH (68)
String Quartet No. 15
Four verses of Capitan
 Lebjadkin, for bass and
 piano
Suite on verses of
 Michelangelo

Buonarroti, for bass
 and piano
BRITTEN (61)
Suite on English Folk
 Tunes, for orchestra
Canticle V, "The death of
 Narcissus", for tenor
 and harp
A Birthday Hansel, for
 voice and harp
DIAMOND (59)
fp. Quartet No. 10
BERNSTEIN (56)
Dybbuk, ballet
ROCHBERG (56)
Imago mundi, for
 orchestra
FRICKER (54)
Spirit Puck, for clarinet
 and percussion
Trio-Sonata for organ
Two Petrarch Madrigals
FOSS (52)
fp. Orpheus, for viola,
 cello (or guitar) and
 orchestra
HAMILTON (52)
The Cataline Conspiracy,
 opera
Piano Sonata No. 2
BERIO (49)
Per la dolce memoria di
CONTINUED

quel giorno, ballet

Après visage, for orchestra
and tape

Calmo, for soprano and
instruments

Chorus, for voices and
instruments

BOULEZ (49)

*Rituel, in memoriam
Maderna,* for orchestra
in eight groups

FELDMAN (48)

Instruments, I

Voice and Instruments, II

KORTE (46)

Libera me, four songs

MUSGRAVE (46)

Space Play, concerto for
nine instruments

STOCKHAUSEN (46)

Atmen gibt das leben . . . ,
for mixed choir

Herbstmusik

Vortrag über Hu, for solo
voice

HODDINOTT (45)

fp. *The Beach of Falesa,*
opera

fp. *Ritornelli,* for solo
trombone, winds and
percussion

WILLIAMSON (43)

The Glitter Gang,
cassation

PENDERECKI (41)

The Dream of Jacob

BIRTWISTLE (40)

*Chorales from a
Toyshop,* for variable
orchestration

DAVIES (40)

*Miss Donnithorne's
Maggot,* for mezzo-
soprano and chamber
orchestra

Dark Angels, for soprano
and guitar

All Sons of Adam, motet
for instrumental
ensemble

BENNETT (38)

Spells, for soprano, chorus
and orchestra

Love Spells, for soprano
and orchestra

Four-piece Suite, for two
pianos

Sonnet Sequence, for
tenor and strings

Time's Whiter Series, for
counter-tenor and lute

BEDFORD (37)

Star's End, for rock
instruments orchestra

Twelve Hours of Sunset,
for chorus and orchestra

*The Golden Wine is
Drunk,* for sixteen solo
voices

*Because he liked to be at
home,* for tenor,
recorder and harp

BLISS (85)
Shield of Faith, cantata
JACOB (80)
Concerto for organ,
    strings and percussion
Rhapsody, for piano
Fantasy Sonata, for organ
HARRIS (77)
Symphony No. 14
SESSIONS (76)
Three Choruses on
    Biblical texts
BERKELEY (73)
Quintet for piano and
    wind
LUTYENS (69)
Eos, for small orchestra
Fanfare for a Festival, for
    three trumpets and
    three trombones
Pietà, for harpsichord
Ring of Bone, for solo
    piano
SHOSTAKOVICH (69)
The Dreamers, ballet
Sonata for viola and
    grand piano
BRITTEN (62)
Phaedra, dramatic cantata
    for mezzo-soprano and
    small orchestra
String Quartet No. 3
BERNSTEIN (57)
Seven Dances from
    Dybbuk
Suite No. 1 from *Dybbuk*
ROCHBERG (57)
Violin Concerto

FRICKER (55)
Symphony No. 5
String Quartet No. 3
HAMILTON (53)
Sea Music, for chorus and
    string quartet
Violin Sonata No. 1
Cello Sonata No. 2
Te Deum
BERIO (50)
Il malato immaginario,
    incidental music
*La ritirata notturna di
    Madrid,* for orchestra
Sequence VIII, for
    percussion
Sequence IX, for violin
FELDMAN (49)
*Piano and Orchestra
Instruments II*
Four Instruments, for
    piano, violin, viola
    and cello
MUSGRAVE (47)
Orfeo I and II, for flute,
    strings and tape
STOCKHAUSEN (47)
Musik im bauch
Tierkreis (Zodiac)
HODDINOTT (46)
fp. Landscapes, for
    orchestra
DAVIES (41)
Ave maris stella
BENNETT (39)
Violin Concerto
Oboe Quartet

This timeline enables the reader to see at a glance when each composer was born and died, as well as who was contemporary with whom. Horizontal lines begin with the year of a composer's birth, and end with that of his death. At the end of each line, the composer's age at death is also given.

Composers are listed chronologically in the left-hand column of each page, according to their dates of birth. Where all the composers born within a century cannot be listed on a single page, the latter part of the century is displayed in full overleaf and any timelines which have to be repeated are printed in gray.

The column following a composer's name shows, in almost every case, the country of his birth. Many composers became citizens of and/or ended their lives in some other country (notably the United States). Stravinsky, for example, achieved the right to four passports—Russian, French, British and American. The compilers feel, however, that the country of a composer's birth is usually of greatest interest.

The abbreviations indicate:

Als:	Alsace	Hol:	Holland
Aust:	Australia	Hun:	Hungary
Aus:	Austria	I:	Italy
Bel:	Belgium	Mex:	Mexico
Braz:	Brazil	Nor:	Norway
Cz:	Czechoslovakia	Pol:	Poland
Den:	Denmark	Rum:	Rumania
Fin:	Finland	R:	Russia
F:	France	Sp:	Spain
G:	Germany	Swe:	Sweden
G.B.:	Great Britain	Swi:	Switzerland
	(including Ireland)	U.S.A.:	United States

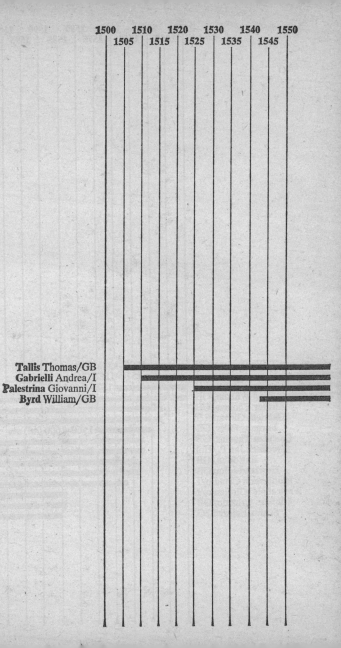

	1550	1555	1560	1565	1570	1575	1580	1585	1590	1595	1600

Tallis Thomas/GB 1505–1585 (80)
Gabrielli Andrea/I 1510–1586 (76)
Palestrina Giovanni/I 1525–1594 (69)
Byrd William/GB
Morley Thomas/GB
Gabrielli Giovanni/I
Farnaby Giles/GB
Campian Thomas/GB 1560–1600 (40)
Sweelinck Jan P./Hol
Bull John/GB
Dowland John/GB
Monteverdi Claudio/I
Frescobaldi Girolamo/I
Gibbons Orlando/GB
Schütz Heinrich/G

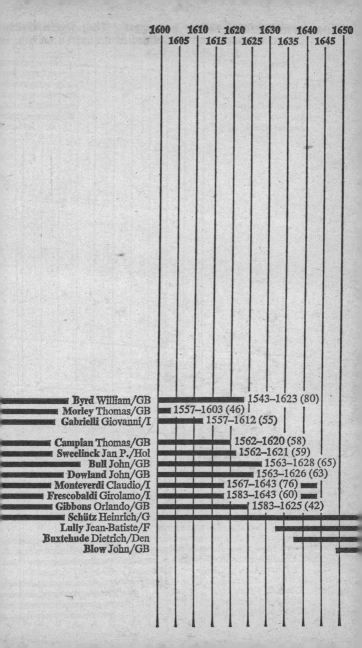

| | 1600 | 1605 | 1610 | 1615 | 1620 | 1625 | 1630 | 1635 | 1640 | 1645 | 1650 |

Byrd William/GB — 1543–1623 (80)
Morley Thomas/GB — 1557–1603 (46)
Gabrielli Giovanni/I — 1557–1612 (55)

Campian Thomas/GB — 1562–1620 (58)
Sweelinck Jan P./Hol — 1562–1621 (59)
Bull John/GB — 1563–1628 (65)
Dowland John/GB — 1563–1626 (63)
Monteverdi Claudio/I — 1567–1643 (76)
Frescobaldi Girolamo/I — 1583–1643 (60)
Gibbons Orlando/GB — 1583–1625 (42)
Schütz Heinrich/G
Lully Jean-Batiste/F
Buxtehude Dietrich/Den
Blow John/GB

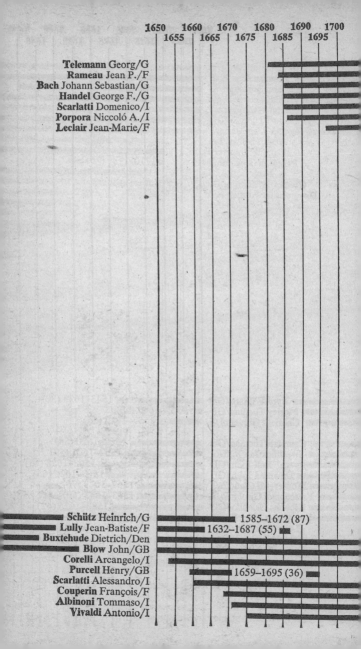

| | 1650 | 1655 | 1660 | 1665 | 1670 | 1675 | 1680 | 1685 | 1690 | 1695 | 1700 |

Telemann Georg/G
Rameau Jean P./F
Bach Johann Sebastian/G
Handel George F./G
Scarlatti Domenico/I
Porpora Niccoló A./I
Leclair Jean-Marie/F

Schütz Heinrich/G   1585–1672 (87)
Lully Jean-Batiste/F   1632–1687 (55)
Buxtehude Dietrich/Den
Blow John/GB
Corelli Arcangelo/I
Purcell Henry/GB   1659–1695 (36)
Scarlatti Alessandro/I
Couperin François/F
Albinoni Tommaso/I
Vivaldi Antonio/I

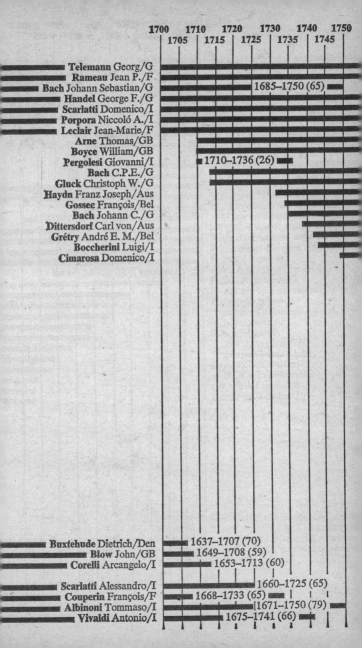

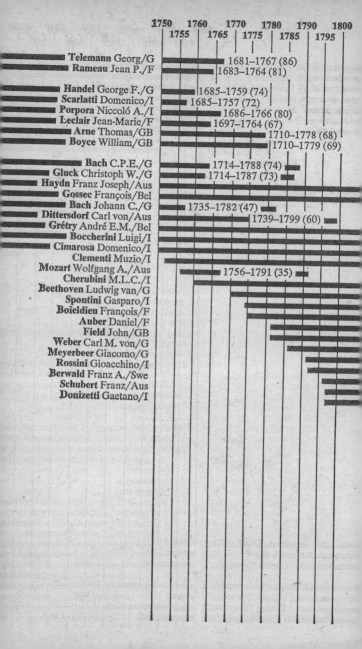

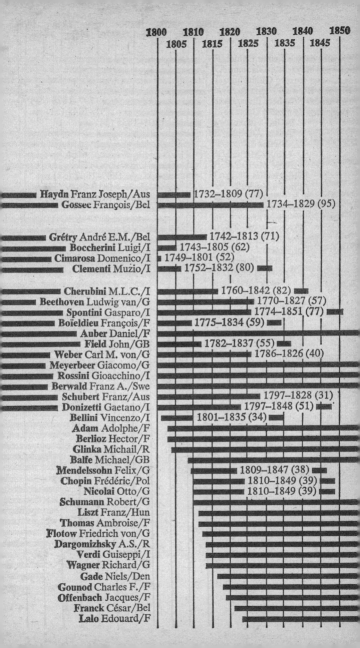

	1800	1810	1820	1830	1840	1850
	1805	1815	1825	1835	1845	

Haydn Franz Joseph/Aus — 1732–1809 (77)
Gossec François/Bel — 1734–1829 (95)

Grétry André E.M./Bel — 1742–1813 (71)
Boccherini Luigi/I — 1743–1805 (62)
Cimarosa Domenico/I — 1749–1801 (52)
Clementi Muzio/I — 1752–1832 (80)

Cherubini M.L.C./I — 1760–1842 (82)
Beethoven Ludwig van/G — 1770–1827 (57)
Spontini Gasparo/I — 1774–1851 (77)
Boïeldieu François/F — 1775–1834 (59)
Auber Daniel/F
Field John/GB — 1782–1837 (55)
Weber Carl M. von/G — 1786–1826 (40)
Meyerbeer Giacomo/G
Rossini Gioacchino/I
Berwald Franz A./Swe
Schubert Franz/Aus — 1797–1828 (31)
Donizetti Gaetano/I — 1797–1848 (51)
Bellini Vincenzo/I — 1801–1835 (34)
Adam Adolphe/F
Berlioz Hector/F
Glinka Michail/R
Balfe Michael/GB
Mendelssohn Felix/G — 1809–1847 (38)
Chopin Frédéric/Pol — 1810–1849 (39)
Nicolai Otto/G — 1810–1849 (39)
Schumann Robert/G
Liszt Franz/Hun
Thomas Ambroise/F
Flotow Friedrich von/G
Dargomizhsky A.S./R
Verdi Guiseppi/I
Wagner Richard/G
Gade Niels/Den
Gounod Charles F./F
Offenbach Jacques/F
Franck César/Bel
Lalo Edouard/F

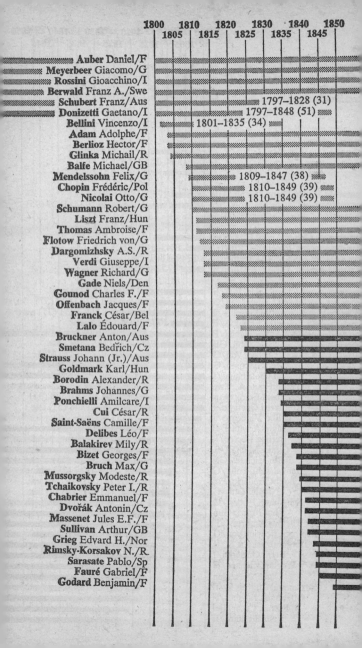

	1800	1810	1820	1830	1840	1850
	1805	1815	1825	1835	1845	

Auber Daniel/F
Meyerbeer Giacomo/G
Rossini Gioacchino/I
Berwald Franz A./Swe
Schubert Franz/Aus — 1797–1828 (31)
Donizetti Gaetano/I — 1797–1848 (51)
Bellini Vincenzo/I — 1801–1835 (34)
Adam Adolphe/F
Berlioz Hector/F
Glinka Michail/R
Balfe Michael/GB
Mendelssohn Felix/G — 1809–1847 (38)
Chopin Frédéric/Pol — 1810–1849 (39)
Nicolai Otto/G — 1810–1849 (39)
Schumann Robert/G
Liszt Franz/Hun
Thomas Ambroise/F
Flotow Friedrich von/G
Dargomizhsky A.S./R
Verdi Giuseppe/I
Wagner Richard/G
Gade Niels/Den
Gounod Charles F./F
Offenbach Jacques/F
Franck César/Bel
Lalo Édouard/F
Bruckner Anton/Aus
Smetana Bedřich/Cz
Strauss Johann (Jr.)/Aus
Goldmark Karl/Hun
Borodin Alexander/R
Brahms Johannes/G
Ponchielli Amilcare/I
Cui César/R
Saint-Saëns Camille/F
Delibes Léo/F
Balakirev Mily/R
Bizet Georges/F
Bruch Max/G
Mussorgsky Modeste/R
Tchaikovsky Peter I./R
Chabrier Emmanuel/F
Dvořák Antonin/Cz
Massenet Jules E.F./F
Sullivan Arthur/GB
Grieg Edvard H./Nor
Rimsky-Korsakov N./R
Sarasate Pablo/Sp
Fauré Gabriel/F
Godard Benjamin/F

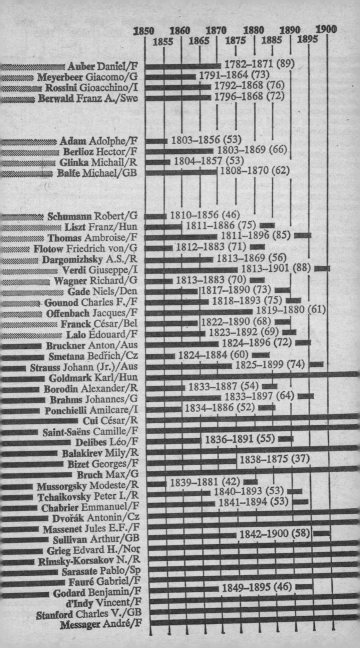

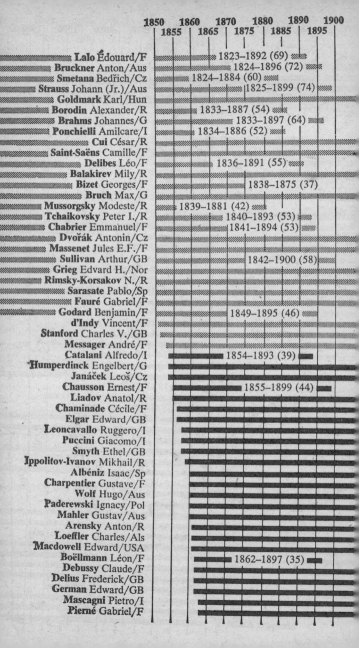

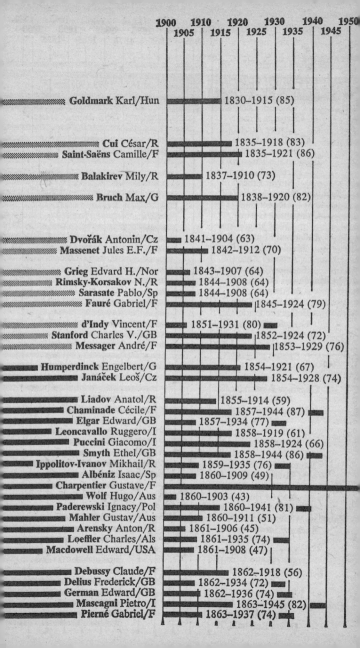

| | 1900 | 1905 | 1910 | 1915 | 1920 | 1925 | 1930 | 1935 | 1940 | 1945 | 1950 |

Goldmark Karl/Hun 1830–1915 (85)

Cui César/R 1835–1918 (83)
Saint-Saëns Camille/F 1835–1921 (86)

Balakirev Mily/R 1837–1910 (73)

Bruch Max/G 1838–1920 (82)

Dvořák Antonin/Cz 1841–1904 (63)
Massenet Jules E.F./F 1842–1912 (70)

Grieg Edvard H./Nor 1843–1907 (64)
Rimsky-Korsakov N./R 1844–1908 (64)
Sarasate Pablo/Sp 1844–1908 (64)
Fauré Gabriel/F 1845–1924 (79)

d'Indy Vincent/F 1851–1931 (80)
Stanford Charles V./GB 1852–1924 (72)
Messager André/F 1853–1929 (76)

Humperdinck Engelbert/G 1854–1921 (67)
Janáček Leoš/Cz 1854–1928 (74)

Liadov Anatol/R 1855–1914 (59)
Chaminade Cécile/F 1857–1944 (87)
Elgar Edward/GB 1857–1934 (77)
Leoncavallo Ruggero/I 1858–1919 (61)
Puccini Giacomo/I 1858–1924 (66)
Smyth Ethel/GB 1858–1944 (86)
Ippolitov-Ivanov Mikhail/R 1859–1935 (76)
Albéniz Isaac/Sp 1860–1909 (49)
Charpentier Gustave/F
Wolf Hugo/Aus 1860–1903 (43)
Paderewski Ignacy/Pol 1860–1941 (81)
Mahler Gustav/Aus 1860–1911 (51)
Arensky Anton/R 1861–1906 (45)
Loeffler Charles/Als 1861–1935 (74)
Macdowell Edward/USA 1861–1908 (47)

Debussy Claude/F 1862–1918 (56)
Delius Frederick/GB 1862–1934 (72)
German Edward/GB 1862–1936 (74)
Mascagni Pietro/I 1863–1945 (82)
Pierné Gabriel/F 1863–1937 (74)

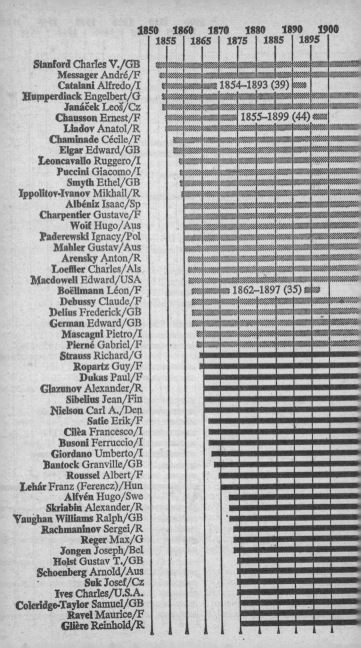

| | 1850 | 1860 | 1870 | 1880 | 1890 | 1900 |
| | 1855 | 1865 | 1875 | 1885 | 1895 | |

Stanford Charles V./GB
Messager André/F
Catalani Alfredo/I — 1854–1893 (39)
Humperdinck Engelbert/G
Janáček Leoš/Cz
Chausson Ernest/F — 1855–1899 (44)
Liadov Anatol/R
Chaminade Cécile/F
Elgar Edward/GB
Leoncavallo Ruggero/I
Puccini Giacomo/I
Smyth Ethel/GB
Ippolitov-Ivanov Mikhail/R
Albéniz Isaac/Sp
Charpentier Gustave/F
Wolf Hugo/Aus
Paderewski Ignacy/Pol
Mahler Gustav/Aus
Arensky Anton/R
Loeffler Charles/Als
Macdowell Edward/USA
Boëllmann Léon/F — 1862–1897 (35)
Debussy Claude/F
Delius Frederick/GB
German Edward/GB
Mascagni Pietro/I
Piern é Gabriel/F
Strauss Richard/G
Ropartz Guy/F
Dukas Paul/F
Glazunov Alexander/R
Sibelius Jean/Fin
Nielson Carl A./Den
Satie Erik/F
Cilèa Francesco/I
Busoni Ferruccio/I
Giordano Umberto/I
Bantock Granville/GB
Roussel Albert/F
Lehár Franz (Ferencz)/Hun
Alfvén Hugo/Swe
Skriabin Alexander/R
Vaughan Williams Ralph/GB
Rachmaninov Sergei/R
Reger Max/G
Jongen Joseph/Bel
Holst Gustav T./GB
Schoenberg Arnold/Aus
Suk Josef/Cz
Ives Charles/U.S.A.
Coleridge-Taylor Samuel/GB
Ravel Maurice/F
Glière Reinhold/R

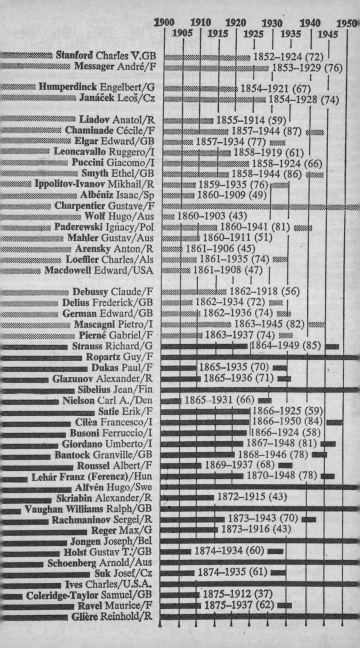

	1875	1880	1885	1890	1895	1900	1905	1910	1915	1920	1925

Charpentier Gustave/F
Strauss Richard/G
Ropartz Guy/F
Dukas Paul/F
Glazunov Alexander/R
Sibelius Jean/Fin
Nielson Carl A./Den
Satie Erik/F — 1866–1925 (59)
Cilèa Francesco/I
Busoni Ferruccio/I — 1866–1924 (58)
Giordano Umberto/I
Bantock Granville/GB
Roussel Albert/F
Lehár Franz (Ferencz)/Hun
Alfvén Hugo/Swe
Skriabin Alexander/R — 1872–1915 (43)
Vaughan Williams Ralph/GB
Rachmaninov Sergei/R
Reger Max/G — 1873–1916 (43)
Jongen Joseph/Bel
Holst Gustav T./GB
Schoenberg Arnold/Aus
Suk Josef/Cz
Ives Charles/U.S.A.
Coleridge-Taylor Samuel/GB — 1875–1912 (37)
Ravel Maurice/F
Glière Reinhold/R
Falla Manuel de/Sp
Wolf-Ferrari Ermanno/I
Carpenter John Alden/U.S.A.
Aubert Louis/F
Dohnányi Ernst von/Hun
Quilter Roger/GB
Ireland John/GB
Respighi Ottorino/I
Bridge Frank/GB
Bloch Ernest/Swi
Medtner Nicholas/R
Pizzetti Ildebrando/I
Bartók Béla/Hun
Enesco Georges/Rum
Grainger Percy Aldridge/Aust
Kodály Zoltán/Hun
Malipiero Gian Francesco/I
Stravinsky Igor/R
Turina Joaquín/Sp
Bax Arnold Trevor/GB
Casella Alfredo/I
Szymanowski Karol/Pol
Webern Anton von/Aus
Griffes Charles/U.S.A. — 1884–1920 (36)
Berg Alban/Aus
Taylor Deems/U.S.A.
Butterworth George/GB — 1885–1916 (31)

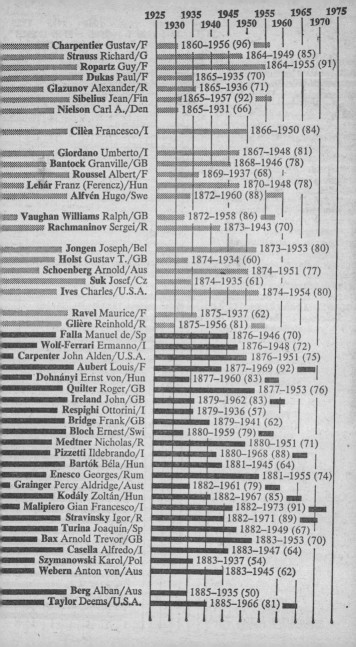

| | 1925 | 1935 | 1945 | 1955 | 1965 | 1975 |
| | 1930 | 1940 | 1950 | 1960 | 1970 | |

Charpentier Gustav/F — 1860–1956 (96)
Strauss Richard/G — 1864–1949 (85)
Ropartz Guy/F — 1864–1955 (91)
Dukas Paul/F — 1865–1935 (70)
Glazunov Alexander/R — 1865–1936 (71)
Sibelius Jean/Fin — 1865–1957 (92)
Nielson Carl A./Den — 1865–1931 (66)

Cilèa Francesco/I — 1866–1950 (84)

Giordano Umberto/I — 1867–1948 (81)
Bantock Granville/GB — 1868–1946 (78)
Roussel Albert/F — 1869–1937 (68)
Lehár Franz (Ferencz)/Hun — 1870–1948 (78)
Alfvén Hugo/Swe — 1872–1960 (88)

Vaughan Williams Ralph/GB — 1872–1958 (86)
Rachmaninov Sergei/R — 1873–1943 (70)

Jongen Joseph/Bel — 1873–1953 (80)
Holst Gustav T./GB — 1874–1934 (60)
Schoenberg Arnold/Aus — 1874–1951 (77)
Suk Josef/Cz — 1874–1935 (61)
Ives Charles/U.S.A. — 1874–1954 (80)

Ravel Maurice/F — 1875–1937 (62)
Glière Reinhold/R — 1875–1956 (81)
Falla Manuel de/Sp — 1876–1946 (70)
Wolf-Ferrari Ermanno/I — 1876–1948 (72)
Carpenter John Alden/U.S.A. — 1876–1951 (75)
Aubert Louis/F — 1877–1969 (92)
Dohnányi Ernst von/Hun — 1877–1960 (83)
Quilter Roger/GB — 1877–1953 (76)
Ireland John/GB — 1879–1962 (83)
Respighi Ottorini/I — 1879–1936 (57)
Bridge Frank/GB — 1879–1941 (62)
Bloch Ernest/Swi — 1880–1959 (79)
Medtner Nicholas/R — 1880–1951 (71)
Pizzetti Ildebrando/I — 1880–1968 (88)
Bartók Béla/Hun — 1881–1945 (64)
Enesco Georges/Rum — 1881–1955 (74)
Grainger Percy Aldridge/Aust — 1882–1961 (79)
Kodály Zoltán/Hun — 1882–1967 (85)
Malipiero Gian Francesco/I — 1882–1973 (91)
Stravinsky Igor/R — 1882–1971 (89)
Turina Joaquín/Sp — 1882–1949 (67)
Bax Arnold Trevor/GB — 1883–1953 (70)
Casella Alfredo/I — 1883–1947 (64)
Szymanowski Karol/Pol — 1883–1937 (54)
Webern Anton von/Aus — 1883–1945 (62)

Berg Alban/Aus — 1885–1935 (50)
Taylor Deems/U.S.A. — 1885–1966 (81)

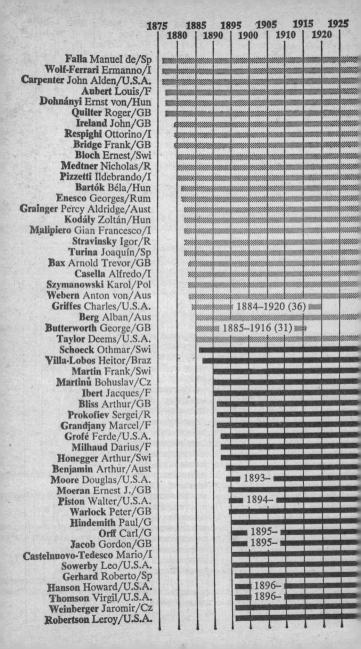

	1875	1885	1895	1905	1915	1925
		1880	1890	1900	1910	1920

Falla Manuel de/Sp
Wolf-Ferrari Ermanno/I
Carpenter John Alden/U.S.A.
Aubert Louis/F
Dohnányi Ernst von/Hun
Quilter Roger/GB
Ireland John/GB
Respighi Ottorino/I
Bridge Frank/GB
Bloch Ernest/Swi
Medtner Nicholas/R
Pizzetti Ildebrando/I
Bartók Béla/Hun
Enesco Georges/Rum
Grainger Percy Aldridge/Aust
Kodály Zoltán/Hun
Malipiero Gian Francesco/I
Stravinsky Igor/R
Turina Joaquín/Sp
Bax Arnold Trevor/GB
Casella Alfredo/I
Szymanowski Karol/Pol
Webern Anton von/Aus
Griffes Charles/U.S.A.　　1884–1920 (36)
Berg Alban/Aus
Butterworth George/GB　　1885–1916 (31)
Taylor Deems/U.S.A.
Schoeck Othmar/Swi
Villa-Lobos Heitor/Braz
Martin Frank/Swi
Martinů Bohuslav/Cz
Ibert Jacques/F
Bliss Arthur/GB
Prokofiev Sergei/R
Grandjany Marcel/F
Grofé Ferde/U.S.A.
Milhaud Darius/F
Honegger Arthur/Swi
Benjamin Arthur/Aust
Moore Douglas/U.S.A.　　1893–
Moeran Ernest J./GB
Piston Walter/U.S.A.　　1894–
Warlock Peter/GB
Hindemith Paul/G
Orff Carl/G　　1895–
Jacob Gordon/GB　　1895–
Castelnuovo-Tedesco Mario/I
Sowerby Leo/U.S.A.
Gerhard Roberto/Sp
Hanson Howard/U.S.A.　　1896–
Thomson Virgil/U.S.A.　　1896–
Weinberger Jaromir/Cz
Robertson Leroy/U.S.A.

	1925	1930	1935	1940	1945	1950	1955	1960	1965	1970	1975

Falla Manuel de/Sp	1876–1946 (70)
Wolf-Ferrari Ermanno/I	1876–1948 (72)
Carpenter John Alden/U.S.A.	1876–1951 (75)
Aubert Louis/F	1877–1969 (92)
Dohnányi Ernst von/Hun	1877–1960 (83)
Quilter Roger/GB	1877–1953 (76)
Ireland John/GB	1879–1962 (83)
Respighi Ottorino/I	1879–1936 (57)
Bridge Frank/GB	1879–1941 (62)
Bloch Ernest/Swi	1880–1959 (79)
Medtner Nicholas/R	1880–1951 (71)
Pizzetti Ildebrando/I	1880–1968 (88)
Bartók Béla/Hun	1881–1945 (64)
Enesco Georges/Rum	1881–1955 (74)
Grainger Percy Aldridge/Aust	1882–1961 (79)
Kodály Zoltán/Hun	1882–1967 (85)
Malipiero Gian Francesco/I	1882–1973 (91)
Stravinsky Igor/R	1882–1971 (89)
Turina Joaquín/Sp	1882–1949 (67)
Bax Arnold Trevor/GB	1883–1953 (70)
Casella Alfredo/I	1883–1947 (64)
Szymanowski Karol/Pol	1883–1937 (54)
Webern Anton von/Aus	1883–1945 (62)
Berg Alban/Aus	1885–1935 (50)
Taylor Deems/U.S.A.	1885–1966 (81)
Schoeck Othmar/Swi	1886–1957 (71)
Villa-Lobos Heitor/Braz	1887–1959 (72)
Martin Frank/Swi	1890–1974 (84)
Martinů Bohuslav/Cz	1890–1959 (69)
Ibert Jacques/F	1890–1962 (72)
Bliss Arthur/GB	1891–1975 (84)
Prokofiev Sergei/R	1891–1953 (62)
Grandjany Marcel/F	1891–1975 (84)
Grofé Ferde/U.S.A.	1892–1972 (80)
Milhaud Darius/F	1892–1974 (82)
Honegger Arthur/Swi	1892–1955 (63)
Benjamin Arthur/Aust	1893–1960 (67)
Moore Douglas/U.S.A.	
Moeran Ernest J./GB	1894–1950 (56)
Piston Walter/U.S.A.	
Warlock Peter/GB	1894–1930 (36)
Hindemith Paul/G	1895–1963 (68)
Orff Carl/G	
Jacob Gordon/GB	
Castelnuovo-Tedesco Mario/I	1895–1968 (73)
Sowerby Leo/U.S.A.	1895–1968 (73)
Gerhard Roberto/Sp	1896–1970 (74)
Hanson Howard/U.S.A.	
Thomson Virgil/U.S.A.	
Weinberger Jaromir/Cz	1896–1967 (71)
Robertson Leroy/U.S.A.	1896–1971 (75)

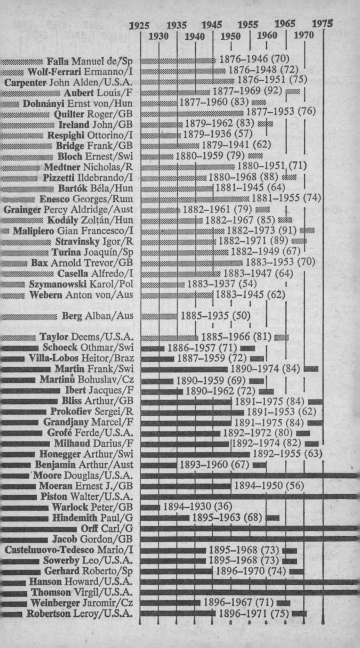

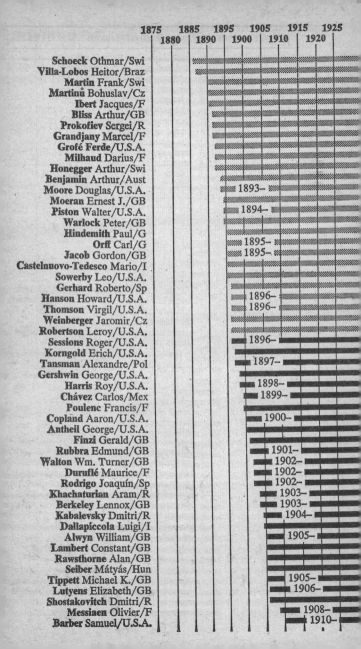

| | 1875 | 1885 | 1895 | 1905 | 1915 | 1925 |
| | 1880 | 1890 | 1900 | 1910 | 1920 | |

Schoeck Othmar/Swi
Villa-Lobos Heitor/Braz
Martin Frank/Swi
Martinů Bohuslav/Cz
Ibert Jacques/F
Bliss Arthur/GB
Prokofiev Sergei/R
Grandjany Marcel/F
Grofé Ferde/U.S.A.
Milhaud Darius/F
Honegger Arthur/Swi
Benjamin Arthur/Aust
Moore Douglas/U.S.A. 1893–
Moeran Ernest J./GB
Piston Walter/U.S.A. 1894–
Warlock Peter/GB
Hindemith Paul/G
Orff Carl/G 1895–
Jacob Gordon/GB 1895–
Castelnuovo-Tedesco Mario/I
Sowerby Leo/U.S.A.
Gerhard Roberto/Sp
Hanson Howard/U.S.A. 1896–
Thomson Virgil/U.S.A. 1896–
Weinberger Jaromir/Cz
Robertson Leroy/U.S.A.
Sessions Roger/U.S.A. 1896–
Korngold Erich/U.S.A.
Tansman Alexandre/Pol 1897–
Gershwin George/U.S.A.
Harris Roy/U.S.A. 1898–
Chávez Carlos/Mex 1899–
Poulenc Francis/F
Copland Aaron/U.S.A. 1900–
Antheil George/U.S.A.
Finzi Gerald/GB
Rubbra Edmund/GB 1901–
Walton Wm. Turner/GB 1902–
Duruflé Maurice/F 1902–
Rodrigo Joaquín/Sp 1902–
Khachaturian Aram/R 1903–
Berkeley Lennox/GB 1903–
Kabalevsky Dmitri/R 1904–
Dallapiccola Luigi/I
Alwyn William/GB 1905–
Lambert Constant/GB
Rawsthorne Alan/GB
Seiber Mátyás/Hun
Tippett Michael K./GB 1905–
Lutyens Elizabeth/GB 1906–
Shostakovitch Dmitri/R
Messiaen Olivier/F 1908–
Barber Samuel/U.S.A. 1910–

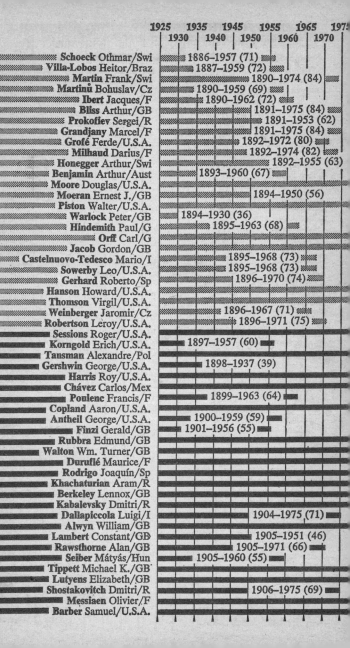

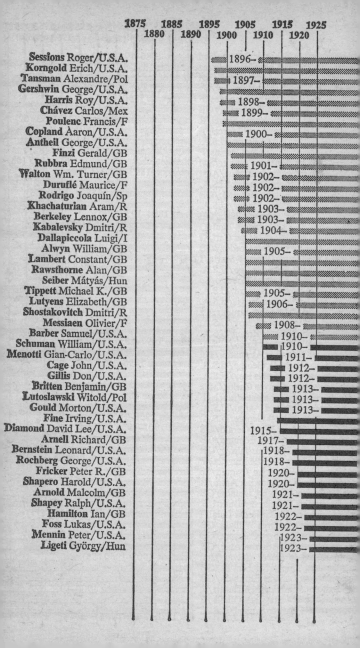

| | 1875 | 1880 | 1885 | 1890 | 1895 | 1900 | 1905 | 1910 | 1915 | 1920 | 1925 |

Sessions Roger/U.S.A. — 1896–
Korngold Erich/U.S.A.
Tansman Alexandre/Pol — 1897–
Gershwin George/U.S.A.
Harris Roy/U.S.A. — 1898–
Chávez Carlos/Mex — 1899–
Poulenc Francis/F
Copland Aaron/U.S.A. — 1900–
Antheil George/U.S.A.
Finzi Gerald/GB
Rubbra Edmund/GB — 1901–
Walton Wm. Turner/GB — 1902–
Duruflé Maurice/F — 1902–
Rodrigo Joaquín/Sp — 1902–
Khachaturian Aram/R — 1903–
Berkeley Lennox/GB — 1903–
Kabalevsky Dmitri/R — 1904–
Dallapiccola Luigi/I
Alwyn William/GB — 1905–
Lambert Constant/GB
Rawsthorne Alan/GB
Seiber Mátyás/Hun
Tippett Michael K./GB — 1905–
Lutyens Elizabeth/GB — 1906–
Shostakovitch Dmitri/R
Messiaen Olivier/F — 1908–
Barber Samuel/U.S.A. — 1910–
Schuman William/U.S.A. — 1910–
Menotti Gian-Carlo/U.S.A. — 1911–
Cage John/U.S.A. — 1912–
Gillis Don/U.S.A. — 1912–
Britten Benjamin/GB — 1913–
Lutoslawski Witold/Pol — 1913–
Gould Morton/U.S.A. — 1913–
Fine Irving/U.S.A.
Diamond David Lee/U.S.A. — 1915–
Arnell Richard/GB — 1917–
Bernstein Leonard/U.S.A. — 1918–
Rochberg George/U.S.A. — 1918–
Fricker Peter R./GB — 1920–
Shapero Harold/U.S.A. — 1920–
Arnold Malcolm/GB — 1921–
Shapey Ralph/U.S.A. — 1921–
Hamilton Ian/GB — 1922–
Foss Lukas/U.S.A. — 1922–
Mennin Peter/U.S.A. — 1923–
Ligeti György/Hun — 1923–

| | 1925 | 1935 | 1945 | 1955 | 1965 | 1975 |
| | 1930 | 1940 | 1950 | 1960 | 1970 | |

Sessions Roger/U.S.A.
Korngold Erich/U.S.A. 1897–1957 (60)
Tansman Alexandre/Pol
Gershwin George/U.S.A. 1898–1937 (39)
Harris Roy/U.S.A.
Chávez Carlos/Mex
Poulenc Francis/F 1899–1963 (64)
Copland Aaron/U.S.A.
Antheil George/U.S.A. 1900–1959 (59)
Finzi Gerald/GB 1901–1956 (55)
Rubbra Edmund/GB
Walton Wm. Turner/GB
Duruflé Maurice/F
Rodrigo Joaquín/Sp
Khachaturian Aram/R
Berkeley Lennox/GB
Kabalevsky Dmitri/R
Dallapiccola Luigi/I 1904–1975 (71)
Alwyn William/GB
Lambert Constant/GB 1905–1951 (46)
Rawsthorne Alan/GB 1905–1971 (66)
Seiber Mátyás/Hun 1905–1960 (55)
Tippett Michael K./GB
Lutyens Elizabeth/GB
Shostakovitch Dmitri/R 1906–1975 (69)
Messiaen Olivier/F
Barber Samuel/U.S.A.
Schuman William/U.S.A.
Menotti Gian-Carlo/U.S.A.
Cage John/U.S.A.
Gillis Don/U.S.A.
Britten Benjamin/GB
Lutoslawski Witold/Pol
Gould Morton/U.S.A.
Fine Irving/U.S.A. 1914–1962 (48)
Diamond David Lee/U.S.A.
Arnell Richard/GB
Bernstein Leonard/U.S.A.
Rochberg George/U.S.A.
Fricker Peter R./GB
Shapero Harold/U.S.A.
Arnold Malcolm/GB
Shapey Ralph/U.S.A.
Hamilton Ian/GB
Foss Lukas/U.S.A.
Mennin Peter/U.S.A.
Ligeti György/Hun
Boulez Pierre/F 1925–
Berio Luciano/I 1925–
Brown Earle/U.S.A. 1926–
Feldman Morton/U.S.A. 1926–
Henze Hans Werner/G 1926–
Musgrave Thea/GB 1928–

| | 1875 | 1885 | 1895 | 1905 | 1915 | 1925 |
| | | 1880 | 1890 | 1900 | 1910 | 1920 |

Schuman William/U.S.A.   1910–

Menotti Gian-Carlo/U.S.A.   1911–

Cage John/U.S.A.   1912–

Gillis Don/U.S.A.   1912–

Britten Benjamin/GB   1913–

Lutoslawski Witold/Pol   1913–

Gould Morton/U.S.A.   1913–

Fine Irving/U.S.A.

Diamond David Lee/U.S.A.   1915–

Arnell Richard/GB   1917–

Bernstein Leonard/U.S.A.   1918–

Rochberg George/U.S.A.   1918–

Fricker Peter R./GB   1920–

Shapero Harold/U.S.A.   1920–

Arnold Malcolm/GB   1921–

Shapey Ralph/U.S.A.   1921–

Hamilton Ian/GB   1922–

Foss Lukas/U.S.A.   1922–

Mennin Peter/U.S.A.   1923–

Ligeti György/Hun   1923–

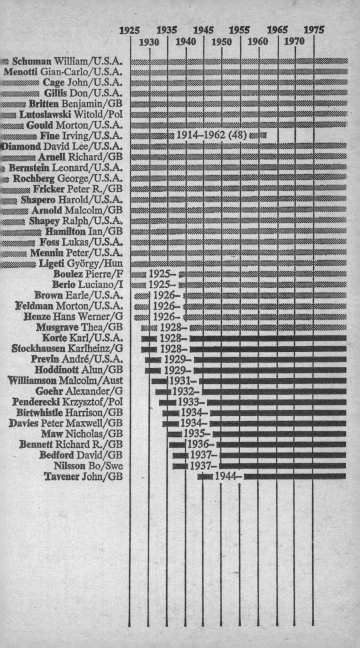

1925	1935	1945	1955	1965	1975
1930	1940	1950	1960	1970	

Schuman William/U.S.A.
Menotti Gian-Carlo/U.S.A.
Cage John/U.S.A.
Gillis Don/U.S.A.
Britten Benjamin/GB
Lutoslawski Witold/Pol
Gould Morton/U.S.A.
Fine Irving/U.S.A.   1914–1962 (48)
Diamond David Lee/U.S.A.
Arnell Richard/GB
Bernstein Leonard/U.S.A.
Rochberg George/U.S.A.
Fricker Peter R./GB
Shapero Harold/U.S.A.
Arnold Malcolm/GB
Shapey Ralph/U.S.A.
Hamilton Ian/GB
Foss Lukas/U.S.A.
Mennin Peter/U.S.A.
Ligeti György/Hun
Boulez Pierre/F   1925–
Berio Luciano/I   1925–
Brown Earle/U.S.A.   1926–
Feldman Morton/U.S.A.   1926–
Henze Hans Werner/G   1926–
Musgrave Thea/GB   1928–
Korte Karl/U.S.A.   1928–
Stockhausen Karlheinz/G   1928–
Previn André/U.S.A.   1929–
Hoddinott Alun/GB   1929–
Williamson Malcolm/Aust   1931–
Goehr Alexander/G   1932–
Penderecki Krzysztof/Pol   1933–
Birtwhistle Harrison/GB   1934–
Davies Peter Maxwell/GB   1934–
Maw Nicholas/GB   1935–
Bennett Richard R./GB   1936–
Bedford David/GB   1937–
Nilsson Bo/Swe   1937–
Tavener John/GB   1944–

ERIC GILDER is a composer, teacher, conductor, pianist and musicologist. Trained at London's Royal College of Music, he studied under such gifted men as John Ireland, Ralph Vaughan Williams, Constant Lambert and Sir Malcolm Sargent. A prolific composer, Gilder has written for the orchestra, voices, the theater and television. He has served as a choral conductor and appeared at London's Royal Festival Hall both as a conductor and as a pianist.

He began his career as a teacher at a private London music college, which was some years later renamed the Eric Gilder School of Music. He continues to teach and lecture on a variety of music subjects.

JUNE G. PORT is a guitarist, cellist, teacher and musicologist. She is currently the administrator of the Eric Gilder School of Music in London and a lecturer on the history of music.